IN THE BLOOD

IN THE BLOOD

CELEBRATING THE RED & WHITE
1874 – 2009

JIM MAIN

ACKNOWLEDGEMENTS

Writing *In The Blood* was a massive task, not only in the actual keying of the manuscript, but also in research and the search and selection of photographs and other illustrations. This book therefore is the work of many and, in particular, I thank Russell Fogarty, Jason Kimberley and Craig Meade for the use of most of the illustrations in this book, all from their private collections, surely the best of any AFL club; Russell Holmesby for his assistance with research and photographic material; Col Hutchinson for his advice on historical matters; Peter Conway for his assistance in the development of the book; Ben Graham for his superb design; Sam Basile for his courage in publishing this massive book; all Sydney Swans executive, staff and players, and especially Rachel Bracken for her magnificent help in tracking down photographs and securing permission for their use; Adam Goodes for granting permission to use his 2006 Brownlow Medal illumination; Mark Branagan and Robert Allan for help with research and, finally, all the men who played in the red and white, coached the club or played any role in its long and proud history. This book is yours.

Published by:
Bas Publishing
ABN 30 106 181 542
PO Box 2052
Seaford Vic 3198
Tel/Fax: (03) 5988 3597
Web: www.baspublishing.com.au
Email: mail@baspublishing.com.au

National Library of Australia Cataloguing-in-Publication entry

Author:	Main, Jim, 1943-
Title:	In the blood : celebrating the red and white 1874 - 2009 / Jim Main.
ISBN:	9781921496011 (pbk.)
Subjects:	Sydney Swans (Football team)--History. Australian football--New South Wales--Sydney--History. Australian football--Victoria--South Melbourne--History.
Dewey Number:	796.336

Photos on the following pages supplied courtesy of The Slattery Media Group:
336, 340, 341, 342, 343, 345, 347, 349, 350, 352, 354, 358, 360, 361,
364, 366, 367, 368, 369, 372, 375, 376, 378, 379, 380, 381, 383.

Design & Layout: Ben Graham

Chairman's Message

Last year we started planning an event that would showcase the extraordinary 135-year history of our club, including the centenary of our first AFL(VFL) premiership of 1909 and culminating in the launch of the club's Hall of Fame.

A key issue was determining the authenticity of much of the accepted history of an organisation that was formed in 1874. How much of what has become accepted as fact was really folklore or urban myth, and how could we fill in some of the void in the club's written history?

This book therefore aims to dispel the myths and present the first comprehensive club history. It will surely be required reading for all Swans supporters.

It is a book for the ages.

I am sure that 135 years from now this book will be the basis of all discussion of the club's provenance and the history of its first 135 years will be resolved.

The lexicon of our game - the argot of Australian football if you like - contains many terms that are synonymous with the human cardio-vascular system.

Players are said to have played with great heart. People are described as the heart and soul of the club. The colloquial term "ticker" is used to describe someone's level of courage. Our supporters are described as having red and white blood coursing through their veins. And there is the age-old maxim that a great club's players bleed for their jumper.

So it is fitting that the term "blood" is the key word in the title of this book.

But the noun "blood" has heightened meaning in our club. The team is consistently referred to with passion and reverence as "the Bloods" (generally accepted as being short for the Blood-Stained Angels).

What would appear to be the case is that the club in its broadest sense is known as the Swans but increasingly the playing group on any given day is referred to as "the Bloods".

For not only do the players refer to themselves as the Bloods, but we hear this from all sections of the crowd at any of our games now played throughout the country. It is the spine-tingling cry of "go the Bloods".

This book's title, "In the Blood", is so simple yet so powerfully captures the essence of the game we love and the club we cherish.

When true believers are asked "why are the Bloods so bloody important", their answer is simple.

"It's in the Blood."

RICHARD COLLESS,
Chairman,
Sydney Swans

FOREWORD

My Grand Final memories date back to 1958. I have missed probably six along the way, which means I have been at the MCG (and VFL Park for 1991) for the climax of the football year about 44 times. I know I was there in '75 when North Melbourne won its first premiership; in 1990 when Collingwood buried the Colliwobbles after 32 years; in 2003 when the Brisbane Lions clinched their hat-trick; in 2007 when the Cats ended a 44-year drought.

Yet my all-time favourite Grand Final was played in 2005.

Outside of the day a dying Ted Whitten was driven around the boundary at the MCG, nursed by his son, Ted jnr, Sydney's premiership win and its aftermath was the most emotional day I have spent at what I call the Temple in more than 1500 visits.

Sydney ... the Swannies ... the Bloods ... South Melbourne.

What a day!

In the end, just four points to spare, yet that probably made it even sweeter.

Leo Barry's mark, the final siren, the outpouring of emotion both on the field and in the stands, and in front of hundreds of thousands of television sets throughout the country, made it special.

The faces of South Melbourne – Skilton, Round, Kimberley and John – of Sydney – Colless, Quade, Weinert, Gerahty, Willesee and Sellers – are forever etched in my mind.

There were others, God, there were thousands of others for whom it was the moment they might happily have gone to their maker.

"Others" including the author of this magnificent and important publication, Jim Main.

Main is a man of passion, yet nothing in his life stirs his passion like the fluctuating fortunes of his footy club, the Swans.

He is not the only one.

I grew up with a special affection for South Melbourne. Perhaps it was because it struggled year after year and never threatened, yet played every next game as if it would prove to be the turning point of its fortunes.

I know I barracked for the Swans in the first semi-final of 1970, when 104,000 people saw them lose to St Kilda. My memory tells me Skilton went into the game with a thigh injury, probably a hamstring.

I remember Clegg and Gunn and Taylor and Dorgan; I loved watching "Mopsy" Rantall and "Wheels" Bedford play, I loved going to the Lake Oval; loved covering games from the old press box, which hung over the ground and allowed us to hear what the players said.

Then came the fight for survival and the move north. I became close friends with Rick Quade, Tony Franklin, Dean Moore and others; I grew to care about their fate.

Fortunately, the right people stayed involved or got involved, and the club has flourished. It is a heartwarming story of faith, persistence, co-operation and triumph.

I am delighted to have watched it unfold for half a century.

MIKE SHEAHAN
Chief Football Writer, Herald Sun

FROM THE AUTHOR

Man and boy, I have followed the Swans for more than half a century. I love the Swans, always will. Writing this book therefore has been an honour. I could even say it was a labour of love, but it was more than that as the hours spent in research and writing would be inestimable.

This is the history of our club, as South Melbourne and the Sydney Swans. One club, two cities. However, it is not the definitive history as I have concentrated on on-field events and, to a certain extent, overlooked some of the internal machinations unless they had a significant bearing on club fortunes. Of course, I could not ignore the "civil war" of 1981 or the complex events swirling around the club over the first decade or so as the Sydney Swans, but I have tried to concentrate on the club's origins and how it has fared from season to season.

This book runs to more than 150,000 words, yet I feel I have hardly scratched the surface. There is so much I have had to overlook and, no doubt, there will be events I have forgotten or failed to find in my research. It has not been possible to record every incident, every suspension, every major injury, every drama. And, if there are any oversights, I beg your forgiveness.

I also have written an extended chapter on the events of 2005. The reason is obvious. That year's premiership erased the pain of decades and we all can take pleasure again and again from the events recorded under the 2005 banner in this book.

Finally, this book has a number of illustrations that, in some respects would not pass muster for publication. They are scratched, torn, age-stained or even blurred. The fact remains, however, that they are historically important and are reproduced here untouched and as found.

Read and enjoy!

JIM MAIN

* * *

Jim Main is one of Australia's most respected journalists and has written more than 50 books. He is a Walkley Award winner, has been inducted into the Melbourne Cricket Club Media Hall of Fame and is a life member of the Australian Football Media Association. He was one of the selectors for the Swans' Team of the Century and, in 2009, was invited to sit on the AFL Hall of Fame selection panel.

BIRTH OF A CLUB

To understand how the South Melbourne Football Club was born it is necessary to look at how the area just south of the Yarra developed. It appears the area was first settled by merchants and dockers and then by those who arrived from Europe, mainly from Ireland, in search of gold in the early 1850s. The area originally was known as Canvas Town but, because of the Irish influx, formally adopted the name of Emerald Hill. By 1861, Emerald Hill had a population of 9000, but then developed so rapidly it was one of Melbourne's most populous areas and later was renamed South Melbourne.

With cricket and the new sport of football spreading across the colony from the late 1850s, it was only natural that Melbourne's

South Melbourne, in the hooped guernseys, clashed with Collingwood in the 1896 VFA Grand Final.

An extremely rare 1890 South membership folder, with coupons for specific matches.

heaviest populated area would become a sports hot spot. Hockey, golf, tennis and bowling also were played in the 600 acres of Albert Park and it was only a matter of time before a football club was formed.

It is believed the first club in the area was Emerald Hill, with founders including early football stars Dick Gray and Theo Marshall. The club played its home games near the Albert Park railway station and, five years later, had a rival club in the area. The Albert Park club was formed in 1864 and played its home games at St Vincent's Gardens. Then, in 1867, Emerald Hill and Albert Park merged to become the South Melbourne Football Club. However, this was not the birth of the club we know today.

The original South Melbourne club played its first game against South Yarra on July 13, 1867, but neither team managed a score. Other games in 1867 were against the Gymnasium Club, Hobson's Bay Railway, Brighton Park and Melbourne, among other clubs. Less than a year later, at a meeting at the Clarendon Hotel on April 17, 1868, the original South Melbourne club changed its name to Emerald Hill, upsetting many of the old Albert Park group.

The new Emerald Hill club played its earliest games at an area known as "Three Chain Road", which now is part of Albert Road and was regarded as one of the strongest clubs in Melbourne. However, there was another attempt to change the name back to South Melbourne in 1869 and after the motion was passed at the club annual meeting, the former Albert Park group walked out. With the club in danger of being torn apart, the original motion was rescinded and a new motion was passed that the club be known as Albert Park.

Early Albert Park stars included Bob Foote, Ernie Cox, Dave and John Chessell, Alex Brown and George Crooke. Albert Park in 1870 played in the foremost competition of the era, the South Yarra Presentation Cup, and significantly, wore red and white uniforms. The striped guernseys were so striking the Albert Park players were known as "those red and white beauties".

Albert Park continued to enjoy modest success over the following seasons but, in June,1874, had a new local rival when a group met at the Temperance Hall in Napier Street to form the Cecil Football Club. This new club less than a month later changed its name to the South Melbourne Football Club. And this is the club we know today, allowing for one further nineteenth century twist.

Despite the rise of the new South Melbourne club, Albert Park remained the most powerful club in the area. Other clubs included South Park, South Melbourne Imperials, Rising Sun, Emerald Hill Standards, St Vincent's, Excelsior and Southern. Then, in 1878, the most powerful clubs in the colony formed the Victorian Football Association (VFA), with Albert Park competing in 11 matches for one win, three defeats and seven described as "unfinished". One match against Melbourne attracted 3000 fans, but the rival South Melbourne club was on the rise.

In fact, South Melbourne was declared a senior side in 1879 and finished third, with Geelong the premier and Carlton runner-up. South's stars in this era were Charles Kellett, John Baragwanath, Bill Collie, Dave Chessell, Bob Hutton and Harry Newman, while Albert Park's stars included Ted Slatter, Matt Minchin and Jack Rosser.

However, Albert Park was on the wane and agreed to amalgamate with South Melbourne in 1880. The merger compromised on name and club colours. South Melbourne was able to retain its name, but had to abandon its blue and white in favour of Albert Park's red and white. The newly merged club's first game was against reigning South Australian premier Norwood at the East Melbourne Cricket Ground, with one unusual twist. Alf Waldron

played for Norwood and his brother Frank for South Melbourne. It was the start of a wonderful era as South finished third with 13 wins, two defeats and five draws. South also played a match against Maryborough and defeated the country side eight goals to nil (behinds were not counted in that era). VFA clubs at that time also played games against "junior" (ie, non-VFA clubs).

The 1881 season was even more significant as the South Melbourne Cricket Club made their ground (the Lake Oval) available to the football club. South was still referred to as "those red and white beauties" and it is believed its first match at the Lake Oval was against Essendon on June 4. However, heavy rain made good play impossible and players were forced from the field before either side could score and the match was declared a draw.

South was the top side for most of the season and clinched its first premiership in defeating Geelong by four goals to one before 10,000 fans at the Lake Oval. South's captain was A.G. Major and stars included defender Jim Young, winger John Gibson, forward Bill Wells and Tom Bushell, regarded as one of the longest kicks of a football in his era.

It was around this time that

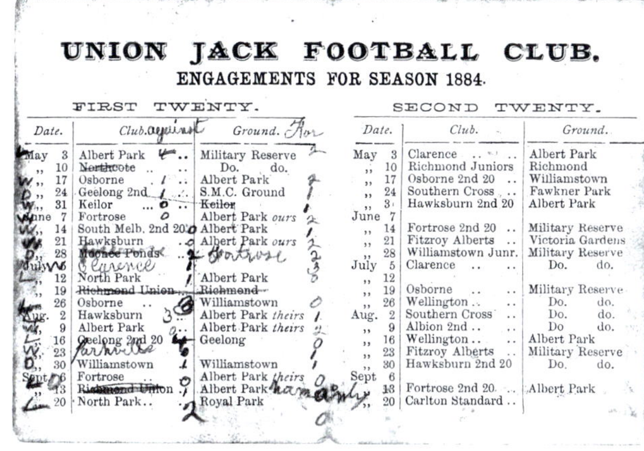

UNION JACK FOOTBALL CLUB.

ENGAGEMENTS FOR SEASON 1884.

FIRST TWENTY.

Date.	Club.	Ground.
May 3	Albert Park	Military Reserve
,, 10	Northcote	Do. do.
,, 17	Osborne	Albert Park
,, 24	Geelong 2nd	S.M.C. Ground
,, 31	Keilor	Keilor
June 7	Fortrose	Albert Park *ours*
,, 14	South Melb. 2nd 20	Albert Park
,, 21	Hawksburn	Albert Park *ours*
,, 28	Moonee Ponds	
July 5		
,, 12	North Park	Albert Park
,, 19	Richmond Union	Richmond
,, 26	Osborne	Williamstown
Aug. 2	Hawksburn	Albert Park *theirs*
,, 9	Albert Park	Albert Park *theirs*
,, 16	Geelong 2nd 20	Geelong
,, 23		
,, 30	Williamstown	Williamstown
Sept. 6	Fortrose	Albert Park *theirs*
,, 13	Richmond Union	Albert Park
,, 20	North Park	Royal Park

SECOND TWENTY.

Date.	Club.	Ground.
May 3	Clarence	Albert Park
,, 10	Richmond Juniors	Richmond
,, 17	Osborne 2nd 20	Williamstown
,, 24	Southern Cross	Fawkner Park
,, 31	Hawksburn 2nd 20	Albert Park
June 7		
,, 14	Fortrose 2nd 20	Military Reserve
,, 21	Fitzroy Alberts	Victoria Gardens
,, 28	Williamstown Junr.	Military Reserve
July 5	Clarence	Do. do.
,, 12		
,, 19	Osborne	Military Reserve
,, 26	Wellington	Do. do.
Aug. 2	Southern Cross	Do. do.
,, 9	Albion 2nd	Do do.
,, 16	Wellington	Albert Park
,, 23	Fitzroy Alberts	Military Reserve
,, 30	Hawksburn 2nd 20	Do. do.
Sept 6		
,, 13	Fortrose 2nd 20	Albert Park
,, 20	Carlton Standard	

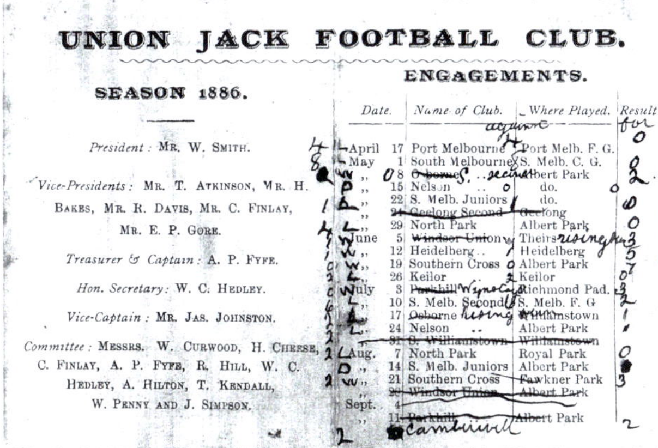

UNION JACK FOOTBALL CLUB.

SEASON 1886.

President: Mr. W. Smith.

Vice-Presidents: Mr. T. Atkinson, Mr. H. Bakes, Mr. R. Davis, Mr. C. Finlay, Mr. E. P. Gore.

Treasurer & Captain: A. P. Fyfe.

Hon. Secretary: W. C. Hedley.

Vice-Captain: Mr. Jas. Johnston.

Committee: Messrs. W. Curwood, H. Cheese, C. Finlay, A. P. Fyfe, R. Hill, W. C. Hedley, A. Hilton, T. Kendall, W. Penny and J. Simpson.

ENGAGEMENTS.

Date.	Name of Club.	Where Played.	Result
April 17	Port Melbourne	Port Melb. F. G.	
May 1	South Melbourne	S. Melb. C. G.	
,, 8	Osborne	Albert Park	
,, 15	Nelson	do.	
,, 22	S. Melb. Juniors	do.	
,, 24	Geelong Second	Geelong	
,, 29	North Park	Albert Park	
June 5	Windsor Union	Theirs	
,, 12	Heidelberg	Heidelberg	
,, 19	Southern Cross	Albert Park	
,, 26	Keilor	Keilor	
July 3	Parkhill	Richmond Pad.	
,, 10	S. Melb. Second	S. Melb. F. G	
,, 17	Osborne	Williamstown	
,, 24	Nelson	Albert Park	
,, 31	S. Williamstown	Williamstown	
Aug. 7	North Park	Royal Park	
,, 14	S. Melb. Juniors	Albert Park	
,, 21	Southern Cross	Fawkner Park	
,, 28	Windsor Union	Albert Park	
Sept. 4			
,, 11	Parkhill	Albert Park	

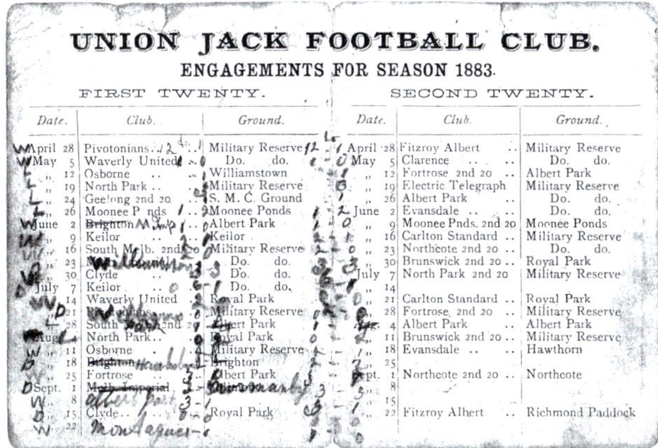

UNION JACK FOOTBALL CLUB.

ENGAGEMENTS FOR SEASON 1883.

FIRST TWENTY.

Date.	Club.	Ground.
April 28	Pivotonians	Military Reserve
May 5	Waverly United	Do. do.
,, 12	Osborne	Williamstown
,, 19	North Park	Military Reserve
,, 24	Geelong 2nd 20	S. M. C. Ground
,, 26	Moonee Ponds	Moonee Ponds
June 2	Brighton	Albert Park
,, 9	Keilor	Keilor
,, 16	South Melb. 2nd 20	Military Reserve
,, 23	[illegible]	Do. do.
,, 30	Clyde	Do. do.
July 7	Keilor	Do. do.
,, 14	Waverly United	Royal Park
,, 21	Pivotonians	Military Reserve
,, 28	South Melb. 2nd 20	Albert Park
Aug. 4	North Park	Royal Park
,, 11	Osborne	Military Reserve
,, 18	Brighton	Brighton
,, 25	Fortrose	Albert Park
Sept. 1	Melb. Imperial	
,, 8		
,, 15	Clyde	Royal Park
,, 22		

SECOND TWENTY.

Date.	Club.	Ground.
April 28	Fitzroy Albert	Military Reserve
May 5	Clarence	Do. do.
,, 12	Fortrose 2nd 20	Albert Park
,, 19	Electric Telegraph	Military Reserve
,, 26	Albert Park	Do. do.
June 2	Evansdale	Do. do.
,, 9	Moonee Pnds. 2nd 20	Moonee Ponds
,, 16	Carlton Standard	Military Reserve
,, 23	Northcote 2nd 20	Do. do.
,, 30	Brunswick 2nd 20	Royal Park
July 7	North Park 2nd 20	Military Reserve
,, 14		
,, 21	Carlton Standard	Royal Park
,, 28	Fortrose 2nd 20	Military Reserve
Aug. 4	Albert Park	Albert Park
,, 11	Brunswick 2nd 20	Military Reserve
,, 18	Evansdale	Hawthorn
,, 25		
Sept. 1	Northcote 2nd 20	Northcote
,, 8		
,, 15		
,, 22	Fitzroy Albert	Richmond Paddock

The Union Jack was a junior club, but played matches against South Melbourne in the 1880s.

South Melbourne Football Club, 1890.

the South Melbourne Football Club was credited with introducing a new word to the English language. The Lake Oval was close enough to the St Kilda Road army barracks for soldiers to attend games and support the local team. Their cheers for South earned them the nickname of "the barrackers".

Although South wore red and white stripes from its amalgamation with Albert Park from 1880, it changed the design to red and white hoops in 1883 and one of its triumphs that season was in "the game of the year" against Geelong. The 1883 season also marked the debut of champion goalkicker Dinny McKay, who went on to score the club's first VFL goal in 1897. Other stars included Henry "Sonny" Elms, Goldie Watsford and Harry Stevens.

Also, South in 1883 played a match in Sydney, almost 100 years before the club relocated there in 1982. The *Maitland Mercury* reported: "This afternoon the important football match between the South Melbourne Club and a Combined Northern team will take place on the Albion ground, West Maitland. Proceedings will begin at a quarter to three o'clock sharp. A numerous attendance of the general public is anticipated … The visitors will arrive by the mail train this morning." The newspaper also reported that the South players that night would be "entertained" at a dinner at the Masonic Hall.

South's next triumphant season was in 1885 when the red and white not only won the VFA premiership but went through the season undefeated. It played 25 games for 22 wins and three draws. Its star recruit was the great Peter Burns, who became a legendary identity in the club's VFA years and later was a Geelong VFL star. Burns, from Ballarat Imperials, was named Champion of the Colony in the premiership season of 1885.

South won its next VFA premiership in 1888, with Geelong runner-up. Almost as significant was South's game against an England rugby side. The match attracted an attendance of 12,000 at the Lake Oval, with gate takings of 202 pounds ($404) — an enormous sum in 1888. South's 20 were: H. Elms (captain), P. Burns (vice-captain), R. Doran, W. Windley, W. Spence, A. Gibson, H. Purdy, R. Kerr, J. McShane, J. Reid, J. Clinton, G. Peters, D. McKay, A. Brown, J. O'Meara, J. Young, E. Hill, F. Greaves, W. Ellis and J. Wyatt. South defeated England seven goals to three. McKay, who kicked an extraordinary (in that era) total of 49 goals in 1888, was named Champion of the Colony.

The club, again under Elms' captaincy, won

the premiership again in 1889, with 14 wins, two defeats and three draws. Stars that season included Burns (who captained a Victorian side), McKay, Edgar Barrett (who topped the VFA goalkicking), Bill Windley, Harry Purdy, Fred McKnight and Bill Lockett (from a local junior club).

The 1888 season was enormously successful in more ways that one as, apart from the premiership, the club also was able to attract a record attendance of 31,672 for a match against Essendon at the Lake Oval. However, a visiting Maori rugby team defeated South six goals to four in a match at the Lake Oval. The 1888 annual meeting was held at the South Melbourne Town Hall for members to see the presentation of premiership caps and trophies valued at 10 guineas ($21) to the successful players.

South completed a hat-trick of premierships in 1890, with 16 wins, two defeats and two draws. There were no Grand Finals in that era and the team on top of the ladder at the end of the home and away series was declared the premier. South romped away with the premiership well before the end of the season and, to celebrate, players and fans went to the final round match against Richmond in horse-drawn vehicles decorated with red and white ribbons, banners and streamers. South then travelled to Adelaide to play South Australian premier club Port Adelaide, but went down seven goals to six. Also, when Victoria played South Australia at the MCG during the 1890 season, South had six representatives in the Victorian team — Elms, Windley, McKay, Purdy, Burns and Jim O'Meara. Victoria defeated South Australia 13 goals to six.

An early South Melbourne team photo. Note the white yoke at the top of several guernseys.

From there, however, South slipped down the ladder to finish fourth in 1891 and sixth the following year. The only consolation was that Burns in 1891 was named Champion of the Colony. Other good players over these seasons included Elms, Windley, McKay, Purdy, Jim Dunn, Bill Spence and "Bolivar" Powell.

The Australian colonies in 1893 were hit by a severe depression and, with many thousands out of work, football also was affected. Attendances slipped and industrial areas like South Melbourne were hardest hit. Despite this, South climbed the ladder to finish fourth in Elms' last season. The depression deepened in 1894 but South, under new captain McKay finished third, behind Essendon and Melbourne.

South in 1895 was dealt a savage blow when McKay crossed to rival VFA club Richmond. He had spent 12 years with South, but returned to the club to play in South's inaugural VFL season of 1897. South's best recruit for 1895 was Bill "Buns" Fraser, from Port Melbourne. South had a mediocre season, with nine wins, seven defeats and two draws. However, the club fared much better the following year.

The 1896 season was the last before the formation of the VFL for the start of the next

South defeats England, played at South Melbourne on June 23, 1888.

season. South had a brilliant season, but so did Collingwood. In fact, there was nothing between them. Both won 14 games, lost three and drew one. They also scored 86 goals each and had 55 kicked against them. Under these remarkable circumstances, the VFA declared the two clubs should play off in a Grand Final. South and Collingwood therefore clashed at the East Melbourne Cricket Ground in the season's decider.

The big match took place on a warm and sunny afternoon in front of 21,289 fans. Collingwood led from the start and although South full-back Dave Adamson was rated the best player on the ground, Collingwood defeated South six goals to five.

The Victorian football world then was torn apart on October 2, 1896, when the stronger VFA clubs met at Buxton's Art Gallery, near the Melbourne Town Hall, to propose a breakaway competition. These clubs felt they were propping up the others, so South Melbourne, Carlton, Collingwood Essendon, Fitzroy, Geelong and Melbourne decided to go their own way. They invited St Kilda to join them and the Victorian Football League was born.

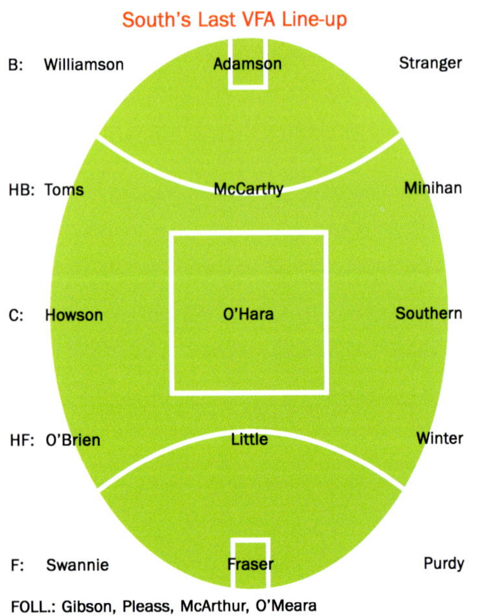

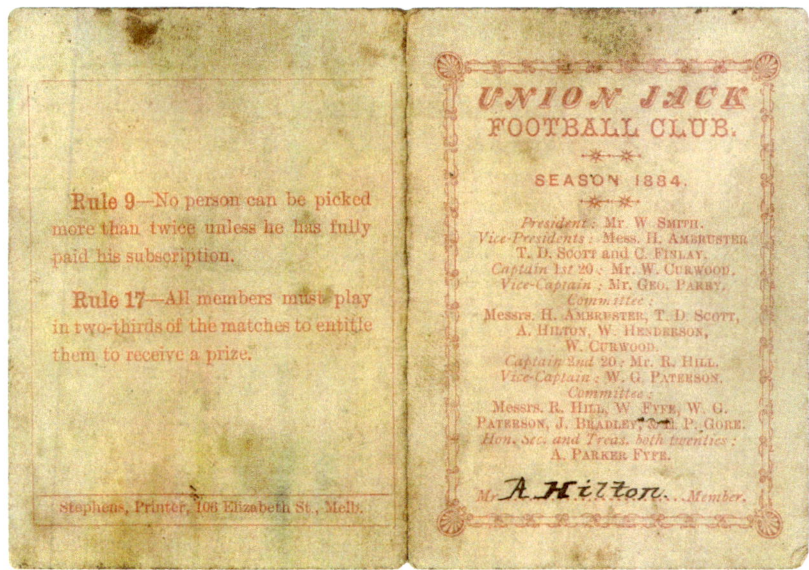

Rule 9—No person can be picked more than twice unless he has fully paid his subscription.

Rule 17—All members must play in two-thirds of the matches to entitle them to receive a prize.

Stephens, Printer, 106 Elizabeth St., Melb.

UNION JACK FOOTBALL CLUB.

SEASON 1884.

President: Mr. W. Smith.
Vice-Presidents: Mess. H. Ambruster, T. D. Scott and C. Finlay.
Captain 1st 20: Mr. W. Curwood.
Vice-Captain: Mr. Geo. Parry.
Committee:
Messrs. H. Ambruster, T. D. Scott, A. Hilton, W. Henderson, W. Curwood.
Captain 2nd 20: Mr. R. Hill.
Vice-Captain: W. G. Paterson.
Committee:
Messrs. R. Hill, W. Fyfe, W. G. Paterson, J. Bradley, E. P. Gore.
Hon. Sec. and Treas. both twenties: A. Parker Fyfe.

Mr A. Hilton Member.

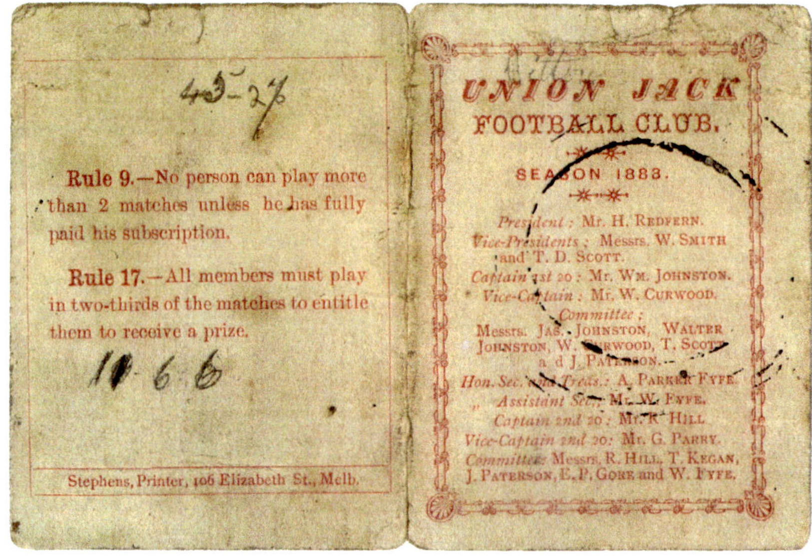

43–27

Rule 9.—No person can play more than 2 matches unless he has fully paid his subscription.

Rule 17.—All members must play in two-thirds of the matches to entitle them to receive a prize.

10 6 6

Stephens, Printer, 106 Elizabeth St., Melb.

UNION JACK FOOTBALL CLUB.

SEASON 1883.

President: Mr. H. Redfern.
Vice-Presidents: Messrs. W. Smith and T. D. Scott.
Captain 1st 20: Mr. Wm. Johnston.
Vice-Captain: Mr. W. Curwood.
Committee:
Messrs. Jas. Johnston, Walter Johnston, W. Curwood, T. Scott and J. Paterson.
Hon. Sec. and Treas.: A. Parker Fyfe.
Assistant Sec.: Mr. W. Fyfe.
Captain 2nd 20: Mr. R. Hill.
Vice-Captain 2nd 20: Mr. G. Parry.
Committee: Messrs. R. Hill, T. Kegan, J. Paterson, E. P. Gore and W. Fyfe.

The front of Union Jack membership tickets, with matches scheduled against South Melbourne in these seasons.

1897

Saturday, May 8, 1897, might have dawned cool and misty but, by mid-afternoon, it was a glorious autumn day. There also was an air of excitement in Melbourne as this day really represented the birth of the Victorian Football League, with four scheduled matches — South Melbourne v Melbourne, Collingwood v St Kilda, Fitzroy v Carlton and Essendon v Geelong. South was runner-up to Collingwood in its last Victorian Football Association season of 1896, with Melbourne fourth and the South-Melbourne clash at the Lake Oval therefore was billed as the highlight of the new competition's first round of matches.

South Melbourne's First VFL Team

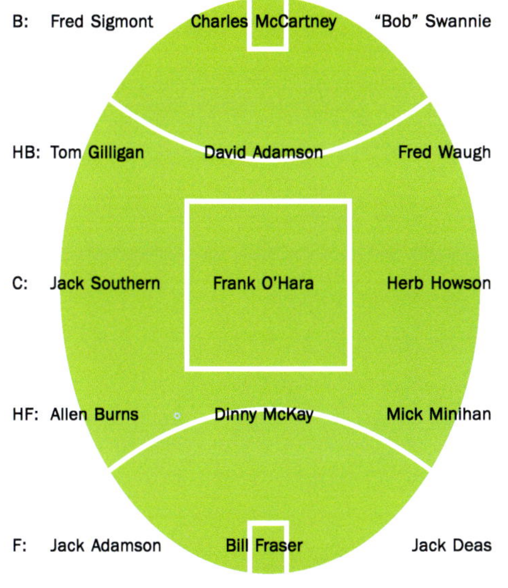

FOLL.: Dick Gibson, "Mick" Pleass, Harry Purdy, Bill Blackwood ROVER: Bill Windley

South fielded an experienced side, captained by veteran Bill "Buns" Fraser, an all-rounder who excelled in the centre or on a half-forward flank (there were 20 players per side in the first two VFL seasons).

The *South Melbourne Record* the following week noted that the ground was "nice and springy after the recent heavy rains", with a good crowd including "a number of ladies". South kicked to the outer end in the first quarter but, despite several early attacks, Melbourne kicked three goals to South's two behinds in this quarter. The Southerners did not score their first VFL goal until late in the second quarter when Denis "Dinny" McKay snapped "smartly", according to the *Record*, and the ball bounced through the goals. Melbourne won by 17 points and the headline in the *Record* read: THE RED AND WHITE DEFEATED.

South made amends the following week when it defeated Carlton by just four points. The *Record* reported that "great excitement attended the play in the last quarter". McKay kicked two of South's six goals and all South players wore back armbands following the death earlier in the week of Dave Adamson, father of players David and Jack Adamson. South the following week thrashed St Kilda by 57 points, also at the Lake Oval, with the Saints scoring just two behinds. Although South defeated Collingwood in the fourth round, its form fell away from there and the Southerners finished the 14-round season in fifth position, half a game behind the Magpies and therefore out of the final four.

The home and away season ended on August 7 and, just four days later, the club was shocked by the sudden death of star forward McKay, who had topped the club goalkicking with 14 in the inaugural VFL season. McKay, 30, had been a reliable forward for the Southerners after joining the club from South Ballarat and also had played in the VFA with Richmond. He had played all 14 games with South that season and his last

Early South star Herb Howson, who also was referred to as "Bert".

MATCH RESULTS

Round 1, at Lake Oval, May 8
Melbourne 6.8 (44) d South Melbourne 3.9 (27)

Round 2, at Lake Oval, May 15
South Melbourne 6.4 (40) d Carlton 5.6 (36)

Round 3, at Lake Oval, May 24
South Melbourne 8.11 (59) d St Kilda 0.2 (2)

Round 4, at Lake Oval, May 29
South Melbourne 5.11 (41) d Collingwood 5.3 (33)

Round 5, at Corio Oval, June 5
Geelong 10.12 (72) d South Melbourne 3.6 (24)

Round 6, at Lake Oval, June 19
Essendon 1.13 (19) d South Melbourne 2.3 (15)

Round 7, at Brunswick Street Oval, June 22
South Melbourne 5.13 (43) drew with Fitzroy 5.13 (43)

Round 8, at MCG, June 26
South Melbourne 11.7 (73) d Melbourne 3.2 (20)

Round 9, at Princes Park, July 3
South Melbourne 11.8 (74) d Carlton 4.4 (28)

Round 10, at Junction Oval, July 10
South Melbourne 8.16 (64) d St Kilda 0.3 (3)

Round 11, at Victoria Park, July 17
South Melbourne 2.15 (27) d Collingwood 0.8 (8)

Round 12, at Lake Oval, July 24
Geelong 6.8 (44) d South Melbourne 5.2 (32)

Round 13, at East Melbourne CG, July 31
Essendon 8.1 (49) d South Melbourne 6.9 (45)

Round 14, at Lake Oval, August 7
South Melbourne 3.12 (30) d Fitzroy 4.5 (29)

game was in the final round when the Southerners pipped Fitzroy by a point at the Lake Oval.

Melbourne newspaper *The Argus* reported in its August 10 edition, under the headline DEATH OF A WELL-KNOWN FOOTBALLER: "Followers of football, and the South Melbourne Club in particular, will learn with regret that D. McKay, the well-known footballer, died in the Melbourne Hospital last night, having suffered for some little time past from an internal ailment. During the past season McKay, although the oldest playing member of the South Melbourne Club, was in very fine form, and appeared to be in vigorous health. He leaves a wife and two children unprovided for, the eldest of the children also being seriously ill. A meeting is to be held in the skittle-alley at the South Melbourne ground this evening to raise funds for their assistance."

McKay had the dubious distinction of being the first VFL footballer to die, from any cause. There had been suggestions for decades that he might have died as a result of a football injury, possibly in his final match. His sudden death, in fact, had nothing to do with football and resulted from a burst appendix and ensuing peritonitis, a commonly fatal illness in a far less sophisticated medical era.

His funeral was held the following week and the *Record* reported that the cortege, a mile long, took half an hour to pass any given point. The hearse, laden with wreaths and other floral tributes, was followed by two mourning coaches and more than 100 other horse-drawn vehicles. South players walked in front of the hearse as the cortege left McKay's house in Iffla Street, South Melbourne, and made its way through the city to the Melbourne General Cemetery, with an outpouring of grief following the death of one of the Southerners' earliest stars. The *Record* noted: "Deceased was buried in the Roman Catholic portion of the cemetery, and an immense concourse of people gathered round the grave. Amongst the most conspicuous of the wreaths were those from the South Melbourne and Richmond football clubs, in both of which Dinny played, Essendon and the League."

The 1897 season might have dawned so brilliantly, but it ended in tragedy for the South Melbourne Football Club.

PLAYER	GAMES	GOALS
ADAMSON, David	13	3
ADAMSON, Jack	1	0
BLACKWOOD, Bill	13	11
BURNS, Allen	13	9
DAVIDSON, George	2	0
DEAS, Jack	2	0
DORAN, Richard	9	0
FLEMING, Jack	5	0
FRASER, Bill	14	1
GIBSON, Dick	13	3
GILLIGAN, Tom	14	9
HOWSON, Herb	14	0
LYONS, Horrie	5	2
McCARTNEY, Charles	13	0
McKAY, Dinny	14	14
O'GORMAN, Mick*	11	13
O'HARA, Frank	13	0
PLEASS, George "Mick"	14	4
PURDY, Harry	13	3
SIGMONT, Fred	6	0
SOUTHERN, Jack	13	0
SWANNIE, Archibald "Bob"	13	4
THOMAS, Alban	1	0
TOMS, Eddie	7	0
WAUGH, Fred	9	0
WILLIAMSON, George	10	0
WINDLEY, Bill	11	2

* Played under the name Mick Minihan

POSITION: Fifth
COACH: -
CAPTAIN: Bill Fraser
BEST AND FAIREST: -
LEADING GOALKICKER: Dinny McKay (14)

1898

Following the disappointment and tragedy of 1897, South was determined to improve the following season and embarked on an extensive recruiting campaign. The Southerners introduced 23 new players — a phenomenal number even in that earliest of football eras — and only 16 remained from the previous season. One of the newcomers was pencil-thin 18-year-old Warwick Armstrong, who later made a name for himself as Australia's Test cricket captain. Armstrong played just one game in his debut VFL season after being recruited from Caulfield and other recruits made bigger impressions, even though he was a magnificent place-kick. It was remarkable considering his light frame that in his cricket heyday in the 1920s, he was known as "the Big Ship" because of his 20-stone build.

The pick of the recruits was Albert Trim, a defender from Beechworth who went on to play 65 games with South to 1901 before joining Carlton. A dashing defender, he represented Victoria and captained the club in 1901. Also, clever winger Henri Jeannerett played all 17 games in his debut season and went on to play 75 games with the Southerners to 1903 and was noted for his speed and brilliant ball-handling.

South prepared for the new season with a practice match against old and local VFA rival Port Melbourne, who defeated the Southerners by 35 points. However, the *South Melbourne Record's* football writer "Rover" noted that South was "trying a number of new men and were, in addition, measuring strides with the 'elect' of last season as far as the Association premiership was concerned".

The Southerners opened the 1898 season against Carlton at Princes Park. In the week leading up to the match South again elected Bill Fraser as captain and the *Record* noted that the captaincy was his reward for "dint of hard work and honest play". South was confident of victory against the previous season's second bottom side (just two wins and above only the winless St Kilda) although the *Record* noted that "the northerners are very strong this year". It added: "The trouble with South today will be to pick the best 18 out of the material at its disposal."

Future Australian Test cricket captain Warwick Armstrong made his VFL debut with South Melbourne in 1898.

When Carlton defeated South by 17 points there was a realisation that the red and white again would struggle to make the finals. South did not notch a win until it defeated Collingwood by 11 points at the Lake Oval in the fourth round and, by then, the horse had bolted. South eventually notched seven wins from its 14 games to finish fifth. South had a long way to go to prove its worth in the new competition as, in its final normal premiership match of the season, went down by 55 points to Fitzroy at the Brunswick Street Oval, kicking just one goal in the process. South's 1.4 (10) will stand forever as its lowest score against Fitzroy and it was no consolation that Fitzroy went on to defeat Essendon by 15 points in the Grand Final.

However, that humiliating defeat was not South's last match of the season as the VFL that season introduced a complicated fixture in which teams finishing first, third, fifth and seventh played each other in one division and second, fourth, sixth and eighth played in the other division. As South finished fifth, it played Essendon (first), Fitzroy (third) and Carlton (seventh) in its sectional matches.

South battled gallantly in going down to Fitzroy by 14 points in the first of these matches and then losing by just 17 points to Essendon. In its final match of the season, South defeated Carlton by 25 points and, with

MATCH RESULTS

Round 1, at Princes Park, May 14
Carlton 6.11 (47) d South Melbourne 3.12 (30)

Round 2, at Lake Oval, May 21
Essendon 5.8 (38) d South Melbourne 3.9 (27)

Round 3, at Corio Oval, May 24
Geelong 7.18 (60) d South Melbourne 1.2 (8)

Round 4, at Lake Oval, May 28
South Melbourne 7.11 (53) d Collingwood 6.6 (42)

Round 5, at Junction Oval, June 4
South Melbourne 7.20 (62) d St Kilda 3.3 (21)

Round 6, at MCG, June 11
South Melbourne 2.3 (15) d Melbourne 1.7 (13)

Round 7, at Lake Oval, June 18
South Melbourne 7.9 (51) d Fitzroy 2.10 (22)

Round 8, at Lake Oval, June 25
South Melbourne 6.8 (44) d Carlton 1.6 (12)

Round 9, at East Melbourne CG, July 9
Essendon 7.12 (54) d South Melbourne 4.6 (30)

Round 10, at Lake Oval, July 16
Geelong 3.11 (29) d South Melbourne 1.3 (9)

Round 11, at Victoria Park, July 23
Collingwood 10.13 (73) d South Melbourne 1.7 (13)

Round 12, at Lake Oval, July 30
South Melbourne 12.15 (87) d St Kilda 3.6 (24)

Round 13, at Lake Oval, August 13
South Melbourne 6.7 (43) d Melbourne 5.8 (38)

Round 14, at Brunswick Street, August 20
Fitzroy 9.11 (65) d South Melbourne 1.4 (10)

Round 1, Section A, at Lake Oval, August 27
Fitzroy 6.11 (47) d South Melbourne 5.3 (33)

Round 2, Section A, at Lake Oval, September 3
Essendon 5.11 (41) d South Melbourne 3.6 (24)

Round 3, Section A, at Lake Oval, September 10
South Melbourne 6.11 (47) d Carlton 3.4 (22)

the top two teams in each group qualifying for the finals, missed the finals. Fitzroy then defeated Essendon by 15 points in what was the first VFL Grand Final. South's big problem the entire season was lack of firepower up forward. Its leading goalkicker, with just 13, was first-year player Charlie Colgan, recruited from West Melbourne. South kicked 10 goals or more in a match just once over the 1898 season, with its best score of 12.15 (87) against St Kilda at the Lake Oval in Round 12.

Warwick Windridge Armstrong might have played just 16 games with South Melbourne from 1898-1900, but achieved sports immortality as an Australian Test cricket captain. He was such a huge man in his cricket prime that it was said his bat looked like a matchstick in his hands. Standing 193cm (six feet, three inches), and with a huge girth, he was known in some circles as "Gulliver in flannels".

Armstrong was born in Kyneton, Victoria, on July 13, 1879, but his family moved to Melbourne when he was less than a year old. The Armstrongs settled in Emerald Hill (now South Melbourne) and then Caulfield. Not only did young Armstrong make his VFL debut with South in 1898 but, just months after the completion of the football season, made his first-class cricket debut for Victoria. He also scored a century for South Melbourne in the 1899-1900 season and made his Test debut against England in the 1901-02 series, therefore ending his football career.

Armstrong played 50 Tests for a batting average of 36.68 and a top score of 159 not out. He also took 87 wickets at 33.59, with best figures of 6/35.

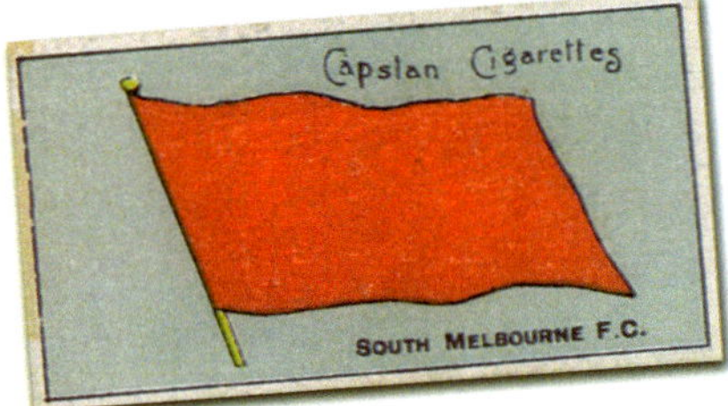

PLAYER	GAMES	GOALS
ADAMSON, Dave	12	1
ADAMSON, Jack	2	0
ARMSTRONG, Warwick	1	0
BROWN, Eddie	5	1
BURNS, Allen	13	7
CHANDLER, Joe	3	2
COLGAN, Charlie	16	13
CORNELIUS, George	16	2
DAVIDSON, George	17	0
DAVIS, Johnny	9	6
FLEMING, Jack	7	0
FRASER, Bill	15	4
GARDNER, Harry	4	0
GIBSON, Dick	16	6
GILLIGAN, Tom	17	12
HOWSON, Herb	11	0
JEANNERETT, Henri	17	0
JOLLY, Jim	7	0
KENNY, Bill	2	0
MACHIN, Archie	3	0
McARTHUR, Jim	1	0
McDERMOTT, John	5	3
McNAIR, Arch	6	0
O'DONNELL, Bob	3	2
O'GORMAN, Mick	1	0
O'HARA, Joe	2	1
PLEASS, George "Mick"	17	5
PURDY, Harry	16	4
RALPH, Jason	5	0
ROBERTSON, Val	6	0
SMITH, Tom	2	0
SOUTHERN, Jack	15	1
SPARROW, Jack	14	2
STRONG, Joe	2	0
TAYLOR, George	1	0
TRIM, Albert	17	0
WILLIAMSON, George	2	0
WINDLEY, Bill	17	1

POSITION: Fifth
COACH: -
CAPTAIN: Bill Fraser
BEST AND FAIREST: -
LEADING GOALKICKER: Charlie Colgan (13)

1899

South Melbourne started with a new slate in 1899, with 17 players from the previous season ending their VFL careers and another two, Michael O'Gorman and George Sparrow, switching to St Kilda. On the other side of the ledger, South introduced 16 new players, including two from rival VFL clubs — Essendon's Jim Cullen and Melbourne's Charlie Goding. Although Cullen played just one game with the Southerners before moving on to Carlton, Goding developed into one of the finest defenders in the competition and represented Victoria in 1901.

The pick of the other newcomers was big former Wagga forward Harry Lampe, who eventually developed into a superb and much feared half-back. He played 137 games with the Southerners to 1907 and had few peers in defence. Lampe played every game in his debut season and was enormously influential when the Southerners made a late push for the flag.

Also, South appointed David Adamson as captain to replace Bill Fraser. The lively ruckman, who had joined South from local club Napier Imperials, was just 24 years of age and in the prime of his career in 1899. Surprisingly, Adamson's appointment as captain was virtually ignored by the newspapers of the time and, for example, the *South Melbourne Record* concentrated on pre-season form.

The Southerners tuned up for the opening round match against Carlton at the Lake Oval with a match against Collingwood Juniors (virtually the Magpie reserves) and the *Record* noted: "On Saturday afternoon last South Melbourne was engaged with the Collingwood Juniors, who put 24 men into the field. For all the good that could be done a dozen might have been added to that number, for half a dozen of the South Melbourne team just did as they liked with the ball." It was hardly the ideal preparation for the opening round as South scored 12.9 (81) to the Collingwood Juniors' 1.1 (7). The *Record,* however, suggested Carlton would not catch South "napping" in the opening round and even said the Southerners' main problem would be selecting the best 18 from the talent available.

The match proved to be a cakewalk for the Southerners as, after Warwick Armstrong kicked South's first goal of the season, the

South Melbourne (hooped guernseys) players defend their goal against Collingwood. Note the caps, and even hats.

MATCH RESULTS

Round 1, at Lake Oval, May 13
South Melbourne 10.13 (73) d Carlton 2.6 (18)

Round 2, at Lake Oval, May 20
Fitzroy 6.6 (42) d South Melbourne 5.8 (38)

Round 3, at East Melbourne CG, May 24
Essendon 1.9 (15) d South Melbourne 0.9 (9)

Round 4, at Lake Oval, May 27
Collingwood 3.11 (29) d South Melbourne 3.4 (22)

Round 5, at Junction Oval, June 3
South Melbourne 10.10 (70) d St Kilda 4.9 (33)

Round 6, at Lake Oval, June 10
South Melbourne 5.5 (35) d Geelong 3.1 (19)

Round 7, at MCG, June 17
Melbourne 7.8 (50) d South Melbourne 6.7 (43)

Round 8, at Princes Park, June 24
Carlton 3.6 (24) d South Melbourne 0.5 (5)

Round 9, at Brunswick Street Oval, July 8
Fitzroy 9.8 (62) d South Melbourne 4.5 (29)

Round 10, at Lake Oval, July 15
Essendon 7.9 (51) d South Melbourne 5.5 (35)

Round 11, at Victoria Park, July 22
Collingwood 5.9 (39) d South Melbourne 5.6 (36)

Round 12, at Lake Oval, July 29
South Melbourne 8.9 (57) d St Kilda 3.6 (24)

Round 13, at Corio Oval, August 5
Geelong 7.12 (54) d South Melbourne 3.9 (27)

Round 14, at Lake Oval, August 12
South Melbourne 6.13 (49) d Melbourne 6.6 (42)

Round 1, Section B, at Corio Oval, August 26
South Melbourne 6.5 (41) d Geelong 5.8 (38)

Round 2, Section B, at Junction Oval, September 2
South Melbourne 12.10 (82) d St Kilda 1.6 (12)

Round 3, Section B, at Lake Oval, September 9
South Melbourne 3.10 (28) d Essendon 2.1 (13)

Grand Final, at Junction Oval, September 16

Fitzroy	0.1	2.4	2.6	3.9 (27)
South Melbourne	2.3	2.3	3.7	3.8 (26)

GOALS: South Melbourne — Lampe 2, Colgan.

Blues offered little resistance. South held Carlton goalless over the first three quarters and although the Blues broke through for two final quarter goals, the red and white triumphed by 55 points. The *Record* reported that South's optimism resulted in every

members' ticket being sold two hours before the start of play and more had to be printed the following week.

However, enthusiasm was dampened the following week when Fitzroy defeated South by four points, also at the Lake Oval. From there, South found it difficult to find any consistency and finished the normal season in sixth position, with five wins and nine defeats. That, however, was not the finish for the Southerners as the VFL again played a round-robin sectional system. The first, third, fifth and seventh teams competed in one section, with the second, fourth, sixth and eighth teams playing each other in the other section. The winners of these sections then played in the final for the premiership.

Although South struggled for much of the home and away season, it hit top form in the sectional matches in defeating Geelong by three points, St Kilda by 70 points and Essendon by 15 points. South therefore topped Section B to face Fitzroy, the Section A winner after topping the home and away ladder, in what was to be the Grand Final.

Fitzroy had been defeated just three times in 1899 and therefore went into the big match at the Junction Oval as firm favourite — until heavy rain threatened to turn the ground into a quagmire and therefore a slog. In fact, VFL officials almost postponed the match and decided to go ahead only after an inspection of the ground. South, meanwhile, had tremendous team problems, with several players unavailable through illness and injury.

Although club president Cr. Tom Craine had organised a team-bonding picnic at Mordialloc the Sunday before the Grand Final, South was devastated when brilliant rover Harry Purdy was declared unavailable because of illness and workhorse ruckman George "Mick" Pleass was forced to play despite a knee injury. The *Record* also reported that Henri Jeannerett had boils on the back of his neck and Fraser had a "stiff neck".

Just 4823 fans attended the big match and the *Record* reported they were "armed against the pluvial visitation with overcoats and umbrellas". South, despite its problems, took it up to the Maroons and led by five points going into the final quarter. Fitzroy kicked with the wind in that quarter and although the South defence stood firm, the Maroons grabbed the lead through a goal by Billy McSpeerin following a dubious free kick paid by umpire Ivo Crapp.

South attacked relentlessly over the final five minutes and, when Lampe sent a long shot towards goal, its efforts seemed certain to be rewarded. But, just as the ball was about to pass the line for a goal, Fitzroy captain Alex Sloan made a desperate lunge and touched it to force a behind. Fitzroy defeated the gallant Southerners by a single point.

In its Saturday, May 6, 1899 edition, *The South Melbourne Record* previewed the season ahead under the headline **FOOTBALL FOSSICKINGS**, written by "Rover" in snippets form. It read:

"The match between South Melbourne and Albert Park last Saturday afternoon was a kind of pipe opener for the red and white boys. The score, South Melbourne 16 goals 20 behinds, Albert Park six behinds, speaks for itself. Some good practice was indulged in, and at times some excellent play was witnessed.

"The only complaint South Melbourne has to find with itself so far this season is a surplus of players. They are simply treading over one another, and the selection committee must find it a pretty difficult matter to pick out the best 18 players from a supply of more than double that number. However, I sincerely hope that playing members will not take umbrage at being left out, but enter upon the season with a determination to do all that is possible in regaining for South its prestige of old.

* * *

"A good man is lost to South Melbourne in the person of Dick Gibson, who has taken to umpiring. Good luck to him!

* * *

"Old players are as a rule in good form, and the new ones are a very promising lot.

* * *

"Armstrong expects to play in a week or so; Adamson can do with a few good gallops; some fast training would suit Burns; Colgan wants to dodge more quickly; Davidson would be more successful if he took his kick; Gilligan is playing in grand form; Fraser should have been on the ball first match; Howson's leg is better and he is in good nick; Jeannerett is improving fast, as also is McNair, but a little more sprinting would do him good.

* * *

"Lampe has, I regret to say, been laid up with influenza, and may not be playing in the match this afternoon with the Collingwood Juniors."

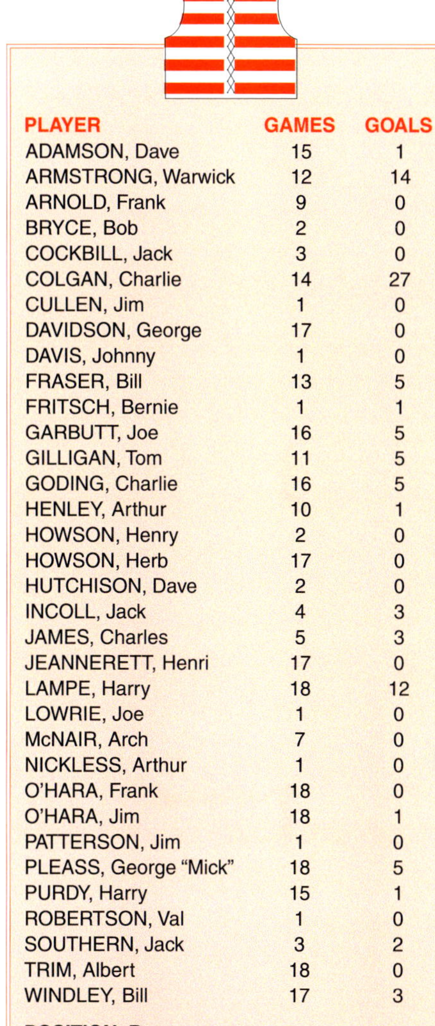

PLAYER	GAMES	GOALS
ADAMSON, Dave	15	1
ARMSTRONG, Warwick	12	14
ARNOLD, Frank	9	0
BRYCE, Bob	2	0
COCKBILL, Jack	3	0
COLGAN, Charlie	14	27
CULLEN, Jim	1	0
DAVIDSON, George	17	0
DAVIS, Johnny	1	0
FRASER, Bill	13	5
FRITSCH, Bernie	1	1
GARBUTT, Joe	16	5
GILLIGAN, Tom	11	5
GODING, Charlie	16	5
HENLEY, Arthur	10	1
HOWSON, Henry	2	0
HOWSON, Herb	17	0
HUTCHISON, Dave	2	0
INCOLL, Jack	4	3
JAMES, Charles	5	3
JEANNERETT, Henri	17	0
LAMPE, Harry	18	12
LOWRIE, Joe	1	0
McNAIR, Arch	7	0
NICKLESS, Arthur	1	0
O'HARA, Frank	18	0
O'HARA, Jim	18	1
PATTERSON, Jim	1	0
PLEASS, George "Mick"	18	5
PURDY, Harry	15	1
ROBERTSON, Val	1	0
SOUTHERN, Jack	3	2
TRIM, Albert	18	0
WINDLEY, Bill	17	3

POSITION: Runner-up
COACH: -
CAPTAIN: Dave Adamson
BEST AND FAIREST: -
LEADING GOALKICKER: Charlie Colgan (27)

1900

The 1900 VFL season opened with football taking second place in public attention to the Boer War. Melbourne's newspapers devoted many columns to the latest information from South Africa, although the *South Melbourne Record* ran a preview of the new season under the simple headline of FOOTBALL — SOUTH MELBOURNE FOOTBALL CLUB. The newspaper indicated that the "serious business of the season" started with the May 5 match against Essendon at the East Melbourne Cricket Ground.

The *Record* reported: "The South Melbourne team was chosen on Thursday evening and represent a force that will, with equal luck, be almost certain to score four points for the red and white colours." The *Record* also reported that, following the Thursday night training session, the players had elected defender George Davidson as club captain. It also noted that he "without doubt" would "handle the task with judgment and success".

Unfortunately, South did not have "equal luck" in this opening match against Essendon and Davidson, who had joined the Southerners from Albert Park, broke a leg in the final quarter and had to be carried from the ground. There were no reserves or interchange players in that era and South therefore had to complete the match one man short. Even worse, Davidson's injury was so severe that he had to retire prematurely. A great club man whose brother Jack also played with South, Davidson the following year donated a one-pound trophy to the "most consistent player at training".

Davidson was not the only South casualty against Essendon as Charlie Robertson twisted an ankle and Martin Gullan so severely injured a knee that he played just one more game before being forced into retirement. *The Age* reported on Davidson's injury: "G. Davidson, a fine footballer who had been playing splendidly, had his leg broken."

Regardless of the injuries, South was no match for Essendon, which led 8.4 to nil at half-time and went on to win by 56 points. It was a bitterly disappointing start to the season, but a 32-point win over St Kilda at the Lake Oval the following week lifted spirits. The Southerners in that match had a new captain in rover Bill Windley, a veteran who had played with South before the inaugural VFL season of 1897. He was 31 years of age when the players elected him captain to replace Davidson, but still an exceptionally talented footballer.

Said to have had "eel-like" evasive qualities, he was a great and extremely popular South identity for most of his life. Windley, who even bought his own membership ticket each season, played 129 VFL games to 1905 and then served the club for many years as the official ball steward.

Despite the easy victory over St Kilda in round two, South went down by 33 points to Fitzroy in its following match (played against a backdrop of enormous public jubilation over the relief of Makefing in the Boer War), on the

Bill "Marked" Windley, club captain in 1900, was a popular South Melbourne identity.

MATCH RESULTS

Round 1, at East Melbourne CG, May 5
Essendon 12.10 (82) d South Melbourne 4.2 (26)

Round 2, at Lake Oval, May 12
South Melbourne 6.21 (57) d St Kilda 3.7 (25)

Round 3, at Brunswick Street Oval, May 24
Fitzroy 6.19 (55) d South Melbourne 3.4 (22)

Round 4, at Lake Oval, May 26
South Melbourne 5.7 (37) d Geelong 3.5 (23)

Round 5, at Lake Oval, June 2
South Melbourne 6.8 (44) d Melbourne 6.5 (41)

Round 6, at Lake Oval, June 9
South Melbourne 4.6 (30) d Carlton 2.6 (18)

Round 7, at Lake Oval, June 23
South Melbourne 4.14 (38) d Essendon 1.4 (10)

Round 8, at Junction Oval, June 30
South Melbourne 5.22 (52) d St Kilda 1.5 (11)

Round 9, at Lake Oval, July 7
South Melbourne 3.8 (26) d Collingwood 2.12 (24)

Round 10, at Lake Oval, July 14
Fitzroy 5.9 (39) d South Melbourne 4.9 (33)

Round 11, at Corio Oval, July 28
Geelong 10.10 (70) d South Melbourne 3.6 (24)

Round 12, at MCG, August 4
South Melbourne 7.6 (48) d Melbourne 6.8 (44)

Round 13, at Princes Park, August 11
Carlton 5.15 (45) d South Melbourne 2.7 (19)

Round 14, at Victoria Park, August 18
Collingwood 5.15 (45) d South Melbourne 3.7 (25)

Round 1, Section A, at Lake Oval, August 25
Essendon 9.5 (59) d South Melbourne 3.1 (19)

Round 2, Section A, at Princes Park, September 1
Carlton 4.7 (31) d South Melbourne 4.6 (30)

Round 3, Section A, Brunswick Street Oval, Sept. 8
Fitzroy 7.9 (51) d South Melbourne 2.8 (20)

Queen's Birthday holiday of Thursday, May 24, before notching six consecutive wins in extraordinary circumstances. Firstly, South became embroiled in a bitter dispute with Geelong when the two teams clashed at the Lake Oval in round four. The South Melbourne Cricket Club, against tradition, charged visiting Geelong women members a fee for admission to the outer. Geelong was so outraged that, in retaliation, it charged all South members admission for the return match at Corio Oval. The VFL intervened and it finally was agreed there would be no charge for a visiting member to any ground.

Also, South's great run of six consecutive victories was helped by the fact that it played four consecutive games at the Lake Oval. This rare run of home games was caused by the postponement of round three, scheduled for May 19, because of heavy rain and flooded grounds. Instead, other rounds were brought forward and the "missing" round was played as round 14. South had been scheduled to play Collingwood at Victoria Park on May 19 and, instead, this game was played on August 18.

South at one stage had a record of six wins and two defeats, but fell away over the final weeks of the season. This slide was bitterly disappointing as the club had embarked on a massive recruiting drive over the previous summer. South in 1900 gave 13 players their VFL debuts, while Sam Brockwell (Geelong), Jack Davidson (Melbourne) and Les Vernon (Carlton) were recruited from rival VFL clubs.

Sadly, most of the 1900 recruits failed to live up to expectation and only defender Tom Wenborn made any real impact with the Southerners. Recruited from Brighton, he won himself a reputation as one of the red and white's best players and played 56 games with the club to 1906.

PLAYER	GAMES	GOALS
ADAMSON, Dave	16	1
ARMSTRONG, Warwick	3	4
BROCKWELL, Sam	15	4
BRYCE, Bob	3	1
CHAPMAN, Alf	2	0
COLGAN, Charlie	5	3
DAVIDSON, George	1	0
DAVIDSON, Jack	7	0
DOWSING, Stan	2	0
FRASER, Bill	17	5
GARBUTT, Joe	2	0
GARDNER, Harry	1	0
GODING, Charlie	8	7
GULLAN, Martin	2	1
HOWSON, Herb	16	0
JAMES, Charlie	8	3
JEANNERETT, Henri	15	7
LAMPE, Harry	17	16
McKEEGAN, Tim	2	0
MONKHOUSE, Fred	2	1
MOODIE, Bill	5	0
NELSON, Ernie	7	0
O'HARA, Frank	11	0
O'HARA, Jim	4	0
O'HEHIR, Mike	6	0
PLEASS, George "Mick"	14	2
PURDY, Harry	16	5
ROBERTSON, Charlie	5	0
ROSE, Albie	4	2
TRIMM, Albert	13	0
VERNON, Les	17	0
WAUGH, Fred	13	3
WENBORN, Tom	10	0
WILLIAMS, Bert	7	1
WILLIAMSON, Jim	13	0
WINDLEY, Bill	17	2

POSITION: Fifth
COACH: -
CAPTAIN: George Davidson, Bill Windley
BEST AND FAIREST: -
LEADING GOALKICKER: Harry Lampe (16)

South completed the premiership season with eight wins and six losses to finish fifth. Then, in its three sectional matches, went down to Essendon (40 points), Carlton (one) and Fitzroy (31) to finish bottom of Section A. The big loss to Essendon in the first of the sectional matches virtually ended South's hopes of reaching a second consecutive Grand Final and the Melbourne Tramway Company recognised the importance of the match as it rostered an extra 40 trams from the city to the Lake Oval. South scored just three goals and all were kicked by Harry Lampe, who scored one goal in the second quarter, one in the third and the other in the final quarter.

The original newspaper caption read ARE SOUTH WINNING? These are young South fans circa 1900, sitting outside the fence, and note the red and white banner two of them are holding.

This is how *The Australasian's* "Markwell" reported South's opening round match against Essendon at the East Melbourne Cricket Ground and George Davidson's career-ending injury:

"The only tally in the opening term was a goal secured by Essendon against the wind. Overwhelming advantage accrued to the home team when ends were changed, and goal upon goal to their credit went up with rapidity until at the interval the one-sided record read: Essendon 8.4, South Melbourne nothing.

"The Southerners' finest efforts were made during the third quarter when they put on 10 points to nothing; but they found the task of recovering the ground they had lost at the start an impossible one. Unfortunately for them, defeat was painfully associated with disaster. The game was not in any sense a rough one, though in the early stages the wind had tended to confine play to the lower half of the ground and the players were at times too closely packed in consequence. It was, however, not whilst the crush was thickest that damage was done, but in the second half, when the wind was weak and the play comparatively open.

"South's first great misfortune was encountered when the ex-Portsman (Port Melbourne), Robertson, sprained his ankle and had to be carried off the ground. The second loss was a veritable calamity, for it robbed them of their finest back player, their newly-elected skipper, G. Davidson, who, falling awkwardly, and by the purest accident, was unlucky enough to break his leg. This regrettable mishap occurred late in the concluding term."

On a more positive note, "Markwell" described the opening of the season as "excellent". He wrote: "All things conspired to make the opening day of the football season a success. The atmosphere was bright, clear and crisp and, save for a stiffish north wind that prevailed only up to half-time, the meteorological conditions were perfect. Ground and ball were pleasingly dry in every instance and, with perhaps the exception of Victoria Park (where Collingwood defeated Fitzroy), where top-dressing had begun a trifle late, the turf upon every enclosure was delightfully springy, and therefore suited to the requirements of the sprinter."

1901

South Melbourne prepared for the 1901 season with a practice match against neighbouring VFA club Port Melbourne, often referred to in that era as "Ports" and had a comfortable win to suggest the Southerners would start the VFL season well against St Kilda at the Junction Oval.

The *South Melbourne Record* in the edition leading up to the match against St Kilda reported that veteran Bill Windley was the players' favourite for the captaincy, but the champion rover declined because he felt a younger player should take charge. Captains at that time also assumed the role of coach and Windley, at 32 years of age, wanted to concentrate on his own game.

With Windley's surprise refusal to accept the captaincy, the job fell to defender Albert Trim, who had joined South from Beechworth in 1898. Regarded as one of the best players in the VFL, Trim had represented Victoria in 1899 and was renowned for his dogged containment of dangerous forwards. The 1901 season was the only one in which he captained South as he returned to the country the following year and moved to Carlton in 1903.

South introduced nine players to VFL football in 1901, but again with limited success. The best of the newcomers was pacy forward Bill Scott, recruited from Brighton and Haileybury College. Scott, whose brother Alf played with St Kilda over the 1900-01 seasons, played 61 games with South to 1906. Another 1901 newcomer, rover Frank Worroll, represented Victoria in his debut season after moving from VFA club Williamstown, but played just 31 games with South to 1903. The only recruit with VFL experience was Harold Rippon, who had played four games with Melbourne in 1898, but he did not play a senior game until 1903.

South was expected to thrash St Kilda in the opening round match as the Saints had tasted victory just once in its first four VFL seasons. That was against Melbourne in the opening round of the 1900 season, but only after a protest. The match originally had been declared a draw, but the Saints successfully protested that one of Melbourne's behinds had been scored after the bell for three-quarter time.

If the South players expected a cakewalk against St Kilda, they would have been stunned by the home side's determination and persistence. Although South led by 22 points at the final change, it scraped home by eight points. The match report in *The Age* the

Fans at a South Melbourne match against Fitzroy at the Brunswick Street Oval. South often found the Maroons a formidable opponent in the VFL's earliest years.

MATCH RESULTS

Round 1, at Junction Oval, May 4
South Melbourne 6.13 (49) d St Kilda 6.5 (41)

Round 2, at MCG, May 9
South Melbourne 5.10 (40) d Melbourne 5.6 (36)

Round 3, at Lake Oval, May 11
South Melbourne 9.4 (58) d Collingwood 6.11 (47)

Round 4, at Princes Park, May 18
Carlton 4.3 (27) d South Melbourne 3.7 (25)

Round 5, at Lake Oval, May 25
Fitzroy 6.5 (41) d South Melbourne 3.7 (25)

Round 6, at Lake Oval, June 1
Essendon 3.23 (41) d South Melbourne 5.5 (35)

Round 7, at Corio Oval, June 3
Geelong 9.11 (65) d South Melbourne 3.4 (22)

Round 8, at Lake Oval, June 8
South Melbourne 7.14 (56) d St Kilda 1.1 (7)

Round 9, at Lake Oval, June 22
Melbourne 9.7 (61) d South Melbourne 6.9 (45)

Round 10, at Victoria Park, June 29
South Melbourne 7.9 (51) d Collingwood 5.1 (31)

Round 11, at Lake Oval, July 6
South Melbourne 10.10 (70) d Carlton 3.2 (20)

Round 12, at Brunswick Street Oval, July 13
South Melbourne 12.7 (79) d Fitzroy 9.11 (65)

Round 13, at East Melbourne CG, July 20
Essendon 6.16 (52) d South Melbourne 8.3 (51)

Round 14, at Lake Oval, July 27
Geelong 6.13 (49) d South Melbourne 6.9 (45)

Round 1, Section A, at Lake Oval, August 10
Essendon 10.9 (69) d South Melbourne 1.3 (9)

Round 2, Section A, at Corio Oval, August 17
Geelong 7.12 (54) d South Melbourne 4.6 (30)

Round 3, Section A, at Princes Park, August 24
South Melbourne 4.13 (37) d Carlton 3.6 (24)

following Monday noted: "Against their heavier South Melbourne opponents the light, smart men of the St Kilda team made such a gallant fight that within a couple of minutes of time they were only two points behind, and then a final goal by South Melbourne left the Saints beaten by eight points." The report suggested that Windley, "who retains all his marvellous vitality", was one of South's best players, along with ruckman/defender Joe Garbutt.

It might have been a narrow escape, but South five days later defeated Melbourne by four points at the MCG. This match, part of round two, was played on the Thursday public holiday to celebrate the opening of the first Commonwealth Parliament. Just two days later, South defeated Collingwood by 11 points at Lake Oval for a hat-trick of wins and was referred to as one of the premiership favourites.

Unfortunately, South's form fell away and four consecutive defeats ruined any hopes of a first VFL flag. The Southerners finished the normal premiership season with seven wins and seven defeats to finish fifth but, for the first time, the three-round sectional matches counted towards an overall ladder and the Southerners therefore still had high hopes of reaching the finals.

There was a week's break before the sectional matches and South took advantage of this to travel to the north of Victoria to play country club Rutherglen. It should have been a romp, yet the locals defeated South by 13 points in a huge upset. The *Rutherglen Sun and Chiltern Valley Advertiser* ran a full match report and indicated that "large numbers" at Barkly Park watched an exciting match. Fans also were entertained by the Rutherglen Brass Band and local businesses shut down for the afternoon, with the match starting at 3.30pm.

The newspaper reported: "The result of the match was a great surprise to the majority of the spectators, as it generally was anticipated that South Melbourne would romp over the local team and that the game would be of a one-sided nature." South had no excuses as all but one of its men had played at least one VFL game. Also, 29 years before the VFL introduced the concept of a nineteenth man, the one player without VFL experience — known only as Noonan — replaced the injured Bill O'Hara (foot) for the second half.

W. SCOTT

South therefore went into the sectional matches with its tail between its legs and played accordingly. Playing in Section A, it went down to Essendon by 60 points at the Lake Oval the week after the Rutherglen humiliation and then by 24 points to Geelong at the Corio Oval. South salvaged some pride with a 13-point win over Carlton at Princes Park in its final sectional match and therefore finished sixth on what was described as "the completed ladder".

South not only had to play two matches in three days over rounds two and three, but also had to play two matches over three days in rounds six and seven. After going down to Essendon by six points at the Lake Oval in round six, the Southerners fronted up against Geelong at the Corio Oval on a public holiday the following Monday. Geelong won by 43 points.

South Melbourne fans in the outer at Fitzroy's Brunswick Street Oval. Fitzroy was South's nemesis club in the early VFL years.

Early football writer "Markwell" produced florid copy and his description of the opening day of the 1901 season was among his most colourful. He wrote under the headline **BRILLIANT OPENING SCENE:**

"A bright and windless afternoon was vouchsafed for the initial premiership encounters and spectators lined the various grounds in numbers almost as great as used to assemble on first days when the game was at the zenith of its popularity. I doubt, indeed, whether on this occasion the aggregate of onlookers fell in any degree short of the best record of the past. That attendances are better distributed than formerly must be admitted.

"Interest in olden times was generally concentrated on a single fixture, where now in senior ranks every match proves sufficiently attractive to draw its thousands; and besides our League and Association tussles, there is an ever-increasing number of junior matches, from those played by clubs connected with the Victoria J.A. (Junior Association) and the Metropolitan J.A. down to the fifth, and perhaps lower raters, all of them commanding the presence and attention of more or less considerable bands of followers.

"A fairly accurate estimate of the number of adult denizens of Melbourne and suburbs for whom football provided an afternoon's pleasurable entertainment this day, would, I am sure, total from 50,000 to 60,000. Add to these the crowds who watched the play at Ballarat, Bendigo and other provincial centres, and include besides attendances at games in less important country places, and the grand total must be set down at not less than 100,000."

PLAYER	GAMES	GOALS
ADAMSON, Dave	16	3
BOWER, Harold	5	7
BURNS, Allen	11	7
COLGAN, Charlie	2	0
CULLEN, Paul	1	0
DOWSING, Stan	4	0
FRASER, Bill	16	1
GARBUTT, Joe	15	5
GODING, Charlie	14	19
HOLLIS, Arthur	4	0
HOWSON, Herb	13	1
JACKSON, Johnny	3	1
JAMES, Charlie	17	1
JEANNERETT, Henri	14	3
LAMPE, Harry	12	20
O'HARA, Frank	3	0
O'HARA, Jim	1	0
O'HARA, J.W. "Bill"	5	2
O'HEHIR, Mike	12	2
PLEASS, George "Mick"	15	11
POWELL, Dave	9	2
PURDY, Harry	12	3
RIPPON, Norm	13	1
ROBERTSON, Charlie	1	0
ROSE, Albie	2	0
SCOTT, Bill	3	0
SMITH, Arthur	9	0
TRIM, Albert	17	0
VERNON, Les	2	0
WENBORN, Tom	17	0
WILLIAMSON, Jim	9	0
WINDLEY, Bill	13	11
WORROLL, Frank	16	6

POSITION: Sixth
COACH: -
CAPTAIN: Albert Trim
BEST AND FAIREST: -
LEADING GOALKICKER: Harry Lampe (20)

1902

South Melbourne again prepared for its new season with a practice match against VFA club Port Melbourne and defeated "Ports" by 15 points. Then, after training the following Thursday night, the players elected veteran Bill Windley club captain, with Dave Adamson his deputy. Windley by now was 33 years of age, but still was one of the best players in the competition. Adamson also was an extremely experienced player and had captained Victoria the previous season.

The *South Melbourne Record* suggested: "As these players were elected without opposition, it remains for players to follow the advice tendered to them, and to rigidly obey orders, to render a good account of themselves throughout the season."

Much depended on Windley and Adamson as there was little other quality and the club gave 17 players VFL debuts in 1902. Both lived up to their reputations, with Windley still one of the best small men in the competition and Adamson as solid and reliable as ever on the ball.

The best of the newcomers was football nomad Harvey Kelly, a brilliant forward from Graham Street Wesley. Kelly played just nine games in 1902 before moving to South Fremantle and then returning to Victoria in 1907 to spend three seasons with Carlton. He moved to Tasmania in 1910 and returned to South in 1913 as coach.

The only recruits from rival VFL clubs were Tom Fogarty, who had played 10 games with St Kilda in 1898, and Alf Wallace, who had played two games with St Kilda in 1899 before seeing service in the Boer War. Wallace played just two games with South, but Fogarty proved an excellent signing as he played 66 games with the Southerners to 1906 before making a comeback with University when it joined the VFL in 1908.

Despite the pre-season optimism, the Southerners played poorly at the Lake Oval in the opening round of the VFL season, going down to Collingwood by 18 points. The Southerners played so poorly that the *Record* noted that good play was "entirely absent".

South, however, improved dramatically the following week to thrash Carlton by 53 points at the Lake Oval and keeping the Blues goalless in the process. The *Record,* after commenting that the chrysanthemums around the cricket ground were in bloom and that Stender's South Melbourne Band entertained the 4000 fans during breaks, reported that South demoralised Carlton with its teamwork.

Although this huge win should have been the springboard for continued success, South fell away over the following weeks and eventually ended the 14-round premiership season in seventh position (above only the winless St Kilda) with just five wins. Wins over Geelong and Fitzroy in three sectional matches lifted South to fifth position, but eight match points behind fourth-placed Melbourne.

The *Record's* unnamed football reporter made this assessment of South's 1902 season: "Out of the 17 matches played, seven were won and 10 lost, their points being 700, with 704 against. Prior to Saturday's game (against Fitzroy), the South were second last, but through the defeat of Carlton and Geelong, together with their fine average (percentage) for the season, they occupy fifth place.

"The players constituting the team this season were a splendid lot, and

MATCH RESULTS

Round 1, at Lake Oval, May 3
Collingwood 5.13 (43) d South Melbourne 3.7 (25)

Round 2, at Lake Oval, May 10
South Melbourne 8.13 (61) d Carlton 0.8 (8)

Round 3, at Brunswick Street Oval, May 17
Fitzroy 8.10 (58) d South Melbourne 8.4 (52)

Round 4, at East Melbourne CG, May 24
Essendon 5.8 (38) d South Melbourne 4.11 (35)

Round 5, at Corio Oval, May 31
Geelong 5.14 (44) d South Melbourne 3.9 (27)

Round 6, at Lake Oval, June 7
South Melbourne 5.13 (43) d St Kilda 1.3 (9)

Round 7, at MCG, June 9
Melbourne 7.5 (47) d South Melbourne 6.10 (46)

Round 8, at Victoria Park, June 14
Collingwood 4.26 (50) d South Melbourne 1.8 (14)

Round 9, at Princes Park, June 21
Carlton 4.7 (31) d South Melbourne 2.6 (18)

Round 10, at Lake Oval, July 5
South Melbourne 6.10 (46) d Fitzroy 4.10 (34)

Round 11, at Lake Oval, July 12
Essendon 6.7 (43) d South Melbourne 5.6 (36)

Round 12, at Lake Oval, July 19
South Melbourne 7.13 (55) d Geelong 6.9 (45)

Round 13, at Junction Oval, July 26
South Melbourne 5.7 (37) d St Kilda 2.10 (22)

Round 14, at Lake Oval, August 2
Melbourne 9.9 (63) d South Melbourne 3.9 (27)

Round 1, Section A, at Victoria Park, August 16
Collingwood 12.12 (84) d South Melbourne 5.14 (44)

Round 2, Section A, at Lake Oval, August 23
South Melbourne 12.12 (84) d Geelong 5.9 (39)

Round 3, Section A, at Brunswick Street Oval, Aug 30
South Melbourne 7.8 (50) d Fitzroy 6.10 (46)

taking the play throughout the season, I have no hesitation in naming N. (Norm) Rippon (centre) as their best player during that period." This was an amazing assessment as Rippon was merely handy, whereas Windley and Dave Adamson played all games and, according to the daily newspapers, both had excellent seasons.

Football writer "Markwell" waxed lyrical over the start of the 1902 season when he wrote in *The Australasian:*

"Nothing has been neglected by League, Association or club executives in their endeavour to make the opening day of season 1902 worthy of the national winter sport of Australia.

"For the past month delegates to either of the two great governing bodies (VFL and VFA) have held almost continuous sittings, working out their plans of campaign, testing and selecting their field and goal umpires, deciding the claims of applicants for transfers from club to club, and giving their best attention to a hundred and one other matters of detail, the overlooking of which might entail consequences disastrous to the life and progress of the game.

"And while delegates have been thus wholesomely engaged, secretaries and committees of clubs have had their energies taxed and their days and nights fully employed in efforts to furnish their teams with recruits of the requisite stamp. To this end search parties were early afoot, and journeys were undertaken, not alone to more or less remote suburbs, but to distant provincial centres as well."

"Markwell" noted that club officials would "undertake any journey" if there was the slightest prospect of signing a future champion and suggested that competition was "keener than ever" to spot talented youngsters.

PLAYER	GAMES	GOALS
ADAMSON, Arthur	13	0
ADAMSON, Dave	17	2
ALLEY, Ned	15	2
BOWER, Harold	8	0
BURNS, Allen	2	0
CORMACK, John	1	1
DOWSING, Stan	3	2
FAHEY, Bill	3	1
FOGARTY, Henry	1	0
FOGARTY, Tom	13	7
FRASER, Bill	9	2
GARBUTT, Joe	6	0
GODING, Charlie	14	19
HAIGBLOOM, Charlie	1	0
HAMMOND, Henry	2	0
HASSETT, Jack	1	0
HICKEY, Bill	5	1
HOWSON, Herb	15	0
JACKSON, Johnny	5	0
JAMES, Charlie	5	0
JEANNERETT, Henri	2	1
JOHNSON, Bill	2	4
KELLY, Harvey	9	4
KELLY, Otto	16	0
KING, Jim	14	0
LAMPE, Harry	8	4
McDONOUGH, Jack	7	0
McDOUGALL, Ernie	3	3
PLEASS, George "Mick"	13	9
POWELL, Dave	12	8
RIPPON, Norm	15	0
ROSE, Albie	6	9
SCOTT, Bill	6	1
SMITH, Len	1	0
STANWORTH, Jim	1	0
WALLACE, Alf	2	4
WILLIAMSON, Jim	8	0
WINDLEY, Bill	17	4
WORROLL, Frank	14	6

POSITION: Fifth
COACH: -
CAPTAIN: Bill Windley
BEST AND FAIREST: -
LEADING GOALKICKER: Charlie Goding (19)

1903

South Melbourne defeated VFA club Port Melbourne by five points in a practice match a week before the opening of the 1903 VFL season and was given a huge boost the following Wednesday night when star recruit Bill Gent was cleared from VFA club Essendon Town. Gent (named as Ghent in the *South Melbourne Record*) was a quality rover who was expected to give the Southerners a touch of class around the packs and lived up to his reputation with a fine VFL debut season. However, he had a controversial career with South as he served a 20-match suspension for striking from late in 1904 and missed the entire 1905 season. He also was suspended for "life" in 1907, although this later was reduced to seven games. Gent retired in 1908 after playing 62 games in the red and white.

A South Melbourne team of 1903, with skipper Tom Fogarty, fifth from the left in the middle row.

Yet again, South recruited far and wide and gave 19 players (including Gent) VFL debuts, although 11 of these newcomers had just the one season at the elite level. Gent undoubtedly was the pick of the recruits, but South also debuted former champion Port Melbourne centreman Bill McGee, who went on to captain the club the following year and whose grandsons Jeff ("Torchy") and Terry later played for the club. Defender Len Incigneri might have played just two games with South over the 1903 and 1905 seasons, but later captained both Richmond and Melbourne.

The players after training on the Thursday night before the start of the season elected follower Tom Fogarty as captain, with full-back Charlie James, recruited locally from Albert Park in 1899, his deputy. The *Record* reported that Fogarty, after being elected, told the players: "We have a good team and with careful attention to training and playing to one

MATCH RESULTS

Round 1, at Lake Oval, May 2
South Melbourne 6.14 (50) d Melbourne 5.13 (43)

Round 2, at Victoria Park, May 9
Collingwood 13.14 (92) d South Melbourne 3.6 (24)

Round 3, at Brunswick Street Oval, May 16
Fitzroy 12.17 (89) d South Melbourne 3.4 (22)

Round 4, at Lake Oval, May 23
Geelong 6.11 (47) d South Melbourne 5.7 (37)

Round 5, at Lake Oval, May 30
Carlton 10.7 (67) d South Melbourne 5.4 (34)

Round 6, at East Melbourne CG, June 6
South Melbourne 6.12 (48) d Essendon 5.11 (41)

Round 7, at Lake Oval, June 8
St Kilda 6.11 (47) d South Melbourne 5.8 (38)

Round 8, at MCG, June 13
Melbourne 6.6 (42) d South Melbourne 3.17 (35)

Round 9, at Lake Oval, June 20
Collingwood 6.6 (42) d South Melbourne 4.11 (35)

Round 10, at Lake Oval, July 4
Fitzroy 7.11 (53) d South Melbourne 5.7 (37)

Round 11, at Corio Oval, July 11
Geelong 9.13 (67) d South Melbourne 3.12 (30)

Round 12, at Princes Park, July 18
Carlton 7.8 (50) d South Melbourne 2.8 (20)

Round 13, at Lake Oval, July 25
Essendon 7.17 (59) d South Melbourne 5.7 (37)

Round 14, at Junction Oval, August 8
St Kilda 12.9 (81) d South Melbourne 4.8 (32)

Round 1, Section B, at Lake Oval, August 15
Geelong 12.14 (86) d South Melbourne 8.8 (56)

Round 2, Section B, at Brunswick Street Oval, Aug 22
Fitzroy 11.17 (83) d South Melbourne 3.5 (23)

Round 3, Section B, at East Melbourne CG, Aug 29
Essendon 14.10 (94) d South Melbourne 5.7 (37)

another on the field, we will come out on top at the end of the season."

South opened the season against Melbourne at the Lake Oval and the *Record* noted: "The season opened under happy conditions on Saturday last, the day being all that could be desired for football. It was indeed a sight to see the people flocking to the ground, all hurrying along to avoid the crush."

South led from the start but, according to the *Record,* "showed little or no system". Regardless, the Southerners defeated Melbourne by seven points to suggest an improvement on 1902. Unfortunately, it proved to be a false dawn as South lost its next four games before defeating Essendon by seven points at the East Melbourne Cricket Ground.

It was South's last win of the season and, with just two wins, collected the club's first VFL wooden spoon, one game and a wide percentage margin behind seventh-placed Melbourne. There were no excuses, even though former captain Dave Adamson played just the one game before being seriously injured and forced into retirement.

The Southerners in round seven even suffered the indignity of going down to St Kilda in a VFL match for the first time. St Kilda defeated South by nine points at the Lake Oval and, to rub salt into the wound, defeated its lakeside neighbour by 49 points at the Junction Oval in the return match.

South endured a miserable 1903 season, but there was one VFL innovation which, in hindsight, was a pointer to the club's long-term future. The VFL, determined to spread the indigenous code north of the Murray, played its first match for premiership points at the Sydney Cricket Ground — 79 years before South flew north to become the Sydney Swans. The pioneer clubs were Fitzroy and Collingwood, who clashed in Sydney in round four on May 23 in front of 18,000 fans. The Maroons defeated the Magpies by seven points and the response was so strong that it was arranged for Fitzroy to play an exhibition match at the SCG two years later — against South Melbourne.

PLAYER	GAMES	GOALS
ADAMSON, Arthur	15	0
ADAMSON, Dave	1	0
ALLEY, Ned	1	0
BAPTISTE, Nick	7	0
BOLES, Joe	1	1
BOURNE, Charles	1	0
BURNS, Allen	1	0
BUTLER, Archie	2	0
BUTLER, Charlie	5	0
CAMERON, Jim	5	0
CAVANAN, Joe	8	7
CORMACK, John	4	2
FOGARTY, Tom	13	0
FOX, Joe	1	0
FRASER, Bill	3	0
GENT, Bill	17	6
GODING, Charlie	10	10
GUY, Harry	4	0
HASSETT, Jack	15	6
HICKEY, Bill	17	0
HOWSON, Herb	16	0
INCIGNERI, Len	1	0
JAMES, Charlie	16	6
JEANNERETT, Henri	10	1
JOHNSON, Bill	8	3
KING, Jim	1	0
LAMPE, Harry	14	5
LITTLER, H. "Joe"	10	9
McCASHNEY, Jim	2	0
McDONOUGH, Jack	14	3
McDOUGALL, Ernie	1	0
McGEE, Bill	9	2
McKELSON, Ollie	1	0
NEWBOLD, Tom	1	0
O'CONNELL, Ossie	1	1
PLEASS, George "Mick"	15	5
POWELL, Dave	6	3
RICHARDS, Chris	1	1
RIPPON, Harold	5	0
RIPPON, Norm	7	1
SCOTT, Bill	14	3
TODD, Jack	7	0
WEST, Charlie	3	0
WINDLEY, Bill	14	0
WORROLL, Frank	1	0

POSITION: Eighth
COACH: -
CAPTAIN: Tom Fogarty
BEST AND FAIREST: -
LEADING GOALKICKER: Charlie Goding (10)

1904

South Melbourne had a major setback in the lead-up to the 1904 season when the VFL Permit Committee refused to endorse a clearance for former Carlton player Bill Monagle, who had played 17 games with the Blues in 1899. South had selected Monagle to captain the club and, instead, turned to centreman Bill McGee, who had joined the Southerners from Port Melbourne the previous season.

The good news for South was that it won a clearance for Brunswick (VFA) forward Charles Clements, regarded as one of the best goalsneaks in Victorian football. However, Clements did not receive his permit until after the opening match of the season, against Essendon at the East Melbourne Cricket Ground, but kicked a season's total of 37 goals to top the club's goalkicking. South's other prize recruit in 1904 was ruckman Bill Strang, who went on to play 69 games in the red and white to 1913 and whose sons Doug, Gordon, Colin and Alan all played in the VFL.

Essendon thrashed South by 41 points in that opening round match and *The Herald* noted that Essendon made the most of kicking with a strong wind behind it in the opening quarter. The Same-Old (as Essendon was known) kicked five goals to South's one behind and, from there, the result was not in doubt, despite gallant efforts by McGee to rally his team.

Clements made his debut the following week against Carlton and kicked his side's only goal (in the first quarter) in the 17-point defeat. South's season had started disastrously and noted football writer "Markwell", of *The Australasian,* suggested South showed "a lack of organisation — exactly the same weakness that for years has kept the Southerners from making headway".

South was a rank outsider to defeat Collingwood at Victoria Park in round three, but defeated the Magpies by 26 points, a huge margin considering it rained heavily for most of the match. "Markwell" wrote that although South's win would have surprised thousands of football fans, "the victory ... was gained unequivocally on merit".

The win inspired South to victories over Geelong, Melbourne and St Kilda over the following three weeks to have the Southerners second on the ladder behind Fitzroy and seemingly headed for the finals. However, the Maroons pipped the Southerners by a point at the Brunswick Street Oval, with champion Fitzroy rover Percy Trotter kicking the winning goal from a free kick.

The seventh round was followed by a week's break that did little to upset South's rhythm. Although some clubs elected to play practice matches on the week the VFL played the VFA and Collingwood even played Castlemaine, South rested its players in preparation for the big clash against Essendon at the Lake Oval. South won by 40 points, thanks largely to the fine roving of Harry Gibson and the strong ruck work of skipper McGee.

Although Carlton defeated South in the following round, the red and white won four of its last five matches, with its only defeat at the hands of Fitzroy — by 12 points — at the Lake Oval in the final round. South therefore was well placed for a crack at the premiership as it had finished the home and away season in third position behind Fitzroy and Carlton with the sectional matches to be played. Interestingly, Victoria defeated Western Australia by 34 points at the MCG in the week before the South-Fitzroy match and one of WA's stars was full-back Bert Franks who joined South in 1906.

Unfortunately for South, it was drawn

MATCH RESULTS

Round 1, at East Melbourne CG, May 7
Essendon 8.10 (58) d South Melbourne 2.5 (17)

Round 2, at Lake Oval, May 14
Carlton 5.6 (36) d South Melbourne 1.13 (19)

Round 3, at Victoria Park, May 21
South Melbourne 7.13 (55) d Collingwood 4.5 (29)

Round 4, at Corio Oval, May 28
South Melbourne 6.16 (52) d Geelong 6.4 (40)

Round 5, at Lake Oval, June 4
South Melbourne 8.16 (64) d Melbourne 5.9 (39)

Round 6, at Lake Oval, June 6
South Melbourne 15.10 (100) d St Kilda 9.4 (58)

Round 7, at Brunswick Street, June 11
Fitzroy 6.9 (45) d South Melbourne 5.14 (44)

Round 8, at Lake Oval, June 25
South Melbourne 10.9 (69) d Essendon 4.5 (29)

Round 9, at Princes Park, July 2
Carlton 9.7 (61) d South Melbourne 5.7 (37)

Round 10, at Lake Oval, July 9
South Melbourne 5.15 (45) d Collingwood 6.6 (42)

Round 11, at Lake Oval, July 16
South Melbourne 6.5 (41) d Geelong 4.15 (39)

Round 12, at MCG, July 23
South Melbourne 11.7 (73) d Melbourne 9.13 (67)

Round 13, at Junction Oval, July 30
South Melbourne 10.5 (65) d St Kilda 6.10 (46)

Round 14, at Lake Oval, August 13
Fitzroy 8.10 (58) d South Melbourne 5.16 (46)

Round 1, Section A, at Brunswick Street, August 20
Fitzroy 4.14 (38) d South Melbourne 3.15 (33)

Round 2, Section B, at Lake Oval, August 27
Essendon 8.11 (59) d South Melbourne 4.3 (27)

Round 3, Section C, at Corio Oval, September 3
South Melbourne 6.8 (44) d Geelong 3.4 (22)

against nemesis club Fitzroy in its opening sectional match and went down by just five points in wet conditions at Brunswick Street. "Markwell" suggested a draw would have been a fairer result and added: "South commanded admiration and applause with its brilliant and persevering efforts."

South was gutted by its third narrow loss to Fitzroy in the one season and went down to Essendon by 32 points at the Lake Oval the following week. Its season virtually was over and not even a 22-point win over Geelong at the Corio Oval in the final sectional match could lift the Southerners into the finals. They finished fifth, behind fourth-placed Essendon only on percentage. To rub salt into South's wounds, Fitzroy defeated Carlton by 24 points in the Grand Final. For South, it was a case of so near, so far. The only consolation was that Clements' 37 goals in 1904 was second only to Melbourne's Vince Coutie (39).

When Bill Strang debuted with South Melbourne as a 20-year-old in 1904, he would not have dreamed he was starting a football dynasty. Strang left the Lake Oval in 1913 to start a business in Albury and raised a family.

Four Strang sons played in the VFL. Alan played 15 games with South in 1947-48, brothers Doug and Gordon joined Richmond and another brother, Colin, played for St Kilda. Gordon Strang played 116 games for the Tigers from 1931-36 and in 1938, while Doug played 64 games from 1931-35. Both Gordon and Doug played in the Tigers' 1932 premiership side, while Doug kicked 14 goals (plus two behinds) in a 1931 match against North Melbourne at the Punt Road Oval. Colin played two games for the Saints in 1933.

Doug's son Geoff also played with Richmond, in 88 games from 1965-71. He bettered his father and uncle by playing in two Tiger premiership sides, in 1967 and 1969. A hard-hitting half-back, Geoff Strang also played in North Adelaide's 1972 SANFL premiership side.

PLAYER	GAMES	GOALS
BRUTON, Henry	2	0
BUTLER, Charlie	1	0
CAMERON, Jim	13	4
CATARINICH, John	4	0
CLEMENTS, Charles	16	37
DARCY, Jim	1	0
DAYKIN, Robert	1	0
FOGARTY, Tom	15	3
FRASER, Bill	1	0
GENT, Billy	14	5
GIBSON, Harry	12	5
GODING, Charlie	1	0
GRIFFITHS, Bill	8	0
HAIGBLOOM, Charlie	5	1
HASSETT, Jack	15	12
HAWKINS, Tom	1	0
HICKEY, Bill	17	0
HOGAN, Con	1	0
HOPE, Les	1	1
HOWSON, Herb	16	0
JAMES, Charlie	16	0
JOHNSON, Edmund	1	0
JOHNSON, Bill	14	0
KIDGELL, Morley	5	0
LAMPE, Harry	17	0
McCANN, Charlie	1	0
McCOLL, David	5	0
McGEE, Bill	14	5
McKAY, Dick	17	0
PERCY, Algy	2	0
PLEASS, George "Mick"	3	0
SCHELLNACK, Jim	7	6
SCOTT, Bill	17	8
SHARPE, Bert	7	6
STRANG, Bill	7	7
WEATE, Bill	2	1
WENBORN, Tom	11	0
WINDLEY, Bill	11	9
WRIGHT, Sam	3	0

POSITION: Fifth
COACH: -
CAPTAIN: Bill McGee
BEST AND FAIREST: -
LEADING GOALKICKER: Charles Clements (37)

1905

South prepared for the 1905 season with a practice match against Leopold (navy blue and white), a local club which later served the Southerners as an ad hoc reserves combination. As South was much stronger, it allowed Leopold to play with an extra two men. It made little difference as South won easily, with several recruits impressing football writer "Markwell", who named South Australian Fred O'Brien, Brunswick's Dick Casey and South Ballarat's Archie Pratt as players to watch.

Unfortunately, neither O'Brien nor Pratt made an impact with the Southerners, but Casey was a wonderfully competitive rover who played with such unfettered aggression that VFL officials in 1906 warned him to curb his ways. He went on to play 112 games with South to 1912, but missed the 1909 premiership side because of injury.

In the week before the opening round of matches, "Markwell" also referred to the reason why former Carlton star Bill Monagle had been refused a clearance to South the previous season. He reported that, just 12 months after the VFL Permits Committee had rejected Monagle's application to join South, it also knocked back a bid by former Fitzroy player Chris Kiernan to join Collingwood.

"Markwell" wrote: "The mere suspicion that

The South Melbourne team and officials, photographed before the SCG match against Fitzroy.

a man is inclined to make a profession of the game almost bars him for life, thus it is that Monagle is unable to play with South and who would have been a master of tactics has been told that League football is not for him. The case of C. Kiernan is on a par with that of Monagle."

South opened the season against Geelong at the Corio Oval and *The Herald* reported a good attendance, although it added that the playing surface was "as hard as a macadamised road". The newspaper also reported that Bill McGee again had been appointed South captain, with Tom Fogarty his deputy.

South, with rover Jack "Paddy" Hasett in fine form, defeated the Pivotonians by 23 points and *The Herald* noted that South seemed fitter than a Geelong team that wilted in the heat after leading by two goals at the main break. The unnamed reporter wrote that some players "were holding out signals of distress".

This rare 1905 card was designed in Germany.

The Southerners continued their winning ways in round two in defeating Melbourne by six points at the Lake Oval, this time in "bracing" weather. Melbourne led with just minutes to play, but South's hero was Charles Clements who sealed victory with his fifth goal. *The Herald* reported: "The applause was deafening."

Although South had started the season well, it faltered in round three in going down to Carlton by 10 points at the Lake Oval, followed by defeats at the hands of Essendon and Collingwood. The Southerners had slipped to sixth position, with nemesis club Fitzroy undefeated on top of the ladder.

South might have defeated St Kilda by 23 points at the Lake Oval in round six, but there were two big occasions looming for the Southerners, both involving Fitzroy. The first of these was against the Maroons at the Brunswick Street Oval and again Fitzroy was South's master in defeating the red and white by 26 points. The following week, South clashed with Fitzroy in an exhibition match at the Sydney Cricket Ground.

The Herald reported there was "a great deal of interest" in the game and that the weather was "very enjoyable". Fitzroy led by 12 points with just minutes to play, with South's Clements kicking a late goal to cut the final margin to six points. Although *The Herald* was warm in its praise of taking the game to Sydney, *The Argus* scoffed: "They have as much chance of supplanting it (rugby) … as they have of superseding cricket with croquet." The newspaper also described the VFL's crusade as "hopeless".

South, following its round seven defeat by Fitzroy, therefore had its work cut out to be in a finals position even before the sectional matches and eventually finished the normal home and away season in fifth position, half a game behind fourth-placed Essendon, but with a much worse percentage anyway.

MATCH RESULTS

Round 1, at Corio Oval, May 6
South Melbourne 8.14 (62) d Geelong 5.9 (39)

Round 2, at Lake Oval, May 13
South Melbourne 11.7 (73) d Melbourne 10.7 (67)

Round 3, at Lake Oval, May 20
Carlton 7.13 (55) d South Melbourne 5.15 (45)

Round 4, at East Melbourne CG, May 27
Essendon 14.11 (95) d South Melbourne 5.9 (39)

Round 5, at Victoria Park, June 3
Collingwood 12.9 (81) d South Melbourne 2.10 (22)

Round 6, at Lake Oval, June 10
South Melbourne 6.11 (47) d St Kilda 3.6 (24)

Round 7, at Brunswick Street, June 17
Fitzroy 9.14 (68) d South Melbourne 6.6 (42)

Round 8, at Lake Oval, July 1
Geelong 6.7 (43) d South Melbourne 4.5 (29)

Round 9, at MCG, July 8
South Melbourne 8.10 (58) d Melbourne 3.8 (26)

Round 10, at Princes Park, July 15
South Melbourne 8.13 (61) d Carlton 7.16 (58)

Round 11, at Lake Oval, July 22
South Melbourne 7.8 (50) d Essendon 6.13 (49)

Round 12, at Lake Oval, July 29
Collingwood 4.5 (29) d South Melbourne 3.3 (21)

Round 13, at Junction Oval, August 5
St Kilda 5.11 (41) d South Melbourne 5.9 (39)

Round 14, at Lake Oval, August 19
South Melbourne 7.8 (50) drew with Fitzroy 7.8 (50)

Round 1, Section A, at Lake Oval, August 26
South Melbourne 13.11 (89) d Melbourne 5.10 (40)

Round 2, Section A, at Princes Park, September 2
Carlton 12.20 (92) d South Melbourne 7.7 (49)

Round 3, Section A, at Victoria Park, September 9
Collingwood 17.16 (118) d South Melb. 5.10 (40)

South Melbourne played Fitzroy at the SCG in 1905, almost 80 years before the club flew north to become the Sydney Swans.

Going into round 14, South needed to defeat Fitzroy at the Lake Oval, while hoping that Collingwood could defeat Essendon at Victoria Park. South got neither wish as it drew with Fitzroy and the Same-Old defeated the Magpies. The draw with Fitzroy was one of South's first in the VFL, but the two match points came in fortunate circumstances as the Maroons' Gerald Brosnan should have had a shot for goal just seconds before the final bell, but made an unsuccessful attempt to pass to a teammate.

South started its sectional matches in style with a 49-point defeat of Melbourne at the Lake Oval, but then went down by 43 points to Carlton at Princes Park before the indignity of Collingwood scoring a then record 17.16 (118) to defeat South by 78 points at Victoria Park. However, "Markwell" noted that South, with no chance of making the finals, "wisely turned its attention" to the following season in giving debuts to three players — Brighton's Des Griffin (who had played one game with St Kilda in 1904), University's Charles Cameron and Leopold Juniors' Percy Pitt (who had played eight games with Carlton in 1904). None played another game for South.

Clements again topped South's goalkicking, this time with 31 to be runner-up to Collingwood's Charlie Pannam (38) in the VFL goalkicking.

PLAYER	GAMES	GOALS
ABERCROMBIE, Percy	12	0
BLENCOWE, Edwin	3	0
BROMLEY, Harry	1	0
CAMERON, Charlie	1	0
CAMERON, Jim	17	4
CASEY, Dick	17	1
CATARINICH, John	3	0
CLEMENTS, Charles	16	31
COFFEY, John	1	0
DOLPHIN, Bill	16	0
FOGARTY, Joe	9	5
FOGARTY, Tom	16	9
GIBSON, Harry	14	3
GRIFFIN, Des	1	0
GRIFFITHS, Bill	1	0
HASSETT, Jack	7	4
HICKEY, Bill	6	0
HOWSON, Herb	15	0
INCIGNERI, Len	1	0
LAMPE, Harry	15	0
McDONNELL, Arthur	4	0
McGEE, Bill	15	5
McKAY, Dick	15	0
O'BRIEN, Fred	2	1
PITMAN, Alf	7	3
PITT, Percy	1	0
PRATT, Archie	7	3
SCOTT, Bill	17	10
SHARPE, Bert	10	11
SMALLHORN, Wal	2	0
STRANG, Bill	15	12
SYKES, Sydney	6	4
THOMAS, Bill	6	0
WEATE, Les	1	0
WENBORN, Tom	14	0
WINDLEY, Bill	12	4

POSITION: Fifth
COACH: -
CAPTAIN: Bill McGee, Tom Fogarty
BEST AND FAIREST: -
LEADING GOALKICKER: Charles Clements (31)

1906

The South Melbourne players elected a new captain for the 1906 season and this, in turn, necessitated a change in tactics. The new captain was Herb Howson, who was 33 years of age but still as nimble as ever. Howson had played all his previous football with South as a winger, but moved to the half-back line after being appointed captain. *The Herald* explained: "Herb Howson, after having played on the wing for 13 years, takes his place on the half-back line henceforward — the position which to a captain is like the conning tower of a battleship."

Alex "Bubs" Kerr was a star South rover of the early VFL years.

This edition of *The Herald,* published the day before the opening round, also reported on two South newcomers, both of whom left indelible marks. Charlie Ricketts joined the Southerners from VFA club Richmond, while Len "Mother" Mortimer crossed from another VFA club, Williamstown. They had stellar careers with South and always will be rated among the club's greatest stars.

Ricketts, however, was the subject of considerable speculation before his first game as rumours swept the football world that he was injured and would miss South's opening match against Essendon at the East Melbourne Cricket Ground. Ricketts quashed the rumour himself in sending South a telegram to say that he was fine and would play against Essendon. He went on to play 82 games with South to 1912 before returning to Richmond. Ricketts achieved immortal South fame as captain of the club's first VFL premiership side, in 1909.

Mortimer, who won his nickname of "Mother" because of the way he cradled the ball when on the run — contemporaries suggested he looked as if he was cradling a baby — became South's first great full-forward. He led the goalkicking in consecutive seasons from 1906-12, a record equalled by Barry Hall from 2002-08. Mortimer played 153 games and kicked 289 goals for South to 1915 and, late in his career suffered such a serious head injury that he later played in a protective skull cap. He also played in the 1909 premiership side.

South's other prize recruit was Bert Franks, who had caught the club's eye when representing Western Australia against Victoria in 1904. Franks was a rough, tough customer who upset the opposition in almost every match he played. A defender/ruckman, he played 99 games with South to 1913 before playing in the VFA with North Melbourne and later serving the Southerners as a committeeman.

Len "Mother" Mortimer had a fine debut season with South in 1906, topping the goalkicking with 24.

MATCH RESULTS

Round 1, at East Melbourne CG, May 5
South Melbourne 9.13 (67) d Essendon 8.12 (60)

Round 2, at Lake Oval, May 12
South Melbourne 12.5 (77) d Collingwood 8.9 (57)

Round 3, at Lake Oval, May 19
South Melbourne 10.14 (74) d St Kilda 9.7 (61)

Round 4, at MCG, May 26
Melbourne 5.9 (39) d South Melbourne 5.4 (34)

Round 5, at Princes Park, June 4
Carlton 10.9 (69) d South Melbourne 10.5 (65)

Round 6, at Corio Oval, June 9
Geelong 8.13 (61) d South Melbourne 3.13 (31)

Round 7, at Lake Oval, June 16
Fitzroy 9.8 (62) d South Melbourne 5.10 (40)

Round 8, at Lake Oval, June 30
Essendon 8.11 (59) d South Melbourne 3.8 (26)

Round 9, at Victoria Park, July 7
Collingwood 14.14 (98) d South Melbourne 5.8 (38)

Round 10, at Junction Oval, July 14
St Kilda 4.11 (35) d South Melbourne 4.4 (28)

Round 11, at Lake Oval, July 21
South Melbourne 12.11 (83) d Melbourne 4.3 (27)

Round 12, at Lake Oval, July 28
South Melbourne 12.12 (84) d Carlton 7.3 (45)

Round 13, at Lake Oval, August 4
South Melbourne 14.17 (101) d Geelong 5.8 (38)

Round 14, at Brunswick Street, August 18
Fitzroy 13.11 (89) d South Melbourne 5.12 (42)

Round 1, Section A, at Lake Oval, August 25
South Melbourne 10.10 (70) d Geelong 7.7 (49)

Round 2, Section A, at East Melbourne CG, Sept. 1
South Melbourne 10.6 (66) d Essendon 3.13 (31)

Round 3, Section A, at Lake Oval, September 8
Carlton 12.14 (86) d South Melbourne 4.15 (39)

South opened the season with a seven-point defeat of Essendon, although *The Australasian* noted that the Same-Old gave eight players their VFL debuts and were nowhere near experienced enough to hold off the Southerners. Then, when South defeated Collingwood and St Kilda over the next two rounds, supporter hopes soared, only for Melbourne to prick the balloon in defeating South by five points at the MCG in round four.

Herb, or "Bert", Howson captained South in 1906.

Melbourne won thanks to a late goal by star forward Vince Coutie, who was knocked unconscious as he took a mark close to goal. *The Herald* reported that Coutie, despite being "terribly shaken" scored the winning goal with virtually the last kick of the game.

The defeat set South back on its heels and six more defeats followed before, ironically, it broke its run of poor form by defeating Melbourne by 56 points at the Lake Oval. Although South then defeated Carlton and Geelong, it was too little too late and the red and white finished the home and away season in fifth position, but three games and a massive percentage margin behind fourth-placed Collingwood.

South defeated Geelong by 21 points at the Lake Oval in the first of its three sectional matches and followed up with a 35-point win over Essendon at the East Melbourne Cricket Ground, but the wins were meaningless as it was impossible to reach the final four.

Besides, Carlton thrashed South by 47 points in the final sectional round to leave South in fifth position, two games out of the final four and Carlton going on to defeat Fitzroy in the Grand Final. As *The Australasian* noted, it was "South's final flutter in a disappointing season".

PLAYER	GAMES	GOALS
ANDERSON, George	6	0
BLENCOWE, Edwin	4	0
BLISS, Dick	1	0
BOURKE, Peter	15	8
BUIST, Ted	11	0
CAMERON, Jim	7	10
CASEY, Dick	14	0
CLARKE, Bill	1	0
CURRAN, George	3	1
DOLPHIN, Bill	17	0
FOGARTY, Tom	9	1
FRANKLIN, Bob	5	1
FRANKS, Bert	13	8
GENT, Bill	14	10
GIBSON, Harry	15	3
HARRISON, Ted	2	1
HOWSON, Herb	17	0
KERR, Alex	5	9
LAMPE, Harry	17	0
McDONNELL, Arthur	2	1
McGEE, Bill	13	17
McKAY, Dick	16	0
MORTIMER, Len	17	24
PASH, Martin	7	8
PETTIT, Tom	1	0
RICKETTS, Charlie	13	10
SCOTT, Bill	4	4
SMALLHORN, Wal	2	0
SMITH, Jim	3	1
STRANG, Bill	17	14
SYKES, Syd	1	1
THOMAS, Bill	13	0
WADE, Ted	17	1
WENBORN, Tom	4	0

POSITION: Fifth
COACH: -
CAPTAIN: Herb Howson
BEST AND FAIREST: -
LEADING GOALKICKER: Len Mortimer (24)

1907

South went into the 1907 season with a new captain in defender Bill Dolphin, who had joined the club from Yarrawonga in 1905. A magnificent kick, Dolphin also was a marvellous defensive general who had a natural instinct for rallying his men. The versatile Harry Lampe was vice-captain, while 1906 captain Bert (often referred to as Herb) Howson decided to concentrate on his role as South's player-secretary.

South's star recruit was Vic Belcher, who crossed from VFA club Brunswick while brother Allan Joined Essendon. Vic Belcher had barracked for South as a boy because a baker in Brunswick would not allow the youngster to hitch a ride at the back of his horse-drawn wagon unless he promised to support the Southerners and, rather than joining nearby VFL clubs Essendon and Carlton, Belcher rode a bike to and from the Lake Oval to play with his beloved South and became one of the club's greatest identities.

The Southerners opened the season with a match against Melbourne at the Lake Oval, but went down by 19 points, with *The Herald* noting that Melbourne "played with much the better judgement". The newspaper also reported that South was hampered by first quarter injuries to Len Mortimer and Charlie Ricketts who, because there were no reserves, had to limp through the match as virtual passengers.

When Fitzroy defeated South by 10 points at the Brunswick Street Oval the following week, the Southerners found themselves above only Geelong on the VFL ladder. South led by six points at the final change, only for Fitzroy to kick the only two goals of the final quarter. South therefore had to wait until round three for its first win of the season, by 28 points over Collingwood at the Lake Oval. South's star was Mortimer, who kicked five of his side's nine goals.

The win over the Magpies was the start of a superb run of five consecutive victories, the sequence coming to an end against Melbourne at the MCG in round eight. Despite going down to Fitzroy by eight points at the Lake Oval the following week, South was able to cling to third position, a game behind Carlton and St Kilda. However, a third consecutive defeat, at the hands of Collingwood, saw the Southerners in a precarious position. A late season rally saw South finish the 14-round home and away season in third position behind Carlton and Collingwood.

Then, in the first of its three sectional matches, South shot into premiership contention with a 17-point win over Carlton at the Lake Oval. Carlton led by six points at the

Spectators held on for dear life in trees around the MCG while watching South play Carlton in the 1907 Grand Final.

MATCH RESULTS

Round 1, at Lake Oval, April 27
Melbourne 9.6 (60) d South Melbourne 6.5 (41)

Round 2, at Brunswick Street, May 4
Fitzroy 7.15 (57) d South Melbourne 7.5 (47)

Round 3, at Lake Oval, May 11
South Melbourne 9.12 (66) d Collingwood 5.8 (38)

Round 4, at East Melbourne CG, May 18
South Melbourne 6.11 (47) d Essendon 6.8 (44)

Round 5, at Princes Park, May 25
South Melbourne 9.7 (61) d Carlton 5.16 (46)

Round 6, at Lake Oval, June 3
South Melbourne 6.9 (45) d Geelong 4.9 (33)

Round 7, at Junction Oval, June 15
South Melbourne 7.2 (44) d St Kilda 4.8 (32)

Round 8, at MCG, June 22
Melbourne 7.10 (52) d South Melbourne 5.10 (40)

Round 9, at Lake Oval, June 29
Fitzroy 7.10 (52) d South Melbourne 6.8 (44)

Round 10, at Victoria Park, July 6
Collingwood 8.9 (57) d South Melbourne 7.8 (50)

Round 11, at Lake Oval, July 13
South Melbourne 8.11 (59) d Essendon 6.11 (47)

Round 12, at Lake Oval, July 20
Carlton 4.12 (36) d South Melbourne 3.9 (27)

Round 13, at Corio Oval, August 3
South Melbourne 7.8 (50) d Geelong 6.6 (42)

Round 14, at Lake Oval, August 10
South Melbourne 8.16 (64) d St Kilda 5.14 (44)

Round 1, Section A, at Lake Oval, August 17
South Melbourne 8.9 (57) d Carlton 4.16 (40)

Round 2, Section A, at MCG, August 24
South Melbourne 10.14 (74) d Melbourne 7.8 (50)

Round 3, Section A, at East Melbourne CG, Aug 31
South Melbourne 15.9 (99) d Essendon 6.7 (43)

First semi-final, at MCG, September 7
South Melbourne 12.10 (82) d Collingwood 6.12 (48)

Grand Final, at MCG, September 21
Carlton 6.14 (50) d South Melbourne 6.9 (45)

final change, only for South to charge home with a five-goal final term. *The Herald* reported: "It was a magnificent finish on the part of the Southerners, who played admirably through this term."

Four rare hand-painted cards of South in action.

South defeated Melbourne by 24 points at the MCG the following week and, in its final sectional match, thrashed Essendon by 56 points to finish second on what was termed the "completed ladder". This meant South would play fourth-placed Collingwood in one semi-final, with Carlton and St Kilda clashing in the other semi-final.

South defeated Collingwood by 34 points at the MCG, while Carlton thrashed St Kilda there by 56 points the following week and fans could not separate the Southerners and the Blues for premiership favouritism, especially as both sides went into the Grand Final with players missing through suspension or injury.

The rugged Bert Franks had been suspended for seven matches for striking earlier in the season, while South teammates Lindsay Main and Bill Goddard were unavailable because of injury. Carlton's problems included the suspension of two of its greatest players, Fred "Pompey" Elliott and Jim Marchbank, with star centreline player Rod McGregor unavailable because of injury. Carlton was so upset with Marchbank's suspension that it presented him with a marble clock and a silk scroll which specifically referred to his "unjust treatment".

The Carlton-South Grand Final on September 21 attracted what *The Herald* estimated was an attendance of 40,000 but, in fact, the official attendance was 45,477, a then record. *The Herald* reported: "Special trains swarming with passengers rattled into Melbourne from Ballarat, Bendigo, Geelong and Castlemaine. There also were furniture vans with bulging loads of people in place of households goods and pony carts, gigs and all sorts of conveyances." South also had one very special supporter, former Australian Test cricketer Harry Boyle, who discharged himself

South defeated Collingwood in this 1907 semi-final at the MCG.

from hospital to see his team play in the Grand Final.

Although Carlton led by 15 points at the final change, South hit back with two early final quarter goals by Bill Strang and, as *The Herald* reported "South was finishing like heroes". South four times reduced Carlton's lead to two points and a late miss by Mortimer proved costly as the Blues held on to win by five points. "Markwell", writing in *The Australasian,* noted that although Carlton won the premiership "I can find no reason for bestowing upon them, for this particular game, more praise that is due South Melbourne".

Four early VFL stars, from left: Henry Young (Geelong), Jim Sharp (Fitzroy), Bob Nash (Collingwood) and Charlie Ricketts (South Melbourne). Bob Nash was the father of South Melbourne champion Laurie Nash.

PLAYER	GAMES	GOALS
ANDERSON, George	19	0
ATKINS, Bert	17	0
BELCHER, Vic	19	7
BOURKE, Peter	2	0
BUIST, Ted	1	0
CALLAN, Hugh	14	6
CAMERON, Jim	15	4
CASEY, Dick	17	23
CURRAN, George	2	0
DOLPHIN, Bill	19	0
DRANE, Horrie	10	0
FRANKS, Bert	15	10
GENT, Bill	13	9
GODDARD, Bill	14	4
HOWSON, Herb	1	1
JACKSON, John	7	2
KERR, Alex	4	6
KERR, Bill	15	8
LACEY, Jim	1	0
LAMPE, Harry	17	0
McKAY, Dick	3	0
MAIN, Jack	1	1
MAIN, Lindsay	13	0
MORTIMER, Len	18	37
MOXHAM, Bill	13	1
RICKETTS, Charlie	13	5
ROACH, Wally	1	0
STRANG, Bill	15	18
THOMAS, Bill	4	0
WADE, Ted	17	1
WEATE, Les	1	0
WILSON, Harry	8	2
WOOD, Phonse	13	0

POSITION: Runner-up
COACH: -
CAPTAIN: Bill Dolphin
BEST AND FAIREST: -
LEADING GOALKICKER: Len Mortimer (37)

1908

The 1908 season was highly significant as the VFL introduced two new clubs, Richmond and University. Richmond, of course, quickly established itself as a formidable opponent, but University bowed out of the competition after the 1914 season. The "Professors" in their seven-year VFL tenure, defeated every other club except Collingwood.

In the new 10-club format, the VFL ruled that all clubs would play each other twice over the home and away season and sectional matches would be consigned to football history. South, with Bill Dolphin captain for a second consecutive season, had high hopes for 1908 after narrowly losing to Carlton in the previous year's Grand Final and had a wonderful recruit in Tom Grimshaw, a reliable defender from Footscray Juniors.

South opened the season with a nine-point win over Fitzroy at the Brunswick Street Oval, with Len Mortimer kicking four of the Southerners' seven goals and Charlie Ricketts named the best player on the ground. Then followed a 19-point win over Geelong at the Lake Oval, with *The Australasian* referring to follower Hugh Callan as "South's brightest star". Tragically, Callan (who had been recruited from Essendon the previous season) was killed in action in World War I.

A South Melbourne team of 1908. Back row, from left: Bert Atkins, Tom Grimshaw, Arthur Hiskins, Hugh Callan, Phonse Wood, George Anderson, Harry Wilson, Bill Thomas, Jim Cameron. Seated, from left: Lindsay Main, Vic Belcher, Charlie Ricketts, Bill Dolphin, Len Mortimer, Henry Paternoster, Ted Wade. Front, Alex Kerr (left), Dick Casey.

Although South had started the season well, its form fluctuated from week to week and, by the completion of the first nine rounds, was struggling to stay in touch with the top clubs. South even had struggled to defeat newcomer University by 11 points at the Lake Oval in round five. South's only consolation was that in going down to Carlton by just two points in the Grand Final "replay" at the Lake Oval in round six, *The Australasian* suggested it was "football of the highest order".

The lowlight of the season was going down to University by two points in extremely heavy conditions at the East Melbourne Cricket Ground in round 14. *The Australasian* noted that "no other team amongst leaguers had during the season suffered defeat by a small margin of points so frequently as South Melbourne" and added that the red and white also had been "severely handicapped by accidents (injuries) to players". South, in fact, lost four matches in 1908 by margins of less than six points, while skipper Dolphin and star rover Charlie Ricketts both missed many games through injury

South's lack of consistency continued over the second half of the season, but it still had a chance of making the finals going into the last round match against Collingwood at Victoria Park. The teams were level on match points, with South holding a percentage advantage. The clash therefore was a "mini" final. Although

MATCH RESULTS

Round 1, at Brunswick Street, May 2
South Melbourne 7.11 (53) d Fitzroy 6.8 (44)

Round 2, at Lake Oval, May 9
South Melbourne 7.9 (51) d Geelong 4.8 (32)

Round 3, at Lake Oval, May 16
St Kilda 7.13 (55) d South Melbourne 4.2 (26)

Round 4, at MCG, May 23
Melbourne 12.3 (75) d South Melbourne 10.13 (73)

Round 5, at Lake Oval, May 30
South Melbourne 12.4 (76) d University 9.11 (65)

Round 6, at Lake Oval, June 6
Carlton 8.5 (53) d South Melbourne 7.9 (51)

Round 7, at Punt Road, June 8
South Melbourne 11.11 (77) d Richmond 9.9 (63)

Round 8, at East Melbourne CG, June 13
Essendon 8.11 (59) d South Melbourne 6.9 (45)

Round 9, at Lake Oval, June 20
South Melbourne 9.11 (65) d Collingwood 6.8 (44)

Round 10, at Lake Oval, June 27
South Melbourne 2.19 (31) d Fitzroy 2.6 (18)

Round 11, at Corio Oval, July 4
South Melbourne 9.12 (66) d Geelong 9.4 (58)

Round 12, at Junction Oval, July 11
St Kilda 5.4 (34) d South Melbourne 4.5 (29)

Round 13, at Lake Oval, July 18
Melbourne 11.8 (74) d South Melbourne 5.10 (40)

Round 14, at East Melbourne CG, July 25
University 11.7 (73) d South Melbourne 10.11 (71)

Round 15, at Princes Park, August 1
Carlton 8.19 (67) d South Melbourne 6.5 (41)

Round 16, at Lake Oval, August 8
South Melbourne 18.12 (120) d Richmond 4.4 (28)

Round 17, at Lake Oval, August 15
South Melbourne 5.8 (38) d Essendon 3.14 (32)

Round 18, at Victoria Park, September 5
Collingwood 12.16 (88) d South Melbourne 3.4 (22)

South was boosted by the return from injury of Callan, Ricketts and Jim Cameron, the versatile Phonse Wood was unavailable after being injured the previous week while representing Victoria in the Jubilee Carnival played in Melbourne. South's other Victorian representative in this Championship of

A South player reaches for a mark against Geelong, but the Southerners appear to be outnumbered.

Australia (with the undefeated Victorians taking the title) was the powerful and fiery Bert Franks, who was named among the Big V's best in the 63-point defeat of Western Australia in the title-deciding final match of the Carnival.

South was no match for Collingwood, who took control with seven goals to two in the first half and went on to win by a thumping 66 points to clinch fourth position. *The Australasian* reported: "Collingwood's system was as good as systems could be; and, to a man, they handled the ball (in wet conditions) with astonishing deftness. *The Australasian* also noted that "the proceedings brought no balm to the visitors' supporters".

Fifth position was a disappointing result after such early season promise. Unfortunately for South, Ricketts' late-season injury robbed the Southerners of momentum and, in fact, *The Australasian's* "Markwell" suggested he would have named the star South rover as "man of the season" ahead of Essendon's Bill Busbridge if he had not missed so much of the season. The 1908 flag went to Carlton, which was aiming for a fourth consecutive premiership the following season.

Bill Dolphin captained South for a second season in 1908. Note, the change of guernsey designs over the early VFL seasons.

PLAYER	GAMES	GOALS
ANDERSON, George	17	0
ATKINS, Bert	15	0
BAIRD, Des	1	0
BELCHER, Vic	18	7
BOWEN, Dave	1	0
CALLAN, Hugh	14	11
CAMERON, Jim	16	5
CASEY, Dick	14	10
CLANCY, Tom	1	0
DOLPHIN, Bill	12	0
DRANE, Horrie	6	1
FRANKS, Bert	15	6
GENT, Bill	4	1
GODDARD, Bill	14	13
GOUGH, Alf	1	0
GRIMSHAW, Tom	18	0
HARRISON, Ted	4	0
HISKINS, Arthur	16	15
HOLLAND, Reuben	1	1
HOSKING, Toner	7	1
HOWSON, Herb	1	0
JONES, Jack	8	3
KERR, Alex	17	14
LARKIN, Joe	2	0
MAIN, Lindsay	3	0
MILLSOM, Charlie	1	0
MORTIMER, Len	17	40
MOXHAM, Bill	4	0
PATERNOSTER, Henry	2	0
RICKETTS, Charlie	12	6
ROBERTS, John	2	0
THOMAS, Bill	15	0
TURNBULL, Jack	12	0
WADE, Ted	14	1
WILSON, Harry	2	0
WOOD, Phonse	17	0

POSITION: Fifth
COACH: -
CAPTAIN: Bill Dolphin
BEST AND FAIREST: -
LEADING GOALKICKER: Len Mortimer (40)

1909

As Carlton had won consecutive premierships from 1906-8 under the coaching of former Fitzroy (VFA) player John Worrall, South Melbourne decided it was time to appoint its first coach. But, in reality, there was little change from the status quo as rover Charlie Ricketts also was appointed captain for 1909 and, under the old system, would have assumed coaching duties anyway.

South recruited extensively for 1909, especially from local clubs. Dave Barry and Jack Scobie joined from Leopold, but the prize recruit was Williamstown winger Jim Caldwell, who went on to play 155 games in the red and white to 1919 and captain the 1918 premiership side.

The Southerners opened the season with a nine-point win over Geelong at the Corio Oval, with *The Australasian* reporting that two train-loads of supporters, numbering 1200, made the return trip to Geelong. The newspaper's "Markwell" congratulated South on its win in stating that it was "well deserved and gained purely on merit". Then, when South defeated reigning premier Carlton by 17 points at the Lake Oval the following week, there were the first suggestions that the Southerners could win the 1909 flag. In heavy conditions, South took control with quick goals from Len Mortimer and Dick Casey in the second quarter. "Markwell" described South's win as "substantial", but warned that Carlton "will still have a big say in the season's proceedings".

South's first defeat of the season was at the hands of Richmond at the Punt Road Oval in round six. South went down by 13 points to the VFL newcomer and *The Australasian*

South's 1909 premiership squad. Back row, from left: J. Marshall (trainer), George Bower, Jack Richardson, Bert Streckfuss, Bert Franks, Bill Thomas, Jack Scobie, A. Swan (trainer). Second back row (from left): Alex Kerr, Hugh Callan, Vic Belcher, Bob Deas, Tom Grimshaw, Len Mortimer, Jack Jones, Ted Wade, Toner Hosking (did not play a game in 1909) . Front row (from left): Herb Howson, Jim Caldwell, Alf Gough, Bill Dolphin (vice-captain), Charlie Ricketts (captain-coach), Arthur Hiskins, Horrie Drane, Dick Casey, Henry Skinner (president). Front: Bill Moxham (left), Alan Pentland.

Vic Belcher, a 1909 premiership hero, also played in the 1918 flag side.

Action shots from the 1909 South Melbourne-Carlton Grand Final.

heralded the victory with the headline RICHMOND'S GREAT FEAT and hinted that South might have been complacent as it described the Southerners as "haughty".

If South had been complacent against a team sitting just eighth on the ladder, the lesson was well learned as the Southerners did not taste defeat again until they went down to Carlton by 24 points at Princes Park in round 11. More than 30,000 fans squeezed into the Carlton ground for the top-of-the-ladder clash and were not disappointed, with the *Herald* reporting the match under the headline MAGNIFICENT FOOTBALL. The newspaper also reported that "trams were taxed to their last inch of carrying capacity" as fans flocked to see what they believed would be a Grand Final preview.

South, despite going down to Carlton, retained top position, but was set back on its heels with consecutive losses to Fitzroy and Collingwood in rounds 13 and 14 respectively. However, wins in

Left: Charlie Ricketts, captain-coach of South's 1909 premiership side. Right: Vic Belcher.

MATCH RESULTS

Round 1, at Corio Oval, May 1
South Melbourne 8.5 (53) d Geelong 6.8 (44)

Round 2, at Lake Oval, May 8
South Melbourne 7.3 (45) d Carlton 4.4 (28)

Round 3, at Lake Oval, May 15
South Melbourne 12.16 (88) d Melbourne 3.6 (24)

Round 4, at Brunswick Street, May 22
South Melbourne 11.10 (76) d Fitzroy 5.7 (37)

Round 5, at Lake Oval, May 29
South Melbourne 6.10 (46) d Collingwood 3.8 (26)

Round 6, at Punt Road, June 5
Richmond 10.11 (71) d South Melbourne 8.10 (58)

Round 7, at East Melbourne CG, June 7
South Melbourne 9.9 (63) d Essendon 9.8 (62)

Round 8, at Lake Oval, June 12
South Melbourne 11.15 (81) d University 2.6 (18)

Round 9, at Lake Oval, June 19
South Melbourne 14.13 (97) d St Kilda 2.8 (20)

Round 10, at Lake Oval, July 3
South Melbourne 17.9 (111) d Geelong 4.7 (31)

Round 11, at Princes Park, July 10
Carlton 9.14 (68) d South Melbourne 6.8 (44)

Round 12, at MCG, July 17
South Melbourne 6.9 (45) d Melbourne 3.6 (24)

Round 13, at Lake Oval, July 24
Fitzroy 5.14 (44) d South Melbourne 4.6 (30)

Round 14, at Victoria Park, July 31
Collingwood 8.6 (54) d South Melbourne 6.7 (43)

Round 15, at Lake Oval, August 14
South Melbourne 18.11 (119) d Richmond 3.8 (26)

Round 16, at Lake Oval, August 21
South Melbourne 6.5 (41) d Essendon 5.7 (37)

Round 17, at East Melbourne CG, August 28
South Melbourne 9.11 (65) d University 5.9 (39)

Round 18, at Junction Oval, September 4
South Melbourne 7.15 (57) d St Kilda 5.5 (35)

Semi-final, at MCG, September 18
South Melbourne 10.8 (68) d Collingwood 6.11 (47)

Preliminary final, at MCG, September 25
Carlton 10.9 (69) d South Melbourne 7.5 (47)

Grand Final, at MCG, October 2

South Melbourne	0.5	2.9	4.12	4.14 (38)
Carlton:	0.5	2.9	3.11	4.12 (36)

GOALS: Franks, Gough, Mortimer, Ricketts.
BEST: Cameron, Franks, Kerr, Mortimer, Thomas, Scobie.

Defender Tom Grimshaw played every game in 1909.

each of the last four rounds saw South finish the season on top of the ladder, a big percentage margin ahead of Carlton.

Under the final four system of that era, South played Collingwood in one semi-final, with Carlton taking on Essendon in the other. *The Herald* reported on the South-Collingwood match, which attracted 35,000 fans: "All roads led to the Melbourne Cricket Ground. People on foot swarmed there. Tens of thousands poured down in train and tram, in motor and cab, and, in fact, every kind of wheeled vehicle bore a human burden".

Collingwood led by two points at half-time, but South played such inspired football to kick six goals in the third quarter that the *Herald* reported: "They (the Southerners) had caught the Collingwood backs napping and their forwards covered themselves with glory. It was a most inspiring series of dashes and roused the spectators to a pitch of great enthusiasm." South won by 21 points and, with Carlton having defeated Essendon by 36 points the previous week, football fans were granted their wish of a South-Carlton final.

When Carlton defeated South by 22 points, the Southerners — as top team — had right of challenge in what was to be the Grand Final. Not only did Carlton dent South's premiership ambitions, but the Southerners were dealt two savage blows in a rough and ready final. Caldwell was reported for striking Carlton's George Bruce and was suspended for nine matches, while dashing full-back Bill Dolphin was injured and missed the Grand Final.

How a Herald *cartoonist saw the South-Collingwood semi-final. The caption for the cartoon on the left reads: "South Melbourne misses the mark, but gets the ball." The other reads: "A Collingwood barracker before and after the match."*

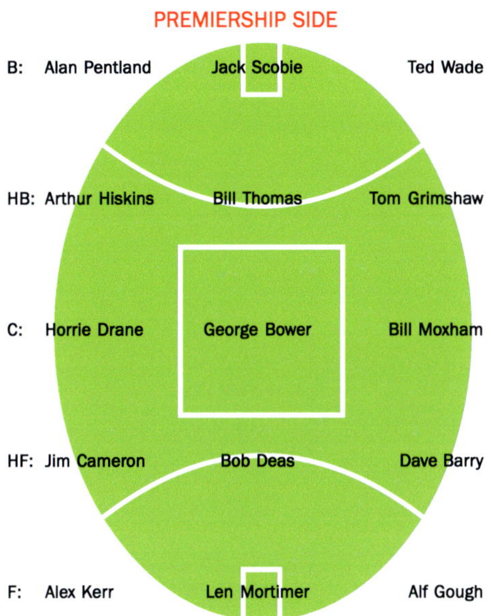

FOLL: Bert Franks, Vic Belcher, Charlie Ricketts (Capt.)

To make South's task even tougher, Carlton welcomed the return of star defender Norman Clark for the Grand Final after he had missed the final because of neuralgia. South, despite its problems, held Carlton over the first half, with scores tied at both quarter and half-time. "Markwell" later noted that whereas South had tried vigour to upset Carlton in the first finals clash, it relied on pace and moving the ball into the open in the Grand Final and its "running with the ball was distinctly the best for the year".

South was helped enormously when Carlton's Jack Bacquie could hardly run in the third quarter after twisting an ankle just before half-time and Martin Gotz had to be carried from the ground with a "sprained foot". South took full advantage of Carlton's problems for Alf Gough to kick a goal just before the three-quarter time bell to give the red and white a seven-point lead.

Carlton attacked relentlessly over the final

A South Melbourne group visited the Blue Mountains in New South Wales in 1909 and are pictured here in their club boaters and ties. Premiership captain Charlie Ricketts is in the middle of the second front row.

quarter, but could manage only one goal, by former South player Harvey Kelly from a place-kick on a tight angle. Although South managed just two behinds in the final term, these were enough to give the red and white victory by two points for a first VFL premiership.

"Markwell" reported: "The excitement that prevailed among the 37,000 spectators was indescribable ... the playing ground was rushed the moment the first tinkle was heard, and a surging multitude of the madly-excited barrackers bore the victors shoulder high from the field. Such a scene of delirious enthusiasm had never before been witnessed at the finish of a football match in Melbourne."

"Markwell" paid tribute to Ricketts when he wrote: "Consummate skill in leadership on the field belongs to few men. It would, perhaps, be an exaggeration to say that captain Ricketts is the possessor of such skill ... His training and judgement have built up a side largely composed of men who, until recently, were junior players, into a company of artists ... To him, therefore, is due chief credit for the team's achievement."

The 1909 season, however, was not quite over for South as the red and white the following week played an exhibition match against country side Hamilton while en route to Adelaide to play for the "premier of premiers" title against West Adelaide. South claimed the title with a 24-point victory, with *The Australasian* naming Bill Thomas, Jack Scobie and Alan Pentland among the best players.

PLAYER	GAMES	GOALS
BAIRD, Des	5	0
BARRY, Dave	10	1
BELCHER, Vic	21	7
BOWER, George	19	5
CALDWELL, Jim	19	2
CALLAN, Hugh	7	0
CAMERON, Jim	15	6
CASEY, Dick	20	20
DEAS, Bob	20	29
DOLPHIN, Bill	14	0
DRANE, Horrie	2	0
FRANKS, Bert	21	13
GOUGH, Alf	18	19
GRIMSHAW, Tom	21	0
HARRISON, Ted	1	0
HISKINS, Arthur	19	7
JONES, Jack	6	5
KERR, Alex	21	9
MOORE, Herbert	1	0
MORTIMER, Len	21	50
MOXHAM, Bill	9	0
PENTLAND, Alan	14	0
RICHARDSON, Jack	1	0
RICKETTS, Charlie	20	11
SCOBIE, Jack	19	0
STRECKFUSS, Bert	2	0
THOMAS, Bill	21	2
WADE, Ted	11	0

POSITION: Premier
COACH: Charlie Ricketts
CAPTAIN: Charlie Ricketts
BEST AND FAIREST: -
LEADING GOALKICKER: Len Mortimer (50)

1910

Although South Melbourne went into the 1910 season as the reigning premier, the club was shocked to learn that flag captain-coach Charlie Ricketts would be unavailable for most of the season because of serious illness. In Ricketts' absence (he played just one game in 1910), South named Bill "Sonna" Thomas as captain-coach.

Thomas, recruited from Rose of Northcote in 1905, was one of the best defenders of his era and, indeed, many rated him best on ground at centre half-back in the 1909 Grand Final win. However, South's new leader not only had to contend with Ricketts' absence, but also the absence on business commitments for most of the season of the talented Hugh Callan. Also, *The Herald* noted: "South Melbourne won the premiership of 1909 with a young team, and they are not troubling the permit committee."

The *Herald* suggested that Les Charge would be the pick of South's recruits and this assessment later was vindicated as Charge went on to play 65 games with South to 1915 and starred in the 1914 Grand Final loss to Carlton. However, *The Herald* neglected to mention that South in 1910 also had recruited a brilliant young follower from VFA club Brighton. Bruce Sloss had played three games with Essendon over the 1907-08 seasons before moving to Brighton and then to South. He went on to play 81 games with South to 1914 and was named Champion of the Colony in 1911 before being killed in action in World War I. Also, South in 1910 picked up St Kilda reject Joe Prince, who went on to play 103 games in the red and white to 1918.

Two great South stars — Bert Franks (left) and Joe Prince. Franks was suspended "indefinitely" in 1910.

The 1909 pennant was unfurled by the wife of club president Henry Skinner before the opening round match against Richmond at the Lake Oval. The president himself unfurled the pennant won by the Albert Park State School as the metropolitan champion. *The Herald* reported that fans "swarmed towards the South Melbourne ground" in great excitement. South defeated Richmond by 46 points to suggest it again would challenge for the flag, only for Collingwood to burst that particular bubble in defeating the Southerners by 41 points at Victoria Park the following week.

South forward Les Charge in a typical pose of the era.

Then, when Essendon defeated South by six points at the Lake Oval in round three, reality hit home. Essendon deserved its surprise victory as it played the last 10 minutes of the match with just 17 men after champion follower Bill Busbridge was injured. When Carlton defeated South by 17 points at Princes Park the following week, the reigning premier languished in eighth position, above only Melbourne and St Kilda. *The Australasian's* "Markwell" wrote: "Matters are not mending rapidly for South Melbourne."

South might have defeated University by two points in round five but, in going down to

MATCH RESULTS

Round 1, at Lake Oval, April 30
South Melbourne 11.12 (78) d Richmond 4.8 (32)

Round 2, at Victoria Park, May 14
Collingwood 13.9 (87) d South Melbourne 5.16 (46)

Round 3, at Lake Oval, May 21
Essendon 11.7 (73) d South Melbourne 10.7 (67)

Round 4, at Princes Park, May 28
Carlton 6.13 (49) d South Melbourne 4.8 (32)

Round 5, at Lake Oval, June 4
South Melbourne 6.14 (50) d University 7.6 (48)

Round 6, at Corio Oval, June 6
Geelong 11.12 (78) d South Melbourne 6.6 (42)

Round 7, at Lake Oval, June 11
South Melbourne 11.15 (81) d Melbourne 6.10 (46)

Round 8, at Junction Oval, June 18
South Melbourne 6.13 (49) d St Kilda 4.5 (29)

Round 9, at Brunswick Street, June 25
South Melbourne 11.6 (72) d Fitzroy 7.13 (55)

Round 10, at Punt Road, July 2
South Melbouurne 10.11 (71) d Richmond 10.7 (67)

Round 11, at Lake Oval, July 9
South Melbourne 13.17 (95) d Collingwood 4.9 (33)

Round 12, at East Melbourne CG, July 16
Essendon 6.9 (45) d South Melbourne 5.4 (34)

Round 13, at Lake Oval, July 23
Carlton 6.8 (44) d South Melbourne 4.7 (31)

Round 14, at East Melbourne CG, July 30
South Melbourne 10.7 (67) d University 3.6 (24)

Round 15, at Lake Oval, August 6
South Melbourne 11.12 (78) d Geelong 3.8 (26)

Round 16, at MCG, August 20
South Melbourne 8.10 (58) d Melbourne 8.6 (54)

Round 17, at Lake Oval, August 27
South Melbourne 11.11 (77) d St Kilda 10.5 (65)

Round 18, at Lake Oval, September 3
South Melbourne 7.10 (52) d Fitzroy 4.5 (29)

Semi-final, at MCG, September 17
South Melbourne 10.5 (65) d Carlton 6.17 (53)

Preliminary final, at MCG, September 24
Collingwood 8.7 (55) d South Melbourne 6.8 (44)

PLAYER	GAMES	GOALS
BARRY, Dave	14	2
BELCHER, Vic	20	15
BIEHL, Francis	3	1
BOWER, George	18	0
CALDWELL, Jim	7	0
CALLAN, Hugh	1	0
CAMERON, Jim	16	7
CARPENTER, Fred	8	7
CASEY, Dick	3	5
CHARGE, Les	6	5
DEAS, Bob	19	26
DOLPHIN, Bill	16	0
FRANKS, Bert	6	4
GOUGH, Alf	20	13
GRIMSHAW, Tom	20	0
HISKINS, Arthur	19	17
HOSKING, Toner	2	0
JONES, Jack	1	1
KERR, Alex	20	17
KIRCHNER, Albie	6	0
LYNCH, Jim	1	0
MORTIMER, Len	18	28
MOXHAM, Bill	3	1
PENTLAND, Alan	20	0
PRINCE, Joe	18	3
PUNSHON, Arthur	4	1
RICKETTS, Charlie	1	0
SCOBIE, Jack	17	2
SLOSS, Bruce	11	5
STRECKFUSS, Bert	16	5
THOMAS, Bill	20	0
WADE, Ted	1	0
WALSH, Jack	5	0

POSITION: Third
COACH: Bill Thomas
CAPTAIN: Bill Thomas
BEST AND FAIREST: -
LEADING GOALKICKER: Len Mortimer (28)

Geelong by 36 points on the King's Birthday holiday Monday two days later, South looked likely to miss the finals altogether. Amazingly, however, the Southerners won their next five games to climb back into contention and eventually finished the home and away season in third position, behind Carlton and Collingwood, with Essendon fourth.

Bill Thomas, South's 1910 captain-coach.

Collingwood thrashed Essendon by 58 points in the first of the semi-finals, with South and Carlton clashing at the MCG the following week. Just one hour before the South-Carlton final, what seemed a relatively minor event threw football into tremendous turmoil and scandal. Carlton removed the names of three players — Alex "Bongo" Lang, Doug Gillespie and Doug Fraser — from its team. Rumours immediately circulated that these players had been "got at" to "play dead" against South.

The Carlton camp was split down the middle and it was no surprise that the Southerners defeated the Blues by 12 points. *The Argus* the following Monday ran Lang's version of events. The Carlton star admitted that although he accepted 10 pounds ($20) to "run a bye", he handed the money to a friend and "never intended for a moment not to push myself in the match".

The VFL met for three hours behind locked doors before announcing it had suspended Lang and Fraser until December, 1915, and that Gillespie had been cleared. It was never suggested South had bribed any player and Lang would only say that he was approached

These two Herald *cartoons depict the battle for the 1910 flag. The first shows Carlton on the canvas after being floored by South Melbourne in a semi-final, with Collingwood about to enter the ring. The other shows Carlton and South in a tug of war before their semi-final.*

"by a man in the street", presumably a bookmaker with an interest in the semi-final result.

Carlton, as minor premier, had the right to challenge the winner of a South-Collingwood preliminary final, played on September 24. South, after trailing by just five points at the final break, went down by 11 points. South was well-served by Arthur Hiskins, who kicked three goals, and "Markwell" wrote: "It must be said of them (the Southerners) that they wound up their season in a way that brought honour and credit upon themselves and their club."

Collingwood defeated the unsettled Carlton by 14 points in the Grand Final and South fans were left with a feeling of "what might have been" because of the suspension earlier in the season of champion follower Bert Franks for what amounted to more than a season and a half. Franks had attended a Tribunal hearing in support of teammate Dick Casey, who had been reported on charges of striking and charging in the round six match against Geelong at the Corio Oval. When Casey was suspended for the rest of the season, Franks vented his feelings towards umpire Lardie Tulloch, who once had played with Collingwood. Franks found himself on charges of assaulting and abusing Tulloch and although the assault charge was dismissed, he was suspended "during the pleasure of the League for insulting language to an umpire".

"Markwell" wrote in *The Australasian:* "It is a pity, both for his club and himself, that so able a player, and one who has behaved himself in the field from the first match of the year, should be found doing off the field an act that necessitated his being stood down indefinitely." Franks' ban was lifted for the start of the 1912 season and he therefore served a total suspension of 33 matches. It remains the longest suspension of any South Melbourne/Sydney Swans player.

THE LEAGUE PREMIERSHIP.

STRUGGLE FOR SUPREMACY.

TWO FINE TEAMS MEET.

SOUTH MELBOURNE AGAINST COLLINGWOOD.

THOUSANDS WATCH THE PLAY.

FINE EXPOSITION OF THE GAME

How The Herald *saw the 1910 South-Collingwood preliminary final.*

1911

South Melbourne re-appointed Bill Thomas as captain-coach for the 1911 season and opened with a comfortable 62-point win over University. The first test of the new season followed in round two, when South played Carlton at Princes Park. Although the Southerners were undermanned through injury, with star follower Bruce Sloss and others missing, they drew with the Blues.

South then won its next two matches before being defeated for the first time in 1911 in going down to Collingwood by just six points at the Lake Oval. This match was played against a background of inter-competition intrigue, with VFL and VFA officials meeting to discuss an amalgamation. Talks broke down, but newspapers relegated the round five matches to the background.

After Richmond defeated South by eight points at the Punt Road Oval in round six, the Southerners hit top form and won their next 10 matches to shoot to premiership favouritism. South even took revenge on Richmond with a 36-point win at the Lake Oval, despite shocking inaccuracy. The Southerners scored 25 behinds, including five "posters".

South Melbourne's Vic Belcher tries to weave his way out of trouble against Carlton.

The VFL went into a 21-day recess following round 15 for the playing of the interstate Carnival, won by South Australia. South took advantage of the break with a "picnic" trip to Sydney and the Blue Mountains. South at this time also organised a testimonial for rugged follower Bert Franks, who had been suspended indefinitely the previous season. One supporter wrote to *The Herald:* "I feel sure that followers of South Melbourne will not permit this opportunity to pass of expressing their appreciation of this player's sterling performances in the past in the interests of his club." The letter was signed "Lest We Forget" and included a five-shilling donation.

South, to the break, had been locked in battle with Essendon for top position and, after defeating Fitzroy, went down to both Geelong (at the Corio Oval) and Essendon (at the East Melbourne Cricket Ground) over the final two rounds. The five-point loss to Essendon might have been heart-breaking, but Essendon had a massive percentage margin over South anyway and the defeat did not cost the Southerners top position. Essendon was minor premier, with South runner-up and Carlton and Collingwood making up the final four.

The Southerners therefore played Collingwood in one of the semi-finals and

MATCH RESULTS

Round 1, at Lake Oval, April 29
South Melbourne 14.18 (102) d University 5.10 (40)

Round 2, at Princes Park, May 6
South Melbourne 10.6 (66) drew with Carl. 10.6 (66)

Round 3, at Junction Oval, May 13
South Melbourne 10.13 (73) d Carlton 2.5 (17)

Round 4, at Lake Oval, May 20
South Melbourne 12.13 (85) d Melbourne 8.11 (59)

Round 5, at Lake Oval, May 27
Collingwood 5.10 (40) d South Melbourne 4.10 (34)

Round 6, at Punt Road, June 3
Richmond 8.14 (62) d South Melbourne 7.12 (54)

Round 7, at Brunswick Street, June 5
South Melbourne 10.11 (71) d Fitzroy 3.5 (23)

Round 8, at Lake Oval, June 10
South Melbourne 7.10 (52) d Geelong 5.9 (39)

Round 9, at Lake Oval, June 17
South Melbourne 6.8 (44) d Essendon 5.11 (41)

Round 10, at MCG, June 24
South Melbourne 9.13 (67) d University 4.5 (29)

Round 11, at Lake Oval, July 1
South Melbourne 12.8 (80) d Carlton 9.11 (65)

Round 12, at Lake Oval, July 8
South Melbourne 12.14 (86) d St Kilda 6.13 (49)

Round 13, at MCG, July 15
South Melbourne 9.8 (62) d Melbourne 7.7 (49)

Round 14, at Victoria Park, July 22
South Melbourne 5.7 (37) d Collingwood 5.6 (36)

Round 15, at Lake Oval, July 29
South Melbourne 8.25 (73) d Richmond 5.7 (37)

Round 16, at Lake Oval, August 19
South Melbourne 5.6 (36) d Fitzroy 4.3 (27)

Round 17, at Corio Oval, August 26
Geelong 10.12 (72) d South Melbourne 10.3 (63)

Round 18, at East Melbourne CG, September 2
Essendon 9.9 (63) d South Melbourne 8.10 (58)

Semi-final, at MCG, September 9
Collingwood 11.11 (77) d South Melbourne 6.11 (47)

Joe Prince, a star South winger.

Bill Thomas was captain-coach in 1911.

PLAYER	GAMES	GOALS
BELCHER, Vic	18	12
BOWER, George	18	5
CALDWELL, Jim	18	2
CAMERON, Jim	16	3
CARPENTER, Fred	17	23
CASEY, Dick	12	14
CHARGE, Les	1	0
DEAS, George	1	0
DOLPHIN, Bill	6	0
FIELDING, Fred	1	0
GEORGE, Ernie	1	0
GOUGH, Alf	16	11
GRIMSHAW, Tom	19	0
HISKINS, Arthur	17	11
KERR, Alex	7	2
MAIN, Ben	1	0
MILNE, Herbert	11	7
MORTIMER, Len	19	44
PENTLAND, Alan	14	0
PRINCE, Joe	17	0
PUNSHON, Arthur	7	1
RICKETTS, Charlie	7	6
SCOBIE, Jack	13	0
SLOSS, Bruce	17	9
STROWNIX, Tom	14	1
TANDY, Mark	3	0
THOMAS, Bill	18	0
WALSH, Jack	18	0

POSITION: Third
COACH: Bill Thomas
CAPTAIN: Bill Thomas
BEST AND FAIREST: -
LEADING GOALKICKER: Len Mortimer (44)

suffered its third consecutive defeat in going down by 30 points in front of 43,575 fans at the MCG. South's premiership dream was over. South had imploded over the final stages of the season and *The Australasian's* "Markwell" suggested South's forwards had been too predictable. He also wrote: "Every year League football gets more vigorous and less skilful, most of the teams adopting the policy of kicking straight ahead, and then it is a man-to-man struggle for the ball — brawn versus brains." South obviously had to play smarter football in 1912 and its only consolation for a disappointing 1911 season was that brilliant follower Bruce Sloss was named Champion of the Colony in a competition run by *The Argus* newspaper.

1912

South was given a massive boost before the start of the 1912 season when the VFL lifted its "indefinite" ban on follower Bert Franks and *The Herald* reported in the lead-up to the season: "Franks is showing much of his old form in practice, and in a week or two should be as brilliant as ever." South also had a new captain-coach. Bill Thomas stepped down in favour of 1909 premiership captain-coach Charlie Ricketts, who had been troubled by an ankle injury and played just seven games in 1911.

However, the season opened on a sad note as club president Henry Skinner MLC died on February 14, 1912, aged 70. Born in London, he arrived in Australia via the United States in 1871 and ran the still-existing Golden Gate Hotel in Clarendon Street, South Melbourne, before establishing himself as one of Melbourne's leading brewers. Skinner was MLC for Melbourne South for just five months before his sudden death. He was replaced as club president by another Parliamentarian, George Elmslie MLA.

The red and white opened the season with a 13-point win over Fitzroy at the Lake Oval and *The Herald* noted that South newcomer Dick Mullaly, from Leopold, made an impressive debut. Centreman Mullaly, who played 69 games with South to 1917, was the first South player to wear number 14, later made famous by Brownlow Medal winners Bob Skilton and Paul Kelly. Although some clubs wore unofficial numbers in some matches over previous seasons, these became official in 1912 with the birth of the *Football Record,* now the *AFL Record.*

Len Mortimer in 1912 topped South's goalkicking for a seventh consecutive season.

South's only other newcomers in 1912 included former Collingwood, Carlton, Richmond and Melbourne full-back Les Abbott, who became the first player to represent five VFL clubs. The only other newcomers were West Australian Frank Comer, Les Rusich (Leopold) and Harry Saltau (Port Melbourne Juniors).

Although Richmond defeated South by three points at Punt Road in round two, the red and white then became a model of consistency and at one stage notched eight consecutive victories. South topped the ladder after 13 rounds and, the following week, Thomas, Joe Prince and Bruce Sloss represented Victoria late in the season, while Vic Belcher, Les Charge and Fred Carpenter represented the VFL against a combined Bendigo side at the

This photograph was taken on a South trip to Sydney in 1912.

MATCH RESULTS

Round 1, at Lake Oval, April 27
South Melbourne 7.5 (47) d Fitzroy 4.10 (34)

Round 2, at Punt Road, May 4
Richmond 5.8 (38) d South Melbourne 2.23 (35)

Round 3, at Lake Oval, May 11
South Melbourne 6.18 (54) d Melbourne 3.4 (22)

Round 4, at Lake Oval, May 18
Essendon 9.8 (62) d South Melbourne 8.8 (56)

Round 5, at Junction Oval, May 25
South Melbourne 7.8 (50) d St Kilda 5.5 (35)

Round 6, at MCG, June 1
South Melbourne 9.16 (70) d University 5.8 (38)

Round 7, at Lake Oval, June 3
South Melbourne 13.15 (93) d Geelong 8.13 (61)

Round 8, at Princes Park, June 8
Carlton 8.16 (64) d South Melbourne 6.10 (46)

Round 9, at Lake Oval, June 15
South Melbourne 4.16 (40) d Collingwood 4.8 (32)

Round 10, at Brunswick Street, June 22
South Melbourne 9.12 (66) d Fitzroy 3.10 (28)

Round 11, at Lake Oval, June 29
South Melbourne 19.12 (126) d Richmond 5.7 (37)

Round 12, at MCG, July 13
South Melbourne 13.8 (86) d Melbourne 0.8 (8)

Round 13, at East Melbourne CG, July 20
South Melbourne 9.11 (65) d Essendon 7.10 (52)

Round 14, at Lake Oval, July 27
South Melbourne 14.7 (91) d St Kilda 7.18 (60)

Round 15, at Lake Oval, August 3
South Melbourne 12.13 (85) d University 7.5 (47)

Round 16, at Corio Oval, August 17
South Melbourne 6.15 (51) d Geelong 4.8 (32)

Round 17, at Lake Oval, August 24
Carlton 7.10 (52) d South Melbourne 6.10 (46)

Round 18, at Victoria Park, August 31
South Melbourne 7.11 (53) d Collingwood 5.7 (37)

Semi-final, at MCG, September 14
Essendon 7.12 (54) d South Melbourne 6.6 (42)

Grand Final, at MCG, September 28
Essendon 5.17 (47) d South Melbourne 4.9 (33)

Lake Oval and Rusich, Arthur Hiskins and Jack Scobie played for the VFL against a combined Ballarat side at Ballarat.

South, despite going down by six points to Carlton at the Lake Oval in the penultimate round, finished the home and away season on top of the ladder on percentage ahead of the Blues, with Essendon and Geelong making up the final four. South therefore played Essendon in a semi-final and, despite starting a hot favourite, went down by 12 points. South skipper Ricketts failed a late fitness test and, in his absence, football history was created when brothers Vic (South) and Allan Belcher (Essendon) led the opposing sides.

Fred Carpenter kicked 24 goals for South in 1912.

Carlton defeated Geelong in the other semi-final and South, as top team, had the right of challenge against the winner of the Essendon-Carlton preliminary final, which Essendon won by just four points.

Ricketts passed a fitness test to take his place in the South side for the Grand Final, but Essendon had to go into the big match without champion rover Ern "Ginger" Cameron, who had broken an ankle in the preliminary final. South therefore was a warm favourite to take its second VFL flag.

A huge attendance of 54,463 watched the action at the MCG and would have been disappointed with the standard of play. There were suggestions that the players were nervous over the first quarter, but the standard did not improve as Essendon led by 11 points at half-time and by a formidable 20 points at the final change. *The Herald* reported: "The game fell short of what was expected. South Melbourne, after the first quarter, never looked to have a chance and played lazy, systemless football." Essendon defeated South by 14 points, but was flattered by this margin as Essendon controlled most of the play and Vic Belcher scored a late goal for the Southerners.

PLAYER	GAMES	GOALS
ABBOTT, Les	3	0
BELCHER, Vic	20	3
BOWER, George	11	1
CALDWELL, Jim	20	1
CARPENTER, Fred	18	24
CASEY, Dick	15	20
CHARGE, Les	18	16
COMER, Frank	2	0
DEAS, George	3	3
DEAS, Bob	9	1
FRANKS, Bert	18	17
GRIMSHAW, Tom	7	0
HISKINS, Arthur	18	5
MILNE, Herbert	20	7
MORTIMER, Len	19	40
MULLALY, Dick	17	1
PENTLAND, Alan	5	0
PRINCE, Joe	14	0
RICKETTS, Charlie	16	9
RUSICH, Les	19	9
SALTAU, Harry	16	0
SCOBIE, Jack	19	0
SLOSS, Bruce	18	10
TANDY, Mark	9	0
THOMAS, Bill	20	0
WALSH, Jack		

POSITION: Runner-up
COACH: Charlie Ricketts
CAPTAIN: Charlie Ricketts
BEST AND FAIRFEST: -
LEADING GOALKICKER: Len Mortimer (40)

1913

Under the club constitution of its earliest VFL years, players (no more than 30) elected a captain and vice-captain, to be approved by the full committee. The players in 1913 elected Vic Belcher as captain, with Harvey Kelly his deputy. It was an unusual arrangement as the committee appointed Kelly coach. Kelly had played with South in 1902, but moved to Western Australia to play with South Fremantle before returning to Victoria to play with Carlton from 1907-09. He played in Tasmania after leaving Carlton and wanted to cross to South in 1912, but the Blues blocked his clearance and he spent that season in the country with Bairnsdale before the talented forward eventually won his release to the Southerners.

South played 10 newcomers in 1913, with the best of them being goalsneak full-forward Jack Freeman (from Rose of Northcote) and defender Arthur Rademacher (Leopold). Freeman later was killed in World War I, while Rademacher played in the 1918 premiership side and notched 101 games with the Southerners to 1920 before being captain-coach of Hawthorn in its VFA years.

The Southerners started the season with a nine-point win over St Kilda at the Lake Oval

and followed-up with a draw against Carlton at Princes Park. South, with Kelly proving he had lost nothing from his years in the football wilderness by twice kicking bags of five goals (against Essendon in round four and University in round 17), finished the home and away season in second position, a game and a half behind Fitzroy, with Collingwood and St Kilda making up the final four.

South therefore played St Kilda in the first of the two semi-finals and, because South had

A postcard featuring a South Melbourne team of 1913.

Bill Strang topped South's goalkicking with 29 in 1913.

MATCH RESULTS

Round 1, at Lake Oval, April 26
South Melbourne 8.15 (63) d St Kilda 8.6 (54)

Round 2, at Princes Park, May 3
South Melbourne 9.7 (61) drew with Carlton 8.13 (61)

Round 3, at Lake Oval, May 10
South Melbourne 8.9 (57) d Richmond 9.2 (56)

Round 4, at East Melbourne CG, May 17
South Melbourne 15.13 (103) d Essendon 7.14 (56)

Round 5, at Corio Oval, May 24
South Melbourne 9.17 (71) d Geelong 7.15 (57)

Round 6, at Lake Oval, May 31
South Melbourne 6.16 (52) d Melbourne 4.4 (28)

Round 7, at Lake Oval, June 7
Fitzroy 11.17 (83) d South Melbourne 7.8 (50)

Round 8, at MCG, June 9
South Melbourne 13.12 (90) d University 10.9 (69)

Round 9, at Lake Oval, June 14
South Melbourne 10.15 (75) d Collingwood 7.9 (51)

Round 10, at Junction Oval, June 21
South Melbourne 13.14 (92) d St Kilda 9.11 (65)

Round 11, at Lake Oval, June 28
South Melbourne 12.16 (88) d Carlton 5.11 (41)

Round 12, at Punt Road, July 5
South Melbourne 8.11 (59) d Richmond 3.17 (35)

Round 13, at Lake Oval, July 19
Essendon 7.20 (62) d South Melbourne 5.12 (42)

Round 14, at Lake Oval, July 26
South Melbourne 12.10 (82) d Geelong 9.12 (66)

Round 15, at MCG, August 2
South Melbourne 5.18 (48) d Melbourne 2.7 (19)

Round 16, at Lake Oval, August 9
Fitzroy 8.11 (59) d South Melbourne 7.14 (56)

Round 17, at Lake Oval, August 23
South Melbourne 17.9 (111) d University 8.13 (61)

Round 18, at Victoria Park, August 30
South Melbourne 8.8 (56) d Collingwood 7.12 (54)

Semi-final, at MCG, September 6
St Kilda 12.12 (84) d South Melbourne 6.15 (51)

defeated St Kilda in both their clashes in 1913, was expected to win comfortably. However, St Kilda pulled off a major upset in defeating South by 33 points. St Kilda's Ernie Sellars kicked six goals, while South's six goals were shared by Belcher, Kelly, Len Mortimer, Bert Franks, Bob Deas and Stan Hiskins.

The great Vic Belcher was South's 1913 captain.

The football world was so shocked that there were immediate suggestions of bribery. The South Melbourne Football Club investigated these claims and, in the annual report released in February, 1914, reported: "The efforts put forward by your committee to secure the best possible team for premiership honours were nullified by the inexplicably poor display in the semi-final match with St Kilda and, whatever the cause, the disappointment has been the topic of severe comment, which may or may not be deserved …

"Allegations of suspicious play both before and after the semi-final matches causes your committee endless worry but, after exhausted and searching enquiry, nothing of a definite nature could be discovered." The annual report tempered this with the comment: "It cannot be denied that in some of the games put up by your team absolutely the finest football for years was shown to the public." It ended this section of the report with the comment that the club hoped that in 1914 the "players will be able to restore the confidence of the supporters".

South in 1913 had 3838 full members, 623 lady and boy members and an annual expenditure of just over 2014 pounds ($4028), with the heaviest expense being player payments of 1192 pounds ($2384).

PLAYER	GAMES	GOALS
ABBOTT, Paddy	4	0
BELCHER, Vic	17	8
BOWER, George	7	0
CAFFYN, Marshall	1	0
CALDWELL, Jim	16	6
CARPENTER, Fred	2	2
CHARGE, Les	17	10
DEAS, Bob	5	1
EASTICK, Bill	13	2
FINCHER, Charlie	9	5
FITZGERALD, Dick	2	0
FRANKS, Bert	11	5
FREEMAN, Jack	3	3
HISKINS, Arthur	17	0
HISKINS, Stan	14	19
KELLY, Harvey	19	27
MORTIMER, Len	19	23
MULLALY, Dick	9	3
PRINCE, Joe	18	2
RADEMACHER, Arthur	19	0
RUSICH, Les	11	8
SALTAU, Harry	12	0
SCOBIE, Jack	7	2
SLOSS, Bruce	17	6
STRANG, Bill	15	29
TANDY, Mark	17	2
THOMAS, Bill	18	0
WEBSTER, Horrie	17	13
WOLFE, Charlie	6	2

POSITION: Third
COACH: Harvey Kelly
CAPTAIN: Vic Belcher
BEST AND FAIREST: -
LEADING GOALKICKER: Bill Strang (29)

1914

The VFL opened the 1914 season with the world at peace, but ended with the greatest conflict known to man. World War I had a devastating effect on Australia, at all levels. The first South Melbourne player to enlist is believed to have been Stan Hiskins, who joined the Mechanical Transport Division, but others quickly followed and South later mourned several of its greatest stars.

No one was to know at the start of the season that Australia would join mother country Britain on August 4 in declaring war on Germany. Australian Prime Minister Joseph Cook famously thundered: "Australia will stand beside her (Britain) to the last man and the last shilling."

Five months earlier, the South players again elected Vic Belcher as captain, with Harvey Kelly his deputy. This time, however, the committee appointed Belcher coach. South also declared before the start of the season that it again would allow the Leopold club to train and play at the Lake Oval. Other junior clubs, including South Melbourne CYMS, South Melbourne District, Howe Crescent and Albert Park Presbyterians also were allowed to train at the Lake Oval.

This seemed only fair as the Leopold club was a prolific recruiting ground and, in 1914, South recruited key forward Aloysius "Alan" O'Donoghue from this local club after he had played with Richmond in 1912. South also recruited a youngster named Herb E. Matthews, who became the first of three generations to represent the club — along with son and Brownlow Medal winner Herb and grandson Herb.

South opened the season with a 54-point win over University at the MCG and, although it drew with Carlton in round four, did not taste defeat until going down to Collingwood by three points at the Lake Oval in round eight. The Southerners also lost to Geelong in round 11 before enduring a horror run of three consecutive defeats (to Carlton, St Kilda and Essendon) over the second round of matches. Then, after defeating Richmond by 14 points at the Lake Oval in round 16, South took full advantage of a two-week break for the national Carnival in Sydney with a "Players' Trip" to Sydney and the Blue Mountains. While Les Charge (who was runner-up for the award for best Victorian player) and Bruce Sloss represented the Big Vee, the other South players visited Katoomba and other tourist

A South Melbourne team of 1914.

MATCH RESULTS

Round 1, at MCG, April 25
South Melbourne 14.14 (98) d University 6.8 (44)

Round 2, at Lake Oval, May 2
South Melbourne 8.14 (62) d Geelong 7.9 (51)

Round 3, at Brunswick Street Oval, May 9
South Melbourne 11.8 (74) d Fitzroy 9.12 (66)

Round 4, at Lake Oval, May 16
South Melbourne 8.4 (52) drew with Carlton 7.10 (52)

Round 5, at Lake Oval, May 23
South Melbourne 11.11 (77) d St Kilda 9.12 (66)

Round 6, at East Melbourne CG , May 30
South Melbourne 5.13 (43) d Essendon 5.11 (41)

Round 7, at Punt Road, June 6
South Melbourne 7.12 (54) d Richmond 4.12 (36)

Round 8, at Lake Oval, June 8
Collingwood 6.10 (46) d South Melbourne 5.13 (43)

Round 9, at MCG, June 13
South Melbourne 13.12 (90) d Melbourne 8.7 (55)

Round 10, at Lake Oval, June 20
South Melbourne 9.16 (70) d University 8.7 (55)

Round 11, at Corio Oval, June 27
Geelong 9.20 (74) d South Melbourne 6.9 (45)

Round 12, at Lake Oval, July 4
South Melbourne 10.4 (64) d Fitzroy 7.12 (54)

Round 13, at Princes Park, July 11
Carlton 11.14 (80) d South Melbourne 9.6 (60)

Round 14, at Junction Oval, July 18
St Kilda 12.7 (79) d South Melbourne 7.15 (57)

Round 15, at Lake Oval, July 25
Essendon 15.14 (104) d South Melbourne 4.8 (32)

Round 16, at Lake Oval, August 1
South Melbourne 8.9 (57) d Richmond 5.13 (43)

Round 17, at Victoria Park, August 22
South Melbourne 8.9 (57) d Collingwood 4.12 (36)

Round 18, at Lake Oval, August 29
South Melbourne 10.18 (78) d Melbourne 5.5 (35)

Semi-final, at MCG, September 5
South Melbourne 5.14 (44) d Geelong 5.8 (38)

Preliminary final, at MCG, September 19
South Melbourne 5.13 (43) d Carlton 3.6 (24)

Grand Final, at MCG, September 26
Carlton 6.9 (45) d South Melbourne 4.15 (39)

points and even were visited in Wagga by former player Harry Lampe.

South in 1914 also visited Maryborough, at the VFL's request. The VFL, to promote goodwill in the country, delegated clubs to various parts of the state to play against local combinations, with South defeating a representative Maryborough team on August 8 on the first Saturday of the two-week break.

The Southerners finished the season in second position behind Carlton, with Fitzroy and Geelong making up the final four. South defeated Geelong by six points in the first of the semi-finals, with Carlton defeating Fitzroy by 20 points. South, in the third week of the finals, defeated Carlton by 19 points but the Blues, as minor premiers, had right of challenge and the two clubs clashed in the Grand Final on September 26.

After Carlton led by 21 points at half-time, South hit back hard at the start of the third quarter and managed to pin the margin back to nine points by the final break. Many of the 30,485 fans at the MCG expected South to close the gap over the final quarter, but Carlton held firm and won by six points.

South's Bruce Sloss played his heart out in the 1914 Grand Final loss to Carlton.

The defeat was heart-breaking but South had the consolation of having the best player on the ground, follower Bruce Sloss. Essendon premiership coach (and former Carlton flag coach) John Worrall wrote in *The Australasian:* "Sloss had no superior on the ground, his glorious efforts in the last quarter stamping him as a great footballer. He possesses all the qualities, but is apt to attempt the impossible on occasions. He marked, kicked and ran like a champion and

Joe Prince was one of South's stars of 1914.

South Melbourne Football Club

THE

Annual General Meeting

Will be held at the South Melbourne Cricket Ground on MONDAY EVENING, 15th FEBRUARY, at 8 o'clock

Polling to be held in the Gymnasium from 6.30 till 9 p.m.

A GRAND

Open Air Concert

Will be held on the Ground

MEMBERS MUST PRESENT LAST SEASON'S TICKET TO SECURE ADMISSION, AND SAME MUST BE SHOWN WHEN VOTING

Admission for Non-Members 6d. Children 3d.

HERBERT HOWSON, Hon. Secretary

almost pulled the match out of the fire by his brilliant efforts".

Sadly, it was Sloss' last match as he already had enlisted in the AIF and was killed in action in France in 1917. Another member of South's 1914 Grand Final side, Jack Freeman, also made the supreme sacrifice. He was South's leading goalkicker in 1914, with 36.

The South Melbourne annual report for the 1914 season said this of team performances: "The season just past is one that will long remain in the minds of football enthusiasts. The games put up by your team during the season won the admiration of friend and foe alike. The semi-final and final game are too fresh in your memory to require to be referred to at any length, but we cannot help drawing your attention to the final and Grand Final matches with our old Carlton rivals. For any club to be able to stop the old Blues scoring only one behind after half-time in one match and only one goal and one behind after half-time in the next match is a record of which any club may be justly proud. "Observer" in *The Argus* remarked that 'although South Melbourne had not won the premiership, they had gained something more'."

The South annual report for the 1914 season referred to the enlistment of Stan Hiskins and added: "The committee and players made him a present for a small token of esteem, and wished him good luck and a safe return.

"Mr George Jackson, one of your trainers, also has gone to the front with the Army Medical Corps, and a small token of esteem was presented to him by players, trainers and committee, with an earnest wish expressed for good health and a safe return.

"The Victorian Football League decided that an extra sixpence be charged on the admission to the semi-final and final games, with the result that the supporters of the noble game contributed 2357 pounds to the Patriotic Funds, a contribution well worthy of the sports following our game.

"The 9th AASC Mechanical Transport were camped adjacent to your ground, and your committee, together with the South Melbourne Cricket Club committee, granted them use of the ground, and the compliment was greatly appreciated by the officers and men. Lieutenant-Colonel Moon expressed the deep debt of gratitude he and his officers and men were under for the kindnesses extended to them during their stay at Albert Park."

The annual report also referred to a trip to Sydney and the Blue Mountains, organised by the Entertainment Committee. The report indicated that, as the players and officials left the Spencer Street station by rail, supporters decorated their carriages with red and white ribbons, streamers and confetti. The report added: "The behaviour of the team whilst on tour was a credit to the game and the club, and the numerous invitations extended to them to again visit the sister State showed their undoubted popularity."

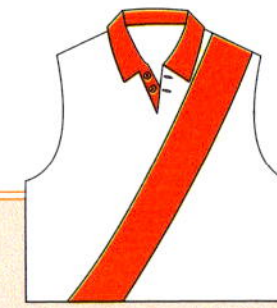

PLAYER	GAMES	GOALS
BELCHER, Vic	21	0
BENNETT, Harold	7	0
BOLLARD, Tom	9	0
BOWER, George	2	0
CALDWELL, Jim	17	4
CHARGE, Les	21	18
DEAS, Bob	19	0
EASTICK, Bill	2	0
FREEMAN, Jack	19	36
HAIR, Ben	18	1
HENNINGTON, Bill	6	1
HISKINS, Arthur	4	1
HISKINS, Stan	16	11
JACKSON, Percy	8	5
JONES, Charlie	4	1
JOOLEN, Herb	1	1
KELLY, Harvey	21	21
LAIDLAW, Wally	2	0
MATTHEWS, Herb E.	1	0
MORGAN, Harry	21	27
MORTIMER, Len	3	1
MULLALY, Dick	18	3
O'BRIEN, Jack	2	2
O'DONOGHUE, Aloysius "Alan"	17	8
PAYNE, George	7	3
PRINCE, Joe	16	0
RADEMACHER, Arthur	21	0
RUSICH, Les	16	7
SALTAU, Harry	16	0
SLOSS, Bruce	18	14
TANDY, Mark	17	3
THOMAS, Claude	8	0

POSITION: Runner-up
COACH: Vic Belcher
CAPTAIN: Vic Belcher
BEST AND FAIREST: -
LEADING GOALKICKER: Jack Freeman (36)

1915

The first round of the 1915 VFL season was played on April 24, the day before the Anzac landings at Gallipoli. Several VFL footballers, including South Melbourne's Charles Fincher, Melbourne's Joe Pearce and Collingwood's Alan Cordner, were killed as they made their away ashore and the South Melbourne Football Club later was to mourn several more of its heroes.

Fincher had played nine games with South in 1913 after he had impressed in a match for the Ballarat League against a VFL combination in 1912. He switched to Essendon VFA in 1914 but enlisted in August that year and trained at the Broadmeadows army camp before sailing for Egypt and then the Dardanelles.

Charles Fincher was killed at the Gallipoli landings.

The 1915 season therefore was played in an atmosphere of enormous debate, with many wanting all sport to go into recess until the end of hostilities. John Worrall, writing in *The Australasian* commented late in the VFL season: "The war news has more intense interest now that our brave boys are giving up their lives for the cause of freedom, rendering it more than ever necessary that there must be some relaxation from the mental strain of poring over the news from the seat of war."

South, with several of its top players already in khaki and on their way to Europe, had a dismal start to the season, losing to St Kilda, Carlton and Richmond over the first three rounds. The big-hearted Vic Belcher again was captain-coach, but champion follower Bruce Sloss was unavailable because he was sent to a musketry school at Port Melbourne.

South's 1915 season was erratic and although it won three of its final four home and away matches, finished fifth and was never a real chance of making the finals. Melbourne claimed fourth position, even though South defeated the Redlegs by seven points in round 16. Melbourne then went down to Essendon in the penultimate round before having a bye in the final round.

The bye was caused by the resignation from VFL ranks of the University club following the 1914 season. It long has been suggested that the war brought about University's demise but, in fact, the Professors (as they were known) relinquished their VFL status because they were unable to field strong enough teams because of studies and other factors. The VFL in 1915 therefore had a nine-team competition.

South's annual report, presented to members on February 21, 1916, said under the heading YOUR TEAM: "Although

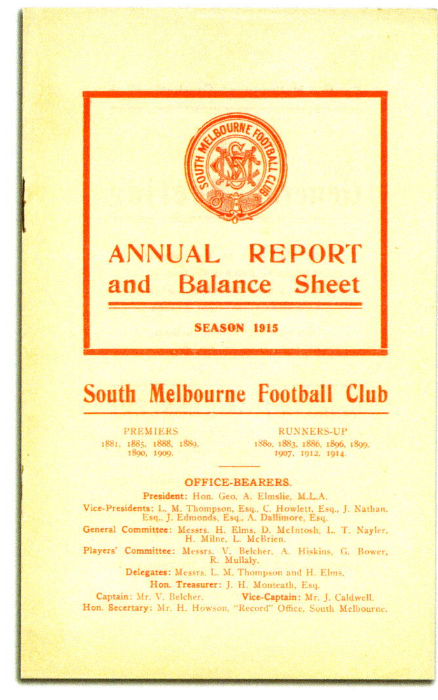

ANNUAL REPORT
and Balance Sheet

SEASON 1915

South Melbourne Football Club

PREMIERS
1881, 1885, 1888, 1889, 1890, 1909.

RUNNERS-UP
1880, 1883, 1886, 1896, 1899, 1907, 1912, 1914.

OFFICE-BEARERS.

President: Hon. Geo. A. Elmslie, M.L.A.

Vice-Presidents: L. M. Thompson, Esq., C. Howlett, Esq., J. Nathan, Esq., J. Edmonds, Esq., A. Dallimore, Esq.

General Committee: Messrs. H. Elms, D. McIntosh, L. T. Nayler, H. Milne, L. McBrien.

Players' Committee: Messrs. V. Belcher, A. Hiskins, G. Bower, R. Mullaly.

Delegates: Messrs. L. M. Thompson and H. Elms.

Hon. Treasurer: J. H. Monteath, Esq.

Captain: Mr. V. Belcher. **Vice-Captain:** Mr. J. Caldwell.

Hon. Secertary: Mr. H. Howson, "Record" Office, South Melbourne.

MATCH RESULTS

Round 1, at Junction Oval, April 24
St Kilda 8.16 (54) d South Melbourne 4.13 (37)

Round 2, at Lake Oval, May 1
Carlton 8.12 (60) d South Melbourne 6.11 (47)

Round 3, at Punt Road, May 8
Richmond 9.15 (69) d South Melbourne 8.19 (67)

Round 5, at Lake Oval, May 22
South Melbourne 8.8 (56) d Fitzroy 6.4 (40)

Round 6, at East Melbourne CG, May 29
South Melbourne 8.16 (64) d Essendon 8.7 (55)

Round 7, at Lake Oval, June 5
Melbourne 10.8 (68) d South Melbourne 7.5 (47)

Round 8, at Lake Oval, June 12
South Melbourne 14.17 (101) d Geelong 13.5 (83)

Round 9, at Victoria Park, June 19
Collingwood 5.13 (43) d South Melbourne 3.10 (28)

Round 10, at Lake Oval, June 26
South Melbourne 9.11 (65) d St Kilda 7.5 (47)

Round 11, at Princes Park, July 3
Carlton 7.15 (57) d South Melbourne 7.5 (47)

Round 12, at Lake Oval, July 10
South Melbourne 10.12 (72) d Richmond 7.11 (53)

Round 14, at Brunswick Street, July 24
Fitzroy 8.6 (54) d South Melbourne 7.6 (48)

Round 15, at Lake Oval, July 31
South Melbourne 13.19 (97) d Essendon 6.4 (40)

Round 16, at MCG, August 7
South Melbourne 5.13 (43) d Melbourne 4.12 (36)

Round 17, at Corio Oval, August 14
South Melbourne 10.14 (74) d Geelong 7.10 (52)

Round 18, at Lake Oval, August 21
Collingwood 7.9 (51) d South Melbourne 4.9 (33)

reductions had to be made (because of the war), attendances at training and their play on the Saturdays were quite worthy of the good old Red and White."

On the war, the report noted: "Your committee is very proud of the prominent part your players are taking in serving their King and Country, and every encouragement is given to any of the players joining the Flag. A roll of honour is to be placed in the gymnasium, with a complete list of the players who have gone to the front.

Jim Caldwell.

"The following members of your team are at present either in the fighting line or in camp: Messrs. S. Hiskins, G. Bower, C. Thomas, B. Sloss, C. Jones, W. Laidlaw, E. Dimsey, N. Bradford, C. Willis, J. Freeman, Les Turner and S. Wootton." Another list included Martin Pash (already wounded), Charles Clements, Hugh Callan, Syd Sykes, Wal Smallhorn (uncle of future Fitzroy Brownlow Medal winner Wilfred "Chicken" Smallhorn), Ted Harrison and Charles Fincher."

The report added: "As it is impossible to obtain the names of all members who have enlisted, it was decided not to publish the names in case some may be unintentionally missed. We tender our best wishes to them all for good health and a safe return, bringing victory with them. It is estimated between 700 and 800 members have joined the colours."

PLAYER	GAMES	GOALS
ADAMS, Arthur	3	0
BELCHER, Vic	14	0
BOLLARD, Tom	9	0
BOYCE, Alf	2	4
BRADFORD, Norm	7	9
CALDWELL, Jim	13	5
CHARGE, Les	2	1
DALY, Bill	13	1
DEAS, Bob	8	1
DOHERTY, Jack	12	6
FARNAN, Pat	2	1
GOUGH, Alf	8	4
HAIR, Ben	13	1
HISKINS, Arthur	14	0
HOWELL, Jack	12	1
JONES, Charlie	3	0
MORGAN, Harry	16	48
MORTIMER, Len	2	2
MULLALY, Dick	15	0
O'DONOGHUE, Aloysius "Alan"	12	1
PAYNE, George	12	7
PRINCE, Joe	8	0
RADEMACHER, Arthur	15	0
RUSICH, Les	8	9
SALTAU, Harry	6	0
STEWART, Jim	16	9
TANDY, Mark	15	0
THOMAS, Claude	5	0
TURNER, Les	1	1
WILLIS, Carl	14	7
WOOTTON, Stan	8	6

POSITION: Fifth
COACH: Vic Belcher
CAPTAIN: Vic Belcher
BEST AND FAIREST: -
LEADING GOALKICKER: Harry Morgan (48)

1916

South Melbourne in 1916 was one of five clubs, along with Melbourne, St Kilda, Essendon and Geelong to pull out of the VFL competition because of the war. They were known as the "patriotic clubs", with Carlton, Collingwood, Fitzroy and Richmond to compete in a severely truncated season. The VFL in July, 1915, had held a special meeting to vote on whether to continue the competition. The delegates (two from each club) voted against the motion of abandonment.

Bruce Sloss before the exhibition match in London.

South was hit particularly hard by the war, with two former players making the supreme sacrifice in 1916 alone. Rover Norman Bradford was killed at Pozieres on August 4, while full-forward Jack Freeman died of wounds in France on November 15.

Bradford had played seven games in the red and white in 1915 after joining South from VFA club Yarraville. He sailed for Egypt and

Lieutenant Bruce Sloss.

ANNUAL REPORT
and Balance Sheet

SEASON 1915

South Melbourne Football Club

PREMIERS
1881, 1885, 1888, 1889, 1890, 1909.

RUNNERS-UP
1880, 1883, 1886, 1896, 1899, 1907, 1912, 1914.

OFFICE-BEARERS.
President: Hon. Geo. A. Elmslie, M.L.A.
Vice-Presidents: L. M. Thompson, Esq., C. Howlett, Esq., J. Nathan, Esq., J. Edmonds, Esq., A. Dallimore, Esq.
General Committee: Messrs. H. Elms, D. McIntosh, L. T. Nayler, H. Milne, L. McBrien.
Players' Committee: Messrs. V. Belcher, A. Hiskins, G. Bower, R. Mullaly.
Delegates: Messrs. L. M. Thompson and H. Elms.
Hon. Treasurer: J. H. Monteath, Esq.
Captain: Mr. V. Belcher. **Vice-Captain:** Mr. J. Caldwell.
Hon. Secertary: Mr. H. Howson, "Record" Office, South Melbourne.

then France late in 1915 and was just one of hundreds of Australians cut down by German artillery and machine-gun fire in the ferocious battle at Pozieres. He had caught up with another South player, Stan Wootton, just days before he was killed and Wootton wrote to *The South Melbourne Record* after hearing of Bradford's death: "Poor young (he was 21) Norman Bradford! He was, as you say, a very fine chap." One of Bradford's former South teammates, Jim Caldwell, paid this tribute published in *The Argus*: "He died as he lived — a hero and a man. To know him was to love him."

Freeman, from the Rose of Northcote club, had played 22 games with South over the 1913-14 seasons and had topped the club goalkicking with 36 in 1914. His last game had been in the 1914 Grand Final defeat by

Carlton. Sapper Freeman, a cabinet-maker, was wounded by a German shell and rushed to a field hospital at Amiens. He wrote to his parents to tell them not to worry as his injuries were not serious. However, he had had both legs amputated and died of his wounds. A tribute in *The Argus* read: "He did his duty and is now resting."

The South Melbourne Record commented: "He was a remarkably fine fellow, and the sympathy of all those who knew him goes out with his sorrowing relatives."

Two South players saw some football action in 1916, with Bruce Sloss and Carl Willis representing the Third Australian Division against the Australian Training Units in an exhibition match in London on October 28, 1916. The match was played in front of 8000 excited Diggers, as well as King Manuel of Spain and the Prince of Wales (later King Edward VIII). Sloss, who captained the Third Division team in blue guernseys with a white map of Australia (the Training Units wore red with a white kangaroo), was killed in action just 10 weeks later.

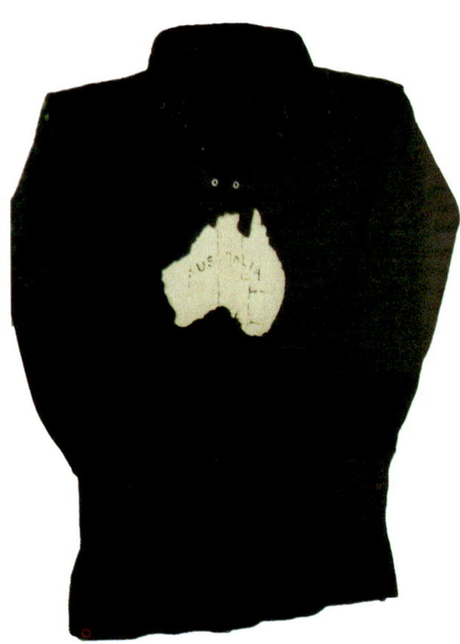

A Third Division guernsey, as worn by Bruce Sloss.

Lieutenant Bruce Sloss (fourth from right) with his men in the 10th Machine Gun Company.

Meanwhile, the four competing clubs in 1916 indicated they would donate part of their gate receipts to the Patriotic Fund and the VFL allowed recruiting officers to address crowds. The season comprised 12 rounds, with the four clubs playing each other three times. Amazingly, there was a "final four" and Fitzroy, which had finished last with just two wins and a draw, not only reached the Grand Final but defeated Carlton by 29 points.

Sapper Jack Freeman, "a remarkably fine fellow".

Three of the men who played in the exhibition match in London late in 1916 later were killed in action. Apart from South Melbourne's Bruce Sloss, Richmond's Les Lee and Fitzroy's Jack Cooper made the supreme sacrifice. Lee had played just two games with Richmond, in 1913, but Cooper not only had played 136 games with Fitzroy from 1907-15, but had captained the Maroons and Victoria.

South also was represented in this exhibition game by Carl Willis who, like Sloss, played for the Third Division side. Willis, who survived the war, played 29 games in the red and white to 1921. He had started with South in 1915, but then missed the next four seasons before returning to VFL action in 1920. He captained South in 1921.

1917

Despite increasing concern over the war, South Melbourne and Geelong rejoined the VFL competition in 1917 for a six-team chase for the flag. In its 1917 annual report, the South committee explained: "After mature consideration your committee decided to again compete in the premiership matches. Your executive considered that it would not be out of the way to place before you what the national sport has done for the great war." It then quoted a State War Council member saying: "If you close everything up you will have a lot of men idle. You will have more men getting into mischief."

South was dealt a massive blow to the heart early in the year when it was reported that former champion Lieutenant Bruce Sloss had been killed in action at Armentieres, France, on January 4. Sloss had been hit by shrapnel and was killed instantly. He was an engineer in civilian life and one of the most popular footballers to have represented the club, and *The South Melbourne Record* reported that, at news of his death, "grown men cried". Sloss had played 81 games in the red and white, was named Champion of the Colony in 1911 and was acclaimed as best on the ground in the 1914 Grand Final.

Also a fine tenor and known as "the Caruso of South Melbourne", Sloss was just 28 years of age when showered by white-hot shrapnel behind the lines. When ambulance bearers emptied his pockets for the return of items to his family, they found a tiny Australian flag, a symbol of his patriotism. Sloss is buried at the Cite Bonjean Cemetery, just out of Armentieres. His headstone reads:

"Whosoever Will Lose His Life For My Sake, The Same Shall Save It."

Other South players to make the supreme sacrifice in 1917 were Hugh Callan (36 games from 1907-10), Teddy "Toiler" Harrison (seven games, 1908-09) and Jack Turnbull (12 games, 1908). Callan, a ruckman, was judged one of South's best players in the 1907 Grand Final loss to Carlton. Harrison was a big, raw-boned footballer who would have played many more games with South if he had not enlisted in the Victoria Police and moved to his native north-east Victoria. Turnbull, sadly, was the father of five children — Edith, Alma, Lylia, Jean and John. Son John was born less than

Bruce Sloss' grave at Armentieres.

Hugh Callan, killed in action.

Private Jack Turnbull had a young family.

MATCH RESULTS

Round 1, at Lake Oval, May 12
South Melbourne 9.18 (72) d Geelong 4.14 (38)

Round 2, at Punt Road, May 19
South Melbourne 8.16 (64) d Richmond 6.16 (52)

Round 3, at Lake Oval, May 26
South Melbourne 5.16 (46) d Carlton 3.13 (31)

Round 4, at Victoria Park, June 2
Collingwood 8.18 (66) d South Melbourne 6.9 (45)

Round 5, at Lake Oval, June 9
Fitzroy 8.7 (55) d South Melbourne 5.20 (50)

Round 6, at Corio Oval, June 16
Geelong 6.14 (50) d South Melbourne 6.11 (47)

Round 7, at Lake Oval, June 23
South Melbourne 9.17 (71) d Richmond 6.3 (39)

Round 8, at Princes Park, June 30
Carlton 9.11 (65) d South Melbourne 7.12 (54)

Round 9, at Lake Oval, July 7
South Melb. 13.12 (90) d Collingwood 10.13 (73)

Round 10, at Brunswick Street, July 14
Fitzroy 9.10 (64) d South Melbourne 8.9 (57)

Round 11, at Lake Oval, July 21
South Melbourne 14.14 (98) d Geelong 6.13 (49)

Round 12, at Punt Road, July 28
South Melbourne 7.14 (56) d Richmond 5.11 (41)

Round 13, at Lake Oval, August 11
South Melbourne 8.7 (55) d Carlton 6.14 (50)

Round 14, at Victoria Park, August 18
Collingwood 6.16 (52) d South Melbourne 2.9 (21)

Round 15, at Lake Oval, August 25
South Melbourne 12.13 (85) d Fitzroy 7.5 (47)

Semi-final, at MCG, September 8
Collingwood 13.17 (95) d South Melbourne 3.17 (35)

four months before Turnbull was mortally wounded by a shell explosion and died on May 2, 1917.

Turnbull died just 10 days before the opening of the 1917 season, with South defeating Geelong by 34 points at the Lake Oval. Although the Southerners won their next two matches, they went down to Collingwood, Fitzroy and Geelong in consecutive matches to slip out of premiership favouritism. With Vic Belcher as captain-coach, South struggled for consistency, mainly because of the huge influx of new players. Of the 30 players used in 1917, 13 were newcomers. The best of these were Harold Robertson, a half-forward flanker from Middle Park CYMS, and City of Northcote winger Artie Wood, who both played in the 1918 flag side.

A black-edged condolence card sent to Bruce Sloss' mother.

South finished the 15-round season in third position, behind Collingwood and Carlton, with Fitzroy making up the final four. South therefore played Collingwood in one of the two semi-finals, but went down by 60 points in poor conditions. Collingwood went on to defeat Fitzroy in the Grand Final and South used its disappointment as a launching pad for the following season.

Meanwhile, South's annual report noted that 18 former players had enlisted for war service, while just over 200 pounds ($400) had been donated to the war effort. Players were paid only expenses and even had to pay for their own entertainment at social gatherings. The report noted: "Our boys at the front are upholding the name won by Australia, and by the numerous letters show they appreciate the way your secretary (Herb Howson) keeps in touch with them."

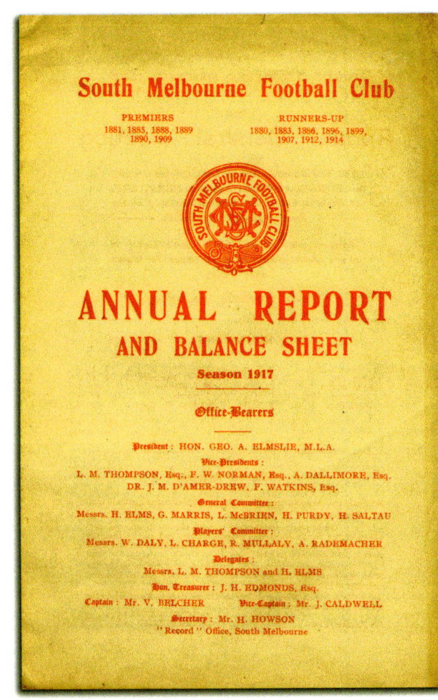

South Melbourne Football Club

PREMIERS
1881, 1885, 1888, 1889
1890, 1909

RUNNERS-UP
1880, 1883, 1886, 1896, 1899,
1907, 1912, 1914

SOUTH MELBOURNE FOOTBALL CLUB

ANNUAL REPORT
AND BALANCE SHEET
Season 1917

Office-Bearers

President: HON. GEO. A. ELMSLIE, M.L.A.
Vice-Presidents:
L. M. THOMPSON, Esq., F. W. NORMAN, Esq., A. DALLIMORE, Esq.
DR. J. M. D'AMER-DREW, F. WATKINS, Esq.
General Committee:
Messrs. H. ELMS, G. MARRIS, L. McBRIEN, H. PURDY, H. SALTAU
Players' Committee:
Messrs. W. DALY, L. CHARGE, R. MULLALY, A. RADEMACHER
Delegates:
Messrs. L. M. THOMPSON and H. ELMS
Hon. Treasurer: J. H. EDMONDS, Esq.
Captain: Mr. V. BELCHER Vice-Captain: Mr. J. CALDWELL
Secretary: Mr. H. HOWSON
"Record" Office, South Melbourne

The inside back cover of the annual report ran a list of the players and officer-bearers to "have given their services to King and Country". Apart from the players listed as already killed in action, the report noted that other former players in Charles Jones, Herbert "Boxer" Milne, Carl Willis and Syd Sykes, along with several former committeemen, were serving in Europe.

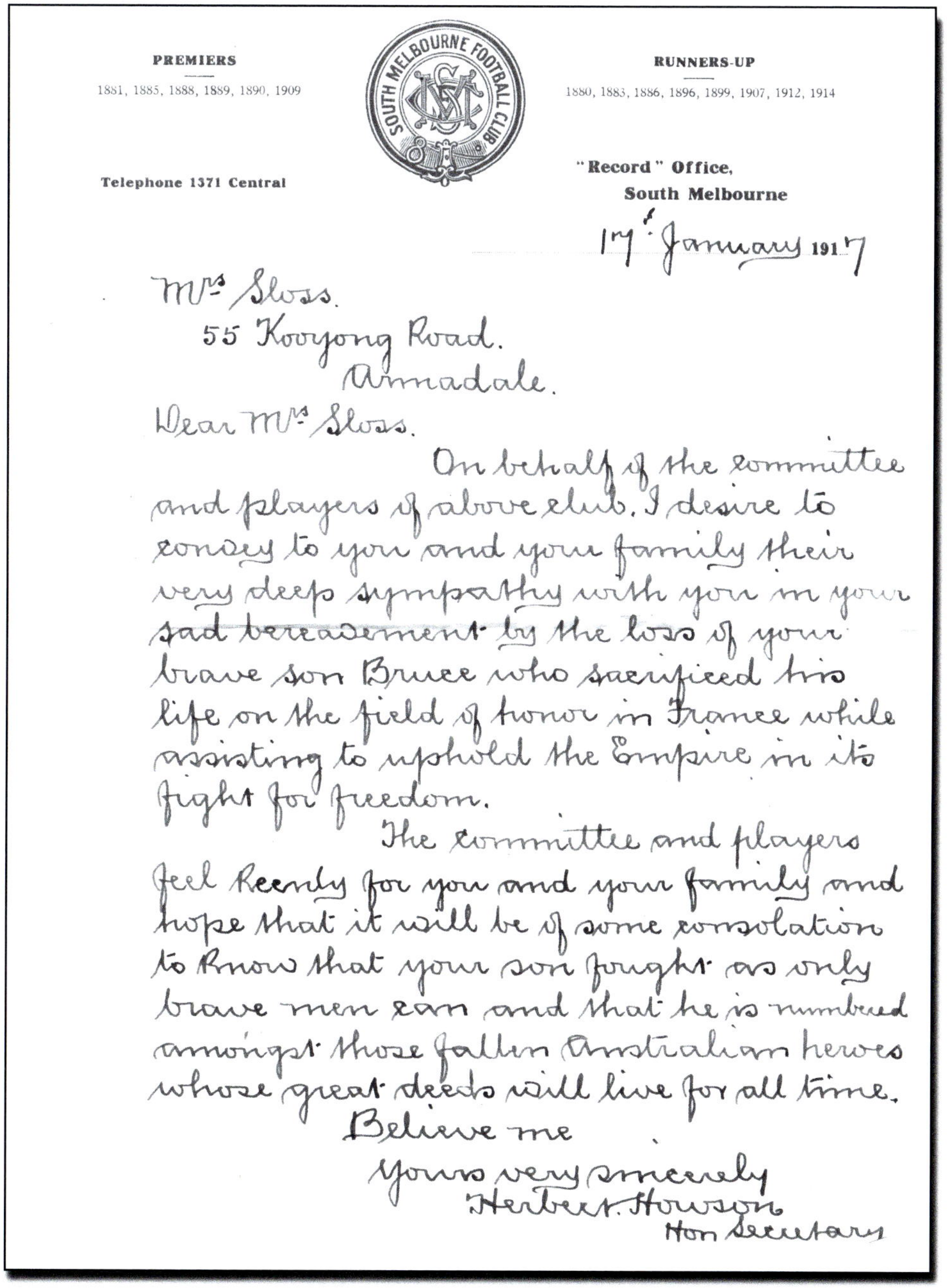

PREMIERS

1881, 1885, 1888, 1889, 1890, 1909

RUNNERS-UP

1880, 1883, 1886, 1896, 1899, 1907, 1912, 1914

Telephone 1371 Central

"Record" Office,
South Melbourne

17th January 1917

Mrs Sloss.
55 Kooyong Road.
Armadale.

Dear Mrs Sloss.

On behalf of the committee and players of above club. I desire to convey to you and your family their very deep sympathy with you in your sad bereavement by the loss of your brave son Bruce who sacrificed his life on the field of honor in France while assisting to uphold the Empire in its fight for freedom.

The committee and players feel keenly for you and your family and hope that it will be of some consolation to know that your son fought as only brave men can and that he is numbered amongst those fallen Australian heroes whose great deeds will live for all time.

Believe me

Yours very sincerely
Herbert Howson
Hon Secretary

South's letter of sympathy to Bruce Sloss' mother.

PLAYER	GAMES	GOALS
ASHTON, Jim	4	0
BELCHER, Vic	16	0
BOLLARD, Tom	6	0
BOYCE, Alf	12	13
BRENNAN, Jack	12	0
CALDWELL, Jim	14	3
DALY, Bill	16	0
DEAS, Bob	16	3
DOHERTY, Jack	10	4
HAIR, Ben	11	0
HOWELL, Jack	15	5
HUTCHINSON, Dick	11	17
JENKINS, Wal	2	0
LAKIN, Harry	1	1
LOWRIE, Mal	4	3
MOLONEY, George	2	0
MORGAN, Harry	15	23
MULLALY, Dick	10	5
O'DONOGHUE, Aloysius "Alan"	5	4
PAYNE, George	7	4
PRINCE, Joe	10	5
PURDY, Harry	7	5
RADEMACHER, Arthur	16	0
ROBERTSON, Harold	16	18
RYAN, Gerald	10	5
SKEHAN, Phil	10	1
STEWART, Jim	3	1
STRONG, Syd	2	0
TANDY, Mark	15	7
WOOD, Artie	10	1

POSITION: Fourth
COACH: Vic Belcher
CAPTAIN: Vic Belcher
BEST AND FAIREST: -
LEADING GOALKICKER: Harry Morgan (23)

1918

The VFL competition was almost back to normal in 1918, with St Kilda and Essendon back in action and with Melbourne the only club still in recess. This meant there were eight teams, with a 14-round home and away season.

The war, meanwhile, still raged and South suffered further losses, with former players Fred Fielding and Claude Thomas making the supreme sacrifice. Fielding had played one game with South in 1911 before playing 13 games with Collingwood in 1913. He joined the Southerners from South Bendigo and his only game in the red and white, in the ruck, was against Collingwood at the Lake Oval. He was killed at Villers-Bretonneaux on August 8, 1918, just three months before armistice.

Thomas played 13 games with South in 1914-15. Recruited from Port Melbourne Juniors, he played on a wing. He was killed in action during a push against the Germans at Hamel on July 5, 1918. A brother, Clarence, was killed in action a month later.

Although many record books indicate that former players Herb Howson and Henry "Sonny" Elms (a champion in the club's VFA years) were joint coaches in 1918 or that Elms took over from Howson during the season, neither version is correct. Howson was appointed coach, with Elms his assistant. The annual report, released in February, 1919, stated: "Mr H. Howson was appointed with the assistance of Mr H. Elms." Champion winger Jim Caldwell, who had joined the club in 1909, was named captain, with follower Vic Belcher vice-captain.

South started the season brilliantly, with big wins over Geelong, Fitzroy and Collingwood before falling to St Kilda by just five points at the Junction Oval in round four. It was South's only defeat of the season and it topped the ladder three games clear of Collingwood, with Carlton and St Kilda making up the final four.

The defeat by St Kilda was unexpected, but there was a reason, even if it could not be used as an excuse. The match was played on the King's Birthday holiday Monday and the South players had spent the previous two days enjoying the hospitality of a club patron at his holiday home in the Dandenongs. Champion rover Mark Tandy years later recalled in *The South Melbourne Record* that "some of the boys were wobbling at the knees when they walked from the St Kilda tram to the St Kilda oval". He added: "Fair dinkum, when some were dressed to go out on the field, they had to be headed in the direction of the arena gate and given a shove-off. That they ever saw the game out was a miracle."

Although South was the raging premiership

The 1918 South Melbourne premiership squad.

MATCH RESULTS

Round 1, at Lake Oval, May 11
South Melbourne 7.15 (57) d Geelong 4.7 (31)

Round 2, at Brunswick Street, May 18
South Melbourne 12.6 (78) d Fitzroy 5.8 (38)

Round 3, at Lake Oval, May 25
South Melbourne 12.13 (85) d Coillingwood 9.13 (67)

Round 4, at Junction Oval, June 3
St Kilda 6.13 (49) d South Melbourne 6.8 (44)

Round 5, at Lake Oval, June 8
South Melbourne 11.10 (76) d Carlton 10.12 (72)

Round 6, at East Melbourne CG, June 15
South Melbourne 7.10 (52) d Essendon 4.8 (32)

Round 7, at Lake Oval, June 22
South Melbourne 12.14 (86) d Richmond 4.10 (34)

Round 8, at Corio Oval, June 29
South Melbourne 7.13 (55) d Geelong 7.8 (50)

Round 9, at Lake Oval, July 6
South Melbourne 12.14 (86) d Fitzroy 8.13 (61)

Round 10, at Victoria Park, July 13
South Melbourne 7.9 (51) d Collingwood 6.8 (44)

Round 11, at Lake Oval, July 20
South Melbourne 14.17 (101) d St Kilda 7.9 (51)

Round 12, at Princes Park, July 27
South Melbourne 8.7 (55) d Carlton 5.13 (43)

Round 13, at Lake Oval, August 3
South Melbourne 12.13 (85) d Essendon 7.10 (52)

Round 14, at Punt Road, August 10
South Melbourne 7.17 (59) d Richmond 7.12 (54)

Semi-final, at MCG, August 31
South Melbourne 8.10 (58) d Carlton 7.11 (53)

Grand Final, at MCG, September 7
South Melbourne 9.8 (62) d Collingwood 7.15 (57)

favourite, it struggled to defeat Carlton in their semi-final two weeks after Collingwood had defeated St Kilda in the other semi-final. A tremendous downpour caused a week's postponement of the South-Carlton semi-final. South squeezed home by five points, thanks to late goals by Tom O'Halloran and Jack

Mark Tandy's 1918 premiership cap.

(sometimes referred to as "Jock") Doherty. O'Halloran was South's hero as he also denied Carlton the chance of a late match-winning goal.

South therefore played Collingwood in the final, with the Southerners having right of challenge if it lost. The red and white looked nervous over the first half and, despite looking the better side, trailed by 16 points at the main break. South still trailed by nine points at the final break and switched Belcher into the ruck for the final quarter. His dominance of the packs lifted teammates and South full-forward Gerald Ryan levelled scores with a late goal. Collingwood scrambled a behind to take the lead and, just when it appeared the Magpies would win, South forward pocket Chris Laird lashed at the ball and kicked the winning goal off the ground with less than a minute to play. South won by five points and with no challenge needed, the red and white had won its second VFL premiership.

The South annual report noted: "In annexing the premiership of 1918, your team have been congratulated from all quarters, and more particularly by their opponents on the field."

Vic Belcher, the only footballer to play in two premiership sides for the red and white.

PREMIERSHIP SIDE

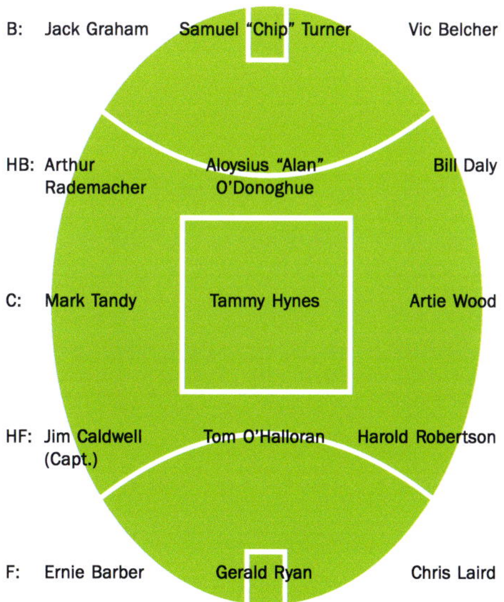

FOLL.: Jack Howell, Phil Skehan, Jack Doherty

South Melbourne Football Club Welfare Committee

CIRCULAR TO THE MEMBERS OF THE S.M.F.C.

A small section of the players are endeavoring to create discontent among the players and members of your Club.

With a view to obtaining control of the management and finances of the Club, they are nominating candidates for office who will assist them in that direction. This section complains that your Committee, by expending £325 in improving your property and comforts, debarred them from dividing that amount among themselves, and consider the Committee have not given them a fair deal. A demand to obtain a bank overdraft to meet renovation expenses on the grounds that this was not a "legitimate expense" during the season, your Committee, in justice to its members, emphatically refused.

Would you welcome a balance sheet with a debt, or find your property sadly neglected and all the finances expended on the players?

The players' allowances show £1,134/2/2, including a bonus of £350. Various social functions and a trip to Ballarat during the season show your players have received excellent treatment—probably the best of any League team.

Your Committee would not agree to the sum of £83, balance from trip fund, being expended on week-end jaunts previous to the opening of the coming season. A majority of the players and supporters requested the Committee to place this sum in trust, to form a fund for a trip for the players at the end of the ensuing season, and this has been done.

If it be your desire that the Club be governed by gentlemen whose services are given gratis for love of the sport, we, as a Committee, having closely reviewed the past season's work, strongly recommend the following gentlemen for your vote—to ensure proper management during the coming season.

L. T. NAYLER,
Chairman.

Election will take place in Gymnasium on Thursday, February 26, from 7 to 9 p.m.

VOTE THUS

COMMITTEE

(Five to be elected.)

DRANE, H. P.
ELMS, H.
~~HOPKINS, J.~~
~~LOCKYER, F. W.~~
MARRIS, G.
McBRIEN, L.
McINTOSH, D.
~~SALTAU, H. C.~~
~~WAGSTAFF, A.~~

PLAYERS' COMMITTEE

(Four to be elected.)

~~DALY, W.~~
HISKINS, A.
LUGG, N.
~~ROBERTSON, H.~~
~~SKEHAN, P.~~
TURNER, S. C.
WOOD, A.

South might have won the 1918 flag but there was dissent at committee level and this circular was inserted in that year's annual report.

PLAYER	GAMES	GOALS
BARBER, Ernie	13	20
BELCHER, Vic	16	1
BOYCE, Alf	4	5
BRENNAN, Jack	6	2
BULPIT, Harry	4	3
CALDWELL, Jim	14	7
CUMMINS, Frank	1	0
DALY, Bill	16	0
DOHERTY, Jack	15	5
GRAHAM, Jack	15	0
HAIR, Ben	1	1
HOWELL, Jack	13	16
HYNES, Tammy	12	1
LAIRD, Chris	12	26
MAGILL, Frank	2	0
MORGAN, Harry	8	2
O'DONOGHUE, Aloysius "Alan"	10	2
O'HALLORAN, Tom	16	5
PRINCE, Joe	2	0
RADEMACHER, Arthur	15	0
ROBERTSON, Harold	14	28
RYAN, Gerald	16	32
RYAN, Mike	1	0
SAMPSON, Reg	2	1
SKEKAN, Phil	15	0
TALBOT, Bill	2	0
TANDY, Mark	15	3
TURNER, Samuel "Chip"	14	0
WOOD, Artie	14	1

POSITION: Premier
COACH: Herb Howson
CAPTAIN: Jim Caldwell
BEST AND FAIREST: -
LEADING GOALKICKER: Gerald Ryan (32)

1919

South's second VFL premiership flag was unfurled immediately before its 1919 opening round match against Collingwood at the Lake Oval. The Magpies, however, rained on the Southerners' parade with a surprise 13-point win. Although *The Herald* admitted South "deserved its symbol of 1918 supremacy", said it could not contain a "better" Collingwood in the opening round clash. John Worrall, writing in *The Australasian,* suggested that "for the losers there was no better man on the ground than little (Jack) Doherty, who mixed roving with attack".

Worrall also praised two South newcomers, Jim Makin and Norm Lugg, but neither made a lasting impression in the red and white. South, unusual for this era, played just seven newcomers this season, with Albert Park recruit Fred Fleiter later becoming part of the famous ruck combination in tandem with Roy Cazaly and Mark "Napper" Tandy. Fleiter played 71 games with South to 1925 and played his role of clearing a path for rover Tandy to perfection.

The 1919 season marked the return of Melbourne following the armistice of the previous November but, with University's resignation after the 1914 season, the VFL was left with nine clubs and a bye system over 18 rounds, with clubs playing each other twice.

South, despite its opening round stumble to Collingwood, defeated the other seven clubs over the next eight rounds (with a bye in round seven), but then went down to Collingwood again in round 10, at Victoria Park. South had kicked shockingly in the previous round's win over Geelong, scoring 5.22 and this was followed by a week's break for a Victoria-South Australia clash at the Adelaide Oval, with a combined VFL side also playing a Ballarat combination that weekend.

Worrall wrote during the break that South was the best team in the competition and "played the cleanest and most scientific football". He singled out skipper Jim Caldwell for his "judgement and coolness", but noted the Southerners were missing premiership players Jack Howell and Harry Morgan, who had crossed to VFA club Footscray.

South was shocked at this stage of the season by the news that former player Bill "Sonna" Thomas had broken a leg so severely (in two places below the knee) while playing with Richmond, as club captain, that he was forced into premature retirement. Worrall wrote of the 1909 South premiership player: "He is an old, tried, valuable and manly player, and deserves well of all football followers."

Worrall, meanwhile, was so impressed with Caldwell's captaincy of South that he paid this special tribute: "It is many years since a more gifted, all-round player or better captain has played the game than Caldwell." Worrall noted that Caldwell, before joining South in 1909, had played with Williamstown CYMS before stints in the VFA with Yarraville and Williamstown. He also wrote: "Caldwell is fairness personified. Force, while a grand

South's Jim Caldwell (left) and Vic Belcher both represented Victoria.

MATCH RESULTS

Round 1, at Lake Oval, May 3
Collingwood 9.8 (62) d South Melbourne 6.13 (49)

Round 2, at MCG, May 10
South Melbourne 10.19 (79) d Melbourne 3.10 (28)

Round 3, at Junction Oval, May 17
South Melbourne 9.13 (67) d St Kilda 4.7 (31)

Round 4, at Lake Oval, May 24
South Melbourne 4.15 (39) d Fitzroy 4.12 (36)

Round 5, at East Melbourne CG, May 31
South Melbourne 9.16 (70) d Essendon 7.8 (50)

Round 6, at Punt Road, June 7
South Melbourne 11.16 (82) d Richmond 7.20 (62)

Round 7, Bye

Round 8, at Lake Oval, June 21
South Melbourne 6.13 (49) d Carlton 6.8 (44)

Round 9, at Lake Oval, June 28
South Melbourne 5.22 (52) d Geelong 5.4 (34)

Round 10, at Victoria Park, July 12
Collingwood 8.11 (59) d South Melbourne 3.18 (36)

Round 11, at Lake Oval, July 19
South Melbourne 13.16 (94) d Melbourne 2.15 (27)

Round 12, at Junction Oval, July 26
South Melbourne 29.15 (189) d St Kilda 2.6 (18)

Round 13, at Brunswick Street, August 9
South Melbourne 14.10 (94) d Fitzroy 7.5 (47)

Round 14, at Lake Oval, August 16
South Melbourne 12.15 (87) d Essendon 8.7 (55)

Round 15, at Lake Oval, August 23
South Melbourne 6.7 (43) d Richmond 4.14 (38)

Round 16, Bye

Round 17, at Princes Park, September 6
Carlton 8.11 (59) d South Melbourne 8.7 (55)

Round 18, at Corio Oval, September 13
Geelong 6.14 (50) d South Melbourne 3.8 (26)

Semi-final, at MCG, September 20
Richmond 10.13 (73) d South Melbourne 9.5 (59)

A studio portrait of Mark Tandy.

PLAYER	GAMES	GOALS
BARBER, Ernie	8	8
BELCHER, Vic	12	2
BRERETON, Harry	8	27
BULPIT, Harry	2	0
CALDWELL, Jim	17	4
CARPENTER, Fred	5	9
DALY, Bill	14	0
DOHERTY, Jack	16	12
FLEITER, Fred	3	0
FROUD, Harry	10	4
HISKINS, Arthur	3	0
HISKINS, Stan	16	1
HYNES, Tammy	16	1
KENNY, Bill	2	0
LAIDLAW, Wally	1	0
LAIRD, Chris	17	28
LUGG, Norm	17	4
MAKIN, Jim	7	0
O'HALLORAN, Tom	16	1
PEARSON, Bill	5	6
POWER, Gladstone	7	5
PURDY, Harry	2	1
RADEMACHER, Arthur	12	0
ROBERTSON, Harold	16	38
SAMPSON, Reg	15	1
SKEHAN, Phil	13	2
STEWART, Jim	3	0
TANDY, Mark	17	3
TURNER, Samuel "Chip"	17	0
WOOD, Artie	9	0

POSITION: Third
COACH: Herb Howson
CAPTAIN: Jim Caldwell
BEST AND FAIREST: -
LEADING GOALKICKER: Harold Robertson (38)

asset, forms no part of his equipment; he trusts to skill, pace, cleverness and judgement."

Meanwhile, the mid-season break appeared to upset South as it went down to Collingwood by 23 points at Victoria Park in round 10 and was defeated in its final two home and away matches by Carlton and Geelong. South therefore finished the season in second position, a game behind Collingwood, with Carlton and Richmond making up the final four.

South played Richmond in the first of the semi-finals, but crashed out of the premiership race in going down by 14 points. Although South had relinquished its crown, there was one massive highlight in 1919 in the mammoth 171-point defeat of St Kilda at the Junction Oval. South's score of 29.15 (189) was a VFL record to that stage, while its final quarter score of 17.4 remains a record for any single quarter. Also, Harold Robertson kicked 14 goals, a club record until Bob Pratt kicked 15 against Essendon at the Lake Oval in 1934. Amazingly, Roberston did not kick a goal in the first quarter and had only three to half-time. He then kicked four in the third quarter and seven in the final term. Worrall wrote that it was "no match" and a headline in *The Australasian* trumpeted SOUTH BREAKS ALL RECORDS.

1920

South had a changing of the guard in 1920, with Arthur Hiskins taking over from Herb Howson as coach, with Vic Belcher returning to the captaincy for the first time since 1917. Again, it was an unusual arrangement as Hiskins was playing coach. A quick, powerful player, "Poddy" Hiskins had joined the Swans from Rutherglen in 1908, had served in the AIF during World War I and returned to the club in 1919. Brother Stan also played for South from 1913-14 and, after war service, from 1919-21.

The Southerners introduced six newcomers in 1920, with easily the best of them being Paddy Scanlan, who played 11 games in his debut season but went on to play 100 games to 1926 before being appointed captain-coach of Footscray. Scanlan, recruited from Leopold, had a delayed start to his VFL career because of war service, but developed into a magnificent utility who excelled in the centre. He made his first appearance for South in the round six match against Richmond at Punt Road and was photographed with teammates Reg Seedsman and Roy Reardon in *The Herald* edition of July 20, 1920, as three returned soldiers recruited by South that season.

South went down to Melbourne by 12 points in a thriller at the MCG in the opening round, with *The Herald* reporting that the final quarter was "a great struggle" and that just six points separated the teams with just minutes to play. The report continued: "The crowd were cheering wildly, but the South barrackers closed down a good deal when (Jack) House scored another goal for Melbourne."

The Southerners went down to Fitzroy the following week before notching their first win of the season in the round three clash with Essendon at the East Melbourne Cricket Ground. However, consistency eluded South even though rover Mark Tandy was in such brilliant form early in the season that he was selected to play

Geelong's Lloyd Hagger, a talented artist, drew this caricature of South's Mark Tandy.

South players wore "boater" hats on club trips in the early '20s and this hat-band featured the SMFC logo.

MATCH RESULTS

Round 1, at MCG, May 1
Melbourne 9.13 (67) d South Melbourne 8.7 (55)

Round 2, at Lake Oval, May 8
Fitzroy 12.7 (79) d South Melbourne 6.13 (49)

Round 3, at East Melbourne CG, May 15
South Melbourne 9.9 (63) d Essendon 7.13 (55)

Round 4, Bye

Round 5, at Lake Oval, May 26
South Melbourne 8.10 (58) d Carlton 4.15 (39)

Round 6, at Punt Road, June 5
Richmond 9.7 (61) d South Melbourne 5.4 (34)

Round 7, at Junction Oval, June 12
South Melbourne 13.10 (88) d St Kilda 7.11 (53)

Round 8, at Lake Oval, June 19
South Melbourne 16.23 (119) d Geelong 5.16 (46)

Round 9, at Lake Oval, June 26
Collingwood 10.7 (67) d South Melbourne 9.9 (63)

Round 10, at Lake Oval, July 3
South Melbourne 12.13 (85) d Melbourne 5.11 (41)

Round 11, at Brunswick Street, July 10
Fitzroy 9.13 (67) d South Melbourne 8.14 (62)

Round 12, at Lake Oval, July 17
South Melbourne 8.14 (62) d Essendon 7.7 (49)

Round 13, at Princes Park, July 31
Carlton 11.14 (80) d South Melbourne 7.11 (53)

Round 14, Bye

Round 15, Lake Oval, August 14
Richmond 14.8 (92) d South Melbourne 9.7 (61)

Round 16, at Lake Oval, August 21
South Melbourne 11.17 (83) d St Kilda 3.14 (32)

Round 17, at Corio Oval, August 28
Geelong 11.10 (76) d South Melbourne 8.25 (73)

Round 18, at Victoria Park, September 4
Coll. 16.12 (108) d South Melbourne 13.13 (91)

against South Australia at the MCG. Tandy also played in the return match in Adelaide later in the season as South's only interstate representative that season. However, South's Reg Sampson kicked two goals for a VFL side against the Goldfields Association in Boulder (WA).

South finished a disappointing fifth, but three games and percentage behind fourth-placed Collingwood. There was further disappointment for South fans when skipper and duel premiership player Belcher announced his retirement on the eve of the finals. Belcher, to 2008 was the only man to play in two premiership sides (1909 and 1918) with South, had played 226 games in the red and white and later was non-playing coach of Fitzroy's 1922 premiership side.

Mark Tandy features in these swap cards of the era.

John Worrall, writing in *The Australasian* paid this tribute to Belcher: "When he began playing senior football, Belcher was a ruckman, being as fine a performer in that position as any man playing. In his latter years he has been a noted defender, his coolness, judgement, fine marking qualities and dash making him an ideal back man and captain. Like the vast majority of champions, Belcher has been fairness personified. He possesses fine spring and determination, was a hard man to beat and was a manly opponent."

PLAYER	GAMES	GOALS
ALLISON, Robert	13	22
BELCHER, Vic	14	0
BRERETON, Harry	1	0
CARPENTER, Fred	2	3
DOHERTY, Jack	13	10
FLEITER, Fred	16	0
HISKINS, Arthur	15	0
HISKINS, Stan	13	2
HYNES, Tammy	8	2
LAIRD, Chris	5	9
LAKIN, Harry	2	0
LANIGAN, Vern	1	1
LUGG, Norm	10	6
O'HALLORAN, Tom	16	6
PEARSON, Bill	7	3
POWER, Gladstone	14	15
RADEMACHER, Arthur	3	0
REARDON, Roy	10	9
ROBERTSON, Harold	11	12
SAMPSON, Reg	5	0
SCANLAN, Paddy	11	6
SEEDSMAN, Reg	16	0
SMITH, Vic	12	2
STEWART, Jim	7	5
TANDY, Mark	16	2
TURNER, Samuel "Chip"	13	0
WILLIS, Carl	3	4
WOOD, Artie	3	4
WOOTTON, Stan	16	28

POSITION: Fifth
COACH: Arthur Hiskins
CAPTAIN: Vic Belcher
BEST AND FAIREST: -
LEADING GOALKICKER: Stan Wootton (28)

1921

South again swung the changes in 1921, with winger Artie Wood taking over as playing coach, with Carl Willis as captain. Wood, who had played in South's 1918 premiership side, was just 25 years of age. Small and fiery, he was a wonderful competitor who played with great commitment. Willis, a dentist, had played in the VFL with University from 1912-14 before moving to South in 1915. He then served in the AIF during World War I before resuming with South in 1920 and making a name for himself as a top forward. Willis also was a fine cricketer who represented Victoria over 15 seasons.

In a pre-season feature on VFL captains, *The Herald* said of Willis: "Only a great love of the game could keep a man of his professional attainments in it every week, more especially as he has been playing under the handicap of a shoulder injury. As a lad he was in the Wesley College XVIII."

The Southerners also started the 1921 season with a star recruit from a rival VFL club. Roy Cazaly, who had wanted to play with Carlton as a boy, had played 99 games with St Kilda from 1911-20 but, because of the frequent rowing at the Junction Oval, switched to the red and white of the Lake Oval to form a superb ruck combination with Fred Fleiter and Mark Tandy. He was already 28 when he joined South, but the move gave him a new football lease of life.

South introduced 14 VFL newcomers as it turned over talent in 1921, with the best of them probably being Martin Brown, a fine half-forward who played 73 games for the club to 1928 and represented Victoria in 1927.

South prepared for the new season with an intra-club practice match, with the "old" players pitted against the "new". Surprisingly, the newcomers held the seasoned players to a margin of 35 points. The following week, South defeated St Kilda by a point in the opening round at the Junction Oval. A goal by Robert Allison gave South a seven-point lead late in the match and although St Kilda managed a late goal of its own, South held on over the final minute in what *The Australasian* described as an "exciting game in front of 15,000 fans".

The great Roy Cazaly crossed from St Kilda in 1921.

It was South's only win over the first seven rounds (including a bye in round seven) and, from there, the Southerners were always going to struggle to make the finals and finished seventh, with five wins and a draw (with Carlton in round five). The only real highlight for South was that Allison was played in a forward pocket for Victoria against South Australia at the interstate Carnival in Adelaide late in the season. Also, Jim Makin played on a half-back flank for a VFL combination against a representative Ballarat side.

In fact, South was so poor in some matches that *The Australasian* suggested the Southerners "had no dash and its defence was much below standard."

Although South had consecutive wins from rounds eight to 10, it was always a long shot to make the finals and all hope disappeared when Collingwood defeated the Southerners by 15 points at the Lake Oval in round 15. *The Football Record* the following week ran the headline OUT OF THE RUNNING —

MATCH RESULTS

Round 1, at Junction Oval, May 7
South Melbourne 9.13 (67) d St Kilda 10.6 (66)

Round 2, at Lake Oval, May 14
Richmond 11.16 (82) d South Melbourne 7.9 (51)

Round 3, at Lake Oval, May 21
Essendon 11.15 (81) d South Melbourne 4.14 (38)

Round 4, at MCG, May 28
Melbourne 10.10 (70) d South Melbourne 9.15 (69)

Round 5, Lake Oval, June 4
South Melb. 10.10 (70) drew with Carlton 10.10 (70)

Round 6, at Victoria Park, June 11
Collingwood 9.13 (67) d South Melbourne 6.8 (44)

Round 7, Bye

Round 8, at Lake Oval, June 25
South Melbourne 10.14 (74) d Geelong 8.5 (53)

Round 9, at Lake Oval, July 2
South Melbourne 8.18 (66) d Fitzroy 6.12 (48)

Round 10, at Lake Oval, July 9
South Melbourne 13.9 (87) d St Kilda 11.8 (74)

Round 11, at Punt Road, July 16
Richmond 9.12 (66) d South Melbourne 8.13 (61)

Round 12, at East Melbourne CG, July 23
Essendon 8.13 (61) d South Melbourne 5.13 (43)

Round 13, at Lake Oval, July 30
South Melbourne 8.21 (69) d Melbourne 7.11 (53)

Round 14, at Princes Park, August 20
Carlton 11.15 (81) d South Melbourne 7.14 (56)

Round 15, at Lake Oval, August 27
Collingwood 8.7 (55) d South Melbourne 5.10 (40)

Round 16, Bye

Round 17, at Corio Oval, September 10
Geelong 10.7 (67) d South Melbourne 3.10 (28)

Round 18, at Brunswick Street, September 17
Fitzroy 10.19 (79) d South Melbourne 6.9 (45)

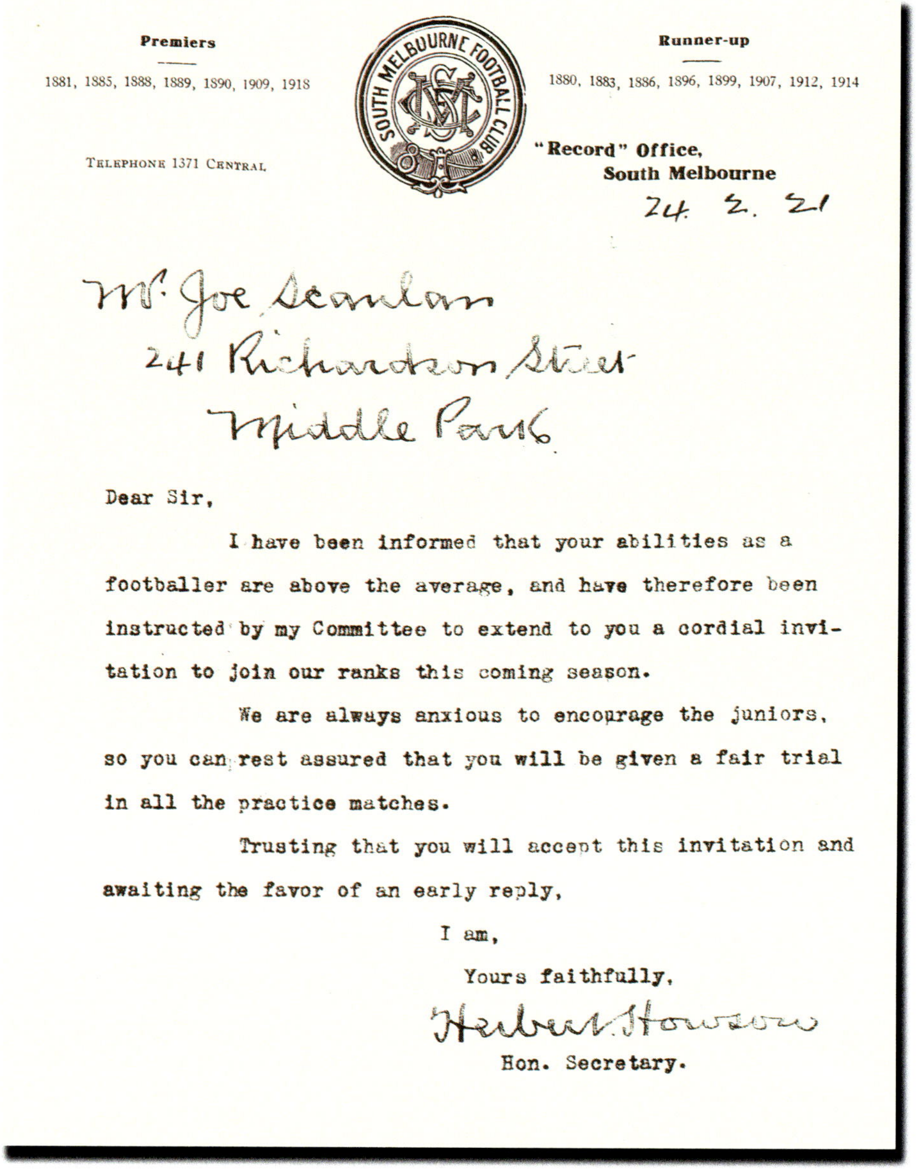

Premiers
1881, 1885, 1888, 1889, 1890, 1909, 1918

South Melbourne Football Club

Runner-up
1880, 1883, 1886, 1896, 1899, 1907, 1912, 1914

Telephone 1371 Central

"Record" Office,
South Melbourne

24. 2. 21

Mr Joe Scanlan
241 Richardson Street
Middle Park

Dear Sir,

I have been informed that your abilities as a footballer are above the average, and have therefore been instructed by my Committee to extend to you a cordial invitation to join our ranks this coming season.

We are always anxious to encourage the juniors, so you can rest assured that you will be given a fair trial in all the practice matches.

Trusting that you will accept this invitation and awaiting the favor of an early reply,

I am,

Yours faithfully,

Herbert Howson

Hon. Secretary.

Joe Scanlan's 1921 invitation to join South.

SOUTH MELBOURNE. Its report, by "Chatterer", read:

"South Melbourne have not beaten Collingwood since 1918. In that season the Scarlet Runners beat them down South and at Collingwood, and again when they met in the final match, although it was considered that South were lucky to have won that day.

"In view of the solid beating of Collingwood by the Tigers it was the opinion of thousands of fans that South Melbourne would whack the Magpies. South had set their minds on winning through to the semi-finals at least, and had paid close attention to training for the great event. They made a good fight of it, but the Magpies were just a bit too good on the centre and forward lines for them … It was a nice, enjoyable match to watch. There was any amount of vigorous play, but never was there any dirty work. The scoring was close for the greater part of the afternoon, but Collingwood shot away with more accuracy, and it was mainly in this advantage that they gained the victory."

South in 1921 introduced a new outfit as they wore red with a white monogram on the chest and carried these colours into 1922.

Martin Brown started with South in 1921.

Carl Willis, South captain in 1921.

PLAYER	GAMES	GOALS
ALLISON, Robert	9	12
BEER, Leon	8	0
BROWN, Martin	9	11
CAZALY, Roy	16	19
DAVENPORT, Harry	1	0
FLEITER, Fred	16	2
GIBB, Bobby	4	0
HISKINS, Arthur	16	0
HISKINS, Stan	7	1
LAIRD, Chris	12	11
LAIRD, Frank	8	10
LANIGAN, Vern	2	0
LAWRENCE, Robert	5	6
McDONALD, Bob	5	2
MAKIN, Jim	11	0
MARSH, Edwin	2	3
MITCHELL, John	1	0
NADORT, Tom	16	1
NICHOLSON, Alex	14	0
O'HALLORAN, Tom	14	0
POWER, Gladstone	2	1
REARDON, Roy	3	2
ROBERTSON, Harold	3	3
RODGERS, Jimmy	11	1
RUSSELL, Bert	1	3
SAMPSON, Reg	3	1
SCANLAN, Paddy	12	5
SEEDSMAN, Reg	15	0
SUTTON, Bert	5	0
TANDY, Mark	15	6
TURNER, Samuel "Chip"	9	1
WILLIS, Carl	12	7
WOOD, Artie	16	1
WOOTTON, Stan	13	8

POSITION: Seventh
COACH: Artie Wood
CAPTAIN: Carl Willis
BEST AND FAIREST: -
LEADING GOALKICKER: Roy Cazaly (19)

A South Melbourne team of 1921.

A South Melbourne team of 1922.

It was thought for decades that South Melbourne wore red guernseys with a white SMFC monogram on the front in just one season, in 1921. However, research has shown that the Southerners wore these guernseys over two seasons — 1921 and 1922. The top hand-painted photograph is of a 1921 team, while the black and white photograph underneath is of the 1922 side.

The coloured photograph shows playing coach Artie Wood in the centre of the front row, with captain Carl Willis to his left. In the 1922 photograph, captain-coach Roy Cazaly is in the middle of the front row, with Artie Wood on the extreme right of the front row.

Apart from adopting a new guernsey design in 1921, South also introduced a new dietary regime and a rule for visitors entering the players' rooms. A club finance committee in May, 1921, asked the club secretary to arrange for the players to have their teas (dinner) at the Café Royal, in the city. The motion agreed: "That tea tickets be given to players living away from South Melbourne, on training afternoons."

The club, wary of strangers being allowed to wander into the players' room, instructed the doorkeepers that "only players and officials are to be allowed in the gymnasium and that other persons desiring to be admitted must be introduced by a member of the committee". Also, South in 1921 travelled to Ballarat to play in a benefit match for an injured Ballarat Imperials player and raised 100 pounds ($200). The club minute book of 1921 reported that the trip was deemed "most satisfactory".

1922

South, after such a poor 1921 season, decided on a raft of changes for the following year, but retained the red guernsey the club had worn in 1921. The new outfit was worn again in the opening round match against Melbourne at the Lake Oval.

The new design was so colourful that *The Herald* reported: "Bolting onto the field like a pack of lively colts, South Melbourne, whose red guernseys were the first to catch the eyes of spectators on the local ground, were given a reception that must have been heart-warming to them. Each and every man looked fit to play for a kingdom, and the South Melbourne contingent of barrackers expected big things accordingly." However, Melbourne defeated South by five points, with Hawthorn recruit Billy Gambetta kicking three goals on debut. Gambetta was a top prospect but returned to Hawthorn the same season after playing just four games with the Southerners.

There also was a dramatic leadership change for South as Roy Cazaly took over as coach and shared the captaincy with rover Mark Tandy. Cazaly, a fitness fanatic, was determined to introduce a heavier training schedule for his players. Artie Wood, coach in 1921, returned to the ranks while Carl Willis, skipper in 1921, indicated that because his dental practice was flourishing he would not be available for many games. In fact, he did not play a single game and South later announced his retirement.

This Victorian side played South Australia in Adelaide in 1922. South was represented by Roy Cazaly (back row, extreme right) and Mark Tandy (from row, extreme right). On the extreme right in the middle row is early South legend Henry "Sonny" Elms, a Victorian selector.

South in 1922 recruited Essendon's Clarrie Woodfield and Collingwood's Basil Smith, but neither made an impression at the Lake Oval. The Southerners also introduced 14 VFL newcomers, including Leopold's Harry Alexander, a follower who later played for Victoria "B" sides. Another recruit, Arthur Hando, achieved unwanted fame after crossing from VFA club Brunswick. Hando was reported and reprimanded in 1924 for shaking a goal-post while an opponent had a shot for goal. He immediately was nicknamed "The Post Wobbler".

South might have defeated Collingwood by six points at Victoria Park in round two, but generally struggled through the 1922 season. The side was unsettled from week to week and there were few genuine stars. Cazaly and Tandy represented Victoria and Paddy Scanlan wore the Big Vee against NSW, but elsewhere the talent was thin. Cazaly topped the goalkicking with a meagre 28, although former Melbourne star Harry Brereton could have solved the club's goalkicking problems if he had not missed so many matches through

MATCH RESULTS

Round 1, at Lake Oval, May 6
Melbourne 8.12 (60) d South Melbourne 7.13 (55)

Round 2, at Victoria Park, May 13
South Melbourne 10.12 (72) d Collingwood 9.12 (66)

Round 3, at Windy Hill, May 20
Essendon 12.12 (84) d South Melbourne 8.13 (61)

Round 4, at Lake Oval, May 27
St Kilda 12.5 (77) d South Melbourne 8.13 (61)

Round 5, at Lake Oval, June 3
South Melbourne 8.15 (63) d Carlton 4.11 (35)

Round 6, Bye

Round 7, at Lake Oval, June 17
Richmond 12.7 (79) d South Melbourne 10.14 (74)

Round 8, at Brunswick Street, June 24
Fitzroy 9.13 (67) d South Melbourne 8.8 (56)

Round 9, at Corio Oval, July 1
Geelong 16.18 (114) d South Melbourne 4.6 (30)

Round 10, at MCG, July 15
Melbourne 15.10 (100) d South Melbourne 9.18 (72)

Round 11, at Lake Oval, July 22
Collingwood 8.16 (64) d South Melbourne 7.14 (56)

Round 12, at Lake Oval, July 29
South Melbourne 14.15 (99) d Collingwood 11.8 (74)

Round 13, at Junction Oval, August 5
South Melb. 11.9 (75) drew with St Kilda 10.15 (75)

Round 14, at Princes Park, August 19
Carlton 14.19 (103) d South Melbourne 10.15 (75)

Round 15, Bye

Round 16, at Punt Road, September 2
Richmond 13.8 (86) d South Melbourne 9.10 (64)

Round 17, at Lake Oval, September 9
Fitzroy 14.9 (93) d South Melbourne 11.12 (78)

Round 18, at Lake Oval, September 16
South Melbourne 21.10 (136) d Geelong 8.10 (58)

Arthur "Poddy" Hiskins was one of South's great early stars.

PLAYER	GAMES	GOALS
ALEXANDER, Harry	14	10
BEER, Leon	6	1
BENCE, Roy	15	6
BRERETON, Harry	8	25
BROWN, Martin	2	1
CAZALY, Roy	16	28
CONLON, Sid	4	3
CONNELL, Maurie	1	0
CULLUM, Jim	2	0
DOHERTY, Jack	1	0
FLEITER, Fred	5	2
GAMBETTA, Billy	4	7
GUNN, Bill	10	1
HANDO, Arthur	11	0
HISKINS, Arthur	12	0
HYNES, Tammy	12	0
LAIRD, Chris	13	25
LAIRD, Frank	15	10
LAW, Tommy	2	1
McDONALD, Bob	14	1
MAKIN, Jim	12	5
MATTHEWS, Wal	12	1
NICHOLSON, Alex	5	0
O'CONNELL, Jack	9	1
PETERS, Bill	4	0
ROSS, Frank	14	0
SCANLAN, Paddy	14	10
SMITH, Basil	6	5
TANDY, Mark	16	5
TEMPLETON, Don	1	0
TURNER, Samuel "Chip"	13	0
WOOD, Artie	15	4
WOODFIELD, Clarrie	1	0
WOOTTON, Stan	4	3

POSITION: Ninth
COACH: Roy Cazaly
CAPTAIN: Roy Cazaly, Mark Tandy
BEST AND FAIREST: -
LEADING GOALKICKER: Roy Cazaly (28)

injury. He kicked 25 goals from just eight games.

The football world was shocked by South's dismal form and *The Sporting Globe* of July 22 even ran the headline SOUTH STILL SLIPPING. Indeed, South was on the bottom of the ladder going into the final round and needed to win its final game of the season, against Geelong at the Lake Oval to have any chance of avoiding the wooden-spoon. South, with Chris Laird kicking six goals, thrashed Geelong by 78 points in front of just 3000 fans. South also needed Richmond to defeat St Kilda at the Junction Oval, only for the Saints to triumph by 27 points. South therefore suffered the indignity of finishing on the bottom of the VFL ladder for the first time since 1903.

There was an interesting footnote to South's final match of the season as *The Australasian* reported: "For over a score of years Peter Burns, the old South Melbourne player, has acted as timekeeper for Geelong. For the first time in that long career he was absent from his post on Saturday. It transpired that the veteran is enjoying a holiday. There were many enquiries for him at the South Melbourne ground by old members of that club, of which he was once a champion."

Meanwhile, Fitzroy landed its seventh VFL flag in defeating Collingwood by 11 points in the Grand Final. South shared some of the Maroons' glory as their non-playing coach was former South champion Vic Belcher.

1923

South reacted savagely to its disastrous 1922 season. It not only scrapped the red guernseys worn the previous season and reverted to white with a red sash, but dumped Cazaly as coach and appointed Collingwood champion Charlie Pannam as captain-coach. However, the Magpies refused to clear Pannam, who had played 97 games in the black and white from 1917-22. Pannam, who had played in Collingwood's 1917 premiership side and had represented Victoria in 1922, was just 25 years of age and the Magpies refused to budge. Pannan therefore was South's non-playing coach until Collingwood released him as a player in 1926.

With Pannam unable to take the field, South appointed the versatile Paddy Scanlan as captain. Scanlan proved to be such a wonderful leader that *The Sporting Globe's* "Truboot" wrote this tribute: "In his make-up as a player and captain Scanlan possesses many excellent qualities. He is before all else a 'heady' footballer, and what he does is done with a purpose … His genial nature makes him popular among the players, and popularity is a great help to a captain. The men respect his opinions and act on his advice without question."

These extraordinary photos are from the match against St Kilda at the Lake Oval in the final round in 1923. The official attendance was 40,441 a ground record.

South's determination to improve in 1923 was reflected in its recruiting. Joe Scanlan joined older brother Paddy at the Lake Oval and became a wonderfully loyal club servant, on and off the field. He played 148 games with South to 1931, captained the club and, on retirement, was a vice-president.

The other star recruit of 1923 was Leopold's Ted Johnson, who joined South as a defender but became a champion goalkicker who topped the club's goalkicking each season from 1923-28. Johnson played on a half-back flank early in the 1923 season but, after being injured against Carlton in round six, was moved to full-forward, with enormous success.

MATCH RESULTS

Round 1, at Lake Oval, May 5
Collingwood 16.5 (101) d South Melbourne 12.7 (79)

Round 2, at Brunswick Street, May 12
Fitzroy 9.11 (65) d South Melbourne 9.9 (63)

Round 3, at Lake Oval, May 19
Essendon 6.13 (49) d South Melbourne 4.15 (39)

Round 4, at MCG, May 26
Melbourne 11.18 (84) d South Melbourne 6.13 (49)

Round 5, at Lake Oval, June 4
South Melbourne 13.11 (89) d Geelong 10.15 (75)

Round 6, at Princes Park, June 9
South Melbourne 7.9 (51) d Carlton 5.19 (49)

Round 7, Bye

Round 8, at Lake Oval, June 23
South Melbourne 12.13 (85) d Richmond 4.10 (34)

Round 9, at Junction Oval, July 7
St Kilda 7.14 (56) d South Melbourne 6.9 (45)

Round 10, at Victoria Park, July 14
South Melbourne 11.11 (77) d Collingwood 8.8 (56)

Round 11, at Lake Oval, July 21
South Melbourne 8.12 (60) d Fitzroy 8.8 (56)

Round 12, at Windy Hill, July 28
Essendon 10.8 (68) d South Melbourne 7.9 (51)

Round 13, at Lake Oval, August 4
South Melbourne 9.13 (67) d Melbourne 5.11 (41)

Round 14, at Corio Oval, August 11
South Melbourne 10.10 (70) d Geelong 8.15 (63)

Round 15, at Lake Oval, August 25
Carlton 13.11 (89) d South Melbourne 10.8 (68)

Round 16, Bye

Round 17, at Punt Road, September 8
South Melbourne 14.16 (100) d Richmond 8.7 (55)

Round 18, at Lake Oval, September 15
South Melbourne 8.20 (68) d St Kilda 7.6 (48)

Semi-final, at MCG, September 29
South Melbourne 10.14 (74) d Essendon 8.9 (57)

Preliminary final, at MCG, October 6
Fitzroy 7.13 (55) d South Melbourne 6.7 (43)

South's great ruck combination of Roy Cazaly (left), Mark Tandy (centre) and Fred Fleiter recall old times in the red and white.

The Southerners therefore were brimming with enthusiasm going into the opening round match against Collingwood at the Lake Oval. However, the Magpies deflated South with a 22-point victory in front of 16,000 fans. South woes continued the next week when defeated by Fitzroy by two points at the Brunswick Street Oval and then by Essendon by 10 points at the Lake Oval. South was on the bottom of the ladder until it defeated Geelong by 14 points at the Lake Oval. *The Herald* indicated that it was "a strenuously contested game" and, despite the result being in the balance in the last quarter, "South was superior".

The win boosted South's confidence and, from there, it launched a late bid for the finals. South won seven of its next 10 matches and, by round 18 (with two bye rounds for each club) the Southerners needed only to defeat St Kilda at the Lake Oval to finish in the final four. It was a tight contest as St Kilda and South were tied on match points and the clash at the Lake Oval therefore was a mini-final.

There was such enormous interest in the South-St Kilda match that a Lake Oval record crowd of 40,441 somehow squeezed into the ground. Fans watched the game from every possible vantage point, even on top of grandstands and hanging from surrounding trees. *The Argus* described the size of the crowd as "immense" and added that at one stage part of the picket fence surrounding the playing arena collapsed under the weight of the crowd. It added: "There were thousands inside the boundary long before the finish, yet they did not seriously interfere with the play."

The huge attendance was even more remarkable considering heavy rain fell before and during the match. South, according to *The Argus,* "were always best" and, despite leading by just seven points at the final change, won by 20 points to clinch a place in the finals. *The Argus* noted that "Cazaly was pretty much at his best again" and indicated that he played a huge part in South's win, along with Mark Tandy and Artie Wood.

South not only made the final four, but finished third, ahead of Geelong on percentage with Essendon on top and Fitzroy second. South therefore had to play Essendon in one of the two semi-finals and stunned the football world in defeating the Dons by 17 points. South's hero was Johnson, who kicked a then VFL finals record of seven goals and was chaired from the ground. *The Argus* headlines read: SOUTH WINS and TERRIFIC STRUGGLE AFTER POOR START. Underneath these lines there was a smaller headline which read DING DONG FIGHT TO LEAD. South later presented Johnson with the match ball.

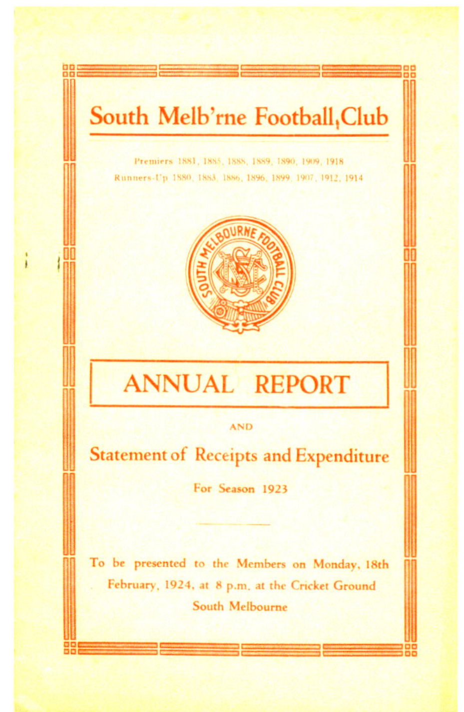

South Melb'rne Football Club

Premiers 1881, 1885, 1888, 1889, 1890, 1909, 1918
Runners-Up 1880, 1883, 1886, 1896, 1899, 1907, 1912, 1914

SOUTH MELBOURNE FOOTBALL CLUB

ANNUAL REPORT

AND

Statement of Receipts and Expenditure

For Season 1923

To be presented to the Members on Monday, 18th February, 1924, at 8 p.m. at the Cricket Ground South Melbourne

South's win was all the more remarkable as half-back flanker Frank Ross had his jaw broken early in the match, but continued playing while in enormous pain. Also, Cazaly sprained an ankle and Bill Condon injured an ankle. South, with so many sore players, went down to Fitzroy by 12 points in the preliminary final. However, its defeat of Essendon in their semi-final clash was all the remarkable considering the Dons defeated the Maroons by 17 points in the Grand Final.

Although South failed to reach the Grand Final, one report from the preliminary final suggested the Southerners had been brilliant against Fitzroy. It said of one piece of play: "In their next lightning dash upon the Fitzroy goal, South Melbourne produced one of the finest pieces of football ever seen on the Melbourne ground (MCG). Commencing from the backline, they handballed the whole length of the field, a display which raised tumultuous applause from all sides of the ground. South Melbourne gave a wonderful exhibition and, although defeated, are deserving of congratulations."

PLAYER	GAMES	GOALS
ALEXANDER, Harry	17	11
ALLISON, Robert	8	9
BEER, Leon	1	1
BILLETT, Bill	3	4
BROWN, Martin	11	6
CAZALY, Roy	17	16
CONDON, Bill	13	11
FLEITER, Fred	4	0
HANDO, Arthur	17	0
HISKINS, Arthur	15	0
HYNES, Tammy	12	0
JAMES, Syd	8	3
JOHNSON, Ted	15	44
JOYCE, Tom	4	0
LAIRD, Frank	15	1
McDONALD, Bob	10	1
MATTHEWS, Herb E.	16	15
MATTHEWS, Wal	8	6
NICHOLLS, Charlie	2	1
O'CONNELL, Jack	15	0
ROBERTS, Bill	1	1
ROBERTSON, Harold	4	4
ROSS, Frank	3	2
RUSSELL, Bert		
SCANLAN, Joe	18	0
SCANLAN, Paddy	17	7
SUTTON, Bert	10	1
TANDY, Mark	18	3
WOOD, Artie	18	3
WOODFIELD, Les		

POSITION: Third
COACH: Charlie Pannam
CAPTAIN: Paddy Scanlan
BEST AND FAIREST: -
LEADING GOALKICKER: Ted Johnson (44)

1924

According to *The Sporting Globe,* the 1924 season opened to "drowning cheers and shouts of excited thousands". South, with Charlie Pannam still sidelined by Collingwood's refusal to clear him to play, again was non-playing coach, with Paddy Scanlan again captain. South opened the season with a 27-point win over Richmond at Punt Road.

South full-forward Ted Johnson kicked 10 goals over the opening three rounds, despite South losing to Fitzroy in round two and then to Essendon, and his form was so impressive that former Geelong player Wally "Jumbo" Sharland, featured him in a special article in *The Sporting Globe.*

Johnson told Sharland he had been born and bred in South Melbourne and had followed the Southerners from the time he was a small boy and saw matches at the Lake Oval as often as possible. Johnson started playing football with the Eastern Road State School, South Melbourne, and then spent three years with Leopold before playing with South.

Sharland also reported that Johnson was such an inaccurate kick in his first game at full-forward for South that former star player Bill "Marked" Windley took him aside and gave him specialised coaching in the place-kick, with remarkable improvement.

Sharland later in the season also featured South winger Jack O'Connell and noted that he was born at Winchelsea, just west of Geelong, and played with Chilwell before joining South. Although O'Connell played under Geelong's nose in the Geelong and District League, the Pivotonians never even approached him and he played in the VFA with North Melbourne before joining South. He played 42 games in the red and white from 1922-24.

South, after the completion of round eight (in which it had the bye) was in third position, behind Fitzroy and Essendon and again seemed likely to play in the finals. South's good form continued after the break and, to the round 13 clash with St Kilda at the Junction Oval, had notched six consecutive wins. However, the Saints defeated the Southerners by four points, with *The Sporting Globe* match report running under the headline SAINTS' DYING EFFORT. St Kilda led by 15 points at the final change and held off a desperate South over the final 10 minutes, with Johnson missing a shot for goal which could have won the match.

It was South's second last defeat of the home and away season and it finished second, behind Essendon, with Fitzroy and Richmond making up the final four. In an extraordinary decision before the start of the season, the VFL decided to revert to the round-robin finals system used in the inaugural season of 1897. South's first challenge was against Richmond at Windy Hill and virtually was knocked out of the premiership race in going down by 28 points.

The South team of 1924, with coach Charlie Pannam on the extreme left in an overcoat.

MATCH RESULTS

Round 1, at Punt Road, April 26
South Melbourne 13.16 (94) d Richmond 10.7 (67)

Round 2, at Lake Oval, May 3
Fitzroy 12.14 (86) d South Melbourne 7.15 (57)

Round 3, at Windy Hill, May 10
Essendon 12.13 (85) d South Melbourne 8.11 (59)

Round 4, at Lake Oval, May 17
South Melbourne 12.9 (81) d St Kilda 7.11 (53)

Round 5, at MCG, May 24
Melbourne 10.16 (76) d South Melbourne 10.9 (69)

Round 6, at Lake Oval, May 31
South Melbourne 9.15 (69) d Collingwood 8.8 (56)

Round 7, at Princes Park, June 7
South Melbourne 11.12 (78) d Carlton 10.12 (72)

Round 8, Bye

Round 9, at Lake Oval, June 21
South Melbourne 7.6 (48) d Geelong 7.3 (45)

Round 10, at Lake Oval, June 28
South Melbourne 9.7 (61) d Richmond 5.13 (43)

Round 11, at Brunswick Street, July 5
South Melbourne 9.10 (64) d Fitzroy 4.17 (41)

Round 12, at Lake Oval, July 12
South Melbourne 9.8 (62) d Essendon 6.13 (49)

Round 13, at Junction Oval, July 19
St Kilda 13.14 (92) d South Melbourne 12.16 (88)

Round 14, at Lake Oval, July 26
South Melbourne 12.13 (85) d Melbourne 5.8 (38)

Round 15, at Victoria Park, August 2
Collingwood 9.16 (70) d South Melbourne 6.15 (51)

Round 16, at Lake Oval, August 23
South Melbourne 13.19 (97) d Fitzroy 4.7 (31)

Round 17, Bye

Round 18, at Corio Oval, September 6
South Melbourne 9.14 (68) d Geelong 9.13 (67)

Semi-final, at Windy Hill, September 13
Richmond 13.7 (85) d South Melbourne 9.3 (57)

Semi-final, at MCG, September 20
Essendon 10.12 (72) d South Melbourne 4.15 (39)

Semi-final, at MCG, September 27
South Melbourne 13.8 (86) d Fitzroy 10.13 (73)

Football legend Roy Cazaly in the Big White Vee.

Then, in the second round, Essendon defeated South by 33 points at the MCG to virtually win the premiership with one round to go. South completed the series with a 13-point win over Fitzroy, also at the MCG. The Dons took the flag even though they went down to Richmond by 20 points in their final round clash at the Lake Oval. Johnson kicked four goals in South's defeat of Fitzroy to set a club record of 60 goals in a season.

South did not have a best and fairest in 1924, but Les Woodfield was presented with a trophy as "most improved" and Johnson was presented with a medallion as leading club goalkicker. Johnson, Bill Condon, Fred Fleiter, Arthur Hando, Frank Laird, Paddy and Joe Scanlan and Mark Tandy were awarded special prizes for not missing a training session. Meanwhile, the VFL in 1924

Pals
Vol. 5. No. 4. [Registered at General Post Office Melbourne, for transmission by post as a Newspaper.] Saturday, September 20, 1924 Price 3d.

THIS WEEK'S PHOTO. CARD. FREE TO READERS

TED JOHNSON, SOUTH MELBOURNE'S GREAT FORWARD

Published Weekly: For Australian Boys

South full-forward Ted Johnson was featured on the front cover of this boys' magazine in 1924.

PLAYER	GAMES	GOALS
ALEXANDER, Harry	19	9
ALLISON, Robert	10	10
BROOKS, Phil	2	1
BROWN, Martin	18	8
CAZALY, Roy	19	32
CONDON, Bill	19	7
DE ARAUGO, Maurie	1	0
FLEITER, Fred	15	6
HANDO, Arthur	17	0
HARRIS, Jack	1	3
HYNES, Tammy	2	0
JOHNSON, Ted	19	60
JOYCE, Tom	16	2
LAIRD, Frank	18	0
McDONALD, Bob	4	0
McDONALD, Charles	16	0
MAHONEY, Harold	2	0
MATTHEWS, Herb E.	15	12
MATTHEWS, Wal	2	0
MILLER, Gil	1	1
NICHOLLS, Charlie	17	2
O'CONNELL, Jack	18	3
O'MEARA, Ted	6	7
ROSS, Frank	2	1
SCANLAN, Joe	19	0
SCANLAN, Merv	2	0
SCANLAN, Paddy	19	1
SIVIES, Ted	1	0
SUTHERLAND, Jim	1	0
SUTTON, Bert	4	1
TANDY, Mark	18	10
WOODFIELD, Les	19	0

POSITION: Fourth
COACH: Charlie Pannam
CAPTAIN: Paddy Scanlan
BEST AND FAIREST: -
LEADING GOALKICKER: Ted Johnson (60)

introduced the Brownlow Medal for each season's fairest and best player in honour of former Geelong official and coach (in the club's VFA years) Charles Brownlow. Brownlow, who also had been VFL president from 1918-19, died on January 23, 1924. The first Brownlow Medal winner was Geelong's Edward "Carji" Greeves, who was voted best on ground in seven matches. South's Mark Tandy was adjudged best on ground in three matches.

1925

The VFL made a momentous decision in the lead-up to the 1925 season, but left it late to get rid of the bye system. The VFL was expected to admit one club to make it a 10-club competition, but shocked the football world by admitting three new clubs — Footscray, Hawthorn and North Melbourne. Footscray looked a certain inclusion as the 1924 VFA premier and then defeating VFL premier Essendon in a Dame Nellie Melba charity match, but the inclusion of the other clubs was totally unexpected.

The VFL had submissions from a number of clubs, including Camberwell and Public Service, but did not make its decision until January 19, less than four months before the start of the new season. South Melbourne's 1924 annual report was released on February 9 and under the heading NEW LEAGUE CLUBS noted: "Opportunity is taken to extend to Hawthorn, Footscray and North Melbourne clubs a cordial welcome on their entry to the Victorian Football League. The inclusion of these three new clubs makes several alterations to the method of playing the coming season's matches, but we feel that the action of the League was a wise one, and the game should benefit to a big extent."

South's 1924 annual report also informed members that a new grandstand would be built at the Lake Oval, funded by both the football and cricket clubs. The report said: "Every effort will be made to have the new structure ready for the opening match of the coming (1925) season."

The Southerners, determined to improve on its fourth position of the previous season, recruited experienced Williamstown (VFA) follower Charlie Stanbridge, who went on to captain South in 1929. South also introduced 15 VFL newcomers in 1925,

The Three Amigos, South's great ruck combination of Roy Cazaly (left), Mark Tandy (centre) and Fred Fleiter.

SOUTH MELBOURNE FOOTBALL CLUB

1874 - 1924

The President and Committee request the pleasure of your Company at the

Jubilee Annual Meeting

to be held on

Monday, 9th February, 1925

at 8 p.m., at the South Melbourne Cricket Ground

PLEASE RETAIN THIS TICKET FOR ADMISSION TO GRANDSTAND

L. H. McBRIEN, SECRETARY

South celebrated its Jubilee in 1924 and this invitation was sent to members for attendance at the Jubilee Annual Meeting of February 9, 1925.

MATCH RESULTS

Round 1, at Lake Oval, May 2
South Melbourne 9.14 (68) d Carlton 4.6 (30)

Round 2, at Western Oval, May 9
Footscray 10.10 (70) d South Melbourne 8.12 (60)

Round 3, at Lake Oval, May 16
South Melbourne 12.10 (82) d North Melb. 8.13 (61)

Round 4, at Punt Road, May 23
Richmond 11.9 (75) d South Melbourne 10.10 (70)

Round 5, at Lake Oval, May 30
South Melbourne 16.9 (105) d St Kilda 10.13 (73)

Round 6, at Victoria Park, June 8
Collingwood 13.14 (92) d South Melbourne 7.11 (53)

Round 7, at Windy Hill, June 13
Essendon 9.11 (65) d South Melbourne 8.9 (57)

Round 8, at Lake Oval, June 20
Melbourne 14.16 (100) d South Melbourne 7.12 (54)

Round 9, at Lake Oval, June 27
South Melbourne 15.14 (104) d Hawthorn 5.7 (37)

Round 10, at Corio Oval, July 11
Geelong 18.13 (121) d South Melbourne 3.10 (28)

Round 11, at Lake Oval, July 18
Fitzroy 12.12 (84) d South Melbourne 6.11 (47)

Round 12, at Princes Park, August 1
South Melbourne 9.20 (74) d Carlton 9.9 (63)

Round 13, at Lake Oval, August 8
South Melbourne 13.14 (92) d Footscray 12.15 (87)

Round 14, at Arden Street, August 22
North Melb. 12.8 (80) d South Melbourne 7.16 (58)

Round 15, at Lake Oval, August 29
Richmond 9.9 (63) d South Melbourne 6.9 (45)

Round 16, at Junction Oval, September 5
St Kilda 11.9 (75) d South Melbourne 9.8 (62)

Round 17, at Lake Oval, September 12
Collingwood 14.11 (95) d South Melbourne 4.6 (30)

including the hugely-talented Peter Reville, who was Christened Henry James, but adopted his father's Christian name. From Moe, he played in South's 1933 premiership side.

South, with Charlie Pannam again non-playing coach and Paddy Scanlan captain, opened the season with an encouraging 38-point win over Carlton at the Lake Oval. However, South went down by 10 points to newcomer Footscray at the Western Oval the following week. *The Herald* headline trumpeted FOOTSCRAY PLAYS GREAT GAME AGAINST SOUTH.

South might have been humiliated, but made sure lightning didn't strike twice. It defeated a second newcomer, North Melbourne, by 21 points at the Lake Oval in round three. Despite's South's comfortable win, *The Herald* headline blared NORTHS GIVE SOUTH GOOD GAME.

The struggle to defeat North was a clear indication that South had slipped dramatically from the previous season and, half-way through the season, *The Herald* suggested "South up against it" and virtually wrote the Southerners off as finals candidates. South lacked any form of consistency and ended the season dismally in going down to Collingwood by 65 points at the Lake Oval.

The lowlight of South's season was going down to Geelong by 93 points at Corio Oval in round 10. Geelong kicked 11.4 to South's nil in the third quarter. To add insult to injury, Geelong was without champion ruckman/defender Tom Fitzmaurice, who was a late withdrawal and replaced by first-year player Frank Mockridge. *The Herald* scoffed: "South were never in the hunt."

South finished eighth, its only consolation being that Johnson kicked 60 goals to equal his club record. Geelong defeated Collingwood by 10 points in the Grand Final to win its first VFL premiership, while St Kilda's Colin Watson won the Brownlow Medal with nine votes (only best on ground performances counted), while Les Woodfield was South's best with three votes. Woodfield, who had joined South from Essendon in 1923, was a tough half-back flanker who represented Victoria eight times and played 76 games in the red and white to 1927.

PLAYER	GAMES	GOALS
ALEXANDER, Harry	16	8
ALLISON, Robert	5	6
ANDERSON, Charlie	8	2
BARLOW, Arthur	4	0
BARNES, Jack	4	4
BROWN, Martin	11	1
BROWNE, Bill	2	2
CONDON, Bill	13	0
CONDON, Fred	6	4
DALY, Albert	1	0
FLEITER, Fred	12	1
FREYER, Bill	12	0
HARRIS, Jack	5	7
HOGG, Syd	14	2
HUME, David	1	1
JACOBSON, Albie	2	0
JOHNSON, Ted	17	60
JOYCE, Tom	8	4
LAIRD, Frank	10	4
LAWRENCE, Robert	2	2
McDONALD, Charles	16	0
MAHONEY, Harold	3	0
NEILL, Harold	2	0
NICHOLAS, Charlie	12	2
O'MEARA, Ted	6	8
REVILLE, Peter	14	12
RUSSELL, Bert	2	0
SCANLAN, Joe	17	2
SCANLAN, Paddy	11	4
STANBRIDGE, Charlie	17	1
STEWART, George	13	1
TANDY, Mark	13	2
WATERHOUSE, George	2	1
WIMBRIDGE, Fred	8	12
WOODFIELD, Les	17	0

POSITION: Eighth
COACH: Charlie Pannam
CAPTAIN: Paddy Scanlan
BEST AND FAIREST: -
LEADING GOALKICKER: Ted Johnson (60)

1926

South Melbourne coach Charlie Pannam finally won his release from Collingwood as a player in 1926, but did not make his debut until the round four match against Carlton at Princes Park. Meanwhile, Paddy Scanlan stood in as club captain until Pannam was able to take his place in the side.

South, despite finishing a disappointing eighth in 1925, recruited only one other player from a rival club. Winger Tom Drummond switched to the Lake Oval after playing 94 games with Collingwood from 1916-22. He might have been a Victorian representative in his time with the Magpies, but played just five games in his only season with the Southerners.

The quality of the other recruits, however, was outstanding. Winger Harry Clarke and defender Hec McKay debuted in the opening round match against Richmond and both went on to have outstanding careers at the Lake Oval. Clarke did not make another appearance for South in 1926, but later established himself as one of the club's greatest centreline players and was named in the Team of the Century. He played 147 games with South to 1935. McKay played 152 games from 1926-35 and won South's best and fairest in 1927. Both Clarke and McKay played in the club's 1933 premiership side. Another winger, Danny Wheelahan, debuted in 1926 and won South's best and fairest in 1929.

South started the season with an eight-point loss to Richmond at the Lake Oval, but broke through the following week in defeating Footscray by 33 points at the Western Oval. *The Herald* suggested South was "in form" , with Roy Cazaly and Robert "Bobby" Allison the best players. However, South had just one more win over the following five rounds, by just two points against North Melbourne at the Lake Oval in round five. *The Herald* reported that South found North "a tough nut" to crack

This is the most iconic photograph in Australian football, of the great Roy Cazaly.

MATCH RESULTS

Round 1, at Lake Oval, May 1
Richmond 12.13 (85) d South Melbourne 11.11 (77)

Round 2, at Western Oval, May 8
South Melbourne 13.12 (90) d Footscray 8.9 (57)

Round 3, at Lake Oval, May 15
St Kilda 6.14 (50) d South Melbourne 6.11 (47)

Round 4, at Princes Park, May 22
Carlton 10.11 (71) d South Melbourne 9.12 (66)

Round 5, at Lake Oval, May 29
South Melbourne 10.15 (75) d North Melb. 11.7 (73)

Round 6, at Victoria Park, June 5
Collingwood 12.16 (88) d South Melbourne 8.11 (59)

Round 7, at MCG, June 7
Melbourne 12.16 (88) d South Melbourne 8.17 (65)

Round 8, at Lake Oval, June 19
South Melbourne 13.15 (93) d Fitzroy 9.5 (59)

Round 9, at Lake Oval, June 26
South Melbourne 9.15 (69) d Essendon 8.9 (57)

Round 10, at Glenferrie Oval, July 3
South Melbourne 11.16 (82) d Hawthorn 8.10 (58)

Round 11, at Lake Oval, July 10
South Melbourne 9.13 (67) d Geelong 8.8 (64)

Round 12, at Punt Road, July 17
South Melbourne 16.12 (108) d Richmond 10.15 (75)

Round 13, at Lake Oval, August 7
South Melbourne 15.17 (107) d Footscray 6.12 (48)

Round 14, at Junction Oval, August 14
South Melbourne 10.21 (81) d St Kilda 7.11 (53)

Round 15, at Lake Oval, August 21
South Melbourne 12.13 (85) d Carlton 9.8 (62)

Round 16, at Arden Street, August 28
South Melbourne 15.16 (106) d North Melb. 9.16 (70)

Round 17, at Lake Oval, September 4
Collingwood 9.9 (63) d South Melbourne 8.9 (57)

Round 18, at Windy Hill, September 11
South Melbourne 10.14 (74) d Essendon 9.17 (71)

and that the VFL newcomers were unfortunate as "their faulty kicking was a handicap to them".

Despite lagging well behind the ladder leaders after seven rounds, South then produced a stunning run of nine consecutive wins and seemed likely to play in the finals. South had rarely been in better form and the Victorian selectors recognised this in nominating Les Woodfield and Peter Reville for matches against NSW and Tasmania and Ted Johnson and Allison for a match against the Ballarat League. Also, Charlie Stanbridge, Arthur Barlow and Hec McKay were selected for a match against the Wimmera League at Horsham.

South's run ended in a six-point defeat by Collingwood at the Lake Oval, and it proved costly. South slipped to fifth position, a game and percentage behind Essendon — and the two clubs clashed at Windy Hill in the final round. South therefore had to defeat Essendon by a huge margin to sneak into the top four.

South defeated Essendon by three points and it was not enough. John Worrall wrote in *The Australasian* the following Monday: "To defeat Essendon for the fourth position in the semi-finals, South required a victory over the 'Same-Old' by at least five goals, but they were lucky to win by three points."

Worrall also suggested that although the match attracted 25,000 fans, there was "no excitement" and "the game was one of the quietest of the season". South might have failed to make the finals but its defeat of

Great South goalkicker Ted Johnson is on the right of this group of South players in Victorian guernseys. The others are Paddy Scanlan (front left) and Harry Alexander (front right).

Harry Clarke started with South in 1926 and this card was designed for wear in a hat-band.

TED JOHNSON
South Melbourne F.C. (Vic.)

PLAYER	GAMES	GOALS
ALEXANDER, Harry	4	2
ALLISON, Robert	9	16
ANDERSON, Charlie	3	0
BARLOW, Arthur	17	5
BERRYMAN, Bill	14	0
CAMERON, Paul	16	28
CAZALY, Roy	18	23
CLARKE, Harry	1	0
CONDON, Bill	12	6
CONDON, Fred	4	0
DRUMMOND, Tom	5	1
ELMER, John	1	1
FERGUSON, Joe	6	2
HOGG, Syd	12	0
JOHNSON, Ted	17	45
McDONALD, Charles	16	3
McKAY, Hec	17	0
MAHONEY, Harold	13	14
NICHOLLS, Charlie	18	3
O'MEARA, Ted	1	0
PANNAM, Charlie	14	1
REVILLE, Peter	13	1
RYDER, Fred	1	0
SCANLAN, Joe	18	2
SCANLAN, Paddy	16	16
STANBRIDGE, Charlie	12	5
SUTTON, Bert	16	18
TANDY, Mark	3	1
WHEELAHAN, Danny	9	0
WOODFIELD, Les	18	0

POSITION: Fifth
COACH: Charlie Pannam
CAPTAIN: Charlie Pannam, Paddy Scanlan
BEST AND FAIREST: Roy Cazaly
LEADING GOAKICKER: Ted Johnson (45)

Essendon was heroic as half-forward Bert Sutton (who later was captain-coach of Hawthorn) was injured early in the match and could not be replaced as a nineteenth man was not introduced until 1930. Also, it was South's first win at Windy Hill.

South in 1926 initiated a best and fairest award and the inaugural winner was the legendary Roy Cazaly. Respected football writer Hec de Lacy wrote of Cazaly in *The Sporting Globe* many years later: "He survived among a race of hard players because he had skilled himself to be hard along with the hard. He matched an electric mind — a split second imagination — against the more obvious tactics of the roughneck."

1927

South maintained the status quo for 1927, with Charlie Pannam again captain-coach. However, there was one major leadership change as the brilliant Paddy Scanlan, who had stood in as captain over the 1923-25 seasons crossed to Footscray as captain-coach. Scanlan had been a wonderfully committed player in 100 games for South from 1920. South's only experienced recruit was former Richmond defender Ted Bourke, but he played just six games in the red and white before crossing to Sandringham and later winning a Recorder Cup as best and fairest in the VFA.

South gave seven players VFL debuts, with three of them — Cecil Pettiona, Austin Robertson and Len Thomas having significant careers at the Lake Oval. Pettiona, a half-forward or winger, played 78 games with South to 1934, Robertson played 154 games to 1937 and was world sprint champion, while Thomas played 187 games to 1938 and was a member of the 1933 premiership side. Thomas, son of former club captain Bill "Sonna" Thomas, made his South debut just 14 years after his father's last game for the club. The Thomases achieved club immortality as South's only father-son premiership combination.

South was featured in this 1927 newspaper pin-up.

The Southerners opened the 1927 season with a one-point victory over Carlton at Princes Park. The match was tight throughout and South led by four points late in the final quarter, only for Carlton to draw level with a string of behinds. South then rushed the ball forward for Ted Johnson to score a behind just

MATCH RESULTS

Round 1, at Princes Park, April 30
South Melbourne 10.10 (70) d Carlton 9.15 (69)
Round 2, at Lake Oval, May 7
South Melbourne 12.11 (83) d Melbourne 7.11 (53)
Round 3, at Junction Oval, May 14
St Kilda 8.15 (63) d South Melbourne 7.13 (55)
Round 4, at Lake Oval, May 21
Coll. 16.10 (106) d South Melbourne 9.13 (67)
Round 5, at Western Oval, May 28
Footscray 7.13 (55) d South Melbourne 6.13 (49)
Round 6, at Lake Oval, June 6
South Melbourne 14.13 (97) d North Melb. 9.9 (63)
Round 7, at Lake Oval, June 11
Richmond 15.17 (107) d South Melbourne 10.11 (71)
Round 8, at Brunswick Street, June 18
Fitzroy 14.11 (95) d South Melbourne 11.14 (80)
Round 9, at Windy Hill, June 25
South Melbourne 15.9 (99) d Essendon 12.12 (84)
Round 10, at Lake Oval, July 2
South Melbourne 13.19 (97) d Hawthorn 5.11 (41)
Round 11, at Corio Oval, July 9
Geelong 10.12 (72) d South Melbourne 9.12 (66)
Round 12, at Lake Oval, July 16
South Melbourne 12.8 (80) d Carlton 8.21 (69)
Round 13, at MCG, July 23
Melbourne 20.20 (140) d South Melbourne 11.5 (71)
Round 14, at Lake Oval, July 30
South Melbourne 13.20 (98) d St Kilda 8.9 (57)
Round 15, at Victoria Park, August 6
Collingwood 18.14 (122) d South Melbourne 6.7 (43)
Round 16, at Lake Oval, August 27
South Melbourne 9.20 (74) d Footscray 10.10 (70)
Round 17, at Arden Street, September 3
South Melbourne 11.12 (78) d North Melb. 8.12 (60)
Round 18, at Lake Oval, September 10
Geelong 15.15 (105) d South Melbourne 14.11 (95)

before the final bell. Jack Barnes kicked five goals for South and *The Sporting Globe* reported that the thrilling finish was "a repetition of the sterling struggles of the past by the old rivals".

When South defeated Melbourne by 30 points at the Lake Oval the following week, *The Sporting Globe* headline read SOUTH'S OVERWHELMING VICTORY OVER MELBOURNE. It might have been a solid win, with Johnson (two goals) and Jack Petchell named South's best players, but the result was misleading as Melbourne was in disarray as star forward Bob Johnson Snr was missing because of influenza and 1926 premiership rover Herbie White because of the death of his brother earlier in the week.

The football world was shocked just a few days later when former Essendon champion Albert Thurgood was killed in a motor accident at the intersection of Kooyong and Toorak Roads, Malvern. The VFL's round three matches therefore were played in a sombre mood, with South and St Kilda clashing at the Junction Oval. St Kilda won by eight points and *The Sporting Globe* declared it was a "brilliant victory over Souths".

South the following week went down by 37 points to Collingwood at the Lake Oval and this was followed by a six-point loss to Footscray at the Western Oval. This left South in a precarious position in the chase for a final four finish and its lack of consistency eventually proved costly and the Southerners finished sixth, three games and a wide percentage margin behind fourth-placed Carlton.

The 1927 season was the great Roy Cazaly's last. He had played 99 games with St Kilda from 1911-20 and then the same number with South from 1921-24 and 1926-27. He had left South to coach Minyip in 1925, but returned the following year. Cazaly crossed to City South (Launceston) and was South's non-playing coach from 1937-38. He also coached Hawthorn in 1942-43.

PLAYER	GAMES	GOALS
AVERY, Bert	5	1
BARLOW, Arthur	14	5
BARNES, Jack	8	19
BERRYMAN, Bill	17	0
BOURKE, Ted	6	1
BROWN, Martin	16	7
CAZALY, Roy	13	10
CLARKE, Harry	12	9
CONDON, Bill	15	8
FAIRLEY, Roland	8	3
FERGUSON, Joe	11	4
HOGG, Syd	5	0
JACOBSON, Albie	2	0
JOHNSON, Ted	15	50
McDONALD, Charles	6	2
McKAY, Hec	18	0
McMAHON, Tom	1	1
NICHOLLS, Charlie	7	2
PANNAM, Charlie	18	19
PETCHELL, Jack	15	19
PETTIONA, Cecil	7	0
REVILLE, Peter	11	5
ROBERTSON, Austin	16	7
SCANLAN, Joe	18	4
STANBRIDGE, Charlie	8	2
SUTTON, Bert	14	14
THOMAS, Len	12	0
WHEELAHAN, Danny	12	0
WOODFIELD, Les	14	0

POSITION: Sixth
COACH: Charlie Pannam
CAPTAIN: Charlie Pannam
BEST AND FAIREST: Hec McKay
LEADING GOALKICKER: Ted Johnson (50)

1928

South's 1927 season might have been disappointing, but Charlie Pannam continued as captain-coach, with follower Joe Poulter and defender Cyril Powell both crossing from Richmond. Poulter, who had been a Tiger star from 1923, played 31 games with South, while Powell managed just 20.

The star recruit was local youngster Terry Brain, from South Melbourne Dictricts. A brilliant rover, he went on to play 141 games to 1937, played in the 1933 premiership side and won the best and fairest in 1934. Collingwood sought a clearance for Brain just before the start of the 1928 season and, in fact, the Magpies had selected him for their opening round match. South secretary Like McBrien told Collingwood there would be no clearance, especially as Brain had been selected to play for South in its opening round match.

South defeated Footscray by just one point at the Lake Oval in that opening match, with star full-forward Ted Johnson kicking eight goals. South might have had a lucky escape, but was without several top players from 1927, including Roy Cazaly, Les Woodfield and Bert Sutton. Cazaly and Woodfield had retired from VFL football, while Sutton had been appointed captain-coach of Hawthorn.

It was obvious the South team needed rebuilding and although *The Sporting Globe* suggested "the red and whites have a fine lot of recruits", the cupboard was near bare and the squad boasted only a handful of quality players. Although South defeated St Kilda by 21 points at the Junction Oval in round two, the early season enthusiasm quickly died off through eight consecutive defeats. One of these defeats was a 76-point thrashing by Richmond at the Punt Road Oval in round nine. Tiger full-forward Jack Baggott kicked 12 goals and *The Sporting Globe* said South was "demoralised".

South broke its horror run of defeats with a lucky five-point win over bottom side Hawthorn at the Glenferrie Oval in round 11. *The Sporting Globe* praised Hawthorn for its "pace and clever anticipation", but there were no words of encouragement for South. After all, Hawthorn did not win a game that season and was the chopping block of the competition.

Pannam retired as a player late in the season, with Joe Scanlan taking over the captaincy, but South's woes continued. The Southerners finished the season with just five wins to finish ahead of only North Melbourne, which also won five games but had a much inferior percentage, and the winless Hawthorn. Although South defeated Fitzroy by 10 points

A South Melbourne side of 1928.

MATCH RESULTS

Round 1, at Lake Oval, April 21
South Melbourne 14.16 (100) d Footscray 15.9 (99)

Round 2, at Junction Oval, April 28
South Melbourne 17.15 (117) d St Kilda 14.12 (96)

Round 3, at Windy Hill, May 5
Essendon 12.13 (85) d South Melbourne 5.11 (41)

Round 4, at Lake Oval, May 12
North Melb. 10.10 (70) d South Melbourne 10.9 (69)

Round 5, at Corio Oval, May 19
Geelong 15.15 (105) d South Melbourne 11.15 (81)

Round 6, at Lake Oval, May 26
Carlton 12.13 (85) d South Melbourne 12.10 (82)

Round 7, at Brunswick Street, June 2
Fitzroy 17.11 (113) d South Melbourne 11.11 (77)

Round 8, at Lake Oval, June 4
Collingwood 13.7 (85) d South Melbourne 9.14 (68)

Round 9, at Punt Road, June 9
Richmond 21.16 (142) d South Melbourne 9.12 (66)

Round 10, at Lake Oval, June 23
Melbourne 13.12 (90) d South Melbourne 11.12 (78)

Round 11, at Glenferrie Oval, June 30
South Melbourne 15.10 (100) d Hawthorn 14.11 (95)

Round 12, at Western Oval, July 7
Footscray 13.13 (91) d South Melbourne 13.11 (89)

Round 13, at Lake Oval, July 14
St Kilda 18.13 (121) d South Melbourne 10.10 (70)

Round 14, at Lake Oval, July 28
Essendon 18.11 (119) d South Melbourne 11.17 (83)

Round 15, at Arden Street, August 4
North Melb. 12.10 (82) d South Melbourne 11.14 (80)

Round 16, at Lake Oval, August 11
South Melbourne 15.14 (104) d Geelong 9.13 (67)

Round 17, at Princes Park, August 18
Carlton 9.20 (74) d South Melbourne 8.8 (56)

Round 18, at Lake Oval, September 1
South Melbourne 14.16 (100) d Fitzroy 13.12 (90)

at the Lake Oval in the final round, *The Sporting Globe* reported that only the closeness of the scores enlivened "dull football". It also reported that the attendance was just 5000, a reflection of how South had lost support in one of its worst seasons to date.

South's only consolation was that Johnson again was in top form and equalled his club record of 60 goals in a season. The versatile Charlie Stanbridge won the best and fairest to add to his Victorian representative honours that season. Winger Harry Clarke polled three votes in the Brownlow Medal to finish equal sixth, with Melbourne's Ivor Warne-Smith taking football's highest individual honour with eight best on ground efforts.

Brothers Paddy (left) and Joe Scanlan were opposing captains in this Footscray-South match at the Western Oval in 1928.

PLAYER	GAMES	GOALS
AVERY, Bert	11	1
BARLOW, Arthur	5	0
BARNES, Jack	16	34
BERRYMAN, Bill	16	0
BOLLMAN, Les	10	0
BRAIN, Terry	11	11
BROWN, Martin	6	4
CAMERON, Paul	6	7
CHURCHILL, Bill	8	11
CLARKE, Harry	18	5
CONDON, George	5	0
CROSSAN, Jim	4	4
FAIRLEY, Roland	2	0
FERGUSON, Joe	3	0
HOGG, Len	9	18
HOGG, Syd	1	0
JACOBSON, Albie	11	2
JOHNSON, Ted	15	60
KENNETT, Fred	1	0
McDONALD, Charles	3	0
McKAY, Hec	15	0
MANNION, Bill	1	0
MURPHY, Tom	1	0
O'BRIEN, Jack	1	0
PANNAM, Charlie	13	11
PETCHELL, Jack	15	11
PETTIONA, Cecil	4	0
POULTER, Joe	13	7
POWELL, Cyril	8	0
REVILLE, Peter	18	15
RICHARDSON, Jack	1	0
ROBERTSON, Austin	3	2
SCANLAN, Joe	17	1
STANBRIDGE, Charlie	18	2
TEBBLE, Pat	3	0
THOMAS, Len	18	0
WHEELAHAN, Danny		

POSITION: Tenth
COACH: Charlie Pannam
CAPTAIN: Charlie Pannam, Joe Scanlan
BEST AND FAIREST: Charlie Stanbridge
LEADING GOALKICKER: Ted Johnson (60)

1929

South, in replacing Charlie Pannam as coach for 1929, looked to its past in appointing 1918 premiership captain Jim Caldwell. However, he stood down late in the season and the recently retired Fred Fleiter filled in over the final weeks of the season. Powerful follower-defender Charlie Stanbridge, who had won the best and fairest the previous season was named captain.

South was conscious of the need to build its side and, during the season, *The Sporting Globe* reported that club secretary Dick Mullaly had made many visits to the country. Meanwhile, South introduced two class recruits in 1929, with Ron Hillis and Hugh McLaughlin achieving lasting fame in the red and white. Hillis, from Middle Park, developed into one the finest full-backs to play for South over 137 games to 1937, but missed the 1933 premiership because of injury. McLaughlin, from Port Melbourne CYMS and originally from country club Dundin, played 96 games for South to 1934 and was a member of the 1933 premiership side.

Expectations were low in 1929, and this was reflected in Melbourne's 32-point defeat of South in the wet in their opening round match at the MCG. However, South did well enough to impress *The Sporting Globe*, which reported: "South showed plenty of dash, but failed to press home the advantage on the forward line." Strangely, South named star full-forward Ted Johnson on a half-back flank, with Jack Barnes at full-forward. Barnes and winger Harry Clarke kicked two goals each, but Johnson looked lost in defence.

Johnson returned to his familiar full-forward post for the round two clash with St Kilda at the Lake Oval and, following South's 26-point victory over its lakeside rival, *The Sporting Globe* suggested in its match headline SOUTH'S FORWARDS IMPROVE. The match report read: "South, taking complete charge in the second half, dominated the game. This was due to the better stamina, condition and determination of South."

The match was marred by an unsavoury incident in which St Kilda captain Bill Cubbins was hit on the head by a stone thrown at him from the crowd during the third quarter. *The Sporting Globe* reported that play was held up while Cubbins' teammates rushed to his aid. The St Kilda skipper was dazed but was able to resume play. The newspaper added: "A hostile demonstration was made against the stone thrower."

Although the win over the highly-rated St Kilda, which made the finals that season, was highly encouraging, South failed to find any real consistency over the rest of the season. According to newspaper reports they "battled manfully" in most matches and, following a 27-point loss to the all-conquering Collingwood at the Lake Oval in round 14, *The Argus'* "Old Boy" commented: "South Melbourne's well-known ability to play dashing, effective football on its own ground attracted an unexpectedly big crowd (18,500) to the match against apparently invincible Collingwood. At half-time it looked as if South would win, for Collingwood needed three goals to go ahead. Then, in five minutes of the third quarter, the ball flew from one Collingwood man to another."

"Chatterer", writing in *The Football Record,* praised South for its bid to make the finals. In reference to Collingwood, Carlton, Richmond and St Kilda making the final four with two rounds to play, he wrote of South: "They did right well. They came along swiftly and confidently until a fortnight ago when Collingwood beat them. Then they died hard last week when beaten by Carlton at Princes Park, but it was comforting to know that they had beaten the team which had won fourth place (Essendon, in round 16)."

The second half of the season was marred by heavy conditions, with Melbourne experiencing a particularly wet winter. The inexperienced Southerners struggled in many of their games, but won praise in *The Argus* for their six-point defeat of Essendon at the Lake Oval in round 16. The newspaper reported: "South Melbourne's victory was well-deserved for, on the day, it was a better disciplined and systematic team." It noted that forward Austin Robertson "gave a grand display". He kicked six goals in appalling conditions and finished the season as South's leading goalicker, with 53.

South won just seven games to finish eighth, but at least it was an improvement on

MATCH RESULTS

Round 1, at MCG, April 27
Melbourne 12.8 (80) d South Melbourne 7.16 (48)

Round 2, at Lake Oval, May 4
South Melbourne 12.17 (89) d St Kilda 9.9 (63)

Round 3, at Victoria Park, May 11
Collingwood 19.20 (134) d South Melb. 4.14 (38)

Round 4, at Lake Oval, May 18
Carlton 10.19 (79) d South Melbourne 9.19 (73)

Round 5, at Windy Hill, May 25
Essendon 10.18 (78) d South Melbourne 7.10 (52)

Round 6, at Lake Oval, June 1
South Melbourne 11.14 (80) d Richmond 10.17 (77)

Round 7, at Glenferrie Oval, June 15
Hawthorn 15.8 (98) d South Melbourne 11.13 (79)

Round 8, at Western Oval, June 22
Footscray 11.9 (75) d South Melbourne 8.13 (61)

Round 9, at Lake Oval, June 29
Geelong 10.15 (75) d South Melbourne 10.13 (73)

Round 10, at Brunswick Street, July 6
South Melbourne 17.8 (110) d Fitzroy 12.14 (86)

Round 11, at Lake Oval, July 13
South Melbourne 17.14 (116) d North Melb. 12.9 (81)

Round 12, at Lake Oval, July 20
South Melbourne 12.10 (82) d Melbourne 9.15 (69)

Round 13, at Junction Oval, July 27
St Kilda 15.9 (99) d South Melbourne 8.8 (56)

Round 14, at Lake Oval, August 3
Collingwood 10.10 (70) d South Melbourne 6.7 (43)

Round 15, at Princes Park, August 10
Carlton 17.17 (119) d South Melbourne 11.15 (81)

Round 16, at Lake Oval, August 17
South Melbourne 14.10 (94) d Essendon 13.10 (88)

Round 17, at Punt Road, August 24
Richmond 18.28 (136) d South Melbourne 10.5 (65)

Round 18, at Lake Oval, August 31
South Melbourne 13.10 (88) d Hawthorn 11.5 (71)

the previous year's tenth position with five wins. Winger Danny Wheelahan, who had been recruited from Bacchus March in 1926, won the club best and fairest. However, no South player featured in the top 12 of the Brownlow Medal count, with the award going to Collingwood's Albert Collier.

Charlie Stanbridge, South 1929 captain.

Norman Le Brun, who played three games with South Melbourne in 1929, played with three other VFL/AFL clubs — Essendon, Collingwood and Carlton, as well as with Richmond reserves.

Le Brun, who never seemed to settle at one club, also played in the VFA with Coburg and with country club South Warrnambool before enlisting in the army in World War II. He continued playing football even in the army and was a star player in regimental matches while training in Queensland.

Trooper Le Brun was with the 2/10 Australian Commando Squadron when he was killed by a Japanese rifleman in New Guinea on November 15, 1944. He is buried at the Lae War Cemetery, Papua New Guinea.

PLAYER	GAMES	GOALS
AVERY, Bert	4	0
BARNES, Jack	13	13
BOLLMAN, Les	7	0
BRAIN, Terry	13	10
CHURCHILL, Bill	9	8
CLARKE, Harry	16	3
FAGAN, Dinny	1	0
FORBES, Jim	1	0
HILLIS, Ron	10	11
HOGG, Len	7	12
HOGG, Syd	7	3
HUTTON, Rupert	7	2
JOHNSON, Ted	6	7
LE BRUN, Norman	3	2
McKAY, Hec	14	0
McLAUGHLIN, Hugh	18	0
O'BRIEN, Jack	6	3
O'CONNOR, Bill	1	0
PETCHELL, Jack	5	6
PETTIONA, Cecil	14	1
POOLE, Eric	4	0
POULTER, Joe	17	7
POWELL, Cyril	12	0
REVILLE, Peter	18	35
RICHARDSON, Jack	10	6
ROBERTSON, Austin	17	53
ROSENBROCK, Edward	1	0
SCANLAN, Joe	15	0
SCOTT, Max	17	0
STANBRIDGE, Charlie	14	2
THOMAS, Len	15	0
TWYFORD, Jack	2	2
WHEELAHAN, Danny	9	2
WILDIE, Edwin	11	0

POSITION: Eighth
COACH: Jim Caldwell, Fred Fleiter
CAPTAIN: Charlie Stanbridge
BEST AND FAIREST: Danny Wheelahan
LEADING GOALKICKER: Austin Robertson (53)

1930

South, desperate to reverse its recent fortunes, changed coaches again for 1930, naming former club captain Paddy Scanlan as non-playing coach. Scanlan had played 100 games with South from 1920-26 before being captain-coach of Footscray over the 1927-28 seasons. His younger brother Joe was nominated South captain and this remains the only case of brothers coaching and captaining a VFL/AFL club in the one season.

South, before the season, cleared Jack Twyford to Richmond and Norman Le Brun (later killed in action in World War II) to Essendon and also lost the services of the big-hearted Charlie Stanbridge, who was appointed captain-coach of VFA club Port Melbourne.

On the positive side, South recruited several youngsters who were to make a big impression at the Lake Oval, and none more so than Mitcham recruit Harold Pratt. Harold Pratt? Yes, the future goalkicking freak's full name was Harold Robert Pratt and was known as "Bob" to avoid confusion with his father Harold. Pratt had attracted the attention of both South and Hawthorn when playing with Mitcham, but the Maybloom dropped off after watching Pratt play poorly in a game marred by a strong wind. South maintained its interest through the insistence of the Mitcham coach, a man named Pollard.

S.M. 2ND XVIII F.C.
SEASON 1930
Five Years Certificate.
This is to certify that G. Brain Esq. has rendered valuable services to the
South Melbourne Football Club
Second Eighteen.
President. Robert S. Houghton
Secretary. Geo Moloney

Paddy Scanlan was South's non-playing coach in 1930, while brother Joe was club captain.

MATCH RESULTS

Round 1, at Lake Oval, May 3
Melbourne 13.17 (95) d South Melbourne 9.16 (70)

Round 2, at Junction Oval, May 10
St Kilda 16.10 (106) d South Melbourne 11.12 (78)

Round 3, at Lake Oval, May 17
Collingwood 16.19 (115) d South Melb. 12.12 (84)

Round 4, at Princes Park, May 24
Carlton 20.18 (138) d South Melbourne 11.18 (84)

Round 5, at Lake Oval, May 31
Essendon 15.14 (104) d South Melbourne 6.15 (51)

Round 6, at Punt Road, June 9
Richmond 11.15 (81) d South Melbourne 9.12 (66)

Round 7, at Lake Oval, June 14
South Melbourne 17.11 (113) d Hawthorn 9.10 (64)

Round 8, at Lake Oval, June 21
South Melbourne 15.19 (109) d Footscray 8.12 (60)

Round 9, at Corio Oval, June 28
Geelong 14.12 (96) d South Melbourne 11.6 (72)

Round 10, at Lake Oval, July 5
South Melbourne 13.16 (94) d Fitzroy 12.12 (84)

Round 11, at Arden Street, July 12
South Melbourne 10.20 (80) d North Melb. 6.9 (45)

Round 12, at Windy Hill, July 19
South Melb. 16.12 (108) d Essendon 15.16 (106)

Round 13, at Lake Oval, July 26
South Melbourne 11.11 (77) d Richmond 10.11 (71)

Round 14, at Glenferrie Oval, August 16
South Melbourne 14.10 (94) d Hawthorn 11.7 (73)

Round 15, at Western Oval, August 23
South Melbourne 11.18 (84) d Footscray 8.18 (66)

Round 16, at Lake Oval, August 30
Geelong 15.14 (104) d South Melbourne 12.16 (88)

Round 17, at Brunswick Street, September 6
Fitzroy 15.19 (109) d South Melbourne 14.8 (92)

Round 18, at Lake Oval, September 13
South Melbourne 15.19 (109) d North Melb. 5.6 (36)

Joe Scanlan and committeemen and former players Fred Fleiter and Tammy Hynes took another look at the young Pratt and jokingly told Pollard that, after the first time they saw Pratt they would have cut Pollard's throat, "only that it would make a mess." Pratt made his debut in the opening round of the 1930 season, against Melbourne at the Lake Oval, on a half-forward flank and developed into one of the greatest full-forwards the game has seen.

The other prize recruits of 1930 were Jack Austin and Ron Shapter. Austin, from South Melbourne Districts, went on to play 140 games with South to 1938 and was a member of the 1933 premiership side. Shapter, a ruckman from Queenscliff, played just 26 games with South before crossing to Fitzroy in 1932 and later to Essendon, but had immense potential. In fact, *The Sporting Globe* early in 1930 predicted he would be a champion and likened him to former South star Bert Franks.

Melbourne, in that opening round match, defeated South by 25 points and, ironically, *The Herald* suggested that South had improved on the previous season "though weak forward". Pratt eventually would solve that problem but did well on debut kicking three goals, along with Bert Avery.

South had started the season poorly, with worse to come. It dropped its next five matches to be bottom of the ladder going into the round seven match against fellow struggler Hawthorn at the Lake Oval. South thrashed the Mayblooms by 49 points and *The Sporting Globe,* under the headline SOUTH'S FIRST — HAWTHORN ALWAYS BEHIND reported: "A complete reversal of form on the part of both teams saw South Melbourne overwhelm Hawthorn ."

Amazingly considering South's run of six straight defeats from the start of the season, the Southerners notched six consecutive wins from rounds 10-15. *The Sporting Globe* ran the following headline after the round 10 defeat of Fitzroy: SOUTHERNERS MOVE UP THE LIST. Pratt showed immense promise in that match, kicking five goals and outshining full-forward Austin Robertson, who kicked four goals.

Austin Robertson won the World Professional Sprint title in 1930.

However, South left its run too late and finished the season in seventh position, with nine wins. The *Sun News-Pictorial* was alert enough to report: "South Melbourne's playing record for the season is a remarkable one. In

18 games it won nine and lost nine, and kicked 1553 points to 1553 kicked against it. Its percentage is, therefore, exactly 100 per cent."

South might have missed the finals yet again in 1930, but a brilliant new dawn was about to break over the Lake Oval, especially with young Pratt showing such outstanding promise. He kicked 43 goals in his debut season and was runner-up to Robertson (54) in the club goalkicking. Full-back Ron Hillis won the best and fairest and polled two votes in the Browlow Medal count, won by Richmond winger Stan Judkins (four votes), who was named the winner after tying with Collingwood's Harry Collier and Footscray's Alan Hopkins because he had played fewer games. Collier and Hopkins were awarded retrospective medals in 1989. South defender Hugh McLaughlin and seven other players polled three votes.

FIXTURES 1930

Date.	Club.	Ground.
May 3	Melbourne	S.M.C.G.
10	St. Kilda	St. Kilda
17	Collingwood	S.M.C.G.
24	Carlton	Carlton
31	Essendon	S.M.C.G.
June 9	Richmond	Richmond
14	Hawthorn	S.M.C.G.
21	Footscray	S.M.C.G.
28	Geelong	Geelong
July 5	Fitzroy	S.M.C.G.
12	North Melb.	North Melb.
19	Essendon	Essendon
26	Richmond	S.M.C.G.
Aug. 2, 9	Carnival Matches	Adelaide
16	Hawthorn	Hawthorn
23	Footscray	Footscray
30	Geelong	S.M.C.G.
Sept. 6	Fitzroy	Fitzroy
13	North Melb.	S.M.C.G.
20, 27, Oct. 4, 11	Semi-Finals and Finals	M.C.G.

"Chatterer", writing in *The Football Record* suggested that one South player promised to eat his hat if the Southerners did not make the final four. "Chatterer" added: "It's up to South Melbourne to shake a leg to better purpose than was the case last season if it is only to save one of their players from eating the most indigestible meal ever thought of. He's so certain that the Southerners will be well amongst the fourers that he has undertaken to eat in public his hat if they do not prove themselves a better side than last year. It goes without saying that if they fail some of the barrackers will insist on his hat being eaten.

"I have no doubt that we shall hear them roaring when matches are being played. 'Remember the hat!', as a stimulating reminder that one of their numbers shall not be called on to swallow his hat or his words. A barracker prefers to see his team win matches to any player dining off his lid." It is not known whether the unnamed player ate his hat when South failed to make the final four.

PLAYER	GAMES	GOALS
AUSTIN, Jack	11	7
AVERY, Bert	5	3
BENNETT, Reg	13	0
BRAIN, Terry	9	11
CALLICK, Alf	1	2
CASSIDY, Roy	1	0
CLARKE, Harry	16	7
CONDON, George	2	0
COUTTS, David	5	0
FAGAN, Dinny	8	0
HILLIS, Ron	17	0
HOGG, Syd	15	1
JOHNSON, Ted	16	30
JORDAN, Bill	3	1
KNIGHT, Tasman	4	0
LAWLER, Stan	1	4
LEFFANUE, Rod	1	1
McKAY, Hec	17	0
McLAUGHLIN, Hugh	16	0
McMAHON, Tom	11	4
MARTIN, Ron	4	3
O'BRIEN, Jack	6	1
O'BRIEN, Bill	2	0
PETTIONA, Cecil	12	2
PRATT, Bob	18	43
REVILLE, Peter	16	26
RICHARDSON, Jack	16	0
ROBERTSON, Austin	13	54
ROSENBROCK, Edward	3	0
SCANLAN, Joe	16	1
SHAPTER, Ron	17	8
SHELTON, Jack	7	2
THOMAS, Len	18	0
TROUGHTON, Charlie	7	6
WHEELAHAN, Danny	9	2
WHEELAHAN, Martin	6	3

POSITION: Seventh
COACH: Paddy Scanlan
CAPTAIN: Joe Scanlan
BEST AND FAIREST: Ron Hillis
LEADING GOALKICKER: Austin Robertson (54)

1931

South retained the services of Paddy Scanlan as coach for 1931, with his brother Joe again captain, with Hec McKay vice-captain. "Jumbo" Sharland, writing in *The Sporting Globe* of March 7 told of how St Kilda officials were convinced the Saints would win the flag and, two weeks later, the former Geelong player reported that South officials declared the Southerners "certain for the four". Sharland also wrote: "South has had many letters from interstate stars desirous of obtaining jobs." However, he added: "The committee will not worry about them because there is scarcely any work."

The Great Depression had hit hard but South did find room for one interstate recruit, Port Adelaide premiership player Jack Wade, who had played for South Australia. However, Wade played just 26 games for South to 1933 and was killed in action in Lebanon in World War II. Of the other newcomers, the most impressive was the rugged Jock McKenzie, who played 55 games with South in three spells at the Lake Oval and was a member of the 1933 premiership side. He also played 48 games with Fitzroy from 1936-39.

Meanwhile, the VFL in 1930 introduced a new finals system, devised by Ken McIntyre and promoted by the Richmond secretary and chairman of the Umpire and Permit committee Percy Page. The Page-McIntyre system involved the third and fourth teams playing off in the first semi-final, with the first and second sides clashing in the second semi-final. The winner of the first semi-final then would play the loser of the second semi-final in a preliminary final to challenge the winner of the second semi-final in a Grand Final. *The Sporting Globe* reported that only Collingwood and St Kilda opposed the change.

South defeated North Melbourne by 52 points at Arden Street in the opening round and *The Sporting Globe* enthused: "In a fast open game, South Melbourne's experience, anticipation and accurate system proved too much for North's dash and persistency." South centreman Len Thomas won "a pat on the back" from *The Sporting Globe,* while the depth of the Depression was reflected in defender Peter Reville being unavailable because he had been searching for work.

Reville took his place in the South side the following week against Footscray at the Lake Oval, but the Southerners went down by 20 points, with *The Sporting Globe* describing it as a "surprise" defeat. Then, when reigning premier Collingwood defeated South by 21 points at Victoria Park in round three, the red and white's finals ambitions already had been dented. South struggled for consistency over the first half of the season and by the completion of eight rounds, had notched just three wins.

The season then was interrupted by a South Australia-Victoria clash in Adelaide and a charity VFL versus VFA clash at the MCG, with proceeds donated to the Blind Association. On resumption of the VFL competition, South defeated Essendon by 10 points to keep its flickering finals hopes alive, but went down to Carlton by just five points at Princes Park the following week. South hovered close to the top four, but without any realistic chance of making the finals.

The Sporting Globe described the round

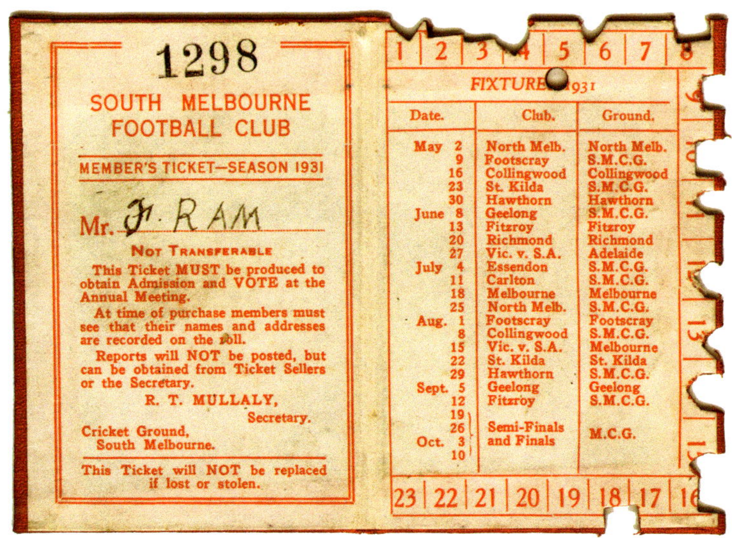

1298

SOUTH MELBOURNE FOOTBALL CLUB

MEMBER'S TICKET—SEASON 1931

Mr. J. RAM

NOT TRANSFERABLE

This Ticket MUST be produced to obtain Admission and VOTE at the Annual Meeting.

At time of purchase members must see that their names and addresses are recorded on the roll.

Reports will NOT be posted, but can be obtained from Ticket Sellers or the Secretary.

R. T. MULLALY,
Secretary.

Cricket Ground,
South Melbourne.

This Ticket will NOT be replaced if lost or stolen.

FIXTURES 1931

Date.	Club.	Ground.
May 2	North Melb.	North Melb.
9	Footscray	S.M.C.G.
16	Collingwood	Collingwood
23	St. Kilda	S.M.C.G.
30	Hawthorn	Hawthorn
June 8	Geelong	S.M.C.G.
13	Fitzroy	Fitzroy
20	Richmond	Richmond
27	Vic. v. S.A.	Adelaide
July 4	Essendon	S.M.C.G.
11	Carlton	S.M.C.G.
18	Melbourne	Melbourne
25	North Melb.	S.M.C.G.
Aug. 1	Footscray	Footscray
8	Collingwood	S.M.C.G.
15	Vic. v. S.A.	Melbourne
22	St. Kilda	St. Kilda
29	Hawthorn	S.M.C.G.
Sept. 5	Geelong	Geelong
12	Fitzroy	S.M.C.G.
19, 26, Oct. 3, 10	Semi-Finals and Finals	M.C.G.

MATCH RESULTS

Round 1, at Arden Street, May 2
South Melb. 19.21 (135) d North Melb. 11.17 (83)

Round 2, at Lake Oval, May 9
Footscray 16.15 (111) d South Melbourne 13.13 (91)

Round 3, at Victoria Park, May 16
Collingwood 13.16 (94) d South Melb. 10.13 (73)

Round 4, at Lake Oval, May 23
South Melbourne 18.19 (127) d St Kilda 16.10 (106)

Round 5, at Glenferrie Oval, May 30
South Melbourne 11.13 (79) d Hawthorn 11.10 (76)

Round 6, at Lake Oval, June 8
Geelong 13.15 (93) d South Melbourne 6.8 (44)

Round 7, at Brunswick Street, June 13
South Melbourne 16.15 (111) d Fitzroy 14.14 (98)

Round 8, at Punt Road, June 20
Richmond 12.12 (84) d South Melbourne 7.15 (57)

Round 9, at Lake Oval, July 4
South Melbourne 10.13 (73) d Essendon 9.9 (63)

Round 10, at Lake Oval, July 11
Carlton 11.11 (77) d South Melbourne 10.12 (72)

Round 11, at MCG, July 18
South Melbourne 12.10 (82) d Melbourne 4.7 (31)

Round 12, at Lake Oval, July 25
South Melbourne 13.16 (94) d North Melb. 9.12 (66)

Round 13, at Western Oval, August 1
Footscray 9.14 (68) d South Melbourne 5.11 (41)

Round 14, at Lake Oval, August 8
Collingwood 8.13 (61) d South Melbourne 6.23 (59)

Round 15, at Junction Oval, August 22
South Melbourne 8.14 (62) d St Kilda 6.18 (54)

Round 16, at Lake Oval, August 29
South Melbourne 12.18 (90) d Hawthorn 9.5 (59)

Round 17, at Corio Oval, September 5
Geelong 16.12 (108) d South Melbourne 8.11 (59)

Round 18, at Lake Oval, September 12
Fitzroy 10.14 (74) d South Melbourne 5.14 (44)

13 Footscray-South match at the Western Oval as "vital" for the Southerners, but the Tricolours ended all South hopes with a 27-point win. *The Sporting Globe* reported: "Though South led off brightly against Footscray, they were shaded in the first half by the play of the spirited and resourceful work of the Tricolours."

South finished the season in seventh position with nine wins in an almost identical repeat of the previous season. South was still using Pratt as a half-forward, with Robertson at full-forward, but change was in the wind. Robertson had represented Victoria in the match against South Australia in Adelaide and was joined in the Big Vee by South teammate Harry Clarke for the return match at the MCG.

Robertson, a professional sprint champion and often referred to as "the fastest man alive", was just one of many speedsters in the South line-up and Sharland in 1931 commented: "In regard to possession of all-round pace there is no faster combination in the game than South Melbourne. Austin Robertson, McLaughlin, Hillis, Brain, Patterson, Harry Clarke, Milburn, McKay and Pratt all have plenty of 'toe'. Even the big men like Wade, Poulter and McPherson can move."

The VFL in 1931 introduced a three, two, one voting system for the Brownlow Medal, with Fitzroy rover Haydn Bunton winning with 26 votes. South's best was Clarke, with nine votes, followed by Cecil Pettiona (six).

PLAYER	GAMES	GOALS
AUSTIN, Jack	18	6
BENNETT, Reg	16	4
BRAIN, Terry	15	23
CLARKE, Harry	18	1
FAGAN, Dinny	10	0
FISHER, Clem	10	1
HARROWER, Eric	3	0
HILLIS, Ron	16	1
JOHNSON, Ted	16	29
LAWLER, Stan	1	2
LEFFANUE, Rod	4	4
McKAY, Hec	14	0
McKENZIE, Jock	1	0
McLAUGHLIN, Hugh	17	0
McMAHON, Tom	7	0
McNAMARA, Cyril	3	0
McPHERSON, Norm	7	0
MIETZCKE, Arthur	1	0
MILBURN, Len	12	3
PATTERSON, Jack	14	14
PETTIONA, Cecil	17	6
POULTER, Joe	7	10
PRATT, Bob	15	23
REVILLE, Peter	12	11
REYNOLDS, Ken	1	0
RICHARDSON, Jack	7	0
ROBERTSON, Austin	18	38
SCANLAN, Joe	10	2
SCOTT, Max	2	0
SHAPTER, Ron	9	6
SIMPSON, Keith	2	0
THOMAS, Len	16	1
THOMAS, Reg	2	0
WADE, Jack	16	2
WHEELAHAN, Martin	5	2

POSITION: Seventh
COACH: Paddy Scanlan
CAPTAIN: Joe Scanlan
BEST AND FAIREST: Len Thomas
LEADING GOALKICKER: Austin Robertson (38)

1932

South, in the lead-up to the 1932 season, realised it needed to be daring. The club had fallen into a rut and looked for new direction. The club therefore offered West Australian Johnny Leonard the job of captain-coach and was delighted when he telegrammed his acceptance. The 30-year-old Leonard had won the 1926 Sandover Medal, Subiaco's best and fairest in consecutive seasons from 1926-30 and, more importantly, had coaching experience, with Victorian country club Maryborough in 1931. Leonard's appointment was just part of a South master-plan for premiership success. Club president Jack Rohan, vice-president Archie Crofts and the committee decided to scour Australia for the best available talent, even though all VFL clubs were restricted to a payment of a maximum three pounds ($6) per player per match under what was termed the Coulter Rule, devised by Gordon Coulter to restrict professionalism.

South's big advantage, however, was that Crofts was able to offer players employment in his state-wide grocery chain. Also, in signing Leonard as captain-coach, South had a great advantage as the West Australian rover had first-hand knowledge of players available in his home state. Leonard's personal contacts therefore helped South sign Subiaco teammates Brighton Diggins and Bill Faul and South Fremantle's Gilbert Beard. All three had significant careers with South and played in the 1933 premiership side.

South also heard that Richmond was unhappy with Richmond ruckman Jack Bisset, a raw-boned ruckman who previously had plied his football trade in the country and in the VFA with Port Melbourne. And South's recruiting did not end there as it also picked up 18-year-old Herbie Matthews from VFA club Northcote. He was the son of former South player Herbie "Butcher" Matthews and had caught Collingwood's attention after he

The South squad of 1932. Back row, from left: J. Howard, W. Gowdie, R. Deane, B. Hair, J. Hudson, C. Hudson, J. Lee, N. Powell. Second back row, from left: Brighton Diggins, Austin Robertson, Peter Reville, Herb Boschen, Gilbert Beard, Ron Hillis, Jack Bisset, J. Marshall. Second front row, from left: Arthur Mietzcke, Hec McKay, Bill Faul, Jock Fahey, Johnny Leonard (capt.-coach), Len Thomas, Hugh McLaughlin, Bob Pratt, Reg Bennett. Front row, from left: Cecil Pettiona, Jack Austin, Herbie Matthews, Reg Thomas, Rod Leffanue, Terry Brain, Harry Clarke.

MATCH RESULTS

Round 1, at Lake Oval, April 30
South Melbourne 11.19 (85) d Melbourne 9.11 (65)

Round 2, at Princes Park, May 7
South Melbourne 17.11 (113) d Carlton 10.15 (75)

Round 3, at Lake Oval, May 14
South Melbourne 10.11 (71) d Footscray 8.12 (60)

Round 4, at Arden Street, May 21
South Melbourne 11.7 (73) d North Melb. 9.16 (70)

Round 5, at Lake Oval, May 28
South Melbourne 14.15 (99) d Essendon 9.11 (65)

Round 6, at Glenferrie Oval, June 4
South Melbourne 16.13 (109) d Hawthorn 11.14 (80)

Round 7, at Lake Oval, June 18
South Melbourne 14.21 (105) d Geelong 14.12 (96)

Round 8, at Punt Road, June 25
South Melbourne 8.9 (57) d Richmond 8.7 (55)

Round 9, at Lake Oval, July 2
South Melbourne 12.10 (82) d Fitzroy 10.15 (75)

Round 10, at Junction Oval, July 9
South Melbourne 9.16 (70) d Fitzroy 10.9 (69)

Round 11, at Lake Oval, July 16
Collingwood 7.8 (50) d South Melbourne 5.17 (47)

Round 12, at MCG, July 23
South Melbourne 13.15 (93) d Melbourne 12.12 (84)

Round 13, at Lake Oval, July 30
Carlton 12.17 (89) d South Melbourne 11.14 (80)

Round 14, at Western Oval, August 6
Footscray 11.14 (80) d South Melbourne 9.14 (68)

Round 15, at Lake Oval, August 13
South Melbourne 9.13 (67) d North Melb. 4.11 (35)

Round 16, at Windy Hill, August 20
Essendon 13.12 (90) d South Melbourne 11.20 (86)

Round 17, at Lake Oval, August 27
South Melbourne 24.13 (157) d Hawthorn 4.10 (34)

Round 18, at Corio Oval, September 3
Geelong 17.23 (125) d South Melbourne 9.15 (69)

First semi-final, at MCG, September 10
Collingwood 17.12 (114) d South Melb. 12.16 (88)

Action from the South-Carlton clash at the Lake Oval. On the left, South's Ron Hillis wards off a Carlton player and, on the right, Bill Faul spoils Carlton's Mickey Crisp.

had moved from the family home in South Melbourne to live with grandparents in Fairfield, close to Victoria Park.

The only problem for South was that Faul, Diggins and Beard were unavailable early in the season because, under the then VFL rules, they had to meet a three-month residential qualification. And Leonard, who was eligible to play from the start of the season, missed the opening round match against Melbourne at the Lake Oval because of illness. This meant that South was unable to field anywhere near its strongest side and, with Bisset acting captain, won by 20 points, with Bob Pratt at full-forward and destined to stay there.

Leonard was able to take his place for the fourth round match against North Melbourne and soon was joined by his fellow Sandgropers. The Bloods looked unbeatable, especially with Pratt in outstanding form. He had kicked 50 goals to round nine as South swept past all sides. However, South got the staggers after losing to Collingwood at the Lake Oval in round 11. It ran into severe injury problems and even went down to Carlton and Footscray in consecutive rounds.

South, after looking assured of the double chance in the finals for most of the season,

Action from the South match against Geelong at the Lake Oval in 1932.

finished a disappointing fourth, behind Carlton, Richmond and Collingwood. It might have been South's first finals series since 1924, but it had set its sights much higher and five defeats over the final eight rounds was hardly the form it wanted going into the first semi-final against Collingwood.

Collingwood rocked South with a stunning burst from the opening bounce. Without the seriously injured Diggins and Peter Reville, South lacked strength when it needed it most and Collingwood went on a rampage over the opening 15 minutes to put the match beyond the Bloods' reach. The Magpies kicked seven goals over the first 15 minutes and led by 46 points at the first break. South then trailed by 40 points at the final change before kicking three quick goals to suggest a belated comeback. However, the Magpies cruised home by 26 points to end South's dream.

West Australian Johnny Leonard was South captain-coach in 1932.

South had improved dramatically from its seventh position of the previous season and the Bloods took consolation from Pratt's 71 goals, breaking the club record of 60 goals in a season by Ted Johnson in each of 1924, 1925 and 1928. Faul had an outstanding debut season to win the best and fairest and was equal runner-up (with Geelong's George Moloney) to Fitzroy's Haydn Bunton in the Brownlow Medal count. Faul and Moloney both polled 16, but Bunton was a runaway winner with 23.

The *South Melbourne Record* reported: "Bill Faull (sic), the son of a Kalgoorlie mining engineer and former Subiaco player, is probably the greatest 'find' of the year. The South Melbourne man tied with George Moloney, another Westerner, for second place in the Brownlow Medal competition."

PLAYER	GAMES	GOALS
AUSTIN, Jack	16	0
BEARD, Gilbert	14	12
BENNETT, Reg	10	1
BISSET, Jack	18	5
BLACK, Austin	1	0
BOSCHEN, Herb	4	0
BRAIN, Terry	18	27
CLARKE, Harry	16	2
COSGRIFF, Joe	1	0
DIGGINS, Brighton	10	2
DOWD, Dinny	2	0
FAHEY, Jock	12	6
FAUL, Bill	17	0
FISHER, Clem	4	3
FLYNN, Bill	2	0
GILMOUR, Alan	2	0
HEARN, Maurie	4	3
HILLIS, Ron	18	0
LEFFANUE, Rod	7	9
LEONARD, Johnny	12	17
McKAY, Hec	17	1
McLAUGHLIN, Hugh	18	1
McPHERSON, Norm	2	0
MATTHEWS, Herbie J.	14	3
MIETZCKE, Arthur	12	6
PETTIONA, Cecil	16	3
PRATT, Bob	17	71
REVILLE, Peter	16	28
ROBERTSON, Austin	18	10
SELLECK, Roy	3	2
THOMAS, Len	17	1
THOMAS, Reg	18	13
WADE, Jack	5	0

POSITION: Fourth
COACH: Johnny Leonard
CAPTAIN: Johnny Leonard
BEST AND FAIREST: Bill Faul
LEADING GOALKICKER: Bob Pratt (71)

1933

South was dealt a savage blow before the start of the 1933 season when captain-coach Johnny Leonard was lured back to Western Australia to work for football manufacturer Ross Faulkner. Leonard might have been with the Bloods just one season, but he had a massive impact and could take much of the credit for rebuilding the side. Just before his departure, Leonard recommended to South that his vice-captain, Jack Bisset, take over as captain-coach.

Meanwhile, the South committee worked tirelessly to raise money to further build the side and club president Jack Rohan urged supporters to dig even deeper as he announced he would step down in favour of grocery magnate Archie Crofts. If rival clubs thought South's recruiting had moved into overdrive in 1932, they were stunned by the Bloods' massive manhunt in 1933.

The Bloods recruited East Perth's Jim "Brum" O'Meara, Subiaco's Johnny Bowe, West Torrens' Wilbur Harris and Ossie Bertram and Tasmanians Laurie Nash and Frank Davies. In fact, South's massive recruiting campaign resulted in the team being labelled "the Foreign Legion", while *The Sporting Globe* wondered how South could attract such a vast array of talent without breaking the Coulter Law "when payments were fixed by the law and theoretically no club could offer a greater financial lure than three pounds ($6) per week".

The most significant signing was that of Nash, who already had played Test cricket for Australia. Nash, the son of former Collingwood captain Bob Nash, had moved from the Melbourne suburb of Richmond to Tasmania primarily to play cricket. To keep himself fit for the summer sport he played football with the City Launceston club, coached by former South star Roy Cazaly.

His cricket career flourished to the extent that he was selected to play a Test for Australia against South Africa in Melbourne and he took

Bob Pratt flying high for a mark.

MATCH RESULTS

Round 1, at Princes Park, April 29
Carlton 12.15 (87) d South Melbourne 11.17 (83)

Round 2, at Lake Oval, May 6
South Melbourne 18.17 (125) d Footscray 14.15 (99)

Round 3, at Victoria Park, May 13
Collingwood 10.11 (71) d South Melbourne 9.3 (57)

Round 4, at Lake Oval, May 20
South Melbourne 11.14 (80) d St Kilda 10.16 (76)

Round 5, at Windy Hill, May 27
South Melbourne 17.15 (117) d Essendon 12.11 (83)

Round 6, at Lake Oval, June 3
South Melbourne 10.13 (73) d Hawthorn 9.6 (60)

Round 7, at Corio Oval, June 10
Geelong 17.14 (116) d South Melbourne 13.15 (93)

Round 8, at Lake Oval, June 17
Richmond 16.12 (108) d South Melb. 15.13 (103)

Round 9, at Brunswick Street, June 24
Fitzroy 15.7 (97) d South Melbourne 11.12 (78)

Round 10, at Lake Oval, July 1
South Melbourne 13.10 (88) d Melbourne 12.9 (81)

Round 11, at Arden Street, July 8
South Melb. 15.13 (103) d North Melb. 13.12 (90)

Round 12, at Lake Oval, July 15
South Melbourne 15.13 (103) d Carlton 9.6 (60)

Round 13, at Western Oval, July 22
South Melbourne 19.15 (129) d Footscray 8.11 (59)

Round 14, at Lake Oval, July 29
South Melb. 13.11 (89) d Collingwood 12.11 (83)

Round 15, at Junction Oval, August 5
South Melbourne 13.15 (93) d St Kilda 8.19 (67)

Round 16, at Lake Oval, August 19
South Melbourne 11.16 (82) d Essendon 6.4 (40)

Round 17, at Glenferrie Oval, August 26
South Melbourne 17.11 (113) d Hawthorn 8.12 (60)

Round 18, at Lake Oval, September 2
South Melbourne 23.17 (155) d Geelong 6.10 (46)

Second semi-final, at MCG, September 16
South Melbourne 14.11 (95) d Richmond 11.11 (77)

Grand Final, at MCG, September 30
South Melbourne 9.17 (71) d Richmond 4.5 (29)

five wickets. He also won City Launceston's best and fairest award in 1931 to have VFL clubs on his trail. City Launceston president

How the Sun News-Pictorial *cartoonist saw South's comeback against Richmond in the second semi-final.*

Hugh Cameron was a close friend of South committeeman and former club captain Joe Scanlan who therefore was given the inside running to sign the precociously talented Nash. Scanlan even was smuggled aboard the trans-Tasman steamer *Nairana* to avoid media attention in his quest to snare Nash.

Finally, Nash agreed to join South in 1933 and he made his VFL debut in the opening round match against Carlton at Princes Park. Nash, as a Test cricketer, was such a drawcard that 38,000 fans squeezed into the ground to see him in football action. Nash, who played on a half-back flank, had a quiet game in Carlton's four-point defeat of South. South easily could have won, but Bob Pratt was woefully inaccurate with 5.9.

South opened its 1933 account with a 26-point defeat of Footscray at the Lake Oval in round two, thanks to a brilliant seven-goal final quarter. Then, before the round three game

South's 1933 premiership squad. Back Row, from left: Jim O'Meara, Jock McKenzie, Dinny Kelleher, Gilbert Beard, Brighton Diggins, Alan Welch, Bill Faul. Second back row, from left: N. Read (who did not play a senior game), Ron Hillis, Maurie Hearn, Wilbur Harris, Arthur Mietzcke, Austin Robertson, Alan Gilmour, Laurie Nash. Seated, from left: Harry Clarke, Hec McKay, Les Thomas, Peter Reville, Jack Bisset (capt.-coach), Hugh McLaughlin, Bob Pratt, Terry Brain, Cecil Pettiona. Front, from left: Fred Backway, Jack Austin, Herbie Matthews, Ossie Bertram.

against Collingwood at Victoria Park, champion utility Austin Robertson announced he would go to the United States to run a series of foot races against American Olympic champion Eddie Tolan. It was a massive blow as Robertson could play in a number of positions and he was so fast that cartoonist Bob Mirams depicted him with wings on his feet. Collingwood defeated South by 14 points and South's critics wondered about the wisdom of the Bloods' recruiting drive.

South had trouble finding any semblance of consistency over the first half of the season and, by the completion of the first nine rounds, had notched just four wins and was in danger of missing the finals altogether. The heavy conditions in some matches did not suit the pacy Bloods, but there could be no excuses. The turnaround, amazingly, resulted from off-field affairs. Crofts resigned as president following what he described as "excess drink expenditure" by guests at a party following the 23-point loss to Geelong at the Corio Oval in round seven. While Crofts went to Queensland for a holiday, the South players responded to go down to the powerful Richmond by just five points at the Lake Oval in round eight.

Crofts returned as president and South reignited its season with a seven-point win over Melbourne at the Lake Oval in round 10. South then went through the rest of the season undefeated. The big test was against Collingwood at the Lake Oval in round 14. South had not defeated Collingwood for 10 years and the Magpies looked like continuing that run in leading by 24 points at the final break.

South, largely through the dominance of Nash at centre half-back, kept ramming the ball forward early in the last quarter and, finally, Collingwood's dam was breached. Scores were level with just seconds to play when South's Brighton Diggins passed to teammate Terry Brain, who marked close to goal as the final bell rang. Brain took his kick after the bell and kicked accurately from 30 metres.

South's confidence rocketed and it finished the home and away season in second position, two games behind Richmond, with Carlton and Geelong making up the final four. South therefore played Richmond in the second semi-final and, after trailing by 29 points at half-time, the Bloods looked a beaten side. The Tigers still led by 28 points at the last change, but Bisset then made several telling moves. He switched Jack Austin to full-back in place of the injured Ron Hillis, moved Jock McKenzie to defence and pushed Pratt out to centre half-forward, with Ossie Bertram at full-forward.

Bisset's moves worked to perfection and quick goals by Pratt, Bertram and Peter Reville put South back in the match. South erased Richmond's lead within 15 minutes of the last quarter and cruised home by 18 points to reach the Grand Final. Richmond then defeated Geelong by nine points in the preliminary final for the Bloods to face the Tigers in the premiership-decider.

An Australian record crowd of 75,754 was at the MCG for the big match, with South starting as if fired from a rocket. The Bloods played ferociously determined football from the first bounce in an effort to unsettle a Richmond side carrying several injured players. South, on the other hand, was without Hillis, who had failed a fitness test after injuring his hip in the second semi-final.

South went into the main break with a 28-

Winger Harry Clarke won South's 1933 best and fairest.

point lead, with Laurie Nash and Hugh McLaughlin the Bloods' best players. The Tigers desperately tried to bridge the gap early in the third quarter, but the Bloods' defence stood firm. South easily brushed aside the Richmond forwards and cruised home by 42 points for the club's third VFL premiership. South's best were Nash, Austin, McLaughlin and Len Thomas. The Bloods celebrated the premiership with a dinner at the South Melbourne Town Hall and, late in the night, rubbed salt into Tiger wounds by riding through the streets of Richmond in a charabanc.

Pratt was idolised by all South fans and they flocked to the Lake Oval and other grounds to see him in action as he headed for the "ton" of goals in a season. He kicked 109 in 1933, but went even better the following season when he kicked a record 150 goals, equalled by Hawthorn's Peter Hudson in 1971.

Laurie Nash is carried from the MCG in triumph after South's Grand Final defeat of Richmond.

PREMIERSHIP SIDE

B:	Jock McKenzie	Hec McKay	Jack Austin
HB:	Bill Faul	Laurie Nash	Hugh McLaughlin
C:	Harry Clarke	Len Thomas	Johnny Bowe
HF:	Jim O'Meara	Brighton Diggins	Peter Reville
F:	Herbie Matthews	Bob Pratt	Ossie Bertram

FOLL.: Jack Bisset (Capt.), Dinny Kelleher, Terry Brain
Res.: Gilbert Beard

PLAYER	GAMES	GOALS
AUSTIN, Jack	11	3
BACKWAY, FRED	1	0
BEARD, Gilbert	14	6
BERTRAM, Ossie	15	28
BISSET, Jack	19	2
BOWE, Johnny	17	0
BRAIN, Terry	17	26
CLARKE, Harry	19	2
DAVIES, Frank	7	3
DIGGINS, Brighton	13	7
FAHEY, Jock	6	4
FAUL, Bill	20	0
GILMOUR, Alan	8	0
HARRIS, Wilbur	3	0
HEARN. Maurie	3	0
HILLIS, Ron	19	1
KELLEHER, Dinny	7	0
McKAY, Hec	20	0
McKENZIE, Jock	9	0
McLAUGHLIN, Hugh	16	0
MATTHEWS, Herbie J.	16	5
MIETZCKE, Arthur	5	2
NASH, Laurie	18	11
O'MEARA, Jim	18	15
PETTIONA, Cecil	7	3
PRATT, Bob	18	109
REVILLE, Peter	20	39
ROBERTSON, Austin	2	2
THOMAS, Len	19	6
WADE, Jack	5	0
WELCH, Alan	8	3

POSITION: Premier
COACH: Jack Bisset
CAPTAIN: Jack Bisset
BEST AND FAIREST: Harry Clarke
LEADING GOALKICKER: Bob Pratt (109)

1934

The South Melbourne players assembled at the Lake Oval six weeks before the opening of the 1934 season, against Collingwood on May 5, but not all its stars were present for the start of the short pre-season campaign. Champion full-forward Bob Pratt trained for just two weeks before the start of the season and played in just one intra-club practice match. He played for a team wearing blue jumpers against a team wearing South jumpers and was so unfit that captain-coach Jack Bisset gave him a run on the ball.

A week later, South unfurled its 1933 premiership flag before the match against Collingwood at the Lake Oval. As Collingwood was expected to be a contender after finishing sixth the previous season, the match attracted a massive attendance of 38,000, with gate takings of 1005 pounds ($2010), more than double the average gate.

South started the season brilliantly, defeating Collingwood by 35 points and Pratt kicking eight goals. The *South Melbourne Record* reported: "Nothing gave South fans greater delight than to see Pratt soaring above the packs. The fruits of victory would not taste so sweet if Pratt failed to reap a bag of half a dozen majors."

Pratt kicked 10 goals against Carlton at Princes Park the following week, but the Swans went down by three points for the *Sporting Globe* to note that "Carlton's physical strength won the day." The three-point margin flattered South as Pratt goaled with almost the last kick of the game from what the *Sporting Globe* suggested was "a dubious mark".

If South expected the premiership to be a cakewalk because of its star-studded line-up, it also was rudely brought back to reality when the powerful Richmond combination defeated the red and white by 44 points at the Punt Road Oval in round six. The Tigers held Pratt to four goals and the *Sporting Globe* headline trumpeted: "Tigers' forwards shine in runaway win" and, in the opening paragraph of the match report South was lashed for showing little good football after the first quarter.

There were no VFL matches the following week as a Victorian team, with South's Bisset as captain-coach, travelled to Adelaide to play South Australia. The Croweaters, wearing the original state colours of turquoise and chocolate brown, defeated the Big V by 11 points and the Melbourne media blasted Bisset for not taking the match seriously enough.

To add to Bisset's woes, Geelong defeated South by 29 points at the Corio Oval the

The 1933 premiership is unfurled at the Lake Oval, but no one would have guessed the club would have to wait another 72 years for the next flag.

MATCH RESULTS

Round 1, at Lake Oval, May 5
South Melb. 19.13 (127) d Collingwood 13.14 (92)

Round 2, at Princes Park, May 12
Carlton 17.20 (122) d South Melbourne 17.17 (119)

Round 3, at Lake Oval, May 19
South Melb. 23.10 (148) d Essendon 15.16 (106)

Round 4, at Western Oval, May 26
South Melbourne 17.18 (120) d Footscray 12.12 (84)

Round 5, at Glenferrie Oval, June 2
South Melbourne 22.12 (144) d Hawthorn 13.14 (92)

Round 6, at Lake Oval, June 9
Richmond 16.12 (108) d South Melbourne 9.10 (64)

Round 7, at Corio Oval, June 23
Geelong 15.16 (106) d South Melbourne 11.11 (77)

Round 8, at Lake Oval, June 30
South Melbourne 13.19 (97) d Fitzroy 13.10 (88)

Round 9, at Arden Street, July 7
South Melbourne 20.18 (138) d North Melb. 7.4 (46)

Round 10, at Lake Oval, July 14
South Melbourne 15.20 (110) d St Kilda 7.4 (46)

Round 11, at MCG, July 21
South Melbourne 22.23 (155) d Melbourne 14.15 (99)

Round 12, at Victoria Park, July 28
South Melb. 21.19 (145) d Collingwood 13.19 (97)

Round 13, at Lake Oval, August 4
South Melbourne 23.13 (151) d Carlton 17.8 (110)

Round 14, at Windy Hill, August 18
South Melbourne 22.14 (146) d Essendon 9.17 (71)

Round 15, at Lake Oval, August 25
South Melbourne 23.18 (156) d Footscray 9.16 (70)

Round 16, at Lake Oval, September 1
South Melbourne 15.11 (101) d Hawthorn 10.10 (70)

Round 17, at Punt Road, September 8
Richmond 14.14 (98) d South Melbourne 13.14 (92)

Round 18, at Lake Oval, September 15
South Melbourne 13.19 (97) d Geelong 8.7 (55)

First semi-final, at MCG, September 22
South Melbourne 11.12 (78) d Collingwood 9.21 (75)

Preliminary final, at MCG, October 6
South Melbourne 15.18 (108) d Geelong 7.6 (48)

Grand Final, at MCG, October 13
Richmond 19.14 (128) d South Melbourne 12.17 (89)

following week to leave the Swans in a precarious fifth position, half a game behind the fourth-placed Cats. From there, however, South notched nine consecutive wins, with Pratt almost unstoppable. He kicked 11 against Carlton and then Essendon in consecutive weeks and followed up with 12 against Footscray the following week.

Pratt, who had kicked a club record 15 goals in the round three match against Essendon at the Lake Oval, reached his "ton" of goals in the third quarter of the round 13 match against Carlton at the Lake Oval. He had started the match on 93 goals and reached the "ton" with a left-foot snap.

It was during this run of nine consecutive victories that South champion Laurie Nash captured the public's imagination with an extraordinary performance against South Australia at the MCG in his debut for the Big V. He kicked two early goals from centre half-forward and, when St Kilda's Bill Mohr was forced off the ground through injury at quarter time, went to full-forward and kicked another 16 goals for a match tally of 18 in Victoria's 105-point win. Typically, Nash claimed he would have kicked 27 if Fitzroy's Haydn Bunton and Melbourne's Percy Beames had not been so greedy.

Then, in round 17, South's run ended at the hands of Richmond at the Punt Road Oval, with the Tigers winning by six points. Even though South defeated Geelong by 42 points at the Lake Oval in the final round, it could not clinch the double chance and finished third, half a game behind third-placed Geelong, with Richmond the minor premier.

The Swans defeated Collingwood by just three points in the first semi-final, with the *Sporting Globe's* J.M. Rohan suggesting that although the points went to South, Collingwood took the honours. Pratt kicked the winning goal from 50 yards with just a minute

Bob Pratt might have kicked just four goals against Richmond in round six, but outmarks the Tigers' Kevin O'Neill in this clash.

SOUTH MELBOURNE
FOOTBALL CLUB

Annual Report
and
Balance Sheet

Centenary Season
1934

R. T. MULLALY, Secretary

Laurie Nash takes a strong mark against Richmond.

This 1934 cartoon shows club president Archie Crofts with an early depiction of South as the Swans.

to play. South two weeks later defeated Geelong by 60 points to reach their second consecutive Grand Final, against Richmond.

The Tigers twice had defeated the Swans in the home and away series, but most experts in the *Sporting Globe* tipped a South win, although Collingwood captain Syd Coventry insisted there was "nothing between them". However, there was a considerable margin and Richmond won in a canter by 39 points. The only consolation for South was that Pratt kicked two goals to give him a season's total of 150.

There were post-match rumours of South players offered and taking bribes and Pratt and the rugged Peter Reville even confronted several teammates. It was a hugely disappointing end to the 1934 season, with further disappointment for Pratt. Despite his 150 goals, he was runner-up to rover Terry Brain in the best and fairest. When he confronted committeeman Charlie McBurnie, he was told: "You were spectacular, Bob, but not very effective."

How a cartoonist saw Laurie Nash's 18 goals for Victoria against South Australia.

PLAYER	GAMES	GOALS
AUSTIN, Jack	17	4
BACKWAY, Fred	3	2
BEARD, Gilbert	7	1
BERTRAM, Ossie	8	15
BISSET, Jack	19	1
BRAIN, Terry	18	33
CLARKE, Harry	19	3
CLEARY, Jim	6	2
DAVIES, Frank	3	1
DIGGINS, Brighton	5	2
FAHEY, Jock	13	1
FAUL, Bill	20	0
HARRIS, Wilbur	5	0
HEARN. Maurie	1	1
HILLIS, Ron	12	0
HUMPHRIES, Reg	16	4
KELLEHER, Dinny	17	7
LEE, Ian	2	0
McKAY, Hec	19	0
McKENZIE, Jock	14	0
McLAUGHLIN, Hugh	11	0
MATTHEWS, Herbie	18	0
NASH, Laurie	17	49
O'MEARA, Jim	20	16
PETTIONA, Cecil	1	0
PRATT, Bob	21	150
REVILLE, Peter	18	35
RICHARDS, Linton	12	0
ROBERTSON, Austin	17	21
THOMAS, Len	21	0
WELCH, Alan	19	8

POSITION: Runner-up
COACH: Jack Bisset
CAPTAIN: Jack Bisset
BEST AND FAIREST: Terry Brain
LEADING GOALKICKER: Bob Pratt (150)

1935

South's enormous accumulation of talent had serious repercussions in the lead-up the 1935 season as several disgruntled players left the club because they felt their opportunities were limited and others were dissatisfied with Jack Bisset's coaching. Brilliant defender Hugh McLaughlin even came to blows with Bisset and subsequently was cleared to Footscray.

Peter Reville was delisted after his 12-month suspension from the 1934 Grand Final, while Gilbert "Blue" Beard was cleared to Footscray after playing just one game in 1935. Ossie Bertram crossed to St Kilda and South even was in danger of losing champion full-back Ron Hillis, who was so outraged at missing selection for the 1934 Grand Final that he trained with Fitzroy in the lead-up to the new season. Cecil Pettiona crossed to Footscray, but did not play a single game with his new club as promised employment fell through and he eventually accepted a position as captain-coach of Birchip.

On the other side of the ledger, South gave debuts to several outstanding youngsters, including Jack Graham and Roy Moore. Graham, from Victorian country club Red Cliffs, went on to play 227 games in the red and white to 1949 and was one of the club's greatest ruckmen. Moore, from Sandhurst, played 66 games with South to 1941 and always will be remembered for standing in at full-forward for the injured Bob Pratt in the 1935 Grand Final.

A South Melbourne team photographed for this post card before a match in 1935.

South prepared for the new season with a practice match against bitter rival Richmond under newly-installed lights at Olympic Park on March 23. The match was a huge success, attracting 20,000 to Olympic Park, with Richmond defeating South by six goals and midget racing cars speeding around the outside of the oval at half-time. South also played practice matches against VFA clubs Port Melbourne and Preston. The match against Preston was arranged as compensation for the Swans recruiting its star centreman, Syd Dineen, who went on to play 28 games with South to 1938.

South therefore was well-prepared for its opening round match against Collingwood at Victoria Park. With Hillis finally abandoning his planned move to Fitzroy, he was named at full-back. The Swans, however, went down by just two points. The Swans had matched the Magpies in every department, but an inaccurate haul of 5.8 by Laurie Nash was a major factor in South's defeat. Collingwood's winning goal was scored from a place-kick by Lou Riley in the dying minutes.

From there, South went on the rampage, racking up win after win. In fact, the Swans notched 12 consecutive wins before going

MATCH RESULTS

Round 1, at Victoria Park, April 27
Collingwood 15.18 (108) d South Melb. 15.16 (106)

Round 2, at Lake Oval, May 4
South Melbourne 17.11 (113) d Footscray 15.9 (99)

Round 3, at Arden Street, May 11
South Melbourne 13.11 (89) d North Melb. 5.14 (44)

Round 4, at Lake Oval, May 18
South Melbourne 13.19 (97) d Carlton 14.6 (90)

Round 5, at Corio Oval, May 25
South Melbourne 17.12 (114) d Geelong 15.10 (100)

Round 6, at Lake Oval, June 1
South Melbourne 23.14 (152) d Fitzroy 10.11 (71)

Round 7, at Punt Road, June 8
South Melbourne 15.15 (105) d Richmond 7.17 (59)

Round 8, at Glenferrie Oval, June 15
South Melbourne 17.14 (116) d Hawthorn 9.23 (77)

Round 9, at Lake Oval, June 22
South Melbourne 13.22 (100) d Essendon 9.7 (61)

Round 10, at Lake Oval, June 29
South Melbourne 13.16 (94) d St Kilda 9.15 (69)

Round 11, at MCG, July 6
South Melbourne 18.14 (122) d Melbourne 11.12 (78)

Round 12, at Lake Oval, July 13
South Melb. 18.16 (124) d Collingwood 10.11 (71)

Round 13, at Western Oval, July 20
South Melbourne 15.8 (98) d Footscray 9.8 (62)

Round 14, at Princes Park, August 10
Carlton 16.26 (122) d South Melbourne 12.9 (81)

Round 15, at Lake Oval, August 17
South Melb. 16.13 (109) d North Melb. 15.10 (100)

Round 16, at Lake Oval, August 24
South Melbourne 21.12 (138) d Geelong 8.14 (62)

Round 17, at Brunswick Street, August 31
South Melbourne 10.15 (75) d Fitzroy 11.8 (74)

Round 18, at Lake Oval, September 7
South Melbourne 14.23 (107) d Richmond 9.9 (63)

Second semi-final, at MCG, September 21
South Melb. 15.14 (104) d Collingwood 11.17 (83)

Grand Final, at MCG, October 5
Collingwood 11.12 (78) d South Melbourne 7.16 (58)

Bob Pratt is on crutches after being knocked down by a truck.

The match program for the South-Collingwood exhibition match in Brisbane in 1935.

down to Carlton by 41 points at Princes Park in round 14. It was South's first game for three weeks as rounds 14 and 15 were spread for an interstate clash. South made the most of the break by sailing up the east coast, culminating in an exhibition match against Collingwood in Brisbane and, several days later, in Newcastle. Collingwood defeated South in Brisbane, but the Swans had their revenge in Newcastle.

The break proved disastrous for South as several key players, including Bob Pratt, Laurie Nash and Jock McKenzie returned with injuries. The Swans, in disarray, had to face a Carlton side which had won its previous nine games. Carlton's big win therefore surprised few football fans, especially as several South stars were hobbling from start to finish.

Despite this setback, South remained flag favourite and went through the rest of the home and away season undefeated. Then, in the second semi-final, the Swans defeated the Magpies by 21 points, thanks largely to Pratt's six goals. His fourth of the match brought up his "ton" for the season and, at the final bell, he had a total of 103. Sadly, he was unable to build on this total because of bizarre circumstances.

Collingwood defeated Richmond by 28 points in the preliminary final for another crack at South, but the Swans remained firm flag favourites — until Pratt stepped off a tram in High Street, Prahran, on the Thursday night before the Grand

This is how a cartoonist for the magazine Table Talk *saw South's 1935 Grand Final defeat. It is titled "Sunday morning after the final".*

Final. As Pratt alighted, a truck driver failed to see the tram come to a stop. There was a squeal of brakes and the swishing of tyres as the truck swerved, but it caught Pratt, who was knocked to the ground. The champion South goalkicker injured an ankle and had lacerations to both legs. Despite seeing a specialist the following day, he already was on crutches and knew he had no hope of playing in the Grand Final.

The South Melbourne Record colourfully commented: "The initial attack on the inhabitants of Adowa by Mussolini's invading army upon Emperor Haile Selassie, is no greater shock than that received by SMFC officials when they learned on Thursday afternoon, through the press, that Bob Pratt had been involved in a collision with a motor truck." Ironically, the truck driver was a South supporter and, on the eve of the Grand Final, went to Pratt's house to present him with a packet of cigarettes.

South, without Pratt, had to reshuffle its side, with Moore moving from a forward pocket to cover for the top Swan at full-forward. The Swans, despite their enormous setback, attacked from the start of the big match, only for the Magpies to lift in the second quarter and go into the main break with a 10-point lead.

However, fortune had completely deserted South as Bisset took a heavy knock early in the match and, despite playing on until the final quarter, later was found to have had a fractured skull. South, despite its gallantry, went down by 20 points. It was a golden opportunity lost.

Although South also made the 1936 Grand Final, it went down again. Then, in 1945, the Swans crashed in another Grand Final. History repeated itself when the club, as the Sydney Swans, went down to North Melbourne in the 1996 Grand Final and long-suffering fans had to wait until 2005 for the club to break its long flag drought. The words of club president Archie Crofts after the 1935 Grand Final therefore rang hollow as he promised supporters the Swans would bounce back from the defeat by Collingwood to "build a dynasty". Crofts told supporters at a smoke night: "I know everyone is downhearted, but luck ran against us before and during the match. I can assure you South will be back and we will add to the premiership we won in 1933."

PLAYER	GAMES	GOALS
AUSTIN, Jack	19	0
BEARD, Gilbert	1	0
BISSET, Jack	16	1
BRAIN, Terry	15	18
CLARKE, Harry	12	2
CLEARY, Jim	14	3
DAVIES, Frank	14	11
DIGGINS, Brighton	20	4
DINEEN, Syd	13	5
EVANS, Owen	1	2
FAUL, Bill	7	2
FLYNNE, Rolton	4	0
GATTI, Lou	4	1
GRAHAM, Jack	3	2
HARRIS, Wilbur	4	1
HILLIS, Ron	20	0
HUMPHRIES, Reg	16	2
KELLEHER, Dinny	20	4
McEACHERN, Roy	14	1
McKAY, Hec	1	0
McKENZIE, Jock	17	0
MATTHEWS, Herbie J.	11	1
MONOGHAN, Leo	2	0
MOORE, Roy	19	52
NASH, Laurie	18	51
O'MEARA, Jim	8	5
PRATT, Bob	18	103
REID, Jim	19	3
RICHARDS, Linton	18	0
ROBERTSON, Austin	18	20
WELCH, Alan	14	10

POSITON: Runner-up
COACH: Jack Bisset
CAPTAIN: Jack Bisset
BEST AND FAIREST: Ron Hillis
LEADING GOALKICKER: Bob Pratt (103)

1936

Although Jack Bisset was reappointed captain-coach for the 1936 season the club committee had looked for a replacement. West Australian Johnny Leonard, who held the position in 1932, rejected an offer to return as non-playing coach, club legend Roy Cazaly apparently was a candidate and 1935 vice-captain Brighton Diggins wanted the job. Then, when it was obvious Bisset again would lead the side, Diggins decided against putting his name forward. Bisset, despite leading South to the 1933 flag, was in the twilight of his playing career and regarded as a poor tactician.

South therefore appeared to be handicapped going into the 1936 season, especially as brilliant winger Harry Clarke had retired after 147 games in the red and white. The Swans, which had lost key players to rival clubs the previous season, turned this around in signing Carlton's Maurie "Mocha" Johnson, a talented and ferociously-competitive follower who had played in Carlton's losing 1932 Grand Final side. South also gave 10 players their VFL debuts, with the best of them being local recruit Keith Smith and Preston's Rex Ritchie, who both had long careers at the Lake Oval. Ritchie won the 1941 best and fairest, while Smith played on a half-forward flank in the losing 1945 Grand Final side.

This much-published photograph of Laurie Nash was taken against Collingwood at Victoria Park in 1936.

The opening round clash with Melbourne at the Lake Oval was expected to be a test of South's resolve as the Redlegs had embarked on their own massive recruiting drive and were expected to be a flag challenger. However, South was thrown into chaos before the match when Bisset failed to turn up at the Lake Oval until just minutes before the first bounce.

A heavy gambler, Bisset had been at the Ascot racecourse to place a bet on a horse in the first race before rushing to the Lake Oval. The enraged South committee refused to allow Bisset to play and he had to watch as his team defeated Melbourne by 21 points. The club told the media that Bisset missed the match because of illness and the furore died.

Bisset continued as captain-coach but the Swans encountered further problems after Bob Pratt failed to kick a goal in the 63-point

defeat of Hawthorn at the Glenferrie Oval. Pratt kicked 0.5, but had a good excuse as his mind was elsewhere. He had been employed by *The Star*, an evening newspaper launched to rival *The Herald* and, when the newspaper suddenly folded, the South champion found himself out of a job in an era of high unemployment.

Pratt then stunned South with a request for a clearance, but without nominating a club. South blocked the request and, after supporter Mr Robert Williams MLC found Pratt employment at a brewery, the crisis passed. Pratt quickly returned to form and South retained its claim to premiership favouritism.

South, despite its off-field woes, was undefeated over the first eight rounds, but then went down by 21 points to Richmond at Punt Road. The Tigers crunched the Swans physically and mentally, leaving the red and white with injuries to key players. South had to make five changes to the side for the match against Collingwood at Victoria Park the

MATCH RESULTS

Round 1, at Lake Oval, May 2
South Melbourne 14.24 (108) d Melbourne 13.9 (87)

Round 2, at Junction Oval, May 9
South Melbourne 12.17 (89) d St Kilda 10.11 (71)

Round 3, at Lake Oval, May 16
South Melbourne 15.17 (107) d Footscray 9.13 (67)

Round 4, at Arden Street, May 23
South Melbourne 18.21 (129) d North Melb. 7.18 (60)

Round 5, at Lake Oval, May 30
South Melbourne 15.21 (111) d Essendon 11.13 (79)

Round 6, at Glenferrie Oval, June 6
South Melbourne 18.20 (128) d Hawthorn 9.11 (65)

Round 7, at Lake Oval, June 13
South Melbourne 13.15 (93) d Fitzroy 7.11 (53)

Round 8, at Lake Oval, June 20
South Melbourne 16.21 (117) d Geelong 15.14 (104)

Round 9, at Punt Road, June 27
Richmond 14.14 (98) d South Melbourne 11.11 (77)

Round 10, at Victoria Park, July 11
South Melb. 14.18 (102) d Collingwood 12.19 (91)

Round 11, at Lake Oval, July 18
South Melbourne 16.11 (107) d Carlton 14.16 (100)

Round 12, at MCG, July 25
Melbourne 22.16 (148) d South Melbourne 14.12 (96)

Round 13, at Lake Oval, August 1
South Melbourne 14.19 (103) d St Kilda 13.11 (89)

Round 14, at Western Oval, August 8
South Melbourne 12.21 (93) d Footscray 11.15 (81)

Round 15, at Lake Oval, August 15
South Melbourne 8.16 (64) d North Melb. 9.9 (63)

Round 16, at Windy Hill, August 22
South Melbourne 11.30 (96) d Essendon 12.16 (88)

Round 17, at Lake Oval, August 29
South Melbourne 16.10 (106) d Hawthorn 15.11 (101)

Round 18, at Brunswick Street, September 5
South Melbourne 11.14 (80) d Fitzroy 11.13 (79)

Second semi-final, at MCG, September 19
Collingwood 12.18 (90) d South Melb. 10.17 (77)

Preliminary final, at MCG, September 26
South Melbourne 13.11 (89) d Melbourne 8.15 (63)

Grand Final, at MCG, October 3
Collingwood 11.23 (89) d South Melb. 10.18 (78)

following week, but pipped the previously undefeated Magpies by 11 points.

This win put South back on top of the ladder but, inexplicably, the Swans crashed by 52 points to Melbourne at the MCG the following week. However, it was the injury-depleted South's last defeat of the home and away season. South finished on top of the ladder a game ahead of Collingwood, with Carlton and Melbourne making up the final four.

South therefore had to play Collingwood in the second semi-final, but had struggled through most of its matches late in the season because of a massive injury toll. Laurie Nash even played in the semi-final with a special guard for an injured wrist. Collingwood, meanwhile, was without champion full-forward Gordon Coventry, who had been suspended for an incident involving Richmond's Joe Murdoch in round 13.

Collingwood defeated South by 13 points in a ferociously contested semi-final in which Brighton Diggins had his jaw smashed and was ruled out for the rest of the season. The Swans therefore played Melbourne in the preliminary final. South, with Pratt kicking five goals, defeated the Redlegs by 26 points to go into a fourth consecutive Grand Final.

After trailing by just two points at quarter-time, South faded over the second quarter as Collingwood kicked 4.10 to 2.3. The Magpies therefore led by 21 points at the main break and seemed assured of the flag. However, South fought back through the good play of Pratt, Jim Cleary and Jack Graham to trail by just seven points at the final break.

When Maurice Johnson goaled early in the final quarter, South trailed by just one point. The Swans, despite playing relentlessly attacking football, just could not bridge the gap and Collingwood led by five points with minutes to play. South hearts finally were broken when Phone Kyne goaled to seal a Magpie victory, by 11 points. South had been defeated in three consecutive Grand Finals.

PLAYER	GAMES	GOALS
ALLEN, Tom	7	2
AUSTIN, Jack	16	3
BISSET, Jack	18	0
BRAIN, Terry	13	25
CLEARY, Jim	18	0
DAVIES, Frank	13	3
DIGGINS, Brighton	17	6
DINEEN, Syd	11	14
EVANS, Owen	17	9
FAUL, Bill	18	0
FLETCHER, Norm	2	0
GEORGE, Jack	11	1
GOLDSMITH, Gordon	1	0
GRAHAM, Jack	17	4
HARRIS, Wilbur	1	0
HILLIS, Ron	11	0
HUMPHRIES, Reg	8	2
JOHNSON, Maurie	8	14
KELLEHER, Dinny	15	3
LEASK, Laurie	6	7
McEACHERN, Roy	3	0
McKENZIE, Jock	3	0
MATTHEWS, Herbie J.	18	1
MITCHELL, Alec	5	8
MOORE, Roy	12	21
MULLANE, Stan	10	1
NASH, Laurie	16	42
O'MEARA, Jim	1	0
PETTIONA, Charlie	8	0
PRATT, Bob	21	64
REID, Jim	17	3
RICHARDS, Linton	9	0
RICHARDS, Reg	3	0
RITCHIE, Rex	3	0
ROBERTSON, Austin	20	39
SMITH, Keith	20	39
THOMAS, Len	15	6
THOMAS, Reg	3	3
WELCH, Alan	3	3

POSITION: Runner-up
COACH: Jack Bisset
CAPTAIN: Jack Bisset
BEST AND FAIREST: Herbie Matthews
LEADING GOALKICKER: Bob Pratt (64)

1937

It was obvious soon after the 1936 Grand Final loss that South would replace Jack Bisset as coach and, after Johnny Leonard again rejected the Swans' overtures, the club turned to former champion Roy Cazaly. South had to act quickly as Fitzroy also was keen to secure his services.

Cazaly might have been the disciplinarian South needed, but its playing stocks were depleted ever further before the start of the 1937 season. Bisset was cleared to be captain-coach of VFA club Port Melbourne, while Dinny Kelleher was cleared to country club Murtoa and Jim Reid crossed the Nullarbor to coach West Australian club Claremont.

Cazaly also had one other major problem as powerful follower Brighton Diggins, rated as one of the best players in the competition, was unsure of his future. Then, when South appointed Laurie Nash captain, Diggins resigned as vice-captain. Diggins had wanted the captaincy and, when he vented his feelings, missed selection for the opening round match against Carlton at Princes Park. He never returned and later applied for a clearance to Carlton. South blocked the move and Diggins had to stand out of football for a year before being appointed Carlton captain-coach for 1938. He took the Blues to the flag in his first year.

South late in the 1937 season reopened negotiations with Diggins but, after talks broke down, the club leaked details of his demands. The club said Diggins wanted full payments for the full 1937 season, a guaranteed place in the South line-up and a clearance to Carlton at the end of the season.

South's opening round match against the Blues was a disaster. It had been years since South had played so poorly and Carlton won by 70 points to suggest the Swans

How cartoonist Gurney saw the Swans in 1937.

MATCH RESULTS

Round 1, at Princes Park, April 24
Carlton 18.21 (129) d South Melbourne 7.17 (59)

Round 2, at Lake Oval, May 1
Collingwood 20.20 (140) d South Melb. 11.19 (85)

Round 3, at Lake Oval, May 8
South Melb. 11.15 (81) drew with Rich. 11.15 (81)

Round 4, at Corio Oval, May 15
Geelong 12.20 (92) d South Melbourne 7.11 (53)

Round 5, at Brunswick Street, May 22
Fitzroy 11.16 (82) d South Melbourne 7.18 (60)

Round 6, at Lake Oval, May 29
South Melbourne 15.11 (101) d Hawthorn 13.20 (98)

Round 7, at Windy Hill, June 5
Essendon 16.12 (108) d South Melbourne 11.10 (76)

Round 8, at Lake Oval, June 14
South Melb. 16.18 (114) d North Melb. 10.10 (70)

Round 9, at Western Oval, June 19
South Melbourne 18.11 (119) d Footscray 10.8 (68)

Round 10, at Lake Oval, June 26
South Melbourne 14.18 (102) d St Kilda 8.12 (60)

Round 11, at MCG, July 3
Melbourne 13.10 (88) d South Melbourne 11.16 (82)

Round 12, at Lake Oval, July 10
South Melbourne 13.9 (87) d Carlton 7.14 (56)

Round 13, at Victoria Park, July 17
Collingwood 18.19 (127) d South Melb. 15.14 (104)

Round 14, at Punt Road, July 24
Richmond 16.23 (119) d South Melbourne 13.11 (89)

Round 15, at Lake Oval, July 31
Geelong 16.11 (107) d South Melbourne 13.10 (88)

Round 16, at Lake Oval, August 7
Fitzroy 15.8 (98) d South Melbourne 10.16 (76)

Round 17, at Glenferrie Oval, August 21
Hawthorn 15.12 (102) d South Melbourne 10.15 (75)

Round 18, at Lake Oval, August 28
South Melbourne 10.16 (76) d Essendon 11.7 (73)

were about to fall from grace. Cazaly reacted by suggesting he would make a VFL playing comeback, at 44 years of age, and VFL clubs were so worried that the former champion was still good enough to make a difference, that they insisted the VFL impose its residence qualification. Cazaly's planned comeback therefore was aborted.

South's second match of the season also was a disaster, and with Bob Pratt sidelined because of illness, Collingwood defeated the red and white by 55 points at the Lake Oval. It was a humiliating home-ground defeat, but the Swans moved above Hawthorn in round three in playing a draw against Richmond at the Lake Oval. South had to wait until round six for its first win of the season, by just three points over Hawthorn at the Lake Oval.

If South's start to the season had been bad enough, there was worse to follow. Champion full-forward Bob Pratt decided to quit after battling an ankle injury and a drop in form. South, rocked to the core, then was enraged when

Laurie Nash takes yet another spectacular mark.

Carlton made Pratt an offer too good to refuse. The Blues offered him a deal in which even if he stood out of football, they would continue to pay him. He applied for a clearance, but South refused to budge.

The Swans were buoyed by Nash's nine-goal effort against Footscray in a 51-point win at the Western Oval, but fans mourned the loss of Pratt. Then, to further deepen the South crisis, another champion forward, Austin Robertson, left the club after accepting a business position in Perth. The Swans, realising his reasons were genuine, cleared him without objection.

South, despite its woes, still had hopes of making the finals when it defeated Carlton by 31 points at the Lake Oval in round 12, but it was a last hurrah. It won just one of its last six games of the season, over Essendon in the final round. South's winter of discontent ended with almost a whimper. The Swans, so powerful over the previous five seasons, won just six games (plus the draw with Richmond) to finish ninth — its worst season since finishing tenth in 1928.

South full-back Jim Cleary was one of the great stars of his era.

Dashing South full-back Ron Hillis played his last game in 1937, and despite being involved in the club's greatest era, did not play in a premiership side. He was injured when the Swans won the 1933 flag and missed selection for the 1934 Grand Final. He played in the 1935-36 Grand Finals, but South lost both.

Hillis had joined South from Middle Park and grew up in South's local area. His father ran a butcher shop in Prahran and young Ron started his career with South as a full-forward. However, he was switched to full-back with tremendous success and his rivalry with champion Collingwood full-forward Gordon "Nuts" Coventry was famous for its intensity.

Hillis was 31 years of age when he decided he wanted to concentrate on his other great sports love — sailing. He had a yacht moored near his Mornington home and rarely attended a VFL game. A magnificent high mark and a long, driving kick, Hillis had yet another string to his bow as he was an Australian ballroom dancing champion. Little wonder his rivals found him light on his feet in the chase for the ball.

PLAYER	GAMES	GOALS
ALLEN, Tom	17	6
AUSTIN, Jack	18	1
BRAIN, Terry	12	14
BRYCE, George	12	2
CLEARY, Jim	17	0
COYLE, Reg	4	0
DINEEN, Syd	4	7
EVANS, Owen	7	14
FAUL, Bill	17	1
FLETCHER, Norm	4	0
GILLETT, Ray	5	0
GRAHAM, Jack	17	4
HACKER, Jack	6	0
HARRIS, Wilbur	16	12
HEDGE, Alf	5	0
HILLIS, Ron	14	3
ILOTT, Percy	7	3
JOHNSON, Maurie	11	13
KENDRICK, Frank	2	0
LEASK, Laurie	5	4
MAHER, Jim	4	3
MATTHEWS, Herbie J.	15	0
McINNES, Ralph	3	0
MITCHELL, Alec	14	7
MOORE, Roy	9	35
MULLANE, Stan	5	0
NASH, Laurie	13	37
PATTERSON, Arthur	11	8
PETTIONA, Charlie	6	0
PRATT, Bob	6	12
RITCHIE, Rex	8	0
ROBERTSON, Austin	12	5
SMITH, Keith	12	0
TAYLOR, Laurie	1	0
THOMAS, Len	18	18
WELCH, Alan	5	3

POSITION: Ninth
COACH: Roy Cazaly
CAPTAIN: Laurie Nash
BEST AND FAIREST: Herbie Matthews
LEADING GOALKICKER: Laurie Nash (37)

1938

If 1937 had been a torturous year for South, there was even worse to follow in 1938. Roy Cazaly, who by now had abandoned any idea of a playing comeback, again was appointed coach, with champion winger Herbie Matthews captain. However, Matthews was seriously injured early in the season and centreman Len Thomas stood in over the rest of the season. Meanwhile, the pre-season football headlines centred on a massive row between the VFL and the VFA.

The VFA wanted a change in the rules to allow throwing of the ball and also declared war on VFL clubs through player payments. VFL clubs had to adhere to the Coulter Law, but the VFA clubs had no such restrictions. They therefore targeted several big-name VFL stars and, in particular, South's Laurie Nash, who told the Swans he had to look after his own financial future.

South therefore was rocked less than a month before the start of the new season when Nash announced that he would be joining VFA club Camberwell. He had been offered eight pounds ($16) a match, an office job with the Camberwell City Council and the position as coach of the Camberwell Cricket Club over the summer months at three pounds ($6) a week. *The South Melbourne Record* reported the news under the headline NASH HURLS BOMB AT SOUTH. South threatened legal action, but it proved to be an empty threat and Nash crossed to Camberwell without a clearance.

SOUTH MELBOURNE FOOTBALL TEAM 1938

Back Row (left to right): R. Moore, P. Farrelly, J. Austin, J. Cleary, W Faul, R. Richards, L. Thomas, R. Humphries, A. Patterson, J. Graham.
Front Row (left to right): J. Hacker, O. Evans, A. Quinn, A. Hedge, H. Matthews (c.), K. Smith, D. Howard, W. Harris.

With the Compliments of "THE LEADER"

A South line-up of 1938.

Champion centreman Len Thomas, pictured here in a posed photograph taken at the Lake Oval, won the 1938 best and fairest.

MATCH RESULTS

Round 1, at Lake Oval, April 23
South Melbourne 14.13 (97) d Footscray 9.14 (68)

Round 2, at Arden Street, April 30
North Melb. 9.10 (64) d South Melbourne 6.8 (44)

Round 3, at Lake Oval, May 7
St Kilda 11.17 (83) d South Melbourne 8.12 (60)

Round 4, at MCG, May 14
Melbourne 23.15 (153) d South Melb. 15.11 (101)

Round 5, at Windy Hill, May 21
Essendon 15.15 (105) d South Melbourne 11.19 (85)

Round 6, at Lake Oval, May 28
Hawthorn 18.12 (120) d South Melbourne 13.16 (94)

Round 7, at Corio Oval, June 4
Geelong 19.32 (146) d South Melbourne 10.10 (70)

Round 8, at Lake Oval, June 13
Richmond 20.15 (135) d South Melbourne 8.14 (62)

Round 9, at Brunswick Street, June 18
Fitzroy 16.12 (108) d South Melbourne 8.8 (56)

Round 10, at Lake Oval, June 25
Carlton 16.13 (109) d South Melbourne 11.7 (73)

Round 11, at Victoria Park, July 2
Collingwood 12.17 (89) d South Melbourne 12.5 (77)

Round 12, at Western Oval, July 9
Footscray 19.19 (133) d South Melbourne 10.10 (70)

Round 13, at Lake Oval, July 23
North Melb. 13.18 (96) d South Melbourne 14.11 (95)

Round 14, at Junction Oval, July 30
St Kilda 10.12 (72) d South Melbourne 7.12 (54)

Round 15, at Lake Oval, August 6
Melbourne 14.15 (99) d South Melbourne 9.16 (70)

Round 16, at Lake Oval, August 13
South Melbourne 13.13 (91) d Melbourne 12.14 (86)

Round 17, at Glenferrie Oval, August 20
Hawthorn 17.15 (117) d South Melbourne 9.20 (74)

Round 18, at Lake Oval, August 27
Geelong 15.12 (102) d South Melbourne 12.8 (80)

Ring MX 1494

Tom Corrigan
Registered Electrician

THE RECORD

SOUTH AND PORT MELBOURNE, ALBERT AND MIDDLE PARK AND GARDEN CITY

W. C. HAWORTH, Ph.C., O.
192 Bridport Street, Albert Park

SATURDAY, APRIL 2, 1938

PRICE 1½D

Nash Hurls Bomb At South

TRANSFERRING TO CAMBERWELL

BIG LEGAL BATTLE IS CERTAIN

After tentative offers since Monday had been rejected, Laurie Nash, captain of South Melbourne football team, on Wednesday decided to transfer to Camberwell (Association) team. This decision has thrown a bombshell into S.M.F.C. circles, for it was thought that, when the club president secured Nash congenial employment some weeks ago, he would be perfectly content to remain with South. Insistent and increasingly attractive offers were made to Nash by Camberwell, and, following a published report that he would definitely "remain with the old club," the next day the South captain succumbed to the Camberwell offer. It is likely, however, that a big legal battle to prevent his appearance with Camberwell will be staged between the League and Association bodies.

ROY MOORE UNDECIDED

With Officials for 2½ Hours

FORWARD WEIGHS OVER 13 STONE

As was anticipated in "The Record" last week, Roy Moore, South's brilliant half-forward, who terminated his association with the club last season to accept promotion in business, visited the S.M.F.C. rooms over last week-end, and in conference with club officials, discussed his intentions for the approaching season.

MISLEADING REPORT

Concerning Bob Pratt

WHY HE DID NOT PRACTISE

"South Melbourne officials were much concerned on Tuesday night when Bob Pratt, full forward, reported that both his ankles were sore and he was unable to train. Until he has had a rest and there is a chance to diagnose exactly what is wrong, there is a fear that Pratt might have suffered a recurrence of the injury which made necessary an operation on his foot half-way through last season."

How the local newspaper reported Laurie Nash's defection.

Champion rover Terry Brain joined Nash at Camberwell, Maurice Johnson and Syd Dineen retired, but Roy Moore agreed to continue after earlier declaring he would retire. The only other good news for South was that Bob Pratt had abandoned his plans to join Carlton. However, even that was tempered by the fact that his start to the new season would be delayed because of his ongoing ankle problems.

Following Nash's departure, VFA clubs now targeted Pratt and *The Sporting Globe* of April 23 reported: "It was learned at the Port Melbourne ground today that an enthusiastic supporter of Preston had made a substantial offer to Pratt, South Melbourne star, to play with Preston. This offer has been made independent of the Preston club. Pratt has until early next week to make a decision."

Nothing came of this rumoured offer and South further was heartened when it defeated Footscray by 29 points in an opening round clash at the Lake Oval. *The Sporting Globe*

Ruck star Jack Graham was a regular Victorian representative.

Len Thomas in full flight.

reported: "South improved during the game and their superiority in the aerial duels enabled them to take the lead at the interval … South outplayed their opponents in the last quarter."

Sadly, however, South did not win another game until it pipped Melbourne by five points at the Lake Oval in round 16. The 14 consecutive defeats was the worst in South history to that time and headlines suggested the Swans had been "thrashed", "humiliated" or "trounced" in most games.

Pratt eventually returned to action to kick 32 goals over seven games and, after a nine-goal haul against Geelong at the Lake Oval in the final round, *The Sporting Globe* ran the headline PRATT BRILLIANT. However, the bottom line told it all as it read BUT GEELONG WIN. The Cats defeated the Swans by 22 points to end South's worst season to date. With just two wins, South collected the wooden-spoon, two games and percentage behind eleventh-placed Hawthorn.

To rub salt into South's wound, Brighton Diggins led Carlton to a 15-point Grand Final win over Collingwood. However, South at least had the satisfaction of Nash's Camberwell failing to make the VFA finals.

PLAYER	GAMES	GOALS
ALLEN, Tom	2	0
AUSTIN, Jack	14	0
BRYCE, George	13	4
CLEARY, Jim	17	0
COLLARD, George	7	3
COOK, Frank	1	1
COYLE, Reg	6	0
DUNN, Les	1	0
EVANS, Owen	13	22
FARRELLY, Pat	6	1
FAUL, Bill	18	1
FLETCHER, Norm	8	2
GRAHAM, Jack	16	10
HACKER, Jack	18	1
HARRIS, Wilbur	10	4
HAYES, Gerry	5	0
HEDGE, Alf	11	3
HORNER, Percy	1	1
HOWARD, Don	6	1
HUMPHRIES, Reg	18	0
LEONARD, Mick	7	1
MASON, Norm	2	0
MATTHEWS, Herbie J.	4	0
MATTHEWS, Norm	6	1
MEEHAN, Joe	2	0
MITCHELL, Alec	8	6
MOORE, Roy	17	34
PATTERSON, Arthur	13	7
PRATT, Bob	7	32
PURVIS, Tom	3	0
QUINN, Jack	7	7
REDSTONE, Jim	4	5
RICHARDS, Reg	8	0
RITCHIE, Rex	6	1
SINCLAIR, Frank	9	6
SMITH, Keith	14	0
TAYLOR, Laurie	3	0
THOMAS, Len	18	22
TIMMS, Arthur	1	1
TIMMS, Syd	12	0

POSITION: Twelfth
COACH: Roy Cazaly
CAPTAIN: Herbie Matthews, Len Thomas
BEST AND FAIREST: Len Thomas
LEADING GOALKICKER: Roy Moore (34)

1939

Following such a dismal season, South replaced Roy Cazaly as coach, with star winger/centreman Herbie Matthews appointed captain-coach for 1939. It was a huge vote of confidence for Matthews as he was just 25 years of age and, just before the start of the season, was featured in a photo-profile of all VFL captains in *The Herald*. Matthews was photographed in his employment as a railways linesman.

Star defender Jack Austin, a member of the 1933 premiership side, retired at 27 to concentrate on his employment with a brewery, while the enormously reliable Bill Faul (also a 1933 premiership player) crossed to VFA club Prahran as captain-coach. Faul returned to South as coach from 1960-61.

The Swans desperately needed new blood and *The Age's* Frank Walsh suggested: "South's difficulty will be to fill the centre half-back and centre half-forward positions ... weak key positions in attack and defence might upset an otherwise improved side. I can't see any recruits making the side and improvement must come from last year's players."

Len Thomas (left) moved to Hawthorn as captain-coach in 1939 and shakes hands with former teammate and Swan captain Herbie Matthews before a match at the Lake Oval.

Jim Cleary was one of South's great stars.

A summary of all clubs' prospects in *The Sporting Globe* disagreed and suggested that South has several good recruits and added: "Bob Pratt, playing in his first practice match, showed that he will be a source of worry to League backmen. Although a trifle overweight, he took many towering marks, and kicked for goal with all his old judgement."

South recruited several players from rival

MATCH RESULTS

Round 1, at Princes Park, April 22
Carlton 20.22 (142) d South Melbourne 13.10 (88)

Round 2, at Lake Oval, April 29
Collingwood 21.20 (146) d South Melb. 15.17 (107)

Round 3, at Lake Oval, May 6
Fitzroy 10.17 (77) d South Melbourne 9.14 (68)

Round 4, at Punt Road, May 13
Richmond 14.24 (108) d South Melbourne 13.7 (85)

Round 5, at Lake Oval, May 20
South Melbourne 18.12 (120) d Footscray 16.6 (102)

Round 6, at MCG, May 27
Melbourne 19.23 (137) d South Melbourne 3.12 (30)

Round 7, at Lake Oval, June 3
St Kilda 13.17 (95) d South Melbourne 8.14 (62)

Round 8, at Windy Hill, June 12
South Melbourne 13.13 (91) d Essendon 9.16 (70)

Round 9, at Lake Oval, June 17
South Melbourne 15.18 (108) d Hawthorn 12.14 (86)

Round 10, at Corio Oval, June 24
Geelong 16.15 (111) d South Melbourne 7.14 (56)

Round 11, at Lake Oval, July 1
North Melb. 14.12 (96) d South Melbourne 7.6 (48)

Round 12, at Lake Oval, July 8
Carlton 16.17 (113) d South Melbourne 12.16 (88)

Round 13, at Victoria Park, July 15
Collingwood 19.11 (125) d South Melb. 8.13 (61)

Round 14, at Brunswick Street, July 22
Fitzroy 15.19 (109) d South Melbourne 9.9 (63)

Round 15, at Lake Oval, August 5
Richmond 18.15 (123) d South Melbourne 12.6 (78)

Round 16, at Western Oval, August 12
Footscray 19.15 (129) d South Melbourne 12.10 (82)

Round 17, at Lake Oval, August 19
Melbourne 12.12 (84) d South Melbourne 11.14 (80)

Round 18, at Junction Oval, September 2
St Kilda 11.13 (79) d South Melbourne 6.16 (52)

VFL clubs, including Melbourne's Pat McNamara and Lou Reiffel, but the Swans had a long injury list when it went into the opening round match against Carlton at Princes Park. Apart from the normal run of knee and ankle injuries, South also lost solidly-built half-forward George Collard for the first six matches of the season after he lost the top of a thumb in a work accident.

The signs were ominous for the Swans when the Blues thrashed them by 54 points in that opening round match, with worse to follow. South did not break through until it defeated Footscray by 18 points in muddy conditions at the Lake Oval in round five. *The Sporting Globe* praised the Swans for their "better system and understanding", but the Bulldogs were rocked by injuries over the first half and played the second half with just 17 men.

When South defeated Essendon by 21 points at Windy Hill in round eight for its second win of the season, *The Sporting Globe* described the Swans' form as "sparkling" and added: "South was never in real danger and ran out comfortable winners. Their win was convicing and resulted from better forward work — with Pratt (six goals) always prominent — solid defence and high marking."

South might have defeated Hawthorn by

Jack Graham, a great ruck champion.

22 points at the Lake Oval the following week, but failed to win another match over the final eight rounds and again finished on the bottom of the ladder, a game and a considerable percentage margin behind eleventh-placed Footscray. The only consolation was that Pratt was back in top form with 72 goals. However, South fans would not have known when Pratt kicked four goals in the final round defeat by St Kilda at the Junction Oval that it would be his last full season with the Swans and that he would play only one more game in the red and white — in 1946.

The 1939 season ended with Australia at war following Germany's invasion of Poland on September 1. The finals series therefore was played with the nation prepared for hardship and heartache. Dozens of VFL footballers made the supreme sacrifice, including South's Melbourne's Alf Hedge, Allan Pearsall, Gordon Sawley, Jack Shelton, Len Thomas, Norman Le Brun and Jack Wade.

The South Melbourne players pre-war took part in several radio and newspaper promotions. In one, ruckman Jack Graham won a prize for being voted the VFL's "most popular player". Readers of *The Argus* newspaper were asked to cast votes through a form published daily.

In a radio competition organised by ABC station 3LO, South players took part in a "footballers' knowledge bee" broadcast every Monday night during the 1939 season. Teams of six players competed against rival VFL teams, with the winning club going into the next round.

South selected its six smartest players but, unfortunately, the Swans went down to Fitzroy in the opening round. There is no record of the players who represented South. Long-kicking competitions also were popular in the 1930s, as was foot-racing, often held between greyhound races at the various courses around Melbourne.

Jack Graham (left) is congratulated by South teammates (from left) Alan Mullenger, Grahame Hall and Rex Ritchie on his win in The Argus' *most popular player contest.*

PLAYER	GAMES	GOALS
BENNISON, Alf	4	1
BRYCE, George	1	0
CLEARY, Jim	16	0
COLLARD, George	12	9
COUPER, Norm	7	3
COYLE, Reg	14	10
DINEEN, Ken	15	10
EVANS, Owen	11	12
GILLETT, Ray	3	0
GRAHAM, Jack	16	10
HACKER, Jack	15	0
HALL, Grahame	9	2
HARRIS, Wilbur	14	0
HUMPHRIES, Reg	10	5
KELLY, Brian	5	5
LEONARD, Mick	18	7
MACKNAMARA, Lindsay	3	1
MATTHEWS, Herbie J.	16	0
MATTHEWS, Norm	9	0
McNAMARA, Pat	10	2
MITCHELL, Alec	14	4
MOORE, Roy	8	2
MULLENGER, Alan	13	5
MULLENGER, Bob	3	0
NEWELL, Albie	2	0
O'CONNOR, Clarrie	5	1
POWELL, Len	1	0
PRATT, Bob	16	72
QUINN, Jack	2	1
REIFFEL, Lou	11	18
RICHARDS, Reg	8	0
RITCHIE, Rex	11	0
SINCLAIR, Frank	4	2
SMITH, Keith	15	16
TIMMS, Syd	7	5
TRAYNOR, Harold	6	0
WHITFIELD, Ted	6	2
WILLIAMS, Jack	2	0

POSITION: Twelfth
COACH: Herbie Matthews
CAPTAIN: Herbie Matthews
BEST AND FAIREST: Herbie Matthews
LEADING GOALKICKER: Bob Pratt (72)

1940

With Australia at war, the public mood was sombre for the opening of the 1940 season. The war had yet to make an impact in Australia, but newspapers carried page after page of events in Europe. Football, however, was still big news and *The Sporting Globe* even ran special weekly features on the playing personnel of each of the 12 clubs. South was featured as No.5 in this series, with pen-pics of all senior players.

The feature noted that Herbie Matthews remained captain, but that former Richmond and Essendon forward Jack Baggott, who had coached the Dons in 1939, had been appointed non-playing coach. Baggott's appointment baffled most football experts as he had resigned early in 1939 when he felt he had lost the confidence of the Essendon committee and, after taking over from Charlie May in 1936, had never taken Essendon to a finals series.

Ken McNaughton played just one game with South but is pictured here in his only game, in 1940, taking a mark while Richmond's Jack Cotter tries to spoil.

The pen-pics also noted that forward Roy Moore had wanted to continue with the Swans, but had retired because of recurring leg injuries. Most player occupations were listed, while the feature stressed that although Owen Evans had been Christened Kenneth Owen, he always was referred to as "KO". His pen-pic described him as a brilliant athlete who once had been a world under-16 high jump champion.

Of course, there was no mention of champion goalkicker Bob Pratt, who had dropped a bomb-shell in announcing he would cross to VFA club Coburg without a clearance. He was just one of a number of VFL stars (including Collingwood's Ron Todd to Williamstown) to move to the rival competition and although he kicked 183 goals for Coburg in 1941, the VFA then went into recess. Pratt joined the RAAF and spent much of the next four years defending airfields in the Pacific, including Borneo.

South went down to Collingwood by 12 points at the Lake Oval in the opening round, but *The Sporting Globe* suggested in its match report headline STH. MELB. HAVE IMPROVED. The report read: "Consensus of opinion at South Melbourne after the game against Collingwood suggested that the Magpies might have been fortunate to win."

Just two days later, *The Age* reported on Austin Robertson's decision to move to VFA club Port Melbourne. The report read: "Austin Robertson received an enthusiastic welcome when he appeared in the members' reserve at South Melbourne on Saturday. As he passed round the reserve there was quite a

South's Don Grossman wins the hitout in this ruck contest with Richmond's Charlie Priestley.

MATCH RESULTS

Round 1, at Lake Oval, April 27
Collingwood 13.14 (92) d South Melb. 11.14 (80)

Round 2, at Princes Park, May 4
Carlton 15.19 (109) d South Melbourne 12.5 (77)

Round 3, at Windy Hill, May 11
Essendon 12.14 (86) d South Melbourne 10.15 (75)

Round 4, at Lake Oval, May 18
South Melbourne 22.13 (145) d Hawthorn 16.10 (106)

Round 5, at Corio Oval, May 25
Geelong 12.21 (93) d South Melbourne 10.12 (72)

Round 6, at Lake Oval, June 1
South Melbourne 16.9 (105) d North Melb. 16.8 (104)

Round 7, at Punt Road, June 8
Richmond 13.16 (94) d South Melbourne 12.13 (85)

Round 8, at Lake Oval, June 15
South Melbourne 12.9 (81) d St Kilda 10.16 (76)

Round 9, at Brunswick Street, June 22
Fitzroy 10.30 (90) d South Melbourne 10.17 (77)

Round 10, at Western Oval, June 29
Footscray 15.15 (105) d South Melbourne 6.10 (46)

Round 11, at Lake Oval, July 6
Melbourne 19.16 (130) d South Melbourne 10.18 (78)

Round 12, at Victoria Park, July 13
Collingwood 19.14 (128) d South Melb. 4.18 (42)

Round 13, at Lake Oval, July 20
South Melbourne 17.11 (113) d Carlton 14.14 (98)

Round 14, at Lake Oval, July 27
South Melbourne 9.6 (60) d Essendon 7.16 (58)

Round 15, at Glenferrie Oval, August 10
Hawthorn 10.19 (79) d South Melbourne 10.13 (73)

Round 16, at Lake Oval, August 17
South Melbourne 12.19 (91) d Geelong 13.9 (87)

Round 17, at Arden Street, August 24
South Melbourne 16.23 (119) d North Melb. 8.5 (53)

Round 18, at Lake Oval, August 31
Richmond 16.12 (108) d South Melbourne 8.13 (61)

stir and young and old hand-clapped him." The newspaper reported that Robertson had been offered 100 pounds ($200) to sign with Port and six pounds ($12) a match.

South did not break through for a win until it defeated Hawthorn by 39 points at the Lake

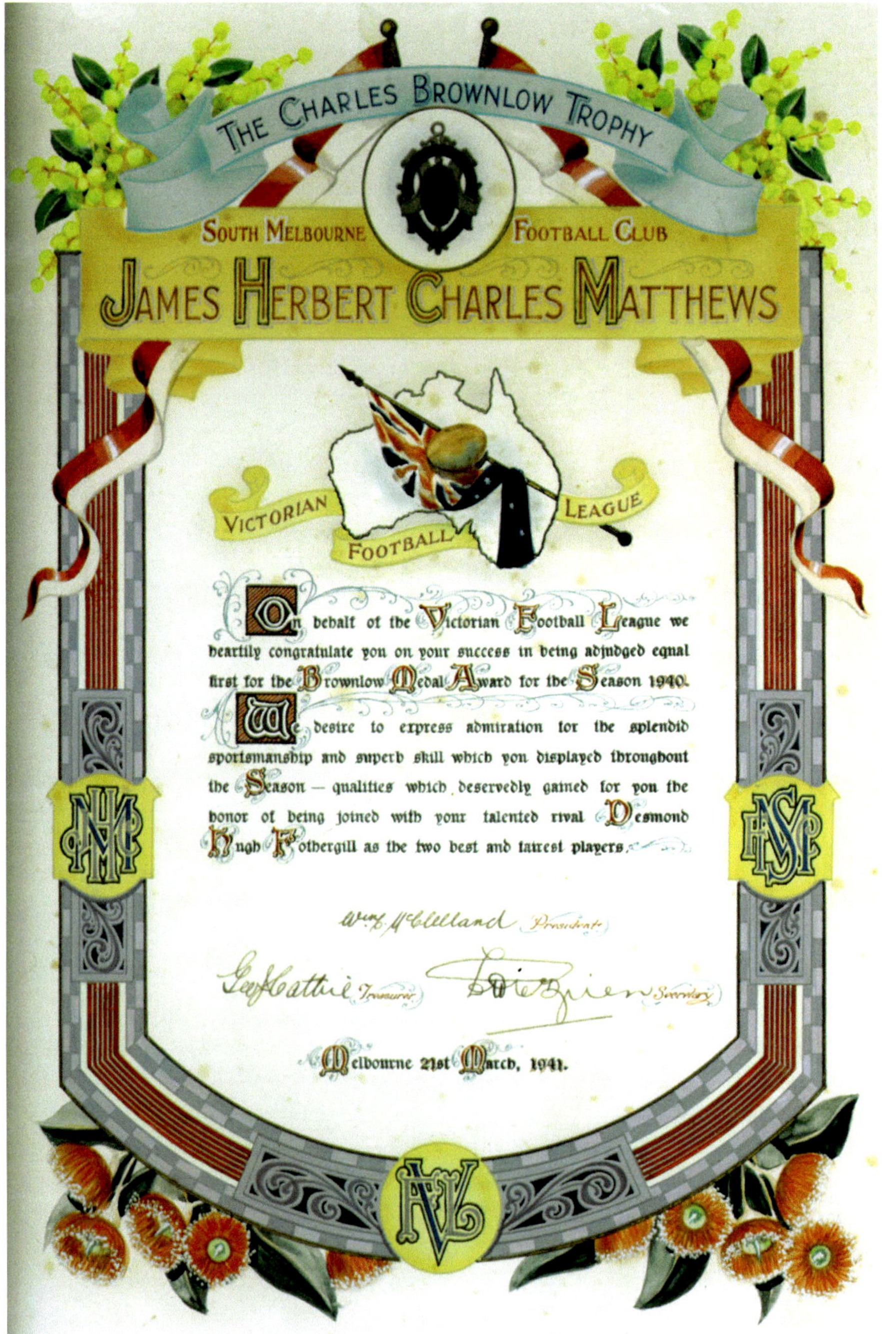

The VFL presented each Brownlow Medal winner with a commemorative illumination and this is the one Herbie Matthews received for his 1940 triumph.

South Melbourne Football Club

MEMBER'S TICKET, SEASON 1940.

OFFICE-BEARERS

President: Mr. J. D. M. Dickson

Vice-Presidents: Mr. H. Burrows, Cr. J. J. Curtain, J.P., Mr. J. Cullen, Cr. R. Morris, Mr. E. F. Norris.

Hon. Treasurer and Assistant Sec.: Mr. F. E. Killingsworth, J.P.

Committee: Messrs. C. Baker, J. J. Gardiner, J. Sullivan, R. Bennett, P. Farnan, J. J. White, F. Ferry, R. Hillis, S. Hogg.

Secretary: Mr. R. O'Brien, 163 William Street, Melbourne, C1.

This Ticket must be produced to obtain Admission and Vote at the Annual Meeting.

This Ticket is issued on the condition that the Club reserves the right to amend the programme of matches in the event of adverse weather or unforeseen circumstances arising.

Ticket, 7/7 plus tax 11d., = **8/6**

Mr.................................

Not Transferable

1940

FIXTURES, 1940

Date	Club	Ground
April 27	Collingwood	S.M.C.G.
May 4	Carlton	Carlton
May 11	Essendon	Essendon
May 18	Hawthorn	S.M.C.G.
May 25	Geelong	Geelong
June 1	Nth. Melb.	S.M.C.G.
June 8	Richmond	Richmond
June 15	St. Kilda	S.M.C.G.
June 22	Fitzroy	Fitzroy
June 29	Footscray	Footscray
July 6	Melbourne	S.M.C.G.
July 13	Collingwood	Collingwood
July 20	Carlton	S.M.C.G.
July 27	Essendon	S.M.C.G.
Aug. 10	Hawthorn	Hawthorn
Aug. 17	Geelong	S.M.C.G.
Aug. 24	Nth. Melb.	Nth. Melb.
Aug. 31	Richmond	S.M.C.G.

Nº 1836

Oval in round four and *The Sporting Globe* headline read SOUTH AT LAST BREAK THE ICE. Former Richmond captain Donald Don wrote: "South Melbourne and Hawthorn staged a delightful game at South Melbourne today … South's magnificent third quarter (nine goals), high marking and clever moves completely overwhelmed their opponents and clinched the game."

The Swans defeated North by a point at the Lake Oval two weeks later to suggest a rebirth, but failed to find any consistency over the rest of the season. It won just seven matches to finish tenth, above St Kilda (five wins) and North Melbourne (four). But at least the Swans had climbed off the bottom of the ladder.

Meanwhile, *The Sporting Globe* of June 8 reported that former champion South centreman and 1933 premiership star Len Thomas had become the first VFL captain to enlist. Thomas had played 187 games with South from 1927-38 before being captain-coach of Hawthorn in 1939 and then appointed captain-coach of North Melbourne in 1940.

The Sporting Globe reported: "Len Thomas, captain and coach of North Melbourne, is the first League captain to enlist. Thomas passed his medical tests this week and will enter camp as soon as business commitments allow." Reporter Hec de Lacy asked him why he had enlisted and Thomas replied: "Well, a man just can't stand out of a thing like this." Sadly, Thomas was killed by the Japanese behind enemy lines in 1943.

Although South had had a dismal run over recent seasons, it had some good reason to celebrate the 1940 season as Herbie Matthews won the club's first Brownlow Medal. Matthews and Collingwood's Des Fothergill both polled 32 votes and, because both had played all 18 games, there was no splitting them on countback. The VFL therefore decided to award each player a replica, while the original was retained at VFL headquarters. Then, in 1989, retrospective medals were awarded. Swan fan and memorabilia collector Russell Fogarty in 2002 paid $35,000 for Matthews' replica and retrospective Brownlow Medals and the original illuminated address.

The original Brownlow Medal won by South's Herbie Matthews.

PLAYER	GAMES	GOALS
BATES, George	3	0
BENNISON, Alf	1	2
BROWN, Stan	3	0
CHINN, Ian	8	11
CHIRGWIN, Dick	1	0
CLEARY, Jim	17	0
COLLARD, George	17	16
COUPER, Norm	5	1
COYLE, Reg	17	0
DINEEN, Ken	11	16
DUDLEY, Merv	3	7
EVANS, Owen	12	28
FERGEUS, Jack	2	1
GRAHAM, Jack	17	18
GRAY, Harry	9	5
GROSSMAN, Don	9	1
HACKER, Jack	13	0
HAMILTON, Gordon	2	0
HARRIS, Wilbur	10	1
HILL, Frank	3	0
JASPER, Howard	5	0
KELLY, Brian	9	0
LEONARD, Mick	2	1
MACKNAMARA, Lindsay	1	3
MATTHEWS, Herbie J.	18	3
MATTHEWS, Norm	13	5
McKENZIE, Jock	11	25
McNAUGHTON, Ken	1	0
MITCHELL, Alec	13	9
MULLENGER, Alan	7	0
MULLENGER, Bob	1	1
O'HALLORAN, Kevin	2	3
PATTERSON, Arthur	2	2
QUINN, Jack	1	0
REIFFEL, Lou	16	33
RICHARDS, Reg	16	6
RITCHIE, Rex	17	0
SMITH, Keith	7	0
TRAYNOR, Harold	2	2
TURNER, Arthur	2	0
VIRTUE, Keith	2	3
WHITFIELD, Ted	2	3

POSITION: Tenth
COACH: Jack Baggott
CAPTAIN: Herbie Matthews
BEST AND FAIREST: Herbie Matthews
LEADING GOALKICKER: Lou Reiffel (33)

1941

South appointed a new coach, former Carlton star Joe Kelly for the 1941 season, with Herbie Matthews again named captain. Kelly, who had played 137 games with the Blues from 1926-34, believed in moving the ball quickly and, a speedster himself in his playing days, favoured quick, running players.

The war by now was starting to take its toll and the VFL was just one of countless bodies to feel the impact. Dozens of players enlisted in the forces and clubs did not know from one week to the next who would be available. There also was a scramble to sign interstate footballers posted to Victoria for military training.

Under the headline FOOTBALLERS IN CAMP, *The Age* of April 25, 1941, reported: "Amongst the men in the AIF and militia camps in Victoria are numbers of prominent footballers, some of them members of League and Association teams. It was announced at Army Southern Command headquarters yesterday that members of League or Association teams who had been selected to play for their clubs would be granted leave from camp."

In the lead-up to the new season *The Age* indicated that Jack Graham had "brought down some splendid marks" in a South intra-club practice match and that a South Fremantle player named Burkett could play with South while in Melbourne with the RAAF. Burkett never played with South, but South in 1941 introduced another serviceman, South Australian Gordon Sawley, who was in Melbourne for pilot training in the RAAF.

South opened the season with a five-point loss to St Kilda at the Junction Oval, with *The Age* declaring that St Kilda had "outlasted" the Swans and that "strength rather than skill was the dominating factor". The opening round drew a total of just 76,000 fans, down 25,000 for the opening round the previous season and football obviously was heading for even tougher times.

Just five days later, South suffered its first casualty of World War II when former player Jack Shelton was killed in northern Africa. Lieutenant Shelton was driving a carrier vehicle when attacked by German tanks and was killed instantly when it was hit by an enemy burst of fire. He had played seven games with South in 1930 after playing 28 games with St Kilda from 1926-29. Later in 1941, on June 11, former South player Jack Wade (26 games from 1931-33) was killed in action in Lebanon while with the 2/27 Battalion. From Port Adelaide, he had represented South Australia in 1929.

South lost its first three matches of the season before breaking through to defeat Fitzroy by 27 points at the Lake Oval. There were no premiership matches the following week and, instead, all clubs played in a Patriotic Carnival lightning premiership (all matches played over two 10-minute halves) at the MCG to raise funds for the war effort. South went down to Essendon by 13 points in the opening round, with Collingwood defeating Melbourne by a point in the Grand Final in front of 19,572 fans.

South the following week played its first match at Kardinia Park. Geelong previously had played at the Corio Oval, but this ground was unavailable from 1941 because it was being used by the military. South defeated Geelong by seven points but, from there, failed to find form consistent enough to make the finals.

Flying Officer Allan Pearsall, killed in 1941, played two games with South in that season.

MATCH RESULTS

Round 1, at Junction Oval, April 26
St Kilda 12.20 (92) d South Melbourne 12.15 (87)

Round 2, at Lake Oval, May 3
Melbourne 14.17 (101) d South Melbourne 13.15 (93)

Round 3, at Western Oval, May 10
Footscray 16.4 (100) d South Melbourne 7.16 (58)

Round 4, at Lake Oval, May 17
South Melbourne 15.19 (109) d Fitzroy 12.10 (82)

Round 5, at Kardinia Park, May 31
South Melbourne 13.25 (103) d Geelong 14.12 (96)

Round 6, at Lake Oval, June 7
Essendon 13.18 (96) d South Melbourne 8.13 (61)

Round 7, at Glenferrie Oval, June 14
South Melbourne 13.12 (90) d Hawthorn 6.20 (56)

Round 8, at Lake Oval, June 21
South Melbourne 8.16 (64) d North Melb. 6.6 (42)

Round 9, at Punt Road, June 28
Richmond 15.13 (103) d South Melbourne 9.16 (70)

Round 10, at Victoria Park, July 5
South Melb. 11.13 (79) d Collingwood 10.12 (72)

Round 11, at Lake Oval, July 12
South Melbourne 16.13 (109) d Carlton 14.9 93)

Round 12, at Lake Oval, July 19
South Melbourne 14.12 (96) d St Kilda 8.6 (54)

Round 13, at MCG, July 26
Melbourne 18.16 (124) d South Melbourne 10.13 (73)

Round 14, at Lake Oval, August 2
Footscray 10.21 (81) d South Melbourne 7.13 (55)

Round 15, at Brunswick Street, August 9
Fitzroy 16.17 (113) d South Melbourne 11.14 (80)

Round 16, at Lake Oval, August 16
South Melbourne 10.10 (70) d Geelong 10.9 (69)

Round 17, at Windy Hill, August 23
Essendon 12.23 (95) d South Melbourne 7.4 (46)

Round 18, at Lake Oval, August 30
Hawthorn 11.17 (83) d South Melbourne 7.12 (54)

The club had to slash player wages from the week after the defeat of Geelong, but the players accepted this as a necessary strategy in dire times. *The Age* reported: "South Melbourne players manifested their loyalty to the football club last night in a splendid manner when they cheered their secretary (Mr T. Cole) at the conclusion of the statement on the club's present financial position, which he said made it necessary for the committee to reduce payments to players from three pounds ($6) to one pound 10 shillings ($3) a match from tomorrow. Accepting the situation as one that called for sacrifice on their part, the players said that they would continue to play with the same enthusiasm that had marked their efforts in the past …

"H. Matthews, the captain, said the players realised that in the present circumstances a reduction of payment was necessary. Officials, members and supporters generally could rest assured that the players would go after the winning of matches with even greater determination." South's membership had dropped from a pre-war level of 6000 to 2000 and gates also were down. For example, the round 16 match against Geelong at the Lake Oval attracted an attendance of just 4000.

The players were as good as their word but South was dealt a blow after a Victoria-South Australia match in Adelaide when the VFL suspended ruck star Jack Graham for failing to travel to Adelaide to represent the Big V. Graham wrote to the VFL to explain that he could not make the journey for family reasons, but his appeal fell on deaf ears. Graham therefore missed a vital match against Carlton in round 11. The Swans, without Graham, defeated the Blues by 16 points at the Lake Oval and *The Age* suggested after South's 42-point defeat of St Kilda at the Lake Oval in round 12 that the Swans were making "a strong bid" for the finals,

South won just one more match in the run home to finish eighth, with just eight wins — with more war heartache to follow.

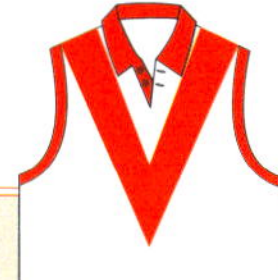

PLAYER	GAMES	GOALS
BARRETT, Kevin	4	6
BAXTER, Archie	11	16
BENNISON, Alf	13	11
BROADLEY, Alan	3	1
CLEARY, Jim	16	0
COLLARD, George	13	12
COYLE, Reg	12	1
DEANS, Billy	1	1
DEMPSEY, Jack	4	2
DINEEN, Ken	13	15
ENGELLENNER, Dave	1	0
EVANS, Owen	3	8
GIBSON, Reg	1	0
GRAHAM, Jack	17	33
GRIEVE, Jeff	11	0
GROSSMAN, Don	2	0
HACKER, Jack	17	0
HALL, Grahame	2	0
HALL, Tom	2	5
HARRIS, Wilbur	6	1
HUXTABLE, Eric	13	1
JASPER, Howard	15	3
KELLY, Brian	18	7
KING, Bill	16	0
LINDEN, Alan	8	3
LUCAS, Bert	4	6
MARTIN, Des	9	6
MATTHEWS, Herbie J.	16	2
McCRORY, Alan	3	2
MOORE, Roy	1	0
MULLENGER, Alan	8	3
MULLIGAN, Jack	8	17
PALMER, Ian	1	0
PEARSALL, Allan	2	0
PORTER, Roy	1	1
REIFFEL, Lou	2	4
RICHARDS, Reg	17	3
RITCHIE, Rex	16	0
SAWLEY, Gordon	7	8
SWEET, Eric	2	1
TRAYNOR, Harold	18	10
WHITFIELD, Ted	3	2
YOUNG, Syd	2	0

POSITION: Eighth
COACH: Joe Kelly
CAPTAIN: Herbie Matthews
BEST AND FAIREST: Rex Ritchie
LEADING GOALKICKER: Jack Graham (33)

1942

With Japan entering the war, Australia was in grave peril in 1942 but football remained as one of the few means of public relief. Although total attendances again dropped, from 1,157,200 in 1941 to a record low of 659,000, the public maintained its interest in the VFL competition and the daily newspapers reported games as extensively as ever.

Also, football was so popular among troops in the Middle East that the Australian Comforts Fund Commissioner, Lieut.-Colonel Gowand, requested the public to donate as many footballs as possible and reported he was astonished by the game's popularity. The VFL sent 1000 footballs overseas and even investigated the possibility of them being manufactured in Palestine.

Pilot Officer Alf Hedge, who played 16 games with South over the 1937-38 seasons, was killed in action over Germany in 1942. He is pictured here as a Flight Sergeant.

South's Alf Hedge (right) waits for any spill of the ball.

The 1942 season saw the temporary resignation of the Geelong Football Club because of war-time travel restrictions. The VFL, with an 11-team competition, organised an unusual home and away season in which five clubs had one bye and the other five having two, with byes worth four match points.

The war again impacted on player availability, with South recruiting two quality footballers from Geelong during the Cats' break from competition. Versatile left-footer Jack Butcher played 32 games with South over the 1942-43 seasons before returning to Geelong and captaining the Cats from 1944-45, while

MATCH RESULTS

Round 1, at Princes Park, May 9
South Melb. 18.25 (133) d Collingwood 14.11 (95)

Round 2, at Princes Park, May 16
South Melbourne 13.21 (99) d Carlton 8.11 (59)

Round 3, at Princes Park, May 23
South Melbourne 22.24 (156) d St Kilda 11.16 (82)

Round 4, at Arden Street, May 30
North Melb. 12.8 (80) d South Melbourne 8.17 (65)

Round 5, at Princes Park, June 6
South Melb. 23.10 (148) d Melbourne 16.19 (115)

Round 6, at Toorak Park, June 13
Fitzroy 11.17 (83) d South Melbourne 9.15 (69)

Round 7, at Punt Road, June 20
South Melbourne 11.20 (86) d Richmond 10.9 (69)

Round 8, bye

Round 9, at Yarraville, July 4
South Melbourne 11.9 (75) d Footscray 7.3 (45)

Round 10, at Punt Road, July 11
South Melbourne 12.19 (81) d Hawthorn 13.10 (88)

Round 11, at Windy Hill, July 18
Essendon 10.15 (75) d South Melbourne 8.7 (55)

Round 12, at Victoria Park, July 25
South Melbourne 15.21 (111) d Essendon 9.15 (69)

Round 13, at Princes Park, August 1
Carlton 12.17 (89) d South Melbourne 10.24 (84)

Round 14, at Toorak Park, August 8
South Melbourne 13.11 (89) d St Kilda 6.10 (46)

Round 15, at Princes Park, August 15
South Melb. 22.13 (145) d North Melb. 12.15 (87)

Round 16, at Punt Road, August 22
South Melbourne 14.23 (107) d Richmond 14.7 (91)

First semi-final, at Princes Park, August 29
South Melbourne 13.13 (91) d Footscray 7.22 (64)

Preliminary final, at Princes Park, September 12
Essendon 19.10 (124) d South Melbourne 14.12 (96)

Champion full-forward Bob Pratt, fourth from the left in the second back row, played with RAAF teams during World War II.

full-forward Lindsay White topped the VFL goalkicking with South in 1942 with 80 goals. Winger Bill Harwood also joined South from Geelong, while Essendon rover Tom Lahiff crossed from Essendon to play six games with South before moving on to Hawthorn.

South in 1942 was devastated to learn that two of its former players had been killed in action. Alf Hedge, who had played 16 games with the Swans from 1937-38, was killed on May 4 when the Halifax bomber he was flying was shot down over Germany. Gordon Sawley, who had played seven games with South while in training with the RAAF in 1941, was killed in a flying accident over Scotland on August 29. He had joined South from Norwood and had been a South Australian representative.

In the week leading up to the opening round of the VFL season, there was a Patriotic Game practice match between Richmond and Fitzroy at the Punt Road Oval. It attracted 15,000 fans, with funds donated to the war cause. The curtain-raiser was a baseball match between two teams of American servicemen.

The 1942 season presented the VFL with ground difficulties as the services occupied Footscray's Western Oval, St Kilda's Junction Oval, Melbourne's MCG and South Melbourne's Lake Oval. South this season therefore had to use Carlton's Princes Park as its home ground, while Footscray played at Yarraville, St Kilda at Prahran's Toorak Park and Melbourne at Punt Road. But even these arrangements presented problems and South, in one of the many venue switches, had to play its round six match against Fitzroy at Toorak Park because Carlton had a "home" game at Princes Park that Saturday.

South, with the status quo of Joe Kelly as coach and Herbie Matthews as captain, opened the season against Collingwood at Princes Park. The Swans won by 38 points and *The Age* match headline read: T.LAHIFF STARS. South then defeated Carlton and St Kilda to be among the early leaders and, despite lacking consistency, started the season with four wins from five games.

One of the season's highlights for South supporters was seeing former stars Bob Pratt and Laurie Nash in inter-services games, Pratt kicked 10 goals in a match for the RAAF against the Navy at the Punt Road Oval, while Nash also had a haul of 10 in an Army No. 4 side against Army No. 3.

South finished the home and away season in third position behind Richmond and Essendon, with Footscray fourth. South played Footscray in the first semi-final at Princes Park and after an even first quarter and the Bulldogs leading by nine points at the main break, won by 27 points. *The Sporting Globe's* Rod McGregor, a former champion Carlton centreman, wrote that a brilliant burst of six goals in 10 minutes during the third quarter lifted the Swans to victory.

As Richmond defeated Essendon in the second semi-final, the Swans played the Dons in the preliminary final, again at Princes Park. South led by five points at half-time, only for Essendon to kick seven goals to two in the third quarter to take control and go on to win by 28 points. *The Sporting Globe* headline read: THIRD TERM FINDS SOUTH OUTPLAYED EVERYWHERE. Reporter Hec de Lacy wrote: "Directly after the break, South started to lose balance against the strength of the Dons' attack and good team work." South at least was able to console itself with Essendon's thrashing of Richmond by 53 points in the Grand Final.

Pilot Officer Alf Hedge's grave at Hamburg, Germany.

Soon after former South Melbourne player Alf Hedge was killed over Germany in 1942, his wife Gwen received a letter from Wing Commander E. Cubally, Commanding Officer, No. 78 Squadron. It read: "I had the highest opinion of your husband both personally as a skilled and able captain and as an individual for his cheerfulness and willingness to undertake any task, however difficult it might be. Your husband was very definitely one of the outstanding characters in the Squadron and I can ill afford to lose men such as he."

Pilot Officer Hedge ordered the crew of their Halifax bomber to "abandon ship" after it was hit by enemy action, but only the tail gunner managed to escape before a wing flew off and the plane plummeted to the ground.

PLAYER	GAMES	GOALS
BENNISON, Alf	16	15
BUTCHER, Jack	17	3
BYWATER, Ron	1	0
CASHION, Terry	5	5
CASTLES, Vic	17	23
CHINN, Ian	9	17
CLEARY, Jim	16	0
COLLARD, George	7	9
CRANE, Tom	2	0
CULPH, Charlie	2	3
DELFS, Len	5	5
ELLENGENNER, Dave	3	0
GOLDING, Bill	3	3
GOLDSMITH, Gordon	11	5
GRAHAM, Jack	16	15
GROSSMAN, Don	14	0
HACKER, Jack	17	0
HARWOOD, Bill	15	5
HUXTABLE, Eric	9	0
KELLY, Brian	10	1
KING, Bill	16	3
LAHIFF, Tommy	6	10
LINDEN, Alan	8	7
MANGAN, Lou	6	1
MARTIN, Des	1	0
MATTHEWS, Herbie J.	14	1
MULLENGER, Alan	16	14
NEENAN, Bernie	3	2
REYNOLDS, Ron	2	1
RITCHIE, Rex	3	0
SMITH, Keith	11	4
TAYLOR, Don	5	0
TETLEY, Laurie	1	0
TRAYNOR, Harold	11	4
TURNER, Arthur	1	0
WHITE, Lindsay	16	80
WILLIAMS, Jack	8	0

POSITION: Third
COACH: Joe Kelly
CAPTAIN: Herbie Matthews
BEST AND FAIREST: Jim Cleary
LEADING GOALKICKER: Lindsay White (80)

1943

With Geelong still in recess in 1943, the VFL came up with a new and more equitable home and away draw. It devised a 16-round season, with each club having a bye to round 11. Then, after round 11, the bottom team dropped out of the competition. This was St Kilda, which finished the season with one win, a draw and eight defeats.

South retained Joe Kelly as coach, with Herbie Matthews again his captain and prepared for the new season with intra-club practice matches. *The Age* reported that South hoped to develop several promising youngsters under the guidance of reserves coach and former player Gilbert "Blue" Beard, with Matthews, Jack Butcher and Lindsay White appearing to be in ominous form. The Swans ended their preparation with a practice match at Northcote. *The Age* reported that the match was umpired by South coach Kelly so that he could get a closer look at his players.

The Swans opened the season with a 25-point loss to the powerful Essendon at Windy Hill. South worried the Dons with a six-goal opening burst, but eventually was overpowered by a stronger team. The match, however, was mired in controversy as police had to break up a final quarter brawl. *The Age* reported: "An ugly scene occurred when, with about 10 minutes to go at Essendon, a dozen players became involved in an all-in mix-up in which blows were exchanged. Umpires, police and a trooper intervened and stopped the

Jim Cleary, one of South's stars during the grim war years.

MATCH RESULTS

Round 1, at Windy Hill, May 8
Essendon 18.9 (117) d South Melbourne 13.14 (92)

Round 2, at Princes Park, May 15
Melbourne 15.19 (109) d South Melbourne 12.14 (86)

Round 3, at Brunswick Street, May 22
Fitzroy 16.17 (113) d South Melbourne 16.16 (112)

Round 4, bye

Round 5, at Princes Park, June 5
Hawthorn 12.13 (85) d South Melbourne 10,15 (75)

Round 6, at Arden Street, June 12
North Melb. 14.7 (91) d South Melbourne 12.18 (90)

Round 7, at Princes Park, June 19
Richmond 17.12 (114) d South Melbourne 12.12 (84)

Round 8, at Western Oval, June 26
Footscray 10.11 (71) d South Melbourne 6.14 (50)

Round 9, at Princes Park, July 3
Carlton 15.13 (103) d South Melbourne 10.13 (73)

Round 10, at Victoria Park, July 10
South Melbourne 16.14 (110) d Collingwood 9.6 (60)

Round 11, at Princes Park, July 17
South Melbourne 16.19 (115) d St Kilda 11.14 (80)

Round 12, at Princes Park, July 31
South Melbourne 14.11 (95) d North Melb. 6.6 (42)

Round 13, at Punt Road, August 7
South Melbourne 21.13 (139) d Melbourne 9.6 (60)

Round 14, at Princes Park, August 14
South Melbourne 12.18 (90) d Collingwood 11.7 (73)

Round 15, at Glenferrie Oval, August 21
Hawthorn 13.10 (88) d South Melbourne 7.14 (56)

Round 16, at Princes Park, August 28
South Melbourne 10.19 (79) d Footscray 10.6 (66)

brawl." Hundreds of spectators jumped the fence to get a closer view of the brawl and South later was severely punished when Matthews was suspended four matches after being found guilty of striking.

Melbourne defeated South by 23 points at Princes Park the following week and *The Sporting Globe* suggested this Swans setback was largely the result of "the absence of several regulars", including the suspended Matthews. To make matters worse, star forward White injured an ankle in the third quarter and had to be replaced by nineteenth man Gordon Goldsmith.

This is how South fans remembered Len Thomas, in action against Hawthorn.

South did not break through until it defeated Collingwood by 50 points at Victoria Park in round 10. The South-St Kilda match at Princes Park in round 11 therefore was critical as the loser dropped out for the rest of the season. St Kilda had defeated Carlton and had drawn with North Melbourne and therefore was two match points above South on the ladder.

The Swans had defeated Collingwood largely through the brilliant form of Jack Graham up forward and the switch of defender Jack Hacker into the ruck and were hoping these big men could hold their form against the Saints. *The Age* described the match as "a dour fight to miss the spoon". But South had St Kilda's measure from the start and skipped to a 26-point lead by quarter-time. The Swans eventually won by 35 points for the right to play out the rest of the season. Amazingly, South then notched consecutive victories over North Melbourne, Melbourne and Collingwood to climb to a more respectable position on the ladder.

Sadly, however, South was devastated late in the season to learn that former champion centreman Len Thomas had been reported as missing in action. Thomas, a member of the 1933 premiership team, had played 187 games with South from 1927-38, and was in the upper echelon of club champions. Corporal Thomas, who had been wounded earlier in the war, had been trapped at Salamaua, about eight kilometres behind enemy lines and killed by the Japanese on August 17.

The South Melbourne Record of September 4 paid this tribute: "Saddest news of the week to South Melbourne residents is the report that Corporal Len Thomas, one of the greatest footballers this district produced, was killed in action on August 17. The sorrowful tidings reached his wife, Mrs Edith Thomas, of 53 Mountain Street, South Melbourne, during the week. Mrs Thomas is left with two children, Barry and Lynette. All admirers of Len Thomas, and there are many, will grieve at the tragic death of this great sportsman and soldier."

Corporal Len Thomas, one of South's greatest players, was killed in New Guinea in 1943.

South's 1943 season therefore ended in grief. The South players wore black armbands when they defeated Footscray by 13 points at Princes Park in round 14. The Swans finished the season in eighth position with six wins and nine defeats.

PLAYER	GAMES	GOALS
BENNISON, Alf	7	3
BLUMFIELD, Max	8	2
BROWN, Mel	1	0
BUTCHER, Jack	15	13
CALLICK, Alf	1	0
CASTLES, Vic	15	16
CLEARY, Jim	15	1
CULPH, Charlie	11	35
EASTMUIR, Bill	4	2
ENGELLENER, Dave	10	0
GOLDSMITH, Gordon	1	0
GRAHAM, Jack	13	12
HACKER, Jack	14	3
HARTRIDGE, Ron	9	7
HAZELWOOD, Les	6	0
ICKE, Bill	2	0
KELLY, Brian	15	0
KING, Bill	13	4
LAMBORN, Chris	1	0
LEAHY, Pat	11	14
LEITH, Merv	14	10
LINDEN, Alan	5	3
MATTHEWS, Herbie J.	11	1
McCRORY, Alan	1	0
MITCHELL, Alec	4	0
MOLONEY, George	3	2
MOLONEY, Vin	6	0
MULLENGER, Alan	13	7
PATTERSON, Fred	1	0
RICHARDS, Reg	10	0
SMITH, Keith	13	4
SOUTHERN, Wally	1	0
SWEET, Eric	2	1
TAYLOR, Percy	7	16
WHITE, Lindsay	9	31
WILLIAMS, Jack	7	0

POSITION: Eighth
COACH: Joe Kelly
CAPTAIN: Herbie Matthews
BEST AND FAIREST: Herbie Matthews
LEADING GOALKICKER: Charlie Culph (35)

1944

The VFL competition returned to full-strength in 1944 when Geelong ended its two-season recession. The VFL therefore was able to revert to its normal 18-round home and away season, with no byes required. However, the war was still raging and, because of war-time restrictions and drop in attendances, the VFL and VFA briefly flirted with the possibility of a merger.

Joe Kelly again was coach, with Herbie Matthews captain and two of South's 1944 interstate "military" recruits, Jack Oatey and Jack Sheedy, later became football legends in their respective states. Oatey coached in South Australia for 38 years, landing 10 SANFL flags. Sheedy, known as "Mr Football" in WA, excelled as both player and coach. He played 210 games with East Fremantle and 122 with East Perth, and coached both clubs.

South opened the season with a 27-point victory over Carlton at its new temporary "home" ground of the Junction Oval. The Lake Oval was still being used by the military, but the move across the Albert Park Lake was much more preferable than spending another season at Princes Park.

Although South was delighted with the team's showing in the opening round, it had serious repercussions for the rest of the season as Matthews badly broke an ankle and missed the rest of the season. *The Herald* reported: "Late in the South Melbourne game, Herb Matthews, South's captain, went down and was carried off on a stretcher. He suffered a fractured ankle." *The Herald* also reported that several South fans jumped the fence when a Carlton player felled Swan forward Charlie Culph.

Jack Graham took over as South captain following Herbie Matthews' injury early in 1944.

There also was drama in South's next match, against Geelong at Kardinia Park. It was Geelong's first "home" game since its resumption and although 8000 fans were at the ground for the opening bounce, there was no sign of the South team. The Swans' train from Melbourne had been delayed and the match, scheduled

A South line-up of 1944.

for a 2.40pm bounce-down, started at 3.12. *The Herald* reported that Geelong "made a gala day of its re-entry to the League" and that there was "an impressive ceremony" in which the opposing teams formed a Vee as the Geelong Highland Band had ushered them onto the ground.

The Herald also noted that former South Melbourne (VFA) star Peter Burns had resumed his duties as Geelong timekeeper. The paper reported: "At Geelong, the most interested spectator was the veteran Peter Burns, 40-year timekeeper for the (Geelong) club. In his heyday he was a champion rover for South in the '80s and came to Geelong in 1892 to maintain his record and later captain Geelong. Despite his 80 years, Peter appeared remarkably fit."

South defeated Geelong by 19 points and continued its winning run to round five when, surprisingly, it went down by a point to North

MATCH RESULTS

Round 1, at Junction Oval, May 6
South Melbourne 13.10 (88) d Carlton 9.7 (61)

Round 2, at Kardinia Park, May 13
South Melbourne 11.18 (84) d Geelong 9.11 (65)

Round 3, at Junction Oval, May 20
South Melbourne 9.10 (64) d St Kilda 7.10 (52)

Round 4, at Victoria Park, May 27
South Melb. 12.18 (90) d Collingwood 11.18 (84)

Round 5, at Junction Oval, June 3
North Melb. 10.13 (73) d South Melbourne 10.12 (72)

Round 6, at Brunswick Street, June 10
Fitzroy 14.7 (91) d South Melbourne 10.17 (77)

Round 7, at Western Oval, June 17
Footscray 9.13 (67) d South Melbourne 8.10 (58)

Round 8, at Junction Oval, June 24
Richmond 17.10 (112) d South Melbourne 11.11 (77)

Round 9, at Junction Oval, July 1
South Melbourne 15.12 (102) d Hawthorn 11.11 (77)

Round 10, at Punt Road, July 8
Melbourne 10.10 (70) d South Melbourne 9.13 (67)

Round 11, at Junction Oval, July 15
Essendon 15.16 (106) d South Melbourne 7.15 (57)

Round 12, at Princes Park, July 22
Carlton 10.14 (74) d South Melbourne 8.12 (60)

Round 13, at Junction Oval, July 29
South Melbourne 8.30 (78) d Geelong 8.8 (56)

Round 14, at Junction Oval, August 5
South Melbourne 10.19 (79) d St Kilda 7.12 (54)

Round 15, at Junction Oval, August 12
South Melb. 16.10 (106) d Collingwood 8.22 (70)

Round 16, at Arden Street, August 19
South Melbourne 13.16 (94) d North Melb. 6.12 (48)

Round 17, at Junction Oval, August 26
Fitzroy 17.14 (116) d South Melbourne 8.13 (61)

Round 18, at Windy Hill, September 2
Essendon 17.24 (126) d South Melbourne 6.8 (44)

Melbourne at the Junction Oval. In an amazing round of results, the top four teams were beaten, with South, Richmond and Carlton suffering their first defeats and Fitzroy slipping out of the four through its second defeat. *The Herald* named North full-back Tom Roulent as

South Melbourne Football Club
70th
Annual Report and
Balance Sheet
Season 1944

best on the ground against South and, ironically, he joined the Swans in 1946 and played 29 games in the red and white to 1947.

The Swans, after such a bright start to the season, slipped out of the top four after going down to Footscray by nine points at the Western Oval in round seven. However, *The Sporting Globe* suggested South was hopeful of defeating Richmond at the Junction Oval in round eight. Former Fitzroy captain Gordon Rattray wrote: "South Melbourne which has not had the best of luck this season, but has shown flashes of brilliance, entered upon its game against Richmond hopeful of retrieving its fortunes." Richmond, however, triumphed by 35 points to severely dent South's finals ambitions.

South notched four consecutive wins from rounds 13-16 but had little chance of making up lost ground over the final two rounds as, at that stage of the season, Carlton held fourth position by two games and a big percentage margin clear of the sixth-placed Swans. It mattered little as Fitzroy and Essendon defeated South over the final two rounds and the Swans finished seventh, with nine wins and nine defeats and a percentage of just 96.9.

PLAYER	GAMES	GOALS
BAXTER, Archie	4	3
BENNISON, Alf	1	0
BLUMFIELD, Max	9	4
BOURKE, Pat	3	0
BROWN, Stan	6	3
BYWATER, Ron	1	0
CASTLES, Vic	17	22
CHURCHETT, Colin	1	0
CLEARY, Jim	14	0
CRANE, Tom	4	1
CULPH, Charlie	6	17
DANCKERT, Jack	4	0
DE MEDICI, Joe	5	3
DEMPSEY, Jack	11	4
DINEEN, Ken	4	6
DUNCAN, Norm	13	10
ENGELLENNER, Dave	13	1
FROST, Lou	6	0
GRACE, Pat	4	0
GRAHAM, Jack	18	16
GROSSMAN, Don	17	6
HACKER, Jack	11	3
HARTRIDGE, Ron	17	31
HAYES, Gerry	1	0
HAZELWOOD, Les	3	2
KEIGHRAN, Lisle	8	3
KELLY, Brian	13	1
KING, Bill	16	2
LINDEN, Alan	18	14
MANGAN, Lou	8	3
MATLOCK, Bob	11	0
MATTHEWS, Herbie J.	1	0
McKNIGHT, Jim	2	0
MOLONEY, George	8	3
MULLENGER, Alan	1	0
OATEY, Jack	5	4
O'SHEA, Len	2	1
RICHARDS, Reg	13	3
RIPPON, Max	4	0
SHEEDY, Jack	6	8
SMITH, Keith	7	9
WHITFIELD, Ted	11	1
WILLIAMS, Jack	15	0

POSITION: Seventh
COACH: Joe Kelly
CAPTAIN: Herbie Matthews, Jack Graham
BEST AND FAIREST: Jim Cleary
LEADING GOALKICKER: Ron Hartridge (31)

1945

World War II was drawing to an end by the time the VFL arranged its draw for the 1945 season and, surprisingly, decided on a 20-round home and away season, the longest in VFL history to that stage. This decision was to make up for "lost" games over the previous seasons, but had a major repercussion for South Melbourne as Carlton needed the 20 rounds to scrape into the final four and then defeated the Swans in the Grand Final.

South in 1945 appointed a new coach to replace Joe Kelly. West Australian Bill "Bull" Adams had joined Fitzroy from South Fremantle in 1924 and had captained the Maroons in 1926 before playing in the VFA with Northcote and Preston and then returning to the VFL with Melbourne for the 1931-32 seasons. Herbie Matthews, after recovering from his ankle injury, again was captain.

The Swans in 1945 were blessed with two recruits of the very highest calibre, both going on to become club greats. Ron Clegg, a local product from the Melbourne Boys League, won the 1949 Brownlow Medal and captained and coached Swans over his 231 games in the red and white. Billy Williams, recruited from Spotswood, originally wanted to play with Essendon, but was tied residentially to South and the Swans held firm. Williams won South's best and fairest three times and he was one of the most brilliant small men to represent the club.

The Swans also were buoyed by the return of champion forward Laurie Nash, who had left the club in acrimonious circumstances at the end of the 1937 season. Nash had played 74 games with VFA club Camberwell from 1938-41, but then played only RAAF representative games for three seasons while the VFA was in recess. The prodigal son returned to the Lake Oval at 35 years of age and not knowing whether the VFL would even issue him a playing permit. He had been disqualified for three years for crossing to Camberwell without a clearance, but it was alleged that Nash had played two games in the Footscray District League while disqualified. He therefore had to appear before the VFL Permits Committee.

A South line-up in the Grand Final year of 1945.

The Swans argued that refusing Nash a clearance would be a gross injustice as he had served his country in New Guinea and merely wanted to end his playing career with the club he had served with such great distinction. Nash was granted a permit on the eve of the new season but earlier, in one intra-club practice match, he proved he had not lost any of his skills in kicking five goals against regular full-back Jim Cleary.

MATCH RESULTS

Round 1, at Junction Oval, April 21
South Melbourne 17.16 (118) d St Kilda 10.17 (77)

Round 2, at Junction Oval, April 28
South Melb. 12.14 (86) d Collingwood 11.10 (76)

Round 3, at Punt Road, May 5
South Melbourne 15.19 (109) d Richmond 13.11 (89)

Round 4, at Kardinia Park, May 12
South Melbourne 10.23 (83) d Geelong 9.13 (67)

Round 5, at Junction Oval, May 19
South Melbourne 15.9 (99) d Footscray 12.11 (83)

Round 6, at Arden Street, May 26
North Melb. 9.12 (66) d South Melbourne 8.10 (58)

Round 7, at Brunswick Street, June 2
South Melbourne 10.15 (75) d Fitzroy 7.23 (65)

Round 8, at Junction Oval, June 9
South Melbourne 12.16 (88) d Melbourne 9.4 (58)

Round 9, at Glenferrie Oval, June 16
South Melbourne 20.10 (130) d Hawthorn 12.10 (82)

Round 10, at Junction Oval, June 23
South Melbourne 12.15 (87) d Essendon 5.11 (41)

Round 11, at Princes Park, June 30
Carlton 8.8 (56) d South Melbourne 7.8 (50)

Round 12, at Junction Oval, July 7
South Melbourne 14.22 (106) d St Kilda 6.14 (50)

Round 13, at Victoria Park, July 14
Collingwood 11.14 (80) d South Melbourne 7.12 (54)

Round 14, at Junction Oval, July 21
South Melbourne 14.11 (95) d Richmond 10.17 (77)

Round 15, at Junction Oval, July 28
South Melbourne 18.27 (135) d Richmond 10.7 (67)

Round 16, at Western Oval, August 4
South Melbourne 8.8 (56) d Footscray 7.13 (55)

Round 17, at Junction Oval, August 11
South Melbourne 21.8 (134) d North Melb. 10.16 (76)

Round 18, at Junction Oval, August 18
Fitzroy 11.16 (82) d South Melbourne 10.13 (73)

Round 19, at Punt Road, August 25
South Melbourne 12.20 (92) d Melbourne 10.13 (73)

Round 20, at Junction Oval, September 1
South Melbourne 16.16 (112) d Hawthorn 11.10 (76)

Second semi-final, at Princes Park, September 15
South Melb. 13.10 (88) d Collingwood 11.11 (77)

Grand Final, at Princes Park, September 29
Carlton 15.13 (103) d South Melbourne 10.15 (75)

Most VFL clubs by now had returned to their original "home" grounds, but South still had to share the Junction Oval with St Kilda, while Melbourne continued to play at Punt Road. The Swans' Lake Oval now was known as Camp Robinson and the MCG as Camp Murphy. South opened the season as the "away" team to St Kilda at the Junction Oval. Nash, wearing his old number 25 guernsey, lined up at centre half-forward and was named in South's best players in its 41-point defeat of the Saints. A headline in *The Herald* blared NASH SHINES FOR SOUTH.

South's Ron Clegg, flattened by Carlton's Bob Chitty in the "Bloodbath" Grand Final.

Nash's comeback was so spectacularly successful that he played a huge role in South's unbeaten run to the completion of round five. However, he missed the round six game against North Melbourne at Arden Street and the Shinboners defeated the Swans by eight points in one of the upsets of the season.

It was a temporary setback for the Swans, only for internal problems to erupt just before South played Collingwood at Victoria Park in round 13. The club suspended skipper Matthews and half-forward Keith Smith for refusing to play in their selected positions the previous week and the Swans therefore were severely handicapped for a match against a club pressing them for top position. Collingwood won by 26 points.

The crisis passed and, with Matthews and Smith resuming, South finished the season on top of the ladder, one game clear of Collingwood, with North Melbourne and Carlton making up the final four. It was the first time the Shinboners had made the finals and their third position was well-deserved. Carlton, on the other hand, scraped into the finals when it defeated fifth-placed Footscray in the final round.

Carlton defeated North by 26 points in the first semi-final at Princes Park and, a week later, South defeated Collingwood by 11 points, also at Princes Park. *The Sporting Globe* reported under the headline SOUTH'S BRILLIANT TRIUMPH IN SEMI-FINAL: "With a dashing third quarter in which they over-ran a stubborn Collingwood, South kicked eight goals to the Magpies' five." Reporter Hec de Lacy named Jack Graham, Vic Castles, Don Grossman, Bob Matlock, Clegg and Smith as South's best players. Nash and Castles kicked four goals each. South had reached its first Grand Final since 1936.

Carlton came from behind to defeat Collingwood by 10 points in a vicious preliminary final and South should have realised from this brutal encounter that the Blues were hell-bent on winning the flag, no matter the cost. One newspaper reported that the game was "marred by vicious incidents", while former Fitzroy captain Gerald Brosnan wrote that Collingwood appeared unsettled by Carlton's physical attacks.

With the war over, the 1945 Grand Final was the most anticipated for years and 62,986 fans somehow squeezed into Princes Park for the big match. *The Herald* reported that the ground was so packed that some fans were carried off on stretchers before the first bounce. South started a warm favourite, but seemed unsettled over the first quarter as Carlton kicked 2.4 to five behinds to lead by 11 points at quarter-time.

The match erupted when Carlton captain Bob Chitty flattened 18-year-old Clegg and, from there, the match developed into what the media labelled "the Bloodbath" Grand Final. Although Carlton led by two points at the main break, it appeared to be worried by Carlton's rough-house tactics, with worse to come.

Fights erupted all over the ground over the second half and one headline in *The Herald* pointed to BOTTLES THROWN BY CROWD. Carlton's Fred Fitzgibbon, who was unavailable for selection because of suspension, jumped the fence to join the brawl, while South's Ted Whitfield pulled his jumper over his head so umpires could not take his number.

Carlton defeated South by 28 points in what was described as the most vicious game in VFL/AFL history. *The Argus'* Percy Taylor commented: "Punching, kicking and deliberate assaults made the League Grand Final at Carlton on Saturday one of the worst in history. Many people left the ground disgusted with what they saw. Officials of the two teams expressed disgust at the unsavoury end of an excellent season. Each blamed the other for starting the brawls." *Truth* described the match as "bash-ball" and suggested in a headline GRAND FINAL WAS GRAND SHAMBLES.

South's Jack "Basher" Williams, Jim Cleary, Don Grossman, Smith, Matthews and Whitfield were reported for various offences, with Whitfield suspended 21 matches, Cleary eight and Williams 12. Matthews was cleared of a charge of deliberately throwing the ball away, while Grossman and Smith were cleared of striking charges.

South Melbourne Football Club
Member's Ticket, Season 1945
★
Office-bearers:
President: Mr. Lionel Newton
Vice-Presidents:
Messrs. J. P. Cullen, C. Everett, P. Farnan, W. King.
Committee:
Messrs. C. Baker, F. Ferry, M. Gardiner, F. Maloney, R. Maslen, L. McIlroy, H. Thomas.
Hon. Treasurer: Mr. J. J. White.
Hon. Asst. Secretary: Mr. H. Thomas.
Hon. Secretary: Mr. J. Kelly.
23 Huntingfield Rd., Mid. Brighton. X5240
Member's Fee 10/6
Mr. ....
Not Transferable.
This Ticket must be produced to obtain Admission and Vote at the Annual Meeting

1945

FIXTURES, 1945

DATE	CLUB	GROUND
April 21	St. Kilda	St. Kilda
28	Collingwood	St. Kilda
May 5	Richmond	Richmond
12	Geelong	Geelong
19	Footscray	St. Kilda
26	North Melb.	North Melb.
June 2	Fitzroy	Fitzroy
9	Melbourne	St. Kilda
16	Hawthorn	Glenferrie
23	Essendon	St. Kilda
30	Carlton	Carlton
July 7	St. Kilda	St. Kilda
14	Collingwood	Collingwood
21	Richmond	St. Kilda
28	Geelong	St. Kilda
Aug. 4	Footscray	Footscray
11	North Melb.	St. Kilda
18	Fitzroy	St. Kilda
25	Melbourne	Richmond
Sept. 1	Hawthorn	St. Kilda

Nº 1623

PLAYER	GAMES	GOALS
BLUMFIELD, Max	1	1
CALDER, Tom	5	0
CASTLES, Vic	21	38
CLEARY, Jim	22	0
CLEGG, Ron	15	6
COYLE, Reg	9	2
CRANE, Tom	1	0
DANCKERT, Jack	5	0
DEMPSEY, Jack	21	4
DINEEN, Ken	4	3
DOUGHERTY, George	10	26
ENGELLENNER, Dave	3	1
GLASS, Max	3	0
GRAHAM, Jack	21	19
GROSSMAN, Don	22	5
GUYATT, Owen	4	1
HARTRIDGE, Ron	22	32
FRANK, Hill	2	0
KELLY, Brian	22	0
KING, Bill	20	3
LEAHY, Pat	1	0
LINDEN, Alan	20	12
MATLOCK, Bob	22	0
MATTHEWS, Herbie J.	19	0
McKNIGHT, Jim	5	0
NASH, Laurie	17	56
PORTER, Roy	4	0
RICHARDS, Reg	20	24
SMITH, Keith	13	12
TIPPETT, Peter	5	0
WHITFIELD, Ted	18	3
WILLIAMS, Jack	21	0
WILLIAMS, Billy	20	33

POSITION: Runner-up
COACH: Bill Adams
CAPTAIN: Herbie Matthews
BEST AND FAIREST: Jack Graham
LEADING GOALKICKER: Laurie Nash (56)

1946

The suspensions imposed after the "Bloodbath" Grand Final seriously impacted South in 1946. Ted Whitfield's 21-match suspension ended his VFL career as he was 32 years of age when he played in the 1945 Grand Final. Full-back Jim Cleary had to sit out most of the first half of the season and Jack "Basher" Williams could play only seven games. Besides, Laurie Nash had retired after playing 99 games with South and moved to Wangaratta as captain-coach.

On the other hand, champion full-forward Bob Pratt agreed to make a comeback with the Swans. Pratt had wanted to return the previous season, but the RAAF posted him north and this delayed any thought of a comeback. South fans looked forward to seeing Pratt back in action, but soon were doomed to disappointment as he broke down in his comeback match.

South, still under the coaching of "Bull" Adams, therefore had to re-stock its list and recruited six players from rival clubs. The best of these proved to be long-kicking North Melbourne full-back Tom Roulent and ruckman Bert Lucas, who had played for Carlton in 1944 before spending a season with VFA club Sandringham. Lucas went on to captain the Swans in 1949.

The Swans also had to name a new captain as the great Herbie Matthews had retired after the losing 1945 Grand Final after 191 games in the red and white from 1932. Ruckman/forward Jack Graham was the logical replacement as he had captained the club for most of the 1944 season after Matthews fractured an ankle in the opening round.

The VFL must have devised its 1946 19-round fixture with a sense of humour as South played Carlton at the Junction Oval (the Lake Oval was still unavailable) in the split open round. The Blues defeated the Swans by eight points to set the tone for a disappointing season. Even worse, Pratt was badly injured after kicking two early goals and he never played again.

Ron Clegg, an emerging super-star in 1946.

In fact, South did not break through until it defeated Hawthorn by 34 points at the Junction Oval in round five. *The Sporting Globe* reported that South held Hawthorn while the Hawks had the wind in the first quarter and that Hawthorn could not cope with South's ruck strength.

The win lifted South's spirits and it won its next four matches to march up the ladder. Although South never looked like making the finals, it finished the season with wins over North Melbourne and St Kilda. However, *The*

MATCH RESULTS

Round 1, at Junction Oval, April 22
Carlton 18.9 (117) d South Melbourne 16.13 (109)

Round 2, at Windy Hill, April 27
Essendon 10.11 (71) d South Melbourne 8.5 (53)

Round 3, at Junction Oval, May 4
Footscray 14.18 (102) d South Melbourne 12.14 (86)

Round 4, at Punt Road, May 11
Melbourne 12.15 (87) d South Melbourne 11.8 (74)

Round 5, at Junction Oval, May 18
South Melbourne 11.21 (87) d Hawthorn 6.17 (53)

Round 6, at Brunswick Street, May 25
South Melbourne 10.12 (72) d Fitzroy 7.21 (63)

Round 7, at Junction Oval, June 1
South Melbourne 10.16 (76) d North Melb. 10.10 (70)

Round 8, at Junction Oval, June 10
South Melbourne 15.22 (112) d St Kilda 7.5 (47)

Round 9, at Junction Oval, June 17
South Melb. 18.16 (124) d Richmond 15.20 (110)

Round 10, at Victoria Park, June 22
Collingwood 18.17 (125) d South Melb. 12.12 (84)

Round 11, at Junction Oval, July 6
South Melbourne 12.19 (91) d Geelong 7.12 (54)

Round 12, at Princes Park, July 13
Carlton 12.13 (85) d South Melbourne 11.18 (84)

Round 13, at Junction Oval, July 20
Essendon 10.8 (68) d South Melbourne 9.13 (67)

Round 14, at Western Oval, July 27
Footscray 12.12 (84) d South Melbourne 4.7 (31)

Round 15, at Junction Oval, August 3
South Melbourne 15.16 (106) d Melbourne 14.11 (95)

Round 16, at Glenferrie Oval, August 10
South Melbourne 16.14 (110) d Hawthorn 12.15 (87)

Round 17, at Junction Oval, August 17
Fitzroy 12.15 (87) d South Melbourne 7.16 (58)

Round 18, at Arden Street, August 24
South Melbourne 15.19 (109) d North Melb. 11.8 (74)

Round 19, at Junction Oval, August 31
South Melbourne 14.10 (94) d St Kilda 6.13 (49)

Sporting Globe noted that the final round match against St Kilda was "spiritless" and that "mistakes were numerous".

South finished the season in seventh position with 10 wins and nine defeats. Essendon defeated Melbourne in the Grand Final and Melbourne's Don Cordner won the first Brownlow Medal since South's Herbie Matthews and Collingwood's Des Fothergill had tied in 1940. No South players finished in the top 10, but rover Harry Mears polled 11 votes after crossing from Collingwood after just two games in the black and white at the start of 1946. The lightly-built Mears also topped South's goalkicking with 32.

Although Mears polled more Brownlow Medal votes than any other South player, Billy Williams won the Swans' best and fairest. Although Williams usually played as a rover for South, he invariably played on a wing in his nine games for Victoria. He also won the club best and fairest in 1947 and in 1950. Williams also topped the Swans' goalkicking in 1947 and 1951. He was named in the club Team of the Century.

PLAYER	GAMES	GOALS
ALLEN, George	4	6
BARNES, Fred	3	2
BARRY, Ron	7	0
BAXTER, Archie	8	7
BLUMFIELD, Max	3	5
BOURKE, Pat	4	0
BYWATER, Ron	8	4
CALLICK, Alf	16	3
CASTLES, Vic	17	25
CHAMBERS, Wylie	11	1
CLEARY, Jim	11	0
CLEGG, Ron	19	21
COTTER, Jack	9	0
DEMPSEY, Jack	8	2
DOWLING, Doug	4	1
DUNCAN, Norm	6	5
GRAHAM, Jack	18	22
GROSSMAN, Don	11	15
HARTRIDGE, Ron	2	1
HOLLAND, Len	15	0
JASPER, Howard	6	0
JONES, Ray	1	0
KING, Bill	18	1
LEITH, Merv	3	0
LINDEN, Alan	18	17
LUCAS, Bert	11	2
LUGG, Jack	2	0
MATLOCK, Bob	2	0
McKNIGHT, Jim	1	0
MEARS, Harry	15	32
MULLENGER, Bob	2	0
NANKERVIS, Vic	4	2
PERRETT, George	10	1
PIGGOTT, Max	4	10
PRATT, Bob	1	2
RICHARDS, Reg	15	18
RITCHIE, Rex	12	0
ROULENT, Tom	19	9
SPOKES, Larry	4	1
STIBBARD, Neville	6	2
THOMAS, Ray	1	0
TIPPETT, Peter	15	2
WILLIAMS, Jack	7	3
WILLIAMS, Billy	19	4

POSITION: Seventh
COACH: Bill Adams
CAPTAIN: Jack Graham
BEST AND FAIREST: Billy Williams
LEADING GOALKICKER: Harry Mears (32)

1947

The 1947 season marked a return to normality for the VFL as South Melbourne at last returned to the Lake Oval and Melbourne was able to play at the MCG. South again had Bill Adams as coach, with Jack Graham as captain, but was without ferociously competitive defender Jack "Basher" Williams, who moved on after 61 games from 1939. Williams, from Maryborough, early in his career preferred to play with South Districts because he could earn more money with the local club. Williams had saved his match payments in 1945 to back the Swans for the flag, but lost it all when Carlton defeated South in the Grand Final.

South had two quality recruits in 1947 in winger Frank Brew, from East Brunswick, and centreman Keith Schaefer, from local club South Surfers. Brew, also a top cricketer, played 87 games with South to 1953 and later became curator at Carlton's Princes Park.

Dashing centreman Keith Schaefer had a wonderful debut season in 1947.

A South line-up from 1947.

MATCH RESULTS

Round 1, at Windy Hill, April 19
Essendon 16.23 (119) d South Melbourne 10.8 (68)

Round 2, at Lake Oval, April 26
South Melbourne 12.12 (84) d Carlton 9.16 (70)

Round 3, at Lake Oval, May 3
North Melb. 12.10 (82) d South Melbourne 10.18 (78)

Round 4, at Victoria Park, May 10
Collingwood 19.24 (138) d South Melb. 12.14 (86)

Round 5, at Lake Oval, May 17
Geelong 15.16 (106) d South Melbourne 13.9 (87)

Round 6, at Brunswick Street, May 24
South Melbourne 15.11 (101) d Fitzroy 8.15 (63)

Round 7, at Lake Oval, May 31
South Melbourne 15.14 (104) d Hawthorn 12.20 (92)

Round 8, at Lake Oval, June 7
Richmond 15.13 (103) d South Melbourne 15.9 (99)

Round 9, at Junction Oval, June 16
South Melbourne 18.13 (121) d St Kilda 11.9 (75)

Round 10, at MCG, June 21
South Melbourne 9.15 (69) d Melbourne 8.11 (59)

Round 11, at Lake Oval, June 28
South Melbourne 15.9 (99) d Footscray 12.10 (82)

Round 12, at Lake Oval, July 5
Essendon 11.17 (83) d South Melbourne 8.14 (62)

Round 13, at Princes Park, July 12
Carlton 10.14 (74) d South Melbourne 9.16 (70)

Round 14, at Arden Street, July 19
South Melbourne 8.18 (66) d North Melb. 8.14 (62)

Round 15, at Lake Oval, July 26
South Melb. 9.15 (69) drew with Collingwood 9.15 (69)

Round 16, at Kardinia Park, August 9
Geelong 13.19 (97) d South Melbourne 7.19 (61)

Round 17, at Lake Oval, August 16
Fitzroy 12.10 (82) d South Melbourne 10.11 (71)

Round 18, at Glenferrie Oval, August 23
South Melbourne 19.14 (128) d Hawthorn 12.11 (83)

Round 19, at Punt Road, August 30
Richmond 16.17 (113) d South Melbourne 11.13 (79)

Schaefer developed into a devastatingly effective footballer who played 102 games with the Swans to 1953 and won the club best and fairest in 1952.

An artist's impression of South defender Bill King.

The Swans went into the opening round match against Essendon at Windy Hill without the injured Clegg and with Schaefer and Alan Strang (Albury) making their VFL debuts. Essendon, the reigning premier, thrashed South by 51 points and *The Herald* noted that the Dons played "systematic, vigorous football", especially over the second half.

South the following week celebrated its return to the Lake Oval with a clash against bitter rival Carlton. Clegg was able to take his place in the side after recovering from a minor injury and lined up at centre half-forward. The Swans, in front of 30,000 fans, defeated the Blues by 14 points, thanks to an

PLAYER	GAMES	GOALS
ALLEN, George	9	2
ANDERSON, Claude	2	0
BARRY, Ron	13	5
BOURKE, Pat	4	0
BREW, Frank	10	2
BYWATER, Ron	19	0
CALLICK, Alf	11	0
CASTLES, Vic	13	15
CHAMBERS, Wylie	1	1
CLEARY, Jim	15	0
CLEGG, Ron	18	19
CRANE, Len	6	0
DANCKERT, Jack	4	0
DEMPSEY, Jack	1	0
DRIVER, Geoff	2	0
GRAHAM, Jack	18	29
GROSSMAN, Don	17	4
HOLLAND, Len	7	1
JENKINSON, Keith	8	0
KEIGHRAN, Lisle	2	3
KING, Bill	18	3
LINDEN, Alan	3	0
LUCAS, Bert	15	11
LUCAS, George	4	1
McTAGGART, Bill	1	0
MEARS, Harry	15	13
MULLANE, Jack	9	0
O'KEEFE, Jack	3	6
PARKER, Ern	1	0
PERRETT, George	3	3
PIGGOTT, Max	4	11
PROWSE, Frank	1	0
RICHARDS, Reg	7	3
RITCHIE, Rex	13	0
ROULENT, Tom	10	7
SCHAEFER, Keith	17	2
SPOKES, Larry	14	11
STRANG, Alan	10	15
TAYLOR, Don	14	19
THOMAS, Ray	1	0
TIPPETT, Peter	9	0
WILLIAMS, Les	10	1
WILLIAMS, Billy	18	38

POSITION: Eighth
COACH: Bill Adams
CAPTAIN: Jack Graham
BEST AND FAIREST: Billy Williams
LEADING GOALKICKER: Billy Williams (38)

unlikely hero in Max Piggott, a late replacement for the injured Strang. He kicked five goals but, sadly, played just three more games with South.

The Swans were brought back to earth the following week in going down by four points to North Melbourne at the Lake Oval. *The Sporting Globe* reported that the Swans tried desperately to make up the leeway after North's Frank Stephens had kicked a goal to give his side a four-goal break, but the late South rally just failed. The newspaper also reported that the Swans' morale was low as Bert Lucas' brother had been killed earlier in the week.

South struggled from there, despite three consecutive wins over rounds nine to 11. The Swans also were shattered by two narrow losses, by four points to Carlton and by four points to North Melbourne in consecutive weeks. South hearts were broken the following week when they believed they had defeated Collingwood by a point at the Lake Oval. However, the scoreboard was incorrect and the score was adjusted by a point in the Magpies' favour for a draw.

A Kornies card of South's Wylie Chambers.

To make matters worse, South captain Graham had a set shot for goal in the final seconds and deliberately kicked the ball out of bounds to deny the Magpies the chance of whisking the ball downfield from the kick-off. In that era, there was no free kick to the opposition from a kick going out of bounds on the full. *The Sporting Globe* described the game as "a magnificent draw", but South felt it had been robbed of two match points which could have put it in the race for the finals.

The disheartened Swans won just one of its final four games to finish eighth with eight wins, a draw and 10 defeats. Carlton pipped Essendon by one point in the Grand Final and the Blues' Bert Deacon won the Brownlow Medal with 23 votes, two more than St Kilda's Harold Bray. South centre half-back Ron Bywater, whose football career had been severely disrupted by World War II (he missed the 1943 and 1945 seasons), was equal third (with Hawthorn's Wally Culpitt) on 18 votes.

A club portrait of Keith Schaefer.

South Melbourne played North Melbourne in an exhibition match at Albury on August 2, 1947. The match was arranged to coincide with a two-week split round while the 1947 Carnival was being played in Hobart. North defeated South by 26 points and *The Argus* reported that "there was very great interest from both sides of the border". On the same weekend, Melbourne defeated a combined Sunraysia team at Millicent. South went down to Geelong by 36 points at Kardinia Park the following week.

South had two representatives in the Victorian Carnival team — Bill King and Jack Graham. The Victorians were led by Collingwood's Phone Kyne, with Graham his deputy. The competing teams were given a civic reception by the Lord Mayor of Hobart (Mr W.W. Osborne) and formed a parade for the opening ceremony, performed by the Governor of Tasmania, Admiral Sir Hugh Binney. Victoria, despite being defeated by Western Australia, won the championship.

Graham, a few weeks before the Carnival, played his 200th VFL game, against Essendon at the Lake Oval. Unfortunately for Graham, the Bombers defeated the Swans by 21 points. However, *The Football Record* reported that "he delighted supporters with one of his best high marking displays". The club presented Graham with a cheque, a silver cake stand and a tray.

1948

South might have started the 1948 season with Bill Adams still coach, but all that changed mid-season, although Jack Graham remained captain for the entire season. The Swans lost a raft of senior players from 1947, with Vic Castles, Jack Danckert, Reg Richards, Rex Ritchie and Tom Roulent among the departures. Also, star defender Ron Bywater missed most of the season following surgery for appendicitis.

On the credit side, South recruited Frank Stephens from North Melbourne and Richmond's Vic Hill. The VFL newcomers included Queenslander Erwin Dornau, Jack Eichhorn (South Districts), Arthur Fox (Red Cliffs), Jack Garrick (Yarraville) and Reg "Motorbike" Harley (Williamstown). All gave South tremendous service.

South opened the season against Richmond at the Lake Oval, with Harley, Dornau, Fox and Garrick making their debuts. It therefore was an extremely inexperienced Swans' line-up, but South shocked Richmond to win by 15 points. *The Sporting Globe* suggested the Swans were "too pacy" and named Keith Schaefer, Graham, Billy Williams and Harley as South's best players. Swan full-forward Don Taylor kicked five goals. Graham told *The Sun News-Pictorial* after the match: "Our form was better than I anticipated and our new men all played right up to their best reputations."

The win proved an aberration as Collingwood thrashed South by 53 points at

South's 1948 captain Jack Graham, from Post *magazine.*

MATCH RESULTS

Round 1, at Lake Oval, April 17
South Melbourne 18.15 (123) d Richmond 17.6 (108)

Round 2, at Victoria Park, April 26
Collingwood 18.17 (125) d South Melb. 10.12 (72)

Round 3, at Arden Street, May 1
South Melbourne 13.16 (94) d North Melb. 10.11 (71)

Round 4, at Lake Oval, May 8
Essendon 20.20 (140) d South Melbourne 11.12 (78)

Round 5, at Junction Oval, May 15
South Melbourne 14.23 (107) d St Kilda 12.12 (84)

Round 6, at Lake Oval, May 22
Melbourne 15.15 (105) d South Melbourne 9.5 (59)

Round 7, at Western Oval, May 29
Footscray 8.12 (60) d South Melbourne 3.10 (28)

Round 8, at Kardinia Park, June 5
South Melbourne 19.12 (126) d Geelong 15.16 (106)

Round 9, at Lake Oval, June 12
Fitzroy 15.11 (101) d South Melbourne 9.12 (66)

Round 10, at Lake Oval, June 19
Essendon 23.11 (149) d South Melbourne 13.9 (87)

Round 11, at Glenferrie Oval, July 3
South Melbourne 12.15 (87) d Hawthorn 9.7 (61)

Round 12, at Punt Road, July 10
Richmond 21.18 (44) d South Melbourne 9.13 (67)

Round 13, at Lake Oval, July 17
Collingwood 13.16 (94) d South Melb. 10.12 (72)

Round 14, at Lake Oval, July 24
North Melb. 15.14 (104) d South Melb. 14.18 (102)

Round 15, at Windy Hill, August 7
Essendon 11.21 (87) d South Melbourne 8.11 (59)

Round 16, at Lake Oval, August 14
South Melbourne 5.11 (41) d St Kilda 5.9 (39)

Round 17, at MCG, August 21
Melbourne 15.13 (103) d South Melbourne 7.12 (54)

Round 18, at Lake Oval, August 28
Footscray 14.16 (100) d South Melbourne 7.7 (49)

Round 19, at Lake Oval, September 4
South Melbourne 21.15 (141) d Geelong 6.9 (45)

Victoria Park in the following round, on the split round Monday. It was a bitterly disappointing result for the Swans as 47,000 fans squeezed into the Collingwood ground hoping to see a thriller. *The Sporting Globe* reported that South "had few men to show out and had no answer for Collingwood's loose-man play".

South then struggled to find consistency, with coach Adams copping the wrath of the South committee. He was sacked mid-season and replaced by former star Carlton rover Jack Hale, who had played 123 games with the Blues from 1933-41 and was forced into premature retirement because of a broken leg and subsequent complications.

Hale was just 34 when he took over as South coach, but immediately showed he was his own man. He switched the South side around and insisted that skipper Graham play at centre half-forward instead of in the ruck. Hale was no miracle worker, but he demanded nothing less than full commitment and plenty of courage.

South's Reg Harley is caught between Collingwood's Geoff Brokenshire (left) and Neil Mann.

Until Hale's appointment, South had meandered through the 1948 season, but finished the season strongly with two wins over the final four rounds. One of those wins was a 96-point thrashing of Geelong at the Lake Oval in the final round. *The Sporting Globe* reported: "Completely overwhelming Geelong from the bounce, South Melbourne played copybook football and had the game won at quarter time (after scoring 6.6 to nil)."

South might have finished the season in tenth position, with seven wins and 12 defeats, but Hale was impressive enough for South to appoint him coach for the 1949 season. One of the few season's highlights for South was Graham's 10 goals against Geelong at Kardinia Park in round eight. And, in a pointer to the following season, South key position star Ron Clegg polled 16 votes in the Brownlow Medal count, behind Richmond's Bill Morris (24 votes), Carlton's Ollie Grieve (21) and Essendon's Bill Hutchison (17).

The Swans were saddened during the 1948 season on news of the death of club stalwart Herb (or Bert) Howson. He played for the club from 1892 to 1908, was club captain in 1906, coach in 1915, 1918 (winning the premiership) and 1919. Howson was a committeeman from 1901-3 and was club secretary from 1904-21. Another great early identity, Bill Windley, in

A Kornies card featuring South winger/rover Arthur Fox.

1948 relinquished the position of ball steward. He played for the club from 1886-1905 and was honorary ball steward for an astonishing 57 years. Windley represented South in a match against a visiting England rugby team at the Lake Oval in 1888. He was made a club life member in 1893.

South Melbourne Football Club

74th
ANNUAL REPORT
AND
BALANCE SHEET

Season 1948

To be presented to Members at the Annual Meeting in the South Melbourne Town Hall, on Tuesday, 21st December 1948, at 8 p.m.

H. LINGWOOD-SMITH, Hon. Secretary

South defender Pat Bourke clears against Collingwood, with teammate Jim Cleary in support.

PLAYER	GAMES	GOALS
ALLEN, George	3	3
BARRY, Ron	9	0
BOURKE, Pat	13	0
BREW, Frank	10	3
BULPIT, Stan	7	5
BYWATER, Ron	4	1
CALLICK, Alf	13	5
CARIS, George	15	0
CHAMBERS, Wylie	12	4
CLEARY, Jim	8	0
CLEGG, Ron	18	30
COLLINS, Kevin	9	11
CRANE, Len	16	0
DORNAU, Erwin	17	2
EICHHORN, Jack	4	1
FOX, Arthur	7	0
GARRICK, Jack	8	5
GRAHAM, Jack	16	33
HARLEY, Reg	19	11
HILL, Vic	17	6
HOLLAND, Len	11	4
JARRY, Les	4	3
KENNEDY, George	5	5
KING, Bill	17	0
LUCAS, Bert	10	4
MEARS, Harry	5	2
MILLER, Allan	3	8
MULLANE, Jack	3	0
READ, Chester	1	0
RYAN, Tom	5	0
SCHAEFER, Keith	12	2
SIMPSON, Harry	5	2
SPOKES, Larry	16	12
STEPHENS, Frank	3	3
STRANG, Alan	5	2
TAYLOR, Don	17	19
WILLIAMS, Les	16	0
WILLIAMS, Billy	17	26

POSITION: Tenth
COACH: Bill Adams, Jack Hale
CAPTAIN: Jack Graham
BEST AND FAIREST: Ron Clegg
LEADING GOALKICKER: Jack Graham (33)

1949

Former Carlton rover Jack Hale made such a good impression as a coaching replacement after the Swans dumped Bill Adams during the 1948 season that he was given the job for 1949. However, the Swans appointed Bert Lucas as captain to replace Jack Graham, who had led the side over the previous three seasons and most of 1944 when Herbie Matthews broke an ankle in the opening round.

The Swans wanted a younger leader, but the move upset the 32-year-old Graham, who had worn the red and white with tremendous commitment since joining the club from Red Cliffs in 1935. He therefore played just four games for South in 1949 before accepting a position as captain-coach of Minyip. Graham, one of the last masters of the place-kick, played 227 games and kicked 233 goals for the Swans and was best and fairest in 1945.

South started the season without veteran full-back Jim Cleary, known to everyone in football as "Gentleman Jim", who joined Port Melbourne as captain-coach after 222 games with South from 1934. He won the Swans' best and fairest in 1942 and 1944 and later became a popular member of Channel Seven's "World of Sport" football panel. Defender Bill King (136 games from 1940) also retired at the end of the 1948 season.

Bert Lucas was South's 1949 captain.

The Swans in 1949 introduced eight VFL newcomers, including future champion Jim Taylor. A high jump champion from Caulfield Grammar School who just failed to win selection for the 1950 Empire Games, Taylor's family lived close to the Lake Oval. He started with South as a 17-year-old and went on to play 153 games with the Swans to 1961.

South champion Ron Clegg won the 1949 Brownlow Medal.

South started the 1949 season disastrously in going down to Carlton by 64 points at Princes Park. *The Sun News-Pictorial* reported that Carlton was "on top in almost every position and virtually was unchallenged", but the big news from the weekend was the 12-goal debut by Essendon's John Coleman against Hawthorn at Windy Hill.

South recovered from the Carlton mauling to defeat St Kilda by three points at the Lake Oval in round two, only to go down to Geelong by 23 points at Kardinia Park the following week. The Swans were hot one week, but cold the next and virtually were knocked out of the finals race with an 88-point thrashing by North Melbourne in round 10. *The Sporting Globe* reported that North was "better everywhere" and added that over the final quarter "all interest had gone out of the game and it was only a question of how many goals North

MATCH RESULTS

Round 1, at Princes Park, April 18
Carlton 16.16 (112) d South Melbourne 6.12 (48)

Round 2, at Lake Oval, April 23
South Melbourne 12.13 (85) d St Kilda 12.10 (82)

Round 3, at Kardinia Park, April 30
Geelong 14.14 (98) d South Melbourne 10.15 (75)

Round 4, at Lake Oval, May 7
South Melbourne 8.11 (59) d Melbourne 7.9 (51)

Round 5, at Lake Oval, May 14
South Melbourne 10.8 (68) d Footscray 6.14 (50)

Round 6, at Punt Road, May 21
Richmond 15.13 (103) d South Melbourne 8.12 (60)

Round 7, at Glenferrie Oval, May 28
South Melbourne 12.15 (87) d Hawthorn 6.12 (48)

Round 8, at Lake Oval, June 4
Fitzroy 14.14 (98) d South Melbourne 12.7 (79)

Round 9, at Lake Oval, June 11
South Melbourne 15.16 (106) d Essendon 12.9 (81)

Round 10, at Arden Street, June 18
North Melb. 18.25 (133) d South Melbourne 6.9 (45)

Round 11, at Victoria Park, July 2
Collingwood 15.16 (106) d South Melb. 6.16 (52)

Round 12, at Lake Oval, July 9
Carlton 11.15 (81) d South Melbourne 6.12 (48)

Round 13, at Junction Oval, July 16
St Kilda 16.15 (111) d South Melbourne 13.13 (91)

Round 14, at Lake Oval, July 23
Geelong 14.13 (97) d South Melbourne 11.15 (81)

Round 15, at MCG, July 30
Melbourne 12.7 (79) d South Melbourne 9.11 (65)

Round 16, at Western Oval, August 6
Footscray 10.14 (74) d South Melbourne 8.10 (58)

Round 17, at Lake Oval, August 13
Richmond 10.17 (77) d South Melbourne 9.13 (67)

Round 18, at Lake Oval, August 20
South Melbourne 14.8 (92) d Hawthorn 8.14 (62)

Round 19, at Brunswick Street, August 27
Fitzroy 19.12 (126) d South Melbourne 10.17 (77)

would get". Reporter Herb Coombes refused to nominate North's best players and, instead, wrote: "To individualise would be doing some players an injustice."

Ron Clegg had reason to smile in 1949.

The following seven rounds were equally disastrous for South, which did not win again until it defeated lowly Hawthorn by 30 points at the Lake Oval in the penultimate round. South, with six wins, finished tenth, above only St Kilda (four wins) and Hawthorn (three).

South's poor run home eventually cost Hale the coaching position amid club uproar, but there was one great club highlight when star key position player Ron Clegg won a Brownlow Medal. Clegg, who could excel at either end of the ground, polled 23 votes to tie with Hawthorn's Col Austen. Clegg was declared the winner on a countback, although Austen was awarded a retrospective Brownlow in 1989.

Clegg was two months shy of his 22nd birthday when he won his Brownlow, but knew nothing of his triumph until he and wife Billye turned on the car radio to hear the news. They then drove to Clegg family's home to celebrate, but there was a hiccup when the South star was presented with his medal in the Melbourne Cricket Club members' dining room during the finals. Billye did not have a ticket and after eventually gaining admission, got to the dining room just a couple of minutes too late.

PLAYER	GAMES	GOALS
BARRY, Ron	11	0
BOURKE, Pat	12	0
BREW, Frank	14	12
BRUCE, Jack	5	2
BULPIT, Stan	4	3
BYWATER, Ron	16	25
CALLICK, Alf	13	1
CARIS, George	3	0
CHAMBERS, Wylie	13	0
CLEGG, Ron	18	16
COLLINS, Kevin	3	1
CRANE, Len	15	1
DAVIS, Syd	1	0
DORNAU, Erwin	4	0
EICHHORN, Jack	10	4
FOX, Arthur	18	4
GARRICK, Jack	4	6
GRAHAM, Jack	4	6
GULL, Jim	11	11
HARLEY, Reg	17	1
HILL, Vic	3	2
JARRY, Les	17	7
JONES, Dick	17	27
LUCAS, Bert	18	5
MILLER, Allan	9	10
PAEZ, Ron	7	0
READ, Chester	11	4
RICHARDSON, Arthur	5	1
RYAN, Tom	18	1
SCHAEFER, Keith	13	5
SIMMS, Fred	2	0
SIMPSON, Harry	4	0
SPOKES, Larry	17	25
TAYLOR, Jim	7	8
WILLIAMS, Les	7	8
WILLIAMS, Billy	18	2

POSITION: Tenth
COACH: Jack Hale
CAPTAIN: Bert Lucas
BEST AND FAIREST: Ron Clegg
LEADING GOALKICKER: Dick Jones (27)

1950

The Swans were in turmoil early in 1950 when the popular Jack Hale was dumped as coach at the end of the previous season. The South committee, convinced it needed a playing coach to lead by example, turned to Essendon centre half-forward Gordon "Whoppa" Lane. The hugely talented Lane had kicked six goals in Essendon's 1942 Grand Final win and seven in the 1946 premiership decider. He was a particularly strong mark and clever on the ground, but had badly injured a knee in 1948 and had lost much of his sharpness. Regardless, South saw him as the man to take the club into a new era.

South in 1950 also introduced several quality youngsters who would carve significant careers at the Lake Oval. Winger Bob Giles

A South line-up of 1950.

MATCH RESULTS

Round 1, at Lake Oval, April 22
South Melb. 14.12 (96) d Collingwood 11.10 (76)

Round 2, at Windy Hill, April 29
Essendon 29.7 (181) d South Melbourne 10.16 (76)

Round 3, at Lake Oval, May 6
St Kilda 15.13 (103) d South Melbourne 11.15 (81)

Round 4, at Brunswick Street, May 13
Fitzroy 16.27 (123) d South Melbourne 8.9 (57)

Round 5, at Arden Street, May 20
North Melb. 14.12 (96) d South Melbourne 14.9 (93)

Round 6, at Lake Oval, May 27
South Melbourne 20.14 (134) d Hawthorn 10.14 (74)

Round 7, at Lake Oval, June 3
Carlton 11.8 (74) d South Melbourne 9.14 (68)

Round 8, at Western Oval, June 10
Footscray 19.11 (125) d South Melbourne 9.8 (62)

Round 9, at Lake Oval, June 17
Melbourne 13.16 (94) d South Melbourne 8.12 (60)

Round 10, at Lake Oval, June 24
South Melbourne 14.17 (101) d Richmond 13.8 (86)

Round 11, at Kardinia Park, July 1
Geelong 19.21 (135) d South Melbourne 8.7 (55)

Round 12, at Victoria Park, July 8
Collingwood 16.21 (117) d South Melb. 9.20 (74)

Round 13, at Lake Oval, July 15
Essendon 22.17 (149) d South Melbourne 8.9 (57)

Round 14, at Junction Oval, July 29
South Melbourne 13.10 (88) d St Kilda 10.18 (78)

Round 15, at Lake Oval, August 5
Fitzroy 11.11 (77) d South Melbourne 11.8 (74)

Round 16, at Lake Oval, August 12
North Melb. 21.14 (140) d South Melb. 13.11 (89)

Round 17, at Glenferrie Oval, August 19
South Melbourne 16.7 (103) d Hawthorn 14.10 (94)

Round 18, at Princes Park, August 26
Carlton 13.4 (82) d South Melbourne 10.10 (70)

Former Essendon centre half-forward Gordon Lane was South captain-coach in 1950.

(South Melbourne Districts) played 67 games to 1955 and would have played many more if he had not moved to the United States for business reasons, ruckman Don Scott (West Perth) played 83 games to 1954 and half-forward Gray "Mick" Sibun (Mt Carmel, Middle Park) played 111 games to 1956 and was vice-captain in 1955.

Highly-respected football writer Alf Brown, in a special Saturday Magazine feature in *The Herald* in the lead-up to the 1950 season listed the VFL stars he rated the competition's best, with South's Ron Clegg the centrepiece of the article headlined THESE CHAMPIONS—WHAT MAKES THEM TICK?

Brown wrote of Clegg: "He clinched the Brownlow Medal last year when he was switched to centre half-back, and this is his

best position. As a centre half-forward I was often disappointed in him. He handled the ball as much as any man on the field, but failed to do enough with it. He did not get many goals himself and his side did not score enough either.

"As a centre half-back Clegg has everything. He is fast, is a grand mark, is strong, and now that he is beginning to use his weight — it is remarkable the number of big men in the League who have never learned to use their hips and shoulders — he looks like being a star defender for many years."

Brown also reported that, at the end of the 1949 season, Clegg had been offered eight pounds ($16) a week to cross to the VFA. Clegg rejected the offer, but subsequently was offered a mammoth deal to sign with Tasmanian club New Norfolk. The offer included a milk bar, rent-free accommodation and wages. South, the VFL and the Australian National Football Council blocked the move.

Lane's coaching career jumped to a spectacular start when South defeated Collingwood by 20 points in the opening round clash at the Lake Oval. Ron Bywater kicked five goals for the Swans and *The Sporting Globe* reported that South's third quarter was "electrifying".

Lane returned to Windy Hill the following week to face Essendon and was brought back to earth in a rush as the Bombers thrashed the Swans by 105 points. Champion Essendon full-forward John Coleman was almost unbeatable with 11 goals. To make matters worse for South, it was left with a long injury list — Len Crane (ankle), Alf Callick (broken ribs), Jack Eichhorn (broken arm), Jim Gull (dislocated fingers) and Ron Paez (leg). *The Sporting Globe* headline read SOUTH SWAMPED BY ESSENDON.

It was the first of four consecutive defeats, although South was unlucky to go down to North Melbourne by just three points at Arden Street in round five. The Swans led with just minutes to play, but two late goals from Don Condon gave the Shinboners a last-gasp win.

South might have smashed Hawthorn by 60 points at the Lake Oval the following week, but the Swans again were doomed to yet another disappointing season. South's only consolation was that Hawthorn had an even worse season and did not win a single game. South's only win late in the season was at Hawthorn's expense, by nine points at the Lake Oval in the penultimate round. *The Sporting Globe* noted that the "Hawks fought hard, but failed again".

In going down to Carlton by 12 points at Princes Park the following week, South ended the season with just five wins to finish above only the hapless Hawks.

PLAYER	GAMES	GOALS
BARRY, Ron	14	1
BREW, Frank	16	5
BULPIT, Stan	1	0
BYWATER, Ron	9	9
CALLICK, Alf	4	0
CARIS, George	1	1
CHAMBERS, Wylie	11	1
CLEGG, Ron	9	3
COLLIHOLE, Ernie	8	0
CRANE, Len	6	0
DAVIS, Syd	3	0
DORNAU, Erwin	6	2
DUNIAM, Urban	1	0
EICHHORN, Jack	2	2
FOX, Arthur	14	10
GARRICK, Jack	18	3
GILES, Bob	18	0
GOODES, Reg	1	0
GULL, Jim	10	9
HARLEY, Reg	14	0
HILET, Kevin	9	0
LANE, Gordon	16	47
LUCAS, Bert	15	9
McDONALD, Brian	6	6
MILLER, Allan	14	21
PAEZ, Ron	14	0
PALMER, Frank	2	1
READ, Chester	4	0
ROHLEDER, Noel	1	1
RYAN, Tom	10	2
SCHAEFER, Keith	17	2
SCOTT, Don	14	7
SIBUN, Gray "Mick"	11	12
SIMMS, Fred	2	0
SIMPSON, Harry	7	1
SPOKES, Larry	10	2
TAYLOR, Jim	13	9
TRAINER, Bob	3	3
WILLIAMS, Les	9	0
WILLIAMS, Billy	17	36

POSITION: Eleventh
COACH: Gordon Lane
CAPTAIN: Gordon Lane
BEST AND FAIREST: Billy Williams
LEADING GOALKICKER: Gordon Lane (47)

1951

With Gordon Lane as captain-coach for a second season, South launched one of the biggest player cleanouts in club history. Almost half the 1950 senior list was either cleared to a rival VFL club, retired or players told their services no longer were required. Chester Read went to St Kilda, Len Crane crossed to Hawthorn and several of the club's more experienced players decided it was time to hang up the boots or move to the country or junior competitions.

The versatile Ron Bywater, third in the 1947 Brownlow Medal, was appointed captain-coach of Corowa, Victorian representative Arthur Fox called it quits after just three years with the Swans and former skipper Bert Lucas retired at just 29 years of age.

On the other hand, South recruiting was the best for many years, with future stars Keith Browning, Ian Gillett, Fred Goldsmith and Eddie Lane all making their VFL debuts. Browning, an elegant centreman or half-forward played 53 games to 1954 and son Mark had an even more distinguished career with the Swans and captained the club. Gillett, from South Melbourne YCW captained the Swans in 1956, Goldsmith won the 1955 Brownlow Medal and Lane won the Swans' best and fairest in 1954.

Billy Williams was an outstanding rover/winger.

The Football Record, in its opening round edition for 1951 said this of Goldsmith: "He hails from Spotswood, is a good mark and kick, and is described as a 'natural'." *The Football Record* also ran this preview of the season: "Away they go. In the race for the Jubilee Premiership. Twelve teams take the field in the strenuous campaign for championship honours." The "Jubilee" was in reference to Australia celebrating the 50th anniversary of Federation, but the match program dismissed South's chances of winning this special premiership as it had "suffered severe losses in transfers and retirements of leading players".

South opened the season against Geelong at Kardinia Park, with the Cats the raging favourites. The tipsters were on the ball as Geelong defeated South by 54 points. South's score of 6.5 (41) was its lowest against Geelong since it managed just 3.10 (28) in 1925. It also was the Cats' biggest win over the Swans for 10 years. *The Football Record* reported: "South had few stars. Keith Schaefer sparkled at centre, but received little support. Frank Brew won well on his wing, completing

MATCH RESULTS

Round 1, at Kardinia Park, April 21
Geelong 13.17 (95) d South Melbourne 6.5 (41)

Round 2, at Lake Oval, April 28
Richmond 14.13 (97) d South Melbourne 5.7 (37)

Round 3, at Lake Oval, May 5
South Melbourne 14.20 (104) d Essendon 14.7 (91)

Round 4, at Arden Street, May 12
North Melb. 12.6 (78) d South Melbourne 9.19 (73)

Round 5, at Lake Oval, May 19
South Melbourne 15.6 (96) d Melbourne 11.12 (78)

Round 6, at Victoria Park, June 2
Collingwood 13.15 (93) d South Melbourne 6.10 (46)

Round 7, at Lake Oval, June 11
South Melbourne 17.14 (116) d Footscray 9.15 (69)

Round 8, at Lake Oval, June 16
South Melbourne 12.14 (86) d Hawthorn 7.11 (53)

Round 9, at Brunswick Street, June 23
South Melb. 12.13 (85) drew with Fitzroy 12.13 (85)

Round 10, at Junction Oval, June 30
South Melbourne 13.15 (93) d St Kilda 7.7 (49)

Round 11, at Lake Oval, July 14
Carlton 7.14 (56) d South Melbourne 7.9 (51)

Round 12, at Lake Oval, July 21
Geelong 18.11 (119) d South Melbourne 9.8 (62)

Round 13, at Punt Road, July 28
South Melbourne 13.17 (95) d Richmond 8.8 (56)

Round 14, at Windy Hill, August 4
Essendon 16.10 (106) d South Melbourne 8.12 (60)

Round 15, at Lake Oval, August 11
South Melbourne 14.16 (100) d North Melb. 15.9 (99)

Round 16, at MCG, August 18
South Melb. 18.17 (125) d Melbourne 15.16 (106)

Round 17, at Lake Oval, August 25
Collingwood 12.10 (82) d South Melbourne 12.9 (81)

Round 18, at Western Oval, September 1
Footscray 13.15 (93) d South Melbourne 6.12 (48)

Ron Clegg won South's best and fairest in 1951.

a solid centreline, but the team was unable to take advantage of that superiority. Eddie Lane is likely to develop into a good rover and Jim Taylor was a stout follower. Kevin Hilet and (Jack) Garrick were others to show out."

The Swans managed just five goals in going down to Richmond by 60 points at the Lake Oval in round two and were given no chance of defeating reigning premier Essendon at the Lake Oval the following week. Essendon had defeated Melbourne and Hawthorn over the first two rounds and was expected to thrash the unsettled Swans. However, South defeated Essendon by 13 points in a huge upset. *The Football Record* headline read SOUTH TOPPLE THE MIGHTY DONS. The report, by "Chatterer", read: "Bewitched! Bothered and bewildered! Unwary Dons were trapped by dashing Southerners.

"What happened to the Dons? That will remain one of the real mysteries of the year. South had been regarded as the Cinderella of 1951. The team was unsettled, and Essendon supporters settled down to what was confidently expected to be an orgy of goalkicking by the Dons. Actually, the boot was on the other foot. And had the Southerners kicked more accurately it would have been a debacle for the visitors. Good work, South. Keep it up." Rover Bill Williams, in his first game of the season, kicked six goals for the Swans. South's win also ended an Essendon 16-game winning streak and, with South notching 14.20 (104), it was the first time in two years that a team had scored 100 points or more against the Bombers.

It should have been the spark for South to climb the ladder but inconsistency cost it dearly as it went down to North Melbourne by five points at Arden Street the following week. It was the Shinboners' first win of the season

and although football writers suggested the Swans had had a moral victory, this counted little. *The Football Record's* "Chatterer" wrote: "South threw away the match with shockingly inaccurate kicking, but their form, following on the good display against the Dons, augurs well for the future."

"Chatterer" proved to be a good judge as South was defeated just once (by Collingwood at Victoria Park) over the following six rounds. The Swans defeated Melbourne, Footscray, Hawthorn and St Kilda and drew with Fitzroy at Brunswick Street in round nine. South, at the completion of round 10, was sixth on the ladder and behind fourth-placed Richmond by just two match points. The football world now regarded the Swans as a finals prospect.

"Chatterer" wrote of the Swans following their round 10 defeat of St Kilda: "Their pace, handball and intelligent backing up paved the way for numerous successful attacks. The defence was sound, the rucks strong. This is definitely a side with a future. It might not be this year, but their turn isn't far off." Unfortunately the Swans' form fell away from there and they won just three more games over the rest of the season to finish eighth.

The VFL played a lightning premiership at the MCG on Wednesday, May 9, with gate money donated to the Women's Hospital. The Victorian government donated a special plaque to the winning club.

This special football carnival was organised to celebrate the one-off public holiday of Jubilee of Commonwealth Government Day. The first match was played at 11.30am, with the final scheduled to start at around 4.30pm.

Adults were admitted to the grandstand for four shillings (40 cents), with outer tickets costing two shillings (20 cents). The overall attendance was 25,882, with gross receipts of 2216 pounds ($4432). All players were paid one pound ($2) per match.

Matches were played over two 10-minutes halves, with Richmond defeating South Melbourne by 11 points in the first round. Collingwood won the premiership, but only after extra time in the final against Melbourne. Scores were level on one goal each at full-time and, under the rules of the competition, the game was restarted with a bounce in the centre. The Magpies rushed the ball forward to score a "golden" goal.

PLAYER	GAMES	GOALS
BREW, Frank	14	2
BROWNING, Keith	6	4
CLEGG, Brian	2	0
CLEGG, Ron	17	0
COLLIHOLE, Ken	9	0
DEAGAN, Pat	16	16
DIGNEY, Ron	1	0
DORGAN, Jim	5	0
DORNAU, Erwin	16	4
EICHHORN, Jack	2	0
GARRICK, Jack	16	4
GILLETT, Ian	18	20
GOLDSMITH, Fred	3	3
HARLEY, Reg	7	0
HILET, Kevin	15	0
JONES, Dick	2	1
LANE, Esmond "Eddie"	18	17
LANE, Gordon	12	14
McDONALD, Brian	5	0
McGUINNESS, Keith	2	0
MILLER, Allan	10	9
MOORE, Harry	13	0
MURRAY, W.W. Bruce	17	1
OWENS, Lou	2	1
PAEZ, Ron	10	26
PATTERSON, Jeff	9	1
RYAN, Tom	17	0
SCHAEFER, Keith	17	5
SCOTT, Don	16	10
SIBUN, Gray "Mick"	17	13
SMITH, Stan	6	0
TAYLOR, Jim	17	3
WALKER, Ron	2	0
WILLIAMS, Les	6	0
WILLIAMS, Billy	15	41

POSITION: Eighth
COACH: Gordon Lane
CAPTAIN: Gordon Lane
BEST AND FAIREST: Ron Clegg
LEADING GOALKICKER: Billy Williams (41)

Ron Clegg won the best and fairest and was runner-up to Geelong's Bernie Smith in the Brownlow Medal count, with Smith polling 23 votes to Clegg's 20.

1952

South went into the 1952 season without one of its greatest stalwarts. Champion rover Billy Williams had accepted the position of captain-coach of VFA club Williamstown after playing 124 games for the Swans from 1945. He won the club best and fairest in 1946, 1947 and 1950, and topped the goalkicking in 1947. A brilliant rover, he was a regular Victorian representative and, in 2003, was named in the Swans' Team of the Century.

The Swans, after such a massive turnover the previous year, introduced just five VFL newcomers in 1952, while rover Marty Lynch moved to the Lake Oval from Geelong. Easily the best of South's new faces for 1952 was the talented Bill Gunn, a local product from Spotswood. Gunn signed for the Swans with his best mate Fred Goldsmith before the start of the 1951 season, but delayed his VFL career for a season as he promised an uncle he would play at least one season with Williamstown. Gunn went on to play 104 games with the Swans to 1959 and was rated one of the best players of his era. He had a stunning debut season and represented Victoria after just a handful of games with the Swans.

South, which had shown tremendous improvement the previous season, started the 1952 season with wins over St Kilda, Carlton and Richmond to suggest it could make the finals for the first time since 1945. The Swans suffered a setback in going down to lowly

Bill Gunn had a superb debut season in 1952.

MATCH RESULTS

Round 1, at Lake Oval, April 19
South Melbourne 11.16 (82) d St Kilda 8.26 (74)

Round 2, at Princes Park, April 26
South Melbourne 13.11 (89) d Carlton 12.12 (84)

Round 3, at Lake Oval, May 3
South Melbourne 14.17 (101) d Richmond 12.9 (81)

Round 4, at Glenferrie Oval, May 10
Hawthorn 11.3 (69) d South Melbourne 8.12 (60)

Round 5, at MCG, May 17
South Melbourne 10.11 (71) d Melbourne 8.9 (57)

Round 6, at Lake Oval, May 31
South Melbourne 14.12 (96) d Fitzroy 9.11 (65)

Round 7, at Lake Oval, June 9
South Melbourne 16.14 (110) d Footscray 11.13 (79)

Round 8, at Albury, June 14
South Melb. 18.10 (118) d North Melb. 14.12 (96)

Round 9, at Kardinia Park, June 21
Geelong 7.13 (55) d South Melbourne 4.11 (35)

Round 10, at Lake Oval, June 28
Collingwood 12.13 (85) d South Melbourne 9.10 (64)

Round 11, at Arden Street, July 5
South Melbourne 10.17 (77) d North Melb. 7.4 (46)

Round 12, at Lake Oval, July 12
Essendon 9.15 (69) d South Melbourne 8.12 (60)

Round 13, at Junction Oval, July 19
South Melbourne 6.8 (44) d St Kilda 5.8 (38)

Round 14, at Lake Oval, July 26
South Melb. 10.16 (76) drew with Carlton 10.16 (76)

Round 15, at Punt Road, August 2
South Melbourne 12.14 (86) d Richmond 10.14 (74)

Round 16, at Lake Oval, August 9
Hawthorn 9.14 (68) d South Melbourne 6.14 (50)

Round 17, at Lake Oval, August 16
South Melbourne 10.14 (74) d Melbourne 8.18 (66)

Round 18, at Brunswick Street, August 23
Fitzroy 9.10 (64) d South Melbourne 7.15 (57)

Round 19, at Western Oval, August 30
Footscray 13.13 (91) d South Melbourne 8.13 (61)

The Swans featured in this 1952 souvenir in The Argus.

Hawthorn by nine points at the Lake Oval in round four, but won their next four games to have a win-loss ratio of 7-1. South fans already were excitedly talking about September.

South's seventh win was in exceptional circumstances as it was part of what the VFL named National Day, but which the media tagged "the Propaganda Round". The VFL, wanting to spread the popularity of the competition, arranged for round eight matches to be played in country centres and interstate. South played North Melbourne at Albury and other matches in the round were: Geelong v Essendon (Brisbane), Richmond v Collingwood (Sydney), Fitzroy v Melbourne

(Hobart), Carlton v Hawthorn (Euroa) and Footscray v St Kilda (Yallourn).

The round coincided with a Victorian team playing Western Australia in Perth. South therefore went into the match against North without interstate representatives Jim Taylor and Gunn. The North-South clash at Albury attracted an attendance of 15,000 and *The Sun News-Pictorial* noted in its match headline the following Monday SOUTH HAS WIN IN ALBURY CROWD-PLEASER.

The report of South's 22-point win read: "South Melbourne lasted better than North in a fast, crowd-pleasing 'away' game at Albury. Every phase of the game was displayed and credit must go to both teams for the good exhibition of fast, play-on football."

South, apart from missing Gunn and Taylor, also was without the injured Ron Clegg, with Goldsmith replacing him at centre half-back and doing well. The *Sun* also reported: "South Melbourne players combined well in attack, with captain-coach Gordon Lane showing out." The newspaper named Keith Schaefer as best on ground. It said of his performance: "Ken (sic) gave a first-class exhibition at centre, rarely wasting a kick." Pat Deagan kicked four goals.

South faced its acid test the following week when it played reigning premier Geelong at Kardinia Park. The Swans, however, were buoyed by Essendon's thrashing of Geelong in Brisbane the previous Monday night. Torrential rain had made play impossible on the previous Saturday and, after the game was rescheduled, there was speculation that Cat and Bomber players who had represented Victoria in Perth could fly to Brisbane to play for their respective clubs.

However, the clubs struck a "gentleman's agreement" that they would stick to the teams they originally had selected. The Cats therefore were without Fred Flanagan and Bruce Morrison, while the Bombers were missing Bill Hutchison and Norm McDonald. The Bombers, however, still had a match-winner in champion full-forward John Coleman, who kicked 13 goals in the Bombers' 69-point thrashing of Geelong.

The Cats were still smarting over this unexpected setback when they lined up against the Swans and, in appalling conditions, won by 20 points. South, which had been sitting second to Collingwood on the VFL ladder to that defeat, therefore started having self-doubts which were reflected by its performances over the rest of the season, especially in going down to Collingwood by 21 points at the Lake Oval in the following round. The race for the finals was tight, with Fitzroy, Carlton and South locked in a battle for third and fourth.

South managed to hold its place in the top four going into the final stages of the season but, inexplicably, crashed to Hawthorn yet again, this time by 18 points at the Lake Oval in round 16. To make matters worse, Fitzroy defeated South by seven points at Brunswick Street in the penultimate round to put the Swans under tremendous pressure in their bid to make the finals.

It all boiled down to the final round as the Swans had to defeat lowly Footscray at the Western Oval and hope that ladder leader Geelong would defeat Carlton at Kardinia Park. The Cats did their bit in defeating the Blues by 45 points and, in the process, keeping the visitors to their lowest score — 3.14 (32) — of the season. The match attracted a ground record attendance of 49,109.

South led Footscray by 21 points at quarter-time in their clash, but faded badly to go down by 30 points. It was just Footscray's fifth win of the season and South missed the finals by just two match points behind fourth-placed Carlton. The Swans might have had their best season since 1945, but it was not enough to save Lane's job as captain-coach.

PLAYER	GAMES	GOALS
BREW, Frank	18	3
BROWNING, Keith	19	0
CLEGG, Ron	6	0
DEAGAN, Pat	12	9
DIGNEY, Ron	7	1
DORGAN, Jim	7	0
DORNAU, Erwin	11	0
EARL, Don	4	0
EICHHORN, Jack	17	17
GARRICK, Jack	18	1
GILES, Bob	7	0
GILLETT, Ian	18	14
GOLDSMITH, Fred	8	1
GREEN, Lindsay	1	0
GUNN, Bill	17	19
HARLEY, Reg	4	0
HILET, Kevin	17	0
LANE, Esmond "Eddie"	19	23
LANE, Gordon	19	33
LYNCH, Marty	8	11
MURRAY, W.W. Bruce	18	5
NOLAN, Bill	7	3
PAEZ, Ron	16	24
PATTERSON, Jeff	11	1
ROSEWARNE, Harold	4	0
RYAN, Tom	11	0
SCHAEFER, Keith	17	4
SCOTT, Don	19	10
SIBUN, Gray "Mick"	17	13
SMITH, Stan	8	0
TAYLOR, Jim	15	2

POSITION: Fifth
COACH: Gordon Lane
CAPTAIN: Gordon Lane
BEST AND FAIREST: Keith Schaefer
LEADING GOALKICKER: Gordon Lane (33)

1953

South, following the "resignation" of captain-coach Gordon Lane at the end of the 1952 season, turned to a past club champion in an effort to lift its fortunes. The Swans appointed Laurie Nash as coach and he did not waste any time in telling the football world he would rejuvenate the club. In fact, he boldly declared the Swans would win a premiership under his guidance.

He told *The Herald's* Alf Brown: "I was in South's last premiership side in 1933; now I expect to be the first old player to coach them to a premiership. With specialised training, I will improve every South player 33 and one-third per cent and we will win the Coronation premiership (Elizabeth II was crowned that year)." Nash told Brown he would have specialised training to bring out the best in players and that he wanted to play centreman/flanker Bill Gunn at centre half-forward.

A South line-up of 1953, with the great Laurie Nash (centre, middle row) as coach.

The former South champion also declared that he wanted South to play the fast-running game Geelong used to win the 1951-52 flags and added: "I want everyone to make this year South's year."

South's annual report for the 1953 season noted: "Taking over from Gordon Lane, who retired at the end of season 1952, Laurie Nash, one of the greatest players ever to don a red and white guernsey, was appointed non-playing coach for season 1953. He needed no introduction to players and supporters and quickly settled down in his new role towards moulding a formidable side for South."

South also was buoyed at the start of the season by the news that champion key position player Ron Clegg had made a full recovery from knee cartilage surgery and had been training brilliantly in the lead-up to the

MATCH RESULTS

Round 1, at Victoria Park, April 18
Collingwood 17.16 (118) d South Melb. 11.11 (77)

Round 2, at Lake Oval, May 2
South Melbourne 13.21 (99) d Essendon 13.11 (89)

Round 3, at Lake Oval, May 9
Fitzroy 12.14 (86) d South Melbourne 10.15 (75)

Round 4, at Glenferrie Oval, May 16
South Melbourne 9.9 (63) d Hawthorn 7.11 (53)

Round 5, at Lake Oval, May 23
North Melb. 9.8 (62) d South Melbourne 8.10 (58)

Round 6, at Kardinia Park, May 30
Geelong 14.16 (100) d South Melbourne 7.5 (47)

Round 7, at Junction Oval, June 6
South Melbourne 18.16 (124) d St Kilda 7.11 (53)

Round 8, at Lake Oval, June 13
South Melbourne 11.11 (77) d Melbourne 9.17 (71)

Round 9, at Western Oval, June 20
South Melbourne 11.6 (72) d Footscray 5.13 (43)

Round 10, at Lake Oval, June 27
South Melbourne 12.7 (79) d Richmond 6.14 (50)

Round 11, at Princes Park, July 4
Carlton 14.13 (97) d South Melbourne 10.13 (73)

Round 12, at Lake Oval, July 18
Collingwood 17.17 (119) d South Melb. 12.9 (81)

Round 13, at Windy Hill, July 25
Essendon 12.11 (83) d South Melbourne 8.14 (62)

Round 14, at Brunswick Street, August 1
Fitzroy 12.18 (90) d South Melbourne 7.19 (61)

Round 15, at Lake Oval, August 8
Hawthorn 9.8 (62) d South Melbourne 7.12 (54)

Round 16, at Arden Street, August 15
South Melbourne 11.21 (87) d North Melb. 8.8 (56)

Round 17, at Lake Oval, August 22
South Melbourne 14.14 (98) d Geelong 8.7 (55)

Round 18, at Lake Oval, August 29
South Melbourne 13.20 (98) d St Kilda 4.12 (36)

opening round match against Collingwood at Victoria Park.

The Swans also were hopeful their recruits would do well and, for example, had gone to considerable trouble to win a clearance for Subiaco (WA) rover Nick Gelavis. Other South newcomers in 1953 included follower Don Keyter (Merbein), who later played for a Victoria "B" side, and highly-rated Murchison full-forward John Svenson. Also, *The Herald* reported that 16-year-old Bob Pratt Junior had trained with the Swans pre-season and would be joining the Swans. The son of the legendary Swan full-forward played 35 games in the red and white from 1955-58.

South coach Laurie Nash introduces the Victorian Governor, Sir Dallas Brooks, to the Swans.

Although Nash painted a rosy scene for the Swans, there was supporter dismay over the state of the football members' grandstand at the Lake Oval. Supporters at the annual meeting held just before the start of the 1953 season described the old wooden stand as "an old cowshed". South president Jack Cullen promised there were plans to improve the stand, but little was done and it burned down a decade later.

Despite Nash's optimism, South's 1953 ambitions were dealt a savage blow in the opening round when the Magpies thrashed the Swans by 41 points. *The Sun News-Pictorial* reported: "Battering-ram tactics, supported by a tough, resilient defence, enabled Collingwood to crush South Melbourne at Victoria Park. The Southerners' attacks were smashed and converted into Magpie drives with ruthless, almost machine-like precision." The *Sun* noted that Clegg was the Swans' "only cheer for the day" and played "good, solid football" at centre half-back. South consoled itself with the fact that number one ruckman Jim Taylor was a late withdrawal because of a jarred heel.

South defeated Essendon by 10 points at the Lake Oval the following week, but Swan supporters were heavily criticised for an incident involving champion Bomber full-forward John Coleman, who kicked 11 goals in a losing side. Coleman at one stage was paid a free kick near the boundary at the grandstand end of the ground. South fans reacted by throwing bottles onto the ground. Gunn was named South's best player.

Fitzroy defeated South by 11 points at the Lake Oval in round three but, after early season inconsistency, South found form to notch four consecutive wins from rounds 7-10. This run, however, coincided with the accidental death of former star South winger/rover Arthur Fox, a Victorian representative. Fox was killed in a motor-bike accident when he was travelling from Rupanyup to visit his mother at Red Cliffs. He was just 29 years of age.

South at that stage looked likely to make the finals, but its form fell away sharply, with five consecutive defeats. Although the Swans finished the season with consecutive wins over North Melbourne, Geelong and St Kilda, it missed the finals by a wide margin, in eighth position and 16 match points behind fourth-placed Essendon.

Jim Taylor won the Swans' 1953 best and fairest.

South's poor run towards the end of the season coincided with controversy over the selection of the Victorian squad for the 1953 Carnival in Adelaide. Taylor and Gunn originally were selected as South's Big Vee representatives, but when Gunn was declared unavailable, the selectors called up Clegg. South complained that this robbed the team of an extra player, but the VFL stood firm.

The Swans in 1953 also were savaged by injuries and were unable to field a full-strength side for any game. The more seriously injured were Jim Dorgan (broken leg), Leo O'Halloran (broken pelvis) and Ray Preston (broken hand). It also appeared Clegg was worried at times after pre-season knee surgery.

Taylor won the best and fairest and South's annual report for the 1953 season noted: "He rightly earns the congratulations of all connected with the club on his sterling performances. Looking back over the years of the Best and Fairest winners, one is struck by the names of truly great players who have fought their way up through the ranks of South's junior teams, and here we have another great clubman adding his name to the list of South's immortals."

Clegg was runner-up in the best and fairest, Keyter won a trophy for the best first-year player, Eddie Lane won the award for most consistent player and Fred Goldsmith was named "most improved".

PLAYER	GAMES	GOALS
ATKINSON, Bob	3	0
BREW, Frank	5	0
BROWNING, Keith	17	0
CLEGG, Ron	17	1
CULLINAN, Ray	2	0
DEAGAN, Pat	12	1
DIGNEY, Ron	1	1
DONALDSON, Dave	5	0
DORGAN, Jim	8	0
EARL, Don	1	0
EICHHORN, Jack	14	5
GARRICK, Jack	14	3
GELAVIS, Nick	14	16
GILES, Bob	16	1
GILLETT, Ian	18	34
GOLDSMITH, Fred	12	0
GREEN, Richie	2	0
GUNN, Bill	17	26
HILET, Kevin	18	1
HOGAN, Pat	4	5
KEYTER, Don	9	4
LANE, Esmond "Eddie"	18	20
LYONS, Maurie	4	0
McDONALD, Gerry	1	0
McPHERSON, Alan	6	10
MEAGHER, Jack	3	4
MURRAY, W.W. Bruce	8	0
NOLAN, Bill	3	1
O'HALLORAN, Leo	9	11
PAEZ, Ron	5	2
PRESTON, Ray	7	0
ROSEWARNE, Harold	5	2
SCHAEFER, Keith	9	2
SCOTT, Don	17	15
SIBUN, Gray "Mick"	17	20
SMITH, Stan	10	0
STEVENS, Jack	3	1
SUMMERS, Frank	2	0
SVENSON, John	4	3
TAYLOR, Jim	16	1
TAYLOR, Ron	4	2

POSITION: Eighth
COACH: Laurie Nash
CAPTAIN: Ron Clegg
BEST AND FAIREST: Jim Taylor
LEADING GOALKICKER: Ian Gillett (34)

1954

The great Laurie Nash made a rod for his own back in declaring he would coach South to a premiership as, after a disappointing 1953 season, he was dumped as coach after just one season in charge and replaced by another club legend, Herbie Matthews. However, South denied it had sacked Nash and, instead, insisted it had advertised the coaching position to ensure it had the best man for the job. Nash, in fact, re-applied for the job after it was advertised, but was overlooked.

Football writer Alf Brown reported in *The Herald:* "Laurie Nash has not been re-appointed coach of South Melbourne Football Club. South's committee met this week (late October, 1953) to discuss the coaching position for 1954 and they decided to call for applications for a playing or non-playing coach … Nash said he would be re-applying for the position although, so far as he understood, he had a two-year contract with the club."

It was obvious South wanted to replace Nash, even though club secretary Joe White denied that advertising the position did not necessarily mean Nash was certain to be replaced. The Brown report concluded: "Some South committeemen would like to see former Brownlow Medal winner Herbie Matthews get the job. Matthews has been coaching South Seconds." Brown suggested that if the Swans wanted a playing coach, they would be looking to champion Essendon rover Bill Hutchison.

Herbie Matthews took over as South coach in 1954.

Matthews, in being appointed coach, made no outlandish promises and, instead, went about his job with a minimum of fuss. The South annual report for the 1953 season said of Matthews' appointment: "Herb is one of the real true red and white old players who have given practically a lifetime of service for the club. Beginning many years ago with the junior eighteens, he commenced his first season in 1932 with the senior eighteen and from there was never out of the side."

The report went out of its way to note that Matthews' appointment was "in the best interests of the club" and added: "In appointing Herbie, it (the committee) stresses that there was no reflection whatever on any of the other

MATCH RESULTS

Round 1, at Lake Oval, April 17
South Melbourne 11.18 (84) d Carlton 11.13 (79)

Round 2, at Windy Hill, April 24
South Melbourne 8.13 (61) d Essendon 5.18 (48)

Round 3, at Western Oval, May 1
Footscray 17.14 (116) d South Melbourne 3.11 (29)

Round 4, at Lake Oval, May 8
South Melbourne 12.9 (81) d Richmond 10.16 (76)

Round 5, at Lake Oval, May 15
Collingwood 14.17 (101) d South Melb. 6.13 (49)

Round 6, at Arden Street, May 22
South Melbourne 12.13 (85) d North Melb. 8.14 (62)

Round 7, at MCG, May 29
Melbourne 15.21 (111) d South Melbourne 14.5 (89)

Round 8, at Lake Oval, June 5
Hawthorn 8.10 (58) d South Melbourne 6.13 (49)

Round 9, at Junction Oval, June 12
South Melbourne 13.18 (96) d St Kilda 2.18 (30)

Round 10, at Brunswick Street, June 26
Fitzroy 11.10 (76) d South Melbourne 10.14 (74)

Round 11, at Lake Oval, July 3
Geelong 17.12 (114) d South Melbourne 9.10 (64)

Round 12, at Princes Park, July 10
Carlton 11.10 (76) d South Melbourne 10.10 (70)

Round 13, at Lake Oval, July 24
Essendon 13.8 (86) d South Melbourne 8.18 (66)

Round 14, at Lake Oval, July 31
Footscray 11.12 (78) d South Melbourne 6.5 (41)

Round 15, at Punt Road, August 7
Richmond 12.15 (87) d South Melbourne 6.16 (52)

Round 16, at Victoria Park, August 14
South Melb. 13.12 (90) d Collingwood 12.16 (88)

Round 17, at Lake Oval, August 21
North Melb. 14.11 (95) d South Melbourne 11.14 (80)

Round 18, at Lake Oval, August 28
Melbourne 14.17 (101) d South Melbourne 7.7 (49)

applicants. It simply means that, in the considered opinion of the committee, he possesses all the qualities which are most likely to benefit the club."

Ron Clegg was appointed captain for a second consecutive season, but South went into pre-season training without several experienced players, including Frank Brew, Keith Schaefer and Ron Paez, their places filled by several promising players. Lightly-framed winger Ken McCormack, ruckman John Ledwidge, rover Kevin Hogan and aptly-named utility Don Star were among 13 players given VFL debuts in 1954.

Champion South full-back Fred Goldsmith gets a rubdown from trainer Bill Mitchell.

South, regarded by many critics as the best team outside the finals the previous season, started 1954 with a five-point win over Carlton at the Lake Oval. South, thanks to a late goal by Eddie Lane, led by 11 points with just a few minutes to play and, when Carlton's Vin English snapped a goal, had to hold tight for the final two minutes. It was a great win as Carlton led by 20 points at half-time and by 12 points at the final break. *The Sporting Globe* headline read SOUTH'S RECOVERY DOWNS BLUES.

The Swans continued their good early form with a 13-point win over Essendon at Windy Hill, but were handed a gift when the Bombers were unable to select the ill (influenza) John Coleman, who had kicked 10 goals the previous week against Hawthorn and also was involved in a collision with former Swan Len Crane. Newcomer Star, in his second match after joining South from Wodonga, kicked three goals and Fred Goldsmith was named in *The Sporting Globe* as best on ground at full-back.

South, after the opening two rounds, was second on the ladder behind Collingwood, with North Melbourne the only other undefeated side. However, the Swans crashed back to earth the following week when Footscray thrashed them by 87 points at the Western Oval. South managed just three goals (two by Eddie Lane and one by Alan McPherson) and *The Sporting Globe* reported that the Bulldogs "overwhelmed" the Swans and held the visitors to just one goal after quarter-time.

The Swans defeated Richmond by five points at the Lake Oval in round four, but had led by 23 points at half-time and were lucky to survive a late Tiger onslaught. In fact, Richmond grabbed the lead with about five minutes to play and South was saved by a late goal from Ian Gillett from a strong mark.

South generally struggled from there and lost six consecutive matches from rounds 10-15 to slip to tenth position. The Swans then pulled off the shock of the season in defeating

Ian "Razors" Gillett was a fine ruckman/ forward who played every game in 1954.

second-placed Collingwood at Victoria Park in round 16. The Magpies went into the game as overwhelming favourites, but the Swans surprised them with their pace and precision after a dismal first half.

Collingwood led by 34 points at the main break and looked set for a huge win. Rover Clarrie Lane sparked South's comeback with an early goal in the third quarter and *The Sporting Globe* reported that South now was "playing with more fire". South at one stage in the third quarter scored 5.4 to a single Collingwood behind and went into the final quarter trailing by just one point. South eventually clinched victory with a goal from Gray "Mick" Sibun, although *The Sporting Globe* suggested Goldsmith was "a tower of strength in the Southern defence and saved them repeatedly".

The Age reported the following Monday that a "fighting speech" by Matthews at half-time had lifted South to play "paralysing" football in the third quarter. The report read: "South's new-found pace, smart handball and the improved play of the following division made the Magpies look a team of hard-striving, but baffled players."

It was South's last win of the season as it went down to North Melbourne and then Melbourne in the final two rounds to finish tenth with six wins, above only Fitzroy and St Kilda, who both had four wins and a draw. Eddie Lane won the best and fairest and was equal third (with Essendon's John Gill and Footscray's Harvey Stevens) behind Richmond ruckman Roy Wright in the Brownlow Medal, with Collingwood ruckman Neil Mann runner-up.

PLAYER	GAMES	GOALS
ATKINSON, Bob	7	1
BROWNING, Keith	11	0
CAMPBELL, Neville	8	0
CHARLESTON, Peter	2	0
CLEGG, Ron	14	9
DEAGAN, Pat	8	0
DONALDSON, Dave	1	0
DORGAN, Jim	18	0
EARL, Don	8	0
EICHHORN, Jack	1	0
GARRICK, Jack	16	3
GELAVIS, Nick	1	0
GILES, Bob	11	2
GILLETT, Ian	18	24
GOLDSMITH, Fred	18	0
GRANT, Trevor	1	0
GREEN, Lindsay	3	1
GUNN, Bill	10	6
HARRINGTON, Pat	7	0
HILET, Kevin	6	0
HOGAN, Kevin	6	0
HOGAN, Pat	6	1
HUDSON, Jack	3	0
KEYTER, Don	16	12
LANE, Clarrie	8	12
LANE, Esmond "Eddie"	17	28
LEDWIDGE, John	6	2
LESLIE, Lewis	6	3
LOGAN, Max	10	0
McCORMACK, Ken	11	0
McDONALD, Gerry	14	0
McPHERSON, Alan	2	2
MEAGHER, Jack	1	0
MURRAY, W.W. Bruce	1	0
NELSON, Daryl	3	0
NOLAN, Bill	8	10
PAYNE. Ernie	3	1
ROSEWARNE, Harold	3	0
SCOTT, Don	17	16
SIBUN, Gray "Mick"	16	15
SMITH, Stan	2	0
STAR, Don	12	13
TAYLOR, Jim	13	3
TAYLOR, Don	2	1
THOMAS, Keith	2	0
TYRELL, Noel	3	0

POSITION: Tenth
COACH: Herbie Matthews
CAPTAIN: Ron Clegg
BEST AND FAIREST: Eddie Lane
LEADING GOALKICKER: Eddie Lane (28)

1955

Despite the disappointment of the previous season's tenth finish, Herbie Matthews retained his position as non-playing coach in 1955, with a new captain in Bill Gunn. The Swans had been shocked over summer when champion key position player and club captain Ron Clegg announced he would be accepting a position as captain-coach of North Albury.

Country and VFA clubs had been chasing Clegg for several seasons and at one stage he rejected an offer of a 500 pound ($1000) signing fee and eight pounds ($16) a match — a huge amount at the time. South reluctantly cleared Clegg to North Albury, hoping he soon would return to the Swans. The Brownlow Medal winner was 27 years of age at the time and South could not afford to lose such a devastatingly effective player.

The Swans' 1955 best and fairest, Ian Gillett.

To compound South's problems, number one ruckman Jim Taylor accepted an offer to play with South Australian club Norwood. He was a huge success with the SA Redlegs as he was best on ground in Norwood's Grand Final loss to Port Adelaide and represented the Croweaters against Victoria.

The Swans also went into the 1955 season without the experienced Keith Browning, Jack Eichhorn, Kevin Hilet and Don Scott. South in 1955 therefore knew it would have to rely on its younger players, with sons of two former champions given chances at VFL level. Bob Pratt Junior and Hugh McLaughlin Junior both debuted in 1955, along with promising rover Brian McGowan.

South opened the season against Geelong at Kardinia Park, a "hoodoo" ground for the Swans as they had not won there since 1948. The trend continued as South, with just one first half goal (by Max Logan) went down by 38 points. The scoreline flattered the Swans as they kicked six of their nine goals in the final quarter when the game virtually was over. Don Keyter kicked three goals and was named best player for South. *The Sporting Globe* suggested Geelong was "too experienced and versatile" for South.

The Swans bounced back to defeat Fitzroy by 38 points at the Lake Oval the following week and *The Sporting Globe* reported that South won across the centre and was "more purposeful around the packs". But, as Fitzroy had finished second last the previous season, no one at the Lake Oval was getting carried

Rover Eddie Lane was runner-up to Ian Gillett in the Swans' best and fairest award.

MATCH RESULTS

Round 1, at Kardinia Park, April 16
Geelong 15.14 (104) d South Melbourne 9.12 (66)

Round 2, at Lake Oval, April 23
South Melbourne 16.11 (107) d Fitzroy 9.15 (69)

Round 3, at Lake Oval, April 30
Hawthorn 15.8 (98) d South Melbourne 7.14 (56)

Round 4, at Punt Road, May 7
Richmond 15.20 (110) d South Melbourne 7.10 (52)

Round 5, at Lake Oval, May 14
South Melbourne 25.16 (166) d St Kilda 4.8 (32)

Round 6, at Princes Park, May 21
South Melbourne 12.11 (83) d Carlton 11.9 (75)

Round 7, at Lake Oval, May 28
Melbourne 11.6 (72) d South Melbourne 10.11 (71)

Round 8, at Windy Hill, June 4
Essendon 13.14 (92) d South Melbourne 7.12 (54)

Round 9, at Lake Oval, June 11
Collingwood 9.18 (72) d South Melbourne 8.15 (63)

Round 10, at Lake Oval, June 25
South Melbourne 10.10 (70) d North Melb. 8.10 (58)

Round 11, at Western Oval, July 2
Footscray 11.16 (82) d South Melbourne 6.13 (49)

Round 12, at Lake Oval, July 9
Geelong 15.9 (99) d South Melbourne 13.10 (88)

Round 13, at Brunswick Street, July 16
Fitzroy 14.16 (100) d South Melbourne 6.10 (46)

Round 14, at Glenferrie Oval, July 23
Hawthorn 10.11 (71) d South Melbourne 6.15 (51)

Round 15, at Lake Oval, July 30
Richmond 13.16 (94) d South Melbourne 14.9 (93)

Round 16, at Junction Oval, August 6
South Melbourne 11.16 (82) d St Kilda 8.5 (53)

Round 17, at Lake Oval, August 13
Carlton 12.7 (79) d South Melbourne 6.12 (48)

Round 18, at MCG, August 20
Melbourne 12.22 (94) d South Melbourne 4.7 (31)

away with this win and, indeed, South lost its next two matches, against Hawthorn and Richmond.

The clash with the Tigers at the Punt Road Oval saw young Pratt make his senior debut and old-time Swan fans flocked there to see the son of the club's most iconic player. They

South Melbourne full-back Fred Goldsmith won the 1955 Brownlow Medal.

A Swan line-up of 1955.

were not disappointed as the youngster goaled very early in the match with his first kick at VFL level after taking a brilliant mark 40 metres from goal. He added another just before quarter-time and finished with an inaccurate 3.6 to be named among South's best players.

Then, in round five, the Swans produced one of their most remarkable performances in club history in defeating a hapless St Kilda by 134 points at the Lake Oval. It was the club's second biggest winning margin, bettered only by the 171-point defeat of St Kilda in 1919. *The Sporting Globe* reported that South "swamped" St Kilda for the Lakeside Premiership. Rover Eddie Lane kicked six goals, Ian Gillett four and Gunn, Don Keyter and John Ledwidge three each, with Gunn, Lane and "Mick" Sibun named South's best players.

South continued its good form in defeating Carlton by eight points at Princes Park the following week, but then had its heart broken with a one-point loss to top side Melbourne at the Lake Oval in round seven. Melbourne was undefeated on top of the ladder, yet South led by 17 points at the final change and looked likely to produce the biggest upset of the season to date.

The Swans dominated play early in the final quarter but, as *The Sporting Globe* reported "could not press home its advantages in attack". Then, when young Pratt snapped a clever left-foot goal, the Swans led by 23 points. Melbourne, however, fought back to creep within five points of South when Bob Johnson goaled late in the match. Then, when the Swans seemed almost certain to hang on, Johnson goaled again to give the Demons the lead just before the final siren.

PLAYER	GAMES	GOALS
ATKINSON, Bob	7	2
BARRY, Des	8	0
DORGAN, Jim	18	0
EARL, Don	2	0
FERGUSON, John	14	0
GARRICK, Jack	12	3
GILES, Bob	15	0
GILLETT, Ian	18	12
GOLDSMITH, Fred	18	0
GRANT, Trevor	3	0
GUNN, Bill	13	16
HOGAN, Kevin	14	14
HUDSON, Jack	4	0
KEYTER, Don	18	22
LANE, Clarrie	4	2
LANE, Esmond "Eddie"	16	36
LEDWIDGE, John	13	4
LESLIE, Lewis	14	3
LOGAN, Max	3	3
McCORMACK, Ken	14	1
McDONALD, Gerry	15	0
McGOWAN, Brian	1	1
McLAUGHLIN, Hugh	10	0
McNEILL, Neil	7	0
NELSON, Daryl	4	0
NOLAN, Bill	1	0
PRATT, Bob Jnr	15	24
PRIMMER, Frank	12	5
REED, Ray	9	1
SIBUN, Gray "Mick"	18	9
STAR, Don	8	3
TAYLOR, Ron	15	10
TRETHOWAN, John	8	1
TYRELL. Noel	1	0
VANCE, Colin	3	5
WOOLLEY, John	5	0

POSITION: Tenth
COACH: Herbie Matthews
CAPTAIN: Bill Gunn
BEST AND FAIREST: Ian Gillett
LEADING GOALKICKER: Eddie Lane (36)

The Sporting Globe reported: "It was an amazing finish. Just when South Melbourne seemed to have the game sewn up the

Demons, beaten all day, suddenly produced a superhuman effort to snatch the game in the last few minutes." Gunn kicked four goals for the Swans, with Eddie Lane, Ken McCormack and Jim Dorgan named among the red and white's best players.

Melbourne's remarkable comeback victory stunned the Swans and they dropped consecutive matches to Essendon and Collingwood before a mid-season break for a Victoria-Western Australia clash at the MCG. Sibun was South's sole representative in the 29-point defeat of the Sandgropers in atrocious conditions as Gunn was a late withdrawal because of an ankle injury.

South might have defeated North Melbourne by 12 points in the round played after the break, but its finals hopes were forlorn as it trailed fourth-placed Footscray, the reigning premier, by 16 match points after the completion of 11 rounds. The Swans' only win over the rest of the season was by 29 points against St Kilda at the Junction Oval in round 16. The Swans led by just 12 points at the final change, but *The Sporting Globe* reported that "a strong finish" lifted South to a big win, with Eddie Lane kicking four goals.

Although South again finished tenth, it had the joy of celebrating yet another Brownlow Medal triumph when full-back Fred Goldsmith polled 21 votes to pip Essendon rover Bill Hutchison by one vote. Goldsmith, a fireman, was on duty at the Eastern Hill station when he was declared the winner. He was playing snooker as the count was broadcast on radio, but did not take any notice until 3KZ commentator Norman Banks called to tell him he was leading. Goldsmith immediately headed for the mess room where he and his mates tuned in for the rest of the count. "The whole place erupted when I was announced the winner," Goldsmith later recalled.

Bill Gunn was a superb footballer, who could play in the centre or at half-forward.

As Goldsmith was rostered on duty until 11pm, he rang Fire Brigade chief L.P. Whitehead, who also was the VFL Tribunal chairman, to ask whether he could knock off early. Whitehead told him he could leave, so Goldsmith drove home to Williamstown. As he pulled up outside the family home, all his friends and neighbours were there to greet the latest member of the Brownlow Medal club. From there, Goldsmith went to the Lake Oval to celebrate with teammates over two barrels of beer donated by the club. Amazingly, however, Goldsmith did not win South's best and fairest in 1955, that honour going to ruckman/forward Ian Gillett, with rover Eddie Lane runner-up.

1956

South was buoyed at the start of 1956 by news that Ron Clegg and Jim Taylor had returned to the Lake Oval. Clegg had spent 1955 as captain-coach of North Albury, but he and wife Billye missed the city and decided to return to Melbourne. Taylor, who had played with South Australian club Norwood in 1955, also decided to resume his career with the Swans. Despite Clegg's return, South appointed ruckman/forward Ian Gillett captain, with Herbie Matthews again coach.

The official South training list for 1956, published in *The Age* in the lead-up to the opening round, therefore not only looked unusual with the return of these stars, but contained one other name destined to become familiar with all football fans — R. Skilton.

South issued this list of newcomers: G. Crough (St Patrick's, Ballarat), R. Clegg (North Wagga), E. Hicks (Stanhope), B. Jeffreys (R.A.N.), D. Matthews (Thirds), J. Monks (Essendon), T. Ryan (Seconds), R. Skilton (Fourths), J. Taylor (Norwood) and M. Younger (St Patrick's, Ballarat).

Of course, Bob Skilton went on to become arguably the greatest player in club history, while Gerald Crough and Marshall Younger were handy players for the Swans. They had signed with the Swans as a pair as they were schoolmates and did not want to play against each other at VFL level. Crough played 56 games to 1962 and Younger 41 games to 1961. Monks, a rover, played just 14 games over the 1956-57 seasons.

The Swans opened the 1956 season against Geelong at the Lake Oval, with Crough, Matthews and Ellis Hicks named for their VFL debuts. Clegg played at centre half-forward and Taylor resumed duties as the club's number one ruckman. After being level with Geelong at half-time,

South eventually went down by 27 points and *The Sporting Globe* suggested that the Cats were "too solid and steady" for the Swans. However, the match report also suggested Fred Goldsmith was in top early form and had the better of Cat full-forward Noel Rayson.

According to *The Sporting Globe,* Collingwood "swept South aside" in round two at Victoria Park to win by 37 points, but

Back pocket Jim Dorgan, the Swans' 1956 best and fairest.

MATCH RESULTS

Round 1, at Lake Oval, April 14
Geelong 11.11 (77) d South Melbourne 7.8 (50)

Round 2, at Victoria Park, April 21
Collingwood 12.18 (90) d South Melbourne 7.11 (53)

Round 3, at Brunswick Street, April 28
Fitzroy 13.16 (94) d South Melbourne 10.13 (73)

Round 4, at Lake Oval, May 5
Hawthorn 8.11 (59) d South Melbourne 6.17 (53)

Round 5, at Western Oval, May 12
Footscray 9.13 (67) d South Melbourne 8.9 (57)

Round 6, at Lake Oval, May 19
South Melbourne 15.8 (98) d Essendon 11.20 (86)

Round 7, at Arden Street, May 26
North Melb. 15.7 (97) d South Melbourne 7.16 (58)

Round 8, at Punt Road, June 4
South Melbourne 12.6 (78) d Richmond 10.15 (75)

Round 9, at Lake Oval, June 9
South Melbourne 14.5 (89) d St Kilda 11.8 (74)

Round 10, at MCG, June 23
Melbourne 12.10 (82) d South Melbourne 8.11 (59)

Round 11, at Lake Oval, June 30
South Melbourne 9.19 (73) d Carlton 7.12 (54)

Round 12, at Kardinia Park, July 7
Geelong 10.7 (67) d South Melbourne 3.8 (26)

Round 13, at Lake Oval, July 14
Collingwood 11.9 (75) d South Melbourne 10.9 (69)

Round 14, at Lake Oval, July 21
Fitzroy 15.15 (105) d South Melbourne 11.15 (81)

Round 15, at Glenferrie Oval, July 28
South Melb. 12.6 (78) drew with Hawthorn 10.18 (78)

Round 16, at Lake Oval, August 4
South Melbourne 10.10 (70) d Footscray 8.15 (63)

Round 17, at Windy Hill, August 11
Essendon 11.10 (76) d South Melbourne 7.16 (58)

Round 18, at Lake Oval, August 18
South Melbourne 13.9 (87) d North Melb. 7.13 (55)

conceded that South showed "great courage in battling it out throughout". Clegg kicked three of South's seven goals and South badly missed star half-forward flanker Bill Gunn, who was injured in the opening round clash with Geelong. It might have been a significant margin, but there was a pointer to the future when the Swans announced the team on the Thursday night. Listed among the three emergencies was the unknown R. Skilton, along with "Mick" Sibun and Neil McNeill.

Then, after South went down to Fitzroy and Hawthorn over the next two rounds, the selectors no longer could ignore Skilton's credentials. He was named first rover for the round five match against Footscray at the Western Oval as one of three team changes. Younger and Bob Pratt also were included, while Jim Taylor was unavailable because of injury and Don Matthews and Clarrie Lane were dropped.

The 17-year-old Skilton had started the season in the Under 19s, but was quickly promoted to the reserves before being named for his debut against the Bulldogs. Skilton won the first kick of the match and never again played in the reserves. The Bulldogs defeated South by 10 points and although Skilton was not named among the Swans' best players, he quickly made a name for himself as an emerging champion.

South notched its first win of the season in defeating Essendon by 12 points at the Lake Oval in round six and, this time, Skilton won rave reviews. *The Age*, under the headline SOUTH DESERVED FIRST VICTORY, noted: "Skilton's aggressive, fearless roving, backed up by deadly accuracy around goals, fully capitalised ruck drive stemming from Keyter, Gillett and Ferguson."

Skilton kicked five goals in just his second match and *The Sporting Globe* named him best player on the ground. The reporter, Cyril Nott, wrote of one Skilton goal: "They (the Swans) found Skilton who, with the confidence of a veteran, scored another goal." The 21,000 fans at the Lake Oval that afternoon saw enough to suggest that the young Skilton one day would be a champion.

The Kia-Ora Sports Parade radio show was enormously popular in the 1950s and featured a different VFL club each week.

Skilton was off-target in scoring just four behinds in the 39-point defeat by North Melbourne at Arden Street the following week, but it was an aberration as he showed over the rest of the season that he truly was "deadly" with either foot. Skilton kicked four goals in the round nine match against St Kilda at the Lake Oval and played a vital part in the Swans' 15-point defeat of the Saints.

Skilton's form was the only ray of sunshine in an otherwise disastrous season for the Swans. South in 1956 was savaged by injuries, with several stars players missing for large chunks of the season. For example, Bill Gunn fractured an elbow after falling heavily over Geelong's Norm Sharp in the round 12 match at Kardinia Park. It was a bitter blow, especially as South kicked just three goals (by Gunn, Skilton and Matthews) in the 41-point loss to Geelong. Gunn, to the time he was injured, was second on the VFL goalkicking list with 28, two fewer than St Kilda's Bill Young.

To add insult to injury, Clegg was reported for allegedly striking Hawthorn's Norm Maginness in the draw at the Glenferrie Oval in round 15. Clegg was cleared by the VFL Tribunal, but it was yet another distraction in a season in which little went right for the Swans except for Skilton's emergence as a future champion.

South finished the season in ninth position,

Ruckman Jim Taylor, runner-up in the Swans' 1956 best and fairest.

only a slight improvement on 1955 when it had been without Clegg and Taylor. Apart from Skilton's emergence, however, there were other highlights. Back pocket Jim Dorgan polled 15 Brownlow Medal votes to finish third behind Footscray's Peter Box (22 votes) and Geelong's Peter Pianto (16). Dorgan had joined the Swans in 1951 after playing three games with Melbourne in 1950 and he and full-back Fred Goldsmith formed a wonderful last-line partnership.

The Swans also won the inaugural night premiership in defeating Carlton by six points in the Grand Final in front of 32,450 fans at the Lake Oval.

PLAYER	GAMES	GOALS
BIGGS, Stan	2	0
CAMPBELL, Neville	1	0
CLEGG, Ron	16	15
CROUGH, Gerald	8	0
DORGAN, Jim	18	0
ELDER, John	16	0
EVANS, Barry	3	1
FERGUSON, John	8	3
GILLETT, Ian	13	7
GOLDSMITH, Fred	16	16
GRANT, Trevor	7	0
GUNN, Bill	8	28
HICKS, Ellis	5	1
HOGAN, Kevin	16	3
HUDSON, Jack	8	0
JEFFREYS, Bernie	4	7
KEYTER, Don	17	16
LANE, Clarrie	6	5
LANE, Esmond "Eddie"	8	5
LEDWIDGE, John	11	2
LESLIE, Lewis	2	0
MATTHEWS, Don	15	7
McCORMACK, Ken	8	2
McDONALD, Gerry	6	0
McLAUGHLIN, Hugh	8	0
McNEILL, Neil	4	1
MELESSO, Neil	3	0
MONKS, Ian	12	7
NELSON, Daryl	4	0
OATEN, Max	5	5
PRATT, Bob Jnr	11	6
PRIMMER, Frank	8	0
REED, Ray	1	0
RYAN, Peter	2	0
SEYMOUR, Ken	6	5
SIBUN, Gray "Mick"	15	6
SKILTON, Bob	14	17
TAGLIABUE, Gerald	5	0
TAYLOR, Jim	15	1
TAYLOR, Ron	1	0
TRETHOWAN, John	16	1
YOUNGER, Marshall	8	2

POSITION: Ninth
COACH: Herbie Matthews
CAPTAIN: Ian Gillett
BEST AND FAIREST: Jim Dorgan
LEADING GOALKICKER: Bill Gunn (28)

1957

Despite a lack of progress over the 1954-56 seasons, Herbie Matthews was coach again in 1957, with Ron Clegg taking over from Ian Gillett as captain. Rover Eddie Lane was cleared to country club Bairnsdale and Gray "Mick" Sibun left for Rupanyup after the 1956 season and this would have left South vulnerable around the packs if it had not been for the emergence of Bob Skilton the previous season.

The Age published the training lists for all 12 VFL clubs in the lead-up to the new season and listed South's newcomers as: P. Appleyard (Wodonga), K. Boyd and B. Faulkner (Thirds), J. Cairns (Spotswood), C. Colquhoun (Emerald), W. Egan, F. Harris and E. Gleeson (Seconds), R. Evans (Newport), J. Heriot (Spotswood), J. Kelton (Hampton Rovers), S. O'Neill (Yarram), J. Phillips (Eaglehawk) and J. Svenson (Murchison). Svenson already had played for the Swans on permit, but was classed as a newcomer, while Boyd and Heriot later left their mark in the red and white.

Fred Goldsmith was a regular selection for Victoria.

Boyd developed into the team "protector" as a hard-hitting follower and played 60 games with the Swans to a sensational incident involving Carlton's John Nicholls in 1961. Heriot, who did not make his senior debut until the following season, developed into a champion full-back who was named in the Swans' Team of the Century. He played 153 games for the Swans to 1968.

South opened its 1957 season with an Easter Saturday match against St Kilda at the Junction Oval. The Swans included two newcomers — Colquhoun at full-back and Stan O'Neill on a half-forward flank. The selection of Colquhoun in the key defensive position was to allow regular full-back Fred Goldsmith to play at centre half-back and, later in the season, on the forward line.

St Kilda defeated South by 29 points and *The Age* reported that "St Kilda's ambitious team of youngsters baffled South Melbourne with initiative in the first half". *The Sporting Globe* described the Saints as "fanatical" and

Full-forward John Svenson was known as the "Blond Bombshell".

MATCH RESULTS

Round 1, at Junction Oval, April 20
St Kilda 12.16 (88) d South Melbourne 7.17 (59)

Round 2, at Lake Oval, April 27
Carlton 10.16 (76) d South Melbourne 6.16 (52)

Round 3, at Lake Oval, May 4
South Melbourne 19.16 (130) d Richmond 13.9 (87)

Round 4, at Victoria Park, May 11
Collingwood 14.9 (93) d South Melbourne 11.17 (83)

Round 5, at Lake Oval, May 18
Essendon 14.16 (100) d South Melbourne 7.16 (58)

Round 6, at MCG, May 25
Melbourne 17.12 (114) d South Melbourne 6.15 (51)

Round 7, at Lake Oval, June 1
North Melb. 11.13 (79) d South Melbourne 11.9 (75)

Round 8, at Lake Oval, June 8
Hawthorn 13.11 (89) d South Melbourne 9.14 (68)

Round 9, at Western Oval, June 17
Footscray 12.15 (87) d South Melbourne 8.12 (60)

Round 10, at Kardinia Park, June 22
South Melbourne 10.10 (70) d Geelong 10.8 (68)

Round 11, at Lake Oval, June 29
South Melbourne 15.19 (109) d Fitzroy 14.12 (96)

Round 12, at Lake Oval, July 6
South Melbourne 11.15 (81) d St Kilda 9.17 (71)

Round 13, at Princes Park, July 13
Carlton 11.15 (81) d South Melbourne 10.5 (65)

Round 14, at Punt Road, July 27
South Melbourne 11.12 (78) d Richmond 10.13 (73)

Round 15, at Lake Oval, August 3
Collingwood 12.19 (91) d South Melbourne 9.13 (67)

Round 16, at Windy Hill, August 10
Essendon 10.15 (75) d South Melbourne 7.13 (55)

Round 17, at Lake Oval, August 17
South Melbourne 11.9 (75) d Melbourne 9.17 (71)

Round 18, at Arden Street, August 24
South Melb. 17.11 (113) d North Melb. 10.20 (80)

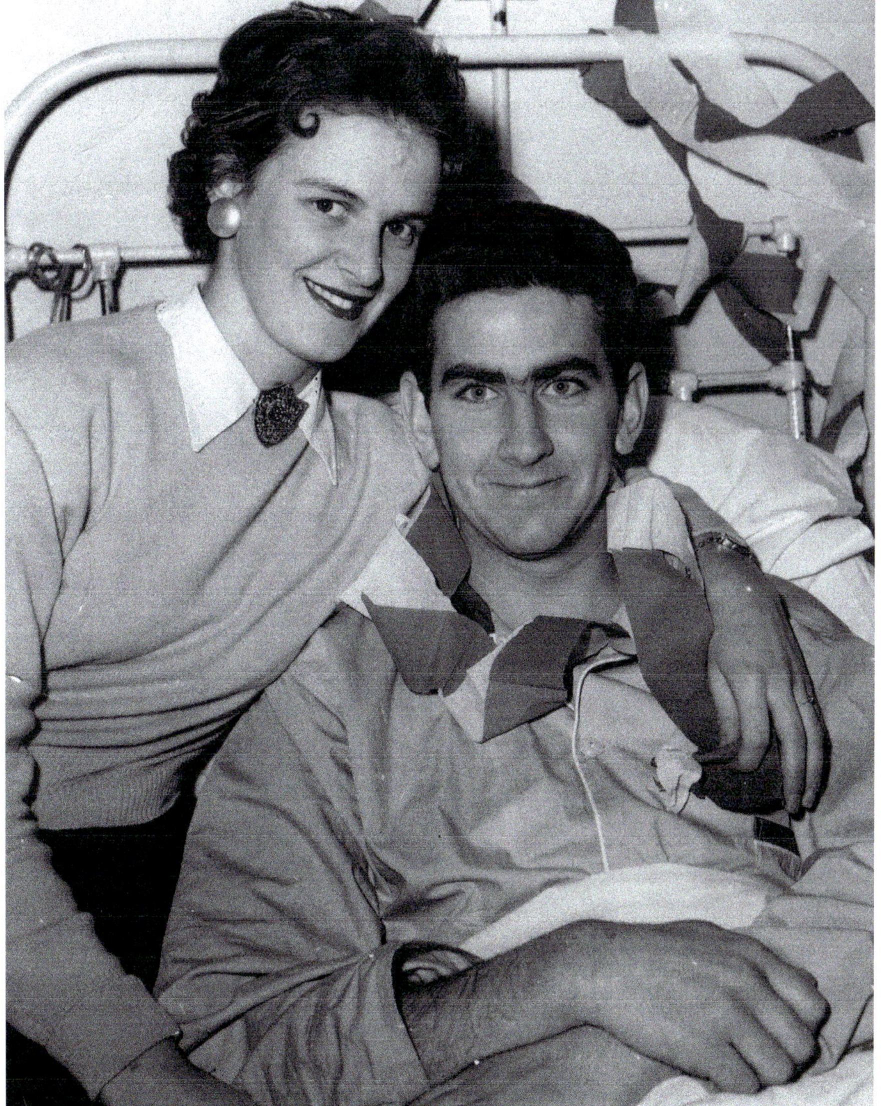

Ruckman John Ledwidge injured a knee in 1957 and is pictured here with fiancée Bev after a cartilage operation.

reporter Peter Bye suggested they would be "one of the glamour teams of the season". However, he praised newcomer Colquhoun in writing — "A great game at full-back and held (Bill) Young early." Rover Brian McGowan, who had played one game in his debut season of 1955, also won praise for his four goals and good play around the ground and Bye suggested he looked "a ready-made star". McGowan went on to form a tremendous roving partnership with Skilton.

The Swans again had started a season poorly and, in going down to Carlton by 24 points at the Lake Oval in round two, *The Sporting Globe* described the Swans as "mediocre". Colquhoun again won praise, as did O'Neill, but the side copped a roasting from Matthews at half-time after scoring just one

goal (by Bill Gunn) to the main break. Goldsmith, who had lined up at centre half-forward, was named South's best player.

South broke through the following week when it defeated Richmond by 43 points at the Lake Oval, with Goldsmith kicking nine goals as full-forward. *The Age* match headline read GOLDSMITH LIFTS SOUTH TO WIN. The copy read: "A scintillating display at full-forward by 1955 Brownlow Medallist Fred Goldsmith meant the difference between victory and defeat for South Melbourne against Richmond on Saturday. Goldsmith lifted what was a hesitant, lumbering group of individuals in the first 15 minutes into a confident, aggressive striking force." McGowan chipped in with three goals, while Clegg and Percy Appleyard kicked two each.

Although South had started slowly and led by just three points at the first break, it kicked six goals to one in the second quarter and Goldsmith, almost unbeatable, had seven goals by the main break. *The Sporting Globe* headline read SWANS KILL TIGERS and reporter Peter Henry described Goldsmith's performance as "inspirational".

The big win should have been a launching pad for a push towards the top, but South then suffered six consecutive losses to wallow at the bottom of the ladder. At the completion of round eight, South had won just the one game and was propping up the rest of the competition and seemingly headed for a wooden-spoon. In fact, the Swans were playing so poorly that Matthews dropped Gunn to the reserves for the round six match against Melbourne. *The Age* described this move as "the team's most drastic shake-up this season".

South's two-point defeat of Geelong at Kardinia Park in round 10 was such a huge upset that *The Sporting Globe's* front page splash headline read SHOCKS GALORE TODAY IN LEAGUE. Inside, there was a full match report under the headline SOUTH HANGS ON FOR TWO POINT WIN. South, after a sluggish start, led from halfway through the second quarter and led by almost three goals with just minutes to play. However, the Cats scored two late goals and only strong marking by Swans Ian Gillett and Jack Hudson held Geelong at bay.

PLAYER	GAMES	GOALS
APPLEYARD, Percy	4	2
BOYD, Ken	9	6
CAIRNS, Jim	1	0
CAMPBELL, Neville	5	0
CLEGG, Ron	17	13
COLQUHOUN, Colin	6	0
CROUGH, Gerald	6	0
DORGAN, Jim	12	2
ELDER, John	1	0
FAULKHEAD, Brian	1	0
FERGUSON, John	3	1
GILLETT, Ian	16	1
GOLDSMITH, Fred	13	43
GUNN, Bill	9	3
HAMILTON, John	9	0
HARRIS, Fred	5	0
HOGAN, Kevin	13	10
HUDSON, Jack	15	0
KELTON, John	6	3
KEYTER, Don	15	16
KITELY, Jeff	2	1
KNIGHT, Alan	3	0
LANE, Clarrie	5	0
LEDWIDGE, John	3	0
MATTHEWS, Don	10	7
McCORMACK, Ken	10	2
McGOWAN, Brian	12	13
McLAUGHLIN, Hugh	17	1
MONKS, Ian	2	0
OATEN, Max	11	10
O'NEILL, Stan	11	4
POWER, Bill	13	2
PRATT, Bob Jnr	2	0
PRIMMER, Frank	5	2
RYAN, Peter	5	0
SEYMOUR, Ken	2	0
SKILTON, Bob	17	22
SVENSON, John	12	11
TAGLIABUE, Gerald	12	2
TAYLOR, Jim	15	2
TRETHOWAN, John	10	0
TRICKEY, Ern	4	4
YOUNGER, Marshall	7	1

POSITION: Tenth
COACH: Herbie Matthews
CAPTAIN: Ron Clegg
BEST AND FAIREST: Jim Taylor
LEADING GOALKICKER: Fred Goldsmith (43)

The win was even more amazing considering South was without Goldsmith and Jim Taylor because of their selection for the Victorian team against South Australia in Adelaide. Goldsmith played at full-back in Victoria's 16-point defeat of the Croweaters, while Taylor started on the bench and replaced Collingwood's Murray Weideman at three-quarter time.

The Swans then climbed off the bottom of the ladder into ninth position when they defeated Fitzroy by 13 points at the Lake Oval the following week. South, despite its woeful early season form, finished with a flourish and won six of its last nine games and even defeated top side Melbourne by four points at the Lake Oval in the penultimate round.

Melbourne was a game and a half on top when it took the field against South, with most commentators tipping a Demon romp. The Swans, however, started brilliantly and led the Demons by 18 points at half-time. Melbourne then kicked five third-quarter goals and went into the final break with an eight-point lead. South had been gallant, but Melbourne looked likely to run away for an easy win.

South hit back with a goal from John Kelton following a brilliant mark, but Melbourne still led by two points deep into time-on. South, in one last, desperate move, rushed the ball forward to the grandstand end of the Lake Oval. Ruckman Don Keyter was replacing a boot with the help of a trainer when he saw the chance to win possession. Brushing the trainer aside, he won possession and snapped a goal a split-second before the siren blared. South had won by four points and Swan fans swamped their heroes in the excitement of a comeback victory against the top side and reigning premier.

The Swans finished the season in tenth position, with seven wins and 11 defeats. The move of Goldsmith to the forward line had been successful, but the Swans lacked depth and consistency. Ruckman Jim Taylor not only won the club best and fairest, but was fourth in the Brownlow Medal. He polled 16 votes and was headed by St Kilda's Brian Gleeson (24 votes), Richmond's Roy Wright (20) and Carlton's John James (19).

South completed the 1957 season with a 51-point defeat of Geelong in the night series Grand Final in front of 25,000 fans at the Lake Oval.

Injured Swan stars Jim Taylor (left), Ron Clegg (centre) and Bill Gunn watch training. Note the cigarette in Taylor's right hand.

1958

After four years as coach without South Melbourne finishing higher than ninth, Herbie Matthews was replaced by Ron Clegg as coach. Clegg, to the start of the 1958 season, had played 184 games with the Swans and was one of only three Swans with 100 games or more experience, along with Ian Gillett (119) and Jim Taylor (111). They were joined during the season by Fred Goldsmith and Jim Dorgan, who both ended the season on 101 games.

South in 1958 desperately lacked experience, but recruited just two players from rival VFL clubs. The Swans, in a desperate bid to bolster their goalkicking, recruited Geelong full-forward Noel Rayson, who had topped the VFL goalkicking with 80 in 1955. However, he played just 12 games over two seasons with the Swans. South also recruited 1954 Footscray premiership defender Ron Stockman, who played 23 games with the Swans to 1961.

Keen to turn over talent, the Swans gave nine youngsters their VFL debuts in 1958, with John Heriot playing seven games in his first season and Terry Brain, son of former champion rover Terry Snr, just the one.

South opened the season against Richmond at the Lake Oval, but was dealt a blow pre-match when Gillett had to pull out of the side because of tonsillitis and was replaced by John Trethowan. The Tigers defeated the Swans by 25 points and *The Sporting Globe* reported that Richmond was "more systematic" that South. The Swans failed to score in the third quarter and, at one stage, scored 11 consecutive behinds. Chief culprit was Fred Goldsmith, who kicked 2.9. Bob Skilton also was inaccurate with 3.4.

St Kilda's Neil Roberts, due to play his 100th VFL game congratulates South's Ron Clegg in the lead-up to the Swan champion's 200th game.

The Swans had gone into the match against Richmond without any first-game players but introduced two newcomers for the round two match against Fitzroy at the Brunswick Street Oval. *The Sporting Globe*, under the headline HOW THE RECRUITS FARED had this to say of the new Swan pair: "Alan Dawson (Flinders Naval Base) — A solid type of player who did better in defence than in the ruck. Could make good. Malcolm Smith (Eaglehawk) — Was paid a wonderful compliment when switched to (Don) Furness in the centre. He looks as if he could develop."

Furness had dominated for the Lions over the first three quarters and *The Sporting Globe* suggested that Fitzroy's centreline brilliance

MATCH RESULTS

Round 1, at Lake Oval, April 12
Richmond 17.18 (120) d South Melbourne 12.23 (95)

Round 2, at Brunswick Street, April 19
Fitzroy 11.18 (84) d South Melbourne 10.15 (75)

Round 3, at Lake Oval, April 26
Footscray 24.13 (157) d South Melbourne 13.18 (96)

Round 4, at Kardinia Park, May 3
South Melbourne 8.12 (60) d Geelong 8.11 (59)

Round 5, at Lake Oval, May 10
St Kilda 13.15 (93) d South Melbourne 14.8 (92)

Round 6, at Glenferrie Oval, May 17
Hawthorn 11.15 (81) d South Melbourne 8.16 (64)

Round 7, at Lake Oval, May 24
South Melbourne 10.19 (79) d Carlton 7.15 (57)

Round 8, at Victoria Park, May 31
Collingwood 20.20 (140) d South Melb. 9.12 (66)

Round 9, at Lake Oval, June 7
Melbourne 16.12 (108) d South Melbourne 11.10 (76)

Round 10, at Arden Street, June 16
North Melb. 12.15 (87) d South Melbourne 8.9 (57)

Round 11, at Lake Oval, June 21
Essendon 15.13 (103) d South Melbourne 8.13 (61)

Round 12, at Punt Road, June 28
Richmond 12.13 (85) d South Melbourne 11.8 (74)

Round 13, at Lake Oval, July 19
South Melbourne 19.6 (120) d Fitzroy 11.22 (88)

Round 14, at Western Oval, July 26
South Melbourne 14.12 (96) d Footscray 8.15 (63)

Round 15, at Lake Oval, August 2
South Melbourne 16.13 (109) d Geelong 14.17 (101)

Round 16, at Junction Oval, August 9
South Melbourne 15.9 (99) d St Kilda 9.23 (77)

Round 17, at Lake Oval, August 16
South Melbourne 6.14 (50) d Hawthorn 6.12 (48)

Round 18, at Princes Park, August 23
Carlton 12.11 (83) d South Melbourne 10.21 (81)

was the main factor in the home side defeating the Swans by nine points. South's forwards again struggled, even though Clegg was named his side's best player at centre half-forward. Skilton, Jim Dorgan and Gerald Tagliabue also were named among the Swans' best.

Clegg did not taste success as captain-coach until the Swans defeated Geelong by just one point at Kardinia Park in round four. South squeaked home courtesy of a late goal by Goldsmith and *The Sporting Globe* reported: "South recorded their first win for the season by defeating the pacy Geelong by a point. A winning ruck and clever rovers enabled South to counter Geelong's speed. Another factor in South's win was the steadiness of their defenders." Skilton (four of South's eight goals), Goldsmith, and Kevin Hogan were named South's best players.

South might have been jubilant following its one-point victory, but was on the wrong end of a one-point result against St Kilda at the Lake Oval the following week. The Saints led by nine points at the final break but a goal by Smith gave the Swans hope of a comeback win. South even levelled the scores through a Gerald Brennan behind in his debut game, but the Saints rushed another score to win by the barest possible margin. Skilton again was South's only reliable goalkicker with four.

Although South defeated Carlton by 22 points at the Lake Oval in round seven, it struggled through the middle stages of the season and, by the completion of round 12, was on the bottom of the ladder. The VFL season then went into recess for the interstate Carnival in Melbourne, with one game — South Australia versus Western Australia — played at South's Lake Oval under lights on a Wednesday night.

Victoria opened the Carnival with a 118-point thumping of SA at the MCG, with Skilton South's sole representative. He kicked two goals and was joined by Goldsmith for the match against WA. The Vics struggled to defeat the Sandgropers by 19 points, but while Goldsmith was named among the Big Vee's best players, Skilton corked a thigh in the second quarter. Unfortunately for Skilton, he could not leave the ground as Victoria already had used its two reserves and Skilton therefore had to hobble near the forward goal square for the entire second half.

Skilton's "corky" was so severe than he was unable to take his place in the South side for the round 13 match against Fitzroy at the Lake Oval. But, even without their star rover, the Swans were able to defeat the Lions by 32 points. Goldsmith starred at centre half-forward and Brian McGowan had a sensational game as first rover in Skilton's place. *The Sporting Globe* match report headline read SOUTH MAKE LIONS MICE. The report said: "South Melbourne, with their big men on top and forwards uncannily accurate, convincingly downed Fitzroy at South Melbourne ... Brian McGowan, who scored four goals, was South's match-winner with his pace and goal sense."

South then climbed off the bottom of the ladder the following week in defeating Footscray by 33 points at the Western Oval. Skilton, back for the Swans, kicked four goals, while McGowan and Goldsmith again were named among South's best players. The victory, described by *The Sporting Globe* as a "shock" result, pushed South above bottom-placed Geelong and the following week at the Lake Oval, made sure of avoiding the wooden-spoon in defeating the Cats by eight points. Amazingly, South notched this victory despite ruckmen Jim Taylor and Don Keyter playing in the reserves match at Kardinia Park that afternoon.

The Swans, using Gillett and Ken Boyd in the ruck, led for most of the match but had to hold off a fast-finishing Geelong. Goldsmith again was named South's best player, while McGowan kicked another four goals. The Swans continued their amazing run in defeating St Kilda by 22 points at the Junction Oval the following week. This game was marked by two Brownlow Medal milestones as Clegg played his 200th VFL game and St Kilda's Neil Roberts, who went on to win the 1958 Brownlow played his 100th game.

South continued its great late-season run with a two-point win over Hawthorn at the Lake Oval to make it five in a row. Rayson kicked the winning goal for South, but the margin could have been greater as a shot by Goldsmith just before the final siren was touched on the line. *The Sporting Globe* reported that "a huge crowd swarmed onto the ground" to cheer the Swans. The newspaper also commented on South: "At last the team is producing the form it showed in pre-season training."

It was all far too late and although the Swans were gallant in going down to Carlton by two points at Princes Park, they finished the season with seven wins and 11 defeats. As a pointer to the future, Skilton polled 19 votes to finish third in the Brownlow Medal, behind St Kilda's Roberts (24 votes) and Hawthorn's Brendan Edwards (22). Amazingly, South's Bill Gunn was the early runaway leader and had polled three best on ground votes before any of the top three had scored. Gunn, however, finished fifth with 16 votes.

PLAYER	GAMES	GOALS
BOYD, Ken	10	5
BRAIN, Terry	1	0
BRENNAN, Gerald	4	2
CAMPBELL, Neville	3	1
CLEGG, Ron	18	5
CROUGH, Gerald	6	1
DAWSON, Alan	2	0
DORGAN, Jim	16	0
GILLETT, Ian	16	0
GOLDSMITH, Fred	18	33
GUNN, Bill	16	2
HAMILTON, John	7	0
HARRIS, Fred	7	0
HERIOT, John	7	1
HOGAN, Frank	3	4
HOGAN, Kevin	10	7
HUDSON, Jack	10	0
KELTON, John	5	1
KEYTER, Don	11	11
KITELEY, Jeff	4	1
LEDWIDGE, John	7	3
LEWIS, Terry	3	0
MATTHEWS, Don	6	0
McCORMACK, Ken	14	2
McGOWAN, Brian	15	22
McLAUGHLIN, Hugh	13	0
OATEN, Max	15	34
POWER, Bill	3	2
PRATT, Bob Jnr	7	5
RAYSON, Noel	6	11
SKILTON, Bob	16	29
SMITH, Mal	5	6
STOCKMAN, Ron	10	0
SVENSON, John	8	2
TAGLIABUE, Gerald	12	4
TAMPION, Ian	9	1
TAYLOR, Jim	9	0
THOMPSON, Don	1	0
THRETHOWAN, John	13	0
YOUNGER, Marshall	14	1

POSITION: Ninth
COACH: Ron Clegg
CAPTAIN: Ron Clegg
BEST AND FAIREST: Bob Skilton
LEADING GOALKICKER: Max Oaten (34)

1959

Veteran Ron Clegg remained as captain-coach for 1959 but, at 31 years of age, was nearing the end of his magnificent career. He was still an inspiration to younger Swans, but no longer was able to win matches off his own boot. Besides, Clegg in 1959 was handicapped by the retirement of several key players of the previous few seasons. Former captain Ian Gillett, ruckman/forward Don Keyter and back pocket specialist Jim Dorgan ended their VFL careers at the end of 1958 and Clegg therefore was left with an inexperienced list.

Gillett, Keyter and Dorgan all joined country clubs, with Gillett going to the NSW club of Coolamon, Keyter to Griffith and Dorgan to Moe. Besides, Bob Pratt Junior returned to his old suburban club Canterbury, John Ledwidge went to Golden Square and Malcolm Smith to Wedderburn. South had five players with 100 or more games' experience in Clegg, Jim Taylor, Fred Goldsmith, Noel Rayson and Bill Gunn but there was little middle-experience and, to fill gaps, the Swans recruited 1956 Richmond best and fairest Laurie Sharp and Footscray's Ray Broadway.

In the week leading up to the opening round, *The Age* published the 12 VFL club final training lists, with South nominating the following newcomers: "P. Brigila (Seconds), R. Burke (Seconds), G. Burgess (Seconds), C. Deacon (Kyneton), R. Evans (Seconds), F. Hepner (Crib Point), R. Landorff (Port Melbourne), R. Marshall (Frankston), R. Munn (Thirds), W. McGrath (Minyip), N. McKenzie (Daylesford), P. Rice (Camberwell), L. Sharp (Richmond), B. Tarrant (Wentworth), L. Walker (Thirds), H. Wills (Minyip) and A. Wilson (Thirds)."

The arrival of Dick Burke and Hedley Wills at the same time led to reporters quipping that South was exploring its future courtesy of Burke and Wills. Burke developed into a fine ruckman for the Swans and played 66 games to 1963 and later served the club as vice-president, while Wills played just three games in the red and white.

Three of South's newly listed players — Ray Landorff, Norm McKenzie and Cliff Deacon — debuted in the opening round against reigning premier Collingwood at Victoria Park. Collingwood proudly unfurled its 1958 flag before the start of play and promptly was thrashed by the rampaging

Four great Swan Brownlow Medal winners, from left, Fred Goldsmith, Ron Clegg, Bob Skilton and Herbie Matthews. Skilton won the first of his medals in 1959.

MATCH RESULTS

Round 1, at Victoria Park, April 18
South Melb. 14.17 (101) d Collingwood 7.18 (60)

Round 2, at Lake Oval, May 2
South Melbourne 13.21 (99) d Fitzroy 12.11 (83)

Round 3, at Lake Oval, May 9
South Melbourne 9.11 (65) d Essendon 7.10 (52)

Round 4, at Glenferrie Oval, May 16
Hawthorn 19.14 (128) d South Melbourne 13.19 (97)

Round 5, at Western Oval, May 23
Footscray 17.11 (113) d South Melbourne 13.8 (86)

Round 6, at Lake Oval, May 30
North Melb. 13.18 (96) d South Melbourne 8.18 (66)

Round 7, at MCG, June 6
Melbourne 14.17 (101) d South Melbourne 8.8 (56)

Round 8, at Lake Oval, June 15
South Melbourne 16.13 (109) d St Kilda 7.11 (53)

Round 9, at Princes Park, June 27
South Melbourne 14.21 (105) d Carlton 14.11 (95)

Round 10, at Punt Road, July 4
South Melbourne 15.16 (106) d Richmond 10.13 (73)

Round 11, at Lake Oval, July 11
South Melbourne 17.16 (118) d Geelong 12.12 (84)

Round 12, at Lake Oval, July 18
Collingwood 12.13 (85) d South Melbourne 6.9 (45)

Round 13, at Brunswick Street, July 25
Fitzroy 13.19 (97) d South Melbourne 10.7 (67)

Round 14, at Windy Hill, August 1
Essendon 10.19 (79) d South Melbourne 8.14 (62)

Round 15, at Lake Oval, August 8
Hawthorn 10.3 (63) d South Melbourne 8.14 (62)

Round 16, at Lake Oval, August 15
Footscray 12.13 (85) d South Melbourne 11.10 (76)

Round 17, at Arden Street, August 22
South Melbourne 19.20 (134) d North Melb. 6.6 (42)

Round 18, at Lake Oval, August 29
Melbourne 10.16 (76) d South Melbourne 8.13 (61)

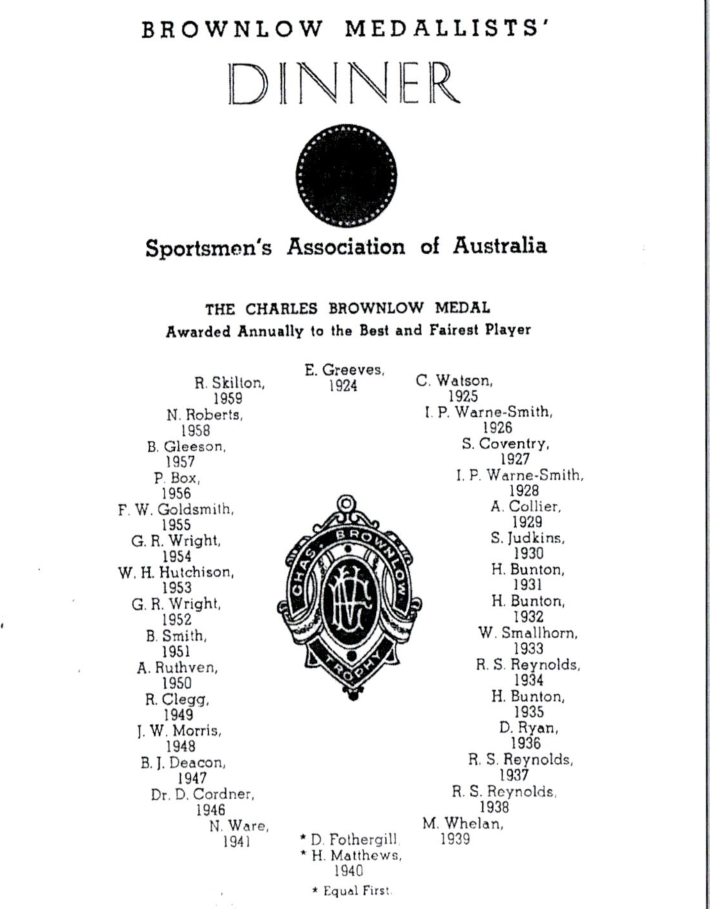

BROWNLOW MEDALLISTS'

DINNER

Sportsmen's Association of Australia

THE CHARLES BROWNLOW MEDAL
Awarded Annually to the Best and Fairest Player

E. Greeves, 1924
C. Watson, 1925
I. P. Warne-Smith, 1926
S. Coventry, 1927
I. P. Warne-Smith, 1928
A. Collier, 1929
S. Judkins, 1930
H. Bunton, 1931
H. Bunton, 1932
W. Smallhorn, 1933
R. S. Reynolds, 1934
H. Bunton, 1935
D. Ryan, 1936
R. S. Reynolds, 1937
R. S. Reynolds, 1938
M. Whelan, 1939
* D. Fothergill,
* H. Matthews, 1940
N. Ware, 1941
Dr. D. Cordner, 1946
B. J. Deacon, 1947
J. W. Morris, 1948
R. Clegg, 1949
A. Ruthven, 1950
B. Smith, 1951
G. R. Wright, 1952
W. H. Hutchison, 1953
G. R. Wright, 1954
F. W. Goldsmith, 1955
P. Box, 1956
B. Gleeson, 1957
N. Roberts, 1958
R. Skilton, 1959

* Equal First.

ST. KILDA TOWN HALL

Monday, September 21st, 1959

The Sportsmen's Association of Australia held a special dinner function to honour South's Bob Skilton after his 1959 Brownlow Medal triumph.

Swans. South scored five goals to one in the first quarter and never released its grip on the match points.

Former Collingwood champion Bill Twomey, writing in *The Sporting Globe*, reported: "It did my old heart good to see the Collingwood president's wife, Mrs Syd Coventry, unfurl the premiership flag to the strain of 'Good Old Collingwood Forever', but I'm afraid I can't let club parochialism creep into my copy. Old 'Smoky' Clegg and his Swans were nervous before the start of the game, but they showed no sign of it when umpire Nash made the first bounce. In the first 15 minutes South surprised Collingwood with fast, vigorous football and the ball seldom reached the Magpies' forward zone."

The Swans maintained the pressure to lead by 31 points at half-time and 40 points at the final break before cruising to a 41-point win. Collingwood fans were stunned and the front

South Melbourne Football Club

MEMBER'S TICKET, SEASON 1959

President: J. P. Cullen Esq.
Vice-Presidents: Messrs. A. Dark, J. McGenniss. R. Powell, R. Skilton and R. Warner.
Committee: Messrs R. Barrand, J. Bishop, K. Capp, R. Giles, P. Horner, H. McKay, R. Maslen, R. Ritchie and R. Tait.
Hon. Treasurer: Mr. C. Uniacke.
Secretary: Mr. J. J. White, 312 Albert Road, South Melbourne. MX2924.

IMPORTANT: Retain this ticket, as it must be produced to gain admission to the Annual Meeting of the Club. Only members whose names appear on the roll of members and who produce their membership tickets shall be entitled to vote at the Annual Meeting. To ensure that your name is recorded on such roll, please complete the address card issued with this ticket and place such card in the box at the entrance to the ground, or forward it to the Secretary.

M. R. L. McRostron

Not Transferable.

FIXTURES, 1959

DATE	CLUB	GROUND
April 18	Collingwood	Collingwood
May 2	Fitzroy	South Melb.
9	Essendon	South Melb.
16	Hawthorn	Hawthorn
23	Footscray	Footscray
30	North Melb.	South Melb.
June 6	Melbourne	Melbourne
15	St. Kilda	South Melb
27	Carlton	Carlton
July 4	Richmond	Richmond
11	Geelong	South Melb.
18	Collingwood	South Melb.
25	Fitzroy	Fitzroy
Aug. 1	Essendon	Essendon
8	Hawthorn	South Melb.
15	Footscray	South Melb.
22	North Melb.	North Melb.
29	Melbourne	South Melb.

No 1582

1959 CANCELLED

page splash headline in *The Sporting Globe* blared MIGHTY MAGPIES CANED! Merv Williams' report read: "South Melbourne caused the shock of the day by thrashing Collingwood, last year's premiers, by 41 points in a fiery game at Collingwood." Brian McGowan kicked four goals and Fred Goldsmith three and both were named in South's best, along with Clegg, Bob Skilton, Bill Gunn and John Heriot. Clegg was so delighted with the Swans' shock triumph that, before the team left Victoria Park, he assigned youngster Skilton to pull down the recently unfurled Magpie premiership flag.

South found itself in the unusual position of being on top of the ladder, with a percentage of 168.33. The win should have been the catalyst for a sustained charge to the finals and South fans were overjoyed when their team defeated Fitzroy by16 points at the Lake Oval in round two. Former Collingwood and Hawthorn rover Kevin Coghlan wrote in *The Sporting Globe:* "South showed that their win over last year's premier, Collingwood, was no fluke when they outpaced and out-thought Fitzroy today. Bob Skilton was the complete master and initiated many moves to keep South attacking."

South, at the completion of the second round was one of four undefeated teams, with Carlton, Melbourne and North Melbourne and continued its amazing run the following week against Essendon at the Lake Oval. The Swans defeated the Bombers by 13 points, but only thanks to a misunderstanding between forward Max Oaten and the selectors. With the Bombers pressing in the final quarter, Oaten was told to move from full-forward to a half-forward flank, but moved to the wrong side of the ground. However, just as he was about to move to the correct position he marked and kicked the sealing goal. South had had its best start to a season for years and was second on the ladder, behind Carlton on percentage.

The Swans then crashed back to earth at the Glenferrie Oval in round four. Hawthorn defeated South by 31 points, with Hawk full-forward John Peck kicking eight goals. South immediately slipped out of the four, to fifth

PLAYER	GAMES	GOALS
BOYD, Ken	14	7
BRIGLIA, Paul	6	5
BROADWAY, Ray	3	0
BURKE, Dick	13	9
CLEGG, Ron	16	8
CROUGH, Gerald	4	0
DEACON, Cliff	4	0
FALLON, Bill	3	0
GOLDSMITH, Fred	13	11
GUNN, Bill	14	1
HARRIS, Fred	7	0
HERIOT, John	18	0
HOGAN, Frank	9	2
HUDSON, Jack	2	1
KELTON, John	2	0
KITELEY, Jeff	6	0
LANDORFF, Ray	14	0
MARSHALL, Bob	8	0
McCORMACK, Ken	17	3
McGOWAN, Brian	18	31
McGRATH, Bill	15	18
McKENZIE, Norm	15	2
McLAUGHLIN, Hugh	17	0
MUNN, Bob	12	6
OATEN, Max	6	9
POWER, Bill	14	11
RAYSON, Noel	6	7
RICE, Peter	2	0
SHARP, Laurie	11	5
SKILTON, Bob	16	60
STOCKMAN, Ron	5	0
SVENSON, John	12	0
TAGLIABUE, Gerald	3	0
TAMPION, Ian	2	0
TAUBE, Greg	4	1
TAYLOR, Jim	14	6
TRETHOWAN, John	12	4
WILLS, Hedley	3	3

POSITION: Ninth
COACH: Ron Clegg
CAPTAIN: Ron Clegg
BEST AND FAIREST: Bob Skilton
LEADING GOALKICKER: Bob Skilton (60)

position, with worse to come over the next three weeks. After defeats by Footscray, North Melbourne and Melbourne, South looked to be out of the finals race in seventh position and with a poor percentage. South thrashed St Kilda by 56 points at the Lake Oval and this was followed by a week's break for a Victoria-Western Australia clash at the MCG on June 20.

Skilton was South's only representative in the 178-point romp in which WA kicked only three goals. However, McGowan and Bill Gunn represented a Victorian "B" side which defeated Tasmania by 55 points at Devonport the same afternoon. South's Jeff Kitely and Greg Taube played for a Victoria Seconds' side which defeated a South Australia Seconds side by 18 points in the curtain-raiser to the Victoria-WA clash at the MCG.

The home and away season resumed on June 27, with South defeating top side Carlton by 10 points at Princes Park in one of the most vicious matches for years. *The Sporting Globe* reported that there were "numerous unnecessary incidents" throughout the match. South's Landorff and Bill McGrath and Carlton's Graham Donaldson were reported, with Landorff and Donaldson both suspended for two matches and McGrath being reprimanded.

South, with that upset win, climbed back into finals contention as it was fifth and out of the top four by one game and percentage. Then, when South defeated Richmond by 33 points at Punt Road in round 10, the Swans were back inside the top four. It all depended on the run home and it all looked so promising when South defeated Geelong by 34 points at the Lake Oval in round 11.

However, Collingwood had taken the opening round defeat by South to heart and had its revenge in trouncing the Swans by 40 points at the Lake Oval the following week. The front page headline in *The Sporting Globe* read: MAGPIES "DROWN" SWANS. South, however, remained in the top four, on percentage ahead of St Kilda. South the following week slipped out of the four and into seventh position in going down to Fitzroy by 30 points at the Brunswick Street Oval and, from there, the Swans fell into freefall. Its only win over the rest of the season was by 92 points over North Melbourne at Arden Street in the penultimate round.

South, after looking likely to make the finals halfway through the season, finished ninth with eight wins and 10 defeats. However, there was unbridled Swan joy when Skilton polled 20 votes to win the Brownlow Medal on countback from St Kilda's Verdun Howell, who later was awarded a retrospective Brownlow. Skilton had had an outstanding season and was one of the favourites for the medal. However, he was doing a plumbing apprenticeship at the time and was at night school when voting started. When he reached home he noticed cars everywhere in his street and asked himself: "What's going on?" Someone told him "you've won the Brownlow Medal". Skilton was presented with his Brownlow, the first of three he won, before the first semi-final between Collingwood and Essendon at the MCG the following week.

The Southerly Bust-up

This is how cartoonist Wells saw South's defeat of Collingwood in the opening round of 1959.

1960

Highly respected football writer Alf Brown wrote in *The Herald* during the 1950s that South Melbourne needed coaching stability to return to a position of strength. After the dumping of Laurie Nash at the end of the 1953 season after just one season in charge, Brown argued that the Swans were too keen to switch coaches.

South seemed to take this advice in retaining Herbie Matthews' services as coach from 1954-57, but then played musical chairs yet again. Veteran Ron Clegg was captain-coach over the 1958-59 seasons, but the Swans felt they needed yet another new direction. They therefore appointed 1933 premiership half-back Bill Faul as coach, with Clegg retaining the captaincy for his final VFL season. Faul had had a wealth of coaching experience with VFA clubs Prahran (captain-coach from 1939-41), Northcote (1948 and 1953-56), Prahran (1949-52) and Moorabbin (1957-58).

Faul's task was monumental as South went into the new season without champion full-back Fred Goldsmith, who moved to captain-coach Albury, and the retired Bill Gunn. South also lost the services of several other players, including Jack Hudson (Ariah Park), John Svenson (South Warrnambool) and Gerald Tagliabue (Drouin).

It was obvious South would have to rely on youngsters and although it had signed talented Tasmanian Darrel Baldock, its hold on him expired and he not only joined St Kilda, but led the Saints to the 1966 premiership. *The Age,* in the lead-up to the 1960 season, listed South's newcomers as: P. Appleyard (Wodonga), K. Barrett (Stratford), B. Bennett (Woomelang), G. Brennan (Ararat), B. Chisholm (Berrigan), A. Dunn (Seconds), F. Johnson (South Warrnambool), J. Woolley (Bayswater), H. Wills (Minyip), M. Williams (North Melbourne) and R. Porta (Footscray). This list was slightly misleading as Percy Appleyard had played with South in 1957, Gerald Brennan had played with the Swans in 1958 and Hedley Wills had played three games in 1959.

The prize recruit was Frank Johnson, a hugely-talented ruckman who finally agreed to play with the Swans after years of rejecting all overtures. Johnson had been a star with VFA club Port Melbourne and had even been captain-coach of the Borough over the 1956-57 seasons before moving to South Warrnambool. He had represented the VFA in two interstate Carnivals and had won the J.J. Liston Trophy as VFA best and fairest in 1952. Johnson was just short of his 28th birthday when he made his debut with South in 1960, but looked as if he had been playing at the elite level for years and won the club best and fairest in his first season.

South opened the 1960 season against St

South coach Bill Faul addresses fans on the radio show Kia-Ora Sports Parade.

MATCH RESULTS

Round 1, at Lake Oval, April 16
South Melbourne 17.12 (114) d St Kilda 8.15 (63)

Round 2, at Kardinia Park, April 30
Geelong 20.14 (134) d South Melbourne 14.6 (90)

Round 3, at MCG, May 7
Melbourne 16.14 (110) d South Melbourne 6.10 (46)

Round 4, at Lake Oval, May 14
South Melbourne 11.12 (78) d North Melb. 5.8 (38)

Round 5, at Punt Road, May 21
Richmond 7.5 (47) d South Melbourne 4.7 (31)

Round 6, at Lake Oval, May 28
South Melbourne 12.8 (80) d Collingwood 11.12 (78)

Round 7, at Princes Park, June 4
South Melbourne 13.13 (91) d Carlton 11.13 (79)

Round 8, at Lake Oval, June 11
Fitzroy 13.13 (91) d South Melbourne 13.12 (90)

Round 9, at Windy Hill, June 18
Essendon 13.10 (88) d South Melbourne 12.15 (87)

Round 10, at Lake Oval, June 25
Hawthorn 13.6 (84) d South Melbourne 11.7 (73)

Round 11, at Western Oval, July 9
South Melbourne 8.9 (57) d Footscray 7.12 (54)

Round 12, at Junction Oval, July 16
St Kilda 11.13 (79) d South Melbourne 9.3 (57)

Round 13, at Lake Oval, July 23
South Melbourne 10.20 (80) d Geelong 11.13 (79)

Round 14, at Lake Oval, July 30
Melbourne 16.13 (109) d South Melbourne 10.10 (70)

Round 15, at Arden Street, August 6
North Melb. 14.16 (100) d South Melbourne 9.20 (74)

Round 16, at Lake Oval, August 13
South Melbourne 13.13 (91) d Richmond 7.12 (54)

Round 17, at Victoria Park, August 20
Collingwood 8.3 (51) d South Melbourne 5.9 (39)

Round 18, at Lake Oval, August 27
Carlton 11.9 (75) d South Melbourne 8.8 (56)

South champion Ron Clegg (right) congratulates newly-appointed coach Bill Faul.

Kilda at the Lake Oval in front of a tremendous attendance of 28,100. The Swans fielded one of its most inexperienced sides for years, even allowing for Clegg playing at centre half-forward and Johnson starting in a back pocket. Johnson shared ruck duties with Cliff Deacon and Jim Taylor and made such a huge impression in South's 51-point win that *The Sporting Globe* singled him out for praise.

The Saturday evening edition read: "Much-discussed former VFA and Port Melbourne ruckman Frank Johnson made a very good impression. Although 28 (sic), Johnson showed he has plenty of pace and ability, but his disposal is erratic." Johnson was named among South's best players, along with John Heriot, Bob Skilton, Max Oaten, Brennan and Clegg. It was a perfect start for Faul's term as coach, but he quickly acknowledged that his team did not have enough depth for continued success.

His words rang true the following week when Geelong defeated South by 44 points at Kardinia Park. Although Skilton kicked four goals and Johnson again played well, the Swans were "outsped" according to *The Sporting Globe.* It reported: "The blistering pace of the Cats all over the field gave the sluggish Swans no hope, either in defence or attack." Then, when reigning premier Melbourne thrashed South by 64 points at the MCG in round three, the red and white again was floundering.

The big loss to the Demons prompted *The Age* to report: "'Where do we go from here?' was the question on the lips of all South Melbourne players and officials after the side's crushing 64-point defeat by a still far from top form Melbourne … The answer, which no one wanted to acknowledge was that the side is

incapable of handling the present heavy conditions and, with so many key men below form, seems unlikely to recover ground lost through two consecutive defeats."

South might have defeated North Melbourne by 40 points at the Lake Oval in round four and then defeated Collingwood and Carlton in rounds six and seven, but could not find any semblance of consistency. To make matters worse, Skilton injured his back in a fall from a ladder and, at one stage, Taylor (ankle), Marshall Younger (shoulder), Hugh McLaughlin (thigh), Ray Landorff (ankle), Bill Power (shoulder) and Deacon (knee) all were sidelined at the same time.

Skilton's injury was not serious and, after returning to action, was named as South's sole representative in the Victorian team to play Western Australia at the MCG on the Queen's Birthday Monday holiday of June 13. Johnson and Max Oaten were selected in the Victorian "B" side to play Tasmania the same afternoon.

South hearts were broken the following week when Essendon defeated the Swans by a point at Windy Hill. Essendon was second on the ladder at that stage of the season and *The Sporting Globe* had nothing but praise for South's gallant effort. It reported that South, after trailing by 34 points at three-quarter time, stormed home with 6.5 to 1.2 in the final quarter. The Swans were moving the ball towards goal when the siren blared and *The Sporting Globe* suggested they were "desperately unlucky".

Skilton and North Melbourne rover Allen Aylett were named Victoria's best players in the return match against Western Australia at Subiaco on June 27 but, without Skilton, the Swans went down to Hawthorn by 11 points at the Glenferrie Oval. Even worse, Clegg pulled a thigh muscle in the third quarter and the Hawks took full advantage in his absence. Clegg returned a couple of weeks later and South introduced yet another newcomer for the round 13 match against Geelong at the Lake Oval. Peter Rice was the fourth player the Swans tried at full-forward to that stage of the 1960 season. He kicked only one goal, but South defeated Geelong by one point, with Henry Gunstone snapping the winning behind in the final minutes of play.

The end of the home and away season coincided with the Rome Olympics. South finished the season in eighth position with seven wins and 11 defeats and the 1960 season also represented the end of the magnificent career of one of the club's greatest champions in Ron Clegg. The 1949 Brownlow Medal winner played 231 games and kicked 156 goals for the Swans from his debut season of 1945. He won three best and fairest awards — in 1948, 1949 and 1951 — and always will be one of the club's favourite sons. He died tragically young, at 62 years of age, in 1990.

South, with Skilton as acting captain, defeated Hawthorn by 13 points in the 1960 night series Grand Final, giving the Swans three night flags since the competition's inception in 1956.

PLAYER	GAMES	GOALS
APPLEYARD, Percy	6	6
BARRETT, Ken	2	0
BENNETT, Brian	12	22
BOYD, Ken	17	9
BRAIN, Terry	3	1
BRENNAN, Gerald	3	1
BRIGLIA, Paul	3	5
BURKE, Dick	9	7
CHISHOLM, Bob	3	2
CHISHOLM, Brian	12	1
CLEGG, Ron	13	10
CROUGH, Gerald	7	2
DEACON, Cliff	10	1
DUNN, Albie	4	0
GUNSTONE, Henry	7	2
HEPNER, Fred	3	0
HERIOT, John	18	0
HOGAN, Kevin	4	0
JOHNSON, Frank	17	6
KELTON, John	8	0
KITELEY, Jeff	16	0
LANDORFF, Ray	5	0
McCORMACK, Ken	18	2
McGOWAN, Brian	18	22
McKENZIE, Norm	11	1
McLAUGHLIN, Hugh	16	0
MUNN, Bob	8	5
OATEN, Max	18	39
PORTA, Ron	16	0
POWER, Bill	12	9
RICE, Peter	12	5
SKILTON, Bob	16	22
TAMPION, Ian	5	0
TAUBE, Greg	1	0
TAYLOR, Jim	8	0
TRETHOWAN, John	4	0
WOOLLEY, John	4	0
YOUNGER, Marshall	11	5

POSITION: Eighth
COACH: Bill Faul
CAPTAIN: Ron Clegg
BEST AND FAIREST: Frank Johnson
LEADING GOALKICKER: Max Oaten (39)

1961

South Melbourne started the 1961 season with Bill Faul coach for a second year and, following the retirement of Ron Clegg at the end of 1960, brilliant rover Bob Skilton stepped into the leadership role. Several players, including Kevin Hogan, Ray Landorff and Ian Tampion, retired from VFL football, with the Swans giving 12 players their senior debuts as Faul looked to strengthen his squad.

Probably the best of the newcomers were rugged defender Clem Goonan, recruited from Whoroully and Myrtleford and key forward Bob Kingston, who worked his way through the ranks after being recruited from Spotswood. Goonan played 50 games for the Swans to 1964, while Kingston played 91 to 1967 after making his debut at just 16 years of age.

The Swans named just one newcomer, Peter Brain, for the opening round match against Hawthorn at the Glenferrie Oval. Brain was just 16 years of age and this was his only VFL game; he was replaced by Henry Gunstone in the final quarter of South's surprise 25-point win. *The Sporting Globe* suggested that South's pace had stunned Hawthorn, with Swan rovers Bob Skilton and Brian McGowan in brilliant touch. *The Sun* reported: "South Melbourne gained great drive through its cheeky rovers, particularly courageous captain Bob Skilton, whose breathtaking exhibition was reminiscent of his Brownlow Medal form."

South might have started the season better than its fans thought possible, but wasted a golden opportunity to remain undefeated when it went down to Geelong by just four points at the Lake Oval in round two. The Swans led by eight points with just minutes to play, only for the Cats to steal victory almost on the final siren. *The Sporting Globe* reported that several players from both sides could count themselves they were not reported in what was described as a "fiery" match. McGowan kicked six goals and he and winger Ken McCormack were named South's best players.

However, the Swans were far from discouraged and bounced back the next round to defeat Richmond by 44 points at the Punt Road Oval, with Skilton and McGowan again dominant. The win lifted South into second position, behind the undefeated Footscray but, after

South's Ken Boyd admitted striking Carlton's John Nicholls and ended his career in 1961.

MATCH RESULTS

Round 1, at Glenferrie Oval, April 15
South Melbourne 11.15 (81) d Hawthorn 7.14 (56)

Round 2, at Lake Oval, April 22
Geelong 12.12 (84) d South Melbourne 12.8 (80)

Round 3, at Punt Road, April 25
South Melbourne 12.17 (89) d Richmond 6.9 (45)

Round 4, at Lake Oval, May 6
Carlton 11.6 (72) d South Melbourne 7.14 (56)

Round 5, at Lake Oval, May 13
South Melbourne 12.12 (84) d Footscray 12.10 (82)

Round 6, at Windy Hill, May 20
Essendon 20.13 (133) d South Melbourne 6.18 (54)

Round 7, at Lake Oval, June 3
Fitzroy 17.15 (117) d South Melbourne 7.8 (50)

Round 8, at Junction Oval, June 10
St Kilda 16.14 (110) d South Melbourne 5.16 (46)

Round 9, at Lake Oval, June 17
Melbourne 14.14 (98) d South Melbourne 8.14 (62)

Round 10, at Victoria Park, June 24
Collingwood 12.12 (84) d South Melbourne 6.8 (44)

Round 11, at Lake Oval, July 1
South Melbourne 9.14 (68) d North Melb. 7.8 (50)

Round 12, at Lake Oval, July 8
Hawthorn 9.11 (65) d South Melbourne 7.7 (49)

Round 13, at Kardinia Park, July 15
Geelong 11.16 (82) d South Melbourne 9.13 (67)

Round 14, at Lake Oval, July 29
South Melbourne 16.9 (105) d Richmond 9.14 (68)

Round 15, at Princes Park, August 5
Carlton 17.9 (111) d South Melbourne 7.10 (52)

Round 16, at Western Oval, August 12
Footscray 14.17 (101) d South Melbourne 5.16 (46)

Round 17, at Lake Oval, August 19
Essendon 16.11 (107) d South Melbourne 11.12 (78)

Round 18, at Brunswick Street, August 26
Fitzroy 25.29 (179) d South Melbourne 11.10 (76)

A 1961 South lineup.

defeating the Bulldogs by two points at the Lake Oval in round five, South's form fell right away. Five consecutive defeats left the Swans with virtually no hope of making the finals and, besides, they later were rocked by a massive controversy following the round 15 defeat by Carlton at Princes Park.

The Blues thrashed the Swans by 59 points and, if that was not bad enough, South ruckman Ken Boyd later admitted that he had struck Carlton ruck champion John Nicholls. There was no mention of any incident in that night's edition of *The Sporting Globe* and no umpire had made a report. However, the football world was rocked when Boyd not only confessed to football writers Peter Bye and Ian McDonald that he had struck Nicholls, but explained why.

Boyd told these reporters, who published the full account in the mid-week edition of *The Sporting Globe:* "I'm not ashamed I hit John Nicholls last Saturday. I've a clear conscience on the whole matter. Early in the last quarter at a centre bounce, I was kicked in the stomach and the groin (here he showed Bye and McDonald stop marks on his stomach). I was in terrific pain and when I recovered I simply went back, turned Nicholls around and dropped him. It's the first time I've ever hit a player behind play, but I'm not ashamed. I draw the line at what happened to me. I'm entitled to protect myself."

He continued: "I've whacked a few players in my day but I've always done it openly. Saturday's incident didn't come as some people think — from when I was reported in the South Melbourne-Carlton game earlier in the year (he was suspended for six matches after being found guilty on two charges). I bore no malice from that game. Too many South players have been 'stopped' and somebody has to look after them … When I was rolling on the ground in pain some Carlton players were having a giggle at me and their supporters were cheering. When Nicholls went down the same people were squealing and their supporters were bellowing, too."

The report proved to be a sensation and the VFL was forced to act on Boyd's admission and ordered him to face a special

South's Bill Faul feels the anguish of coaching. His runner, on the right, is former Swan star Bill Gunn.

investigations committee. Boyd did not give evidence but, in less than half an hour, the South ruckman was found guilty and suspended 12 matches. Boyd told reporters: "Naturally, I am disappointed, but I've got to accept the decision." Asked if he would retire, Boyd replied: "I have got a lot of thinking to do, but I have made no definite decision yet." Boyd eventually decided to end his VFL career and the following season was appointed captain-coach of country club Wangaratta Rovers.

Controversy and on-field incidents seemed to dog the Swans in 1961 as Skilton was the innocent party in a ferocious challenge by St Kilda defender Eric Guy at the Junction Oval in round eight. According to *The Sporting Globe*, Guy "flattened" Skilton, who had to be carried from the ground on a stretcher just 20 minutes into the game. Swan fans boiled with rage and there were fears they would jump the fence to remonstrate with Guy. *The Sporting Globe* reported that Skilton, after running "blindly out of a pack", ran into the St Kilda player known as "the human tank". To make matters worse for the Swans, the Saints defeated them by 64 points. Skilton told reporters: "That's the hardest knock I have ever had."

South, after such a promising start to the season, finished above only North Melbourne and avoided the wooden-spoon by just two match points and had a much worse percentage. Although Skilton won the club best and fairest, ruckman Frank Johnson finished fourth in the Brownlow Medal count with 13 votes, behind Carlton's John James (21 votes), North Melbourne's Laurie Dwyer (19) and Hawthorn's Ian Law (17).

PLAYER	GAMES	GOALS
BENNETT, Brian	11	3
BOYD, Ken	10	10
BRAIN, Peter	1	0
BRAIN, Terry	3	3
BRIGLIA, Paul	7	4
BURKE, Dick	11	8
CARLILE, John	4	0
CHISHOLM, Bob	13	15
CROUGH, Gerald	14	0
DEACON, Cliff	14	0
DUNN, Albie	6	2
ELLIOTT, Morrie	1	0
GOONAN, Clem	3	0
GUNSTONE, Henry	2	0
HANNON, Barry	2	0
HERIOT, John	16	1
HOPKINS, Bill	3	0
HOTCHKIN, Allan	5	0
JOHNSON, Frank	16	0
KINGSTON, Bob	10	4
KITELEY, Jeff	11	0
LEWTHWAITE, Neil	9	0
McCORMACK, Ken	16	3
McGOWAN, Brian	18	38
McKENZIE, Norm	8	2
McLAUGHLIN, Hugh	12	0
MUNN, Bob	10	5
OATEN, Max	14	24
PORTA, Ron	5	0
POWER, Bill	9	3
RICE, Peter	17	1
ROLFE, Ron	8	4
SKILTON, Bob	17	28
SONNLEITNER, Otto	3	1
STOCKMAN, Ron	8	0
TAYLOR, Jim	11	0
TOMLINSON, Brian	11	0
TRETHOWAN, John	5	2
WOOLLEY, John	15	0
YOUNGER, Marshall	1	0

POSITION: Eleventh
COACH: Bill Faul
CAPTAIN: Bob Skilton
BEST AND FAIREST: Bob Skilton
LEADING GOALKICKER: Brian McGowan (38)

1962

South Melbourne announced two significant signings over the summer of 1961-62. One was the appointment of former star Melbourne defender Noel McMahen as coach to replace the retired Bill Faul and the other was the acceptance by the Governor-General of Australia, Lord De L'Isle, of the club's number one membership ticket. The South committee believed that McMahen's experience in 175 games with the Demons from 1946-56 and as captain of the 1955-56 premiership sides would be invaluable. Former champion Swan centreman Keith Schaefer was appointed assistant coach, but had to resign late in the season because of business commitments.

Apart from the premature retirement of Ken Boyd the previous season and his subsequent appointment as captain-coach of Wangaratta, the Swans also cleared Paul Briglia (Brunswick), Terry Brain (Oakleigh), Ken McCormack (Edithvale), Bill Power (Edithvale), Ron Porta (Mordialloc), Ron Stockman (Melton) and Marshall Younger (East Perth), among others.

SOUTH MELBOURNE FOOTBALL CLUB

"Victory or Death"

ANNUAL REPORT

AND

BALANCE SHEET

SEASON 1962

On the other hand, the Swans introduced Harry Alexander (Sale), Trevor Castlehow (Under 19s), Ken Colvin (Rochester), Gordon Dann (Under 19s), Peter Dolling (Mansfield), John Fogarty (Koroit), Neville Forge (Albury), Geoff Heyme (Under 19s), Darryl Howland (Dimboola), Tom Hynes (St Bede's, Mentone), Terry McGee (Fourths), Stuart Magee (Under 19s), Kevin Mithen (Melbourne), John Plumridge (CBC Parade), Bob Porter (Fourths), Jim Pumphrey (Garfield), Elkin Reilly (Wentworth), Alan Self (Spotswood), Pat Thethowan (Rockbank) and Russell Tulloch (Reserves).

Of these newcomers, the Irish-born Magee played 84 games with the Swans to 1968, mainly as a half-forward flanker, and later captained Footscray. Also, Reilly was a talented Aboriginal ruckman who played 51 games in the red and white to 1966.

South rovers Bob Skilton (left) and Brian McGowan represented Victoria in 1962.

Off-field, the Swans launched their first coterie group, the Southerners' Association, with club committeeman Jack Marks its chairman. Marks later was to be a hugely influential club figure as president leading up to South's move to Sydney in 1982. Also, the club on July 16 opened its new room, between the cricket club members' stand and the ancient wooden stand.

The Swans completed their preparation for the new season with an intra-club practice match at the Lake Oval nine days before their opening round match against North Melbourne at the Lake Oval on the Easter

A South line-up from 1962. Back: R. Kingston, C. Deacon, K. Colvin, N. Forge, J. Trethowan, R. Burke, M. Oaten, D. Howland, K. Mithen, J. Heriot. Centre: A. Goodall (Secretary), G. Crough, R. Munn, F. Johnson (Vice-Captain), N. McMahen (Coach), R. Skilton (Captain), H. McLaughlin, R. W. Tait (President). Front: B. Bennett, B. McGowan, H. Alexander, A. Dunn, G. Heyme.

Monday. *The Sporting Globe* was particularly impressed with Magee, who had represented a VFL Under 19s side against South Australia in Adelaide the previous season, winger Heyme and Hynes, son for former South champion Tammy Hynes.

South opened the season with a six-point win over North Melbourne at the Lake Oval, with *The Sun News-Pictorial* reporting that Bob Skilton was best on ground and in Brownlow Medal form. It also praised all South's newcomers, Forge, Colvin, Mithen, Heyme, Howland and Alexander. Unfortunately, however, star South ruckman Frank Johnson injured a knee in the final quarter and did not return to action until the second half of the season.

When the Swans defeated St Kilda by 12 points at the Junction Oval the following Saturday, there were expectations the red and white would improve dramatically on its second-last position of the previous season. Rover Bob Munn kicked the sealing goal after the Swans had led by 16 points at half-time, with a big test against Collingwood at the Lake Oval the following week.

After an even first half, the Magpies raced away to win by 44 points. *The Sporting Globe* reported: "Collingwood gave a display of their old power when they out-bumped and out-played South Melbourne for a convincing win. South wilted before the Magpies' greater physical power in a rugged game in which both sides tore in fearlessly."

It was the start of a disastrous run of 13 consecutive defeats, including several humiliating performances. The worst of these was against Melbourne at the MCG in round six when the Swans scored just one goal in

MATCH RESULTS

Round 1, at Lake Oval, April 23
South Melbourne 14.13 (97) d North Melb. 13.13 (91)

Round 2, at Junction Oval, April 28
South Melbourne 13.7 (85) d St Kilda 10.13 (73)

Round 3, at Lake Oval, May 5
Collingwood 15.10 (100) d South Melb. 7.14 (56)

Round 4, at Western Oval, May 12
Footscray 17.17 (119) d South Melbourne 10.11 (71)

Round 5, at Lake Oval, May 19
Fitzroy 13.16 (94) d South Melbourne 10.13 (73)

Round 6, at MCG, May 26
Melbourne 8.15 (63) d South Melbourne 1.11 (17)

Round 7, at Lake Oval, June 2
Essendon 16.15 (111) d South Melbourne 7.11 (53)

Round 8, at Kardinia Park, June 9
Geelong 9.10 (64) d South Melbourne 6.8 (44)

Round 9, at Lake Oval, June 23
Richmond 11.13 (79) d South Melbourne 10.13 (73)

Round 10, at Lake Oval, June 30
Hawthorn 12.14 (86) d South Melbourne 7.8 (50)

Round 11, at Princes Park, July 7
Carlton 17.14 (116) d South Melbourne 6.12 (48)

Round 12, at Arden Street, July 14
North Melb. 12.22 (94) d South Melbourne 5.15 (45)

Round 13, at Lake Oval, July 21
St Kilda 11.14 (80) d South Melbourne 9.9 (63)

Round 14, at Victoria Park, July 28
Collingwood 11.10 (76) d South Melb. 10.12 (72)

Round 15, at Lake Oval, August 4
Footscray 10.20 (80) d South Melbourne 9.9 (63)

Round 16, at Brunswick Street, August 11
South Melbourne 22.11 (143) d Fitzroy 17.16 (118)

Round 17, at Lake Oval, August 18
Melbourne 9.13 (67) d South Melbourne 7.10 (52)

Round 18, at Windy Hill, August 25
Essendon 13.15 (93) d South Melbourne 13.10 (88)

going down by 46 points in atrocious conditions. South's only goal was scored by Skilton in the first quarter. The heaviest defeat was at the hands of Carlton at Princes Park in round 11, with Carlton thrashing South by 68 points. *The Sporting Globe* reported that Carlton "outclassed the battling Swans".

Defender Clem Goonan won an award for the club's "most determined player".

South finally broke its run of outs in defeating Fitzroy by 25 points in a high-scoring match at the Brunswick Street Oval in round 16. Skilton kicked seven goals and Johnson six. *The Sporting Globe* reported that South had produced its best form of the season and that its pace and teamwork was "too much" for the Lions. However, it was the last of South's three wins of the season and the Swans finished on the bottom of the ladder.

Strangely, however, the club annual report commented: "It is many years since South Melbourne finished a season on such an encouraging note, and it is confidently anticipated that season 1963 will see the Swans commence their rise in search of premiership honours that have eluded the club for so long … There are many who consider that, in time to come, season 1962 will be looked upon and regarded as the year of the revival of the South Melbourne Football Club."

PLAYER	GAMES	GOALS
ALEXANDER, Harry	15	2
BENNETT, Brian	17	1
BURKE, Dick	18	5
CASTLEHOW, Trevor	5	0
CHISHOLM, Bob	6	3
COLVIN, Ken	16	3
CROUGH, Gerald	7	0
DANN, Gordon	2	0
DEACON, Cliff	3	0
DOLLING, Peter	12	1
DUNN, Albie	8	2
FOGARTY, John	4	0
FORGE, Neville	2	0
GOONAN, Clem	17	2
GUNSTONE, Henry	4	2
HERIOT, John	15	14
HEYME, Geoff	5	0
HOPKINS, Bill	2	0
HOTCHKIN, Allan	8	0
HOWLAND, Darryl	3	1
HYNES, Tom	5	1
JOHNSON, Frank	9	14
KINGSTON, Bob	15	7
MAGEE, Stuart	6	2
McGEE, Terry	5	2
McGOWAN, Brian	18	25
McKENZIE, Norm	2	0
McLAUGHLIN, Hugh	15	3
MITHEN, Kevin	4	1
MUNN, Bob	10	13
OATEN, Max	11	12
PLUMRIDGE, John	8	0
PORTER, Bob	3	0
PUMPHREY, Jim	7	2
REILLY, Elkin	12	1
RICE, Peter	8	0
SELF, Alan	5	3
SKILTON, Bob	16	36
TOMLINSON, Brian	4	0
TRETHOWAN, John	13	5
TRETHOWAN, Pat	10	2
TULLOCH, Russell	4	1
WOOLLEY, John	1	0

POSITION: Twelfth
COACH: Noel McMahen
CAPTAIN: Bob Skilton
BEST AND FAIREST: Bob Skilton
LEADING GOALKICKER: Bob Skilton (36)

1963

South Melbourne might have been optimistic about its chances in 1963, but the reality was that the Swans did not have the depth of talent to go even close to claiming a top four position. Noel McMahen again was coach with Bob Skilton captain and Frank Johnson vice-captain. As usual, the Swans prepared for the new season with intra-club practice matches, with the first of these played at Port Melbourne on March 16.

The following Saturday *The Sporting Globe* reported that South was desperately trying to sign star Moorabbin (VFA) centreman Max Papley. However, *The Sporting Globe* added that the Swans were having difficulty snaring their man as Moorabbin had offered Papley 12 pounds ($24) a match. Under the VFL's Coulter Law, clubs could pay players only a total of 160 pounds ($320) a season and this put the VFA club in the box seat in the Papley tug-of-war. Although Papley played in a Swans' intra-club practice match, the Swans had to wait another season for him to join them, but the wait was worth it.

Bob Skilton won his second Brownlow Medal in 1963, a true Swan legend.

A team wearing blue and gold played a team wearing red and black at the Lake Oval in the final practice match, with several youngsters given chances against established South stars. For example, Traralgon's Paul Harrison was pitted against John Heriot and Cobden youngster John Rantall picked up a succession of opponents while being trialled on a half-back flank.

Harrison and Rantall were just two of South's 1963 recruits, while others included Kevin Batch (Box Hill), Des Bethke (Horsham), Ron Cotton (Melbourne), Jim Fuller (Under 19s), Ken Phillips (East Burwood), Fred Rees (Loch), Bill Ross (Williamstown High School), Trevor Somerville (Trafalgar), Bob Strachan (Horsham) and Eric White (Melbourne). The losses from 1962 included Brian Bennett (Coorparoo), Bob Chisholm (Berrigan), Gerald Crough (Sandhurst), Gordon Dann (Port Melbourne), Albie Dunn (Corowa), Henry Gunstone (S. and W. Rovers), Bill Hopkins (Albury), Max Oaten (Nar Nar Goon), Jim Pumphrey (Port Melbourne), Peter Rice (Bayswater), Brian Tomlinson (Warrandyte), John Trethowan (Ballarat), Russell Tulloch (Mordialloc) and John Woolley (East Brighton).

The front cover of South's annual report for the 1963 season shows Bob Skilton being presented with his second Brownlow Medal by VFL president Sir Kenneth Luke.

The Swans opened the season disastrously, going down to Geelong by 59 points at Kardinia Park and the following week crashed by 23 points to Richmond at the Lake Oval in an Anzac Day clash. Then followed big defeats by Carlton (35 points) and Hawthorn (71), with the Swans' only consolation being the form of several of their youngsters and, in particular, Rantall. Also, pocket-sized rover Brian McGowan played his 100th VFL game in the loss to Carlton.

South and Fitzroy were the only two clubs without a win going into round five and the Swans pushed the Lions to the bottom of the ladder in defeating North Melbourne by 38 points at the Lake Oval. *The Sporting Globe* described it as a "shock win" and praised the "elusive play" of Skilton and the "dominance" of ruckmen Johnson and Elkin Reilly. Rantall again was named among South's best players and won Victorian representative honours after just a handful of games.

The Swans, meanwhile, struggled in most matches and notched just four wins for the season. Apart from that round five defeat of North Melbourne, they also defeated Melbourne, Fitzroy and Richmond to finish

SOUTH MELBOURNE FOOTBALL TEAM—1963

BACK ROW—E. Reilly, E. White, D. Howland, R. Kingston, H. Alexander, R. Burke, C. Goonan, N. Smith, K. Wharton, K. Barnes, A. Self, T. Somerville, K. Colvin, P. Quirk.

STANDING—N. Cunningham, F. Rees, D. Bethke, T. Hynes, J. Heriot, P. Harrison, K. Batch, T. McGee, G. Heyme.

SEATED—P. Dolling, J. Rantall, R. Cotton, R. Skilton (Capt.), Mr. R. Warner (President), F. Johnson (Vice-Capt.), B. McGowan, H. McLaughlin, G. Johnston.

FRONT ROW—J. Plumridge, R. Strachan, E. Collings, J. Fuller, R. Porter, S. Magee, K. Phillips, W. Ross.

MATCH RESULTS

Round 1, at Kardinia Park, April 20
Geelong 16.26 (122) d South Melbourne 9.9 (63)

Round 2, at Lake Oval, April 25
Richmond 17.7 (109) d South Melbourne 12.14 (86)

Round 3, at Lake Oval, May 4
Carlton 16.15 (111) d South Melbourne 10.14 (74)

Round 4, at Glenferrie Oval, May 11
Hawthorn 21.25 (151) d South Melbourne 11.14 (80)

Round 5, at Lake Oval, May 18
South Melbourne 17.11 (113) d North Melb. 11.9 (75)

Round 6, at Junction Oval, May 25
St Kilda 13.16 (94) d South Melbourne 8.5 (53)

Round 7, at Lake Oval, June 1
South Melbourne 11.8 (74) d Melbourne 8.22 (70)

Round 8, at Western Oval, June 10
Footscray 6.16 (52) d South Melbourne 5.9 (39)

Round 9, at Lake Oval, June 22
South Melbourne 8.10 (58) d Fitzroy 5.9 (39)

Round 10, at Victoria Park, June 29
Collingwood 19.11 (125) d South Melb. 11.8 (74)

Round 11, at Lake Oval, July 20
Essendon 12.20 (92) d South Melbourne 6.10 (46)

Round 12, at Lake Oval, July 27
Geelong 14.11 (95) d South Melbourne 8.12 (60)

Round 13, at Punt Road, August 3
South Melbourne 20.10 (130) d Richmond 9.10 (64)

Round 14, at Princes Park, August 10
Carlton 17.13 (115) d South Melbourne 8.9 (57)

Round 15, at Lake Oval, August 17
Hawthorn 15.15 (105) d South Melbourne 6.9 (45)

Round 16, at Arden Street, August 24
North Melb. 12.12 (84) d South Melbourne 5.9 (39)

Round 17, at Lake Oval, August 31
St Kilda 19.14 (128) d South Melbourne 8.7 (55)

Round 18, at MCG, September 7
Melbourne 12.19 (91) d South Melbourne 8.8 (56)

Key forward Bob Kingston, runner-up to Bob Skilton in the 1963 Swan best and fairest.

above only Fitzroy, which won just one game. It was yet another disappointing season, but there was one huge consolation as Skilton won his second Brownlow Medal. The champion rover polled 20 votes to defeat Geelong ruckman Graham Farmer and St Kilda centre half-forward Darrel Baldock by three votes.

The club annual report for the 1963 season noted: "Without the slightest doubt, easily the happiest feature of the season's operations was the success enjoyed by club captain Bob Skilton in winning, for the second time, the Brownlow Medal awarded to the best and fairest player in the Victorian Football League. Bob richly deserved this coveted award, and we are grateful to him for the honour and distinction he has once again brought to the

Bob Kingston, a powerful centre half-forward, played many fine games for the Swans.

South Melbourne Football Club." The Swans rewarded Skilton with a club testimonial and expressed "appreciation of the pleasure derived from the superlative and tremendously courageous displays for the club".

Skilton was determined to keep a low profile on the night of the count, but coach McMahen talked him into attending a party at McMahen's Aspendale home to listen to the count on radio. Skilton later recalled: "It was one of the best decisions I made as my teammates were all there. Bob Kingston kindly emptied his beer all over me after I won." Skilton also won the club best and fairest, with Kingston runner-up. Rantall, despite representing Victoria in his debut season, missed out to Harrison for the best first-year player award.

The football world went into mourning post-season when the great Roy Cazaly, who had played 99 games for both South Melbourne and St Kilda, died in Hobart on October 15 following a long illness at 70 years of age.

PLAYER	GAMES	GOALS
ALEXANDER, Harry	11	0
BATCH, Kevin	4	0
BETHKE, Des	6	6
BURKE, Dick	4	4
COLVIN, Ken	18	2
COTTON, Ron	4	0
DEACON, Cliff	2	0
DOLLING, Peter	11	8
FOGARTY, John	2	0
FULLER, Jim	1	0
GOONAN, Clem	17	0
HARRISON, Paul	18	4
HERIOT, John	17	14
HYME, Geoff	5	0
HOTCHKIN, Allan	1	0
HOWLAND, Darryl	6	0
HYNES, Tom	5	0
JOHNSON, Frank	10	13
JOHNSON, Gary	14	0
KINGSTON, Bob	18	18
MAGEE, Stuart	8	8
McGEE, Terry	11	0
McGOWAN, Brian	18	19
McLAUGHLIN, Hugh	7	1
MUNN, Bob	1	0
PHILLIPS, Ken	14	4
PLUMRIDGE, John	4	0
PORTER, Bob	15	10
RANTALL, John	14	2
REES, Fred	1	0
REILLY, Elkin	12	0
ROSS, Bill	15	4
SELF, Alan	9	8
SKILTON, Bob	17	36
SOMERVILLE, Trevor	16	4
STRACHAN, Bob	3	0
TRETHOWAN, Pat	9	1
WHITE, Eric	12	5

POSITION: Eleventh
COACH: Noel McMahen
CAPTAIN: Bob Skilton
BEST AND FAIREST: Bob Skilton
LEADING GOALKICKER: Bob Skilton (36)

1964

The South Melbourne annual report covering the 1963 season noted: "The cause of our lack of success is not easy to pin-point, but after much consideration and deliberation we have been forced to the conclusion that insufficient top-class players was the main reason for our failure to advance." The Swans, admitting their deficiencies, therefore launched a massive recruiting drive in an effort to climb the VFL ladder.

This drive was launched immediately after the 1963 season and the Swans announced just weeks after the Grand Final that it had signed East Perth centre half-forward Graeme John. However, *The Sporting Globe* of Wednesday, October 23 ran a small item carrying the headline JOHN? NO HOPE, SWANS. It read: "There's as much chance of Graeme John being cleared to South as there is of Bob Skilton being cleared to WA. That's what a top East Perth official told Austin Robertson (former champion Swan and journalist) this week."

East Perth must have been bluffing as John won his clearance and joined the Swans for the start of the 1964 season, along with a long list of other newcomers, including Keith Baskin (Moorabbin), Pat Bowd (Under 19s and Clayton YCW), Jeff Bray (West Adelaide), Ray Dawson (Melbourne), Kevin Dore (Bruthen), Reg Edwards (Rutherglen), Charlie Evans (Footscray), Les Heywood (Croydon), Herbie Matthews Jnr (Melbourne), Ed Melai (Geelong), Ray Nilsson (Melbourne), Max Papley (Moorabbin), Terry Tate (Geelong) and Fred Way (Berrigan).

Also listed was West Perth's Mike Willesee, who played reserves football with the Swans, but became more famous as a television journalist and presenter. He also became a club part-owner following the club's move to Sydney in 1982 and played an immense role in club fortunes. Apart from John, there were several huge signings, with barrel-chested South Australian Bray joining the Swans with a big reputation, Papley finally agreeing to join the Swans and Way developing into a quality ruckman who represented Victoria.

The departures included classy rover Brian McGowan, who crossed to South Australian club Glenelg, Bob Munn (Waverley), John Plumridge (East Ballarat), Geoff Heyme (Redan) and Darryl Howland (Dimboola). Ruckman Dick Burke, had announced his retirement during the previous season and later was elected to the club committee, while winger Harry Alexander was transferred to Traralgon in his employment after just three games in 1964.

Stuart Magee, an extremely dangerous half-forward.

South was so confident with its recruiting that club secretary Alby Goodall declared in *The Sporting Globe:* "We won't finish second

SOUTH MELBOURNE FOOTBALL TEAM – 1964

BACK ROW—L. Sullivan, T. Somerville, E. Melai, R. Kingston, F. Way, K. Wharton, K. Barnes, E. White, E. Reilly, P. Trethowan.
STANDING—P. Bowd, R. Strachan, A. Self, K. Colvin, P. Harrison, G. John, K. Batch, T. Hynes, J. Bray, D. Bethke.
SEATED—L. Heywood, M. Papley, J. Rantall, J. Heriot (Vice-Captain), R. Skilton (Captain), E. Collings, R. Cotton, B. Parker, C. Goonan, W. Ross.
FRONT ROW—R. Bollard, H. McLaughlin, C. Evans, S. Magee, K. Phillips, G. Parker, R. Porter, G. Johnston.

last this year", and predicted John, Bray and Papley all would star in the VFL. John was so dominant in South's first intra-club practice match that Swan officials immediately flew to Perth to secure his clearance. *The Sporting Globe* reported: "John was most impressive with his play-on game and co-operation with other forwards." Unfortunately for the Swans, however, one of their other star recruits — Bray — broke a hand in the final practice match against Traralgon and also was told he would not be eligible to play over the first seven rounds because he had not completed residential qualification.

Despite their recruiting coups, the Swans opened the season with a 24-point loss to Hawthorn at the Lake Oval, with the Hawks' John Peck kicking eight goals. Papley kicked four goals on debut, but neither he nor John were named in South's best players. However, the Swans turned it around in defeating Fitzroy by 23 points at Brunswick Street the following Saturday, Anzac Day. *The Sporting Globe* reported that the Swans' "two-man team" of Skilton and Papley did all the damage. Skilton kicked six goals and Papley five.

The Swans faltered badly from there and

MATCH RESULTS

Round 1, at Lake Oval, April 18
Hawthorn 14.13 (97) d South Melbourne 10.13 (73)

Round 2, at Brunswick Street, April 25
South Melbourne 18.10 (118) d Fitzroy 13.17 (95)

Round 3, at Lake Oval, May 2
Richmond 8.15 (63) d South Melbourne 8.7 (55)

Round 4, at Victoria Park, May 9
Collingwood 12.13 (85) d South Melbourne 8.9 (57)

Round 5, at Lake Oval, May 16
Geelong 11.10 (76) d South Melbourne 8.11 (59)

Round 6, at Western Oval, May 23
Footscray 10.22 (82) d South Melbourne 10.9 (69)

Round 7, at Lake Oval, May 30
Essendon 14.12 (96) d South Melbourne 11.18 (84)

Round 8, at Lake Oval, June 6
Carlton 12.14 (86) d South Melbourne 8.13 (61)

Round 9, at Arden Street, June 15
North Melb. 10.15 (75) d South Melbourne 7.9 (51)

Round 10, at Junction Oval, June 27
St Kilda 18.15 (123) d South Melbourne 10.8 (68)

Round 11, at Lake Oval, July 4
Melbourne 18.21 (129) d South Melbourne 12.11 (83)

Round 12, at Glenferrie Oval, July 11
Hawthorn 15.13 (103) d South Melbourne 6.15 (51)

Round 13, at Lake Oval, July 18
South Melbourne 17.15 (117) d Fitzroy 5.14 (44)

Round 14, at Punt Road, July 25
Richmond 13.21 (99) d South Melbourne 5.4 (34)

Round 15, at Lake Oval, August 1
Collingwood 12.13 (85) d South Melbourne 5.13 (43)

Round 16, at Kardinia Park, August 8
Geelong 8.9 (57) d South Melbourne 1.9 (15)

Round 17, at Lake Oval, August 15
Footscray 10.15 (75) d South Melbourne 10.8 (68)

Round 18, at Windy Hill, August 22
Essendon 28.16 (184) d South Melbourne 2.7 (19)

lost its next 10 games before defeating Fitzroy again, by 73 points, this time at the Lake Oval. *The Sporting Globe* suggested that the Swans, in victory, "passed on their chances for the wooden-spoon". Again, Papley and Skilton were South's best players. However, it was South's last win of the season and, despite Goodall's prediction, the Swans again finished second-last, with the winless Fitzroy on the bottom.

South's low-point of the season was scoring just one goal in the round 16 clash with Geelong at Kardinia Park. That goal was scored by Ian Randle in the final quarter. Geelong won by 42 points in heavy rain and, amazingly, *The Sporting Globe* paid this tribute to the Swans: "Although South had been well beaten on the scoreboard, never for one minute did they cease trying to match their more experienced opponents." In scoring the late goal, Randle saved the Swans severe embarrassment. Recruited from Diamond Creek it was his only goal in his only VFL game. The Swans' only excuse for yet another disappointing season was that Skilton was restricted to just 10 games because of a knee injury and subsequent surgery.

South's annual report for the 1964 season therefore posed the following question:

"As history reveals the meagre success attained in 1964 was even less than that recorded in 1963. What was the reason for this lack of success? Where did the club fail?" The report suggested the reasons were many and varied, but that the committee vowed to work hard to rectify weaknesses. Skilton, despite playing just 10 games, won the best and fairest, with Heriot runner-up and Magee third (plus an award for most improved player). Winger Glen Parker won the award for best first-year player, but played just one more season with the Swans.

PLAYER	GAMES	GOALS
ALEXANDER, Harry	3	1
BARNES, Ken	4	0
BASKIN, Keith	2	0
BATCH, Kevin	1	0
BETHKE, Des	18	22
BOWD, Pat	7	0
BRAY, Jeff	3	0
COLLINGS, Ted	1	0
COLVIN, Ken	16	0
DAWSON, Ray	4	0
EDWARDS, Reg	1	1
EVANS, Charlie	8	0
GOONAN, Clem	13	0
HARRISON, Paul	17	0
HERIOT, John	16	6
HEYWOOD, Les	5	0
HYNES, Tom	4	0
JOHN, Graeme	17	16
JOHNSON, Frank	12	5
JOHNSON, Gary	13	1
KINGSTON, Bob	16	5
MAGEE, Stuart	16	22
MATTHEWS, Herbie Jnr	8	5
MELAI, Ed	7	2
NILSSON, Ray	8	2
PAPLEY, Max	16	25
PARKER, Glen	9	0
PARKER, Kevin	5	0
PHILLIPS, Ken	13	6
PORTER, Bob	3	2
RANDLE, Ian	1	1
RANTALL, John	18	0
REILLY, Elkin	8	0
ROSS, Bill	5	0
SELF, Alan	7	1
SKILTON, Bob	10	23
SOMERVILLE, Trevor	9	0
STANLEY, Don	4	0
STRACHAN, Bob	1	0
TATE, Terry	7	7
TRETHOWAN, Pat	11	0
WAY, Fred	6	1
WHARTON, Ken	4	2

POSITION: Eleventh
COACH: Noel McMahen
CAPTAIN: Bob Skilton
BEST AND FAIREST: Bob Skilton
LEADING GOALKICKER: Max Papley (25)

1965

After taking South Melbourne to a highest position of eleventh over three seasons as coach, Noel McMahen did not seek reappointment. South had a ready-made replacement in its own backyard, with Bob Skilton named captain-coach. Skilton was 26 years of age and in the prime of his playing career, but his appointment was overshadowed by massive developments at other clubs. Ron Barassi left Melbourne to be captain-coach of Carlton, Richmond switched its home games from the Punt Road Oval to the MCG, St Kilda moved from the Junction Oval to Moorabbin and North Melbourne boldly experimented with a shift from Arden Street to the Coburg City Oval.

The Swans lost several important players from 1964, with Frank Johnson and Hugh McLaughlin retiring and others moving to country and suburban clubs. Johnson might have played just 64 games with the Swans, but his contribution had been immense. McLaughlin had played 116 games and was a wonderful club servant following in the footsteps of his father Hugh Senior, a 1933 premiership player.

South in 1965 introduced just 12 first-year players, down four on the previous season and there was just one recruit from a rival VFL club — Richmond ruckman Gary Williamson. The newcomers included West Australians Ray Lucev and Eric Sarich, South Australian John Long and Yarraville's Noel Orange. On paper, the Swans looked capable of climbing the ladder.

Skilton had his first good look at his charges in action in an intra-club practice match on March 13. Skilton did not play and sat on the sidelines with assistant coach and mentor Tom Lahiff and reserves coach Ken McCormack. The match involved mainly junior players, with most of the seniors in action the following day. *The Sporting Globe* reported that the following week's practice match was poor and Skilton consequently revved his players up for the third practice match. *The Sporting Globe* headline read SKILTON SPEECH SET SOUTH PACE. The newspaper reported: "South Melbourne players tore into the play with scant regard for injury following a pep talk by coach Bob Skilton. Skilton himself was in great form and capitalised on some great ruck play by Elkin Reilly and Ken Barnes."

The Swans opened the season against North Melbourne in appalling conditions at Coburg. Heavy rain lashed the ground from start to finish and South slogged through the mud and slush marginally better than the Kangaroos to win by 10 points. It might have been an encouraging start to the season, but it was back

Centre half-forward Graeme John was runner-up to Bob Skilton in the Swans' 1965 best and fairest award.

to earth for the Swans in going down to St Kilda by 33 points at the Lake Oval in round two. South bounced back to defeat Barassi's Carlton by 15 points at the Lake Oval the following week, but then had its heart broken against reigning premier Melbourne at the MCG.

Again, heavy rain lashed the ground, but the Swans handled the atrocious conditions better than the Demons to lead by a point at the final break. As the teams broke from their three-quarter time huddle, Swan half-back Orange ran towards South fans huddled at the back of the Great Southern Stand to get them to cheer on their team for what would have been an important win. The Swans, despite everything the Demons threw at them, held them — until almost the last kick of the match. Melbourne's Barry Bourke somehow kicked a freakish goal to give his side a three-point win. *The Sporting Globe* reported: "With 18 seconds left to play Melbourne rover Barry Bourke kicked the winning goal after unselfish play by his skipper, Hassa Mann."

Victory would have given the Swans a 3-1 win-loss ratio and there was worse the following week when Footscray pipped the Swans by a point at the Western Oval. Brownlow Medallist Neil Roberts, writing in *The Sporting Globe*, indicated that the Bulldogs managed to fight off a late South

South Melbourne Football Team—Season 1965

Back Row: K. Batch, P. Trethowan, G. John, E. White, G. Williamson, K. Barnes, R. Kingston, T. Somerville, L. Sullivan, N. Orange.

Standing: R. Strachan, J. Long, B. Parker, R. Tenabel, P. Harrison, R. Lucev, A. Self, J. Bray, K. Dore, K. Pedrotti.

Seated: K. Parker, D. Bethke, J. Heriot (Vice-Captain), T. Lahiff (Asst. Coach), R. Skilton (Captain-Coach), K. McCormack (Reserves' Coach), M. Papley, E. Sarich, C. Goonan, I. Davison.

Front Row: R. Nilsson, D. Stanley, H. Matthews, H. McAuliffe, S. Magee, G. Davey, P. Higgins, G. Parker, G. Gemmill, J. Rantall.

MATCH RESULTS

Round 1, at Coburg Oval, April 19
South Melbourne 6.10 (46) d North Melb. 4.12 (36)

Round 2, at Lake Oval, April 24
St Kilda 12.12 (84) d South Melbourne 7.9 (51)

Round 3, at Lake Oval, May 1
South Melbourne 12.14 (86) d Carlton 10.11 (71)

Round 4, at MCG, May 8
Melbourne 12.8 (80) d South Melbourne 11.11 (77)

Round 5, at Western Oval, May 15
Footscray 11.11 (77) d South Melbourne 11.10 (76)

Round 6, at Lake Oval, May 22
South Melbourne 14.12 (96) d Essendon 12.16 (88)

Round 7, at Victoria Park, May 29
Collingwood 15.11 (101) d South Melb. 10.12 (72)

Round 8, at Lake Oval, June 5
South Melbourne 13.24 (102) d Hawthorn 12.19 (91)

Round 9, at Lake Oval, June 12
South Melbourne 20.9 (129) d Geelong 17.13 (115)

Round 10, at Brunswick Street, June 26
Fitzroy 14.16 (100) d South Melbourne 14.10 (94)

Round 11, at MCG, July 10
Richmond 23.20 (158) d South Melbourne 12.10 (82)

Round 12, at Lake Oval, July 17
South Melbourne 8.8 (64) d North Melb. 6.17 (53)

Round 13, at Moorabbin, July 24
St Kilda 18.9 (117) d South Melbourne 6.12 (48)

Round 14, at Princes Park, July 31
South Melbourne 13.12 (90) d Carlton 9.19 (73)

Round 15, at Lake Oval, August 7
South Melbourne 11.12 (78) d Melbourne 5.9 (39)

Round 16, at Lake Oval, August 14
Footscray 13.14 (92) d South Melbourne 10.18 (78)

Round 17, at Windy Hill, August 21
Essendon 14.13 (97) d South Melbourne 4.7 (31)

Round 18, at Lake Oval, August 28
South Melbourne 13.16 (94) d Collingwood 12.6 (78)

challenge after goals from Des Bethke and then Graeme John.

Although South turned around its run of poor luck in defeating Essendon by eight points at the Lake Oval in round six, it could not find the consistency to maintain a challenge for the top four. However, its wins over Hawthorn and Geelong in rounds eight and nine were the club's first consecutive triumphs since rounds six and seven in 1960. The Swans, after that 14-point defeat of the Cats at the Lake Oval in round nine, were eighth but just one game outside the top four. However, it had to wait a week to see whether it could maintain its challenge for a finals position as Victoria played South Australia at the MCG on the Saturday before the Swans were scheduled to play Fitzroy at Brunswick Street. Skilton and John were South's representatives in the Big Vee's 59-point romp.

The Swans were red-hot favourites to defeat the Lions in round 10, but went down narrowly yet again, by six points. However, it could have been a different result if Skilton had not been forced out of the South side after failing a late fitness test. Fitzroy's winning goal was kicked by Peter Woods with just a minute or so to play.

The VFL then had a split round, with matches played over two Saturdays, with Victoria playing Western Australia in Perth on a Tuesday and, on the way home, South Australia in Adelaide. South and Geelong took advantage of the break by playing an exhibition match at the SCG on July 3. The Swans were without Skilton and John because of interstate duties and went down by 22 points in front of an estimated attendance of 20,000.

Still without Skilton and John for the round 11 clash with Richmond at the MCG, the Swans crashed by 76 points. The huge defeat ended South's slim finals hopes as it trailed fourth-placed Essendon by two games and a massive percentage margin. The Swans

finished the season on a high note, winning three of its last five games, including a final round victory over high-flying Collingwood at the Lake Oval.

South's 16-point defeat of Collingwood prompted *The Sporting Globe* to suggest the Swans had turned the final round into an "anti-climax" as the Magpies almost lost the double chance to Geelong. *The Sporting Globe* also suggested South's "blistering pace" had upset Collingwood and that the Swans won well around the packs. Not surprisingly, Skilton was named in South's best players, along with Matthews and John.

The Swans finished eighth, with nine wins and nine defeats. It was a huge improvement on the previous few seasons and, for the first time in years, there was a mood of genuine optimism at the Lake Oval. Skilton again won the club best and fairest and polled 14 Brownlow Medal votes, six fewer than St Kilda's Ian Stewart and North Melbourne's Noel Teasdale.

PLAYER	GAMES	GOALS
BARNES, Ken	7	2
BATCH, Kevin	10	0
BETHKE, Des	9	7
BRAY, Jeff	13	1
COLVIN, Ken	5	1
DAVEY, Geoff	9	2
DAVISON, Ian	11	5
DORE, Kevin	1	0
HARRISON, Paul	18	4
HERIOT, John	15	0
HIGGINS, Paul	2	1
JOHN, Graeme	17	27
KINGSTON, Bob	18	48
LONG, John	5	2
LUCEV, Ray	15	2
MAGEE, Stuart	18	15
MATTHEWS, Herbie Jnr	17	14
McAULIFFE, Haydn	3	4
NILSSON, Ray	13	8
ORANGE, Noel	16	3
PAPLEY, Max	13	9
PARKER, Brian	1	0
PARKER, Glen	16	2
PARKER, Kevin	8	0
PEDROTTI, Kevin	2	0
RANTALL, John	18	1
REILLY, Elkin	13	1
SARICH, Eric	6	4
SELF, Alan	1	0
SKILTON, Bob	16	26
SOMERVILLE, Trevor	17	0
STRACHAN, Bob	3	0
TATE, Terry	2	1
TENABEL, Quirinus "Ron"	7	0
WHITE, Eric	7	2
WILLIAMSON, Gary	8	3

POSITION: Eighth
COACH: Bob Skilton
CAPTAIN: Bob Skilton
BEST AND FAIREST: Bob Skilton
LEADING GOALKICKER: Bob Kingston (48)

Winger Ian Davison was named South's best first-year player in 1965.

1966

During a summer holiday in his hometown of Perth, star South Melbourne centre half-forward Graeme John declared that the Swans should make the finals in 1966. With the Swans signing West Australian Austin Robertson Junior for the new season, John said: "I expect South to go close to repeating their 1933 performance when they won the premiership with about five West Australians in the side."

Journalists took up the "new Foreign Legion" theme and, in a pre-season feature in *The Herald* football writer John Craven listed South's 10 1966 "interstate" players and profiled each. The 10 were John (East Perth), Robertson (Subiaco), Eric Sarich (Swan Districts), Ray Lucev (West Perth), Eric Wilson (Swan Districts), Jeff Bray (West Adelaide), John Long (Glenelg), Fred Way (Berrigan, NSW), Doug Priest (Holbrook, NSW) and Greg Lambert (Corowa, NSW).

Austin Robertson topped South's goalkicking in his only VFL season.

Champion rover Bob Skilton again was South captain-coach and, following the highly-promising 1965 season, was able to retain most of his list. Apart from Robertson, Lambert and Priest, the Swans welcomed other promising newcomers in Tony Haenen (Mildura Imperials), Russell Cook (Portland) and John Sudholz (Rupanyup). All left their mark at the Lake Oval, with Haenen proving himself a more than handy ruckman, Cook winning the 1972 best and fairest and the burly Sudholz topping the goalkicking in consecutive seasons from 1967-70.

Austin Robertson, pictured here in a Subiaco guernsey, played just the one season with the Swans, in 1966.

South expected a protracted wrangle with the Subiaco club for Robertson's clearance but, after the WA club discussed the matter for two and a half hours, he won his release to play with the Swans early in March. The committee took into account that Robertson, a tall and quick full-forward, had been transferred to Melbourne in his employment as a journalist and had not missed a game in four years with Subiaco. Robertson said: "I'm very pleased that I'll be with the club for which my father played and of which he is a life member."

Skilton prepared his side for the opening of the season with a series of intra-club practice matches, with Way particularly impressive in the ruck and Paul Harrison outstanding at centre half-back. Then, in the final hit-out, Sudholz was so impressive that the Swans sent country club Rupanyup an urgent request to either clear him or provide him with match permits. Rupanyup, in turn, wanted a clearance for former South player Don Stanley, who had been transferred to the Wimmera as a schoolteacher. However, Stanley wanted to play with Murtoa.

Sudholz finally won his release to play with the Swans and he was named at centre half-forward for the opening round match against Fitzroy at the Lake Oval. South defeated Fitzroy by 53 points, with Robertson and Sudholz both kicking three goals on debut.

South Melbourne League Football Team—Season 1966

Back Row: I. PRICE, R. LUCEV, K. BATCH, G. JOHN, J. SUDHOLZ, K. BARNES, E. WILSON, T. HAENEN, N. ORANGE, R. TENABEL.

Standing: J. LONG, B. PARKER, R. STRACHAN, K. PEDROTTI, R. COOK, D. PRIEST, P. HARRISON, A. ROBERTSON, J. BRAY, A. SELF

Seated: T. LAHIFF (Asst. Coach), C. PASQUILL, K. PHILLIPS, R. KINGSTON (Vice-Captain), W. RICHARDS (Chairman of Selectors), R. SKILTON (Captain-Coach), E. SARICH, D. BETHKE, J. RANTALL, K. McCORMACK (Reserves' Coach).

Front Row: IAN DAVISON, S. MAGEE, H. MATTHEWS, G. PARKER, G. LAMBERT, M. PAPLEY, A. DUNN, H. McAULIFFE, G. DAVEY, A. CAMILLERI.

MATCH RESULTS

Round 1, at Lake Oval, April 23
South Melbourne 16.19 (115) d Fitzroy 9.8 (62)

Round 2, at Kardinia Park, April 30
Geelong 13.16 (94) d South Melbourne 11.8 (74)

Round 3, at Lake Oval, May 7
South Melbourne 14.22 (106) d Hawthorn 7.15 (57)

Round 4, at MCG, May 14
South Melbourne 17.17 (119) d Melbourne 12.17 (89)

Round 5, at Lake Oval, May 21
St Kilda 13.17 (95) d South Melbourne 7.11 (53)

Round 6, at MCG, May 28
Richmond 12.16 (88) d South Melbourne 9.9 (63)

Round 7, at Lake Oval, June 4
South Melb. 17.16 (118) d North Melb. 15.16 (106)

Round 8, at Princes Park, June 11
Carlton 7.15 (57) d South Melbourne 8.6 (54)

Round 9, at Lake Oval, June 18
Collingwood 13.20 (98) d South Melbourne 11.7 (73)

Round 10, at Western Oval, June 25
Footscray 8.19 (67) d South Melbourne 8.7 (55)

Round 11, at Lake Oval, July 9
Essendon 13.12 (90) d South Melbourne 12.10 (82)

Round 12, at Brunswick Street, July 16
South Melbourne 10.15 (75) d Fitzroy 8.5 (53)

Round 13, at Lake Oval, July 23
Geelong 9.17 (71) d South Melbourne 9.11 (65)

Round 14, at Glenferrie Oval, July 30
South Melbourne 14.17 (101) d Hawthorn 10.16 (76)

Round 15, at Lake Oval, August 6
South Melb. 18.17 (125) d Melbourne 15.19 (109)

Round 16, at Moorabbin, August 13
St Kilda 19.19 (133) d South Melbourne 10.6 (66)

Round 17, at Lake Oval, August 20
Richmond 10.12 (72) d South Melbourne 10.11 (71)

Round 18, at Arden Street, August 27
North Melb. 12.16 (88) d South Melbourne 11.5 (71)

Yet again, however, South's best player was Skilton, who kicked four goals, including the first of the season.

Robertson continued to impress with six goals against Geelong at Kardinia Park the next week, but the Cats defeated the Swans by 20 points. *The Sporting Globe* reported: "Austin Robertson, with six goals to his credit, lifted his team, but the Swans could not keep the ball up to him." Robertson, Bray, Harrison and Skilton were named South's best players.

The Swans, in defeating Hawthorn by 49 points in round three and then Melbourne by 30 points in round four, jumped to third position, level on match points with second-placed Collingwood and St Kilda undefeated on top. South therefore faced a huge test in the round five match against the Saints at the Lake Oval. However, St Kilda not only defeated South by 42 points, but put the skids under the Swans for the rest of the season. Although South defeated North Melbourne by 12 points at the Lake Oval in round seven, it was all downhill from there and the Swans won only three more times over the rest of the season.

Skilton again had his season interrupted by injury, with Max Papley winning the best and fairest. Robertson finished the season with 60 goals, the best by a South player since Skilton kicked the same total in 1959, but returned to Subiaco at season's end, never again to play with the Swans. He had joined the Swans in the same season as Tasmanian Peter Hudson made his VFL debut with Hawthorn and both kicked 60 goals in 1966. The Swans, after promising so much, finished a disappointing eighth, with seven wins and 11 defeats.

Skilton was so disappointed with the Swans' progress that he declared late in the season he would be stepping down as coach after the final round, indicating that he could not devote himself fully to either his coaching or captaincy duties.

Paul Harrison brings down the 'Mark of the Season' in a match against Melbourne.

Centreman Max Papley won South's 1966 best and fairest award.

PLAYER	GAMES	GOALS
BARNES, Ken	3	0
BATCH, Kevin	1	0
BETHKE, Des	7	5
BRAY, Jeff	18	1
COOK, Russell	4	0
DAVEY, Geoff	5	0
DAVISON, Ian	8	4
DORE, Kevin	5	0
DUNN, Albie	13	8
HAENEN, Tony	1	0
HARRISON, Paul	16	8
HERIOT, John	12	1
JOHN, Graeme	13	16
KINGSTON, Bob	10	9
LAMBERT, Greg	6	1
LONG, John	2	2
LUCEV, Ray	15	12
MAGEE, Stuart	14	10
MATTHEW, Herbie Jnr	17	3
McAULIFFE, Haydn	7	8
ORANGE, Noel	8	0
PAPLEY, Max	16	14
PARKER, Glen	7	3
PASQUILL, Clive	6	0
PEDROTTI, Kevin	11	0
PHILLIPS, Ken	6	2
PRIEST, Doug	8	0
RANTALL, John	14	0
REILLY, Elkin	6	0
ROBERTSON, Austin	18	60
SARICH, Eric	17	17
SELF, Alan	2	0
SKILTON, Bob	13	18
SOMERVILLE, Trevor	5	0
SUDHOLZ, John	12	10
TENABEL, Quirinus "Ron"	3	0
WAY, Fred	18	0
WILSON, Eric	6	0

POSITION: Eighth
COACH: Bob Skilton
CAPTAIN: Bob Skilton
BEST AND FAIREST: Max Papley
LEADING GOALKICKER: Austin Robertson (60)

1967

Following Bob Skilton's resignation as coach towards the end of the previous season, South Melbourne had to find a new coach for 1967. The Swans even advertised the coaching position and, for example, *The Sporting Globe* of October 1, 1966, indicated that South specifically wanted a non-playing coach and that applicants should give details of experience and other information. Just above this headline there was a report headlined TOP COACH JOB BID.

The report read: "South Melbourne Under 19 coach Allan Miller on Tuesday night told his boys that he'd apply for the Swans' top coaching job. Talk in today's footy circles makes Allan favourite for the job, but the position wasn't advertised until this weekend."

Miller had never played at VFL level and, instead, played junior football in the South Melbourne area before accepting a coaching position with Albert Park in the Melbourne Sunday Association. He took the club to two premierships before being appointed coach of the Swan Under 19s. Miller resigned his position to take a position on the club committee, but returned to the Under 19s in 1966.

Miller, despite his lack of senior experience, was appointed coach and immediately had to restart building the list as 1966 leading goalkicker Austin Robertson returned to Western Australia and other interstaters Jeff Bray, Ray Lucev and John Long ended their VFL careers. The Swans therefore lost a tremendous amount of key position experience and tried a huge batch of youngsters in practice matches leading up to the 1967 season.

However, the Swans still had Skilton as captain and former North Melbourne champion rover Allen Aylett, writing in *The Sporting Globe* suggested the South super-star could win a third Brownlow Medal. Aylett wrote that Skilton would be a much better player now that he had relinquished the coaching position and ended his report with the line: "I would be happy to see Bobby Skilton's name bracketed with triple Brownlow Medallists (Haydn) Bunton and (Dick) Reynolds." Aylett was just one year out with this prediction.

SOUTH MELBOURNE FOOTBALL CLUB

AUT VINCERE AUT MORI

REPORT OF SEASON 1967

The senior list of 1967, with coach Allan Miller fifth from the left, second front row.

MATCH RESULTS

Round 1, at Glenferrie Oval, April 15
Hawthorn 20.12 (132) d South Melbourne 15.12 (102)

Round 2, at Lake Oval, April 22
South Melbourne 15.13 (103) d Fitzroy 10.5 (65)

Round 3, at Western Oval, April 29
South Melbourne 11.13 (79) d Footscray 6.5 (41)

Round 4, at Lake Oval, May 6
South Melbourne 18.19 (127) d Essendon 13.10 (88)

Round 5, at Victoria Park, May 13
Collingwood 13.25 (103) d South Melb. 7.15 (57)

Round 6, at Kardinia Park, May 20
Geelong 16.12 (108) d South Melbourne 13.11 (89)

Round 7, at Lake Oval, May 27
South Melb. 11.12 (78) drew with Carlton 11.12 (78)

Round 8, at Lake Oval, June 3
South Melbourne 20.18 (138) d St Kilda 14.25 (109)

Round 9, at MCG, June 12
Melbourne 19.14 (128) d South Melbourne 12.17 (89)

Round 10, at Arden Street, June 24
North Melb. 16.11 (107) d South Melbourne 14.7 (91)

Round 11, at Lake Oval, July 1
Richmond 14.25 (109) d South Melbourne 8.9 (57)

Round 12, at Lake Oval, July 8
Hawthorn 13.12 (90) d South Melbourne 10.17 (77)

Round 13, at Princes Park, July 22
Fitzroy 19.21 (135) d South Melbourne 12.10 (82)

Round 14, at Lake Oval, July 29
South Melbourne 10.11 (71) d Footscray 5.10 (40)

Round 15, at Windy Hill, August 5
Essendon 14.15 (99) d South Melbourne 7.16 (58)

Round 16, at Lake Oval, August 12
Collingwood 16.14 (110) d South Melbourne 5.6 (36)

Round 17, at Lake Oval, August 19
Geelong 21.13 (139) d South Melbourne 9.9 (63)

Round 18, at Princes Park, August 26
Carlton 10.22 (82) d South Melbourne 7.7 (49)

Miller, as coach, demanded speed, speed and more speed and in the lead-up to the new season insisted that as many of his players as possible should take up professional running. Four Swans — Kevin Pedrotti, Haydn McAuliffe, Brian Parker and Greg Lambert — combined to win a special footballers' 4 x 100 yards relay at Lilydale in a meeting record of 43.9 seconds. The Swans obviously were determined to have a flying start in 1967.

The Swans, in their intra-club practice match late in March, impressed keen observers with their early form and *The Sporting Globe's* Bruce Matthews noted that ruckman Fred Way was "impressive" despite being unable to train because of business (trucking) commitments in southern New South Wales. South then was rocked by injuries in the lead-up to the opening round clash with Hawthorn at the Glenferrie Oval. Defender Doug Priest strained knee ligaments, ruckman Trevor Somerville strained a shoulder and Eric White twisted an ankle. To complicate matters for the Swans, key forward Bob Kingston had moved to Adelaide for work and was unable to get away for the final practice match.

South went into the match against Hawthorn with an inexperienced line-up and went down by 30 points. To add to the Swans' woes, full-back John Heriot was concussed in the first half and Eric Sarich (leg) also had to be replaced before the main break. Skilton started the season brilliantly with four goals, but had little support.

Despite its inexperience, South turned its form around over the next three weeks in defeating Fitzroy, Footscray and Essendon in consecutive matches. It was the first time the red and white had won three in a row since 1958. Amazingly, however, South could not break into the top four and, after defeating Essendon by 39 points, was in sixth position with three wins and one defeat. *The Sporting*

Stewart Bennett was named South's best first-year player in 1967.

Globe reported that the Swans had "swamped the Bombers" and, for a change, Skilton was not dominant. Max Papley was named best on ground, while John Sudholz kicked four goals.

Collingwood ended South's run the following week in defeating the Swans by 46 points at Victoria Park and, from there, the Swans won just two more games, plus a draw with ladder leader Carlton at the Lake Oval. The undefeated Blues virtually pinched two match points with a rushed behind in the final seconds of play. South defeated St Kilda by 29 points at the Lake Oval the following week, but then had to wait six rounds for its next win, by 31 points over Footscray at the Lake Oval.

John Sudholz, leading goalkicker in 1967.

Russell Cook was named the 'Most Improved Player' for 1967.

South finished a disappointing ninth, with five wins, a draw and 12 defeats. Skilton, who represented Victoria again in 1967, polled 11 votes in the Brownlow Medal and, at season's end travelled to Ireland via Rumania to play for an Australian side against Gaelic teams. The tour was sponsored by former VFL umpire Harry Beitzel and, because the players wore slouch hats with feathers in club colours, they were mockingly known as the Galahs.

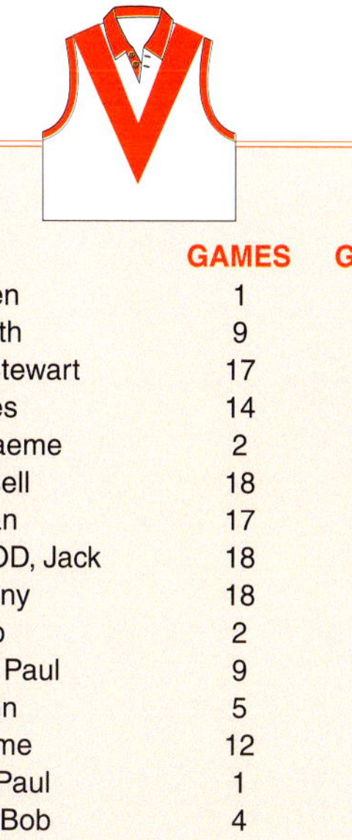

PLAYER	GAMES	GOALS
BARNES, Ken	1	0
BASKIN, Keith	9	8
BENNETT, Stewart	17	6
BETHKE, Des	14	2
BRADLY, Graeme	2	1
COOK, Russell	18	0
DAVISON, Ian	17	7
GREENWOOD, Jack	18	0
HAENEN, Tony	18	5
HANDO, Bob	2	0
HARRISON, Paul	9	2
HERIOT, John	5	2
JOHN, Graeme	12	17
KENNELLY, Paul	1	0
KINGSTON, Bob	4	11
LAMBERT, Greg	9	0
MAGEE, Stuart	18	13
MAGOR, Doug	7	0
MALLETT, Bob	4	0
MATTHEWS, Herbie Jnr	15	0
McAULIFFE, Haydn	18	16
McGEE, Jeff	5	7
MORRIS, Wayne	5	0
MULLIGAN, Mick	12	20
PAPLEY, Max	14	18
PASQUILL, Clive	3	0
PEDROTTI, Kevin	2	0
PHILLIPS, Ken	18	14
PRICE, Ian	1	0
PRIEST, Doug	7	0
RANTALL, John	6	0
ROCHE, Kevin	6	0
SARICH, Eric	17	9
SKILTON, Bob	13	11
SOMERVILLE, Trevor	2	0
SUDHOLZ, John	18	35
TENABEL, Quirinus "Ron"	7	0
VAN LINT, Wennie	2	0
WILCOX, Dick	2	2
WILLIAMS, Rod	1	0
WILSON, Eric	1	0

POSITION: Ninth
COACH: Allan Miller
CAPTAIN: Bob Skilton
BEST AND FAIREST: Bob Skilton
LEADING GOALKICKER: John Sudholz (35)

1968

Although South Melbourne in 1967 had slipped slightly from the previous season, the club kept faith with coach Allan Miller, while Bob Skilton was captain for an eighth consecutive season. The Swans' annual report for the 1967 season, in announcing Miller would coach the seniors for a second season, said: "His drive, enthusiasm, dedication and strength of character transmits itself to all players coming under his care. It was the enthusiasm of Mr Miller, more than any other factor, which enabled a young and very inexperienced side to win four of their first eight games. Unfortunately, injuries upset the structure of the team in the latter half of the season … the committee of management has unanimously appointed Mr Miller as coach in 1968."

BOB SKILTON
CAPTAIN, STH. MELBOURNE

The Swans also were forced into several off-field changes as club president Colin Ridgeway stepped down because of ill-health after serving almost five years and was replaced by barrister Brian Bourke. Also, secretary Alby Goodall resigned for business reasons following a six-year term and was replaced by Noel Brady.

South listed 16 newcomers on its 1968 list, with Port Melbourne's Peter Bedford easily the pick of the bunch. Bedford had been a star centreman with the VFA club, but crossed to the Swans without a clearance after the Borough rejected all approaches. Bedford went on to captain the Swans and win the 1970 Brownlow Medal. He always will be remembered as one of the club's greatest players. Other top 1968 recruits included Richmond ruckman Neil Busse, who later became the AFL Tribunal chairman and Melbourne pair Graeme Jacobs and Terry Leahy.

South champion Bob Skilton after being presented with his third Brownlow Medal. On the left is Footscray's Ted Whitten and, on the right, is Hawthorn's Peter Hudson. Note the two black-eyes.

However, there was one key player missing for the 1968 campaign. Hugely-talented centreman Max Papley walked out on the Swans to be captain-coach of VFA club Williamstown. *The Sporting Globe* of March 27 reported: "Max Papley will be Williamstown's captain-coach for the next three years although South have turned down

MATCH RESULTS

Round 1, at Lake Oval, April 15
South Melbourne 18.17 (125) d St Kilda 13.22 (100)

Round 2, at Glenferrie Oval, April 20
South Melb. 19.12 (126) drew with Haw. 17.24 (126)

Round 3, at Lake Oval, April 27
Melbourne 14.14 (98) d South Melbourne 13.10 (88)

Round 4, at Windy Hill, May 4
Essendon 16.19 (115) d South Melbourne 10.15 (75)

Round 5, at Lake Oval, May 11
Richmond 13.25 (103) d South Melbourne 8.10 (58)

Round 6, at Lake Oval, May 18
Carlton 12.11 (83) d South Melbourne 10.11 (71)

Round 7, at Arden Street, May 25
South Melbourne 8.13 (61) d North Melb. 7.15 (57)

Round 8, at Western Oval, June 8
South Melbourne 11.9 (75) d Footscray 9.8 (62)

Round 9, at Lake Oval, June 15
South Melb. 19.10 (124) d Collingwood 15.9 (99)

Round 10, at Kardinia Park, June 22
Geelong 13.15 (93) d South Melbourne 8.15 (63)

Round 11, at Lake Oval, June 29
South Melbourne 17.15 (117) d Fitzroy 13.12 (90)

Round 12, at Moorabbin, July 6
St Kilda 15.19 (109) d South Melbourne 6.9 (45)

Round 13, at Lake Oval, July 13
Hawthorn 15.11 (101) d South Melbourne 12.10 (82)

Round 14, at MCG, July 20
South Melbourne 12.8 (80) d Melbourne 10.10 (70)

Round 15, at Lake Oval, July 27
Essendon 14.13 (97) d South Melbourne 7.12 (54)

Round 16, at MCG, August 3
Richmond 15.21 (111) d South Melbourne 10.11 (71)

Round 17, at Princes Park, August 10
Carlton 18.14 (122) d South Melbourne 11.14 (80)

Round 18, at Lake Oval, August 17
North Melbourne 11.13 (79) d South Melb. 9.14 (68)

Round 19, at Lake Oval, August 24
Footscray 11.16 (82) d South Melbourne 11.12 (78)

Round 20, at Victoria Park, August 31
Collingwood 23.19 (157) d South Melb. 14.14 (98)

his first application for a clearance. He says he's disappointed South did not honour the transfer promise they guaranteed when he switched over from Moorabbin." South refused to budge and Papley crossed to Williamstown without a clearance. Despite the wrangle, Papley wished the Swans the best of luck and said he would miss playing alongside Skilton.

Miller started his 1968 campaign with an intra-club practice match on March 9 and warned his players that several of them would be chopped from the list to make way for newcomers. Then, after the second practice match, *The Sporting Globe* described the Swans as "snappy", with Miller and reserves coach Ken McCormack telling players they would not be selected for senior action if they were "not willing to go in hard for the ball".

South's 1968 interstate representatives – Bob Skilton (left) and Eric Sarich.

There was no let-up for the Swans and, after four practice matches, opened the season against St Kilda at the Lake Oval and, in the lead-up, former St Kilda star Neil Roberts wrote in *The Sporting Globe* that the Swans were "cocky" about their chances of upsetting the Saints and suggested star South forward Graeme John would be St Kilda's "bogey" player and warned his old side that the Swans always were dangerous on their home turf.

South named five newcomers, with Busse, Jacobs and Leahy already having VFL experience and Ron Viney (Spotswood) and Bruce Reid (Leeton) given their senior debuts. South led from start to finish to win by 25 points, with *The Sporting Globe* naming Skilton (seven goals) best on ground. Roberts wrote in *The Sporting Globe:* "Bobby Skilton magnificently skippered a brilliant, confident, explosive South as they trounced the Saints." Skilton kicked four of his seven goals in the final quarter and, after he kicked the last goal of the match, excited Swan fans rushed onto the ground believing the final siren had sounded. Umpires and police had to clear the ground for the final two minutes of play.

The Swans introduced Bedford the following week against Hawthorn at the Glenferrie Oval and he immediately stamped himself as a future champion. He not only was named among South's best players, but kicked the last goal of the match to give the Swans a draw. Hawthorn had led by 34 points at the final break, but South stormed him to kick eight last-quarter goals to salvage a draw. Skilton was named best on ground for the second time in two rounds. Amazingly, however, Skilton was knocked out in that match against Hawthorn and, on being revived, the trainers asked him to read the scoreboard to check whether he was all right. Skilton had been smart enough to glance at the scoreboard a

1968 SENIOR LIST.
Top Row: I. Davison, J. Rantall, J. Sudholz, D. Priest, R. Elwin, R. Giblett, E. Sarich, K. Pedrotti, R. Svoronich.
Second Row: J. Heriot, R. Cook, N. Anderson, R. Mohr, P. Harrison, G. Jacobs, R. Viney, T. Leahy, K. Phillips.
Third Row: R. Anderson, D. Brookes, G. Lambert, K. Baskin, R. Skilton (capt.), G. John (vice-capt.), J. Greenwood, R. Mallett, N. Busse, J. Luscombe.
Bottom Row: B. Reid, P. Bedford, D. Dey, P. McCracken, R. Williams, H. Matthews, H. McAuliffe, G. Notman.
Absent: A. Miller, S. Bennett, A. Haenan, R. Wilcox.

split second before he was crunched and was allowed to keep playing.

Although the Swans had started the season better than most critics expected, they soon fell into a hole and, by the completion of round six, had been defeated in four consecutive games to slip to tenth position, above only Hawthorn and Footscray. Then, remarkably, they won their next three matches — against North Melbourne, Footscray and Collingwood — to jump to seventh position. *The Sporting Globe* described South's 25-point defeat of Collingwood at the Lake Oval as "courageous" and described Skilton's best on ground performance as "lion-hearted".

Skilton was in magnificent form and, in the middle of South's three consecutive wins, was South's sole representative in Victoria's 53-point defeat of South Australia at the MCG. And he was able to hold his form over the rest of the season, even though the Swans found it difficult to find consistency over the second half of the season. In fact, South's only win over the final nine rounds was by 10 points over Melbourne at the MCG in round 14.

The Swans again finished a disappointing ninth, but had a huge reason to celebrate the week after the final home and away round as Skilton won his third Brownlow Medal. He polled 24 votes to defeat Geelong centreman Denis Marshall by three votes, with Fitzroy's Kevin Murray third with 18 votes. Despite Skilton's blistering season, he was not the Brownlow favourite. *The Sporting Globe* nominated Richmond rover Kevin Bartlett as the player most likely to win the medal, with Skilton, St Kilda's Carl Ditterich, Hawthorn's Peter Hudson and Carlton's Sergio Silvagni also tipped to poll well.

Dinner at the Chevron Hotel in honour of Bob Skilton's third Brownlow medal.
From left: J.W. Meehan, Justice McInerney, Bob Skilton, B.J. Bourke, Hon. V.F. Wilcox M.P. and N.S. Brady.

The Sporting Globe, in its Wednesday edition two days after the medal count described Skilton in its front page headline as "MR BROWNLOW". The newspaper reported that Skilton was unable to go to work the day after the Brownlow, not because of the celebrations, but because he had two black eyes and a severe headache, courtesy of collisions in the Swans' two final matches, against Footscray and Collingwood.

Skilton was reported as saying: "This is the best of the three. It's been worth all the pain." He also thanked wife Marion for her support and "keeping me going when I've been injured". The South champion had been in bed on the night the votes were broadcast on radio after originally planning to be at a sports night at Pentridge jail. And how did Skilton celebrate his third Brownlow Medal? He went into hospital to have an operation on his broken nose.

Skilton won the club best and fairest, with Bedford runner-up and Keith Baskin third. Bedford also won the best first-year player award, Tony Haenen was named "most improved" and Russell Cook was presented with a trophy for "the most serviceable player".

PLAYER	GAMES	GOALS
ANDERSON, Ray	7	2
BASKIN, Keith	19	17
BEDFORD, Peter	19	24
BENNETT, Stewart	13	8
BETHKE, Des	2	1
BROOKES, Don	6	0
BUSSE, Neil	17	2
COOK, Russell	19	8
DAVISON, Ian	15	11
ELWIN, Ross	8	5
GREENWOOD, Jack	4	0
HAENEN, Tony	20	13
HARRISON, Paul	16	9
HERIOT, John	14	0
JACOBS, Graeme	20	11
JOHN, Graeme	9	9
LAMBERT, Greg	13	1
LEAHY, Terry	12	4
LUKE, Richard	15	4
LUSCOMBE, John	1	0
MAGEE, Stuart	4	2
MALLETT, Bob	3	1
MATTHEWS, Herbie Jnr	15	0
MOHR, Rod	1	0
MULLIGAN, Mick	1	0
PEDROTTI, Kevin	2	0
PHILLIPS, Ken	7	2
PRIEST, Doug	9	0
RANTALL, John	18	0
REID, Bruce	2	0
SARICH, Eric	19	7
SKILTON, Bob	17	35
SUDHOLZ, John	19	36
VINEY, Ron	5	3
WILCOX, Dick	12	2
WILLIAMS, Rod	2	1

POSITION: Ninth
COACH: Allan Miller
CAPTAIN: Bob Skilton
BEST AND FAIREST: Bob Skilton
LEADING GOALKICKER: John Sudholz (36)

1969

South Melbourne, in its annual report for the 1968 season, thanked coach Allan Miller, but expressed its "regret" that the man who had been in charge for two seasons "would be unable to continue in this capacity for health and business reasons". The Swans in fact, had axed Miller and had a much bigger name in mind for the job from 1969 — former Melbourne premiership coach Norm Smith, who had taken the Demons to the 1955-57, 1959-60 and 1964 flags. The vastly-experienced Smith had played 210 games for Melbourne from 1935-48 and then 17 as captain-coach of Fitzroy in 1949-50.

The Lake Oval had become known as a coaches' graveyard by the time the Swans first approached Smith, with club secretary Noel Brady visiting the former Demon legend at his home in the inner northern Melbourne suburb of Pascoe Vale. Brady was so convinced Smith would agree to coach South that he rang club president Brian Bourke to tell him to get to Smith's house as soon as possible.

Bourke, in the book *The Red Fox*, told author Ben Collins he explained South's position to Smith, who then replied: "Well, if you agree to certain conditions, but they're because of my health — I'll coach you. I can't get out on the ground now like I used to, and like all the other coaches do these days. But if you get Ian Thorogood to be my assistant, Clyde Laidlaw to coach the seconds and Donny Williams to coach the thirds, I'll coach them for you."

Smith wanted to surround himself with his former Melbourne charges and Bourke told him "you're the man". After agreeing to take on one of football's toughest jobs, Smith said he was not interested in money, but Bourke settled the coaching fee at $25,000 a year. Bourke told Collins for *The Red Fox:* "The deal was done within about 20 minutes of me arriving, I'd had no idea Norm Smith was interested in coaching again, so it was a complete fluke that we got him."

Getting Smith to commit himself to the Swans was the easy part as the club then had to stump up the money to pay him. Several key Swan coterie members, including lingerie

MATCH RESULTS

Round 1, at Arden Street, April 5
North Melb. 15.20 (110) d South Melb. 14.17 (101)

Round 2, at Lake Oval, April 12
Fitzroy 15.10 (100) d South Melbourne 14.14 (98)

Round 3, at Kardinia Park, April 19
Geelong 19.20 (134) d South Melbourne 11.8 (74)

Round 4, at Lake Oval, April 26
Richmond 19.22 (136) d South Melbourne 13.13 (91)

Round 5, at Princes Park, May 3
Carlton 20.17 (137) d South Melbourne 17.10 (112)

Round 6, at Lake Oval, May 10
South Melbourne 14.9 (93) d St Kilda 7.14 (56)

Round 7, at Western Oval, May 17
South Melbourne 9.12 (66) d Footscray 8.10 (58)

Round 8, at Lake Oval, May 24
Collingwood 18.22 (130) d South Melb. 11.8 (74)

Round 9, at MCG, May 31
South Melbourne 14.10 (94) d Melbourne 9.15 (69)

Round 10, at Lake Oval, June 14
Essendon 18.15 (123) d South Melb. 15.13 (103)

Round 11, at Glenferrie Oval, June 21
Hawthorn 25.13 (163) d South Melbourne 14.21 (105)

Round 12, at Lake Oval, June 28
South Melbourne 12.11 (83) d North Melb. 11.14 (80)

Round 13, at Princes Park, July 5
Fitzroy 18.21 (129) d South Melbourne 11.14 (80)

Round 14, at Lake Oval, July 12
Geelong 17.11 (113) d South Melbourne 12.15 (87)

Round 15, at MCG, July 19
Richmond 22.12 (144) d South Melbourne 11.11 (77)

Round 16, at Lake Oval, July 26
Carlton 19.12 (126) d South Melbourne 11.8 (74)

Round 17, at Moorabbin, August 9
South Melbourne 15.10 (100) d St Kilda 9.14 (68)

Round 18, at Lake Oval, August 16
South Melbourne 16.17 (113) d Footscray 13.18 (96)

Round 19, at Victoria Park, August 23
Collingwood 19.15 (129) d South Melb. 6.22 (58)

Round 20, at Lake Oval, August 30
South Melbourne 17.18 (120) d Melbourne 13.7 (85)

king Leon Worth, agreed to make donations, while Smith himself donated $500. Smith, as coach, then laid down the law to his players from the very start, not even allowing triple Brownlow Medallist Bob Skilton to escape his attention.

Skilton turned up late for the annual general meeting at the South Melbourne Town Hall and, despite the Swan champion winning rapturous applause as he took his seat, Smith later told him: "Bobby, I'm coach here now. Never be late for another function at South Melbourne. Understand?" Skilton got the message and so did the rest of the team as Smith brought discipline to a club with a reputation for laxity.

Smith had little material at the Lake Oval and was asked to transform pigs' ears to silk. Besides, champion full-back John Heriot had accepted the job as captain-coach of VFA club Yarraville, defender Des Bethke retired and later became Town Clerk for the Melbourne City Council and several players were chopped from the list.

However, the Swans produced several outstanding recruits in 1969, thanks partly to country zoning, which was introduced the previous season, but did not have any real effect until the following season as, in the lead-up to this new zoning scheme, clubs signed just about every promising country youngster. Club names were placed in the premiership cup and, as the zones were called, these names were pulled out. South drew the short-straw of southern New South Wales.

Regardless, South's first batch of country zone recruits included Steve Hoffman (Pyramid Hill), David McLeish (Wodonga) and John Pitura (Wagga Tigers). Hoffman became a star rover, McLeish was a solid and reliable defender and Pitura enjoyed considerable success with the Swans before becoming embroiled in an ugly clearance wrangle with Richmond. The Swans also won a release for Richmond centreman Wayne Walsh and, during the season, the Tigers' Alan "Bull" Richardson. Tasmanian Arthur Budd also joined the Swans in 1969 as a "boom" recruit but, after showing great form over just seven games in his debut season, had to abandon his VFL career because of illness.

Norm Smith was appointed South coach in 1969.

Also, the Swans lured ruckman Fred Way back to the club after he originally had indicated he would stay in the country to concentrate on his trucking business. The Swans allowed Way to stay in Berrigan for most of the week, as long as he travelled down to train on a Thursday night and then play on the Saturday,

Former Collingwood champion Bill Twomey, in *The Sporting Globe* of March 19, wrote under the headline SOUTH NEED A

WAND: "South will have to rely heavily on the Norm Smith 'magic' if they're going to make the four this year. The talk in football circles is that there'll be a big improvement in the Swans. Smithy himself won't be satisfied with anything less than an appearance on the MCG in September. Admittedly, there could be a big improvement, but they'd have to have some trump cards up their sleeve."

Disaster then struck the Swans just a week before the opening round match against North Melbourne at Arden Street. Skilton snapped an Achilles tendon in a practice match against the Port Adelaide Magpies in Adelaide and was ruled out for the entire season. *The Sporting Globe* reported: "Bob Skilton fell heavily and was helped from the ground with a leg injury in the first quarter against Port Adelaide today." To make matters worse, Port defeated South. Defender John Rantall therefore assumed the captaincy for the 1969 season.

Fred Way, a quality ruckman.

South opened the season with four newcomers. Apart from Walsh and former Melbourne player Rob Dowsing, the Swans introduced Budd and Graham Brandt (South Bendigo). The Roos jumped the Swans to lead by 35 points at half-time and, despite a late South surge, won by nine points. Smith would have liked better in his first game as South coach, but South had fine players in Rantall, Graeme Jacobs (five goals) and Keith Baskin (four).

Besides, there were encouraging signs the following week when South went down to Fitzroy by just two points at the Lake Oval. The Swans had a late chance to win the game, but Baskin missed a set shot from 50 metres. This narrow defeat was followed by losses to Geelong, Richmond and Carlton and Smith therefore was waiting for his first victory as South coach when the red and white hosted St Kilda at the Lake Oval in round six.

Finally, the Swans broke through, defeating the Saints by 37 points. *The Sporting Globe* reported: "The youthful Swans reduced the

PLAYER	GAMES	GOALS
ANDERSON, Ray	2	0
BASKIN, Keith	12	16
BEDFORD, Peter	19	26
BENNETT, Stewart	7	8
BRANDT, Graham	12	2
BUDD, Arthur	7	2
BUSSE, Neil	1	0
CATLIN, Sid	7	10
COGHLAN, John	2	1
COOK, Russell	20	8
COOPER, Reuben	2	0
DAVISON, Ian	4	2
DOWSING, Rob	4	6
DOYLE, Robert	10	3
HAENEN, Tony	18	0
HARRISON, Paul	19	0
HARTREE, John	1	1
HOFFMAN, Steve	12	24
JACOBS, Graeme	18	24
JOHN, Graeme	9	12
LAMBERT, Greg	18	1
LEAHY, Terry	19	3
LUKE, Richard	4	0
LUSCOMBE, Ken	7	0
MATTHEWS, Herbie Jnr	10	0
McAULIFFE, Haydn	19	31
McCRACKEN, Peter	5	0
McLEISH, David	9	0
MOHR, Rod	6	1
PAGE, Graham	1	0
PHILLIPS, Ken	2	0
PITURA, John	12	14
PRIEST, Doug	2	0
RANTALL, John	20	3
REID, Bruce	3	0
RICHARDSON, Alan	6	9
SUDHOLZ, John	15	35
SVORINICH, Robert	7	7
WALSH, Wayne	16	0
WAY, Fred	19	8
WETZEL, Ron	12	0
WILLIAMS, Gary	2	0

POSITION: Ninth
COACH: Norm Smith
CAPTAIN: John Rantall
BEST AND FAIREST: Peter Bedford
LEADING GOALKICKER: John Sudholz (35)

powerful Saints to a mediocre side as they raced away with their first win for new coach Norm Smith at the Lake Oval today." Walsh and Peter Bedford starred for the Swans, while Graeme John kicked three goals. South defeated Footscray by eight points the following week, but the football world was looking further ahead, to Smith's tangle with his old club at the MCG in round nine.

South president Bourke, realising how much this game meant to Smith, asked the coach if he could address the team before the start of play. The players, revved up for their coach, scored 8.1 to 3.5 in the first quarter and went on to win by 25 points. *The Sporting Globe* match report headline read SWANS ALL THE WAY! Full-forward John Sudholz kicked seven goals and rover Haydn McAuliffe three. South's best players were Sudholz, Hoffman, McAuliffe, Bedford, Paul Harrison and Way.

Herb Matthews Jnr. His father, Herb Matthews Snr, played 191 games with South from 1932-1945.

After defeating North Melbourne by three points at the Lake Oval in round 12, key forward John retired because of recurring shoulder and knee injuries. He briefly played in the VFA with Port Melbourne the following year, but abandoned his football career after just a few games with the Borough when he had to travel to the United States on business.

The Swans won three more over the rest of the season and, appropriately defeated Melbourne by 35 points in the final round to give Smith a double over his old side. South finished ninth for a third consecutive season, but there were brighter days ahead. The club's annual report for the 1969 season noted: "A great deal of work still remains to be done, and our ultimate goal can only be achieved by all associated with the club contributing to the best of his ability without any thought of reward, apart from success that will belong to the South Melbourne Football Club."

Bedford won the best and fairest, with Way runner-up and McAuliffe third. Walsh won the best first-year player award and Rantall the club's Outstanding Service Award as captain in the absence of Skilton.

Peter Bedford, South's 1969 best and fairest.

1970

The ladder position of ninth in 1969 was no reflection of the vast improvement South Melbourne showed under the coaching of Norm Smith. Good football judges therefore suggested the Swans would climb the ladder. Besides, the Swans were confident they would regain their brilliant skipper, Bob Skilton, after missing the entire 1969 season through snapping an Achilles tendon in a practice match in Adelaide. Skilton had had his injured leg in plaster for 14 weeks and spent 16 weeks on crutches. He put on 20kg during his lay-off and therefore had to work harder than any other Swan on the training track in the lead-up to the 1970 season.

South retained most of the players they saw as necessary for the rebuilding of the side, although winger Ian Davison, defender Herb Matthews and the versatile Ken Phillips retired from VFL football. However, the Swans picked up several promising players, including Reg Gleeson (Lockhart), Gary Brice and Shane McKew (Port Melbourne), John Murphy (Sturt) and Rick Quade (Ariah Park). Gleeson, Brice, McKew, and Murphy all had fine debut seasons, but Quade injured an anterior cruciate ligament on debut and missed the rest of the season.

Quade's brothers Tom and Mick had played for North Melbourne and young Rick barracked for the Kangaroos. In fact, he wanted to join North before country zoning was introduced but his father believed Rick, at 17, was too young to play in the VFL. The Roos' loss was the Swans' gain as Quade not only developed into a champion ruck-rover, but captained and coached the Swans before serving the club as a director.

The young Quade had built an enormous reputation in the country and Smith believed his star recruit would be as good as the great Ron Barassi. *The Sporting Globe* agreed and, after the newcomer starred in a practice match, it reported: "At South Melbourne, Ricky Quade, from Ariah Park, had supporters comparing him with Austin Robertson Junior. Quade is a similar build and, like Robertson, shoots accurately for goal with drop punts. He looks like filling the spearhead position for South."

South champion Bob Skilton leads his side onto the MCG in his only finals match, the 1970 first semi-final against St Kilda.

South opened the season against Melbourne at the MCG with Brice, McKew, Murphy, Quade and Tasmanian Jim Wilkinson making their VFL debuts. Quade lined up at full-forward but, after winning four first-quarter possessions and taking two marks, injured his knee and was replaced by Wilkinson. It was a savage blow to both player and club, especially as the Demons defeated the Swans by 25 points. Quade had a knee reconstruction and was sidelined 12 months. South's best in the disappointing start to the season were ruckman Fred Way and centreman Wayne Walsh.

The Swans, however, were still without Skilton and he made his long-awaited return

MATCH RESULTS

Round 1, at Lake Oval, April 4
Melbourne 14.9 (93) d South Melbourne 9.14 (68)
Round 2, at Arden Street, April 11
South Melbourne 8.12 (60) d North Melb. 8.11 (59)
Round 3, at Lake Oval, April 18
Essendon 15.10 (100) d South Melbourne 12.17 (89)
Round 4, at Waverley Park, April 25
South Melbourne 11.11 (77) d Footscray 9.6 (60)
Round 5, at MCG, May 2
South Melbourne 10.11 (71) d Richmond 6.13 (49)
Round 6, at Lake Oval, May 9
South Melbourne 9.25 (79) d St Kilda 9.8 (62)
Round 7, at Lake Oval, May 16
South Melbourne 23.12 (150) d Carlton 10.13 (73)
Round 8, at Glenferrie Oval, May 23
Hawthorn 21.20 (146) d South Melbourne 12.12 (84)
Round 9, at Lake Oval, May 30
South Melbourne 19.14 (128) d Geelong 10.18 (78)
Round 10, at Junction Oval, June 6
Fitzroy 14.9 (93) d South Melbourne 12.19 (91)
Round 11, at Lake Oval, June 15
South Melb. 16.15 (111) d Collingwood 16.14 (110)
Round 12, at Waverley Park, June 20
South Melbourne 12.10 (82) d Melbourne 12.6 (78)
Round 13, at Lake Oval, June 27
South Melbourne 16.9 (105) d North Melb. 14.12 (96)
Round 14, at Waverley Park, July 4
South Melbourne 11.5 (71) d Essendon 5.10 (40)
Round 15, at Western Oval, July 11
South Melbourne 13.10 (88) d Footscray 6.4 (40)
Round 16, at Lake Oval, July 18
Richmond 12.17 (89) d South Melbourne 11.9 (75)
Round 17, at Moorabbin, July 25
St Kilda 13.14 (92) d South Melbourne 11.6 (72)
Round 18, at Princes Park, August 1
Carlton 11.17 (83) d South Melbourne 10.19 (79)
Round 19, at Lake Oval, August 8
South Melbourne 16.7 (103) d Hawthorn 13.8 (86)
Round 20, at Kardinia Park, August 15
South Melbourne 11.15 (81) d Geelong 10.14 (74)
Round 21, at Lake Oval, August 22
South Melbourne 14.15 (99) d Fitzroy 10.20 (80)
Round 22, at Victoria Park, August 29
Collingwood 22.15 (147) d South Melbourne 7.9 (51)
First semi-final, at MCG, September 5
St Kilda 22.11 (143) d South Melbourne 13.12 (90)

The front cover of the club's annual report for the 1970 season.

in the round two match against North Melbourne at Arden Street. Despite his long absence, he looked as if he had not missed a beat and picked up 31 possessions. He also kicked two goals and *Footy Week* named him the Swans' best player in the one-point defeat of the Kangaroos. Skilton spent most of the first half in the forward pocket, but later was moved on to the ball, with devastating effect. North could have stolen victory in the final minute, but Roo forward Maurie Wood kicked into the man on the mark from a set shot.

After going down to Essendon by 11 points at the Lake Oval in round three, South notched four consecutive wins to be rated a definite finals chance. The most stunning of these wins was by 77 points over Carlton at the Lake Oval in round seven. *Footy Week* reported: "Smithy's Swans beat Barassi's baffled Blues at South Melbourne with a display that must have delighted South fans." The report suggested Peter Bedford "had the ball on a string" and that Russell Cook dominated at centre half-forward.

South jumped into rarified air with this win as it was second on the ladder behind Collingwood. However, stumbling against Hawthorn and Fitzroy meant the clash against Collingwood at the Lake Oval became vital. South was still second but three games behind Collingwood and inside the top four by just a game from fifth-placed St Kilda. The top of the ladder Swans-Magpies clash attracted a massive attendance of 35,567 and most observers believed it was the Swans' acid test for making the finals for the first time in 25 years.

The Swans started nervously but, recovering their poise, led by five points at half-time. Collingwood, however, took control early in the final quarter before South hit back to take the lead with just two minutes to play. South fans were so overjoyed they rushed onto the ground in their excitement in the mistaken belief the final siren had blared. Then, after umpires and police cleared the ground, the Swans held on to win by a point.

It was one of several close South wins in 1970 and easily the most extraordinary was against Geelong at Kardinia Park in round 20. The Swans, clinging desperately to fourth position, led the Cats by eight points with just a few minutes to play when Geelong's Doug Wade had a shot for goal. The ball seemed certain to go through the goals, but hit an apple in mid-flight and slewed offline for a behind. The apple had been thrown by a South fan, but there was little umpire Jeff Crouch could do about it. In another extraordinary incident, South at one stage had 19 men on the ground and Crouch had to order McKew to the bench.

South's Peter Bedford receives the 1970 Brownlow Medal from the Governor of Victoria, Sir Rohan Delacombe.

PLAYER	GAMES	GOALS
BASKIN, Keith	15	19
BEDFORD, Peter	23	50
BENNETT, Stewart	16	3
BRICE, Gary	23	20
CATLIN, Sid	8	4
COOK, Russell	23	18
DAVIS, Bruce	1	1
DOYLE, Robert	2	0
ELWIN, Ross	2	1
GLEESON, Reg	18	2
HAENEN, Tony	23	1
HARRISON, Paul	6	0
HOFFMAN, Steve	7	8
JACOBS, Graeme	19	0
LAMBERT, Greg	16	0
LEAHY, Terry	8	2
LUKE, Richard	20	12
McAULIFFE, Haydn	22	18
McCRACKEN, Peter	1	0
McKEW, Shane	18	4
McLEISH, David	22	2
MILLER, Neville	6	0
MURPHY, John	20	13
PAVONE, Mick	6	7
PITURA, John	23	0
QUADE, Rick	1	0
RANTALL, John	22	1
RICHARDSON, Alan	1	0
SKILTON, Bob	20	33
SUDHOLZ, John	20	60
WALSH, Wayne	19	0
WAY, Fred	18	0
WETZEL, Ron	6	1
WILKINSON, Jim	1	0
WILLIAMS, Gary	4	6

POSITION: Fourth
COACH: Norm Smith
CAPTAIN: Bob Skilton
BEST AND FAIREST: Peter Bedford
LEADING GOAKICKER: John Sudholz (60)

Swans Bob Skilton (left) and John Pitura have it all covered in the 1970 first semi-final.

McKew just a minute earlier had been injured and, while he was being treated, reserve Haydn McAuliiffe ran on to the ground.

The Swans clinched their finals position before a final round thrashing by Collingwood at Victoria Park. Meanwhile, South was overjoyed when Bedford won the Brownlow Medal at the first televised dinner, at the Sir Dallas Brooks Hall in East Melbourne. Ironically, the site once had been where Bedford had gone to school, at CBC Parade. Bedford polled 25 votes to defeat Footscray ruckman Gary Dempsey by four votes, with Carlton's Alex Jesaulenko (20 votes) third.

South was the raging sentimental favourite for the first semi-final against St Kilda at the MCG. The Saints were hardened finals campaigners as they had won the flag just four years earlier, while the Swans were in their first final since going down to Carlton in the 1945 "Bloodbath" Grand Final. A massive crowd of 104,329 roared as Skilton, in his only finals match, led the Swans on to the MCG.

The young Swans took it up to the Saints over the first half and even went into the main break with a five-point lead. However, it was obvious St Kilda's greater physical strength would tell. St Kilda took control in the third quarter and went on to win by 53 points. The Swans were far from disgraced, but found Saint ruckmen Carl Ditterich and Brian Mynott too strong. Former VFL umpire Harry Beitzel, wrote in *Footy Week*: "St Kilda's big-man strength and a bad case of finals 'jitters' were the undoing of South Melbourne in the first semi-final."

South's best were Walsh, Hoffman, Brice, Murphy, Skilton, Haenen and Way. Hoffman kicked four goals and Bedford three. The South annual report for the 1970 season ran the line THE 25-YEAR DROUGHT IS BROKEN on the front cover. Inside, it said: "Respect is a hard quality to earn in the field of League football; for 25 years the South Melbourne Football Club earned nothing but sympathy. They were painful years that just had to come to an end. They did this season when the club won the praise and congratulations of the Victorian football public by reaching fourth place on the premiership ladder and playing its first finals match for a quarter of a century."

Swan centre half-forward Russell Cook leans back to take a mark against North Melbourne in 1970.

1971

The South Melbourne committee knew that one swallow did not make a summer and that the Swans had to have continuous success to win full credibility after breaking the finals drought in 1970. The club annual report for 1970 said: "The future! It is what we make it. We know the congratulations of this season will turn to envy as we continue to succeed, and succeed we must. But South Melbourne making the top four has set for itself a standard that must be maintained because any VFL side that doesn't make the finals today is considered to have failed and is penalised accordingly. South already is looking forward and planning the year ahead and realises it must overcome the restrictions on obtaining ready-made League players, whether they be from interstate of metropolitan zones."

The Swans were having a discreet swipe at the VFL country zoning scheme as they had to develop a sparsely populated region while clubs like Carlton (Bendigo) and Hawthorn (Mornington Peninsula and parts of Gippsland), in particular, had easily accessible zones with large populations. South therefore had few quality recruits for 1971, although Ariah Park's Jim Prentice was a handy key forward who went on to play 58 games with the Swans to 1974.

South, to add experience and height to its list, also recruited two players from rival VFL clubs — Richmond's Ray Ball and Collingwood's Ernie Hug. Ball played 43 games, mainly at full-back in the red and white to 1974 while Hug played just the 15 games with the Swans in 1971. Although Hug might not have left a lasting on-field impression at the Lake Oval, he surely must have been the only player in club history to arrive at training in a Rolls Royce.

Despite the scarcity of talent in South's country zone, it welcomed the return of boom country recruit Rick Quade following his severe knee injury in the opening round of the 1970 season. Quade made his comeback against Melbourne in the opening round of 1971 and picked up 11 possessions, He took four marks and kicked a goal to suggest he certainly would have an impact at VFL level.

The downside was that South lost a vast amount of experience over the summer of 1970-71, with ruckman Stewart Bennett, Paul Harrison, Graeme Jacobs and Terry Leahy ending their VFL careers. To make matters more difficult for the Swans, full-forward John Sudholz retired after just two games in 1971. These departures left the Swans desperately short of quality and height in the ruck and in key positions.

South, for a second consecutive season, opened with a match against Melbourne at the MCG. The Demons gave the Swans a taste of what to expect over the rest of the season with a 105-point thumping. It was a far cry from the gallant efforts of the previous season. Inimitable former Collingood captain Lou Richards was so underwhelmed by

Ray Ball was a handy full-back for the Swans after crossing from Richmond.

MATCH RESULTS

Round 1, at MCG, April 3
Melbourne 24.21 (165) d South Melbourne 7.18 (60)

Round 2, at Lake Oval, April 10
Geelong 16.14 (110) d South Melbourne 12.20 (92)

Round 3, at Western Oval, April 17
Footscray 14.15 (99) d South Melbourne 14.9 (93)

Round 4, at Lake Oval, April 24
Richmond 20.13 (133) d South Melbourne 5.9 (39)

Round 5, at Waverley Park, May 1
Hawthorn 12.21 (83) d South Melbourne 6.9 (45)

Round 6, at Lake Oval, May 8
Carlton 14.10 (94) d South Melbourne 13.14 (92)

Round 7, at Windy Hill, May 15
South Melbourne 16.9 (105) d Essendon 12.17 (89)

Round 8, at Lake Oval, May 22
Fitzroy 19.19 (133) d South Melbourne 13.11 (89)

Round 9, at Victoria Park, May 29
Collingwood 15.10 (100) d South Melb. 10.6 (66)

Round 10, at Lake Oval, June 5
St Kilda 18.23 (131) d South Melbourne 9.6 (60)

Round 11, at Arden Street, June 14
South Melbourne 13.20 (98) d North Melb. 12.17 (89)

Round 12, at Waverley Park, June 19
Melbourne 6.13 (49) d South Melbourne 2.6 (18)

Round 13, at Kardinia Park, June 26
Geelong 13.9 (87) d South Melbourne 9.12 (66)

Round 14, at Lake Oval, July 3
Footscray 19.11 (125) d South Melbourne 18.15 (123)

Round 15, at MCG, July 10
Richmond 12.18 (90) d South Melbourne 11.13 (79)

Round 16, at Lake Oval, July 17
Hawthorn 11.16 (82) d South Melbourne 3.15 (33)

Round 17, at Princes Park, July 24
Carlton 24.16 (160) d South Melbourne 11.7 (73)

Round 18, at Lake Oval, July 31
Essendon 13.18 (96) d South Melbourne 13.8 (86)

Round 19, at Junction Oval, August 7
Fitzroy 11.17 (83) d South Melbourne 8.10 (58)

Round 20, at Waverley Park, August 14
Collingwood 18.18 (126) d South Melbourne 9.8 (62)

Round 21, at Moorabbin, August 21
St Kilda 18.14 (122) d South Melbourne 6.14 (50)

Round 22, at Lake Oval, August 28
South Melbourne 19.17 (131) d North Melb. 8.11 (59)

Bob Skilton after his final game, against North Melbourne, with his father Robert (centre) and Swan supporter and future Australian Prime Minister Bob Hawke.

South's performance that he wrote in *The Sun* that Melbourne would win the 1971 flag and South would win one in 1972 — in the VFA. He described the match as a "slaughter" and suggested the Swans "didn't have a feather to fly with".

South's woes deepened when 1970 Brownlow Medal winner Peter Bedford cracked ribs in the round three defeat by Footscray. South was winless after three rounds and Richmond compounded its misery with a 94-point thrashing at the Lake Oval.

SOUTH MELBOURNE
FOOTBALL CLUB
ANNUAL REPORT 1971

South Melbourne commissioned this oil painting of triple Brownlow Medal winner Bob Skilton. A photograph of this painting was used on the front cover of the 1971 annual report.

South reacted by making six changes to the side to play Hawthorn at Waverley Park in round five. Centreman Wayne Walsh, who had been dropped the previous week for disciplinary reasons, returned to the side, but the Hawks defeated the Swans by 38 points.

PLAYER	GAMES	GOALS
BALL, Ray	8	0
BASKIN, Keith	8	7
BEDFORD, Peter	18	44
BELL, Robert	2	0
BRANDT, Graham	1	0
BRICE, Gary	21	13
BROWN, Peter	8	0
CARRODUS, Trevor	2	2
COOK, Russell	8	4
DAVIS, Bruce	11	1
DOYLE, Robert	12	4
DROSCHER, Dave	2	2
GLEESON, Reg	22	0
GRIMA, Robert	5	6
HAENEN, Tony	13	8
HAINES, Jim	9	0
HAY, Robert	7	0
HOCKING, Graham	1	0
HOFFMAN, Steve	18	31
HUG, Ernie	15	0
LAMBERT, Greg	9	0
MATTHEWS, Dennis	1	0
MacGREGOR, Duncan	1	0
McAULIFFE, Haydn	9	6
McCRACKEN, Peter	9	1
McHENRY, Russ	9	7
McKEW, Shane	1	0
McLEISH, David	19	3
MILLER, Neville	12	14
MURPHY, John	21	6
OFFICER, Steve	5	2
PAGE, Ron	3	1
PAVONE, Mick	4	2
PAYNE, John	1	0
PITURA, John	20	8
PRENTICE, Jim	12	8
QUADE, Rick	18	20
RANTALL, John	22	1
ROBERTSON, Garry	4	0
SARICH, Eric	3	1
SKILTON, Bob	19	16
SUDHOLZ, John	2	0
SVORINICH, Robert	1	0
WALSH, Wayne	20	4
WAY, Fred	20	5
WILKINSON, Jim	4	0

POSITION: Twelfth
COACH: Norm Smith
CAPTAIN: Bob Skilton
BEST AND FAIREST: Peter Bedford
LEADING GOALKICKER: Peter Bedford (44)

Despite their woeful start to the season, the Swans almost upset reigning premier Carlton at the Lake Oval in round six. The Blues scraped home by two points. This performance was highly encouraging and, in the next round, the Swans broke through to defeat Essendon by 16 points at Windy Hill. It was South's first win at Essendon's home ground for 26 years. Recruit full-forward Neville Miller (Wagga) kicked five goals and Bedford was rated best on ground.

Rick Quade has given the Swans a lifetime of devotion, as player, coach and director.

The Swans defeated North Melbourne by nine points at Arden Street in round 11 but, at the halfway mark of the season was eleventh on the ladder, one game clear of bottom side Geelong. But, with the Cats staging a late-season revival, the Swans were doomed to collect the wooden-spoon.

South turned in several woeful performances, including a score of just 2.6 (18) in going down to Melbourne by 31 points at Waverley Park in round 12. Rover Steve Hoffman kicked both goals and it was the most recent occasion in which a South/Sydney Swans player kicked the entire goals tally in a match. South also scored a woeful 3.15 (33) in going down to Hawthorn by 49 points at the Lake Oval in round 16.

The Swans went into the final round match against North Melbourne at the Lake Oval without any hope of avoiding last position, but had a massive incentive to defeat North as their greatest champion, Bob Skilton, earlier in the season had announced this would be his last in the VFL and the match against the Roos therefore was his last hurrah.

Skilton's teammates did him proud in sending him off in style with a 72-point thrashing of the Roos. Bedford kicked seven goals and Quade four, while Skilton set the standard for his teammates with eight possessions in the first quarter. He racked up 23 possessions in his final match and kicked one goal. The South players surrounded Skilton at the final siren and carried him from the ground to the applause of fans from both sides. Skilton had played 237 games and kicked 412 goals with the Swans from his debut in 1956 and, apart from his three Brownlow Medals, won the Swans' best and fairest nine times. Truly a club legend!

Peter Bedford, a wonderfully loyal club servant.

1972

With the retirement of Bob Skilton at the end of the 1971 season, South Melbourne appointed the experienced John Rantall as captain for 1972. Rantall, of course, had stood in for Skilton when the triple Brownlow Medallist missed the 1969 season with an Achilles injury. There was no doubt the Swans would miss Skilton's enormous class but they had another Brownlow Medal winner in Peter Bedford. Elsewhere, however, the cupboard was bare. Ruckman Tony Haenen crossed to VFA club Port Melbourne and there was little talent emerging from the Swans' country zone.

The best of South's country zone recruits in 1972 was centre half-back Max Robertson but, unfortunately, he seriously injured a knee after moving from Cohuna Union. Centre half-forward Stewart Gull, whose father Jim had played for the Swans, moved from North Ballarat and went on to play 87 games to 1978, while classy rover Norm Goss was recruited from Port Melbourne. Goss played 121 games with South to 1977 before crossing to Hawthorn. South also recruited Melbourne's George Lakes, Richmond's Eric Moore and Hawthorn's Lance Morton during the season.

South started its pre-season campaign with a practice match against Carlton at Princes Park on March 4. The Blues defeated the Swans by seven points and, the following week, Skilton announced that he might make a comeback — with Port Melbourne. He explained that when he retired the previous season he never intended playing again, but admitted he had developed "itchy feet" over the summer and had kept himself fit "just in case".

The Swans opened their season with a split round Monday match against Geelong at the Lake Oval and Lou Richards, writing in *The Sun,* predicted the Cats would "eat" the home team. He asked: "How could anyone bar (South coach) Norm Smith go for South Melbourne ... they have been so bad at South that yesterday the tide went out and didn't come back. Even the artificial flowers in the clubrooms have died."

South rubbed egg all over Richards' face as it defeated Geelong by 12 points, with Goss kicking three goals on debut. Bedford was named best on ground and *The Sun's* Bob

South key forward Stewart Gull drives the ball forward against Collingwood.

MATCH RESULTS

Round 1, at Lake Oval, April 3
South Melbourne 10.13 (73) d Geelong 9.7 (61)

Round 2, at Windy Hill, April 8
Essendon 16.11 (107) d South Melbourne 7.18 (60)

Round 3, at Lake Oval, April 15
Carlton 18.18 (126) d South Melbourne 14.10 (94)

Round 4, at MCG, April 22
Melbourne 18.19 (127) d South Melbourne 8.8 (56)

Round 5, at Lake Oval, April 29
St Kilda 9.16 (70) d South Melbourne 5.17 (47)

Round 6, at Waverley Park, May 6
South Melb. 14.22 (106) d North Melb. 13.13 (91)

Round 7, at Glenferrie Oval, May 13
Hawthorn 13.14 (92) d South Melbourne 9.20 (74)

Round 8, at Lake Oval, May 20
Fitzroy 18.11 (119) d South Melbourne 9.7 (61)

Round 9, at Western Oval, May 27
Footscray 12.9 (81) d South Melbourne 9.10 (64)

Round 10, at Lake Oval, June 3
Collingwood 19.14 (128) d South Melb. 8.11 (59)

Round 11, at MCG, June 10
Richmond 14.11 (95) d South Melbourne 2.19 (31)

Round 12, at Kardinia Park, June 24
Geelong 15.14 (104) d South Melbourne 10.13 (73)

Round 13, at Lake Oval, July 1
Essendon 13.9 (87) d South Melbourne 12.12 (84)

Round 14, at Lake Oval, July 8
Melbourne 14.9 (93) d South Melbourne 10.9 (69)

Round 15, at Princes Park, July 15
Carlton 20.8 (128) d South Melbourne 8.15 (63)

Round 16, at Waverley Park, July 22
St Kilda 14.11 (95) d South Melbourne 9.5 (59)

Round 17, at Arden Street, July 29
North Melb. 12.15 (87) d South Melbourne 11.12 (78)

Round 18, at Lake Oval, August 5
Hawthorn 23.10 (148) d South Melbourne 13.11 (89)

Round 19, at Junction Oval, August 12
Fitzroy 14.14 (98) d South Melbourne 6.17 (53)

Round 20, at Lake Oval, August 19
Footscray 11.13 (79) d South Melbourne 9.12 (66)

Round 21, at Victoria Park, August 26
Collingwood 22.17(149) d South Melbourne 11.6 (72)

Round 22, at Waverley Park, September 2
Richmond 23.20 (158) d South Melbourne 12.10 (82)

Stewart Gull was an extremely good mark.

Peter Bedford squirts out a handpass at training.

Crimeen reported: "Big-hearted Russell Cook never stopped trying to combat Geelong's heavyweight rucks." The Swans, after such a dismal 1971 season, were in fourth place, but facing a tough test against Essendon at Windy Hill in round two.

With the Bombers thrashing the Swans by 47 points, reality hit home — that the red and white again would struggle, despite the wizardry of coach Smith. The Swans the next week paid Hawthorn $5000 to release Morton, but still went down to Carlton by 32 points at the Lake Oval. Defeat followed defeat, but the Swans broke through to defeat North Melbourne by 15 points in front of just 9000 fans at Waverley Park in round six to suggest they could avoid the wooden-spoon. The Roos had yet to win a game to that stage of the season and, as it turned out, won just once in 1972 — against the Swans at Arden Street in round 17. The Roos won by nine points to virtually end Smith's coaching career at the Lake Oval.

South finished the season with just two wins, losing its last 16 games. The low point of the dismal season was the 64-point defeat by Richmond at the MCG in round 11. The hiding was tough to take, but South's miserable score of 2.19 (31) was pathetic. South's goals came from Robert Hay and Peter Brown, both in the second half.

This feeble effort came the week after Wayne Walsh walked out on the club after rowing with Smith and eventually was cleared back to Richmond, apparently without Smith's approval. Smith felt that Walsh had not been paying attention at a half-time address during the round 10 match against Collingwood at the Lake Oval. Smith blew up and, after he berated Walsh at training the following week, the former Tiger

PLAYER	GAMES	GOALS
BALL, Ray	16	0
BASKIN, Keith	6	6
BEDFORD, Peter	21	28
BELL, Robert	9	0
BRICE, Gary	7	5
BROWN, Peter	14	1
CARRODUS, Trevor	1	1
COOK, Russell	20	2
DAVIS, Bruce	11	9
DEMPSTER, Graham	2	1
DOYLE, Robert	10	2
EWIN, Wayne	7	1
GLEESON, Reg	21	0
GOSS, Norm	17	16
GRIMA, Robert	2	0
GULL, Stewart	5	7
HAINES, Jim	10	2
HAY, Robert	7	1
HOFFMAN, Steve	13	17
KERR, Peter	1	0
LAKES, George	6	2
LAMBERT, Greg	4	0
McAULIFFE, Haydn	1	0
McCRACKEN, Peter	1	0
McHENRY, Russ	8	7
McKEW, Shane	13	3
McLEISH, David	18	5
MILLER, Neville	10	10
MOORE, Eric	11	19
MORTON, Lance	12	23
MURPHY, John	11	2
NORRIS, Michael	3	2
OFFICER, Stephen	17	1
PITURA, John	19	6
PLANT, Michael	4	1
PRENTICE, Jim	18	6
QUADE, Rick	21	15
RANTALL, John	22	0
ROBERTSON, Garry	5	0
ROBERTSON, Max	7	0
STIBBARD, Neville	2	0
WALSH, Wayne	8	1
WILKINSON, Jim	10	1
WOODMAN, Brian	5	3

POSITION: Eleventh
COACH: Norm Smith
CAPTAIN: John Rantall
BEST AND FAIREST: Russell Cook
LEADING GOALKIICKER: Peter Bedford (28)

responded by saying he would never again play under Smith.

There were fears the Walsh-Smith row would split the club and Rantall addressed all players at a special meeting in the clubrooms. A headline in *The Sun* the following day read SWANS STICK WITH SMITH. The report, by the highly-respected Scot Palmer read: "South Melbourne captain John Rantall last night made an emotional plea to every senior player to 'finish and forget' the Wayne Walsh affair. And the players responded by pledging their full support for veteran coach Norm Smith.

"With special club permission, Rantall called the team together before Smith took charge of training and said: 'We must stop the knocking. We owe it to the club, we owe it to Smithy and we owe it to ourselves.' Nearly 40 players sat silent in the upstairs room while Rantall went through his toughest ordeal since taking over the captaincy from Bob Skilton this year."

Peter Bedford shows his classical kicking style.

There was considerable speculation over Smith's tenure at the Lake Oval over the last few weeks of the season, but club president Stan Keane assured Smith he would be reappointed for 1973. However, in the week after the final round, Smith was told the club would advertise the coaching position. Amazingly, the letter Smith received from the club expressed the hope he would reapply for the job he already held. It was a smack in the face for the veteran and hugely successful coach and his reign at the Lake Oval was over.

Author Ben Collins, writing in the Smith biography *The Red Fox,* told of how Smith believed there was "a sickness within the committee". Smith had told *The Herald's* Alf Brown: "Too many committeemen are arguing among themselves about who should be president." Smith told *Inside Football* he had "never known a club with supporters who show such tremendous loyalty, even when their side is losing game after game". However, he added that he had never come across a club with "so many people so critical of what goes on".

Collins wrote that the Swan players held a farewell function for Smith at the George Hotel, South Melbourne, as "the Last Supper for Norm Smith and His Disciples". Pointedly, the committee was not invited.

1973

Although South Melbourne indicated after it had sacked Norm Smith at the end of the 1972 season that it wanted to appoint a playing coach, it finally settled on a non-playing coach. It therefore was ironic that the Swans settled on former star centre half-forward Graeme John, who had played 77 games with South from 1964-69 and ended his career while Smith was coach. There was speculation that John ended his VFL career because of personal difficulties with Smith but, rather, was forced into retirement because of injuries and business commitments.

A senior trucking executive and later Managing Director of Australia Post, John brought passion for the club to his coaching position and wore his heart on his sleeve. He later served the club as president (1978-80) and was appointed an AFL Commissioner in 2000. It is doubtful if anyone has served the club and football so diversely and with so much loyalty and dedication.

South retained most of its senior players for 1973, but the loss of club captain John Rantall to North Melbourne was a savage blow. The Kangaroos exploited the short-lived 10-year rule to woo Rantall and other star veterans to Arden Street and, without the cement holding the defence together, South looked likely to leak goals in 1973. South, following Rantall's departure, appointed Peter Bedford captain. On the other hand, the Swans introduced badly needed height through the recruitment of Port Melbourne ruckman Vic Aanensen, Ormond key forward Barry Beecroft and East Perth centre half-back Ian Thomson.

John started his VFL coaching career disastrously, with Collingwood thrashing the Swans by 76 points at Victoria Park. The season then went further downhill as the Swans struggled to get even close to winning. Their best effort over the first half of the season was pushing Footscray to 17 points at the Lake Oval in round three. After North Melbourne defeated the Swans by 44 points at Waverley Park in round six, *The Sun's* Greg Hobbs asked John if the Swans would win a game in 1973. John replied: "There's no worries about that."

Graeme John took over as South coach in 1973.

The South coach added: "The potential is there. So far we've just lacked the experienced player to kick the vital goal. I am not disappointed I took the job. I would be if I could see no light through the forest. You must remember we have had a bad run of injuries. Russell Cook has had a bad knee and young Wayne Ewin has been out, too."

John's patience was rewarded when the Swans broke through to defeat Geelong by 45 points at the Lake Oval in round 14. Jim Prentice kicked five goals for the Swans, while Bedford chimed in with three. *The Sun* the following

MATCH RESULTS

Round 1, at Victoria Park, April 7
Collingwood 17.22 (124) d South Melb. 6.12 (48)

Round 2, at Lake Oval, April 14
Essendon 21.20 (146) d South Melb. 15.19 (109)

Round 3, at Lake Oval, April 23
Footscray 20.15 (135) d South Melbourne 17.16 (118)

Round 4, at Kardinia Park, April 28
Geelong 17.16 (118) d South Melbourne 12.14 (86)

Round 5, at Lake Oval, May 5
St Kilda 10.16 (76) d South Melbourne 6.12 (48)

Round 6, at Waverley Park, May 12
North Melb. 18.16 (124) d South Melb. 11.14 (80)

Round 7, at MCG, May 19
Melbourne 17.10 (112) d South Melbourne 12.11 (83)

Round 8, at Lake Oval, May 26
Carlton 19.16 (130) d South Melbourne 7.9 (51)

Round 9, at Junction Oval, June 4
Fitzroy 16.8 (104) d South Melbourne 7.15 (57)

Round 10, at Lake Oval, June 9
Richmond 13.14 (92) d South Melbourne 9.8 (62)

Round 11, at Waverley Park, June 16
Hawthorn 17.17 (119) d South Melbourne 11.10 (76)

Round 12, at Lake Oval, June 23
Collingwood 15.9 (99) d South Melbourne 12.5 (77)

Round 13, at Windy Hill, June 30
Essendon 20.19 (139) d South Melb. 16.14 (110)

Round 14, at Lake Oval, July 7
South Melbourne 18.15 (123) d Geelong 12.6 (78)

Round 15, at Western Oval, July 14
South Melbourne 20.21 (141) d Footscray 12.7 (79)

Round 16, at Moorabbin, July 21
St Kilda 14.16 (100) d South Melbourne 13.15 (93)

Round 17, at Lake Oval, July 28
South Melbourne 19.16 (130) d North Melb. 14.7 (91)

Round 18, at Waverley, Park, August 4
South Melbourne 12.14 (86) d Melbourne 11.12 (78)

Round 19, at Princes Park, August 11
Carlton 20.17 (137) d South Melbourne 11.14 (80)

Round 20, at Lake Oval, August 18
Fitzroy 14.21 (105) d South Melbourne 15.11 (101)

Round 21, at MCG, August 25
Richmond 22.11 (143) d South Melbourne 13.16 (94)

Round 22, at Glenferrie Oval, September 1
Hawthorn 16.20 (116) d South Melbourne 11.13 (79)

SOUTH MELBOURNE

The Swans

SOUTH MELBOURNE

PREMIERS

1909
1918
1933

RUNNERS-UP

1899
1907
1912
1914
1934
1935
1936
1945

CLUB SONG *Tune: "Notre Dame March"*

Cheer, cheer, the Red and the White,
Honour the name, by day and by night;
Lift that noble banner high,
Shake down the thunder from the sky.
What though the odds be great, or small,
South will go in and win over all;
While her loyal sons are marching
Onward to victory.

Monday reported that, after losing their first 13 matches of the season to add to the 16 at the end of 1972 to make it 29 defeats in a row, the Swans finally were able to sing "Cheer, Cheer, the Red and the White".

It reported: "You can imagine the decibels they rang up after Saturday's crushing home win over Geelong! There they were, still in their battle-scarred red and white, singing their glad hearts out, with a very happy Graeme John roaring them along … The frustration built up by the morale-shattering succession of losses disappeared in voice as players, coach and supporters beefed it out." The report added

Graeme John addresses his Swans at Geelong's Kardinia Park.

that John, mobbed by well-wishers, quipped: "The theme song is reserved for victories, Maybe we'll be hoarse by the end of the season."

And John proved to be a clairvoyant as the Swans won three of their next four matches, over Footscray at the Western Oval, North Melbourne at the Lake Oval and Melbourne at Waverley Park. South's form over this period was so good that *The Sunday Observer* praised the "scintillating Swans" following the 39-point defeat of North Melbourne. Bedford kicked six goals, with Prentice and Stewart Gull contributing four each.

Sadly, however, the coach South had sacked at the end of the 1972 season — Norm Smith — died at his home of a brain tumour the day after this South victory. Smith had been gravely ill for six months, but his death still was a shock to the football community. Smith's funeral, at the St John's Presbyterian Church, Essendon, was held on August 1 and was attended by hundreds of football identities.

South, three days after Smith's funeral, defeated Melbourne by eight points. *The Sun* suggested that the Swans would be the competition spoilers over the rest of the season and could upset premiership hopefuls over the final four rounds. It suggested John had transformed his team from an ugly duckling to a glamorous Swan. However, South did not win any of its final four matches and finished on the bottom, two games behind eleventh-placed Geelong.

The Swans might have gone down to Hawthorn by 37 points in the final round, but shared a slice of history as it was the last premiership game played at Glenferrie Oval. The Hawks the following year moved its "home" games to Princes Park and, according to critics, not before time. Ground staff had to work overtime to prepare the gluepot playing surface fit for its final game and *The Sun* noted that the Hawks would do football a disservice if they ever played there again. The final match there attracted an attendance of just 9932.

PLAYER	GAMES	GOALS
AANENSEN, Vic	18	14
BALL, Ray	16	0
BASKIN, Keith	4	5
BEDFORD, Peter	19	52
BEECROFT, Barry	20	1
BRICE, Gary	14	10
BROWN, Peter	10	1
COOK, Russell	17	7
CRAIGHEAD, Geoff	7	0
DAVIS, Bruce	13	4
DEMPSTER, Graham	11	0
DOYLE, Robert	20	8
EWIN, Wayne	6	1
GLEESON, Reg	21	0
GOSS, Norm	22	20
GULL, Stewart	14	29
HARLEY, Gary	2	0
HODGES, Russell	2	0
HOFFMAN, Steve	19	22
LAMBERT, Greg	18	4
McAULIFFE, Haydn	14	6
McKEW, Shane	1	0
McLEISH, David	16	0
MILLER, Greg	5	0
MOORE, Eric	7	9
MURPHY, John	6	0
NORRIS, Michael	2	0
OBUDZINSKI, Ted	2	0
PITURA, John	19	19
PRENTICE, Jim	22	27
QUADE, Rick	15	14
STIBBARD, Neville	10	7
THOMSON, Ian	20	2
WOODMAN, Brian	22	0

POSITION: Twelfth
COACH: Graeme John
CAPTAIN: Peter Bedford
BEST AND FAIREST: Peter Bedford
LEADING GOALKICKER: Peter Bedford (52)

1974

With Graeme John in his second season as coach in 1974 and Peter Bedford again his captain, South Melbourne should have been looking forward to the new season as it showed distinct promise over the final stages of 1973. However, the Swans were embroiled in a bitter dispute with winger John Pitura, who wanted a clearance to Richmond. The Pitura saga was a running sore for the Swans as the long-kicking left-footer insisted he would stand out of football unless and until the Swans cleared him and there was weekly media speculation about his future even before the start of the season. Pitura to that stage had played 93 games with the Swans after being recruited from the Wagga Tigers and Richmond saw him as a player ideally suited to a wing at the MCG.

In a special preview of the season, *The Sunday Press* commented on all clubs' chances and had this to say of the Swans: "Wood-spooners South Melbourne once again face a long heartache battle to move up the ladder. The young Swans last year spent a depressing 22 rounds in either eleventh or twelfth position. And for a long time it seemed the Swans might go through the season without a win — but they finally broke through for their first win in the fourteenth round against Geelong. This was one of their only four wins of the season, Added to their worries is the reluctance of top utility player John Pitura to play this season. He has made it clear he has finished with South, and so far has kept to his word.

"Coach Graeme John, who took over the reins last season, realises the job ahead of him but feels the pace and teamwork of his smaller players will help offset the lack of big key men. John, who played 82 (it was actually 77) games with South is in charge of a team that has only reached the finals once since 1945 and they have not won a premiership since 1933. When South did get to the first semi-final in 1970 they promptly shot back down the list the following year and have stayed there since.

"Tremendous onus once again rests on the shoulders of their captain and most brilliant forward, Peter Bedford. But overall South's scoring power is not strong. Bedford kicked 33 goals (it was 52), but then the goalkickers fell away to the 20s, with the restless Pitura in second spot with 20 (incorrect). South have also had their internal problems, but a new look committee under the presidency of leading businessman, Mr Keith Hooker, may see a lift in performances this year."

South therefore started the season without Pitura and the only other significant loss was rover Haydn McAuliffe, who crossed to South Fremantle after 105 games for the Swans after being recruited from Spotswood in 1965.

MATCH RESULTS

Round 1, at Lake Oval, April 6
South Melb. 15.10 (100) d North Melb. 11.14 (80)

Round 2, at Windy Hill, April 15
Essendon 21.24 (150) d South Melbourne 10.18 (78)

Round 3, at Lake Oval, April 20
Hawthorn 20.15 (135) d South Melbourne 8.18 (66)

Round 4, at Western Oval, April 27
Footscray 15.6 (96) d South Melbourne 7.9 (51)

Round 5, at Lake Oval, May 4
South Melb. 14.16 (100) drew with Fitzroy 15.10 (100)

Round 6, at Princes Park, May 11
Carlton 19.21 (135) d South Melbourne 12.9 (81)

Round 7, at Lake Oval, May 18
South Melbourne 13.16 (94) d Melbourne 11.10 (76)

Round 8, at Waverley Park, May 25
St Kilda 10.10 (70) d South Melbourne 8.9 (57)

Round 9, at Kardinia Park, June 1
South Melbourne 17.7 (109) d Geelong 16.12 (108)

Round 10, at Lake Oval, June 8
Richmond 23.9 (147) d South Melbourne 9.13 (67)

Round 11, at Lake Oval, June 15
Collingwood 15.14 (104) d South Melb. 10.13 (73)

Round 12, at Arden Street, June 22
North Melb. 28.17 (185) d South Melbourne 12.7 (79)

Round 13, at Lake Oval, June 29
Essendon 14.12 (96) d South Melbourne 11.16 (82)

Round 14, at Lake Oval, July 6
South Melbourne 19.27 (141) d Footscray 12.19 (91)

Round 15, at Princes Park, July 13
Hawthorn 16.14 (110) d South Melbourne 4.7 (31)

Round 16, at Junction Oval, July 20
South Melbourne 19.19 (133) d Fitzroy 10.13 (73)

Round 17, at Lake Oval, July 27
South Melbourne 14.17 (101) d Carlton 11.14 (80)

Round 18, at Waverley Park, August 3
South Melbourne 14.13 (97) d Melbourne 11.17 (83)

Round 19, at Moorabbin, August 10
South Melbourne 13.15 (93) d St Kilda 9.13 (67)

Round 20, at Lake Oval, August 17
Geelong 12.14 (86) d South Melbourne 13.7 (85)

Round 21, at MCG, August 24
Richmond 23.24 (162) d South Melb. 17.27 (129)

Round 22, at Waverley Park, August 31
South Melb. 15.10 (100) d Collingwood 13.15 (93)

David McLeish takes a spectacular mark over teammate Gary Brice.

Amazingly, the Swans played just three newcomers in 1975 — Tasmanian Tony Franklin (Penguin), defender Alf Beus (Springvale YCW) and utility Graeme Wilson (University Blues). Franklin might have played just 32 games with the Swans, but briefly coached the club in 1984 and gave the club many years of loyal service as a committeeman and chairman of selectors. Franklin had impressed South the previous season when, playing at full-back for Tasmania, kept Victorian full-forward Peter Hudson to five goals.

The Swans opened the season with a 20-point win over North Melbourne at the Lake Oval, but then lost its next three matches before a draw with Fitzroy at the Lake Oval. South's second win was by 18 points against Melbourne at the Lake Oval and, by this time, the Pitura drama was bubbling in the background, with almost daily media speculation. Then, in the lead-up to the Swans' round 16 clash with Fitzroy at the Junction Oval, the matter looked like being resolved.

Pitura met with South officials at the Lake Oval and *The Sun's* Scot Palmer reported that Pitura and his solicitor, Brian Ward, had tried to reach an agreement for his return to the club on the proviso that he would be cleared the following year. Neither Ward nor Pitura would comment after the meeting, but Pitura eventually agreed to return to the Swans and was named in the side to play Carlton at the Lake Oval in round 17. The Swans defeated the Blues by 21 points and Pitura kicked two goals. The rangy winger played out the rest of the season in the red and white before the saga took further twists the following year.

With Pitura back in the fold, even if only temporarily, the Swans backed up their win over the Blues with victories over Fitzroy, Carlton, Melbourne, St Kilda and Collingwood over the final seven rounds. South's seven-point defeat of Collingwood at the Lake Oval was particularly significant as the Magpies were rated a premiership contender and finished fourth. Ian Thomson kicked four goals for the Swans, with Stewart Gull kicking three and Pitura two in what was to be his last game for the Swans.

The Swans, with nine wins, a draw and 12 defeats, finished ninth, above St Kilda, Fitzroy and Melbourne. It had been an encouraging season in more ways than one. Apart from its biggest total of match points (38) since making the finals in 1970, the Swans showed they would not be pushovers in player dealings. South played hard-ball on the Pitura issue and refused to settle on anything but its own terms, with considerable benefits the following season.

South had even played hard-ball over the pre-season release of former champion Bob Skilton to coach Melbourne. The Swans held up Skilton's clearance until the Demons agreed to release an untried youngster who wanted to play with the Swans but was residentially bound to the Demons. The young footballer never played a senior game, but the Swans had made their point.

PLAYER	GAMES	GOALS
AANENSEN, Vic	13	9
BALL, Ray	3	0
BEDFORD, Peter	19	34
BEECROFT, Barry	18	6
BELL, Robert	2	0
BEUS, Alf	5	0
BRICE, Gary	17	8
BROWN, Peter	16	0
COOK, Russell	17	6
DEMPSTER, Graham	4	0
DOYLE, Robert	16	11
FRANKLIN, Tony	16	2
GLEESON, Reg	19	0
GOSS, Norm	22	37
GRIMA, Robert	5	10
GULL, Stewart	21	25
HODGES, Russell	18	9
HOFFMAN, Steve	20	23
LAMBERT, Greg	22	3
McLEISH, David	22	2
MILLER, Greg	17	0
NORRIS, Michael	5	2
PITURA, John	6	14
PRENTICE, Jim	6	3
QUADE, Rick	18	18
ROBERTSON, Max	22	0
STIBBARD, Neville	11	14
STIBBARD, Robert	6	1
THOMSON, Ian	22	24
WILSON, Graeme	10	13
WOODMAN, Brian	22	0

POSITION: Ninth
COACH: Graeme John
CAPTAIN: Peter Bedford
BEST AND FAIREST: Norm Goss
LEADING GOALKICKER: Norm Goss (37)

1975

With Graeme John in his third season as coach in 1975, the Swans were hopeful of building on the good form towards the end of the previous season when they won five of their last seven games. Peter Bedford again was captain and player losses were minimal. John had a young side, but the Swans were still trying to resolve the John Pitura saga as the disgruntled winger/half forward threatened to take the club to court if he did not get his clearance to Richmond after agreeing to play six games with South at the end of the 1974 season.

The Swans in 1975 introduced several outstanding prospects, including Beverley Hills youngster Mark Browning, son of former South star Keith Browning, who played 53 games from 1951-54. Mark Browning went on to play 251 games with the Swans to 1987 and captained the club from the middle of the 1984 season until the end of the following season. A regular Victorian representative, Browning won the Swans' best and fairest in 1983 and was one of the club stalwarts in the traumatic shift to Sydney in 1982.

South in 1975 also introduced brilliant rover Colin Hounsell (Collingullie) and handy key position player Terry O'Neill (Narrandera) from its country zone and picked up reliable North Melbourne defender Denis Pagan who, of course, went on to become a coaching legend in taking the Kangaroos to the 1996 and 1999 premierships. Pagan played 23 games with

Defender Francis Jackson proved his worth after crossing from Richmond.

MATCH RESULTS

Round 1, at Victoria Park, April 5
Collingwood 12.19 (91) d South Melbourne 8.7 (55)

Round 2, at Lake Oval, April 12
Essendon 19.17 (131) d South Melb. 15.12 (102)

Round 3, at Moorabbin, April 19
St Kilda 11.21 (87) d South Melbourne 9.17 (71)

Round 4, at Lake Oval, April 26
Hawthorn 13.21 (99) d South Melbourne 9.15 (69)

Round 5, at MCG, May 3
Richmond 19.23 (137) d South Melbourne 12.14 (86)

Round 6, at MCG, May 10
Melbourne 22.23 (155) d South Melbourne 13.12 (90)

Round 7, at Lake Oval, May 17
Carlton 19.14 (128) d South Melbourne 11.11 (77)

Round 8, at Junction Oval, May 24
Fitzroy 13.13 (91) d South Melbourne 11.12 (78)

Round 9, at Lake Oval, May 31
South Melbourne 11.26 (92) d Geelong 7.13 (55)

Round 10, at Waverley Park, June 7
Footscray 13.11 (89) d South Melbourne 12.15 (87)

Round 11, at Lake Oval, June 16
North Melb. 16.12 (108) d South Melb. 12.16 (88)

Round 12, at Waverley Park, June 21
Collingwood 12.13 (85) d South Melb. 11.11 (77)

Round 13, at Windy Hill, June 28
Essendon 19.18 (132) d South Melb. 17.12 (114)

Round 14, at Waverley Park, July 5
Hawthorn 9.10 (64) d South Melbourne 5.9 (39)

Round 15, at Lake Oval, July 12
St Kilda 19.16 (130) d South Melbourne 10.10 (70)

Round 16, at Lake Oval, July 19
Richmond 26.11 (167) d South Melbourne 8.12 (60)

Round 17, at Waverley Park, July 26
Melbourne 13.13 (91) d South Melbourne 11.9 (75)

Round 18, at Princes Park, August 2
Carlton 19.17 (131) d South Melbourne 15.13 (103)

Round 19, at Lake Oval, August 9
Fitzroy 16.19 (115) d South Melbourne 13.20 (98)

Round 20, at Kardinia Park, August 16
South Melbourne 15.15 (105) d Geelong 12.16 (88)

Round 21, at Lake Oval, August 23
Footscray 18.7 (115) d South Melbourne 10.15 (75)

Round 22, at Arden Street, August 30
North Melb. 15.19 (109) d South Melb. 12.15 (87)

Coach Graeme John (right) celebrates a win with Graham Teasdale (left) and Peter Bedford.

the Swans to the following season before being appointed captain-coach of VFA club Yarraville. The Swans also recruited several other key players from rival VFL clubs following the resolution of the Pitura squabble.

Clubs had barely started playing practice matches before the Pitura row flared and *The Herald's* Alf Brown reported on March 14: "This is a weekend of decision for star South half-forward John Pitura. He will train with a League club next week but had not decided which one. All clubs like Pitura, but have to be careful. If Pitura trains with them without permission from South Melbourne they could be reported to the League." Brown also reported that Pitura had signed an agreement late in 1974 that stipulated that if he and the Swans could not reach an agreement by March 1 he could go to another League club. However, any offer had to go through through solicitors for both parties.

Just three days later Brown wrote that

South's 1975 coach, Graeme John.

Geelong had taken the front running to sign Pitura, with Collingwood later joining the queue. Meanwhile, South tuned up for the new season with a four-point practice match win over the Port Adelaide Magpies before pulling out of a scheduled practice match against Essendon in the week leading up to the opening round. John cited injury problems and the fear of adding to South's long list of walking wounded.

Then, virtually on the eve of the 1975 season, Pitura trained with Richmond wearing a Tiger guernsey. Pitura was introduced to Richmond coach Tom Hafey and then jogged laps before doing ball-work. This move angered the Swans, who immediately asked the VFL to investigate as Pitura was alleged to have trained with the Tigers without South's permission. South president Keith Hooker described Richmond's action as "cheeky" and added: "It certainly won't endear them to South." The Swans next day lodged an official

PLAYER	GAMES	GOALS
AANENSEN, Vic	8	6
BEDFORD, Peter	21	36
BEECROFT, Barry	16	3
BEUS, Alf	1	0
BLAIR, John	1	0
BRAND, Alan	2	0
BRICE, Gary	18	19
BROWN, Peter	16	0
BROWNING, Mark	13	14
CARLTON, Phil	10	2
COELLI, Rod	3	0
COOK, Russell	18	1
COWMEADOW, Gary	3	0
DEAN, John	4	0
DEMPSTER, Graham	8	1
DOYLE, Robert	7	8
EWIN, Wayne	4	1
FRANKLIN, Tony	16	9
GLEESON, Reg	20	3
GOSS, Norm	22	37
GULL, Stewart	10	11
HODGES, Russell	8	0
HOFFMAN, Steve	18	13
HOUNSELL, Colin	3	1
JACKSON, Francis	9	1
LAMBERT, Greg	20	0
McLEISH, David	19	2
MILLER, Greg	20	0
OFFICER, Steve	2	2
O'NEILL, Terry	4	0
PAGAN, Denis	7	0
QUADE, Rick	3	2
ROBERTS, Brian	15	2
ROBERTSON, Max	16	0
RUSS, Steve	5	1
SCOTT, Garry	6	7
STIBBARD, Neville	2	1
STILO, Mick	10	3
TEASDALE, Graham	15	38
THOMSON, Ian	13	13
WILSON, Graeme	3	1
WOODMAN, Brian	21	12

POSITION: Twelfth
COACH: Graeme John
CAPTAIN: Peter Bedford
BEST AND FAIREST: Peter Bedford
LEADING GOALKICKER: Graham Teasdale (38)

complaint with the VFL but, meanwhile, had the opening round clash with Collingwood at Victoria Park in mind.

South went into the match against Collingwood without any new players and went down by 36 points in a spiteful encounter in which Bedford and Tony Franklin were reported. Bedford was charged with allegedly striking Collingwood newcomer Phil Carman, while Franklin was booked for allegedly attempting to strike Collingwood's Ian Cooper. *The Sun* described the match as "footbrawl" and, after being found guilty, Bedford was "severely reprimanded". However, teammate Franklin was not so fortunate as he was suspended for two matches.

After Essendon defeated South by 29 points at the Lake Oval in round two, the Pitura saga flared again, with four Richmond officials — Hafey, president Ian Wilson, secretary Alan Schwab and team manager Graeme Richmond — ordered to face the VFL Complaints Committee, which met on April 24. The VFL eventually fined the Tigers $2000 and, on May 13, South finally agreed to talk with Richmond through an intermediary, VFL president Sir Maurice Nathan. Pitura, who had been training with VFA club Camberwell in the interim, could see light at the end of a long and dark tunnel.

South agreed to allow Pitura to train with Richmond on the eve of round seven, but insisted the Tigers insure him for $100,000. Pitura was cleared one week later in exchange for two players — Brian "The Whale" Roberts and full-forward Graham Teasdale — plus $40,000. In a separate deal, the Swans picked up young Tiger defender Francis Jackson. It was a huge coup for the Swans as Roberts was the ruckman the Swans so desperately needed, while Teasdale went on to win the 1977 Brownlow Medal. Jackson also became a fine centre half-back for the Swans.

The Swans named their three new players in their line-up for the round eight match against Fitzroy at the Junction Oval, but the Lions defeated the Swans by 13 points, with only Roberts (23 hit-outs) having any impact. Pitura was named Richmond's best player in its eight-point loss to North Melbourne. Pitura failed to make a lasting impression at Tigerland and played just 40 games with the Tigers to 1977 before heading to Sydney as captain-coach of North Shore.

Brian "The Whale" Roberts enjoys a post-match cigarette as he and Peter Bedford listen to coach Graeme John.

Roberts played superb football over the rest of the 1975 season, while Teasdale and Jackson also made their mark. Teasdale kicked 38 goals in his 15 games and thrilled Swan fans with his spectacular high marking. Jackson might have played just nine games in his first season with South, but went on to play 100 wonderfully competitive games for the club to 1982. Roberts was so effective that he polled 17 Brownlow Medal votes, just three fewer than the winner, Footscray's Gary Dempsey. He was left to wonder what might have been if he had been cleared to South earlier.

South, despite its coup over the Pitura affair, won just two games — against Geelong at the Lake Oval in round nine and against the Cats in the return match at Kardinia Park. The Swans were back on the bottom, but at least with three new highly-talented players in Jackson, Teasdale and Roberts.

South Melbourne Football Club

MEMBER'S TICKET SEASON 1975

Retain this ticket as it must be produced to obtain admission to the Annual Meeting of the Club.

To ensure that your name is recorded on the Roll, please complete the enclosed card and forward to

M. LINGWOOD-SMITH
Secretary/Manager,
P.O. Box 384
South Melbourne, 3205.

M.........................

Not transferable
This Ticket admits to home matches only.

"PENSIONER"

FIXTURES—1975

DATE	CLUB	GROUND
Apri[illegible] 5	Collingwood	Away
Ap[illegible]2	Essendon	Home
A[illegible]19	St. Kilda	Away
A[illegible]6	Hawthorn	Home
[illegible] 3	Richmond	Away
[illegible]y 10	Melbourne	Away
[illegible]ay 17	Carlton	Home
[illegible]ay 24	Fitzroy	Away
May 31	Geelong	Home
June 7	Footscray	Waverley
June 16	North Melb.	Home
June 21	Collingwood	Waverley
June 28	Essendon	Away
July 5	Hawthorn	Waverley
July 12	St. Kilda	Home
July 19	Richmond	Home
July 26	Melbourne	Waverley
August 2	Carlton	Away
August 9	Fitzroy	Home
August 16	Geelong	Away
August 23	Footscray	Home
August 30	North Melb.	Away

1976

There was speculation during Grand Final week in 1975 that Graeme John would resign as South Melbourne coach after three years in charge. John's burgeoning business career made it difficult for him to continue and he finally resigned. The Swans immediately cast around for a replacement and finally nominated former Richmond and St Kilda centreman Ian Stewart. The triple Brownlow Medal winner had played 127 games with the Saints from 1963-70 and 78 with the Tigers from 1971-75. However, here was a huge hurdle to clear before he could take charge of the Swans.

Richmond, still rankling over the John Pitura saga of the previous two seasons, refused to clear Stewart unless it was paid a $5000 fee. The Swans refused and club vice-president Des Moody declared that Stewart would coach the Swans from the other side of the fence if necessary. "There's no way we'll pay Richmond one red cent," he declared. The Swans eventually got their man, but there was one other major problem in the lead-up to the new season.

Stewart had a massive decision to make as he felt huge ruckman Brian Roberts was not pulling his weight at training. Stewart dumped him and, at one stage the Swans even tried to sell the man known as "the Whale" back to Richmond. Roberts retired and the Swans went into the new season without a player who had made an enormous impact over the second half of the previous season.

South 1976 best and fairest Rick Quade, all determination.

MATCH RESULTS

Round 1, at Lake Oval, April 3
Geelong 25.7 (157) d South Melbourne 23.15 (153)

Round 2, at Victoria Park, April 10
South Melb. 20.14 (134) d Collingwood 16.27 (123)

Round 3, at Western Oval, April 17
Footscray 20.14 (134) d South Melbourne 14.11 (95)

Round 4, at Lake Oval, April 24
South Melb. 22.11 (143) d Essendon 16.13 (109)

Round 5, at Princes Park, May 1
Carlton 8.19 (67) d South Melbourne 9.12 (66)

Round 6, at Lake Oval, May 8
Melbourne 21.10 (136) d South Melb. 16.12 (108)

Round 7, at Junction Oval, May 15
Fitzroy 11.22 (88) d South Melbourne 12.15 (87)

Round 8, at Princes Park, May 22
Hawthorn 20.16 (136) d South Melbourne 11.10 (76)

Round 9, at Lake Oval, May 29
South Melbourne 13.18 (96) d Richmond 13.10 (88)

Round 10, at Moorabbin, June 5
South Melbourne 19.10 (124) d St Kilda 12.27 (99)

Round 11, at Lake Oval, June 12
North Melb. 18.13 (121) d South Melb. 14.11 (95)

Round 12, at Kardinia Park, June 19
Geelong 23.17 (155) d South Melbourne 6.15 (51)

Round 13, at Waverley Park, June 26
South Melb. 17.19 (121) d Collingwood 11.16 (82)

Round 14, at Windy Hill, July 3
Essendon 13.15 (93) d South Melbourne 12.6 (78)

Round 15, at Lake Oval, July 10
South Melbourne 20.16 (136) d Footscray 17.14 (116)

Round 16, at Lake Oval, July 17
Carlton 15.10 (100) d South Melbourne 14.10 (94)

Round 17, at Waverley Park, July 24
South Melbourne 14.9 (93) d Melbourne 11.13 (79)

Round 18, at Lake Oval, July 31
South Melbourne 16.11 (107) d Fitzroy 11.14 (80)

Round 19, at Waverley Park, August 7
Hawthorn 13.19 (97) d South Melbourne 12.11 (83)

Round 20, at MCG, August 14
Richmond 16.14 (110) d South Melbourne 12.12 (84)

Round 21, at Lake Oval, August 21
South Melbourne 15.18 (108) d St Kilda 10.6 (66)

Round 22, at Arden Street, August 28
North Melb. 19.14 (128) d South Melb. 12.19 (91)

On the credit side, the Swans welcomed back the enormously loyal John Rantall after he had achieved his football ambition of playing in a VFL premiership side, with North Melbourne in 1975. Rantall's heart had never left the Lake Oval and the Swans welcomed him back with open arms. And, to replace Roberts, they wooed Footscray ruckman Barry Round to the Lake Oval. Round, who originally was going to cross to Geelong, became an enormously important player for the Swans as club captain and winner of a Brownlow Medal in 1981. North Melbourne ruckman Barry Goodingham joined the Swans before the round two match against Collingwood and Collingwood forward Robert Dean also crossed to the Swans in 1976 and, among the country recruits, was Ungarie's Terry Daniher.

Along with Rantall, South named five newcomers — Round, Dean, former Footscray utility Peter Morrison, defender

Syd Anderson (Port Melbourne) and rover Chris Elliott (Benalla) for the opening round match against Geelong at the Lake Oval. Geelong defeated the Swans by four points in a high-scoring match, but most critics named Dean best on ground. He not only kicked eight goals, but took several outstanding high marks. Elliott also made a fine debut with 18 possessions.

Goodingham made his Swans' debut in the round two match against Collingwood at Victoria Park, and the Swans triumphed by 11 points, with Dean kicking another six goals to top the VFL goalkicking. The *Sunday Press'* Ian McDonald wrote: "They were crying in their beer at the Collingwood Social Club last night after last year's wooden-spooner South Melbourne had upset the Magpies ... at Victoria Park. It was a triumph for triple Brownlow Medallist Ian Stewart in his second game as coach. He said the Swans would start flying this season — and they have."

South's Graham Teasdale often took big pack marks, this time against St Kilda, with Rick Quade waiting for any spill.

PLAYER	GAMES	GOALS
AANENSEN, Vic	1	1
ANDERSON, Syd	4	0
BEDFORD, Peter	19	31
BEECROFT, Barry	8	0
BLAIR, John	12	15
BRICE, Gary	21	13
BROWN, Peter	13	7
BROWNING, Mark	22	15
DANIHER, Terry	1	0
DEAN, Robert	20	37
DEMPSTER, Graham	18	5
ELLIOTT, Chris	5	0
GLEESON, Reg	7	6
GOODINGHAM, Barry	20	9
GOSS, Norm	17	23
GULL, Stewart	15	36
HODGES, Russell	5	0
HOFFMAN, Steve	14	17
HOUNSELL, Colin	10	13
JACKSON, Francis	4	0
LAMBERT, Greg	13	5
McLEISH, David	21	3
MILLER, Greg	13	5
MORRISON, Peter	10	4
O'NEILL, Terry	7	4
PAGAN, Denis	16	0
QUADE, Rick	22	16
RANTALL, John	21	0
ROBERTSON, Max	16	0
ROUND, Barry	14	12
RUSS, Steve	3	0
STILO, Mick	2	1
TEASDALE, Graham	15	11
THOMSON, Ian	19	22
WILSON, Graeme	1	0
WOODMAN, Brian	18	17

POSITION: Eighth
COACH: Ian Stewart
CAPTAIN: Peter Bedford
BEST AND FAIREST: Rick Quade
LEADING GOALKICKER: Robert Dean (37)

The Swans might have gone down by 39 points to Footscray at the Western Oval, but bounced back to defeat Essendon by 34 points at the Lake Oval the following week. This meant that South already had equalled its record of two wins of the previous season, with more victories to come. However, the victory over the Bombers came at a price as star South ruckman/forward Graham Teasdale was reported for allegedly kneeing Bomber hard man Ron Andrews and subsequently was suspended for two matches. The Tribunal described the incident as "stupid, not vicious".

South then could have been flying high, but a one-point loss to Carlton at Princes Park in round five not only was costly, but had coach Stewart grinding his teeth in fury over umpiring decisions. He stormed: "The umpires (David Leavens and Neville Nash) kept them in the game." When warned he could be fined for speaking out, he fumed: "Don't tell me I'll get fined for telling the truth — it's not Russia, is it?" The VFL fined Stewart $200 and, even worse, Melbourne defeated South by 28 points at the Lake Oval the following Saturday.

Although the Swans defeated Richmond and St Kilda in rounds nine and 10, the finals were out of the question. However, the eight-point defeat of the Tigers at the Lake Oval was particularly satisfying considering the bad blood between the two clubs. South also disclosed after the match that Rick Quade, Ian Thomson and Dean (three goals) had played after battling influenza during the week.

Off-field, the Swans were considering their future at the Lake Oval and there was media speculation the club would relocate to share the Junction Oval with Fitzroy. Lion president Frank Bibby even declared he would make a formal approach to the Swans at the end of the season. However, nothing came of this suggestion and Swan president Craig Kimberley indicated there were "no plans" for South to leave the Lake Oval.

According to *The Age,* South officially fell out of the finals race in going down by 26 points to North Melbourne at the Lake Oval in round 11. South at that stage was seventh on the ladder, but two games and a considerable percentage behind fifth-placed Footscray. Then, when Geelong thrashed the Swans by 104 points at Kardinia Park in round 12, the *Sunday Press* suggested the game was "a one-sided massacre that could only serve as a confidence booster for Geelong and a headache for Ian Stewart".

Coach Ian Stewart congratulates Graham Teasdale after a win.

The Swans might have pulled off what the *Sunday Press* described as a "miracle" in defeating Collingwood by 39 points at Waverley Park in round 13, but South's eyes now were firmly on 1977. However, there was one huge bonus for the Swans to the completion of the 1976 season when Quade became the first player to be awarded the full 10 points in the *Sun* player ratings. Quade won this extraordinary accolade for a superb performance in the 27-point win over Fitzroy at the Lake Oval in round 18. The *Sunday Press* suggested: "If ever a man was entitled to sit back and pull quietly on a cigar as reward for a day's work well done, it was South Melbourne's dynamic ruck-rover Ricky Quade. And that is just what Quade did at the Lake Oval early tonight."

South finished eighth, with nine wins and 13 defeats. It was a massive improvement on the two wins and the wooden-spoon of the previous season and, on August 28, *The Herald* reported that Stewart would meet with club officials to decide on which players he wanted to retain for 1977. However, the club insisted in this report that it was not interested in signing Collingwood's Phil Carman, whose name had been linked with the Swans.

1977

South Melbourne coach Ian Stewart had built himself an enviable reputation as a tactician and disciplinarian in his debut season of 1976 and was determined to lift the Swans even higher in 1977. He had a young side, with Rick Quade taking over as captain following Peter Bedford's release to Carlton at 30 years of age. Stewart also was able to go quietly about preparing his team for the new season as most of the sports headlines in March, 2007, centred on cricket's Centenary Test between Australia and England.

South named just two newcomers for the opening round match against Melbourne at the MCG. Small utility Wayne Evans was from Grong Grong Matong, while rover Peter Carter joined the Swans from Brentwood. The Swans, with Graham Teasdale in top form with eight goals, defeated the Demons by 69 points to prompt critics to suggest South would be one of the big improvers of 1977. In fact, a headline in *The Sun* blared IT'S THE YEAR OF THE SWAN, with veteran journalist Jack Dunn suggesting this was the "logical conclusion" to be drawn from the Swans' easy romp at the MCG.

Then, when South thrashed Essendon by 77 points at the Lake Oval the following week, the football media raved about Stewart's "promising Swans". Teasdale again was in top form with nine goals, while Quade and Norm Goss dominated around the packs. The *Sunday Press* reported: "A storm warning went up over the South ground for the top sides yesterday. It read: 'Be prepared for anything when you come down here because the Swans mean business.' The Swans, whipped into a tornado, have found out what the big time is all about."

Yet, inexplicably, South went down to Richmond, Geelong and Carlton over the next three rounds before rekindling its season with a 19-point defeat of Fitzroy at the Lake Oval and then playing a draw with St Kilda at Moorabbin the following week. This left South in sixth position, one game behind fifth-placed Richmond, but with a better percentage. When Hawthorn thrashed South by 60 points at the Lake Oval the following week it looked as if a finals berth had been but a wild dream. However, the Swans then won its next four matches, the fire to succeed ignited by Stewart, who lashed his players after the Hawthorn match. "They let the club down and themselves," he fumed.

The turnaround was remarkable and coincided with Stewart's master-stroke of switching Teasdale from full-forward to the ruck. Playing with much greater freedom,

Swans Steve Hoffman (left), Gary Brice (centre) and Terry Daniher celebrate making the 1977 finals, thanks to a last-round win over North Melbourne.

MATCH RESULTS

Round 1, at MCG, April 2
South Melbourne 21.15 (141) d Melbourne 10.12 (72)

Round 2, at Lake Oval, April 9
South Melbourne 27.13 (175) d Essendon 15.8 (98)

Round 3, at Lake Oval, April 16
Richmond 13.13 (91) d South Melbourne 11.13 (79)

Round 4, at Waverley Park, April 25
Geelong 16.18 (114) d South Melbourne 12.15 (87)

Round 5, at Princes Park, April 30
Carlton 21.8 (134) d South Melbourne 16.11 (107)

Round 6, at Lake Oval, May 7
South Melbourne 21.19 (145) d Fitzroy 19.12 (126)

Round 7, at Moorabbin, May 14
South Melb. 14.14 (98) drew with St Kilda 14.14 (98)

Round 8, at Lake Oval, May 21
Hawthorn 18.7 (115) d South Melbourne 7.13 (55)

Round 9, at Lake Oval, May 28
South Melbourne 14.14 (98) d Footscray 11.13 (79)

Round 10, at Victoria Park, June 4
South Melb. 20.16 (136) d Collingwood 15.20 (110)

Round 11, at Lake Oval, June 11
South Melbourne 12.9 (81) d North Melb. 9.11 (65)

Round 12, at Lake Oval, June 18
South Melbourne 8.22 (70) d Melbourne 9.10 (64)

Round 13, at Windy Hill, June 25
Essendon 9.9 (63) d South Melbourne 6.15 (51)

Round 14, at Kardinia Park, July 2
South Melbourne 9.10 (64) d Geelong 7.15 (57)

Round 15, at Waverley Park, July 9
Richmond 14.16 (100) d South Melbourne 10.11 (71)

Round 16, at Lake Oval, July 16
Carlton 13.7 (85) d South Melbourne 12.4 (76)

Round 17, at Junction Oval, July 23
South Melbourne 16.21 (117) d Fitzroy 7.13 (55)

Round 18, at Lake Oval, July 30
South Melbourne 21.12 (138) d St Kilda 12.11 (83)

Round 19, at Waverley Park, August 6
South Melbourne 16.7 (103) d Hawthorn 10.18 (78)

Round 20, at Western Oval, August 13
South Melbourne 14.12 (96) d Footscray 9.19 (73)

Round 21, at Lake Oval, August 20
Collingwood 12.17 (89) d South Melbourne 8.9 (57)

Round 22, at Arden Street, August 27
South Melbourne 15.13 (103) d North Melb. 14.9 (93)

Elimination final, at Waverley Park, September 3
Richmond 13.10 (88) d South Melbourne 7.12 (54)

Teasdale was able to use his mobility and extraordinary aerial skills to dominate game after game. South was back as a finals contender, even though its free-running game was hampered by heavy grounds in one of the wettest Melbourne winters for years.

The Swans, after several stutters, finally climbed into the top five after defeating Hawthorn by 25 points at Waverley Park in round 19. Meanwhile, however, the Swans had to ride out an off-field drama. South was struggling to make ends meet at the Lake Oval and St Kilda stepped in with an offer to share the Moorabbin Oval with the Swans. St Kilda president Graham Huggins told *The Sun:* "If South came to Moorabbin it would move into a new vigorous area close to its metropolitan areas of Springvale and Noble Park". South president Craig Kimberley was unimpressed and said: "We are aware that St Kilda is interested in sharing its premises with South Melbourne, but I've told them that winning a place in the finals is all we are thinking about at the moment."

South's finals ambition all boiled down to its final round match against North Melbourne at Arden Street. South had to defeat third-placed North Melbourne and hope that Footscray could defeat fifth-placed Carlton at the Western Oval. *The Age* preview of the North-South match was headlined SOUTH SET TO GO WEST AT NORTH. Highly respected journalist Ron Carter wrote: "South supporters may be willing to throw something Footscray's way if it wins."

Swan fans tuned into the Footscray-Carlton clash as they watched their team play the Roos and were jubilant when the Bulldogs roared into the final break with a 38-point lead. South, however, trailed North by 23 points at the final break but must have realised that one last, huge effort could lift them into finals. The Swans dug deep to defeat North by 10 points, while Footscray defeated Carlton by 18 points. South had made the finals for the first time since 1970.

South's remarkable effort was front page news the following day. The *Sunday Press* splash lead announced SWANS ARE IN FIVE. A report by Greg Hobbs inside read: "August 27: This was the day that South's number came up. At Arden Street yesterday everything fell into place beautifully for the Swans ... The look on the South Melbourne faces after the match told the story. You'd have thought they all had won Tattslotto."

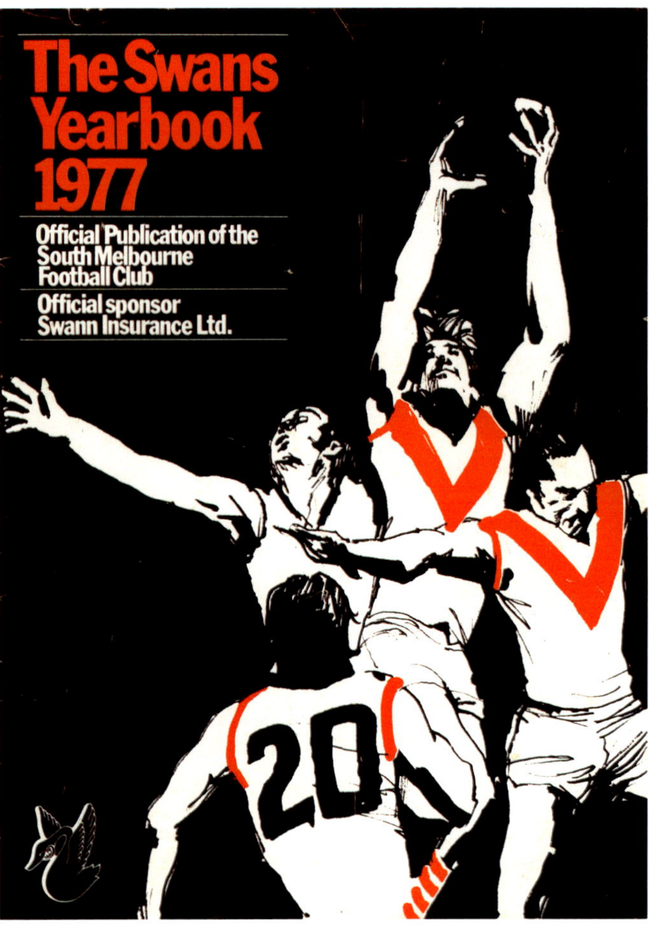

There was even better news the following Monday night when Teasdale romped home with the Brownlow Medal. The South ruckman polled 59 votes (both field umpires cast votes) to defeat Richmond's Kevin Bartlett by 14 votes. Teasdale, wearing a rented chocolate brown velvet suit, admitted immediately after the count that he had thought of quitting football when his form was down at one stage in 1977. "I was very uncertain about my career," he said. "I was very disappointed with the way I was playing and I thought, well, Sydney or the bush."

South, however, had a setback in the lead-up to the elimination final against Richmond at Waverley Park as forward David Young pulled a thigh muscle at training and was ruled out of the side. The Swans went into the big match as huge underdogs and just could not cope with the Tigers' strength, vigour and experience. Richmond took control in the first quarter and never let the nervous Swans into the match. The final margin was just 34 points, but some critics described South's effort as "one of the worst" in a finals match for several years. It was a sad end to what otherwise had been a reasonably successful season.

PLAYER	GAMES	GOALS
BEECROFT, Barry	2	0
BLAIR, John	11	11
BRICE, Gary	18	6
BROWNING, Mark	22	6
CARTER, Peter	2	0
DANIHER, Terry	18	22
DEAN, Robert	17	26
DEMETRIOU, Andrew	1	0
DEMPSTER, Graham	13	13
ELLIOTT, Chris	3	1
EVANS, Wayne	11	7
GOODINGHAM, Barry	10	3
GOSS, Norm	21	28
GULL, Stewart	12	17
HODGES, Russell	5	1
HOFFMAN, Steve	12	14
HOUNSELL, Colin	15	10
JACKSON, Francis	15	2
JAMIESON, Ray	4	5
LAMBERT, Greg	14	6
McLEISH, David	18	1
MORRISON, Peter	22	22
MORWOOD, Paul	4	2
O'NEILL, Terry	23	1
QUADE, Rick	22	5
RANTALL, John	23	0
ROBERTSON, Max	9	1
ROUND, Barry	23	12
SCARLETT, John	10	0
SMITH, Michael	2	5
TEASDALE, Graham	22	38
WOODMAN, Brian	15	14
YOUNG, David	19	23
ZANTUCK, Shane	22	15

POSITION: Fifth

COACH: Ian Stewart
CAPTAIN: Rick Quade
BEST AND FAIREST: Graham Teasdale
LEADING GOALKICKER: Graham Teasdale (38)

1978

South Melbourne was dealt a massive blow before the start of the 1978 season when Carlton swooped to sign Swan coach Ian Stewart, who had taken the red and white to the finals the previous season. Carlton obviously saw Stewart, who had been with South for two years, as one of the best young coaches in the competition and the ideal replacement for former South assistant coach Ian Thorogood. However, Stewart had health problems early in the 1978 season and, after stepping down at Princes Park, was replaced by Alex Jesaulenko as captain-coach.

Meanwhile, South replaced Stewart with former Collingwood and Essendon star half-forward Des Tuddenham, who had been Bomber captain-coach from 1972-75. Tuddenham, who had started his VFL playing career with the Magpies in 1962, brought a blood and thunder approach to the Lake Oval and insisted on players attacking the ball at all times.

South fans also were shocked to learn that young key forward Terry Daniher was to be traded to Essendon. Daniher was told of the club's decision just weeks before the start of the season and he became part of a deal in which Bomber centreman Neville Fields arrived at the Lake Oval. Incredibly, the Swans also cleared Daniher's brother Neale to Essendon sight unseen. It was one of the greatest clearance blunders in football history.

The Swans finalised their preparation for the 1978 season with a practice match against reigning premier North Melbourne, with the Roos winning by 30 points. However, North coach Ron Barassi fielded youngsters over the final quarter and this allowed the Swans to kick nine goals to save themselves from humiliation. Hawthorn captain Don Scott, writing in *The Australian*, suggested: "The loss, one week before the VFL competition, has dented South's hopes of kicking on from their fine form of last season."

South the day after the North defeat named its training squad for the new season. It revealed that Daniher had crossed to Essendon and that ruckman Barry Goodingham had been cleared to South Adelaide, while rover Norm Goss was cleared to Hawthorn. South, after making the finals in 1977, shed vital players and part of its future. Newcomers included Fields and Noble Park youngster Tony Morwood, who was to have a remarkably successful career with the Swans, sometimes alongside brothers Paul and Shane. The Swans also listed Port Melbourne's Bernie Evans and Port Adelaide's Max James, subject to clearances.

Fields and Evans were the only new faces named in the South line-up for the opening round game which, ironically, was against Essendon at Windy Hill. The Swans, however, indicated they would rush James into the line-up if they could win a last-minute release from the Port Magpies. The James clearance

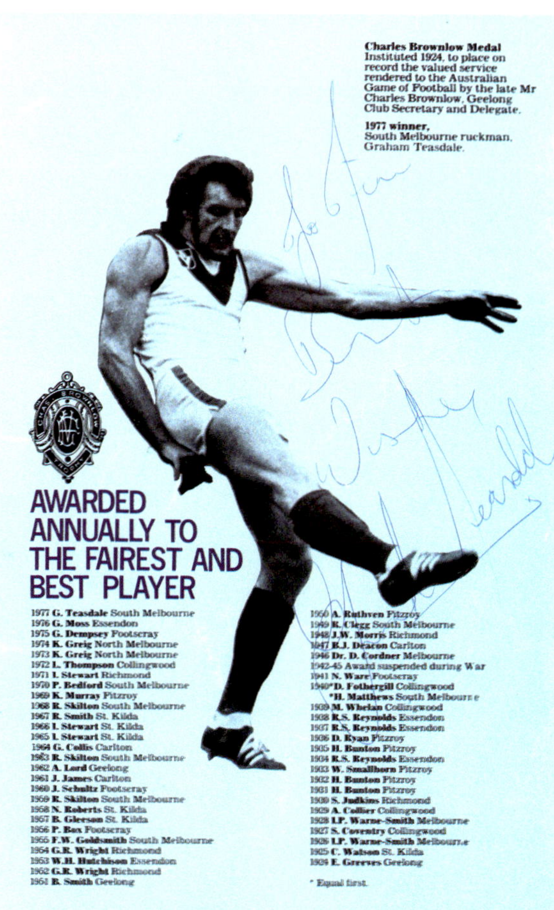

This 1978 Brownlow Medal dinner menu is signed on the back by the previous year's winner, South's Graham Teasdale.

MATCH RESULTS

Round 1, at Windy Hill, April 1
Essendon 19.9 (123) d South Melbourne 14.18 (102)

Round 2, at Lake Oval, April 8
Hawthorn 18.24 (132) d South Melbourne 16.8 (104)

Round 3, at Lake Oval, April 15
South Melb. 18.11 (119) d Collingwood 14.18 (102)

Round 4, at Junction Oval, April 22
Fitzroy 21.17 (143) d South Melbourne 18.16 (124)

Round 5, at Lake Oval, April 29
South Melbourne 18.9 (117) d Carlton 17.14 (116)

Round 6, at Waverley Park, May 6
South Melbourne 18.15 (123) d Footscray 16.9 (105)

Round 7, at MCG, May 13
South Melbourne 19.11 (125) d Richmond 14.14 (98)

Round 8, at Lake Oval, May 20
South Melbourne 20.16 (136) d St Kilda 4.13 (37)

Round 9, at Kardinia Park, May 27
Geelong 16.13 (109) d South Melbourne 14.11 (95)

Round 10, at Lake Oval, June 5
South Melbourne 24.18 (162) d Melbourne 14.8 (92)

Round 11, at Waverley Park, June 17
North Melb. 17.15 (117) d South Melbourne 15.7 (97)

Round 12, at Lake Oval, June 24
Essendon 17.18 (120) d South Melbourne 13.19 (97)

Round 13, at Princes Park, July 1
Hawthorn 21.14 (140) d South Melbourne 18.11 (119)

Round 14, at Lake Oval, July 8
South Melbourne 22.11 (143) d Fitzroy 13.15 (93)

Round 15, at Victoria Park, July 15
Collingwood 17.12 (114) d South Melb. 12.22 (94)

Round 16, at Princes Park, July 22
Carlton 16.16 (112) d South Melbourne 9.17 (71)

Round 17, at Lake Oval, July 29
South Melbourne 15.15 (105) d Footscray 13.13 (91)

Round 18, at Waverley Park, August 5
South Melbourne 14.9 (93) d Richmond 9.16 (70)

Round 19, at Moorabbin, August 12
St Kilda 13.7 (85) d South Melbourne 3.19 (37)

Round 20, at Lake Oval, August 19
Geelong 26.11 (167) d South Melbourne 24.11 (155)

Round 21, at MCG, August 26
Melbourne 15.16 (106) d South Melbourne 11.19 (85)

Round 22, at Arden Street, September 2
North Melb. 16.15 (111) d South Melb. 12.15 (87)

arrived just in time for him to take his place in the Swans' line-up and football writers were quick to make a meal of the Daniher-Fields swap and of Tuddenham coaching the Swans.

The Sun's Lou Richards wrote in his match preview: "There's a Biblical touch to the Essendon-South Melbourne match today. Two Prodigal Sons in Des Tuddenham and Neville Fields are returning to Windy Hill in Swans' clothing. And you could say — if you had the nerve — that there is a (Terry) Daniher in the Bombers' Den." Richards also pointed out that it was easier to get a camel through the eye of a needle than to win at Essendon, and he was proven right. The Bombers defeated the Swans by 21 points. Fields had just four possessions and was taken from the ground in the final quarter. Daniher was the best player on the ground until he copped a heavy knock in the second quarter.

South's wheeling and dealing over summer also was criticised after a 28-point defeat by Hawthorn at the Lake Oval the following week as Goss kicked three goals against his old side and many football writers named him best on ground. Mike Sheahan wrote in The *Sunday Press:* "Former South coach Ian Stewart, now in charge of the hapless Carlton, decided after the 1977 season that Goss was dispensable. But the little left-footer had South officials rueing the decision yesterday."

Des Tuddenham coached the Swans in 1978.

Max James joined the Swans from Port Adelaide.

Even though the season was just two weeks old, the Swans already had a lengthy injury list, with 15 players sidelined. Captain Rick Quade had damaged a knee cartilage, Tasmanian recruit Graham Fox had broken a bone in his left hand and Graham Dempster, Peter Morrison and Stewart Gull also had

Neville Fields was involved in the controversial player swap which saw Terry Daniher cross to Essendon in 1978.

injury problems. South therefore went into the round three match against Collingwood at the Lake Oval without Quade, Dempster, Fox, James and Hounsell. However, the underdog Swans notched their first win of the season in defeating the Magpies by 17 points. Michael Davis wrote in the *Sunday Press:* "Injury-hit South Melbourne patched up their wounds with a gutsy win over Collingwood yesterday. Head 'surgeon' was coach Des Tuddenham,

PLAYER	GAMES	GOALS
BLAIR, John	3	5
BRICE, Gary	22	7
BROWNING, Mark	20	20
CAMPBELL, Russell	1	1
CARTER, Peter	2	0
DEAN, Robert	18	9
DEMPSTER, Graham	1	3
EVANS, Bernie	22	28
FIELDS, Neville	14	14
FOX, Graham	3	2
GULL, Stewart	10	26
HALL, Peter	1	0
HOFFMAN, Steve	16	18
HOUNSELL, Colin	16	22
JACKSON, Francis	17	2
JAMES, Max	18	17
JAMIESON, Ray	1	0
LAMBERT, Greg	3	1
McLEISH, David	22	3
MORRISON, Peter	21	27
MORWOOD, Paul	2	0
MORWOOD, Tony	15	17
MURPHY, John	16	31
O'NEILL, Terry	22	7
PLUMB, Phillip	1	0
QUADE, Rick	14	3
RANTALL, John	21	0
ROUND, Barry	21	26
SCARLETT, John	19	2
SMITH, Michael	11	9
TEASDALE, Graham	22	22
WOODMAN, Brian	1	0
WRIGHT, Michael	12	3
YOUNG, David	21	17
ZANTUCK, Shane	11	5

POSITION: Eighth
COACH: Des Tuddenham
CAPTAIN: Rick Quade
BEST AND FAIREST: John Murphy
LEADING GOALKICKER: John Murphy (31)

assisted by giant ruckmen Graham Teasdale and Barry Round."

South then became embroiled in yet another clearance dispute, this time over its wooing of star Fitzroy centreman John Murphy. The Lions refused to budge and the matter eventually went to the VFL Appeals Board, which placed a $70,000 fee on Murphy's head. South indicated it would refuse to pay the fee and threatened legal action. South president George Camakaris met with the VFL to try and resolve the row and insisted "there was absolutely no way" the Swans would pay $70,000 for Murphy's release.

Murphy even threatened to move to South Australian club Norwood but, on April 28, finally won his release to the Swans. The breakthrough followed a meeting between South and Fitzroy officials, with the VFL acting as an intermediary. No details of the settlement were disclosed, but it was believed South had paid a substantial fee. Alf Brown, writing in *The Herald* suggested the fee was "about half the $70,000 set by the Appeals Board".

Murphy took his place in the South line-up for the following Saturday's game against Carlton at the Lake Oval. The Swans defeated the Blues by just one point, with Murphy the best player on the ground with 22 possessions. However, the victory came at a cost as the Swans again copped a horror run of injuries. Full-back John Scarlett, who was on "lease" from Geelong, had his jaw broken, James broke a hand bone, Jackson strained a hamstring and Quade strained a thigh. Murphy told reporters after the game: "I was whacked out after a quarter, but I couldn't do anything about it because there were a lot more deserving cases before me who had to leave the field."

The Swans, with so many injuries, struggled to string together enough wins to hold a place in the top five over the final rounds. Going into the round 20 clash with

John Murphy might have had problems crossing to South but won the 1978 best and fairest.

Geelong at the Lake Oval, the Swans were eighth, but trailed the fifth-placed Cats by just four match points. The Swans-Cats clash therefore was a mini-final and the red and white was rocked during the week when star ruckman Barry Round had to be admitted to hospital with a poisoned arm. However, the courageous Swan was able to take his place in the side for the big match.

It was South's last chance to stay alive in the race for the finals and, despite a huge team effort by the injury-depleted Swans, the Cats won by 12 points in a high-scoring match. Gull and Geelong full-forward Larry Donohue each kicked eight goals. Murphy kicked three goals and Tuddenham after the match described his efforts as "a magnificent performance by a champion".

South finished the season in eighth position, 12 match points behind fifth-placed Geelong. It had been a disappointing season after making the finals in 1977, but the Swans could console themselves with their fighting spirit in the face of such a terrible run of injuries. Murphy, despite his delayed start to the season, won the club best and fairest and was top goalkicker with 31. However, he did not stay long with the Swans and eventually was cleared to North Melbourne.

John Scarlett joined the Swans on "lease" from Geelong.

1979

South Melbourne was on the horns of a dilemma going into the 1979 season as Des Tuddenhan had been coach the previous year, while Ian Stewart again was available after ill-health forced him to resign as Carlton coach just a few weeks into the 1978 season. Stewart had made an enormous impression in taking the Swans to the 1977 finals, so the club had to make a decision. Tuddenham or Stewart as senior coach?

The situation eventually became ridiculous as both men turned up to take charge of training; Tuddenham claimed he was contracted, yet the club had appointed Stewart coach. The matter finally was resolved, with Stewart as coach for a second term. Meanwhile, there also was media speculation on who would captain the Swans. In fact, one newspaper report suggested John Murphy would take over from Rick Quade, with ruckman Graham Teasdale an outside chance to be skipper. The Swans did not announce their choice until the Sunday before the opening round and maintained the status quo in naming Quade as captain.

The Swans also shocked the football world by recruiting Collingwood ruckman and 1972 Brownlow Medal winner Len Thompson, who had played 270 games with the Magpies from 1965. Thompson and former Richmond, Melbourne and North Melbourne rover Daryl Cumming were the only newcomers selected for the opening round match against Richmond at the Lake Oval. Although Thompson kicked two goals and Cumming was named South's best player, Richmond won by 14 points.

This opening round defeat was bad enough, but there was worse news the following day when defender Francis Jackson had to have knee reconstruction surgery after rupturing knee ligaments. Although South president Graeme John suggested Jackson might be available if the Swans made the finals, it was an extremely optimistic assessment and Jackson did not play again in 1979.

Despite this setback, South defeated Fitzroy by 53 points at the Junction Oval the following week. The Lions led by 21 points early in the match, but the Swans dominated after half-time, with Thompson, Max James and Neville Fields each kicking four goals. South the following week defeated Melbourne by seven points at the Lake Oval to jump into fifth position, ahead of Footscray on percentage.

However, South faced an acid test in round four as it was pitted against second-placed Hawthorn at Waverley Park. The Hawks went into the match as overwhelming favourite, yet Lou Richards wrote in *The Sun* that he "wouldn't give a pie for Hawthorn's chances" and suggested "the Blood-Stained Angels will make mince meat of the Hawks". Hawthorn used the taunt to its advantage and crushed South by 94 points. The Hawks scored 11.6 over the last quarter to overwhelm the Swans.

John Rantall, a great club stalwart.

South's woes continued the following week when it went down to North Melbourne by 50 points at Arden Street. To add to the Swans' woes, star utility Mark Browning had to be rushed to Melbourne's Eye and Ear Hospital after the football had been kicked into his face during the second quarter. His left eye filled with blood and he was in hospital for the next five days.

Although South thrashed bottom side St Kilda by 89 points at the Lake Oval in round

MATCH RESULTS

Round 1, at Lake Oval, April 7
Richmond 19.11 (125) d South Melb. 15.21 (111)

Round 2, at Junction Oval, April 14
South Melbourne 21.13 (139) d Fitzroy 12.14 (86)

Round 3, at Lake Oval, April 21
South Melb. 18.10 (118) d Melbourne 16.15 (111)

Round 4, at Waverley Park, April 25
Hawthorn 29.15 (189) d South Melbourne 15.5 (95)

Round 5, at Arden Street, May 5
North Melb. 19.24 (138) d South Melb. 12.16 (88)

Round 6, at Lake Oval, May 12
South Melbourne 26.19 (175) d St Kilda 11.20 (86)

Round 7, at Western Oval, May 19
Footscray 22.17 (149) d South Melbourne 14.17 (101)

Round 8, at Lake Oval, May 26
Collingwood 20.11 (131) d South Melbourne 6.8 (44)

Round 9, at Waverley Park, June 2
Geelong 18.15 (123) d South Melbourne 17.8 (110)

Round 10, at Windy Hill, June 9
Essendon 16.19 (115) d South Melbourne 14.15 (99)

Round 11, at Lake Oval, June 18
Carlton 20.12 (132) d South Melbourne 18.18 (126)

Round 12, at MCG, June 23
Richmond 25.16 (166) d South Melb. 16.14 (110)

Round 13, at Lake Oval, June 30
Fitzroy 20.16 (136) d South Melbourne 15.20 (110)

Round 14, at Lake Oval, July 7
South Melbourne 13.11 (89) d Hawthorn 10.14 (74)

Round 15, at MCG, July 14
Melbourne 24.23 (167) d South Melb. 24.10 (154)

Round 16, at Waverley Park, July 21
North Melb. 12.16 (88) d South Melbourne 8.18 (66)

Round 17, at Moorabbin, July 28
St Kilda 19.14 (128) d South Melbourne 16.12 (108)

Round 18, at Lake Oval, August 4
South Melbourne 31.9 (195) d Footscray 15.16 (106)

Round 19, at Victoria Park, August 11
Collingwood 14.11 (95) d South Melbourne 13.9 (87)

Round 20, at Lake Oval, August 18
South Melbourne 16.6 (102) d Geelong 10.12 (72)

Round 21, at Waverley Park, August 25
Essendon 13.17 (95) d South Melbourne 10.16 (76)

Round 22, at Princes Park, September 1
Carlton 23.16 (154) d South Melbourne 17.19 (121)

South's Wayne Carroll stretches for a mark against St Kilda.

six, it was a rare highlight for the red and white, especially as the club had yet again been embroiled in controversy over the previous week. The Swans reacted to their poor start to the season by parting company with club secretary Oberon Pirak and dumping South Australian forward David Young. South president Graeme John told the media that the club would be willing to clear Young to a rival club and, soon after, Collingwood snapped him up. Pirak resigned after being told the club wanted him to move to a recruiting role.

South, in the lead-up to the round 10 clash with Essendon at Windy Hill, shocked the football world by dropping veterans Thompson, Murphy and James. Murphy soon after was cleared to North Melbourne and, while Thompson crossed to Fitzroy the following year, James continued playing with the Swans to 1982.

Swan president Graeme John thumps out the club song with Michael Wright. Note the cigarette in Wright's right hand.

The Swans even declared that from now on they would concentrate on youth and were as good as their word. They selected 18-year-old David Ackerly for his first game after training with the Under 19s the previous week. Ackerly went on to win the Swans' best and fairest the following season, and in 1982. He had 15 possessions and kicked a goal against Essendon on debut, but the Bombers won by 16 points.

The Swans won just three more matches over the rest of the season. They defeated Hawthorn by 15 points at the Lake Oval in round 14, Footscray by 89 points at the Lake Oval in round 18 and Geelong by 30 points, again at the Lake Oval, in round 20. The huge defeat of the Bulldogs was remarkable as it was the first time South had scored 30 or more goals in a match. Its score of 31.9 (195) was a club record to that stage, bettering the 29.15 (189) against St Kilda in 1919. The *Sunday Press* headline shouted THE SWANS RUN RIOT. Four players — Tony and Paul Morwood, Peter Morrison and Barry Round — kicked four goals each.

South finished the season a disappointing tenth, with just six wins. It finished above only Melbourne (also six wins) and St Kilda (three). It might have been a dismal season, but the

PLAYER	GAMES	GOALS
ACKERLY, David	11	1
BRICE, Gary	10	0
BROWNING, Mark	13	2
CARROLL, Wayne	1	1
CARTER, Peter	4	2
CUMMING, Daryl	10	4
DEAN, Robert	9	7
DEMPSTER, Graham	7	1
EVANS, Bernie	12	15
FIELDS, Neville	21	33
FRASER, Mark	4	0
HALL, Peter	4	0
HOUNSELL, Colin	12	6
HUMMEL, Jon	14	20
JACKSON, Francis	1	0
JAMES, Max	16	22
KOOP, Doug	2	2
KRUSE, Max	8	7
LAMB, Robert	7	10
LAMBERT, Greg	2	0
McLEISH, David	19	1
MORRISON, Peter	18	21
MORWOOD, Paul	20	29
MORWOOD, Tony	22	56
MURPHY, Dale	5	0
MURPHY, John	7	9
O'NEILL, Terry	16	2
PLUMB, Phillip	1	0
QUADE, Rick	21	14
RANTALL, John	21	0
ROBERTS, John	10	3
ROUND, Barry	22	8
SMITH, Michael	10	16
TARPEY, Howard	1	0
TEASDALE, Graham	8	4
THOMPSON, Len	20	39
WILLIAMS, Garry	3	0
WRIGHT, Michael	17	0
WRIGHT, Stevie	11	9
YOUNG, David	4	0
ZANTUCK, Shane	16	11

POSITION: Tenth
COACH: Ian Stewart
CAPTAIN: Rick Quade
BEST AND FAIREST: Barry Round
LEADING GOALKICKER: Tony Morwood (56)

The Swans in celebratory mood, from left, Garry Williams, coach Ian Stewart, David McLeish, Max Kruse and Colin Hounsell.

Swan cause was not helped by star ruckman Graham Teadale's walk-out during the season. Teasdale declared he would never play for the Swans again and his absence over the second half of the season proved to be a severe handicap as the Swans lacked ruck depth. Meanwhile, there were enormous off-field developments that were to be critical to the club's future.

The VFL in 1979 waged a running battle with the Victorian government over the possibility of playing Sunday games and, to make its point, played a Sunday match in Sydney. The guinea pig clubs were Hawthorn and North Melbourne, the two Grand Final teams of the previous season. Hawthorn defeated North by 51 points in their round 10 clash, but the VFL was the big winner as it realised there was enormous potential in playing games in Sydney.

Veteran football writer Ron Carter suggested in *The Age* that, with 31,395 at the SCG, "the last bastion has fallen". He added: "At last Sydney looks ready to accept Australian football. The people of this rugby city turned out in their thousands for the start of regular VFL games at the Sydney Cricket Ground." He quoted VFL president Dr Allen Aylett as saying: "We are not getting carried away. There is still a very long way to go, but we have taken step one." Then, later in the season, Richmond defeated Fitzroy by 17 points in a Round 15 match at the SCG. Both games proved pointers to the future.

1980

The Swans, who had been involved in one controversy after another the previous two seasons, had a low profile start to the 1980 season. Ian Stewart again was coach, with Barry Round captain following Rick Quade's decision to stand down in his final season. The Swans, hoping their injury woes of the previous season were behind them, opened their campaign with a practice match against North Melbourne at Wagga. The Swans defeated the Roos by 22 points, with Barry Round and Stevie Wright kicking five goals each.

Two days later, veteran South ruckman Len Thompson declared he wanted to be released, with Fitzroy stepping in to sign the former Collingwood Brownlow Medal winner. Thompson the previous season had kicked 39 goals as a permanent forward pocket for the Swans and the Lions indicated they wanted to use him in a similar role.

The Swans indicated they would not stand in Thompson's way and, besides, had convinced 1977 Brownlow Medal winner Graham Teasdale to return to the club after he had walked out on it during the previous season. Teasdale, who said when he quit the Swans in an effort to join Collingwood the previous June that he would "never return", signed a new two-year contract.

However, the Swans' aim of adopting a low profile was shattered in the lead-up to the new season when Stewart declared that veteran John Rantall should be dumped from the playing list. Rantall, immensely loyal to the Swans, was 36 years of age and Stewart felt the club needed to inject youth. However, the Swan players backed Rantall and Mark Browning even offered to step aside to allow Rantall to break the VFL games record of 333 games by Fitzroy's Kevin Murray from 1955-64 and 1967-74. Rantall, to the end of the 1979 season, had played 260 games with South and 70 with North Melbourne for a total of 330.

The Age on March 27 even ran an editorial headed SO MUCH FOR LOYALTIES. It read: "Loyalty is a flexible word in football ... John Rantall could claim to be a loyal South Melbourne man. True, he used the 10-year rule to fly a bit higher with North, bagging a premiership there. However, everyone knew where his heart really lay ... Yesterday, Rantall's loyalty was rewarded with all the graciousness of a slap in the face with a wet football sock. He was given, in the jargon of the game, the flick pass."

An anguished Stewart reacted by telling *The Herald's* Mike Sheahan: "How do you tell a great player he's not good enough to be in the team any more? It was a match committee decision and the executive knew it was coming. They'd known it for some time. It's worried me since last football season. I knew he wouldn't be in our best side. But I

Geelong's John "Sam" Newman tackles the Swans' Ricky Quade, who claims he does not have the ball.

MATCH RESULTS

Round 1, at Kardinia Park, March 29
South Melbourne 13.10 (88) d Geelong 12.13 (85)

Round 2, at Lake Oval, April 7
South Melbourne 14.17 (101) d Footscray 10.13 (73)

Round 3, at Waverley Park, April 12
Essendon 24.12 (156) d South Melb. 14.17 (101)

Round 4, at Princes Park, April 19
Carlton 22.18 (150) d South Melbourne 13.15 (93)

Round 5, at Lake Oval, April 26
South Melbourne 17.20 (122) d St Kilda 7.15 (57)

Round 6, at MCG, May 3
South Melb. 19.16 (130) d Melbourne 15.14 (104)

Round 7, at Lake Oval, May 10
South Melb. 17.13 (115) d Collingwood 13.12 (90)

Round 8, at Arden Street, May 17
North Melb. 15.19 (109) d South Melb. 16.10 (106)

Round 9, at Junction Oval, May 24
South Melbourne 16.25 (121) d Fitzroy 14.16 (100)

Round 10, at Lake Oval, May 31
South Melbourne 28.15 (183) d Hawthorn 14.15 (99)

Round 11, at Waverley Park, June 7
Richmond 18.13 (121) d South Melbourne 10.8 (68)

Round 12, at SCG, June 15
Geelong 21.21 (147) d South Melbourne 12.12 (84)

Round 13, at Western Oval, June 21
Footscray 15.14 (104) d South Melbourne 12.15 (87)

Round 14, at Lake Oval, June 28
Carlton 10.18 (78) d South Melbourne 5.9 (39)

Round 15, at Moorabbin, July 12
South Melbourne 6.14 (50) d St Kilda 5.6 (36)

Round 16, at Windy Hill, July 19
South Melbourne 19.19 (133) d Essendon 20.9 (129)

Round 17, at Lake Oval, July 26
South Melbourne 17.22 (124) d Melbourne 13.12 (90)

Round 18, at Victoria Park, August 2
Collingwood 11.24 (90) d South Melbourne 8.9 (57)

Round 19, at Lake Oval, August 9
South Melbourne 12.13 (85) d North Melb. 11.7 (73)

Round 20, at Lake Oval, August 16
South Melbourne 20.14 (134) d Fitzroy 17.15 (117)

Round 21, at Waverley Park, August 23
Hawthorn 16.17 (113) d South Melbourne 12.11 (83)

Round 22, at Lake Oval, August 30
South Melbourne 16.11 (107) d Richmond 7.11 (53)

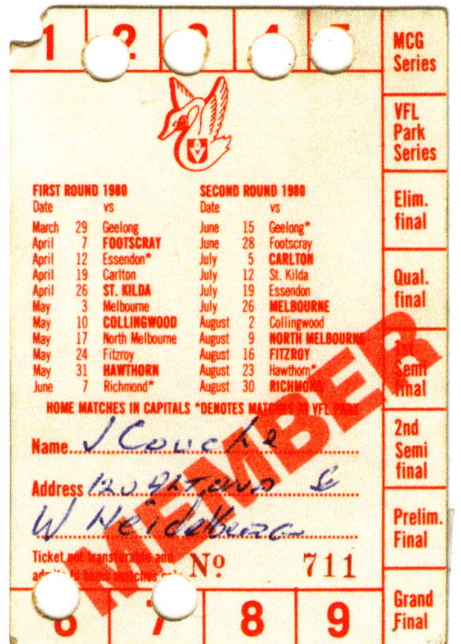

never asked him to retire. He was told every encouragement would be given him to break the record. I've certainly never said I don't want him around the place." Rantall briefly retired before crossing to Fitzroy where he broke Murray's VFL games record in his fourth game with the Lions. He retired two games later on 336 games.

South, meanwhile, had its opening round match against Geelong at Kardinia Park to worry about. Teasdale was back in the side following his half-season absence and South named five newcomers — former Footscray centre half-back Robert McGhie, former Richmond full-back Noel Jenkinson, Victor Hugo (Narrandera), John Roberts (Woodville) and Kevin Goss (Port Melbourne). The inclusions promised to give the Swans considerably more key position strength than they had for years and Roberts repaid the Swans' faith in him right from the start.

Geelong raced to a 16 points lead by half-time, only for the Swans to gradually peg them back. With Neville Fields best on ground, the Swans and the Cats went goal for goal in the final quarter. With just seconds to play, Roberts marked and then goaled after the siren to give the Swans a three-point win. Hundreds of fans were on the ground as he took his kick, but the new South full-forward was so close to goal it would have been a shock if he had missed.

The Swans, buoyed by this win, defeated Footscray by 28 points at the Lake Oval in round two and were briefly third on the ladder, with Carlton and Melbourne also undefeated. Although the Swans went down to Essendon (55 points) and Carlton (57 points) over the following two rounds, they remained in finals contention with wins over St Kilda (65 points) in round five and Melbourne (26 points) in round six.

The Sun's Peter Simunovich was so impressed with South's four-two win-loss ratio that he wrote: "This time last year South Melbourne was in a shambles. The club went through a change in administration, its local and country recruiting was virtually non-existent and its balance sheet looked like an Essendon jumper except it was predominantly

Coach Ian Stewart pats skipper Barry Round for yet another big-hearted effort. On Round's right is Shane Zantuck.

red. But, under the leadership of president Graeme John and coach Ian Stewart the Swans knuckled down to a summer of sweat and some hard talking at executive level. The dedication, sacrifices and hard work shown by the administrators has finally rubbed off on the players."

Unfortunately for the Swans, they could not find consistency and, despite several excellent wins, slowly slipped out of finals contention. Four consecutive defeats over rounds 11-14 were costly, but South at least found several stars mid-season. Centreman Greg Smith made his debut after being recruited from East Wagga, centre half-back Doug Green joined the Swans from Western Australia and full-back Rod Carter, who had been playing in the VFA after being dumped by Fitzroy. Smith and Carter had long and distinguished careers with the Swans, but former WA captain Green played just the six games with South in 1980.

South's final five hopes were all but extinguished when it went down Collingwood by 33 points at Victoria Park in round 18. The defeat left the Swans an almost impossible task as they trailed the Magpies by six match points. Although the Swans won three of their last four games, they missed the finals by that six match points margin. It had been a much improved season for the Swans and finishing sixth was no disgrace considering the problems and controversy early in the season.

PLAYER	GAMES	GOALS
ACKERLY, David	22	1
BROWNING, Mark	20	5
CALLERY, Paul	1	0
CAMPBELL. Russell	3	2
CARROLL, Wayne	8	11
CARTER, Peter	2	0
CARTER, Rod	19	0
DEAN, Robert	2	2
EATHER, Stephen	2	0
EVANS, Bernie	18	20
FIELDS, Neville	19	8
FRASER, Mark	6	0
GOSS, Kevin	15	4
GREEN, Doug	6	0
HUGO, Victor	2	0
JACKSON, Francis	22	1
JAMES, Max	5	4
JENKINSON, Noel	5	0
KOOP, Doug	9	12
KRUSE, Max	9	3
McGHIE, Robert	15	1
McLEISH, David	8	0
MORRISON, Peter	18	21
MORWOOD, Paul	22	14
MORWOOD, Tony	21	47
MURPHY, Dale	7	0
OATEN, Michael	1	0
O'NEILL, Terry	1	0
PLUMB, Phillip	2	0
QUADE, Rick	9	3
RHYS-JONES, David	4	3
ROBERTS, Ian	7	5
ROBERTS, John	22	67
ROUND, Barry	21	21
SMITH, Greg	18	9
SMITH, Michael	7	8
TEASDALE, Graham	22	8
WRIGHT, Michael	11	11
WRIGHT, Stevie	22	20
ZANTUCK, Shane	7	5

POSITION: Sixth
COACH: Ian Stewart
CAPTAIN: Barry Round
BEST AND FAIREST: David Ackerly
LEADING GOALKICKER: John Roberts (67)

David Ackerly thumps the ball clear as he crashes into teammate Max Kruse.

Meanwhile, the VFL continued its Sydney experiment with more games at the SCG. North Melbourne thrashed Footscray there by 122 points in round five and Essendon defeated Carlton there by 37 points in round nine. More significantly, however, South clashed with Geelong at the SCG in round 12 as a forerunner to events less than two years down the track. Geelong defeated the Swans by 63 points in front of 13,209 fans.

John Roberts kicked the winning goal on his debut for the Swans.

It was around this time that Fitzroy president Frank Bibby declared that the Lions were broke and considering a relocation to Sydney. Fitzroy eventually rejected the possibility of a move and when Bibby stood down at the end of the 1980 season, new president Leon Wiegard said: "A move to Sydney or to any other capital city would be the end of the Fitzroy Football Club." The VFL was keen to relocate a club to Sydney and, the following year, South was ripped apart by the proposed move to the Harbour City.

South finished the 1980 season on a high note, defeating top side Richmond by 54 points at the Lake Oval. The Swans played superb football in a howling northerly gale to push the Tigers down to third position. It could have been costly for Richmond, but it defeated Carlton and Geelong in finals matches before thrashing Collingwood in the Grand Final. South finished sixth, but out of the top five behind fifth-placed Collingwood by six match points.

1981

Although South Melbourne fans did not know it at the time, there were moves very early in 1981 for the VFL to have a club based in Sydney. Fitzroy had rejected a proposed move but, on January 29, 1981, VFL vice-president Graham Huggins resigned to take up a position as a VFL consultant in Sydney. He immediately gathered support for a possible thirteenth VFL club and, at the same time, the South Melbourne board realised the club was fighting a losing battle trying to keep its head above a sea of red ink.

Huggins' move to Sydney followed the tabling of a report commissioned by the VFL on the possibility of a club being based in Sydney. This report was titled "The Sydney Solution! VFL at the Crossroads" and was prepared by consultant John Hennessy. Also known as the Hennessy Report, it listed the needs of any club based in Sydney and these included at least 6000 members, a national sponsor, average attendances, after a settling period, of 17,500 and special VFL assistance towards establishment costs.

The Swans, well aware they were fighting for their survival at the Lake Oval, had several meetings with the VFL, but managed to keep discussions in-house until a report in *The Australian* of June 20 spilled the beans. The report, written by Jim Main (author of this book) stunned the football world. It bluntly read: "South Melbourne is considering making a bid to become the Victorian Football League's Sydney-based club next year." Channel 10 reporter Rob Astbury also broke the news, the biggest in football for decades.

South officials immediately posted a letter to all members. It explained the reasons for the proposed move and said:

• "The club will win a much larger recruiting zone in NSW, increasing the existing zone to include Broken Hill.

• "Rich sponsorship deals have been offered by Melbourne and Sydney companies which see the advantages of backing a club which has all of its games televised.

Young Swan Mark Browning swoops for the ball despite being under pressure.

MATCH RESULTS

Round 1, at Arden Street, March 28
North Melb. 21.19 (145) d South Melb. 12.25 (97)

Round 2, at Lake Oval, April 4
Richmond 22.13 (145) d South Melb. 16.14 (110)

Round 3, at Waverley Park, April 11
South Melbourne 21.13 (139) d Hawthorn 18.9 (117)

Round 4, at Junction Oval, April 18
Fitzroy 25.19 (169) d South Melbourne 14.16 (100)

Round 5, at Lake Oval, April 25
South Melbourne 18.22 (130) d Footscray 9.14 (68)

Round 6, at Waverley Park, May 2
South Melbourne 15.13 (103) d St Kilda 13.15 (93)

Round 7, at Victoria Park, May 9
Collingwood 18.15 (123) d South Melb. 7.16 (58)

Round 8, at Lake Oval, May 16
South Melbourne 17.25 (127) d Melbourne 12.11 (83)

Round 9, at Princes Park, May 23
Carlton 25.22 (172) d South Melbourne 11.7 (73)

Round 10, at Kardinia Park, May 30
Geelong 14.8 (92) d South Melbourne 10.10 (70)

Round 11, at Lake Oval, June 8
Essendon 15.18 (108) d South Melbourne 12.8 (80)

Round 12, at Waverley Park, June 13
Richmond 19.12 (126) d South Melb. 16.15 (111)

Round 13, at Princes Park, June 20
Hawthorn 20.18 (138) d South Melbourne 15.16 (106)

Round 14, at Lake Oval, June 27
Fitzroy 14.9 (93) d South Melbourne 9.16 (70)

Round 15, at Western Oval, July 11
South Melbourne 17.12 (114) d Footscray 7.9 (51)

Round 16, at Lake Oval, July 18
South Melbourne 22.19 (151) d St Kilda 16.4 (100)

Round 17, at SCG, July 26
South Melb. 18.13 (121) d Collingwood 15.13 (103)

Round 18, at MCG, August 1
South Melbourne 17.13 (115) d Melbourne 12.14 (86)

Round 19, at MCG, August 9
Carlton 13.7 (85) d South Melbourne 8.14 (62)

Round 20, at Lake Oval, August 15
Geelong 21.13 (139) d South Melbourne 12.14 (86)

Round 21, at Windy Hill, August 22
Essendon 26.23 (179) d South Melbourne 10.8 (68)

Round 22, at Lake Oval, August 29
North Melb. 15.17 (107) d South Melb. 10.14 (74)

• "A combination of the new finance and the larger recruiting zone will improve playing performance and could have South back on top by 1984 (it is 48 years since South's last premiership).

• "The coach and players have assured the board of directors of their unqualified support for the proposal.

• "Club colours will not be changed.

• "South Melbourne Cricket Club will play District games at the Lake Oval."

The letter also outlined the following alternatives if the club remained at the Lake Oval:

• "Continue to operate at a loss and go out of existence.

• "Be 'driven off' the Lakeside Oval by the VFL decision to freeze ground funds and therefore let the ground deteriorate to an unacceptable standard. This would lead South to joining another VFL club to share facilities and as a consequence loss of identity.

• "Voluntary liquidation. If this proposal is not supported there is a strong possibility that the club's financial guarantors will choose to withdraw their substantial guarantees. If that happens the club would go into voluntary liquidation."

Ian Roberts was a wonderfully reliable defender.

South captain and Brownlow Medal winner Barry Round.

The letter ended: "The board of directors has taken into account all the advantages and alternatives and believe that the proposal to the VFL is South Melbourne's only chance of survival as a force in the VFL."

The Age reported that the proposal was "designed to prevent the club from going bankrupt and avoid being forced to amalgamate with another VFL club". There was talk at the time that St Kilda wanted South to join it at Moorabbin and a new club would be known as the Southern Saints. Under the Swans' proposal, the club would play 11 games a season under lights at the SCG and the other 11 at Waverley Park, Melbourne. South officials also pointed out that coach Ian Stewart and the players had backed the proposal.

Two great mates, Barry Round and Bernie Quinlan (in Footscray guernsey) fly in opposition for a mark. They shared Brownlow Medal honours in 1981, but Quinlan had moved to Fitzroy. At the front is South forward David Young.

PLAYER	GAMES	GOALS
ACKERLY, David	19	0
ALLENDER, Stephen	10	8
BOYSE, Maurice	5	5
BROWNING, Mark	12	13
CARROLL, Dennis	14	6
CARROLL, Wayne	8	7
CARTER, Rod	21	0
CONLEN, Bernie	2	0
COWTON, Gary	8	0
DANIHER, Anthony	9	0
EATHER, Stephen	3	0
EVANS, Bernie	20	19
FIELDS, Neville	6	0
FOSCHINI, Silvio	17	37
FRASER, Mark	10	1
GOSS, Kevin	9	2
HOUNSELL, Colin	16	13
JACKSON, Francis	17	2
JAMES, Max	12	12
JENKINSON, Noel	1	0
KOOP, Doug	4	1
KRUSE, Max	12	1
McGHIE, Robert	1	0
MELESSO, Peter	1	0
MOIR, Phillip	3	3
MORRISON, Peter	1	0
MORWOOD, Paul	16	4
MORWOOD, Shane	4	4
MORWOOD, Tony	20	21
OATEN, Michael	1	0
PLUMB, Phillip	5	1
RHYS-JONES, David	18	1
ROBERTS, Ian	6	1
ROBERTS, John	21	51
ROUND, Barry	22	12
SCOTT, Brett	7	0
SMITH, Greg	19	13
SMITH, Michael	2	5
TAYLOR, Kevin	14	24
TEASDALE, Graham	17	17
WHITZELL, Mark	1	0
WINBANKS, David	4	0
WRIGHT, Stevie	22	23

POSITION: Ninth
COACH: Ian Stewart
CAPTAIN: Barry Round
BEST AND FAIREST: Barry Round
LEADING GOALKICKER: John Roberts (51)

South's John Roberts attempts to spoil North's Gary Cowton, who also played with the Swans.

Many South fans reacted to the news with shock and outrage, with a Keep South at South (KSAS) committee being formed. However, South triple Brownlow Medal winner Bob Skilton was quoted as saying: "I don't like the thought of if (a move) happening and I have mixed feelings. But I don't like the alternatives because I can't see any future in the way things are going. Any action taken must be for the good of the club. There doesn't seem to be any light at the end of the tunnel. Maybe South can start something."

South's planned move was big news for weeks and, on July 13, the KSAS group, headed by committee chairman John Keogh, outlined its objections. Keogh made a speech from the steps of the South Melbourne Town Hall in which he claimed 90 per cent of club members were opposed to the move. He also claimed the KSAS group had received legal advice that neither South Melbourne nor the VFL had the authority to move the club to Sydney.

Although it was obvious the club's 1200 members would be aghast at the news, South Melbourne Club Ltd's three top officials — chairman Jack Marks, vice-chairman Graeme John and club director Craig Kimberley — indicated the members would have little say if the VFL supported the proposed move. Under the proposal, South would continue to use the Lake Oval as its training and administrative headquarters as it had another 20 years to run on the ground's lease. VFL president Dr Allen Aylett told *The Age:* "South Melbourne's submission is feasible, reasonable and well researched. No one else has given any indication they would want to play in Sydney."

The South civil war ran for weeks, with claim and counter-claim and, finally, the KSAS group forced a extraordinary general meeting of club members on the night of September 22. The Caulfield Town Hall was packed for the meeting, with most fans decked in red and white. Both sides presented their cases before a vote was taken on the proposed relocation. The KSAS group won by a mere 10 votes. John Keogh became club president, but the war was far from over.

The VFL had voted two months earlier to allow South to play 11 matches in Sydney in 1982 and the KSAS group had to convince the VFL that it should reverse this decision. This, of course, would have been contrary to the VFL's planned expansion of the competition and there seemed little or no way the KSAS group could convince a two-thirds majority to rescind the previous decision.

Keogh's KSAS group also ran into difficulties with the players, most of whom were keen for the club to play its home matches in Sydney. The KSAS group met with the players, but were shocked when told they would go on strike if necessary. The KSAS group appointed club great John Rantall as coach, but most of the players believed Rick Quade would be coaching the club in 1982. The two groups were diametrically opposed and Keogh wrote to members: "It is with great personal sorrow that I must advise you that I and all other members of the board consider that we must accept the VFL decision to play 11 games in Sydney in 1982 on a trial basis, and we will continue to fight on your behalf that South will have a definite say as to where it plays in 1983 and thereafter."

However, that was not the end of the matter as the two factions kept locking horns and there even were fears the VFL would cut the Swans from the competition altogether. Some players had indicated they would seek clearances to other clubs and, all the while, some players trained under Rantall. The situation looked impossible but, on December 11, the KSAS group resigned and racing broadcaster Bill Collins, a whole-hearted Swans man, took over as club chairman. This move was designed to bring both parties together but, when the new board reconfirmed Rantall as coach, the war erupted yet again.

Finally, the VFL called an emergency

meeting and this time meant business. Dr Aylett insisted the Swans were going to play their home games in Sydney in 1982. No arguments would be tolerated. Rantall stood down as coach and Quade took over. The VFL's Alan Schwab was loaned to the Swans for three months to facilitate a smooth transition and, finally, the players were able to sigh in relief. The civil war was over and the Swans would play in Sydney after all.

The Swans played for half a season with controversy their daily companion, even though they had started 1981 blissfully unaware of the impending civil war. Ian Stewart again was coach, with Rick Quade his captain yet again. South tuned up for the new season with a practice match against Collingwood at Ararat, but went down by 29 points. Meanwhile, South was involved in a tug of war for highly promising Port Melbourne ruckman/forward Stephen Allender, the 1980 VFA best and fairest. Allender was residentially bound to Carlton, but he insisted he would not play for the Blues as he had barracked for the Swans all his life. South took Supreme Court action to win his release but withdrew its action when it agreed to pay Carlton $60,000 for Allender's clearance.

South also introduced several other notable players in 1981, with none better than Dennis Carroll, who went on to captain the club from 1986-92. Goalsneak Silvio Foschini created a huge impression in his debut season, Shane Morwood joined brothers Tony and Paul in the red and white, Anthony Daniher played nine games in his debut season and Brett Scott briefly coached the club in 1993 after a brilliant, but injury-riddled playing career.

South went down to North Melbourne by 48 points at Arden Street in the opening round and then by 35 points to Richmond at the Lake Oval in round two. The Swans managed to break through to defeat Hawthorn by 22 points at the Lake Oval in round three, but the finals always looked out of the question, especially after six consecutive defeats from rounds nine to 14. Amazingly, however, the Swans turned it all around with four consecutive wins from rounds 15 to 18, all while the civil war swirled and raged around them.

Two games late in the season were highly significant as one was played at the SCG as part of the VFL's push for games in Sydney and other was the second Sunday VFL game in Victoria. South played Collingwood at the SCG in round 17 on July 26 and not only did the Swans defeat the Magpies by 18 points, but the match attracted an extremely healthy attendance of 22,238. The Swans two weeks later played Carlton at the MCG on a Sunday in the middle of an umpires' strike. The Blues defeated the Swans by 23 points and the game attracted 24,388 fans. One of the field umpires called in for senior duty to replace the men on strike was Brad Beitzel, son of umpires' director Harry Beitzel. The first Sunday match was played at the MCG the previous week, with Essendon defeating Collingwood by 19 points.

The Swans went into the final round not knowing where they would be playing the following season. They were pitted against North Melbourne at the Lake Oval and, despite intense speculation that this was likely to be the last game at the Lake Oval, the clash attracted just 8485 fans. The weather was atrocious and, to make the players' mood even darker, the cheer squad held up a black crepe banner for the team to run through before the start of play; Round instructed his team to run around it.

North defeated South by 33 points in what was Stewart's last game as coach. The curtain was drawn on South's association with the Lake Oval from its earliest years, even though the Swans continued to use the ground as a training venue for several more seasons.

The Swans might have been downhearted after that loss to North, but soon cheered up when big-hearted ruckman Barry Round shared Brownlow Medal honours with his good mate, Fitzroy's Bernie Quinlan. The pair had been close friends at Footscray and even had played their 250th games on the same day during the 1981 season. Round and Quinlan polled 22 votes each to pip Carlton rover Rod Ashman by one vote. The Swans celebrated that night in a suite at the Southern Cross Hotel, where the Brownlow dinner had been held. It had been the toughest of seasons, but had ended with the Swans winning one last slice of glory while still known as South Melbourne.

South Melbourne's last team at the Lake Oval

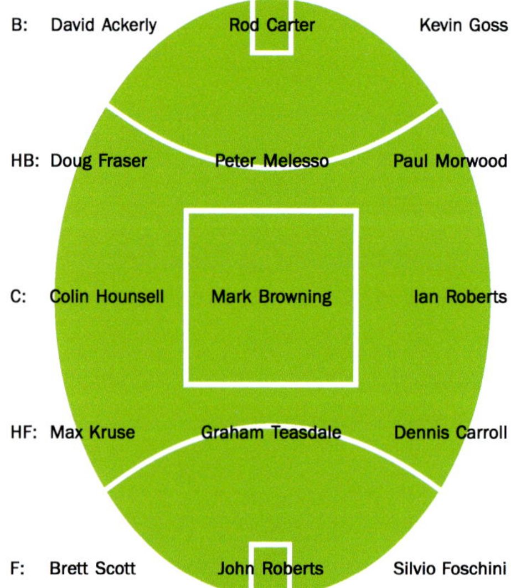

FOLL.: Barry Round, Greg Smith, Stevie Wright
RES.: Bernie Conlen, Peter Morrison

1982

The decision to play "home" games in Sydney in 1982 was irreversible. The draw had been made very early over the summer of 1981-82 and finally, everyone accepted the decision. Well, almost everyone. Many diehard South Melbourne supporters refused to have anything to do with the move, while newspapers still referred to the club as South Melbourne. The club in this season wanted to be known simply as the Swans but, when the teams for the first round were announced the only reference to Sydney was in terms of the playing venue.

For example, *The Sun* and the *Age* both listed the club's opening round match as South Melbourne v Melbourne, with the additional line of "Sydney, Sunday". The Swans' only newcomer was key position player Barry Beecroft, who had returned to the club after a stint in Western Australia with Claremont. It was Ricky Quade's debut as Swan coach, with Barry Round the club's first captain in Sydney. The game also marked Ron Barassi's debut as coach of Melbourne.

The match attracted a respectable attendance of 15,764 and the Swans, despite starting favourites, had to work hard to defeat the Demons by 29 points. In fact, the Demons challenged strongly early in the final quarter and only Round's strong marking in defence held them at bay. The Swans that night celebrated at a party at the harbourside home of Sydney socialite Lady Mary Fairfax. It was a glittering start to the club's new image, but there were mighty tough times ahead, even in this first year in Sydney.

In realily, the club had two homes in 1982 as it played its "home" games at the SCG but continued to train at the Lake Oval. It was obvious this arrangement would take its toll on players, staff and committee but, with the opening round win, *The Age* suggested this was "a relief for the VFL". It reported: "The pressure on the Swans to win their first game in Sydney was so great that a couple of times it seemed as if the occasion

Skipper Barry Round leads the Swans onto the SCG for the opening round game against Melbourne.

MATCH RESULTS

Round 1, at SCG, March 28
Sydney Swans 20.17 (137) d Melbourne 16.12 (108)

Round 2, at Arden Street, April 3
North Melb. 24.13 (157) d Sydney Swans 16.21 (117)

Round 3, at Moorabbin, April 10
Sydney Swans 20.22 (142) d St Kilda 17.14 (116)

Round 4, at SCG, April 18
Sydney Swans 24.18 (162) d Fitzroy 14.22 (106)

Round 5, at Kardinia Park, April 24
Geelong 12.12 (84) d Sydney Swans 11.16 (82)

Round 6, at SCG, May 2
Essendon 18.9 (117) d Sydney Swans 15.21 (111)

Round 7, at Western Oval, May 8
Sydney Swans 20.11 (131) d Footscray 15.20 (110)

Round 8, at SCG, May 16
Sydney Swans 15.25 (115) d Collingwood 13.19 (97)

Round 9, at Princes Park, May 22
Carlton 27.23 (185) d Sydney Swans 12.11 (83)

Round 10, at SCG, May 30
Hawthorn 24.13 (157) d Sydney Swans 15.13 (103)

Round 11, at MCG, June 5
Richmond 20.14 (134) d Sydney Swans 18.25 (133)

Round 12, at SCG, June 13
North Melb. 16.15 (111) d Sydney Swans 15.15 (105)

Round 13, at SCG, June 20
Sydney Swans 30.19 (199) d St Kilda 15.13 (103)

Round 14, at Junction Oval, June 26
Sydney Swans 20.13 (133) d Fitzroy 16.16 (112)

Round 15, at SCG, July 4
Sydney Swans 18.18 (126) d Geelong 12.15 (87)

Round 16, at Windy Hill, July 17
Sydney Swans 17.13 (115) d Essendon 12.10 (82)

Round 17, at SCG, July 25
Sydney Swans 14.27 (111) d Footscray 15.8 (98)

Round 18, at Victoria Park, July 31
Sydney Swans 13.12 (90) d Collingwood 12.13 (85)

Round 19, at SCG, August 8
Sydney Swans 15.16 (106) d Carlton 9.18 (72)

Round 20, at Princes Park, August 14
Hawthorn 18.18 (126) d Sydney Swans 8.14 (62)

Round 21, at SCG, August 22
Richmond 19.13 (127) d Sydney Swans 16.14 (110)

Round 22, at MCG, August 28
Melbourne 25.13 (163) d Sydney Swans 22.16 (148)

Defender Max Kruse was one of the Swans' best in the Escort Cup Grand Final.

would get to them. Besides being a victory for South, it was a massive win for the VFL's venture into this rugby city."

North Melbourne defeated the Swans by 40 points in their round two match at Arden Street and the poor attendance of 14,097 was a reflection of the red and white's loss of some support. However, there remained a large contingent of faithful Swan supporters and they were rewarded when their team defeated St Kilda by 26 points at Moorabbin in round three. The Swans went into the St Kilda match almost at full strength after winger David Rhys-Jones was cleared of a striking charge laid during the match against North, while rover Stevie Wright was reprimanded over an incident in the same match.

The Swans defeated Fitzroy by 56 points in their second match at the SCG, in front of 13,617 fans. The Swans' hero was brilliant goalsneak Silvio Foschini, who kicked seven goals to give him a tally of 51 from 21 games after making his debut the previous season. The 18-year-old was happy to train and play with the Swans, but there was heartache all round when the club insisted that players shift to Sydney for the following season.

Meanwhile, the Swans' fortunes fluctuated over the first half of the 1982 season, but they turned this around with seven consecutive wins from rounds 13-19. The Swans even defeated Collingwood by five points at Victoria Park, holding the Magpies at bay when they almost stole victory after

David Rhys-Jones was an early Sydney favourite.

PLAYER	GAMES	GOALS
ACKERLY, David	22	1
ALLENDER, Stephen	14	18
BEECROFT, Barry	7	0
BRADDY, Craig	12	13
BROWNING, Mark	22	7
CARROLL, Dennis	22	17
CARROLL, Wayne	13	22
CARTER, Rod	22	0
DANIHER, Anthony	18	8
EVANS, Bernie	18	23
FOSCHINI, Silvio	21	42
HOUNSELL, Colin	18	15
JAMES, Max	3	2
KRUSE, Max	22	6
LUCAS, Jack	2	1
MORWOOD, Paul	21	12
MORWOOD, Shane	13	9
MORWOOD, Tony	20	45
MUSTEY, Trevor	1	0
NEESHAM, Gerard	9	1
OATEN, Michael	4	8
REID, John	5	0
RHYS-JONES, David	21	3
ROBERTS, Ian	3	0
ROBERTS, John	7	17
ROUND, Barry	21	18
SCOTT, Brett	21	22
SMITH, Greg	21	22
TAUBERT, Steve	12	21
WINBANKS, David	5	1
WRIGHT, Stevie	22	27

POSITION: Seventh
COACH: Rick Quade
CAPTAIN: Barry Round
BEST AND FAIREST: David Ackerly
LEADING GOALKICKER: Tony Morwood (45)

trailing by 27 points. The Swans therefore went into their next match, against Carlton at the SCG, with high hopes. However, a report in *The Age* the day before the match suggested the Swans were in dire financial difficulties yet again.

The report, by Ron Carter and Mike Coward, indicated that the VFL had given the Swans $60,000 in advance of their season's allocation, on top of a $400,000 loan from earlier in the season. The VFL now wanted the Swans to supply it with "a precise financial statement". The Swans, in turn, argued that it needed special assistance if they were to survive in Sydney. There also were suggestions some Swan identities were working behind the scenes to unsettle the club's plan to move lock, stock and barrel to Sydney from 1983.

This report did not seem to ruffle the players as the Swans defeated Carlton by 34 points to move into sixth position, just one game behind fifth-placed North Melbourne and therefore a real chance to make the final five. However, Hawthorn thrashed the Swans by 64 points at Princes Park to shatter the finals dream. The Swans then went down to Richmond and Melbourne in the final two rounds to finish seventh, two games outside the final five.

There was one huge highlight during the 1982 season when the Swans defeated North Melbourne by 32 points in the night series (Escort Cup) Grand Final. The match, played in front of 20,082 fans, was a remarkable achievement considering the club was still being torn apart. Director Kevin Campbell resigned during the season and the VFL even had to appoint assistant general manager Alan Schwab to oversee the thrust to move everyone to Sydney from 1983.

Mike Coward reported in *The Age* of the Swans' night series success: "It was a triumph for coach Ricky Quade and his young team. The start of the year saw the club in turmoil and suggestions that it would even disband ... The Swans had to wait longer than anticipated for their moment of glory when hundreds of supporters from the crowd of 20,082 invaded the ground with five minutes to play." It was obvious the Swans still had plenty of support in Melbourne and they proved it by turning up to the celebrations at the Lake Oval that night. Foschini kicked four goals, with Tony Morwood and Bernie Evans kicking three each. Max Kruse, Colin Hounsell and Rod Carter were named as the Swans' best players.

Barry Round holds aloft Sydney's first trophy, the 1982 Escort Cup.

1983

The Swans fully relocated to Sydney in 1983, with tremendous associated trauma. Again, the Swans were split. Many players relished the opportunity, but several refused to make the move. Silvio Foschini insisted he would not be leaving his closely-knit Italian family and Paul and Shane Morwood also were reluctant to shift. Other players shifted to Sydney not knowing what to expect or even where they would live. Football manager Dean Moore often would meet players at Sydney airport with a street directory or even guides to hospitals for pregnant player wives.

All this drama was being played out against a backdrop of intrigue as there was a push for more Sydney influence on the board. The Swans also appointed former Melbourne wing champion Brian Dixon as CEO. Dixon, who also had coached North Melbourne and had been a Victorian member of parliament, was seen as having the perfect credentials for running a football club. There also was talk that the club could be privately owned, but nothing came of it — at the time.

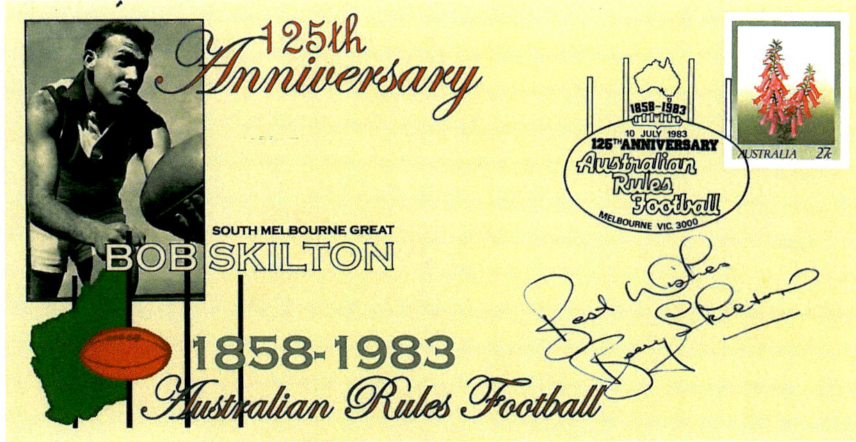

Australia Post celebrated the 125th anniversary of Australian football with this first-day cover. It is signed by Swan great Bob Skilton.

The season had not even started when the Swans were rocked by an application by Foschini for a clearance to Sydney. Despite legal advice that the Swans should clear the goalsneak, the club refused to budge. Foschini took legal action and the matter eventually went before the Supreme Court of Victoria. On April 15, Justice Crockett ruled there had been a restraint of trade and that the VFL rules and regulations regarding player movements were invalid. In another off-field drama, Sir James Hardy resigned as president in January, 1983, and was replaced by entrepreneur Michael Edgley.

The Swans opened the season with a one-point win over Essendon at the SCG, in heroic circumstances. The Swans copped injury after injury and finished the match with just 15 fully fit players and one, John Reid, had to stay on the ground even though he could barely hobble. The Swans dropped their next three matches, but little wonder considering the off-field drama swirling around the club. There was disquiet over Dixon's man management style and he was offered the opportunity to resign. When he refused, the club issued the following statement: "Today (May 7) at a board meeting of the South Melbourne Club Limited (the club still was not officially referred to as the Sydney

MATCH RESULTS

Round 1, at SCG, March 27
Sydney Swans 17.9 (111) d Essendon 15.20 (110)

Round 2, at Princes Park, April 4
Hawthorn 9.16 (70) d Sydney Swans 5.15 (45)

Round 3, at SCG, April 10
North Melb. 27.23 (185) d Sydney Swans 5.15 (45)

Round 4, at Junction Oval, April 16
Fitzroy 17.23 (125) d Sydney Swans 6.16 (52)

Round 5, at SCG, April 24
Sydney Swans 24.16 (160) d St Kilda 21.11 (137)

Round 6, at MCG, April 30
Melbourne 18.18 (126) d Sydney Swans 12.21 (93)

Round 7, at SCG, May 8
Carlton 22.17 (149) d Sydney Swans 18.10 (118)

Round 8, at Kardinia Park, May 14
Sydney Swans 16.14 (110) d Geelong 11.18 (84)

Round 9, at SCG, May 22
Syd. Swans 18.13 (121) d Collingwood 14.16 (100)

Round 10, at MCG, May 28
Richmond 16.10 (106) d Sydney Swans 14.10 (94)

Round 11, at SCG, June 5
Sydney Swans 17.19 (121) d Footscray 15.12 (102)

Round 12, at Windy Hill, June 11
Essendon 23.18 (156) d Sydney Swans 13.5 (83)

Round 13, at SCG, June 19
Hawthorn 15.20 (110) d Sydney Swans 11.12 (78)

Round 14, at Arden Street, June 25
North Melbourne 11.16 (82) d Sydney Swans 7.8 (50)

Round 15, at SCG, July 3
Sydney Swans 23.9 (147) d Fitzroy 17.15 (117)

Round 16, at Moorabbin, July 16
St Kilda 20.9 (129) d Sydney Swans 14.16 (100)

Round 17, at SCG, July 24
Sydney Swans 18.17 (125) d Melbourne 16.16 (112)

Round 18, at Princes Park, July 30
Carlton 17.17 (119) d Sydney Swans 11.9 (75)

Round 19, at SCG, August 5
Geelong 20.21 (141) d Sydney Swans 10.15 (75)

Round 20, at Victoria Park, August 13
Collingwood 28.14 (182) d Syd. Swans 18.12 (120)

Round 21, at SCG, August 21
Richmond 15.24 (114) d Sydney Swans 10.13 (73)

Round 22, at Western Oval, August 27
Footscray 17.12 (114) d Sydney Swans 10.12 (72)

Swans), it was unanimously resolved to terminate the services of Mr Brian Dixon, the executive director."

Also, the VFL finally agreed to subsidise the Swans with an additional $900,000 and even appointed an eight-man board to run the club. This comprised VFL president Dr Allen Aylett, general manager Jack Hamilton, assistant general manager Alan Schwab, company secretary Ralph Lane, media manager Ian McDonald and corporate planner John Hennessey. The Swan representatives were Michael Edgley and John Keogh. It also was agreed that the club would enter a scheme of arrangement to settle debts. Finally, the club's name was changed to Sydney Swans Limited.

Little wonder the players found it difficult to find consistency and, besides, there was considerable on-field drama early in the season because of the Foschini-Paul Morwood situation. St Kilda decided it would play both of them in a round four match against Geelong at Waverley Park, without clearances. The Saints smuggled the pair into the rooms pre-match and there was stunned silence when the former Swans ran onto the ground. They then lined up against their old side the following week at the SCG and, amid predictions of "mayhem and revenge", the Swans defeated the Saints by 23 points. There were no incidents and, remarkably, brothers Tony and Paul Morwood played on opposite sides as Tony had been happy to relocate to Sydney.

The VFL was forced to adopt interim player movement rules following the Foschini-Morwood controversy, while the Swans eventually cleared Morwood to the Saints for $75,000 and later sold Foschini for a similar fee. Swan coach Ricky Quade

Wayne Carroll was a fine competitor in the Swans' earliest Sydney years.

Max Kruse played with great commitment.

was jubilant but cautious following the win over St Kilda and admitted to the media that his victory speech had been vetted by lawyers. He said: "We won out on the ground and all their lawyers can't take the four points from us. It's a shame football has come to this." St Kilda president Lindsay Fox was not invited to the Swans' official pre-match luncheon and, instead, ate a pie and sauce. He said after the match: "We all ate pies for lunch, and now we eat humble pie."

Fortunately, the Swans were able to stay out of the headlines over the second half of the season, although *The Age* reported in its June 29 edition that the club was thinking of novel ways to raise money "to stay alive". The plan followed a decision by Justice Murphy to refuse permission to call a meeting of creditors to discuss the scheme of arrangement. The judge described the club as "hopelessly insolvent", but the Swans vowed to continue their fight for survival.

Terry Thripp was the first local product to play with the Sydney Swans.

The Swans did well to remain competitive through all this drama and carved themselves a small slice of history when they played Geelong in the first VFL night match at the SCG on August 5. The Cats defeated the Swans by 66 points, but the game paved the way for what now are regular Friday night matches across the country.

The Swans finished eleventh, above only St Kilda, with seven wins and 15 defeats. It had been one of the toughest years in the club's long and proud history, but it was still alive and breathing. Just! One of the few highlights of a forgettable season was skipper Round's 300th VFL game, in the round 21 game against Richmond at the SCG. Unfortunately, the Swans were unable to help him celebrate as they went down by 41 points.

PLAYER	GAMES	GOALS
ACKERLY, David	20	0
ALLENDER, Stephen	4	2
BAKER, Garry	6	5
BOYSE, Maurice	11	11
BRADDY, Craig	21	48
BROWNING, Mark	22	15
CAPPER, Warwick	1	0
CARROLL, Dennis	17	6
CARROLL, Wayne	9	4
CARTER, Rod	22	0
CATOGGIO, Vin	8	9
DANIHER, Anthony	22	11
EVANS, Bernie	17	27
FRANGALAS, Gary	15	13
HEDLEY, Steve	1	1
HENDERSON, Darryl	3	0
HOUNSELL, Colin	15	10
JACKSON, Francis	15	1
KRUSE, Max	22	12
LUCAS, Jack	12	2
MALONI, Peter	1	0
McBROOM, Stephen	3	1
MUSTEY, Trevor	1	0
REID, John	5	2
RHYS-JONES, David	14	9
ROBERTS, Ian	22	9
ROUND, Barry	22	7
SCOTT, Brett	3	3
SMITH, Greg	19	14
STIRLING, David	7	5
SUTTON, Darryl	14	25
TAUBERT, Steve	11	4
THRIPP, Terry	3	1
VERNON, Daryl	4	2
WALL, Mark	1	0
WHITZELL, Mark	4	0
WINBANKS, David	6	1
WRIGHT, Stevie	16	12

POSITION: Eleventh
COACH: Rick Quade
CAPTAIN: Barry Round
BEST AND FAIREST: Mark Browning
LEADING GOALKICKER: Craig Braddy (48)

1984

By the time the Sydney Swans started preparations for the 1984 season, it was disclosed that the VFL already had provided loans amounting to $1.4 million. However, the Swans believed they needed a "marquee" player to attract fans and, with this in mind, recruited Collingwood centre half-back Bill Picken. The 27-year-old defender had played in four losing Grand Final sides and was expected to give the Swans the experience and glamour they needed to thrive in Sydney.

Picken ran into injury problems and played just 28 games over two seasons with the Swans, who also picked up North Melbourne's Craig Holden in the lead-up to the new season. Holden became a great club servant over 80 games in the red and white to 1988 and then in off-field roles over the next two decades. Although the Swans had been delighted to win Picken's signature, they were far from happy in being forced to pay $155,000 for his clearance.

Arthur Chilcott was recruited locally.

Two other recruits, one from the club's Melbourne metropolitan zone and the other from its country area, made huge impacts. Rover Barry Mitchell joined the Swans from Mulgrave, while winger David Murphy came from Turvey Park (NSW). Mitchell played 170 games with the Swans to 1992 and Murphy 156 to 1993. Both were wonderfully whole-hearted competitors and, while Mitchell won the best and fairest in 1991, Murphy in 2003 was named in the club's Team of the Century.

Rick Quade again was coach, with Barry Round the club captain, and the Swans prepared for the season with several practice matches, including one against Melbourne at Wagga. The Swans defeated the Demons by 40 points, with local youngster Arthur Chilcott (Western Suburbs) impressing with four goals and Round and Greg Smith named as the Swans' best players. The Swans then went down by 23 points to Essendon at Waverley Park in their final practice match, with Chilcott (three goals) again impressing.

The Swans in 1984 might have been based in Sydney, but a rump of players still lived in Melbourne and trained at the Lake Oval under reserves coach, former Richmond rover Peter Hogan. Among them were Rod Carter, Bernie Evans, Gary Frangalas, Warwick Capper and Mark Whitzell. Hogan was responsible for the Swans retaining Capper after VFA club Port Melbourne almost won his clearance. Hogan told the club committee Capper had enormous potential and advised the Swans against a clearance.

Picken, Chilcott and the Wagga Tigers' Paul Hawke were named in the Swan line-up for the opening round match against Hawthorn at Princes Park. It was a tough first-up assignment, and the Hawks had little trouble in defeating the Swans by 35 points. David

Swan full-back Rod Carter was both mean and reliable.

MATCH RESULTS

Round 1, at Princes Park, March 31
Hawthorn 17.22 (124) d Sydney Swans 13.11 (89)

Round 2, at SCG, April 8
Sydney Swans 16.16 (112) d Melbourne 13.20 (98)

Round 3, at Moorabbin, April 14
Sydney Swans 22.13 (145) d St Kilda 18.8 (116)

Round 4, at Victoria Park, April 21
Sydney Swans 17.4 (116) d Collingwood 15.13 (103)

Round 5, at SCG, April 29
Sydney Swans 17.17 (119) d Fitzroy 15.14 (104)

Round 6, at Western Oval, May 5
Footscray 11.18 (84) d Sydney Swans 11.11 (77)

Round 7, at SCG, May 13
Richmond 18.21 (129) d Sydney Swans 17.20 (122)

Round 8, at Arden Street, May 19
Sydney Swans 19.20 (134) d North Melb. 18.19 (127)

Round 9, at SCG, May 27
Sydney Swans 16.15 (111) d Geelong 7.27 (69)

Round 10, at SCG, June 3
Carlton 20.19 (139) d Sydney Swans 12.15 (87)

Round 11, at Windy Hill, June 9
Essendon 20.15 (135) d Sydney Swans 14.10 (94)

Round 12, at MCG, June 16
Melbourne 21.17 (143) d Sydney Swans 5.16 (46)

Round 13, at SCG, June 24
St Kilda 19.12 (126) d Sydney Swans 15.11 (101)

Round 14, at SCG, July 1
Collingwood 19.17 (131) d Syd. Swans 14.16 (100)

Round 15, at Junction Oval, July 7
Sydney Swans 14.12 (96) d Fitzroy 9.14 (68)

Round 16, at SCG, July 15
Sydney Swans 16.17 (113) d Footscray 12.15 (87)

Round 17, at MCG, July 28
Richmond 12.19 (91) d Sydney Swans 3.10 (28)

Round 18, at SCG, August 5
North Melb. 18.15 (123) d Sydney Swans 17.6 (108)

Round 19, at Kardinia Park, August 11
Geelong 16.17 (113) d Sydney Swans 14.8 (92)

Round 20, at SCG, August 19
Hawthorn 25.24 (174) d Sydney Swans 11.19 (85)

Round 21, at SCG, August 26
Sydney Swans 23.17 (155) d Essendon 14.15 (99)

Round 22, at Princes Park, September 1
Carlton 20.19 (139) d Sydney Swans 15.13 (103)

Rhys-Jones kicked six goals for the Swans and was named among the Swans' best, along with rover Evans and ruckman Steve Taubert.

The Swans opened their account in defeating Melbourne by 14 points at the SCG the following week and then defeated St Kilda, Collingwod and Fitzroy over consecutive weeks to be branded potential finalists. However, there was one major hiccup over this period. The Swans' flight to Melbourne for a Sterling Cup night series match against Fitzroy at Waverley Park was delayed several hours during a national airline dispute. They did not arrive in Melbourne until 8pm and the VFL had no option but to postpone the match and thousands of fans were turned away from the ground. The Swans eventually defeated Fitzroy, but went down to Essendon in the competition Grand Final.

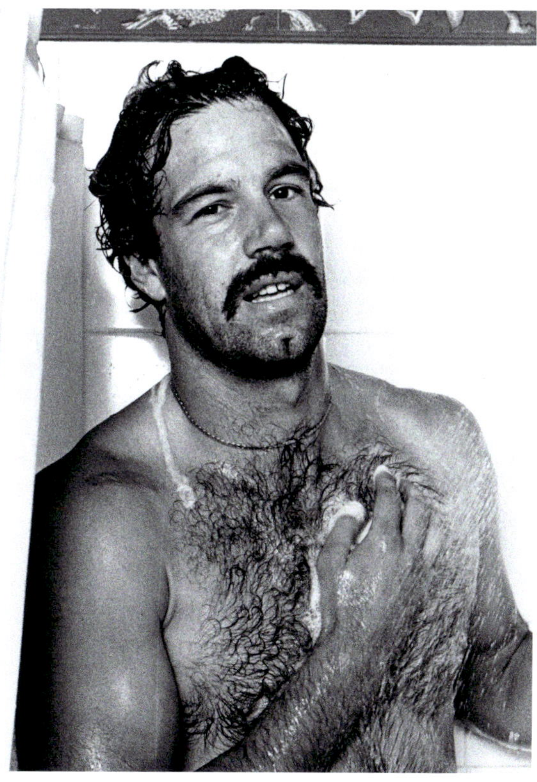
Ruckman Steve Taubert was fourth in the 1984 Brownlow Medal count.

The golden run of four consecutive wins came to an end when Footscray defeated the Swans by seven points at the Western Oval and, from there, the red and white struggled for consistency. They were out of the top five on percentage after going down to Carlton by 52 points at the SCG in round 10, and *The Age* suggested SWANS MISS BIG CHANCE. Essendon defeated the Swans by 41 points at Windy Hill the following week and the club from there fell apart.

A headline in the *Sunday Press* screamed THE LAST ROUND? The front-page article suggested Round should retire as he had just four kicks and took only two marks against the Bombers. The Swans dropped Round for the match against Collingwood and he immediately announced his retirement. He had been a magnificent player for the Swans in 193 games from 1976. Mark Browning was named the replacement captain, but the Swans were rocked again just after the defeat by the Magpies.

Quade announced that he would be resigning as coach because of ill health. Quade had been taken to hospital with stomach ulcers and club general manager Barry Lyons said: "We have to wait and see how his condition is. Rick is still our senior

Swan centreman Greg Smith was known as the "Bionic Man" because of his ability to play through injuries.

coach at the moment." However, the Swans immediately launched a search for a new coach, with chairman of selectors and former player Tony Franklin appointed interim coach. Franklin's appointment was short-term as he explained to the media that he was based in Melbourne and, besides, did not want the job permanently.

There even were suggestions Round would return to the club as coach, but Swan officials on July 3 flew to Adelaide to interview South Australian Bob Hammond, who had coached Norwood from 1974-79. Hammond accepted the position and immediately flew to Sydney to meet the players. Asked why he took the job, Hammond told *The Herald's* Peter Stone: "I must be crazy, but I love football and see the Swans as the first step to a national competition." A visionary, Hammond years later was appointed an AFL Commissioner.

Hammond made a huge impression with the Swans but, at season's end, indicated he did not want the job permanently. The Swans finished tenth with just nine wins. The club desperately needed stability, but lost several administrators at season's end. Franklin resigned as chairman of selectors, and general manager Lyons and football manager Dean Moore followed suit. At the same time, there were the first hints that the VFL would consider private ownership of the Swans.

PLAYER	GAMES	GOALS
ACKERLY, David	22	5
BRADDY, Craig	18	21
BROWNING, Mark	22	22
CAPPER, Warwick	15	39
CARROLL, Dennis	14	3
CARROLL, Wayne	12	10
CARTER, Rod	19	0
CHILCOTT, Arthur	11	14
DANIHER, Anthony	22	4
DAVIS, Michael	1	1
EVANS, Bernie	22	36
FOY, Pat	7	1
FRANGALAS, Gary	14	12
HAWKE, Paul	22	23
HOLDEN, Craig	16	3
HOUNSELL, Colin	9	7
HUGHES, Tony	2	2
KRUSE, Max	12	1
LUCAS, Jack	5	3
McBROOM, Steve	3	1
MITCHELL, Barry	7	6
MORWOOD, Tony	20	30
MURPHY, David	6	2
PICKEN, Bill	15	0
POTTER, Craig	3	0
RHYS-JONES, David	19	23
ROBERTS, Ian	21	4
ROUND, Barry	15	28
SCOTT, Brett	9	5
SIDDONS, Jamie	2	1
SMITH, Greg	19	6
TAUBERT, Steve	21	1
THRIPP, Terry	2	1
VERNON, Daryl	4	0
WHITZELL, Mark	3	0
WRIGHT, Stevie	6	6

POSITION: Tenth
COACH: Rick Quade, Bob Hammond
CAPTAIN: Barry Round, Mark Browning
BEST AND FAIREST: Bernie Evans
LEADING GOALKICKER: Warwick Capper (39)

1985

With Bob Hammond rejecting overtures for him to be appointed full-time coach of the Sydney Swans, the club had to search for a replacement. Although the media made numerous suggestions, the club appointed former Richmond half-forward John Northey, who had impressed while coaching in Victorian country football. He also had spent the 1978 season as an assistant coach at St Kilda. He had played 118 games with the Tigers from 1963-70 and had a reputation for bonding his players. It might have been a surprise appointment, but Northey did well enough in his only season with the Swans to later coach Melbourne, Richmond and the Brisbane Bears.

The Swans also had a new-look administration, with former SANFL general manager Don Roach appointed chief executive and former Hawthorn player and Geelong coach Rod Olsson football director and chairman of selectors. However, the Swans were dealt a savage blow just before Christmas when star winger David Rhys-Jones walked out on the club after he was asked to take a pay cut. Rhys-Jones, who had played 76 games with the Swans from 1980, joined Carlton. He played 106 games with the Blues to 1992 and won the Norm Smith Medal as best on ground in the 1987 Grand Final and his loss to the Swans was inestimable.

However, the Swans did land two star recruits in 1985, with Mark Bayes and John Ironmonger making their debuts. Bayes' signing was a masterstroke by former Swan official and player Greg Miller as the youngster had been tied residentially to Footscray. Miller convinced the Bulldogs that if they did not release Bayes, the Noble Park teenager would wait until their hold on him expired. Bayes went on to play 246 games with the Swans to 1998, won the best and fairest in 1989 and was named in the club's Team of the Century. Ironmonger had won the 1983 Sandover Medal with East Perth and his bulk promised to boost the Swans' big-man

Winger Merv Neagle was one of the prize recruits of the Edelsten era and signed late in 1985.

MATCH RESULTS

Round 1, at Moorabbin, March 30
Sydney Swans 26.20 (176) d St Kilda 8.18 (66)

Round 2, at MCG, April 6
Sydney Swans 13.14 (92) d Richmond 12.16 (88)

Round 3, at SCG, April 14
Fitzroy 26.15 (171) d Sydney Swans 18.12 (120)

Round 4, at SCG, April 21
Hawthorn 8.15 (63) d Sydney Swans 5.14 (44)

Round 5, at Victoria Park, April 27
Collingwood 15.15 (105) d Sydney Swans 13.12 (90)

Round 6, at SCG, May 5
Sydney Swans 25.11 (161) d Footscray 11.17 (83)

Round 7, at SCG, May 12
Carlton 12.16 (88) d Sydney Swans 11.17 (83)

Round 8, at MCG, May 18
North Melbourne 11.8 (74) d Sydney Swans 6.10 (46)

Round 9, at SCG, May 26
Geelong 16.21 (117) d Sydney Swans 13.11 (89)

Round 10, at MCG, June 1
Melbourne 15.19 (109) d Sydney Swans 14.8 (92)

Round 11, at Windy Hill, June 8
Essendon 17.11 (113) d Sydney Swans 11.5 (71)

Round 12, at SCG, June 16
Sydney Swans 23.21 (159) d St Kilda 13.14 (92)

Round 13, at SCG, June 23
Sydney Swans 19.23 (137) d Richmond 8.12 (60)

Round 14, at Victoria Park, June 29
Fitzroy 13.17 (95) d Sydney Swans 11.14 (80)

Round 15, at Princes Park, July 6
Hawthorn 23.18 (156) d Sydney Swans 12.11 (83)

Round 16, at SCG, July 21
Collingwood 29.11 (185) d Syd. Swans 17.21 (123)

Round 17, at Western Oval, July 27
Footscray 15.15 (105) d Sydney Swans 11.13 (79)

Round 18, at Princes Park, August 3
Carlton 19.13 (127) d Sydney Swans 14.9 (93)

Round 19, at SCG, August 11
North Melb. 14.15 (99) d Sydney Swans 12.22 (94)

Round 20, at Kardinia Park, August 17
Geelong 13.13 (91) d Sydney Swans 9.10 (64)

Round 21, at SCG, August 25
Sydney Swans 24.21 (165) d Melbourne 14.13 (97)

Round 22, at SCG, September 1
Essendon 24.21 (165) d Sydney Swans 11.12 (78)

The Swans' Anthony Daniher started on a wing and developed into a fine defender.

depth. He played 45 games with the Swans to 1987 before crossing to Fitzroy.

Mark Browning was given his first full season as captain but, even before the start of the season, there was news that Sydney medico Dr Geoffrey Edelsten was willing to buy the Swans. His offer included the repayment of the club's $1.4 million VFL debt and a fee for the purchase of a licence. Dr Edelsten's announcement brought other parties into play and it soon became obvious the club would be sold, to the right purchaser. Other interested parties included Melbourne businessman and former Carlton reserves player Dick Pratt and international businessman Basil Sellers. Edelsten immediately upped his offer to the repayment of debt AND $3 million.

All three parties met with the VFL soon after the start of the season and, after Pratt withdrew his offer, there was an attempt to involve Edelsten and Sellers in a joint venture. The ownership saga dragged on for most of the season but, finally, the VFL agreed to the sale of the club to Edelsten. The announcement was made on July 31 and the bid was reported to total $6 million. It was the start of one of the Swans' most dramatic eras, with Edelsten raising the club's profile in rebuilding the playing stocks through the recruitment of stars from rival clubs.

On-field, the Swans started the season brilliantly in thrashing St Kilda by 110 points at Moorabbin in the opening round and then defeating Richmond by four points at the MCG. Veteran football writer Jack Dunn in the *Sunday Press* described the Swans as "sizzling" in their demolition of the Saints and named Bernie Evans as best on ground after the rover and Swan favourite kicked nine goals. The Swans' David Ackerly was named best on the ground in the defeat of the Tigers at the MCG.

The Swans were aiming for top position on the ladder when they were scheduled to play Footscray at the SCG in round six, but ran into trouble in the week leading up to the game when the SCG Trust banned the Swans from training on their home ground. It mattered little as the Swans thrashed the Bulldogs by 78 points, and from there, the Swans won only a handful more games. Their season was overshadowed by the speculation surrounding the private ownership battle, with the deal finalised after the Bulldogs defeated the Swans in their return match at the Western Oval in round 17.

On the eve of the VFL's decision, *The Age* ran a list of "pros and cons" for both the Edelsten and Sellers bids. The article described Edelsten as "flamboyant and entrepreneurial" and Sellers as having "the ability to turn troubled waters around". *The Age* said it believed the Edelsten bid was slightly higher than the Sellers bid and added that Edelsten had warned the VFL that there would be an "exodus" of players if the rival camp won the bid. This, of course, was merely a tactical ploy but, next day, *The Age* headline read VFL GOES FOR THE DOCTOR. Edelsten had won the bidding war. Sellers' only comment was "that's the way it goes". Although the Edelsten years were dramatic, with some success, it was short-lived, whereas Sellers remained staunchly committed to the Swans as a major benefactor in the rebuilding of the club after the flamboyant doctor walked away.

The main terms of the agreement were: (1) Repayment of the Sydney Swans' debt of $1.4 million (owed to other clubs); (2) An additional payment (licence fee) of $1.5 million, to be shared by the other clubs; (3) A further licence fee payment amounting to five per cent of each yearly profit; (4) A payment

PLAYER	GAMES	GOALS
ACKERLY, David	22	4
BAYES, Mark	18	11
BRADDY, Craig	5	1
BROWNING, Mark	21	7
CAPPER, Warwick	14	45
CARROLL, Dennis	19	19
CARROLL, Wayne	5	2
CARTER, Rod	21	0
CHILCOTT, Arthur	2	0
DANIHER, Anthony	22	19
DUURSMA, Jamie	18	3
EVANS, Bernie	19	44
FAVIER, John	2	0
FRANGALAS, Gary	22	5
HAWKE, Paul	14	14
HOLDEN, Craig	17	12
HOUNSELL, Colin	8	1
HUGHES, Tony	4	0
IRONMONGER, John	15	1
KOTZUR, Hilton	1	0
KRUSE, Max	3	2
McASEY, Darren	11	0
MITCHELL, Barry	18	25
MORWOOD, Tony	17	29
MURPHY, David	17	12
PICKEN, Bill	13	0
PROSSER, Robbie	2	1
ROBERTS, Ian	15	2
ROBERTS, Mark	6	4
ROUND, Barry	12	13
RUSSELL, Mark	14	13
SAGGERS, Robbie	2	2
SCOTT, Brett	5	5
SCOTT, Malcolm	1	1
SINCLAIR, Tony	2	1
SMITH, Andrew	4	1
SNEDDON, Lindsay	2	0
WHITZELL, Mark	2	0
WRIGHT, Stevie	22	16
YONSON, Rudy	3	3

POSITION: Tenth
COACH: John Northey
CAPTAIN: Mark Browning
BEST AND FAIREST: Stevie Wright
LEADING GOALKICKER: Warwick Capper (45)

of 10 per cent of any gains in the event of the licence being sold; (5) The granting of a licence being conditional on approval by the Swans board and membership; (6) The licensee (Edelsten) assumed all other liabilities of the Sydney Swans, present and future. *The Age* also published a logo depicting the new club image, with a dollar sign over a swan. *The Herald* the next day declared SWANS: NOW FOR ACTION. It ran a photograph of Edelsten with wife Leanne near a car registration plate which read SWANS.

Edelsten's first public appearance after the announcement was as a special guest at Carlton's official pre-match function when the Swans played the Blues at Princes Park the following Saturday. Carlton defeated the Swans by 34 points but there was such bonhomie that Carlton president John Elliott promised the new Swan owner that the Blues would make available any player who was surplus to requirements at Princes Park. Just a few years later Elliott was plotting the demise of the Swans so that Carlton could play all its away games in Sydney.

Just days after the announcement of the sale, West Australian company Westeq was disclosed as the power behind the Edelsten bid and, shortly later, Olsson was sacked as football manager and Northey was told he would not be reappointed coach for the following season. The Swans, in fact, had interviewed former Richmond premiership coach Tom Hafey and Essendon's Kevin Sheedy. After Sheedy re-signed with the Bombers, the Swans settled on Hafey, with the announcement made on October 21.

The Swans had finished the 1985 season in tenth position, but all supporters expected far better seasons ahead, especially as Edelsten was as good as his word in signing a clutch of players from rival clubs over the following summer.

Ian Roberts - safe, reliable and courageous.

1986

With former Richmond premiership coach Tom Hafey installed as coach in October, 1985, the Sydney Swans embarked on one of the greatest recruiting drives in football history, rivalling the club's own massive efforts of the 1930s and North Melbourne's spree under the short-lived 10-year rule in the mid-1970s. Hafey was seen as the man most likely to lift the Swans and to give it the profile the club needed in the difficult Sydney market. Hafey had played just 67 games with the Tigers from 1953-58, but coached the club to four premierships before having stints with Collingwood and then Geelong.

Forward Jim Edmond, recruited from Footscray.

Hafey had been Cat coach from 1983-85 and therefore had intimate knowledge of the players he believed he could lure to Sydney. The Swans therefore raided Kardinia Park to sign Greg Williams, Bernard Toohey and David Bolton. All served the Swans exceptionally well, with Williams in particular a major drawcard. However, the recruiting did not end there as the Swans also signed Essendon's Merv Neagle, Melbourne's Gerard Healy, Footscray's Jim Edmond, Fitzroy's Glenn Coleman and Richmond's Maurice Rioli. Williams and Healy won Brownlow Medals with the Swans, but Rioli never pulled on the red and white as the VFL ruled that the club could not fit him in the salary cap. Former player Paul Morwood also rejoined the Swans after a controversial stint with St Kilda but, after 10 games in 1986, also had to be released because of salary cap restrictions.

Training under Hafey started on November 11, 1985, but the Swans were dealt a blow a few days later when Essendon ruckman Simon Madden announced he would be staying with the Bombers. Madden many years later told of how Edelsten offered him a small fortune to sign with the Swans. When Edelsten asked him what he did for a living, Madden told him he was a schoolteacher. According to Madden, Edelsten replied: "Well, I'll buy you your

Star Swan centreman Greg Williams at Victorian state training in 1986.

MATCH RESULTS

Round 1, at MCG, March 31
Sydney Swans 20.6 (126) d North Melb. 15.11 (101)
Round 2, at SCG, April 6
Syd. Swans 19.20 (134) d Collingwood 15.10 (100)
Round 3, at Kardinia Park, April 12
Sydney Swans 19.18 (132) d Geelong 15.15 (105)
Round 4, at SCG, April 20
Sydney Swans 20.22 (142) d Footscray 9.12 (66)
Round 5, at MCG, April 25
Sydney Swans 16.14 (110) d Melbourne 14.17 (101)
Round 6, at SCG, May 4
Sydney Swans 18.12 (120) d Carlton 13.20 (98)
Round 7, at Princes Park, May 10
Hawthorn 18.25 (133) d Sydney Swans 15.10 (100)
Round 8, at SCG, May 18
Richmond 16.16 (112) d Sydney Swans 16.15 (111)
Round 9, at Moorabbin, May 24
Sydney Swans 6.11 (47) d St Kilda 5.8 (38)
Round 10, at SCG, June 1
Sydney Swans 18.18 (126) d Fitzroy 14.17 (101)
Round 11, at Windy Hill, June 9
Sydney Swans 10.18 (78) d Essendon 9.4 (58)
Round 12, at SCG, June 13
North Melb. 14.11 (95) d Sydney Swans 13.13 (91)
Round 13, at Victoria Park, June 21
Sydney Swans 14.12 (96) d Collingwood 14.11 (95)
Round 14, at SCG, June 29
Sydney Swans 17.11 (113) d Geelong 13.13 (91)
Round 15, at Western Oval, July 5
Sydney Swans 12.14 (86) d Footscray 11.4 (70)
Round 16, at SCG, July 13
Sydney Swans 24.18 (162) d Essendon 15.13 (103)
Round 17, at SCG, July 27
Sydney Swans 29.15 (189) d Melbourne 9.11 (65)
Round 18, at Princes Park, August 2
Carlton 15.14 (104) d Sydney Swans 12.15 (87)
Round 19, at SCG, August 10
Hawthorn 27.9 (171) d Sydney Swans 10.13 (73)
Round 20, at MCG, August 16
Sydney Swans 21.18 (144) d Richmond 14.12 (96)
Round 21, at SCG, August 24
Sydney Swans 20.20 (140) d St Kilda 16.15 (111)
Round 22, at Victoria Park, August 30
Fitzroy 9.19 (73) d Sydney Swans 8.15 (63)
Qualifying final, at MCG, September 7
Carlton 18.12 (120) d Sydney Swans 15.14 (104)
Semi-final
Fitzroy 13.16 (94) d Sydney Swans 13.11 (89)

Paul Morwood briefly rejoined the Swans in 1986.

own school." Regardless, Madden probably was the missing link and the Swans might have won a premiership under Hafey if he had signed to move to Sydney.

The Swans also were rocked by the revelation that Edelsten was not the sole owner of the club and that the VFL licence to operate the club was held by Powerplay, a public company with links to Westeq. On the playing side, the Swans were sad to lose champion rover Bernie Evans, whose personal commitments made it impossible to move to Sydney. He had played 148 games for the Swans from 1978 and was wonderfully reliable. Finally, the VFL fined the Swans for "poaching" the Geelong stars. Edelsten

Winger David Murphy was named in the Swans' Team of the Century.

Dashing Swan half-forward Tony Morwood takes yet another spectacular mark.

relocated by saying it was a only a "technicality". However, Williams, Bolton and Toohey were released to play with the Swans only on the eve of the new season.

An opening round match against North Melbourne at the MCG on Easter Monday, on March 31, saw the Swans unveil their new-look combination, with defender Dennis Carroll the new club captain. The star recruits had had little time to bond, but they were too

PLAYER	GAMES	GOALS
BARTHOLOMAEUS, Grant	2	0
BAYES, Mark	20	12
BOLTON, David	20	16
BROWNING, Mark	21	4
CAPPER, Warwick	24	92
CAPRIOLI, Robert	1	0
CARROLL, Dennis	21	4
CARTER, Rod	22	1
COLEMAN, Glenn	20	6
DANIHER, Anthony	22	20
DUURSMA, Jamie	7	1
EDMOND, Jim	17	19
HAWKE, Paul	19	19
HEALY, Gerard	22	26
HOLDEN, Craig	20	2
IRONMONGER, John	17	0
JONES, Graham	1	0
McASEY, Darren	4	8
MITCHELL, Barry	24	27
MORWOOD, Tony	22	44
MORWOOD, Paul	10	4
MURPHY, David	16	9
NEAGLE, Merv	14	4
ROBERTS, Ian	23	2
ROBERTS, Mark	12	1
SCOTT, Brett	2	0
SMITH, Tony	4	0
TOOHEY, Bernard	24	4
WHITZELL, Mark	2	0
WILLIAMS, Greg	24	28
WRIGHT, Stevie	23	32

POSITION: Fourth
COACH: Tom Hafey
CAPTAIN: Dennis Carroll
BEST AND FAIREST: Gerard Healy
LEADING GOALKICKER: Warwick Capper (92)

strong for North and won by 25 points. It was the start of an exciting new era and, the following week, the Swans defeated Collingwood by 34 points at the SCG. Williams, Bolton and Toohey then were booed when they lined up against Geelong at

Kardinia Park in round three, but had the last laugh in the Swans' 27-point victory.

Even then there seemed little doubt the Swans would play in the finals and the undefeated run continued until the red and white tackled Hawthorn at Princes Park in round seven. The Hawks defeated the Swans by 33 points and the following week, Richmond pipped the Swans by a point at the SCG. These were temporary setbacks as the Swans regrouped to win eight of their next 11 games. The massive 124-point defeat of Melbourne at the SCG in round 17 was significant as the winning margin remains as the club's greatest against the Demons. The Swans' score of 29.15 (189) also is their highest against Melbourne. Finally, Swan full-back Rod Carter kicked his only VFL goal in this match.

The Swans were certain finalists by the time they played Fitzroy at Victoria Park in the final round, but were almost dealt a savage blow. Champion centreman Greg Williams was reported on a striking charge and was in danger of being suspended. However, the Swans breathed a sigh of relief when he was cleared. However, the Swans went into the finals series without skipper Carroll, who had injured a knee late in the season.

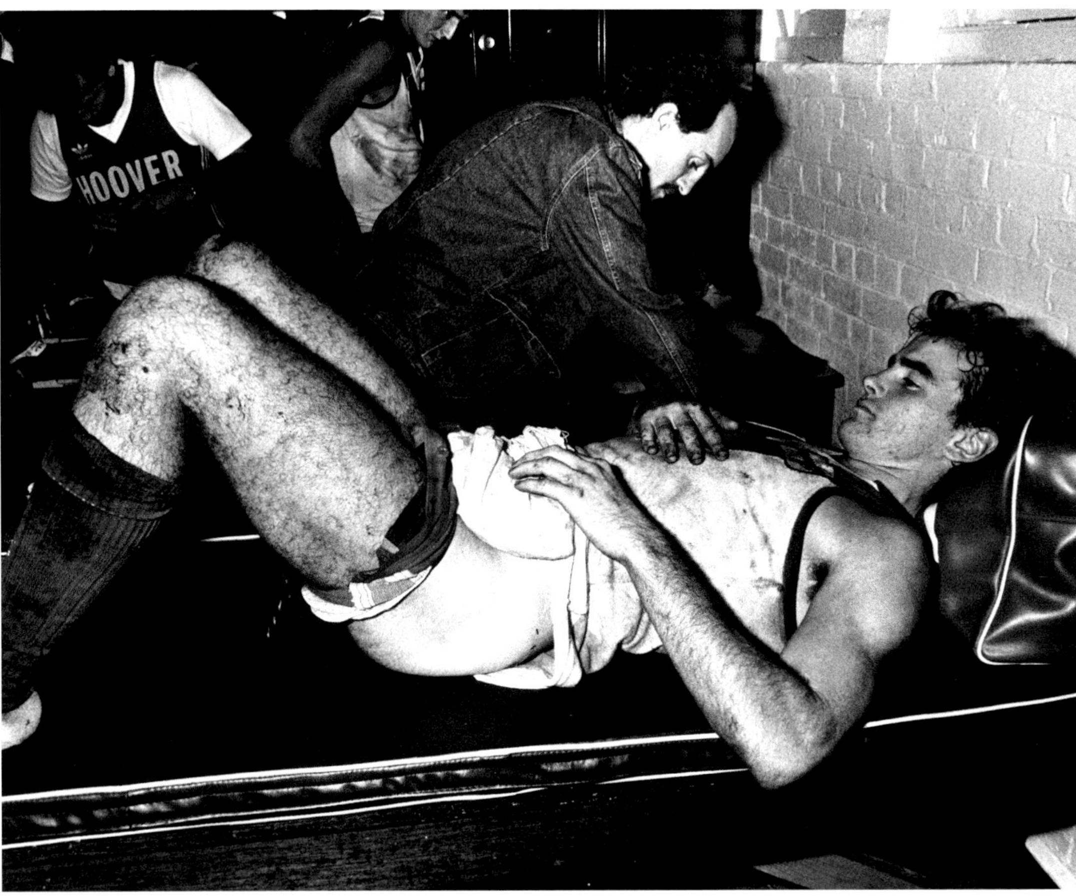

Swan rover Barry Mitchell is exhausted after a game against Hawthorn at Princes Park in 1986. Next to him is Mark Browning.

In finishing second behind Hawthorn, the Swans were drawn to play Carlton in a qualifying final at the MCG. Although the Swans at times looked capable of defeating the Blues, they went down by 16 points. Then, in the following week's semi-final against Fitzroy at the MCG, the Swans looked likely winners until the Lions fought back to kick two late goals for a five-point win. The Swans, after such a brilliant season, had bowed out of the finals in straight sets.

However, there was one major triumph in 1986 as Williams shared Brownlow Medal honours with Hawthorn's Robert DiPierdomenico. Each polled 17 votes, one more than Fitzroy's Paul Roos. Williams and DiPierdomenico might have been fortunate as Roos missed out in the final round against the Swans, even though most media experts rated him best on ground. Williams, however, missed out on the club best and fairest award in 1986, that honour going to Healy.

Also, glamour full-forward Warwick Capper went close to the "ton" of goals in a season, kicking 92, including a bag of 10 in the one-point loss to Richmond at the SCG in round eight. It was the first time a Swan player had kicked double figures since Jack Graham booted 10 against Geelong at Kardinia Park in round eight, 1948.

1987

The Sydney Swans endured more drama over the summer of 1986-87 which, in reality, ended the Dr Geoffrey Edelsten era. The Swans' owner had resigned as chairman in July, 1986, and was replaced

Swan full-forward Warwick Capper drew fans to the SCG.

Barry Mitchell gets his kick despite pressure from Carlton's David Glascott.

by the Lord Mayor of Sydney, Doug Sutherland. Powerplay in October, 1986, bought all Edelsten's shares in the club and yet another new era started for the Swans. Powerplay was determined to lift the club's profile even higher in Sydney and, to make sure the club reflected its new base rather than the old South Melbourne, designed a new club guernsey of white with a red yoke in which the outline of the Sydney Opera House was depicted.

The 1987 season also saw the birth of two new clubs, West Coast and the Brisbane Bears, in the development of a national competition. This meant a 14-team competition, although the VFL retained its 22-round home and away season. The VFL in late 1986 also introduced the national draft and the Swans' first choice was Barooga's John Brinkkotter as the overall number 10 selection. Brinkkotter played just five games

MATCH RESULTS

Round 1, at Victoria Park, March 28
Sydney Swans 25.15 (165) d Collingwood 11.8 (74)
Round 2, at SCG, April 5
Sydney Swans 27.25 (187) d Footscray 11.13 (79)
Round 3, at Subiaco, April 12
Sydney Swans 18.16 (124) d West Coast 14.13 (97)
Round 4, at Windy Hill, April 20
Essendon 17.11 (113) d Sydney Swans 9.12 (66)
Round 5, at MCG, April 25
Sydney Swans 21.20 (146) d Richmond 19.12 (126)
Round 6, at SCG, May 1
Sydney Swans 13.16 (94) d Carlton 12.15 (87)
Round 7, at SCG, May 10
Sydney Swans 18.14 (122) d Hawthorn 17.12 (114)
Round 8, at SCG, May 15
Fitzroy 16.20 (116) d Sydney Swans 13.9 (87)
Round 9, at Kardinia Park, May 24
Geelong 15.14 (104) d Sydney Swans 11.13 (79)
Round 10, at SCG, May 31
North Melb. 23.7 (145) d Sydney Swans 20.16 (136)
Round 11, at Carrara, June 7
Sydney Swans 19.23 (137) d Bris. Bears 9.10 (64)
Round 12, at MCG, June 13
Sydney Swans 17.10 (112) d Melbourne 11.10 (76)
Round 13, at SCG, June 21
Sydney Swans 20.14 (134) d St Kilda 11.9 (75)
Round 14, at SCG, June 26
Sydney Swans 14.17 (101) d Collingwood 10.14 (74)
Round 15, at Waverley Park, July 4
Sydney Swans 16.10 (106) d Footscray 10.13 (73)
Round 16, at SCG, July 19
Sydney Swans 30.21 (201) d West Coast 10.11 (71)
Round 17, at SCG, July 26
Sydney Swans 36.20 (236) d Essendon 11.7 (73)
Round 18, at SCG, July 31
Sydney Swans 31.12 (198) d Richmond 15.17 (107)
Round 19, at Princes Park, August 8
Carlton 17.21 (123) d Sydney Swans 8.7 (55)
Round 20, at Princes Park, August 15
Hawthorn 20.22 (142) d Sydney Swans 15.7 (97)
Round 21, at SCG, August 23
Geelong 18.23 (131) d Sydney Swans 18.14 (122)
Round 22, at Princes Park, August 29
Sydney Swans 20.21 (141) d Fitzroy 20.13 (133)
Qualifying final, at Waverley Park, September 5
Hawthorn 23.18 (156) d Sydney Swans 8.9 (57)
Semi-final, at MCG, September 13
Melbourne 21.23 (149) d Sydney Swans 10.13 (73)

Swan defender Neil Cordy reaches for the ball against Fitzroy. In the background is the Lions' Paul Roos, a future Swan premiership coach.

for the Swans, but none of their other selections managed a game between them. They were Tasmanian Lyndon Dakin, Albury's Donald Thompson, the ACT's Craig Elias and Tocumwal's Laurie Menhenut.

The Swans cleared Anthony Daniher to Essendon, Paul Morwood to Collingwood and Mark "Fridge" Roberts to Brisbane and introduced even more players from rival VFL clubs. Neil and Graeme Cordy crossed from

PLAYER	GAMES	GOALS
BARTHOLOMAEUS, Grant	2	0
BAYES, Mark	23	38
BOLTON, David	21	15
BROWNING, Mark	21	8
BYRNE, Michael	11	9
CAPPER, Warwick	22	103
CARROLL, Dennis	20	6
CARTER, Rod	24	0
COLEMAN, Glenn	15	8
CORDY, Graeme	10	5
CORDY, Neil	19	0
HAWKE, Paul	17	16
HEALY, Gerard	20	22
HENWOOD, Wayne	24	3
HIGGINS, Leon	1	0
HOLDEN, Craig	23	4
IRONMONGER, John	13	0
LLOYD, Matt	1	0
MITCHELL, Barry	20	37
MORWOOD, Tony	23	46
MURPHY, David	16	14
NEAGLE, Merv	18	15
PHYLAND, Michael	5	2
POTTER, Craig	10	8
QUIRK, Peter	7	1
ROBERTS, Ian	8	2
SCOTT, Brett	7	11
SMITH, Tony	3	0
THRIPP, Terry	16	7
TOOHEY, Bernard	18	2
WILLIAMS, Greg	22	21
WRIGHT, Stevie	19	34

POSITION: Fourth
COACH: Tom Hafey
CAPTAIN: Dennis Carroll
BEST AND FAIREST: Gerard Healy
LEADING GOALKICKER: Warwick Capper (103)

Glamour full-forward Warwick Capper takes a spectacular mark over Carlton's Warren McKenzie, who later joined the Swans.

Footscray and Michael Byrne from Hawthorn. Neil Cordy in particular gave the Swans great service as he played 96 games with the Swans to 1993 and was an exceptionally reliable defender. The Swans also snared Glenelg key position player Wayne "Moose" Henwood and, from their old country zone, Tocumwal's Leon Higgins.

With Hafey again coach and Carroll in his second year as captain, the Swans opened the season against Collingwood at Victoria

Park. It should have been a daunting prospect, but the Swans triumphed by a massive 91 points. The margin and the Swans' score of 25.15 (165) remain club records against the Magpies. Then followed wins over Footscray at the SCG and the first defeat of West Coast in Perth. The Swans defeated the Eagles by 27 points at Subiaco and were hailed as potential premiers, until they went down to Essendon by 47 points at Windy Hill in round four.

The Swans had a 6-4 win-loss ratio at the completion of round 10, but then produced one of the most incredible bursts of form in club history. The Swans not only notched eight consecutive wins, but rewrote records along the way. With Greg Williams and Gerard Healy two of the best midfielders in the competition and Warwick Capper kicking swags of goals, the Swans went on the rampage in consecutive SCG matches against Essendon, West Coast and Richmond.

It all started in the round 16 clash with the Eagles. The Swans scored a briefly-held club record 30.21 (201) to defeat the hapless Eagles by 130 points. It was the first time the club had scored 200 or more points in a match yet, amazingly, the Swans repeated the effort against Essendon the following round. The Swans led by just two points at quarter-time, but then produced truly scintillating form to defeat the Bombers by 163 points. They scored a mammoth 36.20 (236) to smash the previous round's effort by a whopping 35 points. Bomber coach Kevin Sheedy said after the match he was sick and tired of seeing the home club's cheer group, the Swanettes, going through their routine after every goal.

It was the first time a club had scored 200 points or more in consecutive matches and the media wondered whether the Swans could make it three in a row. They almost made it. They scored 31.12 (198) to defeat Richmond by 91 points. It was the first time any VFL team had kicked 30 or more goals in even two, let alone three consecutive matches. The Swans now were red-hot premiership favourites, only to fall right away almost immediately. They went down to Carlton by 68 points at Princes Park in round 19 and then lost to Hawthorn and Geelong before defeating Fitzroy at Princes Park in the final round, only to lose Carroll through injury yet again on the even of a finals series.

The Swans finished the home and away season in third position and played the second-placed Hawthorn in a qualifying final at Waverley Park. It proved a disaster for the Swans as they went down by 99 points. The only consolation was that Capper reached his "ton" of goals and finished the season with 103 in bagging four against the Hawks. However, Capper then missed the following week's semi-final against Melbourne at the MCG through injury. The Demons thrashed the tired Swans by 76 points amid rumours that Hafey had trained his players the night before the match. It was a bitterly disappointing end to a season in which the Swans rewrote the record books.

Swan Gerard Healy was a midfield genius who won the club best and fairest in 1987.

The match program from a Swans' post-season match against Melbourne in Vancouver, Canada.

1988

The Sydney Swans started the 1988 season behind the eight-ball. Owner Powerplay, in financial difficulty, off-loaded players against the express wishes of coach Tom Hafey, in his third season with the Swans. The most damaging was the clearance of glamour full-forward Warwick Capper to the Brisbane Bears. In many ways Capper had been the face of the Swans and, in clearing its main drawcard, the club consigned itself to a miserable season. The Swans also cleared ruckman John Ironmonger to Fitzroy and midfielder Paul Hawke to Collingwood.

Champion Swan centreman Greg Williams.

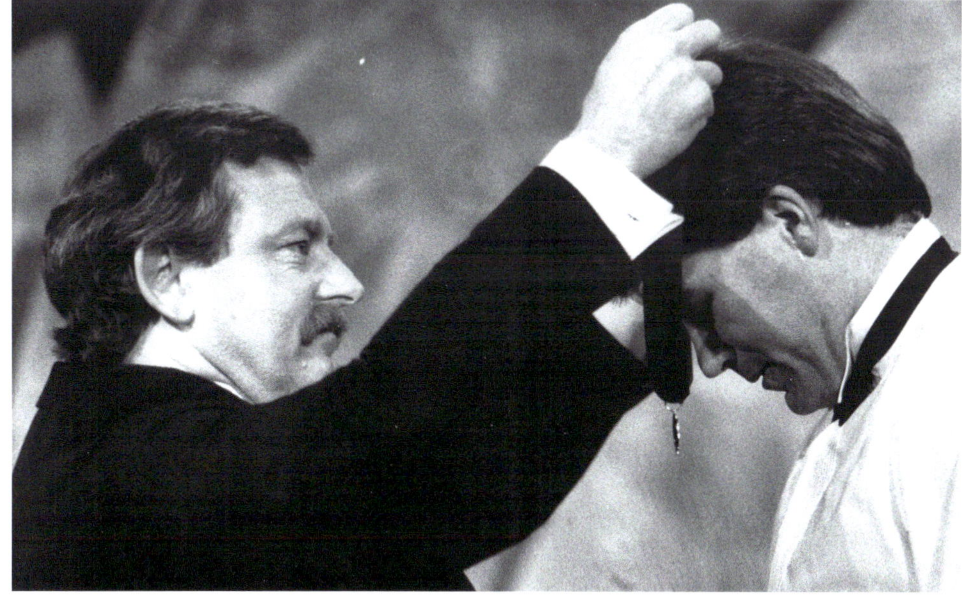

VFL boss Ross Oakley presents Swan Gerard Healy with the 1988 Brownlow Medal.

Former captain Mark Browning retired at the end of the 1987 season and the powerful Swan line-up was breaking up at an alarming rate.

Indeed, the situation was so dire that assistant coach Craig Davis agreed to make a comeback. The former Carlton, North Melbourne and Collingwood forward had not played since 1983, but bravely put his body on the line in his loyalty to Hafey. Besides, the 1987 national draft had given the Swans little comfort. Ruckman Michael Parsons (North Adelaide) was nominated as the overall number 10 selection and immediately joined the Swans for the 1988 season, but elsewhere, there was little talent available to help the Swans.

The Swans were so short of talent that Davis lined up against Footscray at Waverley Park in the opening round. He was almost 34 years of age, but was one of the Swans' few good players in the 26-point defeat. Although the Swans defeated St Kilda by 11 points at the SCG the following week, they struggled from there and rarely looked like making the finals.

To make matters worse, Powerplay announced that it was prepared to sell the club. There were no offers and, to save the club, the VFL bought it back for $10. The

MATCH RESULTS

Round 1, at Waverley Park, April 4
Footscray 16.6 (102) d Sydney Swans 11.10 (76)

Round 2, at SCG, April 10
Sydney Swans 9.12 (66) d St Kilda 7.13 (55)

Round 3, at Princes Park, April 16
Hawthorn 17.12 (114) d Sydney Swans 13.15 (93)

Round 4, at SCG, April 24
Carlton 24.22 (166) d Sydney Swans 10.20 (80)

Round 5, at SCG, May 1
Melbourne 17.14 (116) d Sydney Swans 12.17 (89)

Round 6, at Kardinia Park, May 8
Sydney Swans 17.12 (114) d Geelong 16.15 (111)

Round 7, at Princes Park, May 14
Fitzroy 15.16 (106) d Sydney Swans 9.13 (67)

Round 8, at SCG, May 20
Brisb. Bears 17.13 (115) d Sydney Swans 11.21 (87)

Round 9, at MCG, May 28
Sydney Swans 20.16 (136) d Richmond 10.13 (73)

Round 10, at SCG, June 3
Sydney Swans 11.11 (77) d Essendon 8.7 (55)

Round 11, at SCG, June 10
Sydney Swans 18.24 (132) d North Melb. 19.11 (125)

Round 12, at SCG, June 19
Sydney Swans 14.20 (104) d West Coast 8.13 (61)

Round 13, at Victoria Park, June 25
Collingwood 9.14 (68) d Sydney Swans 2.11 (23)

Round 14, at SCG, July 1
Richmond 19.17 (131) d Sydney Swans 13.18 (96)

Round 15, at MCG, July 9
Sydney Swans 19.16 (130) d Melbourne 8.9 (57)

Round 16, at MCG, July 17
Sydney Swans 24.19 (163) d Hawthorn 16.16 (112)

Round 17, at Moorabbin, July 23
Sydney Swans 13.21 (99) d St Kilda 14.8 (92)

Round 18, at SCG, July 29
Geelong 22.19 (151) d Sydney Swans 12.16 (88)

Round 19, at Waverley Park, August 6
Sydney Swans 15.17 (107) d Carlton 11.13 (79)

Round 20, at SCG, August 14
Sydney Swans 24.16 (160) d Fitzroy 14.13 (97)

Round 21, at MCG, August 19
North Melb. 16.17 (113) d Sydney Swans 14.17 (101)

Round 22, at Carrara, August 28
Sydney Swans 10.21 (81) d Bris. Bears 11.11 (77)

The 1988 Brownlow Medal winner, the Swans' Gerard Healy.

Swan winger David Murphy on the move against Collingwood.

League appointed an interim board, but this did little to lift player morale as they were worried about the Swans' and their own futures. The new board included the VFL's Greg Durham, TV identity and former club reserves player Mike Willesee, businessman Graham Galt and former Swan president Craig Kimberley.

Despite the gloom surrounding the club, the Swans notched several notable wins. They had four consecutive wins from round 9-12 and later defeated Melbourne by 73 points and Hawthorn by 51 points. The Swans finished the season in seventh position, with 12 wins and 10 defeats. Despite their problems, they missed the finals by just one game, a two-goal defeat by North Melbourne at the MCG in the penultimate round costly.

The Swan players were still coming to terms with missing the finals when news broke that the club had sacked Hafey. The axe fell on September 7, but it was no surprise to insiders as there were rumours the players were unhappy with his almost relentless training. The VFL now had another task on its hand, to find someone else to take over the running of the troubled club.

There was, however, one huge highlight for the Swans in 1988 as champion midfielder Healy won the Brownlow Medal. He polled 20 votes to defeat Essendon ruckman Simon Madden and Hawthorn full-forward Jason Dunstall by four votes. It was an amazing achievement as Healy was troubled by a hernia complaint for most of the season and,

PLAYER	GAMES	GOALS
BATTISTON, Adrian	7	3
BAYES, Mark	19	3
BOLTON, David	15	8
BRINKKOTTER, John	2	1
BROWN, David	5	14
BYRNE, Michael	8	3
CARROLL, Dennis	21	3
CARTER, Rod	20	0
COLEMAN, Glenn	16	32
CORDNER, David	5	6
CORDY, Graeme	10	1
CORDY, Neil	20	4
DAVIS, Craig	9	17
EUSTICE, Mark	5	0
HEALY, Gerard	20	26
HENWOOD, Wayne	16	12
HIGGINS, Leon	13	17
HOLDEN, Craig	4	1
KELLETT, Mark	11	0
LLOYD, Matt	9	0
LOCKMAN, Michael	11	1
McASEY, Darren	2	0
MITCHELL, Barry	21	35
MORWOOD, Tony	13	21
MURPHY, David	21	14
NEAGLE, Merv	2	0
PARSONS, Michael	12	6
PHYLAND, Michael	4	0
POTTER, Craig	14	6
ROBERTS, Ian	16	2
SILVESTRO, Jim	8	7
SMITH, Tony	10	1
THRIPP, Terry	5	1
TOOHEY, Bernard	22	13
WILLIAMS, Greg	18	20
WILLIS, David	8	0
WRIGHT, Stevie	18	23

POSITION: Seventh
COACH: Tom Hafey
CAPTAIN: Dennis Carroll
BEST AND FAIREST: Gerard Healy
LEADING GOALKICKER: Barry Mitchell (35)

in one match, wore a girdle. His training also was limited to very brief Thursday night runs. The Brownlow triumph was especially emotional for Healy as his grandfather, Bill O'Brien, was seriously ill. Healy also won the Swan best and fairest for a third consecutive season.

Meanwhile, the search was on for a new owner and a new coach. The VFL was determined there would be no more ownership mistakes and, in hindsight, it probably should have granted the Basil Sellers group the licence ahead of Dr Geoffrey Edelsten. Regardless, it was the end of an exciting yet wasteful and disappointing era which almost ended in disaster for the Swans. Yet, despite the VFL's diligence, there were many more problems ahead and the Swans again had to fight for their survival.

Swan captain Dennis Carroll led by example.

Swan coach Tom Hafey congratulates Bernard Toohey after a win in 1988.

1989

The Sydney Swans rolled the dice in selecting a coach to replace Tom Hafey from the 1989 season. They rejected pleas to name another experienced coach and, instead, named a man who had never played in the VFL and had never coached at the elite level. Colin Kinnear, however, had been an enormously successful coach with VFA club Coburg and as an assistant coach with North Melbourne and then Carlton. His stint with Carlton was particularly successful as he guided the Blues reserves to four consecutive Grand Finals. Kinnear, despite his lack of senior VFL experience, had a superb football background and his father Joe played 47 games with Melbourne from 1932-37.

Off-field, a new ownership consortium was trying to ease its way through troubled financial waters. The 16 consortium members, including Peter Weinert, Craig Kimberley, Mike Willesee and Basil Sellers, pumped millions into the club to erase debt and pay the AFL licence. In reality, it was a licence to burn money and the new consortium, after budgeting to make $400,000 in 1989, ended up losing almost $1.5 million. But, as Weinert later recalled: "It might have been the last chance for the club to survive."

Kinnear started his VFL coaching career with a pre-season Panasonic Cup match against Melbourne at Waverley on February 11. The Demons defeated the Swans by 17 points and went on to defeat Geelong in the Grand Final. Then, in the opening round of the home and away season, Kinnear and his Swans celebrated after defeating Richmond by 16 points at the SCG. However, the match was played in appalling conditions as heavy rain swept the ground throughout the match and made good play almost impossible. The Swans, however, did well to kick away from Richmond with five third-quarter goals after trailing by 10 points at half-time.

The Swans were brought back to earth when thrashed by the Brisbane Bears at Carrara in round two. The Bears, after leading by just 15 points at the main break, cruised home by 58 points. Then, in a topsy-turvy start to the season, the Swans defeated West Coast by 51 points at the SCG. The Swans kicked nine goals to two in the final quarter to leave them with a unique record as the only club not to have been defeated by the Eagles since they joined the competition in 1987.

When the Swans defeated Fitzroy by 74 points at Princes Park in round four, they jumped into fourth position on the ladder behind Hawthorn, Geelong and Collingwood. The Swans toyed with the Lions and although Greg

David Murphy was brilliant on a wing.

MATCH RESULTS

Round 1, at SCG, April 2
Sydney Swans 12.17 (89) d Richmond 11.7 (73)

Round 2, at Carrara, April 9
Bris. Bears 18.15 (123) d Sydney Swans 8.17 (65)

Round 3, at SCG, April 16
Sydney Swans 20.14 (134) d West Coast 11.17 (83)

Round 4, at Princes Park, April 22
Sydney Swans 23.15 (153) d Fitzroy 11.13 (79)

Round 5, at SCG, April 30
Sydney Swans 10.17 (77) d Collingwood 9.12 (66)

Round 6, at Moorabbin, May 6
St Kilda 13.17 (95) d Sydney Swans 9.13 (67)

Round 7, at SCG. May 12
North Melbourne 9.13 (67) d Sydney Swans 7.16 (58)

Round 8, at Princes Park. May 20
Hawthorn 22.25 (157) d Sydney Swans 12.11 (83)

Round 9, at SCG, May 28
Melbourne 6.16 (52) d Sydney Swans 6.7 (43)

Round 10, at Western Oval, June 3
Footscray 14.14 (98) d Sydney Swans 10.6 (66)

Round 11, at SCG, June 9
Carlton 12.13 (85) d Sydney Swans 8.9 (57)

Round 12, at Windy Hill, June 17
Sydney Swans 7.13 (55) d Essendon 7.8 (50)

Round 13, at SCG, June 25
Geelong 16.15 (111) d Sydney Swans 14.19 (103)

Round 14, at MCG, July 8
Richmond 10.15 (75) d Sydney Swans 7.8 (50)

Round 15, at SCG, July 16
Sydney Swans 16.21 (117) d Footscray 10.17 (77)

Round 16, at Subiaco, July 23
West Coast 16.16 (112) d Sydney Swans 9.16 (70)

Round 17, at SCG, July 30
Sydney Swans 12.23 (95) d Footscray 9.16 (70)

Round 18, at Victoria Park, August 5
Sydney Swans 12.13 (85) d Collingwood 11.15 (81)

Round 19, at SCG, August 13
Sydney Swans 25.9 (159) d St Kilda 16.13 (109)

Round 20, at MCG, August 19
Melbourne 14.14 (98) d Sydney Swans 12.15 (87)

Round 21, at SCG, August 25
Sydney Swans 15.20 (110) d Essendon 15.14 (104)

Round 22, at MCG, September 1
Sydney Swans 21.10 (136) d North Melb. 13.15 (93)

Mark Bayes won the Swans' 1989 best and fairest.

Williams and Gerard Healy were the stars of the match, the Swans' 23 goals were shared by 12 players. Then, when the Swans defeated Collingwood by 11 points at the SCG the following week, they claimed second position behind Hawthorn and were tipped to make the finals. Williams was the dominant player on the ground with 32 possessions. More importantly, the match attracted a healthy attendance of 22,490.

Swan rover Stevie Wright receives his guernsey from coach Col Kinnear before the start of the 1989 season.

From there, however, it all came crashing down as the Swans lost their next six matches, and consequently, their right to be considered a genuine finals threat. Healy played his 200th VFL game in the round eight clash with Hawthorn at Princes Park, but had little else to celebrate as the Hawks dumped the Swans by 74 points. But there was much worse in store for the Swans following Carlton's sacking of coach Robert Walls immediately after former Swan Warwick Capper kicked the winning goal for the Brisbane Bears in the round 10 clash with the Blues at Princes Park. The Blues named former club champion Alex Jesaulenko as Walls' replacement and his first match in his second coming at Princes Park was against the Swans at the SCG on the following Friday night.

It was a critically important match for both sides as the Swans wanted to stay in touch with the top five, while Carlton was looking for respect after the humiliating loss to the Bears. The clash was a powder-keg waiting for a spark and it all blew up when Williams clashed with former Swan David Rhys-Jones. Williams injured a shoulder in a collision with Rhys-Jones who, in turn, had his jaw broken. Both players were cited, with Williams being suspended five matches and Rhys-Jones found not guilty on two charges and given a suspended sentence on a third charge.

Williams had been in superb form and his

PLAYER	GAMES	GOALS
BARLING, Tim	5	2
BATTISTON, Adrian	2	0
BAYES, Mark	20	12
BOLTON, David	11	1
BRINKKOTTER, John	3	0
BROWN, David	5	3
BYRNE, Michael	2	0
CARROLL, Dennis	19	14
CARTER, Rod	20	0
COLEMAN, Glenn	10	11
CORDY, Graeme	1	0
CORDY, Neil	11	0
EUSTICE, Mark	20	7
HEALY, Gerard	8	6
HENWOOD, Wayne	11	9
HIGGINS, Leon	20	15
HOLDSWORTH, Paul	6	3
KELLETT, Mark	15	0
LLOYD, Matt	4	1
McASEY, Darren	10	11
MITCHELL, Barry	20	17
MORWOOD, Tony	15	16
MURPHY, David	22	3
NEAGLE, Merv	18	0
OGIER, Darren	8	16
PAGE, Glenn	1	0
PARSONS, Michael	10	8
PHYLAND, Michael	9	3
POTTER, Craig	5	1
ROBERTS, Ian	12	0
SCOTT, Brett	7	5
TEAL, Robert	17	18
THRIPP, Terry	22	22
TOOHEY, Bernard	22	27
WHEELER, Sanford	2	1
WILLIAMS, Greg	17	19
WILLIS, David	13	3
WRIGHT, Stevie	17	11

POSITION: Seventh
COACH: Col Kinnear
CAPTAIN: Dennis Carroll
BEST AND FAIREST: Mark Bayes
LEADING GOALKICKER: Bernard Toohey (27)

suspension was a hammer-blow for the Swans. He returned for the round 17 match after the Swans went down to the Eagles, who notched their first win over the Swans, by 42 points. From there, the Swans meandered through the rest of the season, with only a handful of highlights. One of these included Bernard Toohey's eight goals in the six-point defeat of Essendon at the SCG in round 21. It might have been the Swans' fourth win in five games, but they had no hope of making the finals as they trailed fifth-placed Collingwood by two games and a big percentage margin with just one round to play.

The Swans defeated North Melbourne by 43 points at the MCG in the final round and, after storming home over the final six rounds, finished seventh with 11 wins and 11 defeats. The ineligible Williams polled 16 votes in the Brownlow Medal to finish equal third (with Hawthorn's Jason Dunstall, Essendon's Tim Watson and St Kilda's Nicky Winmar) behind Geelong's Paul Couch (22 votes) and Hawthorn's John Platten (20) and must have pondered on what might have been if he had not been suspended for five matches for that angry mid-season tangle with Rhys-Jones. After all, he had been in brilliant form for most of the season and in the round 19 clash with St Kilda at the SCG racked up an incredible 53 possessions. He also had more handballs (258) than any other player in the competition.

Centre half-back Mark Bayes won the 1989 club best and fairest but there was some controversy over the leading goalkicker award. Toohey, who normally played on a half-back flank but was a marvellous pinch-hitter close to goal, topped the list with 27 goals but was not presented with a trophy as it was felt it was too meagre a total for special recognition.

Bernard Toohey topped the 1989 goalkicking as a "pinch-hitter" up forward.

1990

The 1990 season represented Col Kinnear's second as coach, with Dennis Carroll again captain. The Swans had done well to finish seventh the previous season, but knew there were stern tests ahead. Brilliant half-forward Tony Morwood had retired after playing 229 games in the red and white from 1978 and centreman Brett Scott finally succumbed to a string of injury problems after playing 59 games with the Swans from 1981. Both later played significant off-field roles with the club — Morwood as head of the Swans' operations in Melbourne and Scott as an assistant coach who filled in as senior coach in 1993 following the sacking of Gary Buckanara.

The Swans recruited Geelong's Darren Denneman, Carlton's Michael Kennedy, Collingwood's Matthew Ryan and North Melbourne's Robbie Kerr and picked quality utility Dale Lewis as the overall number two selection at the mid-season draft. Ruckman Brad Tunbridge joined the Swans from East Fremantle and the tall and mobile Gareth John, son of former player, coach and president Graeme John, joined the club under the father-son rule. Other notable newcomers in 1990 included Troy Luff, Craig Nettelbeck, Jim West and Tasmanian Shane Fell.

All pre-season Foster's Cup matches were

The Swans' Bernard Toohey has the front running ahead of Hawthorn's Chris Langford in a pre-season match at Canberra in 1990.

MATCH RESULTS

Round 1, at Princes Park, March 31
Sydney Swans 15.14 (104) d Carlton 14.15 (99)

Round 2, at SCG, April 8
Footscray 20.20 (140) d Sydney Swans 10.18 (78)

Round 3, at Victoria Park, April 16
Collingwood 20.8 (128) d Sydney Swans 12.21 (93)

Round 4, at SCG, April 22
St Kilda 19.17 (131) d Sydney Swans 13.19 (97)

Round 5, at Subiaco, April 29
West Coast 19.14 (128) d Sydney Swans 10.7 (67)

Round 6, at SCG, May 6
Sydney Swans 14.14 (98) d Melbourne 12.21 (93)

Round 7, at Carrara, May 13
Brisb. Bears 14.12 (96) d Sydney Swans 13.10 (88)

Round 8, at SCG, May 18
Sydney Swans 15.17 (107) d Geelong 13.20 (98)

Round 9, at MCG, May 27
Richmond 20.19 (139) d Sydney Swans 9.6 (60)

Round 10, at SCG, June 3
Essendon 25.14 (164) d Sydney Swans 11.8 (74)

Round 11, at Princes Park, June 9
Hawthorn 19.18 (132) d Sydney Swans 11.17 (83)

Round 12, at SCG, June 17
Fitzroy 17.14 (116) d Sydney Swans 10.11 (71)

Round 13, at MCG, June 30
North Melb. 18.23 (131) d Sydney Swans 5.11 (41)

Round 14, at SCG, July 8
Carlton 25.12 (162) d Sydney Swans 13.12 (90)

Round 15, at Western Oval, July 14
Footscray 17.10 (112) d Sydney Swans 13.18 (96)

Round 16, at SCG, July 22
Collingwood 21.21 (147) d Sydney Swans 19.9 (123)

Round 17, at Moorabbin, July 28
St Kilda 22.16 (148) d Sydney Swans 10.13 (73)

Round 18, at SCG, August 5
West Coast 12.11 (83) d Sydney Swans 10.8 (68)

Round 19, at MCG, August 11
Melbourne 27.11 (173) d Sydney Swans 15.16 (106)

Round 20, at SCG, August 17
Sydney Swans 11.20 (86) d Brisbane Bears 7.13 (55)

Round 21, at Kardinia Park, August 25
Sydney Swans 14.8 (92) d Geelong 12.18 (90)

Round 22, at SCG, September 2
Richmond 20.19 (139) d Sydney Swans 15.19 (109)

Swan rover Barry Mitchell is about to pounce on the ball in a match against Richmond in 1990.

played at Waverley Park in 1990, except for the Sydney Swans-Hawthorn clash at the Bruce Stadium, Canberra, in the first round. The Swans defeated the Hawks by 10 points, but then went down to Carlton by just one point in the second round. There were encouraging signs and the Swans therefore went into the opening round match against Carlton at Princes Park reasonably confident. The match was billed as a potentially explosive encounter as the Swans' Greg Williams and the Blues' David Rhys-Jones had clashed heavily the previous year at the SCG. Williams was left with a busted shoulder and Rhys-Jones a broken jaw.

Carlton looked a class above the Swans over the first half and led by 39 points at the main break. Although the Swans bounced back to cut the margin to 24 points by the final break, the Blues looked almost certain winners. The Swans, however, refused to concede and reduced the margin to just one point with just 34 seconds to play. With almost 24,000 fans roaring on both sides, the Swans' Mark Bayes won possession and shot a quick handpass to teammate Barry Mitchell. The

Swan rover snapped from 30 metres and his last-gasp goal gave the Swans a five-point victory, their first over the Blues at Princes Park for 25 years.

The Swans were favourites to defeat Footscray at the SCG, but went down by 62 points. It was the Bulldogs' first win in Sydney and, from there, the Swans struggled to regain confidence. Collingwood defeated them by 35 points at Victoria Park in round three to push the Swans down to twelfth position in the 14-club competition, with the match notorious for two controversies. In the first, Mitchell was penalised for running too far with the ball, even though he clearly had bounced it mid-run. In the second, Collingwood's Craig Kelly crashed Bayes into the boundary fence, dislocating the Swan's shoulder; Kelly was suspended for two matches.

Defeats to St Kilda and West Coast followed before the Swans broke through for their second win of the season in defeating Melbourne by five points at the SCG. The Swans' hero was Carroll, who showed great leadership in continually driving the Swans forward with his long kicking from defence. The Swans went down to the Bears at Carrara the following week and almost immediately were told the players would have to take pay cuts. Swan executive director Geoff Slade met the media in the middle of the SCG to explain the club's financial predicament. It was sinking in a sea of red ink and Slade explained that the owners were $7.5 million out of pocket. Slade was quoted as saying: "We are just not in a position to keep funding mediocrity."

Swan players were distraught, but vowed to stick together, even though there were suggestions that if the latest round of cost-cutting did not succeed the club would consider relocating to Canberra. This might

South Australian Jim West topped the Swans' goalkicking in 1990.

PLAYER	GAMES	GOALS
BARLING, Tim	9	0
BAYES, Mark	13	8
BOLTON, David	20	6
BROWN, David	2	1
CARROLL, Dennis	16	10
CARTER, Rod	7	0
CORDY. Neil	16	0
DENNEMAN, Darren	3	0
EUSTICE, Mark	17	2
FELL, Shane	15	30
HEALY, Gerard	11	7
HENWOOD, Wayne	19	19
HIGGINS, Leon	19	15
JOHN, Gareth	7	0
KELLETT, Mark	11	1
KELLY, Paul	10	2
KENNEDY, Michael	15	3
KERR, Robbie	4	1
LEWIS, Dale	2	3
LLOYD, Matt	7	4
LUFF, Troy	6	8
McASEY, Darren	4	4
MITCHELL, Barry	16	19
MURPHY, David	15	7
NEAGLE, Merv	4	0
NETTELBECK, Craig	5	0
O'DWYER, Chris	5	0
PAGE, Brett	10	3
PARSONS, Michael	3	0
PHYLAND, Michael	4	1
POTTER, Craig	10	1
ROBERTS, Ian	7	1
RYAN, Matthew	10	8
SCOTT, Dion	4	0
STARBUCK, Paul	1	0
TEAL, Robert	1	0
THRIPP, Terry	13	8
TOOHEY, Bernard	22	19
TUNBRIDGE, Brad	7	3
WEST, Jim	22	34
WHEELER, Sanford	11	2
WILLIAMS, Greg	11	17
WILLIS, David	3	0

POSITION: Thirteenth
COACH: Col Kinnear
CAPTAIN: Dennis Carroll
BEST AND FAIREST: Stevie Wright
LEADING GOALKICKER: Jim West (34)

have been a throwaway line, but it created headlines around Australia and the Swans' future again was put under scrutiny. There also were suggestions that some players were asked to take bigger cuts than others and the Swans therefore went into the round eight game against Geelong at the SCG with their very futures in doubt. The Swans, against all the odds, defeated the Cats by nine points, with Fell kicking six goals.

The club's decision to order 20 per cent pay cuts across the player list resulted in player agent/manager Peter Jess threatening legal action if the Swans did not honour contracts, but all players eventually accepted the position as it was declared that if the club did not save $600,000 on all operations its future could not be guaranteed. Just days later the Swans were rocked by news that star winger Merv Neagle would miss the rest of the season because of a severe groin injury. Neagle at the end of the season announced his retirement after 56 games with the Swans from 1986 and 147 with Essendon from 1977-85.

There also was tragic news in June when the Swans' 1940 Brownlow Medal winner Herbie Matthews died at his Apollo Bay, Victoria, home. He was 76 years of age and the Swans wore black armbands in their next match, against Hawthorn at Princes Park. The Hawks defeated the Swans by 49 points to leave the red and white above only the Bears. The season was going from bad to worse, especially when veteran full-back Rod Carter temporarily ended his career. Carter had started the season hoping to reach 300 VFL games, but when the Swans indicated they would not be prepared to nurse him to the milestone, he announced his retirement. Although Carter returned, he finished his career at the end of the season on 293 games — 76 with Fitzroy and 217 with the Swans.

To end a truly miserable season for the Swans, old-time supporters were heartbroken at news of the death of former club champion and 1949 Brownlow Medal winner Ron Clegg on August 24. Sadly, 1945 Grand Final teammate Bill King died on the same day. The Swans had lost two of their Brownlow Medal winners in the one year. On-field, the Swans limped to season's end with just five wins to finish above only the Bears.

The Swans' last win of the season was against Geelong at Kardinia Park in round 21. The Swans won by just two points in one of their most courageous performances of the season. Several players went into the match carrying injuries, with ruckman David Willis and winger Terry Thripp adding to the Swans' injury woes early in the match. Geelong led by four points with a minute to play, but a running goal by defender Ian Roberts snatched victory for the Swans. Richmond in the final round defeated the Swans by 30 points at the SCG, with the miserable attendance of just 7180 a fair reflection on a season the Swans would rather forget.

Swan rover Stevie Wright with wife Kerri celebrates his 1990 best and fairest triumph.

Then, during Grand Final week (in which Collingwood defeated Essendon in the big game), Swan general manager Barry Breen resigned and was replaced by club stalwart Barry Rogers, who had previously served the Swans as an administrator and had been president of the St George rugby league club.

1991

Although Col Kinnear again was coach in 1991, the Sydney Swans rung the changes in other areas, particularly on-field. The biggest loss was through the retirement of brilliant midfielder Gerard Healy. The Brownlow Medal winner had decided he could not continue playing after having broken a wrist against Footscray in 1990 as it would put his career as a physiotherapist as risk. This, however, did not stop Collingwood from nominating him in the pre-season draft. Healy was flattered but never played again.

Other departures included ruckman Tim Barling, Shane Fell, Mark Kellett, Merv Neagle and Rod Carter. Barling had shown enormous promise but was cut down by knee injuries, while Kellett and Fell decided to end their AFL careers. Neagle and Carter in particular had made significant contributions to the Swans and their retirements left the Swans severely exposed as one of the most inexperienced sides in the competition. Off-field, the Swans parted company with team manager John Reid.

On the credit side, the Swans lured glamour full-forward Warwick Capper back from the Brisbane Bears. Capper had played 34 games with the Bears over the previous three seasons but had never really settled at Carrara. The Swans felt the return of the white-booted drawcard would give the club a significant boost.

Star winger David Murphy on the burst in a match against St Kilda at the SCG in 1991.

MATCH RESULTS

Round 1, Bye

Round 2, at Princes Park, April 1
Hawthorn 25.16 (166) d Sydney Swans 10.15 (75)

Round 3, at SCG, April 7
Adelaide 19.18 (132) d Sydney Swans 15.18 (108)

Round 4, at MCG, April 13
Sydney Swans 24.20 (164) d Richmond 19.13 (127)

Round 5, at SCG, April 19
Essendon 24.17 (161) d Sydney Swans 19.16 (130)

Round 6, at MCG, April 25
North Melb. 27.26 (188) d Sydney Swans 21.8 (134)

Round 7, at SCG, May 5
Sydney Swans 20.24 (144) d Geelong 14.14 (98)

Round 8, at Princes Park, May 11
Sydney Swans 21.21 (147) d Fitzroy 10.10 (70)

Round 9, at SCG, May 19
St Kilda 18.11 (119) d Sydney Swans 16.17 (113)

Round 10, at Subiaco, May 26
West Coast 15.16 (106) d Sydney Swans 10.12 (72)

Round 11, at SCG, June 2
Brisb. Bears 26.12 (168) d Sydney Swans 18.13 (121)

Round 12, at Western Oval, June 8
Sydney Swans 5.5 (35) drew with Footscray 4.11 (35)

Round 13, at SCG, June 16
Sydney Swans 18.16 (124) d Carlton 17.8 (110)

Round 14, at Victoria Park, June 23
Collingwood 20.23 (143) d Sydney Swans 6.8 (44)

Round 15, at SCG, June 30
Melbourne 26.21 (177) d Sydney Swans 14.10 (94)

Round 16, Bye

Round 17, at SCG, July 14
Hawthorn 15.24 (114) d Sydney Swans 14.19 (103)

Round 18, at Football Park, July 21
Sydney Swans 19.8 (122) d Adelaide 16.22 (118)

Round 19, at SCG, July 28
Sydney Swans 14.15 (99) d Richmond 12.20 (92)

Round 20, at Windy Hill, August 3
Essendon 22.19 (151) d Sydney Swans 12.12 (84)

Round 21, at SCG, August 11
North Melb. 20.16 (136) d Sydney Swans 13.22 (100)

Round 22, at Kardinia Park, August 17
Geelong 17.13 (115) d Sydney Swans 13.10 (88)

Round 23, at SCG, August 23
Sydney Swans 21.14 (140) d Fitzroy 13.16 (94)

Round 24, at Moorabbin, August 31
St Kilda 24.14 (158) d Sydney Swans 17.17 (119)

Paul Kelly was in just his second season with the Swans in 1991.

Capper was just one of a raft of recruits in yet another massive player turnover. Two of the newcomers, Belconnen's Ben Aulich and Eastlake's Robbie Neill, were part of a concession allowing the Swans to take two players from the ACT. Incredibly, the Swans overlooked another youngster, James Hird, who had played well for Ainslie in the 1990 ACT Grand Final against Queanbeyan. Former Swan Paul Hawke, who had been

Warwick Capper drew the fans to the SCG.

playing with Collingwood, was nominated in the pre-season draft and the Swans at the 1990 national draft swapped their number two selection for Carlton premiership player Warren McKenzie. The Swans also snapped up full-forward Jason Love as a pre-draft selection.

Kinnear therefore had virtually a new-look line-up for the Swans' first game of the season. The Swans had a bye in the opening round, but then played Hawthorn at Princes Park in round two. The Hawks humiliated the Swans by 91 points after kicking 10 goals in the opening quarter. The only consolation for the Swans was that Capper kicked four goals in his comeback match in the red and white.

Then, in the following round, AFL newcomer Adelaide defeated the Swans by 24 points at the SCG. Capper, this time wearing white boots with pink stripes, kicked another four goals, but it was obvious the Swans were heading for another lean season. However, the Swans broke through with an encouraging 37-point defeat of Richmond at the MCG in round four. One of the Swans' best was defender Ian Roberts, who had retired after the previous season but had been talked into leading the reserves to help groom younger players. After good performances in the reserves, Roberts was selected for senior duty against the Tigers.

The Swans might have boosted their morale with the defeat of the Tigers, but were savaged by a severe blow in the following Friday night's match against Essendon at the SCG. Hugely-promising young ruckman Gareth John, the son of former Swan star and coach Graeme John, had his larynx crushed in a freakish collision with Essendon ruckman Simon Madden at a centre bounce. John also had his vocal chord severed and he was rushed to Sydney's St Vincent's Hospital for surgery. To add insult to injury, the Bombers defeated the Swans by 31 points.

Swan morale was further damaged in the following round when North Melbourne came from behind to defeat the red and white by 54 points in an amazing Anzac Day match at the MCG. The Swans kicked 19 first-half goals to lead by 30 points at the main break, but were

PLAYER	GAMES	GOALS
ATHORN, Mark	15	7
BAYES, Mark	2	28
BOLTON, David	8	0
BRUNTON, Neil	3	0
CAPPER, Warwick	13	38
CLARKSON, Justin	3	0
CORDY, Neil	22	0
DOOLAN, Ben	13	4
EUSTICE, Mark	4	0
HAWKE, Paul	1	0
HENWOOD, Wayne	8	2
HIGGINS, Leon	22	13
HOLMES, Darren	7	1
JOHN, Gareth	4	1
KELLY, Paul	20	14
KERR, Robbie	6	1
LAWSON, Jamie	16	8
LEWIS, Dale	22	27
LLOYD, Matt	1	0
LOVE, Jason	21	52
LUFF, Troy	5	4
McASEY, Darren	3	0
McKENZIE, Warren	17	12
MITCHELL, Barry	22	30
MURPHY, David	20	15
NETTELBECK, Craig	15	10
O'DWYER, Chris	3	1
PAGE, Glenn	7	0
ROBERTS, Ian	7	2
STANISLAUS, Brian	1	0
THRIPP, Terry	8	1
TOOHEY, Bernard	21	11
TUNBRIDGE, Brad	17	5
WEST, Jim	9	11
WHEELER, Sanford	1	0
WILLIAMS, Greg	15	13
WILLIS, David	1	0
WRIGHT, Stevie	17	11

POSITION: Twelfth
COACH: Col Kinnear
CAPTAIN: Dennis Carroll
BEST AND FAIREST: Barry Mitchell
LEADING GOALKICKER: Jason Love (52)

swamped over the second half. North at one stage kicked 12 consecutive goals and finished with 27.26 (188), a then record score against the Swans.

Although the Swans defeated Geelong by 46 points at the SCG in the next round and then Fitzroy by 77 points at Princes Park, there were few other highlights in a dismal season. Nothing seemed to go right for the Swans and, in the round nine loss to St Kilda at the SCG, even had 19 men on the field at one stage. Swan Dale Lewis took the field without any teammate going to the bench but, fortunately for the Swans, no official picked up the infringement at the time. Had St Kilda been more alert, the Swans would have been deprived of their score of 9.9 (63) to that stage of the game.

The defeat by St Kilda was one of three in a row mid-season for the Swans, who finally scrambled two match points in forcing a draw with Footscray in appalling conditions at the Western Oval in round 12. Most of the Western Oval was under water and Sydney was denied a win when the Bulldogs' Steve Macpherson scored a behind in the final seconds. The Swans, however, made amends in defeating Carlton by 14 points the following week. The afternoon game started an hour late because of television commitments and finished under lights.

The Swans then had to wait another four games for its next win, over Adelaide at Football Park in extraordinary circumstances. The Crows snatched the lead with just a minute to play and Adelaide fans turned to Swan coach Kinnear to give him "the raspberry". However, the Swans swung into attack from the bounce for Barry Mitchell to kick a goal just seconds before the final siren. The Swans won by four points.

Following the round 21 defeat by North Melbourne, the Swans had to ride another shock wave. Kinnear announced his retirement as coach, effective from the last game of the season. Kinnear declared that his resignation before the end of the season was because "speculation was putting pressure on the team". He added: "The young players were being questioned about it (the coaching position) and it was better to get out of the way. The players don't need this sort of hassle, so I wanted to put an end to it now."

Kinnear's last win as coach was when the Swans defeated Fitzroy 46 points in a penultimate round match at the SCG. However, there was one more controversy for the Swans in 1991. The flamboyant Capper was alleged to have leaned over a fence to slap a female St Kilda supporter in a final round match at Moorabbin. Capper tried to apologise at half-time, but the woman refused to accept it. Regardless, it was Capper's last game for the Swans. He had played 90 games and kicked 317 goals in the red and white and undoubtedly was the Swans' major drawcard in the exciting mid-'80s.

Greg Williams, who won a Brownlow Medal with the Swans, played his last game for the club in 1991.

The Swans finished the season in twelfth position, but it was obvious their playing talent was thinly-spread and, besides, the club was still in a parlous financial position and desperate to appoint the right coach for 1992 and beyond. Love topped the goalkicking in 1991 with 52 goals, Mitchell won the best and fairest and Dennis Carroll polled 11 votes in the Brownlow Medal, but well behind the winner, Melbourne's Jim Stynes (25 votes).

1992

Following Col Kinnear's resignation as coach late in the 1991 season, the Sydney Swans' first task at the completion of the season was the appointment of a new coach. The Swans yet again targeted Essendon coach Kevin Sheedy but when he rejected the Swans' overtures they turned to former Hawthorn half-forward Gary Buckenara. Although untried as a coach, Buckenara had had a stellar playing career with the Hawks. Originally from West Australian club Subiaco, he played 154 games for Hawthorn from 1982-90 and, more importantly, had been coached by the great Allan Jeans.

Buckenara must have known the Swans' playing stocks were low as several key players had moved on, with Warwick Capper, David Bolton and Ian Roberts retiring. Young ruckman David Willis was forced into retirement because of a broken neck and Brownlow Medal winner Greg Williams moved to Carlton, but only after a long and bitter clearance wrangle.

Williams had made it clear at the end of the 1991 season that he wanted to leave the Swans and Carlton and St Kilda vied for his services. Williams eventually signed with the Blues but, on February 12, the AFL deregistered him until April 30 and fined him $25,000 over payment irregularities with the Swans in 1990. The Swans were fined $50,000, half of which was suspended. In a complicated deal, the Swans landed Carlton

Swan full-back Andrew Dunkley, safe and reliable.

MATCH RESULTS

Round 1, Bye

Round 2, at SCG, March 29
Sydney Swans (14.14 (98) d West Coast 14.11 (95)

Round 3, at Victoria Park, April 4
Collingwood 17.14 (116) d Sydney Swans 13.19 (97)

Round 4, at SCG, April 12
Footscray 25.15 (165) d Sydney Swans 17.17 (119)

Round 5, at Princes Park, April 18
Sydney Swans 14.10 (94) d Carlton 10.13 (73)

Round 6, at SCG, April 24
North Melb. 18.17 (125) d Sydney Swans 11.10 (76)

Round 7, at MCG, May 2
Sydney Swans 13.18 (96) drew with Melb. 13.18 (96)

Round 8, at SCG, May 8
Sydney Swans 19.21 (135) d Bris. Bears 8.13 (61)

Round 9, at MCG, May 17
Richmond 19.20 (134) d Sydney Swans 14.18 (102)

Round 10, at SCG, May 24
Hawthorn 21.20 (146) d Sydney Swans 12.13 (85)

Round 11, at MCG, May 31
Essendon 16.20 (116) d Sydney Swans 10.13 (73)

Round 12, Bye

Round 13, at Moorabbin, June 13
St Kilda 24.13 (157) d Sydney Swans 15.14 (104)

Round 14, at SCG, June 21
Geelong 24.14 (158) d Sydney Swans 11.17 (83)

Round 15, at Football Park, June 26
Adelaide 22.17 (149) d Sydney Swans 13.4 (82)

Round 16, at SCG, July 5
Fitzroy 21.10 (136) d Sydney Swans 11.17 (83)

Round 17, at Subiaco, July 12
West Coast 16.11 (107) d Sydney Swans 8.6 (54)

Round 18, at SCG, July 17
Collingwood 17.12 (114) d Sydney Swans 14.12 (96)

Round 19, at Western Oval, July 25
Footscray 15.13 (103) d Sydney Swans 8.9 (57)

Round 20, at SCG, August 2
Carlton 21.13 (139) d Sydney Swans 20.10 (130)

Round 21, at MCG, August 7
North Melb. 15.21 (111) d Sydney Swans 11.14 (80)

Round 22, at SCG, August 16
Melbourne 21.13 (139) d Sydney Swans 13.10 (88)

Round 23, at Carrara, August 22
Bris. Bears 19.15 (129) d Sydney Swans 9.16 (70)

Round 24, at SCG, August 28
Richmond 18.17 (125) d Sydney Swans 13.17 (95)

Rover Stevie Wright (number 26) in the thick of the action against Carlton in a game during his final season in 1992.

full-forward Simon Minton-Connell, who went on to head the Swans' goalkicking from 1992-94.

The Swans also traded to secure defender Stuart Wigney from Footscray, Darren Kappler from Fitzroy and West Australian Gavin Rose. Wigney broke a leg and played just one game with the Swans, but Kappler and Rose both had fine careers in Sydney. The Swans also took a gamble at the 1991 national draft in nominating North Launceston's Andrew Dunkley as the overall number 56 selection. Dunkley originally had been rejected by St Kilda as a junior, but the Swans liked his marking skills and vigorous approach, even though his kicking was poor. He went on to play 217 games for the club to 2002 and was one of the best full-backs of his era.

The Swans pulled off another coup in the 1992 mid-season draft when it nominated North Hobart centreman Daryn Cresswell as the overall number 39 selection. Cresswell originally had been drafted by Geelong, but returned to Tasmania before being snapped up by the Swans. He went on to play 244 games in the red and white, won the best and fairest in 1994 and was named in the Swans' Team of the Century.

Buckenara could not have wished for a better start to his coaching career as the Swans demolished Essendon by 61 points in their first round clash in the pre-season Foster's Cup in front of 13,500 fans at Lavington. The Swans had a bye in the opening premiership round, but started the home and away season brilliantly in defeating West Coast by three points at the SCG in round two. The Eagles led by 10 points with just minutes to play, but late goals from Warren McKenzie and David Strooper lifted the Swans to victory. It was a huge surprise as the Eagles had defeated the Swans by 137 points in a practice match in Perth just two weeks earlier.

The Swans then were gallant in going down to Collingwood by 19 points at Victoria Park in round three, but not without controversy. Magpie Craig Kelly was suspended five matches for striking Sydney's Ben Doolan and Collingwood president Allan McAlister was fined $3000 for comments made following the report.

Footscray defeated the Swans by 46 points at the SCG in round four, but the Swans bounced back with a mighty 21-point defeat of powerful Carlton at the SCG the following week. There was tremendous ill-feeling between the clubs over the Williams controversy and although Carlton led by 23 points at the final break, the Swans stormed home, mainly through the superb ruck work of Brad Tunbridge, who finished the match with 24 possessions and had 18 hitouts. It was the Swans' most satisfying win of the season, and, in fact, there was just one more over the rest of the season.

Sydney drew with Melbourne at the MCG in round seven and defeated the Brisbane Bears by 74 points at the SCG the following week, but lost their next 15 games. The Swans, apart from losing match after match, also were embroiled in controversy over a two-match suspension of rover Barry Mitchell for "conduct unbecoming" in a match against Essendon in round 11. The Swans took legal action to allow Mitchell to continue playing and, on August 17, the Victorian Supreme Court ruled the suspension "void and of no effect". It was the Swans' only victory over the second half of the season.

This Swans' banner celebrates milestones for Paul Kelly and Darren Kappler in 1992. It was Kappler's first game at the SCG after he reached the 100-game milestone.

PLAYER	GAMES	GOALS
ANGOVE, Damien	4	0
ATKINS, Paul	2	0
BAYES, Mark	20	6
BRUNTON, Neil	22	4
CARROLL, Dennis	13	11
CORDY, Neil	7	0
CRESSWELL, Daryn	8	4
DOOLAN, Ben	12	0
DUNKLEY, Andrew	18	0
GRAY, Troy	12	7
HIGGINS, Leon	16	6
HOLMES, Darren	19	3
JOHN, Gareth	6	2
KAPPLER, Darren	16	22
KELLY, Paul	22	8
LAWSON, Jamie	18	12
LEWIS, Dale	20	17
LOVE, Jason	2	2
LUFF, Troy	8	6
McGOVERN, Andrew	12	5
McKELLAR, Allan	2	0
McKENZIE, Warren	4	1
MINTON-CONNELL, Simon	16	60
MITCHELL, Barry	22	18
MOONEY, Jason	8	0
MURPHY, David	12	2
NEILL, Robbie	1	0
NETTELBECK, Craig	21	15
ROSE, Gavin	10	0
SCOTT, Dion	2	0
STEVENS, Gary	4	0
STROOPER, David	22	44
THORPE, Alan	3	5
THRIPP, Terry	9	2
TUNBRIDGE, Brad	21	8
WEST, Jim	6	9
WHEELER, Sanford	10	2
WIGNEY, Stuart	1	0
WRIGHT, Stevie	9	2

POSITION: Fifteenth
COACH: Gary Buckenara
CAPTAIN: Dennis Carroll
BEST AND FAIREST: Paul Kelly
LEADING GOALKICKER: Simon Minton-Connell (60)

The Swans at this stage were in turmoil and, on September 1, the club informed the AFL that it could not continue with being restructured and there was a real possibility the owners would not continue to maintain the club. The Swans therefore were in grave peril of folding. Swan fans feared the worst and, when the AFL Commission met on October 14, it gave the Swans one week to find a solution. It was a dire ultimatum, but club chairman Peter Weinert and president Mike Willesee refused to concede. They worked tirelessly to provide the AFL with a rescue plan and found an unlikely ally in Collingwood at death's door.

The Swans asked the AFL to waive part of the licence fee of $1.95 million and, at a special meeting of AFL delegates, Weinert and director and former club president Craig Kimberley worked tirelessly to present the Swans' case. Collingwood's delegate was former Magpie player Errol Hutchesson, with Collingwood president McAlister an interested observer. Weinert and Kimberley saved the club, with only a tiny bit of help from McAlister, through their unwavering devotion and enormous effort.

Delegates then were given an alternative scenario to throwing the Swans a lifeline. McAlister, in his book "Big Al — Collingwood, the Untold Story", wrote of a remarkable turnaround: "The delegates were told that Carlton could fill the vacuum left by the Swans by playing all its 'away' games at the SCG. I just could not believe my ears as this meant Carlton virtually would never have to play an 'away' game. Carlton would be able to play all its Melbourne games at Princes Park and all other games at the SCG. What a fantastic deal for Carlton, apart from getting an enormous playing advantage.

"The Blues also would have been able to tie up all the Sydney sponsorship and would have been laughing all the way to the bank. It was the most lopsided suggestion I had ever heard and my antennae worked overtime. I stood up and said: 'Excuse me. I am not Collingwood's delegate at this meeting, but I would like the opportunity to say something.'" McAlister argued that the Swan debt was not enormous and it represented little more than $100,000 each to the other clubs. He therefore pleaded for the Swans' survival and, with the magnificent ground work by Weinert and Kimberley, succeeded in saving the Swans. The club, thrown the lifeline it so desperately needed, therefore had to succeed over the next few years — or else.

Midfielder Daryn Cresswell, who started with the Swans in 1992, wore number 28 until he switched to number eight in 1996.

1993

Although the Sydney Swans' future seemed to be assured — for the time being, at least — late during the previous year, the 1993 season still presented the club with enormous challenges. It had dropped its last 15 matches of the 1992 season as the Swans continued to bleed playing talent. The Swans went into the new season without classy rover Barry Mitchell, who originally had wanted to return to Victoria to play with Carlton but, instead, found himself at Collingwood. Mitchell had been a wonderful rover for the Swans in 170 games from 1984, had won the club's 1991 best and fairest and had represented both Victoria and New South Wales.

The Swans also were hit by the AFL retirement of another class rover in Stevie Wright, who had played 246 games in the red and white from 1979. The best and fairest winner in 1985 and 1990, he had been a tremendously competitive small man for the Swans and later carved himself a successful career as a coach in Tasmania. Another retiree was winger Terry Thripp, who had created history as the first Sydney (Pennant Hills) player to represent the Swans, in 1983.

With so much loss of talent and experience, the Swans had to recruit heavily from rival AFL clubs, but found the cupboard largely bare, even though they managed to take star Fitzroy forward Richard Osborne as the number one selection at the pre-season draft. The Swans traded frantically in an effort to bolster its playing

Swan captain Paul Kelly won the 1993 best and fairest.

Swan midfielder Daryn Cresswell used the ball well, with hand or foot.

stocks, with West Coast's Scott Watters, North Melbourne's Dean McRae, Essendon's Ed Considine and Michael Werner and St Kilda's Jayson Daniels making some impact in the red and white. However, none of the Swans' selections at the national draft had long careers in Sydney, although back pocket Scott Direen (New Norfolk) played 50 games with the Swans.

The Swans announced pre-season that long-serving club captain Dennis Carroll would stand down and the identity of his replacement as skipper took everyone by surprise. The Swans plumped for youngster Paul Kelly, who had played just 52 AFL games to that stage of his career. It was an inspired choice as Kelly grew into the position and became acclaimed as one of the most inspirational leaders in football history.

The Swans again had the bye in the opening round before crashing by 57 points to Hawthorn at the SCG in the second round. Amazingly, the Swans led by 17 points late in the third quarter and looked set for a major upset, only for the Hawks to kick 10 last quarter goals to cruise home. Swan coach Gary Buckenara sniffed: "The last quarter was disgraceful". Then, after St Kilda defeated the

MATCH RESULTS

Round 1, Bye

Round 2, at SCG, April 4
Hawthorn 22.17 (149) d Sydney Swans 12.20 (92)

Round 3, at Waverley Park, April 10
St Kilda 20.12 (132) d Sydney Swans 13.16 (94)

Round 4, at SCG, April 18
Essendon 28.13 (181) d Sydney Swans 14.11 (95)

Round 5, at Princes Park, April 24
Fitzroy 24.23 (167) d Sydney Swans 11.8 (74)

Round 6, at Princes Park, May 1
North Melb. 35.19 (229) d Sydney Swans 16.9 (105)

Round 7, at SCG, May 9
Carlton 21.13 (139) d Sydney Swans 13.17 (95)

Round 8, at the Gabba, May 16
Brisbane Bears 33.21 (219) d Sydney Swans 8.9 (57)

Round 9, at SCG, May 23
Geelong 19.15 (129) d Sydney Swans 15.14 (104)

Round 10, at MCG, May 29
Richmond 17.20 (122) d Sydney Swans 14.9 (93)

Round 11, at SCG, June 13
West Coast 17.18 (120) d Sydney Swans 10.3 (63)

Round 12, at Western Oval, June 19
Footscray 13.16 (94) d Sydney Swans 10.9 (69)

Round 13, at SCG, June 27
Sydney Swans 23.11 (149) d Melbourne 16.13 (109)

Round 14, at SCG, July 2
Adelaide 18.18 (126) d Sydney Swans 12.10 (82)

Round 15, at Victoria Park, July 10
Collingwood 25.19 (169) d Sydney Swans 11.11 (77)

Round 16, Bye

Round 17, at Waverley Park, July 25
Hawthorn 24.15 (159) d Sydney Swans 9.13 (67)

Round 18, at SCG, August 1
St Kilda 24.11 (155) d Sydney Swans 17.16 (118)

Round 19, at MCG, August 6
Essendon 18.9 (117) d Sydney Swans 13.18 (96)

Round 20, at SCG, August 13
Fitzroy 17.12 (114) d Sydney Swans 15.9 (99)

Round 21, at SCG, August 22
North Melb. 25.10 (160) d Sydney Swans 14.14 (98)

Round 22, at Princes Park, August 28
Carlton 16.15 (111) d Sydney Swans 16.14 (110)

Swans by 38 points in the following round, there were rumblings about Buckenara's tenure as coach. When Essendon thrashed the Swans by 86 points at the SCG in round four, Buckenara declared: "Today was rock bottom. We're scratching our heads for answers and we're not going to find them in the text-books or video-tapes."

The humiliating defeat brought matters to a head and, in the week leading up to the Swans' round five match against Fitzroy at Princes Park, Buckenara was sacked. The Swans had lost 19 consecutive matches and their patience had worn thin. There were immediate signs that the Swans would appoint former Carlton and North Melbourne premiership coach Ron Barassi but, in the interim, former star Swan centreman Brett Scott was appointed stand-in coach.

Meanwhile, Barassi sat at the back of a grandstand and took notes as the Lions demolished the Swans by 93 points. To make matters worse for the Swans, Carroll announced his retirement after just two games in 1993. His body no longer could stand up to the rigours of football and he bowed out after 219 games from 1981. He had been a wonderful club servant and was the Swans' captain from 1986-92.

Scott again was in charge when North Melbourne humiliated the Swans even further with yet another lopsided contest at Princes Park. The Kangaroos kicked a club record score of 35.19 (229) to defeat the Swans by a massive 124 points. Barassi knew he had a monumental task on his hands and when asked by the media how he would lift the demoralised Swans, he replied: "To play with spirit and be competitive via the heart." He added: "You can worry about methods and tactics, they're head things, which you've got to have as well. But to gain respect from your opponents you need to give a spirited performance— and that's my task."

Barassi's reign started against Carlton at the SCG in round seven and, under his guidance, the Swans performed relatively well in going down by 44 points. The Swans earlier had been saddened by the news of the death of former champion full-back Jim Cleary at 78 years of age. Cleary had played 222 games for the Swans from 1934-48 and had been a much-respected early football panellist on television.

If Barassi expected the Swans would improve from week to week, he was sadly mistaken as the Brisbane Bears walloped the Swans by 162 points at the Gabba in round eight. The Bears scored 19.10 to just four behinds to half-time. However, Barassi remained undaunted and declared: "Today didn't change my mind in any way, except that the task may now be even bigger than I first thought."

If that afternoon at the Gabba had been horrendous, there was worse to follow the following week against Geelong at the SCG as star forward Richard Osborne was involved in a sickening accidental collision. Fans feared for the worst as Osborne started convulsing and an ambulance had to be ushered onto the ground. Osborne at one stage had stopped breathing, but a brain scan later revealed no permanent damage. Although one medical specialist declared Osborne should retire, the courageous Swan returned to action and, just a few weeks later, was an on-field hero yet again.

The Osborne injury was sad enough, but the football world was shocked on June 19 when the body of AFL official Alan Schwab was found in a Sydney hotel room. The AFL had appointed its executive commissioner to oversee the rebuilding of the Swans. In the aftermath, the Swans appointed former North Melbourne administrator Ron Joseph as Chief Executive Officer. A Swans supporter as a boy, he played a huge role in lifting the Sydney club to heights it never dreamed possible.

By the time the Swans were scheduled to play Melbourne at the SCG in round 13, its losing run had extended to 26 games. The Demons therefore went into this clash as red-hot favourites, only for the Swans to match them goal for goal over the first half. The Swans went into the break with a three-point lead and then produced a stunning 10-goal third quarter with Osborne in sensational form close to goal.

Two great Swans, Andrew Dunkley (back) and Paul Kelly.

Because the Swans led by 66 points at the final break, it was obvious they were going to break their long drought and the tears flowed as they cruised home by 40 points. Although there were just 8250 fans at the SCG, they erupted as one to applaud their long-suffering players. It had been 415 days since they last had tasted victory and, to make the victory even sweeter, Osborne finished the match with 10 goals. Barassi was overwhelmed by the reaction to the win and admitted to the media: "I cried a little. I feel extra good. I haven't been here as long as these other guys. They're really crying."

Although the Swans did not win another game in 1993 and collected the wooden-spoon, they were much more competitive in the run home. In fact, the Swans pushed power side Carlton to one point at Princes Park in the final round. Besides, fans at times during the season could see the funny side of the Swans' predicament. Umpires had to stop play in the match against St Kilda at the SCG in round 18 when a fan released a piglet with the name "Plugga" painted on one side and the number four on the other. It was a clear reference to St Kilda's Tony Lockett but, after the Swans' Darren Holmes caught and put the piglet on the other side of the fence, how many Sydney fans would have guessed they would be cheering Lockett from 1995?

PLAYER	GAMES	GOALS
AMBROSE, Richard	3	1
BAYES, Mark	20	6
BEGOVICH, Tony	5	0
BRUNTON, Neil	20	2
BRYCE, Paul	17	14
CARROLL, Dennis	2	0
CONSIDINE, Ed	7	1
CORDY, Neil	1	0
CRESSWELL, Daryn	18	29
DANIELS, Jayson	16	0
DIPETTA, Aldo	2	0
DIREEN, Scott	11	6
DUNKLEY, Andrew	18	1
GRAY, Troy	7	3
HIGGINS, Leon	10	4
HOLMES, Darren	10	4
HUTTON, John	5	9
IRVIN, Nathon	1	0
JOHN, Gareth	4	0
KAPPLER, Darren	5	7
KELLY, Paul	20	11
LAWSON, Jamie	12	4
LEWIS, Dale	16	13
LUFF, Troy	2	0
McGOVERN, Andrew	8	2
McMAHON, Gavin	2	0
McRAE, Dean	18	10
MALAKELLIS, Tony	5	3
MINTON-CONNELL, Simon	10	41
MOONEY, Jason	11	3
MURPHY, David	11	4
NEILL, Robbie	5	2
NETTELBECK, Craig	2	0
OSBORNE, Richard	16	39
ROSE, Gavin	9	0
STAFFORD, Greg	8	4
STEVENS, Gary	1	1
STROOPER, David	10	14
THOMSON, Andrew	2	1
TUNBRIDGE, Brad	5	1
WATTERS, Scott	18	10
WERNER, Michael	15	19
WHEELER, Sanford	12	1

POSITION: Fifteenth
COACH:
Gary Buckenara, Brett Scott, Ron Barassi
CAPTAIN: Paul Kelly
BEST AND FAIREST: Paul Kelly
LEADING GOALKICKER:
Simon Minton-Connell (41)

1994

The 1994 season represented Ron Barassi's first full campaign as coach. He again had Paul Kelly as captain but, again, there was a huge turnover of players. Gallant defender Neil Cordy had retired after just one game in 1993 and brilliant winger David Murphy retired at the end of that season. Murphy was one of the best wingers to represent the club and later was named in the Swans' Team of the Century. He had played 156 games with the club from 1984 after being recruited from Turvey Park and was named All-Australian in 1988.

The Swans at the end of 1993 refused to trade its early draft picks and nominated West Australian defender Darren Gaspar as the overall number one selection, the Geelong Falcons' Glenn Gorman at number four, South Australian Adam Heuskes at five and the Geelong Falcons' Wade Chapman at 20. The Swans also picked up Stefan Carey (Pennant Hills), Brad Seymour (Wagga Tigers) and Damian Lang (Leeton) as NSW priority selections.

To complete their recruiting for 1994, the Swans nominated former Hawthorn champion Dermott Brereton as the overall number one selection at the pre-season draft, Essendon rover Peter Filandia at six and fellow Bomber Derek Kickett at 21. This trio promised to supply the experience to help the many Swan youngsters and although Filandia and Kickett proved good pickups in the long-term, Brereton ran foul of the AFL Tribunal in his only season with the Swans and played only seven games in the red and white.

Brereton might have been keen to prove a point to the Hawks, but he was reported in a practice match against his old club after a video showed him appearing to stand on the head of young Hawk Rayden Tallis. Brereton was suspended for the first seven matches of the season, ruining any chance of the Swans being able to use him as a marquee signing.

The Swans opened the season with a 10-point loss to the Brisbane Bears at the Gabba. It might have been yet another in a long list of defeats from 1992, but it was a huge improvement on the 162-point hiding by the Bears at the Gabba the previous season. The Swans, still short of talent, at least now were playing with plenty of heart and commitment. Barassi told the media: "I asked the boys for a gutsy, 100-minute effort and I can't really complain." The Swans' gallant effort, however, was soured by a five-match suspension imposed on Michael Werner for a challenge which left the Bears' Gilbert McAdam with a broken jaw.

Paul Kelly might have been all sinews and bones, but he was a marvellously inspirational Swans leader.

Following a bye in round two, the Swans pushed Adelaide to 19 points at the SCG, with Darren Kappler and Dale Lewis both kicking four goals. Then, in round four, the Swans broke through for their first win of the season in defeating Richmond by 14 points at the SCG. Simon Minton-Connell, whose 1993 season had been marred by injury, kicked six goals for the Swans. After several seasons in the doldrums, the Swans found themselves in ninth position.

However, Fitzroy defeated the Swans by eight points at the Western Oval in round five and the red and white did not win again until Brereton played his first official AFL match in the red and white against Melbourne at the MCG in round nine. And what a debut! Brereton might have had just nine kicks and three handballs, but he kicked the winning goal. With the Swans leading by less than a kick with just four minutes to play, Brereton marked strongly in a contest with Demon ruckman Jim Stynes and kicked a goal from just outside the 50-metre arc.

It was the Sydney Swans' first win away from the SCG since they had defeated Carlton at Princes Park in round five, 1992. Brereton might have been scratchy in his Swan debut, but he was the difference between victory and defeat and said afterwards: "I've got a lot better games of football than that left in me."

From there, the Swans were competitive in most games, but one of their only other wins of the season was in downing Adelaide by 12 points at Football Park in round 18. Kickett not only celebrated his 100th AFL game with a victory, but also kicked four goals in the Swans' triumph. The Swans were inspired by a Crow decision to suspend star full-forward Tony Modra for one match after missing a training session. The Swans felt insulted as they

The Swans' Andrew Dunkley was one of the best full-backs of his era.

MATCH RESULTS

Round 1, at the Gabba, March 27
Bris. Bears 13.21 (99) d Sydney Swans 12.17 (89)

Round 2, Bye

Round 3, at SCG, April 10
Adelaide 24.10 (154) d Sydney Swans 21.9 (135)

Round 4, at SCG, April 15
Sydney Swans 11.20 (86) d Richmond 10.12 (72)

Round 5, at Western Oval, April 23
Fitzroy 20.17 (137) d Sydney Swans 20.9 (129)

Round 6, at Princes Park, April 30
Carlton 20.14 (134) d Sydney Swans 11.8 (74)

Round 7, SCG, May 8
St Kilda 16.14 (110) d Sydney Swans 17.7 (109)

Round 8, at SCG, May 15
Geelong 25.15 (165) d Sydney Swans 9.17 (71)

Round 9, at MCG, May 21
Sydney Swans 16.10 (106) d Melbourne 14.13 (97)

Round 10, at WACA, May 27
West Coast 14.17 (101) d Sydney Swans 10.15 (75)

Round 11, at SCG, June 5
North Melb. 19.12 (126) d Sydney Swans 16.10 (106)

Round 12, at SCG, June 12
Hawthorn 21.15 (141) d Sydney Swans 13.5 (83)

Round 13, at Western Oval, June 19
Footscray 20.14 (134) d Sydney Swans 9.6 (60)

Round 14, at MCG, June 26
Essendon 19.15 (129) d Sydney Swans 14.11 (95)

Round 15, at SCG, July 3
Collingwood 13.15 (93) d Sydney Swans 10.13 (73)

Round 16, at SCG, July 10
Bris. Bears 21.9 (135) d Sydney Swans 15.20 (110)

Round 17, Bye

Round 18, at Football Park, July 22
Sydney Swans 13.9 (87) d Adelaide 10.15 (75)

Round 19, at MCG, July 31
Richmond 14.11 (95) d Sydney Swans 9.8 (62)

Round 20, at SCG, August 7
Fitzroy 13.16 (94) d Sydney Swans 9.12 (66)

Round 21, at SCG, August 14
Sydney Swans 9.16 (70) d Carlton 8.14 (62)

Round 22, at Waverley Park, August 20
St Kilda 17.12 (114) d Sydney Swans 11.15 (81)

Round 23, at Kardinia Park, August 27
Geelong 16.15 (111) d Sydney Swans 15.9 (99)

Round 24, at SCG, September 4
Melbourne 27.5 (167) d Sydney Swans 18.13 (121)

Daryn Cresswell was a wonderful competitor for the Swans.

believed the Crows had taken them lightly and would not have suspended him if they had been playing a top side.

The Swans won only three games in 1994, but it should have been four as only a remarkable performance by St Kilda's Tony Lockett cost them victory in the round seven clash at the SCG. The Swans led by 23 points at half-time and, when they extended this lead to 38 points by the final break, victory seemed certain. Quick goals in the final quarter extended the Swans' lead to 48 points, but they hadn't counted on Lockett.

The big St Kilda full-forward went on a one-man rampage to destroy the Swans after he earlier had been involved in one of football's most controversial incidents. Lockett collected Swan defender Peter Caven with an errant elbow and Swan fans bellowed in rage. Caven's nose was so badly smashed that he had to have corrective surgery.

To make matters worse for the Swans, Lockett kicked goal after goal over the final 20 minutes and his eleventh gave the Saints the lead for the first time. St Kilda pipped the Swans by one point and Lockett later copped an eight-match suspension. However, the Swan hierarchy knew that Lockett would be out of contract at season's end and almost immediately made a vow to get him into the red and white.

In another highly controversial match, against Richmond at the MCG in round 19, the Swans were savaged by suspension and injuries. Brereton's Sydney career was ended after he was found guilty of striking Tiger captain Tony Free and was suspended another seven matches. In the same game, wing speedster Jamie Lawson broke his left leg so severely that he never played again and Swan captain Kelly copped two matches on a striking charge.

Off-field, there were massive developments as, at the start of the year, the AFL approached former West Coast chairman Richard Colless to head the Swans. Colless had moved to Sydney for business reasons and he agreed to the AFL overture — on specific terms. He successfully argued that the Swans needed meaningful assistance in terms of recruiting concessions, a revamped administration and general AFL support. Colless also argued that the AFL needed a strong team in Sydney to be the linch-pin of a national competition and, with AFL agreement, he became the Sydney Swan chairman.

The Sydney Swans finally looked as if they had found calmer waters and, under Colless' leadership, were determined to succeed rather than merely survive. To do this, the Swans wanted to start with the recruitment of one of the biggest names in football, and few marquee players came bigger than Lockett.

PLAYER	GAMES	GOALS
AHMAT, Matthew	2	0
BAYES, Mark	20	3
BRERETON, Dermott	7	7
BRUNTON, Neil	15	2
CAVEN, Peter	9	3
CHAPMAN, Wade	9	0
CONSIDINE, Ed	15	3
CRESSWELL, Daryn	21	15
DANIELS, Jayson	20	1
DIREEN, Scott	7	1
DUNKLEY, Andrew	17	2
FILANDIA, Peter	20	21
GARLICK, Simon	7	1
GASPAR, Darren	5	0
GRAY, Troy	9	2
HEPBURN, Mark	7	3
HEUSKES, Adam	10	1
HIGGINS, Leon	12	4
HOLMES, Darren	6	2
KAPPLER, Darren	18	25
KELLY, Paul	18	15
KICKETT, Derek	17	29
LANG, Damian	5	4
LAWSON, Jamie	15	5
LEWIS, Dale	22	43
LUFF, Troy	11	4
McMAHON, Gavin	3	0
McPHERSON, Daniel	2	0
McRAE, Dean	18	6
MINTON-CONNELL, Simon	20	68
MOONEY, Jason	14	3
NEILL, Robbie	15	7
NETTELBECK, Craig	2	2
ROSE, Gavin	17	2
SEYMOUR, Brad	9	0
SMITH, Shayne	4	1
STAFFORD, Greg	2	0
WATTERS, Scott	19	1
WERNER, Michael	5	1
WHEELER, Sanford	7	1

POSITION: Fifteenth
COACH: Ron Barassi
CAPTAIN: Paul Kelly
BEST AND FAIREST: Daryn Cresswell
LEADING GOALKICKER:
Simon Minton-Connell (68)

1995

The Fremantle Dockers joined the AFL for the 1995 season, adopting purple, red, green and white as their colours. This meant the AFL now had 16 clubs and no longer needed byes each week. The Sydney Swans, far more settled than they had been for years, relished the start of the new season under the coaching of Ron Barassi and the captaincy of the inspirational Paul Kelly. The Swans might have collected yet another wooden spoon in 1994, but were determined to climb the ladder.

There had been no significant player losses from 1994, apart from Jamie Lawson's forced retirement because of a broken leg and Dermott Brereton's move to Collingwood for one last hurrah and, on the other hand, the Swans again recruited well, with one particularly spectacular coup. The Swans knew they were on the cusp of an exciting era and landed the biggest fish of them all over the summer leading up to the 1995 season.

Swan CEO Ron Joseph made a huge play to sign uncontracted St Kilda full-forward Tony Lockett, only for Collingwood and Richmond to jump to the front of the queue. The Magpies finally dropped off when the board decided, by just one vote, not to pursue Lockett's services, which left the Swans in a two-club battle with the Tigers. Joseph, relentless in pursuit of the champion goalkicker, virtually lived on Lockett's front doorstep until the big man signed with the Swans.

It was one of the most exciting coups in

The Swans' new glamour full-forward Tony Lockett shoots for goal against his old side St Kilda at the SCG in 1995.

MATCH RESULTS

Round 1, at Western Oval, April 2
Footscray 15.12 (102) d Sydney Swans 12.13 (85)
Round 2, at SCG, April 9
Geelong 11.14 (80) d Sydney Swans 10.15 (75)
Round 3, at the Gabba, April 16
Brisb. Bears 15.14 (104) d Sydney Swans 14.15 (99)
Round 4, at SCG, April 22
Sydney Swans 17.14 (116) d Fitzroy 12.12 (84)
Round 5, at SCG, April 30
Sydney Swans 20.24 (144) d Adelaide 12.15 (87)
Round 6, at WACA, May 7
Fremantle 25.13 (163) d Sydney Swans 16.9 (105)
Round 7, at Victoria Park, May 13
Collingwood 13.19 (97) d Sydney Swans 11.10 (76)
Round 8, at SCG, May 19
Sydney Swans 21.6 (132) d Carlton 8.12 (60)
Round 9, at SCG, May 28
Richmond 17.14 (116) d Sydney Swans 14.6 (90)
Round 10, at MCG, June 3
Melbourne 15.12 (102) d Sydney Swans 11.11 (77)
Round 11, at Waverley Park, June 12
Hawthorn 17.11 (113) d Sydney Swans 9.17 (71)
Round 12, at Subiaco, June 25
West Coast 11.7 (73) d Sydney Swans 10.12 (72)
Round 13, at SCG, July 2
Sydney Swans 21.12 (138) d Essendon 17.17 (119)
Round 14, at SCG, July 9
St Kilda 17.17 (119) d Sydney Swans 14.10 (94)
Round 15, at MCG, July 15
Sydney Swans 16.17 (113) d North Melb. 12.12 (84)
Round 16, at SCG, July 22
Footscray 21.8 (134) d Sydney Swans 12.7 (79)
Round 17, at Kardinia Park, July 29
Geelong 23.13 (151) d Sydney Swans 11.8 (74)
Round 18, at SCG, August 6
Brisb. Bears 19.12 (126) d Sydney Swans 17.9 (111)
Round 19, at Western Oval, August 13
Sydney Swans 27.8 (170) d Fitzroy 6.8 (44)
Round 20, at Football Park, August 19
Sydney Swans 22.7 (139) d Adelaide 13.15 (93)
Round 21, at SCG, August 27
Fremantle 20.24 (144) d Sydney Swans 19.13 (127)
Round 22, at SCG, September 3
Sydney Swans 19.13 (127) d Collingwood 15.14 (104)

football history, not only because of Lockett's immense ability, but also because he represented enormous marketing possibilities. He was to become the club's marquee player and fans flocked to the SCG to see him in action. Joseph later recalled: "Plugger's preference always was to stay in Melbourne but we chased him at 100 miles an hour. It was relentless. I even went to his home in Cranbourne (east of Melbourne) on one rush trip in a pair of slippers."

The Swans' final hurdle was to arrange a trade with St Kilda and, finally, got their man by trading their number five draft selection (Joel Smith) and youngster Robbie Neill. It was a win-win situation as many at Moorabbin, despite being unhappy at losing Lockett, felt he had gone stale with the Saints.

The Swans pulled off yet another coup when they snared former Fitzroy captain Paul Roos with its number one pre-season draft selection. The Swans not only had recruited a champion goalkicker, but also a wonderful defender who later would land the club the greatest prize of all after a wait of 72 years. However, the recruiting did not end there as the Swans nominated Anthony Rocca as the overall number two selection at the 1994 national draft and took Shannon Grant at number three. The Swans also drafted South Australian youngster Michael O'Loughlin with the overall number 40 selection and he went on to become one of the club's most decorated players and the club games record-holder. Also, one of the Swans' unsung heroes over the following seasons joined the club as the overall number 21 selection, although Matthew Nicks had to wait to make his mark because of a broken leg. The icing on the cake was

the nomination of New South Wales youngster Leo Barry (Deniliquin) as a zone selection.

Following the best summer of recruiting for many years it was only natural for Swan fans to look excitedly to what they believed would be a much brighter future. Lockett and Roos were the big drawcards and Swan fans flocked to the Western Oval to see their new players in action against Footscray in the opening round. Although Lockett kicked six goals in his first game in the red and white, the Bulldogs won by 17 points after leading by just four points at the last change.

Lockett was expected to make his SCG debut against Geelong the following Sunday afternoon, but was a late withdrawal because of illness. The Swans went down by just five points, courtesy of a last gasp goal by ace

The Swan "book-ends", full-back Andrew Dunkley (rear) and Tony Lockett.

Cat full-forward Gary Ablett from a dubious free kick. The lead had changed 15 times and the Swans were desperately unlucky not to open their account for 1995.

Lockett was still sidelined for the round three clash with the Brisbane Bears at the Gabba, but the Swans were delighted that week when Rocca finally agreed to play with the Swans after initially indicating he would stand out of football for two years rather than play with Sydney. The big key forward made his red and white debut in a reserves match against North Melbourne and showed immense promise. The Swans agreed that he could remain in Melbourne for the 1995 season to complete his schooling. The Swans could have done with Lockett's powerful marking against the Bears as they went down by just five points, with Mark Bayes kicking seven goals.

The Swans finally were able to select Lockett for the round four match against Fitzroy and he kicked seven goals in the 32-point defeat of the Lions. It was the start of a love affair as SCG fans immediately took to the huge man with the strongest hands in the game. Then, in round five, the Swans defeated Adelaide by 57 points at the SCG, even though Lockett was restricted to just three goals. The Swans were on their way, even if it would take more than one season to prove they were about to climb the ladder to the very top.

Although Lockett kicked eight goals in a Friday night 72-point demolition of ladder leader Carlton at the SCG in round eight, the star performer was young O'Loughlin, who showed with his four goals that he would be a star of the future. It was one of only two Carlton defeats that season and the Blues romped away with the 1995 flag. The Swans' win helped Barassi celebrate his 500th game as

Paul Kelly was a popular winner of the 1995 Brownlow Medal.

a VFL/AFL coach and, with Rocca making his senior debut, the Swans clearly were looking to a brighter future.

Richmond defeated the Swans by 26 points at the SCG the following week, but the result was overshadowed by a serious knee injury suffered by Tiger forward Matthew Richardson when he accidentally crashed into the boundary fence. As a result, the boundary line was moved in to give players more room. The length of the playing arena was shortened by two metres and the wings brought in one metre.

Despite the Swans' improvement and the superb form of Lockett and skipper Kelly, the Swans were out of the finals race by the halfway mark of the season. At the completion of round 18, the Swans were third from the bottom, above St Kilda and Fitzroy, and even though Lockett already had bagged 74 goals, he was a long shot to reach the "ton" over the final four rounds — until the following Sunday.

The Swans played Fitzroy at the Western Oval in round 19 and it was obvious from the start that the Lions would be unable to stop the rampaging Lockett. The Swan champion had 12 goals by three-quarter time, even though he took himself from the ground at one stage in the second quarter when the Swans runner ordered him to "cool it" in a tangle with Fitzroy defender Mark Zanotti. Lockett misinterpreted the instruction and was off the ground for several minutes.

Lockett kicked four more goals in the final quarter to give him 16 (without one miss) in the Swans' 126-point romp. His haul broke the club record of 15 set by the legendary Bob Pratt against Essendon in 1934 and, if he had not taken himself off the ground, he might have equalled or even broke the League record of

PLAYER	GAMES	GOALS
ARNOTT, Simon	5	2
BARRY, Leo	1	1
BAYES, Mark	19	16
BRUNTON, Neil	11	2
CAVEN, Peter	9	1
CHAPMAN, Wade	11	2
CONSIDINE, Ed	6	2
CRAWFORD, Justin	10	7
CRESSWELL, Daryn	22	17
DANIELS, Jayson	22	3
DIREEN, Scott	19	2
DUNKLEY, Andrew	22	4
GARLICK, Simon	16	16
GASPAR, Darren	16	1
GRANT, Shannon	10	9
GRAY, Troy	19	11
HEUSKES, Adam	17	2
HIGGINS, Leon	8	6
KAPPLER, Darren	19	20
KELLY, Paul	22	15
KICKETT, Derek	21	26
LEWIS, Dale	18	7
LOCKETT, Tony	19	110
LUFF, Troy	10	11
McPHERSON, Daniel	3	0
McRAE, Craig	21	14
MOONEY, Jason	11	7
MYLES, Dion	3	0
O'LOUGHLIN, Michael	11	12
ROCCA, Anthony	12	8
ROOS, Paul	21	7
ROSE, Gavin	13	1
SCOTT, Tim	1	0
SEYMOUR, Brad	7	1
STAFFORD, Greg	7	0

POSITION: Twelfth
COACH: Ron Barassi
CAPTAIN: Paul Kelly
BEST AND FAIREST: Tony Lockett
LEADING GOALKICKER: Tony Lockett (110)

18 goals by Melbourne's Fred Fanning against St Kilda at the Junction Oval in the final round of the 1947 season.

The 16-goal haul took Lockett to 90 for the season and the "ton" now looked certain. He kicked his 100th goal in the round 21 clash with Fremantle at the SCG. Lockett reached the target with his fourth goal of the match and was mobbed by adoring Swan fans. Unfortunately, however, the Dockers defeated the Swans by 17 points to rain on Lockett's parade.

Three days earlier, Barassi announced that he was resigning as Swan coach, but would stay with the club as the club's Melbourne-based director. Club president Richard Colless paid tribute to Barassi by telling the media: "What Ron inherited was a bankrupt football club that was bankrupt in almost every sense of the word. There are few people in Australia who could have done what he has done. This place was on its knees. It was basically gone for all money and we bought a bit of time in the second half of 1993 on the back of Ron's reputation."

Barassi indeed had saved the club and the players showed him what they thought of his contribution by defeating Collingwood by 23 points at the SCG in his final game as coach. The Swans finished a much-improved twelfth, with eight wins and the promise of plenty more the following season. Lockett kicked seven goals against the Magpies to finish the season with 110.

Lockett's contribution had been enormous, but skipper Kelly sparked even greater Swan celebrations when he polled 21 votes to win the Brownlow Medal, with Hawthorn's Darren Jarman runner-up on 18 votes. He polled three best on ground votes, four two-votes and four single votes. Kelly, who had averaged 13 kicks and seven handballs in his 22 games, won countless thousands of admirers with a victory speech which paid tribute to Barassi. He said: "We (the Swans) might not have been here if it was not for him." Kelly also was voted the AFL Players' Association Most Valuable Player, but was runner-up to Lockett in the club best and fairest. But, as AFL CEO Ross Oakley said immediately after the Brownlow presentation: "This win was hugely popular and gives great credibility to the Brownlow Medal."

Swan skipper Paul Kelly sends the ball downfield during his 1995 Brownlow Medal season.

1996

With the resignation of Ron Barassi as coach late in the 1995 season, the Sydney Swans had to find a coach capable of building on foundations well laid by the old master. Barassi had given the Swans credibility and, more importantly, a future. There no longer was any talk of the club folding or even struggling. It had an extremely promising young list and the selection of the new coach would be one of the most important decisions for years.

Names included home-town hero Dennis Carroll, who had coached the Swan reserves to a Grand Final in 1995, former Essendon stars Simon Madden and Tim Watson, Geelong reserves coach Jeff Gieschen and, finally, North Melbourne assistant coach Rodney Eade, who had played 229 games for Hawthorn from 1976-87 and 30 with the Brisbane Bears from 1988-90. He had played in four Hawk premiership sides and had coached the Bear reserves to the 1991 premiership. Eade's credentials therefore were impeccable and Swan CEO Kelvin Templeton contacted him during the 1995 finals series.

Eade expressed his interest in the position but, at the same time, Fitzroy was interested in appointing him coach. The Swans interviewed Eade three times and, after the third (in Sydney) he no sooner had walked off the plane at Tullamarine than his mobile telephone rang. The Swans were offering him the job and he accepted on the spot. Eade knew little about the Swans, but was aware

Stuart Maxfield was a wonderful signing for the Swans in 1996.

they had two marvellous players in Tony Lockett and Paul Roos and a gaggle of promising youngsters.

The Swans at that stage also were involved in wooing Richmond's Stuart Maxfield as an uncontracted player selection and this really was the cream on top of the coffee as Maxfield had an enormously positive influence on the

MATCH RESULTS

Round 1, at Football Park, March 31
Adelaide 20.10 (130) d Sydney Swans 6.4 (40)
Round 2, at SCG, April 7
Fremantle 13.22 (100) d Sydney Swans 9.17 (71)
Round 3, at SCG, April 14
Sydney Swans 15.17 (107) d Collingwood 10.13 (73)
Round 4, at Waverley Park, April 21
Sydney Swans 10.11 (71) d Richmond 9.16 (70)
Round 5, at SCG, April 27
Sydney Swans 13.10 (88) d Hawthorn 11.10 (76)
Round 6, at SCG, May 3
Syd. Swans 14.6 (90) drew with Essendon 12.18 (90)
Round 7, at MCG, May 11
Sydney Swans 12.10 (82) d Melbourne 5.8 (38)
Round 8, at WACA, May 18
West Coast 14.16 (100) d Sydney Swans 9.10 (64)
Round 9, at SCG, May 26
Sydney Swans 21.6 (132) d Bris. Bears 10.14 (74)
Round 10, at Western Oval, June 8
Sydney Swans 21.11 (137) d Fitzroy 10.7 (67)
Round 11, at Princes Park, June 15
Sydney Swans 24.8 (152) d North Melb. 10.13 (73)
Round 12, at SCG, June 23
Sydney Swans 18.15 (123) d Footscray 11.11 (77)
Round 13, at Princes Park, June 29
Sydney Swans 15.12 (102) d Carlton 13.13 (91)
Round 14, at SCG, July 7
Sydney Swans 18.17 (125) d Geelong 11.8 (74)
Round 15, at Waverley Park, July 13
Sydney Swans 14.12 (96) d St Kilda 11.13 (79)
Round 16, at SCG, July 21
Sydney Swans 16.14 (110) d Adelaide 12.16 (88)
Round 17, at Subiaco, July 28
Fremantle 15.14 (104) d Sydney Swans 12.6 (78)
Round 18, at SCG, August 4
Sydney Swans 17.13 (115) d Melbourne 6.16 (52)
Round 19, at SCG, August 11
Sydney Swans 20.10 (130) d Richmond 12.10 (82)
Round 20, at Waverley Park, August 17
Sydney Swans 9.18 (72) d Hawthorn 7.7 (49)
Round 21, at MCG, August 24
Essendon 14.16 (100) d Sydney Swans 12.10 (82)
Round 22, at SCG, August 31
Sydney Swans 12.13 (85) d West Coast 6.14 (50)
Qualifying final, at SCG, September 7
Sydney Swans 13.12 (90) d Hawthorn 12.12 (84)
Preliminary final, at SCG, September 21
Sydney Swans 10.10 (70) d Essendon 10.9 (69)
Grand Final, at MCG, September 28
North Melb. 19.17 (131) d Sydney Swans 13.10 (88)

playing group over many years. He played 200 games with the Swans to his retirement during the 2005 season and his contribution could never be over-estimated. It was immense in terms of professional attitude and dedication. Melbourne's Kevin Dyson also joined the Swans as an uncontracted player selection and he too made a big impact, even if not rated one of the game's stars. He was an in-and-under midfielder who gave the Swans grunt. The Swans also traded defender Jayson Daniels back to St Kilda in exchange for tough small forward Craig O'Brien, who also made a big impact in 1996.

Eade's first game as Swans coach was a disaster. The players were still coming to terms with their coach's demands and looked hesitant against Adelaide at Football Park. The Swans scored just 1.0 to half-time and eventually went down by an embarrassing 90 points. Then, the following week, Fremantle defeated the Swans by 29 points. The Swans, so hopeful pre-season, were above only Melbourne and Footscray on the ladder.

Club chairman Richard Colless later reflected: "It was the worst possible start to the season, but there was no question of us questioning the coach. We knew he knew what he was doing and although we were a little stunned by the results, we were confident Eade would sort it all out. We regarded it all as something of a learning process under a new coach."

The Swans learned well and defeated Collingwood by 34 points at the SCG in round three. Lockett kicked eight goals, with skipper Paul Kelly chipping in with three. It was the start of a magnificent run, even though there were several hiccups along the way and who knows what might have been if the Swans had not squeaked past Richmond by just one point at Waverley Park in round four.

The narrow defeat of the Tigers was extremely fortunate as Richmond's Chris Bond kicked what appeared to be a goal in the final seconds of play, only for field umpire Haydn Kennedy to rule that Tiger full-forward Matthew Richardson had illegally crashed into Swan defender Andrew Dunkley as the ball sailed through the goals. Lockett kicked six goals, while Maxfield racked up 24 possessions in his first game against his old club.

There was considerable media speculation in the lead-up to the round five clash with Hawthorn at the SCG over whether the Swans could notch three consecutive wins for the first time since rounds three-five in 1989. No worries! The Swans defeated the Hawks by 12 points, with O'Brien kicking six goals and Daryn Cresswell collecting 27 possessions. The win pushed the Swans into the top eight, but they faced another crunch match against Essendon at the SCG in the following round.

Essendon had struggled over the first five rounds, but the Swans desperately needed credibility to push their finals claims and the clash with the Bombers represented a huge test of maturity. It all looked like doom and gloom for the Swans early in the final quarter when the Bombers led by 29 points. However, Sydney fought back magnificently to snatch a one-poind lead before Essendon's James Hird bombed a long torpedo for a behind just before the final siren. The Swans might have had to share the match points, but they were winners in the eyes of their fans.

Paul Kelly and Tony Lockett lead the Swans out for their AFL Centenary match against Melbourne at the MCG. The Swans in this match wore replicas of guernseys from the club's early VFL years.

The Swans the next week against Melbourne ran onto the MCG wearing replicas of the red and white striped guernseys they wore in their earliest VFL years as South Melbourne. It was all part of the AFL Centenary celebrations and the Swans made it a celebration of their own in defeating Melbourne by 44 points. Lockett kicked six goals and Kelly collected 23 possessions in the lopsided contest in which the Demons scored just three goals to three-quarter time and never looked like upsetting the Swans.

Swan fans could hardly contain their delight as the red and white cut a swathe through the opposition week after week to stamp themselves as near certain finalists. The Swans even thrashed early flag favourite North Melbourne by 79 points at Princes Park in round 11 to climb into fifth position. Lockett kicked 10 goals and the media at last rated the Swans a danger to the top sides. It was a big day for the Swans as they helped champion defender Paul Roos celebrate his 300th game. And he played a huge role in the Swans' massive win as he had 18 kicks and 12 handballs, took 11 marks and kicked two goals.

The Swans had climbed into second position, behind North, at the completion of round 14 and then grabbed top spot in defeating St Kilda by 17 points at Waverley Park. The Swans had trailed by two goals at the main break, but stunned the Saints with eight goals to nil in the third quarter. Lockett kicked six goals and with 87 to that stage of the season, looked certain to reach the "ton".

However, the Swans hit a hurdle in round 17 when Fremantle notched a double in defeating the red and white by 26 points at Subiaco. The Swans surrendered top spot to North and were rocked even further when O'Brien was suspended for three matches after being found guilty of striking the Dockers' Dale Kickett.

Lockett went into the round 19 match against Richmond at the SCG needing six goals for his "ton" for the season. He did it with ease, bagging 12 goals in the 48-point

PLAYER	GAMES	GOALS
ARNOTT, Simon	10	4
BARRY, Leo	5	2
BAYES, Mark	8	7
CAREY, Stefan	4	1
CHAPMAN, Wade	15	8
CRAWFORD, Justin	7	4
CRESSWELL, Daryn	24	11
DIREEN, Scott	13	1
DUNKLEY, Andrew	25	0
DYSON, Kevin	22	1
FILANDIA, Peter	13	1
GARLICK, Simon	19	9
GRANT, Shannon	25	11
GRAY, Troy	4	1
HEUSKES, Adam	22	3
KELLY, Paul	25	18
KICKETT, Derek	25	18
KING, Clinton	5	3
LEWIS, Dale	12	10
LOCKETT, Tony	22	121
LUFF, Troy	23	20
MAXFIELD, Stuart	24	14
McPHERSON, Daniel	19	3
McRAE, Dean	3	0
MYLES, Dion	2	1
NICKS, Matthew	6	2
O'BRIEN, Craig	18	34
O'LOUGHLIN, Michael	25	21
ROCCA, Anthony	10	3
ROOS, Paul	24	4
ROSE, Gavin	6	1
SEYMOUR, Brad	24	0
STAFFORD, Greg	22	3

POSITION: Runner-up
COACH: Rodney Eade
CAPTAIN: Paul Kelly
BEST AND FAIREST: Paul Kelly
LEADING GOALKICKER: Tony Lockett (121)

defeat of the Tigers. Lockett reached the "ton" in the second quarter and continued to demoralise a succession of Richmond defenders assigned to play on him. Lockett's big haul, however, was overshadowed by a 14-goal effort by Hawthorn's Jason Dunstall against Footscray at Waverley Park.

The Swans, in thrashing the Tigers, reclaimed top position, but faced an acid test against a resurgent Essendon at the MCG in round 21. The match, billed by some sections of the media as a possible Grand Final preview, attracted a massive attendance of 69,237 — a record for any non-finals Swans match to that stage. Although the Swans took a 10-point lead into the first break, it all went pear-shaped in the second quarter when Lockett tangled with Essendon defender Barry Young. Field umpire Chris Mitchell reported Lockett on a striking charge and many Swan fans from there lost interest in the result. They were more concerned with how Lockett would fare at the AFL Tribunal. Essendon won a fiery match by 18 points and the Swans slipped to second, behind the Brisbane Bears. However, Lockett was cleared and therefore eligible to play in the final round against West Coast and in the finals.

As Collingwood defeated the Bears on the Saturday afternoon at Victoria Park, the Swans knew they could claim top position if they defeated the Eagles in that night's clash at the SCG. However, the weather was foul and, in driving rain and a gale-force wind, it was anyone's guess how the Swans would fare. Swan fans need not have worried as their team kicked five goals to one in the first quarter to have the Eagles chasing them all night. Although the Swans led by just four points at half-time, they won by 35 points to finish on top of the ladder.

The Swans went into the match without Lockett, who had a groin strain, but he still managed to win the John Coleman Medal as the AFL's leading goalkicker over the home and away season. He had kicked 114 goals to that stage of the season and added another seven during the finals. He had had a magnificent season but he, Kelly and Roos took votes from each other in the Brownlow Medal count. They each polled 14 votes, with the Bears' Michael Voss and the Bombers' James Hird sharing honours with 21 votes each. North's Corey McKernan also polled 21 votes but was ineligible because of a suspension early in the season.

Meanwhile, the Swans were scheduled to play Hawthorn at the SCG in one of four qualifying finals. Under the final eight system operating at that time, the top team (Swans) played the eighth team (Hawks). The match was scheduled for the Saturday night and, as fans streamed into the ground, there was an announcement that Lockett would not play because of his groin injury. Swan fans groaned collectively, but the local team remained the firm favourite.

Hawthorn surprised the Swans with their dash over the first half and went into the main break with a nine-point lead. The Hawks tried to press home their advantage in the third quarter, but were dealt a massive blow when Dunstall seriously injured a knee and had to be stretchered off the ground. He had torn a cruciate ligament and later had a knee reconstruction. Hawthorn's misfortune kept the Swans in the match, but the red and white still trailed by nine points at the final break.

The Swans eventually snatched the lead through a Jason Mooney goal, only for Hawk Tony Wood to restore his side's lead. Then, with scores level and time running out, Maxfield won possession and drove the ball forward where Cresswell somehow took an overhead mark from behind Hawk defender Nick Holland in the goal square. His conversion gave the Swans a six-point win, their first in a final since defeating Collingwood in the 1945 second semi-final.

The Swans then had a week off before playing Essendon at the SCG in one of the two preliminary finals. North Melbourne that afternoon defeated the Bears by 38 points in the other preliminary final at the MCG and it therefore would be the Swans or the Bombers to challenge the Roos for the premiership. This time, however, Lockett was able to take his place in the Swans' side, even though it was obvious he was still troubled by his groin injury.

On a still night in front of 41,731 fans at the SCG, Lockett pre-match was presented with his Coleman Medal, but the early signs in the match were ominous for the Swans, who looked extremely nervous. Essendon raced to a 19-point lead and although the Swans pulled this back to 12 points by half-time, the Bombers looked the better side. Then, when Kelly goaled early in the third quarter, the Swans were back in the match and even led by a point at the final break.

The final quarter was frantic, with neither side able to grab an advantage until Bomber Michael Symonds goaled on the run to give his side a 12-point lead. The Swans, in desperate trouble, moved the ball to Dale Lewis who marked and goaled from 10 metres. When Cresswell goaled from 40 metres, scores were level. With less than a minute to play, the Swans swept the ball from deep in defence to the gutsy Wade Chapman. Instead of rushing his kick in the dying seconds, he found Lockett with a perfect pass. The big man marked 55 metres from goal and, as he was lining up the goals, the siren blared.

Lockett kicked and the ball tumbled and tumbled — through for a behind. The Swans had won by a point to reach their first Grand Final since going down to Carlton in the infamous 1945 "Bloodbath".

The Swans might have been delirious, but were shattered the following Wednesday when they learned that full-back Andrew Dunkley would be cited for allegedly striking Essendon's Hird. The Swans were horrified at this late development and immediately took legal action on the grounds that this late development would severely hamper the team's preparation. The Supreme Court of Victoria's Mr Justice Hempl, after listening to arguments from both sides, ruled on the Thursday afternoon that Dunkley could play in the Grand Final.

Although the Swans were the underdogs, they looked by far the better side in the first quarter to lead by 18 points and then stretch this to 25 points before the Roos' Glenn Freeborn bobbed up to lift his side with a brilliant burst close to goal. The Roos not only closed the gap to go into the main break with a two-point lead, but had all the momentum. Although the Swans battled gallantly, they were no match for the Roos over the second half and went down by 43 points. Lockett kicked six goals to give him a season's total of 121, while Roos, Kelly, Cresswell, Dyson and Michael O'Loughlin were named the Swans' best players.

The defeat might have been bitterly disappointing, but die-hards recalled that the Swans were in danger of extinction just a few years earlier. They did not know it at the time, but that long elusive premiership was less than a decade away.

Top of the heap, and now a Grand Final

SYDNEY v NORTH MELBOURNE

Where: MCG.
When: Saturday, 2.45pm.
Odds *(City Index, ACT)*: North 4-11, Sydney 9-4. Points in (evens), North (minus 27½), Sydney (plus 17½). Under 39 points: North (10-9), Sydney (7-2). Over 39 points: North (3-1), Sydney (7-1).

Tickets: Sydney, North members at any Bass agency from 9am today. North's coterie members can obtain tickets today from the Bass agency at the MCG's Northern Stand.
Training: North: today, MCG, 4pm; tomorrow, Arden St, 4.30pm; Thursday, Arden St 3.30pm. Sydney: today, tomorrow and Thursday, all 4pm, SCG.

This is how the Melbourne Herald Sun *featured the Swans' entry to the 1996 Grand Final.*

1997

The AFL had a new look for 1997, with South Australian Wayne Jackson taking over from Ross Oakley as CEO, Port Adelaide joining the competition and Fitzroy and the Brisbane Bears merging to become the Brisbane Lions. The AFL also announced that it would have a new stadium by 2000, at Melbourne's Docklands. Also, former Swans chairman Craig Kimberley joined the AFL commission in one of the most significant years of the competition — 100 years after the inaugural season.

However, it was status quo for the Sydney Swans, with Rodney Eade again coach and Paul Kelly captain. Bookmakers had the 1996 runners-up as fifth favourite (behind North Melbourne, the Brisbane Lions, West Coast and Essendon) at 10/1 for the flag. They were generous odds as the Swans made considerable changes to its playing list for 1997 and traded the highly-promising Anthony Rocca to Collingwood. Rocca, who had played 22 games with the Swans over the previous two seasons, always had indicated he wanted to play with the Magpies alongside brother Saverio.

The Magpies traded Mark Orchard for Rocca, along with two draft choices and the Swans used these to nominate Brett O'Farrell at number 14 and Will Sangster at 33. However, O'Farrell played just eight games with the Swans in 1998 before being traded to Hawthorn and Sangster played two games in the AFL. The Swans also used its number 10 selection at the pre-season draft to nominate a "smokey" in Old Ivanhoe Grammarians winger John Stevens. It was an inspired choice as Stevens proved himself a quick and classy competitor over 78 games in the red and white.

Bookmakers also would have been aware that champion Swan full-forward Tony Lockett would not be available for the early rounds because of pre-season surgery for several injuries. The Swans therefore needed a flying start in the absence of their star goalkicker as they could not afford to play catch-up football after his return.

The Swans opened the season against West Coast in the first night match at Subiaco. The Swans won plenty of the ball but looked lost up forward without Lockett and managed just five goals in the 41-point drubbing. The Swans had no multiple goalkickers and, the following week, the forwards fared little better when the Swans went down to the Western Bulldogs at Princes Park. The Swans scored just 12 goals in going down by seven points, with Craig O'Brien leading the scoring with three goals.

It was a bitterly-contested match and Kelly left the ground with welts and marks all over

Swan Andrew Dunkley is about to handball to a teammate against St Kilda in 1997.

MATCH RESULTS

Round 1, at Subiaco, March 29
West Coast 12.6 (78) d Sydney Swans 5.7 (37)
Round 2, at Princes Park, April 5
Western Bull. 13.12 (90) d Sydney Swans 12.11 (83)
Round 3, at SCG, April 11
Sydney Swans 15.9 (99) d Melbourne 14.7 (91)
Round 4, at Waverley Park, April 19
Sydney Swans 18.19 (127) d St Kilda 12.9 (81)
Round 5, at Waverley Park, April 26
Hawthorn 15.9 (99) d Sydney Swans 11.8 (74)
Round 6, at SCG, May 4
Sydney Swans 21.16 (142) d Carlton 11.17 (83)
Round 7, at Kardinia Park, May 10
Geelong 11.10 (76) d Sydney Swans 6.8 (44)
Round 8, at Football Park, May 17
Adelaide 22.12 (144) d Sydney Swans 8.7 (55)
Round 9, at SCG, May 24
Sydney Swans 16.15 (111) d Collingwood 11.8 (74)
Round 10, at the Gabba, June 1
Bris. Lions 13.14 (92) d Sydney Swans 13.11 (89)
Round 11, at Football Park, June 7
Sydney Swans 10.16 (76) d Port Adelaide 4.17 (41)
Round 12, at SCG, June 13
Sydney Swans 26.8 (164) d Richmond 16.14 (110)
Round 13, at SCG, June 29
Sydney Swans 8.17 (65) d North Melbourne 7.13 (55)
Round 14, at WACA, July 5
Fremantle 6.12 (48) d Sydney Swans 3.15 (33)
Round 15, at SCG, July 13
Sydney Swans 11.13 (79) d Essendon 11.12 (78)
Round 16, at SCG, July 19
Sydney Swans 15.22 (112) d West Coast 11.9 (75)
Round 17, at SCG, July 26
Sydney Swans 22.17 (149) d Western Bull. 7.10 (52)
Round 18, at MCG, August 2
Sydney Swans 25.19 (169) d Melbourne 7.11 (53)
Round 19, at SCG, August 10
St Kilda 18.20 (128) d Sydney Swans 17.17 (119)
Round 20, at SCG, August 17
Sydney Swans 20.15 (135) d Hawthorn 11.11 (77)
Round 21, at Princes Park, August 23
Carlton 11.10 (76) d Sydney Swans 5.11 (41)
Round 22, at SCG, August 30
Geelong 15.10 (100) d Sydney Swans 13.12 (90)
Qualifying final, at MCG, September 6
Western Bull. 18.11 (119) d Sydney Swans 12.12 (84)

Two Swans defend against the Bulldogs while another Swan, Paul Kelly, waits for any spoils.

his body. Fingers were pointed at the Bulldogs' Tony Liberatore, but no action was taken. In fact, Bulldog coach Terry Wallace praised the AFL's smallest player for his job in keeping Kelly quiet. However, the Swans left Princes Park fuming over Liberatore's alleged tactics.

Stevens made his debut for the Swans in the round three match against Melbourne at the SCG, at 25 years of age. Stevens finally had reached his goal after trialling with Collingwood, Geelong, Fitzroy and Richmond, apart from having to undergo heart and knee surgery. He provided the Swans with plenty of run and kicked two goals in the red and white's opening win of the season. The margin was just eight points, but the Swans had to wait until the following week for Lockett's return.

Lockett was named on the bench for the round four clash with his old club St Kilda at Waverley Park and, although most fans believed he would start the match, he did not take the field until the 10 minutes into the third quarter. He kicked three goals in the Swans' 46-point win and looked as dangerous as ever. However, he started on the bench again the next week when Hawthorn defeated the Swans by 25 points. He kicked just two goals as the Swans slipped to third last on the ladder, ahead of only St Kilda and Melbourne

It's another goal for Tony Lockett and Michael O'Loughlin congratulates the Swan full-forward.

The Swans desperately needed to defeat Carlton at the SCG in round six, and did it in style, with a 59-point margin even though Lockett kicked only one goal and appeared to injure a thigh. The game coincided with a joint AFL-Sydney Swans announcement that they planned for some Swan games to be played at the 80,000 seat Olympic Stadium at Homebush the year after the 2000 Games. Both the AFL and the Swans had convinced Homebush Stadium management to configure the ground to suit Australian football.

Although Geelong defeated the Swans by 32 points at Kardinia Park in round seven, Swan fans saw first-hand the raw courage of midfielder Daryn Cresswell. After taking a heavy knock to a knee, Cresswell sat on the ground trying to punch his dislocated kneecap into place. It at first was thought Cresswell would be sidelined for months, but he made a remarkable recovery to be available for selection the following week.

When Adelaide thrashed the Swans by 89 points at Football Park in round eight, few critics gave them any chance of making the

PLAYER	GAMES	GOALS
AHMAT, Robert	14	16
ARNOTT, Simon	11	8
BARRY, Leo	10	12
BAYES, Mark	15	21
CAREY, Stefan	20	18
CHAPMAN, Wade	13	8
COOK, Troy	20	7
CRESSWELL, Daryn	23	16
DUNKLEY, Andrew	21	0
FILANDIA, Peter	5	3
GREEN, Brent	2	0
KELLY, Paul	23	26
KINNEAR, Mark	3	1
LEWIS, Dale	21	28
LICURIA, Paul	4	1
LOCKETT, Tony	12	37
LUFF, Troy	11	5
MATHEWS, Ben	4	1
MAXFIELD, Stuart	22	9
McPHERSON, Daniel	5	0
MOONEY, Jason	18	14
NICKS, Matthew	20	6
O'BRIEN, Craig	11	16
O'LOUGHLIN, Michael	23	26
ORCHARD, Mark	20	4
ROOS, Paul	21	6
SCHWASS, Wayne	20	7
SEYMOUR, Brad	21	2
STAFFORD, Greg	22	5
STEVENS, John	19	10
WARFE, Rowan	12	0
WILSON, Ben	4	0

POSITION: Seventh
COACH: Rodney Eade
CAPTAIN: Paul Kelly
BEST AND FAIREST: Paul Kelly
LEADING GOALKICKER: Tony Lockett (37)

finals and wrote them off as one-season wonders. The Swans, without the injured Lockett, looked a far cry from the team that had played in the previous year's Grand Final and Crow coach Malcolm Blight criticised them for using flooding tactics which he claimed were ruining the game. It was the first, but not the last, criticism of this style of game.

Lockett returned for the round nine game against Collingwood at the SCG and although he kicked just three goals, his mere presence helped lift his side to an important 37-point win. It was the Swans' 15th consecutive win at its home ground and critics started writing about the SCG as being the "Sydney fortress".

The Swans, however, could not find the same form away from Sydney until they defeated newcomer Port Adelaide by 35 points at Football Park. It was a dour slog, but from there the Swans started climbing the ladder, even though Lockett had to undergo mid-season groin surgery. The Swans were seventh and out of the top eight only on percentage when they played bogey side Fremantle in atrocious conditions at the WACA. The Swans kicked just three goals in going down by 15 points and Eade had to face the law when fans complained of his language from the coach's box. Police warned him: "You might find that you don't catch the same plane back as your team." Eade merely replied: "Fair enough."

Kelly notched his 100th game as Swan captain in the one-point win over Essendon at the SCG in round 15, the win coming courtesy of Lockett's return from surgery. He kicked three goals. The win pushed the Swans to seventh position and was the launching pad for a second consecutive finals series. However, Lockett was reported for allegedly striking Melbourne's Shaun Smith in the 116-point thrashing of the Demons at the MCG in round 18. His two-match suspension was his first in his three years with the Swans.

Lockett returned for the round 21 clash with Carlton at Princes Park but kicked just one of the Swans' five goals in the 35-point defeat by the Blues. The Swans at that stage were assured of playing in the finals but even though they were fifth on the ladder they could slip to seventh. The problem was that there was a bottleneck from fifth to ninth, with Port Adelaide just out of the top eight on percentage from the Brisbane Lions.

The Swans' worst fears were realised when Geelong breached the "Sydney Fortress" to win by 10 points in the final round. This left the Swans in sixth position and scheduled to play the Western Bulldogs in a qualifying final at the MCG. Because of the ill-feeling between the clubs from their early season match at Princes Park, the Bulldogs' Wallace declared: "Hey, we're not going into a Holyfield-Tyson fight. It's a game of football."

Daryn Cresswell clears downfield during the 1997 season.

The sore and tired Swans limped into the elimination final with several key players carrying injuries, and it showed. The Bulldogs kicked nine goals to nil in the first quarter and the game was as good as over. Although the Swans fought back to reduce the final margin to 35 points, it was a sad end to an injury-riddled season. To make matters worse, full-back Andrew Dunkley was suspended for two matches after being found guilty of striking the Bulldogs' James Cook. The only consolation for a disappointing season was that Kelly was runner-up (with West Coast's Peter Matera) to St Kilda's Robert Harvey in the Brownlow Medal. The Bulldogs' Chris Grant polled one more vote than Harvey, but was ineligible because of a one-match suspension imposed after the round seven game with Hawthorn.

1998

When the Swans made the 1997 finals after playing off in the previous year's Grand Final, it was the first time the club had made consecutive finals series since the Tom Hafey-coached seasons of 1986-87. But could the Swans make the finals in three consecutive seasons for the first time since their golden era of the 1930s, when they made the finals each season from 1932-36? The Swans in 1998 had every reason for optimism as Rodney Eade was in just his third season as coach and the Swans still had plenty of star quality, with glamour full-forward Tony Lockett expected to have a greater impact following his injury-riddled 1997 season.

The Swans, as aggressive as ever in their recruiting, made sure they were fully compensated when young midfielder Shannon Grant indicated he wanted to return to Victoria to play with North Melbourne. The Swans therefore were able to woo classy midfielder Wayne Schwass in exchange. Although Schwass was older than Grant, he was just the type of midfielder the Swans needed — fast, aggressive and experienced. He became an invaluable player for the Swans before retiring during the 2002 season after playing 98 games in the red and white.

Other new faces on the list in 1998 included Brisbane's Simon Hawking and Brent Green, but Hawking never played a senior game with the Swans, while Green managed just seven. The Swans, at the 1997 national draft, nominated the Eastern Ranges' Jason Saddington at number 11 and, almost unbelievably in hindsight, North Ballarat's Adam Goodes at number 43. Goodes had starred in the 1997 under 18s Grand Final, but inexplicably was a late bargain basement pickup for the Swans as he developed into one of the club's most decorated champions, even if he did not make his AFL debut until 1999.

The Swans opened 1998 with an unusal assignment, against Melbourne in an Ansett Cup pre-season match in Wellington, New Zealand. It was an entirely appropriate fixture considering that the Swans' star 1998 recruit, Wayne Schwass, was a Kiwi. The Demons defeated the Swans by 12 points at Basin Reserve, Wellington, and the Swans then concentrated on their first-up premiership

Rodney Eade was in his third season as Swan coach in 1998.

MATCH RESULTS

Round 1, at Football Park, March 29
Sydney Swans 20.4 (124) d Port Adel. 17.15 (117)
Round 2, at SCG, April 4
Sydney Swans 20.15 (135) d Bris. Lions 14.13 (97)
Round 3, at SCG, April 12
Sydney Swans 24.16 (160) d Geelong 7.15 (57)
Round 4, at WACA, April 18
Sydney Swans 18.10 (118) d West Coast 14.15 (99)
Round 5, at SCG, April 26
Sydney Swans 14.15 (99) d Western Bull. 12.11 (83)
Round 6, at SCG, May 3
Melbourne 12.8 (80) d Sydney Swans 8.13 (61)
Round 7, at MCG, May 8
Sydney Swans 18.7 (115) d Collingwood 12.7 (79)
Round 8, at MCG, May 16
Kangaroos 15.15 (105) d Sydney Swans 14.11 (95)
Round 9, at SCG, May 24
Sydney Swans 17.15 (117) d Hawthorn 11.14 (80)
Round 10, at SCG, May 30
St Kilda 24.10 (154) d Sydney Swans 8.5 (53)
Round 11, at MCG, June 5
Essendon 24.16 (160) d Sydney Swans 15.10 (100)
Round 12, at Princes Park, June 13
Carlton 14.16 (100) d Sydney Swans 11.8 (74)
Round 13, at SCG, June 21
Sydney Swans 16.6 (102) d Richmond 13.13 (91)
Round 14, at SCG, June 28
Adelaide 18.,16 (124) d Sydney Swans 12.15 (87)
Round 15, at Subiaco, July 5
Sydney Swans 13.4 (82) d Fremantle 10.9 (69)
Round 16, at SCG, July 19
Sydney Swans 18.10 (118) d Port Adel. 12.12 (84)
Round 17, at the Gabba, July 26
Sydney Swans 22.17 (149) d Bris. Lions 14.5 (89)
Round 18, at Kardinia Park, August 1
Sydney Swans 19.7 (121) d Geelong 12.15 (87)
Round 19, at SCG, August 9
Sydney Swans 10.14 (74) d West Coast 9.14 (68)
Round 20, at Waverley Park, August 15
Western Bull. 15.9 (99) d Sydney Swans 15.7 (97)
Round 21, at MCG, August 24
Melbourne 17.12 (114) d Sydney Swans 12.11 (83)
Round 22, at SCG, August 30
Sydney Swans 18.11 (119) d Collingwood 16.11 (107)
Qualifying final, at SCG, September 5
Sydney Swans 12.17 (89) d St Kilda 13.9 (87)
Semi-final, at SCG, September 12
Adelaide 14.10 (94) d Sydney Swans 10.7 (67)

Matthew Nicks could play at either end of the ground.

assignment, against Port Adelaide at Football Park, Adelaide. The Swans went into the game without Schwass and full-back Andrew Dunkley, who were carrying over suspensions from the previous season, but had little trouble winning by seven points after the Power had trailed by 39 points at the final break.

Schwass made his Swans' debut against the Brisbane Lions in the round two match at the SCG and was one of the side's best in the 38-point victory. The Swans had had the perfect start to the season and remained undefeated until they went down to Melbourne by 19 points at the SCG in round six. The Swans, in the previous week's defeat of the Western Bulldogs, thought they would have to play the Demons without the inspirational Paul Kelly, who had been reported for striking the Bulldogs' Paul Dimattina. Although Kelly was cleared, Melbourne shocked the Swans with their pace and aggression.

Although the Swans defeated Collingwood by 36 points at Waverley Park in round seven, the victory came at a cost as goalsneak Craig O'Brien injured a knee and missed the rest of the season. Lockett kicked 10 goals and there already was talk he would top the "ton" in 1998. North Melbourne defeated the Swans by 10 points at the MCG the following week and, to add insult to injury, Dunkley was suspended for three matches following an incident involving the Roos' Wayne Carey. From there, the Swans struggled to find consistency until they strung together consecutive wins from Round 15-19.

One of the highlights over the first half of the season was Lockett kicking his 1200th goal, against Hawthorn at the SCG in round nine. The goal came after he won the ball on the ground and he slotted home from 35 metres. He finished the game with 11 goals and played a huge role in the 37-point defeat of the Hawks.

The Swans' run of five consecutive wins from round 15-19 was marred by Kelly's shocking knee injury in the round 16 match against Port Adelaide at the SCG. Kelly's knee gave way as he tried to tackle an opponent, but he refused to concede to the inevitable. However, the diagnosis at half-time was that he had injured a cruciate ligament and he would have to have a full knee reconstruction. It took all the gloss from the 34-point defeat of the Power and the media wondered whether the Swans could win the flag without the most inspirational captain in the competition.

Although the Swans won their next three matches, their form spluttered from there. However, there was one huge highlight as Lockett went into the round 21 match against Melbourne at the MCG needing just two goals for his "ton". However, the Swans also went into the match without ruckman Stefan Carey, who had broken a leg at training during the week. Lockett reached his "ton" after being paid a free kick in the third quarter. He drilled the goal from just 25 metres to spark an avalanche of fans spilling onto the hallowed MCG turf. It was the third time in four seasons Lockett had kicked 100 goals in a season for the Swans.

A win over Collingwood at the SCG in the final round sealed third position for the Swans and they took on St Kilda in a qualifying final at the SCG. The Swans won by just two points in a ferociously contested match and therefore earned the right to play Adelaide in a semi-final at the SCG the following week. This match was played in heavy rain and the Swans were dealt an early blow when star midfielder Daryn Cresswell had his jaw busted.

The Crows defeated the Swans by 27 points in what was Paul Roos' last game. The champion defender had played 87 games with the Swans from 1995 after playing 269 with Fitzroy from 1982-94. Lockett finished the season with 109 goals and won the Coleman Medal for leading AFL goalkicker. Lockett also was named in the 1998 All-Australian team and polled 15 votes in the Brownlow Medal.

PLAYER	GAMES	GOALS
AHMAT, Robert	12	7
BARRY, Leo	16	9
BOMFORD, Andrew	13	5
CAREY, Stefan	5	0
CHAPMAN, Wade	1	1
COOK, Troy	18	4
CRESSWELL, Daryn	24	21
CROUCH, Jared	18	0
DUNKLEY, Andrew	20	0
FILANDIA, Peter	14	6
KELLY, Paul	16	27
KINNEAR, Mark	3	0
LEWIS, Dale	17	17
LOCKETT, Tony	23	109
LUFF, Troy	24	9
MAXFIELD, Stuart	24	5
McPHERSON, Daniel	16	4
NICKS, Matthew	24	10
O'BRIEN, Craig	6	6
O'CONNOR, Ryan	14	8
O'LOUGHLIN, Michael	24	40
RUSSELL, Scott	15	5
SADDINGTON, Jason	22	8
SCHWASS, Wayne	22	23
SEYMOUR, Brad	18	1
STAFFORD, Greg	18	8
STEVENS, John	24	12
WARFE, Rowan	21	1

POSITION: Fifth
COACH: Rodney Eade
CAPTAIN: Paul Kelly
BEST AND FAIREST: Michael O'Loughlin
LEADING GOALKICKER: Tony Lockett (109)

1999

Going into the 1999 season, the Sydney Swans were chasing a record considered impossible over the previous 50 years. They were chasing a fourth consecutive finals series for the first time since the golden years of 1932-36, a string of five. Again, Rodney Eade was coach with Paul Kelly captain. The Swans now had had several years of off-field stability and the squad was still relatively young. The critics pre-season suggested the Swans would finish anywhere from sixth to tenth, even though the Sydneysiders again had recruited well.

The Swans this time were on the other end of the trading boot, swapping players to secure low picks at the 1998 national draft. They traded Paul Licuria and Mark Orchard to Collingwood for the overall number three selection and nominated Norwood youngster Nic Fosdike. The Swans also traded ruckman Brett O'Farrell to Hawthorn for the number four selection and nominated South Adelaide forward Ryan Fitzgerald. They secured the Calder Cannons' Jude Bolton at number eight and picked up the Port Adelaide Magpies' Heath James under the father-son rule as his father Max James had played 55 games with the Swans from 1978-82.

Then, in the pre-season draft, the Swans nominated Collingwood's Scott Russell at number eight. Fosdike played 164 games with the Swans before retiring on the eve of the 2009 season and, like Bolton, played in the 2005 premiership side. Fitzgerald showed enormous potential in his debut season of 2000, but had his football career savaged by injuries and he was traded to Adelaide, where he again ran into injury problems. James also showed great promise, but injuries restricted him to just 18 games from 1999-2005.

The Swans were dealt a blow even before the start of the 1999 season when veteran

The Sydney Swans' squad of 1999.

MATCH RESULTS

Round 1, at SCG, March 26
Port Adel. 17.13 (115) d Sydney Swans 12.14 (86)
Round 2, at MCG, April 3
Richmond 15.18 (108) d Sydney Swans 13.18 (96)
Round 3, at MCG, April 10
Essendon 22.17 (149) d Sydney Swans 9.14 (68)
Round 4, at SCG, April 17
Sydney Swans 10.12 (72) d Kangaroos 10.10 (70)
Round 5, at Football Park, April 25
Adelaide 23.17 (155) d Sydney Swans 11.8 (74)
Round 6, at SCG, May 2
Sydney Swans 15.10 (100) d Fremantle 11.9 (75)
Round 7, at SCG, May 9
Sydney Swans 20.11 (131) d Hawthorn 16.7 (103)
Round 8, at Kardinia Park, May 16
Sydney Swans 21.15 (141) d Geelong 14.16 (100)
Round 9, at SCG, May 23
West Coast 14.10 (94) d Sydney Swans 11.15 (81)
Round 10, at SCG, June 6
Sydney Swans 22.13 (145) d Collingwood 14.10 (94)
Round 11, at Waverley Park, June 12
Sydney Swans 15.12 (102) d St Kilda 10.13 (73)
Round 12, at Princes Park, June 20
Sydney Swans 12.16 (88) d Carlton 8.13 (61)
Round 13, at SCG, June 27
Bris. Lions 20.13 (133) d Sydney Swans 15.8 (98)
Round 14, at SCG, July 4
Western Bull. 18.15 (123) d Sydney Swans 14.17 (101)
Round 15, at MCG, July 10
Sydney Swans 18.17 (125) d Melbourne 10.14 (74)
Round 16, at Football Park, July 18
Port Adelaide 10.12 (72) d Sydney Swans 9.10 (64)
Round 17, at SCG, July 24
Sydney Swans 14.12 (96) d Richmond 8.7 (55)
Round 18, at SCG, July 31
Essendon 15.3 (93) d Sydney Swans 11.13 (79)
Round 19, at SCG, August 7
Kangaroos 17.9 (111) d Sydney Swans 15.11 (101)
Round 20, at SCG, August 15
Sydney Swans 25.9 (159) d Kangaroos 5.11 (41)
Round 21, at WACA, August 21
Sydney Swans 15.19 (109) d Fremantle 10.16 (76)
Round 22, at Waverley Park, August 29
Hawthorn 23.15 (153) d Sydney Swans 11.2 (68)
Qualifying final, at MCG, September 5
Essendon 18.15 (123) d Sydney Swans 7.12 (54)

Dale Lewis broke a wrist and, in the opening round match at the SCG, Port Adelaide defeated the Swans by 29 points. The Power stunned the Swans with a six goals to one behind opening quarter. The Swans' only consolation was that Kelly took the field from the bench to prove that he had recovered from the knee reconstruction he underwent after the previous year's SCG match against Port Adelaide.

Richmond defeated the Swans by 12 points at the MCG the following week and the start to the season went from bad to worse when Essendon thrashed the Swans by 81 points at the MCG in round three. Bomber full-forward Matthew Lloyd kicked 13 goals in front of 50,324 fans and the Swans, at the completion of the round, found themselves on the bottom of the ladder, with Fremantle and Collingwood the only other clubs still chasing a win.

If the Swans were to make the finals, they had to find form in a hurry, and did just that in sensational style against the Kangaroos in round four. The Roos led the Swans by 48 points just before half-time and, even worse, ruckman Greg Stafford had strained a medial ligament early in the match. The Swans managed to reduce the margin to six goals by half-time and then reduced the margin to 11 points by the final break. The red and white dug deep in the final quarter, with a Stuart Maxfield goal putting the Swans within range of a remarkable comeback victory. Kelly then won the match for the Swans with one of the most brilliant goals scored at the SCG. He shrugged off two Roo tackles before slotting the goal from a pocket.

Eade immediately after the game said of Kelly: "I don't think there would be a more inspirational player in the history of the game."

The Swans' two-point victory not only lifted the club off the bottom of the ladder, but was a psychological win against a club trying to muscle in on the Sydney market. The Roos had scheduled "home" games in Sydney and there was considerable ill-feeling between the clubs before the first bounce, In fact, the Swan banner gave a clear indication of club feelings. It read: SWANS NUMBER ONE TEAM IN SYDNEY.

The Swans had a 4-5 win-loss ratio going to the match against Collingwood at the SCG and, apart from the four match points, there was another great prize at stake as Tony Lockett was within range of the all-time 1299-goal record set by Collingwood's Gordon "Nuts" Coventry from 1920-37. "Plugger" at 1.35pm on Sunday, June 6, accepted a pass from his great mate Kelly and, as the football world held its collective breath, the big man kicked for goal. The ball wobbled and wobbled, but the kick was straight and Lockett had notched his 1300th goal. Thousands of fans swarmed onto the ground and, after order finally was restored, Lockett continued his goalkicking ways to finish the match with nine in the Swans' 51-point win.

Kelly said after the match of his pass to Lockett for the record-breaking goal: "I always liked to think that I'd be the one who'd give it to him. I gave him one early and he dropped it. I was a bit dirty on that." Ironically, Lockett played against his old club St Kilda at Waverley Park the following round and the Saints' pre-match banner paid tribute to his goalkicking record. The Swans then defeated the Saints by 29 points to climb into the top eight, in seventh position.

The Swans' form fluctuated from week to week from there and, late in the season, the red and white army heard the news they never wanted to hear — that Lockett was going to

Tony Lockett and the Swans celebrate his 1300th goal.

retire at season's end. The Swans reacted by defeating the Kangaroos by 118 points in the round 20 match at the SCG. As the Swans left the ground, Lockett held the match ball aloft to acknowledge the applause from the home fans as the Swans' last two games of the home and away season were at the WACA and then at Waverley Park.

Although the Swans defeated Fremantle by 33 points at the WACA, they then crashed by 85 points to Hawthorn in what was the last premiership game played at Waverley Park. A massive crowd of 72,130 watched the Hawks demoralise the Swans, who scored just three goals to half-time. Lockett, with four goals, was the only shining light for the Swans and the huge defeat cast a pall over the club on the eve of the finals.

The Swans finished eighth and, under the final eight system operating at that time, had to play top side Essendon in a qualifying final at the MCG. It was an unmitigated disaster for the Swans, in more ways than one. Not only did the Bombers crush the Swans by 69 points, but Kelly fractured a kneecap. Fans also believed it was Lockett's last game and had not counted on him making a comeback in 2002. He quipped immediately after the final against Essendon: "I'm going to a 7-Eleven to get an Eskimo Pie."

However, there was one consolation for the Swans as the highly-promising Adam Goodes won the Norwich Union AFL Rising Star award. The young Swan had created an enormous impression in his 20 games over the 1999 season, collecting 256 possessions and taking 90 marks. He undoubtedly had stamped himself as a future champion. Goodes had been nominated for the award for his second round performance against Richmond and polled 33 votes, nine more than runner-up, Adelaide's Brett Burton, with the Brisbane Lions' Simon Black third with 22 votes.

PLAYER	GAMES	GOALS
AHMAT, Robert	4	5
BARRY, Leo	17	10
BENNETT, Gerrard	6	3
BOLTON, Jude	9	3
BOMFORD, Andrew	9	3
CAMPBELL, Fred	5	3
CAREY, Stefan	16	3
CHAPMAN, Wade	2	0
COOK, Troy	5	0
CRESSWELL, Daryn	23	18
CROUCH, Jared	23	6
DUNKLEY, Andrew	21	2
FEAST, Simon	5	0
FILANDIA, Peter	15	6
FOSDIKE, Nic	13	8
GOODES, Adam	20	19
JAMES, Heath	4	0
KELLY, Paul	21	28
KIRK, Brett	5	5
LEWIS, Dale	11	9
LOCKETT, Tony	19	82
LUFF, Troy	22	6
MATHEWS, Ben	17	4
MAXFIELD, Stuart	22	19
McPHERSON, Daniel	16	4
NICKS, Matthew	23	9
O'BRIEN, Craig	2	0
O'CONNOR, Ryan	17	1
O'LOUGHLIN, Michael	18	26
RUSSELL, Scott	16	8
SADDINGTON, Jason	23	10
SANGSTER, Will	2	0
SCHWASS, Wayne	23	9
SEYMOUR, Brad	14	3
STAFFORD, Greg	11	5
STEVENS, John	13	7
WARFE, Rowan	14	1

POSITION: Eighth
COACH: Rodney Eade
CAPTAIN: Paul Kelly
BEST AND FAIREST: Wayne Schwass
LEADING GOALKICKER: Tony Lockett (82)

2000

The Sydney Swans went into the 2000 season with twin difficulties as champion full-forward Tony Lockett had retired at the end of the previous season and club captain Paul Kelly was still recovering from the kneecap fracture he suffered in the final match of 1999. Also, all clubs had a shorter preparation as the season started far earlier than usual because the AFL did not want the Grand Final to coincide with the 2000 Sydney Olympics. The first match of the season, between Richmond and Melbourne under lights at the MCG, was played on March 8.

The Swans had two ready-made recruits for 2000, trading for West Coast's Jason Ball and Collingwood's Andrew Schauble. Both proved astute signings as Ball played a big-hearted ruck role in the 2005 premiership triumph while Schauble won the Swans' best and fairest in 2000. The Swans at the national draft at the end of 1999 picked up South Adelaide's Stephen Doyle under the father-son rule as his father Robert had played 77 games with the Swans from 1969-75. Finally, there was the bargain-basement draft number 56 selection of the Calder Cannons' Ryan O'Keefe, who also became a 2005 flag hero.

Despite being without their two champions, the Swans defeated the Brisbane Lions by 28 points at Cairns in the opening round of the pre-season competition, the Ansett Cup. Adam Goodes starred with four goals but the Kangaroos defeated the Swans by 23 points

Ruckman Jason Ball was an important signing for the Swans in 2000.

MATCH RESULTS

Round 1, at Docklands, March 12
Sydney Swans 21.8 (134) d St Kilda 15.10 (100)

Round 2, at Subiaco, Match 19
Sydney Swans 12.10 (82) d West Coast 10.10 (70)

Round 3, at SCG, March 26
Sydney Swans 19.12 (126) d Melbourne 17.12 (114)

Round 4, at SCG, April 1
Collingwood 15.16 (106) d Syd. Swans 15.11 (101)

Round 5, at SCG, April 9
Kangaroos 19.14 (128) d Sydney Swans 18.12 (120)

Round 6, at SCG, April 16
Richmond 17.10 (112) d Sydney Swans 16.10 (106)

Round 7, at SCG, April 22
Geelong 17.6 (108) d Sydney Swans 15.9 (99)

Round 8, at Princes Park, April 30
Carlton 16.13 (109) d Sydney Swans 9.10 (64)

Round 9, at SCG, May 7
Sydney Swans 16.15 (111) d Port Adel. 11.19 (85)

Round 10, at SCG, May 14
Western Bull. 21.11 (137) d Sydney Swans 12.7 (79)

Round 11, at SCG, May 21
Bris. Lions 16.14 (110) d Sydney Swans 15.17 (107)

Round 12, at Football Park, May 27
Adelaide 14.14 (98) d Sydney Swans 7.6 (48)

Round 13, at SCG, June 4
Sydney Swans 16.13 (109) d Hawthorn 11.12 (78)

Round 14, at SCG, June 11
Essendon 12.17 (89) d Sydney Swans 11.10 (76)

Round 15, at Subiaco, June 18
Fremantle 20.3 (123) d Sydney Swans 14.12 (96)

Round 16, at SCG, June 24
Sydney Swans 14.9 (93) d St Kilda 10.5 (65)

Round 17, at SCG, July 2
Sydney Swans 22.19 (151) d West Coast 12.8 (80)

Round 18, at MCG, July 8
Melbourne 19.11 (125) d Sydney Swans 15.9 (99)

Round 19, at MCG, July 16
Sydney Swans 15.14 (104) d Collingwood 12.12 (84)

Round 20, at SCG, July 22
Sydney Swans 21.19 (145) d Kangaroos 14.7 (91)

Round 21, at Docklands, July 29
Sydney Swans 12.12 (84) d Richmond 12.11 (83)

Round 22, at Kardinia Park, August 5
Geelong 18.16 (124) d Sydney Swans 18.12 (120)

Brett Kirk was inspirational, even from his earliest seasons with the Swans.

in their second round clash at the Manuka Oval, Canberra.

With Lockett's retirement, the Swans knew they had to find goal alternatives and hoped young South Australian Ryan Fitzgerald would fill the big shoes. Fitzgerald, who had been nominated as the overall number four selection at the 1998 national draft, was named to make his debut against St Kilda at Docklands in the opening round. It also was the Swans' first game at the new football stadium, which had been opened for AFL action just three nights earlier for an Essendon-Port Adelaide clash. Gangly, with a huge leap, Fitzgerald made an enormous impression in contributing five goals to the Swans' 34-point defeat of the Saints. This equalled the club record for goals on debut, by Mike Smith against Collingwood in 1977, Kevin Taylor against North Melbourne in 1981 and Shane Fell against Carlton in 1990.

The Swans continued their fine start to the season in defeating West Coast by 12 points at Subiaco the following week. Midfielder Wayne Schwass racked up 35 possessions and stand-in captain Andrew Dunkley had a superb game at full-back. Then, when the Swans defeated Melbourne by 12 points at the SCG in round three, they were fourth on the ladder. However, the win was soured by yet another serious injury, with veteran utility Dale Lewis breaking an arm.

From there, the Swans' season went into free-fall, starting with a desperately unlucky run of four consecutive defeats at the SCG. This horror run at home started with former Swan Anthony Rocca kicking the winning goal for Collingwood from 55 metres right on the final siren. The Magpies won by five points and, the following week, the Kangaroos defeated the Swans by eight points and, in round six, Richmond breached the once-impregnable SCG fortress in defeating the Swans by just six points. When Geelong defeated the Swans by nine points at the SCG the following week, the Swans had lost four home games by a collective margin of just 28 points.

Amazingly, the Swans were still clinging to a top eight position going into the round eight clash with Carlton at Princes Park but this time there was no heartbreak of a narrow loss as the Blues won by a healthy margin of 45 points. The Swans slid to eleventh position and looked like missing the finals for the first time under coach Rodney Eade.

Although the Swans managed to end their disastrous run with a 26-point defeat of Port Adelaide at the SCG in round nine, they could not recapture the form of previous

Defender/tagger Ben Mathews always played with total commitment.

seasons and desperately missed Lockett's goalkicking and Kelly's inspirational leadership. However, the Swans did produce something like their best form in pushing the undefeated Essendon to 13 points at the SCG in round 14. In fact, the Swans looked like notching the upset of the season until the Bombers scored two late goals to continue their extraordinary winning run.

This heartbreaking defeat left the Swans in twelfth position and with very little hope of making the finals. Then, in the round 15 match against Fremantle at Subiaco, the Swans produced one of the selection shocks of the season. Kelly, who had not been expected to play any games in 2000, was flown to Perth unannounced and was rushed into the Swan line-up. He started on the bench but, soon after taking the field, took one of the marks of the season and helped lift the Swans after they trailed by 43 points at quarter-time. Despite Kelly's heroics, the Dockers won by 22 points.

Just four days earlier, after a Swan training session, Eade said of Kelly: "That was his first full session on the training track. I'm not even setting goals for his return. He'd need two or three lead-up games and he's still some way off that. I think it's too late for this year." Sydney's Captain Courageous insisted on playing and little wonder that at season's end he won an AFL Players' Association award as the competition's most courageous player.

The Swans at that stage of the season were above only Port Adelaide and St Kilda but, buoyed by Kelly's return, won five of their last seven matches of the season. However, these all came far too late for the Swans to make the finals and they therefore had to concentrate on other achievements. For example, Kelly played his 200th game in the 71-point thrashing of West Coast at the SCG in round 17 and was carried from the ground to rapturous applause from red and white diehards. The match also marked a club coaching record as Eade's 112th game in charge was one more than Ian Stewart (1976-77 and 1979-81).

Going into the final round match against Geelong at Kardinia Park (known as Shell Stadium in 2000), the Swans were tenth, one game behind eighth-placed Hawthorn as well as ninth-placed Richmond, but with a better percentage than either the Hawks or the Tigers. The Swans therefore needed a miracle in the final round as they not only had to defeat the Cats, but had to rely on the Western Bulldogs defeating Hawthorn and Carlton defeating Richmond.

All Swan hopes disappeared when the Hawks defeated the Bulldogs by 15 points at Docklands on the Friday night to lock away the eighth position in the finals. It didn't matter as Geelong defeated the Swans by four points. Apart from Hawthorn's win, nothing went right for the Swans as their team bus broke down 25 kilometres from Geelong and the players had to hitchhike to Kardinia Park. The Swans finished a disappointing tenth, with 10 wins and 12 defeats. Forward Michael O'Loughlin capped a fine season in topping the club goalkicking with 53 and polling 16 Brownlow Medal votes.

PLAYER	GAMES	GOALS
AHMAT, Robert	19	23
BALL, Jason	9	9
BARRY, Leo	17	15
BENNETT, Gerrard	6	0
BOLTON, Jude	16	15
CRESSWELL, Daryn	22	23
CROUCH, Jared	22	4
DOYLE, Stephen	2	0
DUNKLEY, Andrew	15	1
FEAST, Simon	4	3
FITZGERALD, Ryan	10	15
FIXTER, Ben	2	0
FOSDIKE, Nic	17	9
GOODES, Adam	22	40
KELLY, Paul	8	10
KIRK, Brett	7	1
LEWIS, Dale	12	6
LUFF, Troy	20	11
MATHEWS, Ben	22	2
MAXFIELD, Stuart	22	8
McPHERSON, Daniel	10	6
NICKS, Matthew	19	13
O'KEEFE, Ryan	5	1
O'LOUGHLIN, Michael	22	53
SADDINGTON, Jason	21	6
SCHWASS, Wayne	22	12
SEYMOUR, Brad	13	2
STAFFORD, Greg	20	14
STEVENS, John	14	9
WARFE, Rowan	13	2

POSITION: Tenth
COACH: Rodney Eade
CAPTAIN: Paul Kelly
BEST AND FAIREST: Andrew Schauble
LEADING GOALKICKER: Michael O'Loughlin (53)

2001

Missing the 2000 finals was a savage blow to the Swans. After decades of mediocrity and failure, the Swans had made the finals in consecutive seasons from 1996-99 and there was a new-found determination to make up for lost time. The 2000 season therefore stuck in the craw of most Swan fans and the club was determined to make amends in 2001. Rodney Eade was coach for a sixth consecutive season, equalling the record set by Charlie Pannam from 1923-28. But whereas Pannam had taken the Swans to just two finals series (third in 1923 and fourth in 1924), Eade already had taken the Swans to four finals series. Also, Paul Kelly in 2001 was Swan captain for a ninth consecutive season, breaking Bob Skilton's record of eight years as skipper from 1961-68.

The Swans at the end of 2000 farewelled a number of experienced players, including Brett Allison, Andrew Bomford, Peter Filandia, Craig O'Brien, Ryan O'Connor and Scott Russell but recruited exceptionally well. The Swans, realising they needed pace in the midfield, traded with Collingwood to sign the brilliant Paul Williams. They also did well at the 2000 national draft, nominating Luke Ablett at 24 and Amon Buchanan at 52. Williams, Ablett and Buchanan all played in the Swans' 2005 premiership side. The Swans also picked up Melbourne's Stephen Tingay in the pre-season draft, but the former Demon was unable to shake off injury problems and did not play a senior game before he announced his retirement late in the 2001 season.

The Swans opened their 2001 campaign with an Ansett Cup pre-season match against Geelong at Marrara Park, Darwin, on February 16. The Swans defeated the Cats by 13 points in torrential rain and, at the same time discovered a future star. Irishman Tadhg Kennelly, who had been recruited from County Kerry, made his first appearance in the red and white and announced after the match that he

Dual Swan best and fairest winner Paul Williams was a great pickup from Collingwood.

MATCH RESULTS

Round 1, at SCG, April 1
Sydney Swans 19.12 (126) d Adelaide 10.14 (74)
Round 2, at Subiaco, April 8
Sydney Swans 15.14 (104) d West Coast 13.11 (89)
Round 3, at SCG, April 14
Sydney Swans 23.13 (151) d Kangaroos 11.5 (71)
Round 4, at SCG, April 20
Essendon 15.12 (102) d Sydney Swans 6.19 (55)
Round 5, at MCG, April 29
Melbourne 18.11 (119) d Sydney Swans 15.14 (104)
Round 6, at Docklands, May 5
St Kilda 18.12 (120) d Sydney Swans 14.10 (94)
Round 7, at SCG, May 13
Brisb. Lions 15.22 (112) d Sydney Swans 12.8 (80)
Round 8, at SCG, May 20
Western Bull. 18.14 (122) d Sydney Swans 15.11 (101)
Round 9, at SCG, May 27
Sydney Swans 12.12 (84) d Fremantle 10.5 (65)
Round 10, at Docklands, June 3
Sydney Swans 11.7 (73) d Collingwood 7.13 (55)
Round 11, at SCG, June 10
Sydney Swans 18.17 (125) d Port Adel. 10.18 (78)
Round 12, at Docklands, June 23
Richmond 12.14 (86) d Sydney Swans 8.12 (60)
Round 13, at SCG, July 1
Geelong 12.12 (84) d Sydney Swans 9.11 (65)
Round 14, at SCG, July 8
Sydney Swans 12.19 (91) d Carlton 12.9 (81)
Round 15, at MCG, July 14
Sydney Swans 14.14 (98) d Hawthorn 11.11 (77)
Round 16, at Football Park, July 22
Sydney Swans 16.9 (105) d Adelaide 7.14 (56)
Round 17, at SCG, July 29
Sydney Swans 11.17 (83) d West Coast 6.12 (48)
Round 18, at SCG, August 4
Sydney Swans 22.11 (143) d Kangaroos 3.18 (36)
Round 19, at Docklands, August 12
Essendon 11.13 (79) d Sydney Swans 11.11 (77)
Round 20, at SCG, August 19
Melbourne 19.17 (131) d Sydney Swans 14.14 (98)
Round 21, at SCG, August 26
Sydney Swans 21.16 (142) d St Kilda 8.7 (55)
Round 22, at the Gabba, September 1
Brisbane Lions 13.15 (93) d Sydney Swans 9.8 (62)
Elimination final, Docklands, September 9
Hawthorn 19.15 (129) d Sydney Swans 11.8 (74)

was "delirious with excitement". Kennelly developed into one of the finest rebounding defenders of his era and also played in the 2005 premiership side.

Port Adelaide defeated the Swans by five points at Football Park in the second round of the Ansett Cup, but the Swans were well-prepared for the opening of the premiership season, with a first-up game against Adelaide at the SCG. The Swans thumped the Crows by 52 points, with Daryn Cresswell not only controlling the midfield but also kicking three goals. Cresswell racked up 27 possessions, while tag specialist Jared Crouch locked potential Crow matchwinner Andrew McLeod out of the game.

However, it was believed Adelaide was on the slide in 2001 and the Swans' big test came against West Coast at Subiaco the following week. The Eagles might not have been one of the fancied sides of 2001, but were always difficult to topple on their home turf. The Swans defeated them by 15 points, with Williams proving his worth with a best on ground effort. Eade should have been delighted with his side's win, but criticised his team for relaxing after leading by 47 points at half-time. When the Swans thrashed the Kangaroos by 80 points at the SCG on the Easter Saturday in round three, they were well on their way to another finals series. The Swans led by 28 points at the final break and then blew the match apart with 10 final-quarter goals.

The rampaging Essendon, premiers in 2000 with just one defeat over the entire season, set the Swans back on their heels with a 47-point demolition at the SCG in round four, while a 15-point loss to Melbourne at the MCG the following week caused the Swans to rethink their finals credentials, even though they were without skipper Kelly and ruckman Greg Stafford. When St Kilda defeated the Swans by 26 points at Docklands in round six, the Swans were back to square one.

Consecutive defeats by the Brisbane Lions and the Western Bulldogs left most pundits to believe the Swans were on the slide, but the defeat of Fremantle by 19 points at the SCG in round nine restored faith and confidence. The Swans knew they had to gather momentum and the round 10 match against Collingwood at Docklands was critical to their finals chances. The match was one of the most notable of the season, but for all the wrong reasons. Eade, in his bid to strangle the Magpies, adopted what became infamous as "flooding" tactics. The Swans at times had all 18 players in the Magpies' forward zone and eventually choked the life out of the opposition to win by 18 points.

The Swans were back in business and, in defeating Port Adelaide by 47 points at the SCG the following week, again were rated a strong chance to make the finals. Despite their inconsistency, the Swans finished seventh and were scheduled to play Hawthorn in an elimination final at Docklands in the first week of the finals. The Swans, heavily criticised for their "flooding" tactics had gone down to the Brisbane Lions by 31 points in pouring rain at the Gabba in the final round and were slight outsiders against the young Hawk side.

The Swans started brilliantly to lead by 20 points early in the second quarter. The Hawks looked nervous and unsettled and the Swans could have built a much greater lead if it had not been for inaccuracy in front of goal. However, injuries took their toll on the Swans. Young Ryan O'Keefe, in his first final, injured

Troy Luff, a great favourite with Swan fans, retired in 2001.

McPherson and gambled on the fitness of other players. For example, Williams went into the match with a fractured bone in one foot and Cresswell had a broken hand. The Swans' best player in the disappointing final game of the season was the hard-working Wayne Schwass, who racked up 22 possessions. Brett Kirk had 21 possessions and kicked three goals.

Williams proved himself to be an inspired recruiting target in winning the club best and fairest, but no Swan player featured in the top 20 in the 2001 Brownlow Medal count. Also, no Swan was named in the All-Australian team. The Swans might have made the finals for the fifth time in six years, but they lacked the goalkicking of the Tony Lockett era and there were suggestions the club could plummet over seasons ahead.

One of the few highlights in an up and down season for the Swans was the emergence of Kennelly, who made his premiership debut in the round 14 match against Carlton at the SCG. The Irishman might have had just seven possessions, but did not look over-awed and even took three marks. Kennelly played eight games in his debut season and grew in stature with every appearance to become a firm favourite with Swan fans. He racked up 49 possessions and took 11 marks in his eight games in 2001, and kicked three goals. He also made his AFL finals debut in that elimination final against Hawthorn.

a knee and Kelly tore a hamstring trying to "soccer" the ball through for a goal. The Swans faded badly after leading by five points at half-time and the Hawks won by 55 points.

Although the Swans might have been humiliated, there were extenuating circumstances. Apart from the O'Keefe and Kelly injuries, they went into the match without the injured Matthew Nicks and Daniel

PLAYER	GAMES	GOALS
AHMAT, Robert	7	11
BALL, Jason	20	24
BARRY, Leo	19	1
BENNETT, Gerrard	7	5
BOLTON, Jude	23	14
CRESSWELL, Daryn	18	16
CROUCH, Jared	23	6
DOYLE, Stephen	5	0
DUNKLEY, Andrew	22	0
FEAST, Simon	5	0
FIXTER, Ben	5	2
FOSDIKE, Nic	17	4
GOODES, Adam	23	34
JAMES, Heath	1	0
KELLY, Paul	11	13
KENNELLY, Tadhg	8	3
KIRK, Brett	19	14
LEWIS, Dale	9	6
LUFF, Troy	13	1
MATHEWS, Ben	23	4
MAXFIELD, Stuart	23	9
McPHERSON, Daniel	22	13
NICKS, Matthew	18	26
O'KEEFE, Ryan	13	18
O'LOUGHLIN, Michael	23	35
PILTZ, Brent	1	0
SADDINGTON, Jason	23	2
SCHAUBLE, Andrew	15	6
SCHWASS, Wayne	22	12
SEYMOUR, Brad	12	0
STAFFORD, Greg	20	19
STEVENS, John	8	7
WARFE, Rowan	5	0
WILLIAMS, Paul	23	25

POSITION: Seventh
COACH: Rodney Eade
CAPTAIN: Paul Kelly
BEST AND FAIREST: Paul Williams
LEADING GOALKICKER: Michael O'Loughlin (35)

2002

The 2002 season was one of the most significant in club history, but no one knew it when the players gathered for pre-season training. Rodney Eade was about to enter his seventh season as coach, with Paul Kelly in his tenth season as captain. The Swans over the summer had lost club stalwarts Dale Lewis and Troy Luff to retirement, while ruckman Greg Stafford was traded to Richmond and injury-plagued forward Ryan Fitzgerald crossed to Adelaide.

The Swans were determined to rebuild their list and traded with St Kilda to sign key forward Barry Hall and small Richmond forward Nick Daffy. Although Daffy played just the one game for the Swans, Hall became one of the most influential players in club history and was joint captain of the 2005 premiership side. Other 2002 newcomers included NSW zone selection Lewis Roberts-Thomson and midfielder/forward Adam Schneider as the overall draft selection number 60. Roberts-Thomson and Schneider also played in the 2005 premiership side.

However, there was also one other significant recruit for 2002 as former champion goalkicker Tony Lockett announced he would be making a comeback. As one Swan fan quipped to the media: "I prayed and he returned." Lockett went through the pre-season draft process and, because he indicated he would play only with the Swans, was named at number six. He was 36 years of age at the start of the season, but the Swans were hopeful he had lost little of his goalkicking skills.

The Swans opened their 2002 campaign with a Wizard Cup pre-season match against Collingwood at the Manuka Oval, Canberra. After thumping the Magpies by 80 points, the Swans went down to the Kangaroos by 21 points in the second round, also in Canberra. This series was played under a round-robin format and the Swans had to defeat Hawthorn in the third round to move into the semi-finals and, after defeating the Hawks by 42 points at Princes Park, went down to Port Adelaide by 14 points at Football Park.

The tough pre-season campaign was an ideal prelude to the season proper, but the Swans faced a daunting prospect against the reigning premiers, the Brisbane Lions, at the Gabba in the opening round. This match marked the Swan debut for Hall and, despite the club's new glamour forward kicking four goals, the Lions defeated the Swans by 23 points. Lockett, in his comeback match, started on the bench and took the field halfway through the second quarter. He kicked a goal from a free kick, but it was his only possession of the game.

Lockett, who was nursed carefully back to full action, missed the following week's game against Carlton at Princes Park, but it didn't really matter as Hall took the Blues apart. He kicked seven goals and the Swans cruised home by 78 points. Hall pulled in 11 marks, but he was not the Swans' only star as Daryn Cresswell had 28 possessions and Jude Bolton was not far behind with 26. The big win should have boosted the Swans' confidence, but they went down to nemesis club Adelaide by 30 points at the SCG in round three. The Swans' old problem of inconsistency had returned and, from there, they struggled to maintain their bid for a finals position.

The Swans also had critics on their back after they struggled to force a draw with the injury-depleted St Kilda at Docklands in round five. The Swans managed just one goal (to St Kilda's two) to half-time and there were howls that the Swans were too defensive and too reliant on flooding. The Swans were indignant and insisted that St Kilda had started the flooding because of their injury woes, but the mud had stuck and the Swans had to carry the negative tag over the rest of the season and beyond.

After struggling to win just three games over the first 11 rounds, matters came to a head after the two-point loss to Geelong at the SCG in round 12, on June 15. Eade, in the final year of his contract, sought clarification over his coaching position. The Swan board indicated that he would not be offered a new contract and Eade resigned the following Monday. By sheer coincidence, Lockett the same day announced his retirement for a second time. His comeback had yielded just three goals from three games.

The Swans, with Eade, club chairman Richard Colless and CEO Kelvin Templeton

MATCH RESULTS

Round 1, at SCG, March 31
Brisb. Lions 17.8 (110) d Sydney Swans 12.15 (87)

Round 2, at Princes Park, April 6,
Sydney Swans 17.9 (111) d Carlton 4.9 (33)

Round 3, at Football Park, April 12
Adelaide 17.12 (114) d Sydney Swans 13.6 (84)

Round 4, at SCG, April 20
Sydney Swans 15.13 (103) d North Melb. 14.16 (100)

Round 5, at Docklands, April 27
Sydney Swans 8.8 (56) drew with St Kilda 8.8. (56)

Round 6, at SCG, May 5
Sydney Swans 15.9 (99) d Melbourne 10.11 (71)

Round 7, at Docklands, May 11
Richmond 13.10 (88) d Sydney Swans 12.10 (82)

Round 8, at SCG, May 19
Western Bull. 24.15 (159) d Sydney Swans 11.24 (90)

Round 9, at Stadium Australia, May 25
Essendon 12.13 (85) d Sydney Swans 11.17 (83)

Round 10, at Docklands, June 1
Collingwood 14.11 (95) d Sydney Swans 12.12 (84)

Round 11, at Subiaco, June 8
West Coast 15.12 (102) d Sydney Swans 13.11 (89)

Round 12, at SCG, June 15
Geelong 15.11 (101) d Sydney Swans 15.9 (99)

Round 13, at SCG, June 30
Sydney Swans 20.19 (139) d Fremantle 9.8 (62)

Round 14, at MCG, July 6
Hawthorn 11.8 (74) d Sydney Swans 9.10 (64)

Round 15, at SCG, July 14
Port Adelaide 14.10 (94) d Sydney Swans 13.14 (92)

Round 16, at the Gabba, July 21
Brisb. Lions 17.15 (117) d Sydney Swans 12.7 (79)

Round 17, at Stadium Australia, July 27
Sydney Swans 13.14 (92) d Carlton 10.9 (69)

Round 18, at SCG, August 4
Adelaide 17.14 (116) d Sydney Swans 15.8 (98)

Round 19, at SCG, August 10
Sydney Swans 22.12 (144) d Kangaroos 15.7 (97)

Round 20, at SCG, August 18
Sydney Swans 12.15 (87) d St Kilda 12.8 (80)

Round 21, at MCG, August 24
Sydney Swans 23.7 (145) d Melbourne 11.11 (77)

Round 22, at Stadium Australia, August 31
Sydney Swans 17.14 (116) d Richmond 11.10 (76)

Ryan O'Keefe, a wonderful late draft selection.

PLAYER	GAMES	GOALS
ABLETT, Luke	4	0
BARRY, Leo	13	0
BENNETT, Gerrard	13	3
BOLTON, Jude	19	9
BROCKMAN, Leigh	10	0
BUCHANAN, Amon	6	1
CRESSWELL, Daryn	22	17
CROUCH, Jared	22	4
DAFFY, Nick	1	1
DOYLE, Stephen	9	10
DUNKLEY, Andrew	18	1
FIXTER, Ben	17	5
FOSDIKE, Nic	21	14
GOODES, Adam	22	21
HALL, Barry	17	55
KELLY, Paul	18	13
KENNELLY, Tadhg	20	7
KIRK, Brett	18	6
LOCKETT, Tony	3	3
MATHEWS, Ben	21	4
MAXFIELD, Stuart	12	4
McPHERSON, Daniel	15	5
MOTT, Ricky	17	3
NICKS, Matthew	21	28
O'KEEFE, Ryan	9	12
O'LOUGHLIN, Michael	19	30
SADDINGTON, Jason	22	7
SCHAUBLE, Andrew	14	10
SCHWASS, Wayne	9	1
SEYMOUR, Brad	13	3
STEVENS, Scott	14	12
SUNDQVIST, Jarred	1	0
WARFE, Rowan	5	0
WILLIAMS, Paul	19	21

POSITION: Eleventh
COACH: Rodney Eade, Paul Roos
CAPTAIN: Paul Kelly
BEST AND FAIREST: Paul Williams
LEADING GOALKICKER: Barry Hall (55)

Andrew Schauble won a best and fairest after joining the Swans from Collingwood.

in attendance, announced the Eade resignation at a press conference. Eade had coached the Swans for a club record 152 games from 1996 and, after thanking the Swans for their support during his tenure, left the club with the task of finding a replacement.

This proved to be one of the most difficult tasks to confront the Swans for years as there were any number of candidates. The board's first task, however, was to appoint a caretaker coach for the rest of the season. Assistant coach and former player Paul Roos might have been an obvious choice, but the Swans also considered rotating the position between Roos and two other assistant coaches, Steve Malaxos and John Longmire. The board finally settled on Roos, whose first game in charge was against Fremantle at the SCG.

The Swans had lost their previous six games, but there were signs early in the match against the Dockers that they would play with much more freedom under Roos. The Swans kicked six first-quarter goals, led by 19 points at half-time and went on to win by 77 points. Hall kicked six goals, Nic Fosdike and Michael O'Loughlin kicked three each and the Swans' total of 139 was its highest score of the year. However, one swallow did not make a summer and the Swans lost their next three matches under Roos, to Hawthorn, Port Adelaide and the Brisbane Lions.

Meanwhile, the board was casting around for a permanent replacement for Eade. Roos certainly was one of the candidates, but there also were suggestions it would try to woo the Kangaroo's Denis Pagan or the Bulldogs' Terry Wallace. Roos' cause was helped enormously when the Swans defeated Carlton, went down narrowly to Adelaide and then notched consecutive wins, over the Kangaroos, St Kilda and Melbourne. By the time the Swans went into their final round match against Richmond at Stadium Australia, there seemed a clear-cut choice — Roos or Wallace. The intrigue surrounding Wallace increased enormously after he resigned as the Bulldogs' coach and many observers jumped to the conclusion that he would get the Swans' job.

Roos and his Swans therefore went into the match against Richmond in a swirl of controversy and innuendo. No one knew who would be coaching the Swans in 2003, but Swan fans and even the players made their feelings known. Many fans waved pro-Roos banners before, during and after the game, while the players ran their hearts out not knowing whether it would be the popular Roos' last game as coach. The Swans defeated the Tigers by 40 points to give Roos a 6-4 record as stand-in coach. Players mobbed him after the match and, with fans sending a message to the board, there now was little doubt Roos would be given a permanent appointment. He took charge in his own right for the following season and, of course, he guided the Swans to the 2005 premiership. The board, the players and the fans got it right.

The final round match against the Tigers also was Kelly's last match. He had played 234 games for the Swans from 1990 and always will be remembered as a club legend. "Captain Courageous", as he was known, did Bob Skilton's famous number 14 proud yet, remarkably, had to be talked into pursuing an AFL career. He once said of his early days: "I was just cruising along doing my plumbing. I thought if I went up to Sydney I'd be there for 12 months, play a few games and they'd send me back and I'd come home with nothing."

Kelly wrote in his autobiography *SwanSong* of his last match: "I finished the way I wanted to finish, still playing at a standard that I wanted to play at … that night was amazing. My head was spinning from the time the siren went until I went down to the dressing-room. I was battling to keep my emotions in check. I just wanted to enjoy it … to go out like that — at home — was ideal. We had won the game and everyone was feeling good; we'd had a great finish for the season and the club was starting to head in the right direction." Kelly was as effective as ever in his final game, winning 16 possessions.

Paul Roos took over as coach in 2002.

The Swans finished the 2002 season in eleventh position, with nine wins, a draw and 12 defeats. It was their lowest position since finishing twelfth in 1995 but, to the end of the 2008 season, it also was the last time they missed the finals and Roos went on to become the club's longest serving coach. Paul Williams won his second consecutive club best and fairest award and polled 16 votes in the Brownlow Medal, won by the Brisbane Lions' Simon Black (25 votes).

2003

With Paul Roos named the Sydney Swans' coach after his 10 games as stand-in coach in 2002, there was promise of a bright new dawn for the red and white. Former St Kilda key forward Barry Hall had settled in well the previous season, but the Swans had to find a replacement for 10-year club captain Paul Kelly. Fortunately, the Swans had a ready-made replacement in midfielder Stuart Maxfield, who had joined the Swans in 1996 after playing 89 games with Richmond from 1990-95. Maxfield led by example, not only in games but also at training and as a role model for younger players. He played a pivotal role in the development of the "Bloods" work ethic and was integral to the club's eventual premiership success.

Apart from Kelly, reliable defender Andrew Dunkley also retired, while Wayne Schwass and Tony Lockett had announced their retirements during the previous season. With the loss of so many senior players, the 2002 trade period therefore had been enormously important to the Swans. They used their selections well. The Swans nominated local youngster Jarrad McVeigh at number five and the Eastern Ranges' Nick Malceski at number 64. Both became important players for the Swans, with McVeigh winning the 2008 best and fairest and Malceski developing into a fine running defender.

The Swans also picked up Gippsland Power defender Sean Dempster under the father-son rule (father Graham had played 64

A first Brownlow Medal triumph for Adam Goodes.

MATCH RESULTS

Round 1, at Stadium Australia, March 29
Sydney Swans 22.14 (146) d Carlton 10.12 (72)
Round 2, at Subiaco, April 5
Fremantle 12.14 (86) d Sydney Swans 8.12 (60)
Round 3, at SCG, April 13
Adelaide 15.13 (103) d Sydney Swans 11.10 (76)
Round 4, at MCG, April 19
Hawthorn 17.8 (110) d Sydney Swans 10.8 (68)
Round 5, at SCG, April 25
Sydney Swans 17.7 (109) d Melbourne 13.7 (85)
Round 6, at Docklands, May 3
Sydney Swans 17.7 (109) d Collingwood 13.11 (89)
Round 7, at SCG, May 11
Sydney Swans 15.8 (98) d Brisbane Lions 11.13 (79)
Round 8, at SCG, May 18
Sydney Swans 17.10 (112) d Geelong 11.7 (73)
Round 9, at Manuka Oval, May 25
Kangaroos 12.12 (84) d Sydney Swans 8.11 (59)
Round 10, at MCG, May 31
Sydney Swans 16.8 (104) d Richmond 10.12 (72)
Round 11, at Stadium Australia, June 7
Sydney Swans 21.7 (133) d Essendon 12.7 (79)
Round 12, at SCG, June 14
Sydney Swans 19.13 (127) d Western Bull. 9.9 (63)
Round 13, at Football Park, June 28
Port Adelaide 14.15 (99) d Sydney Swans 8.12 (60)
Round 14, at SCG, July 6
Sydney Swans 13.14 (92) d West Coast 12.12 (84)
Round 15, at SCG, July 12
Sydney Swans 15.22 (112) d St Kilda 9.7 (61)
Round 16, at Princes Park, July 19
Sydney Swans 18.7 (115) d Carlton 12.12 (84)
Round 17, at SCG, July 27
Sydney Swans 17.9 (111) d Fremantle 14.13 (97)
Round 18, at Football Park, August 3
Adelaide 14.13 (97) d Sydney Swans 14.9 (93)
Round 19, at SCG, August 9
Hawthorn 17.8 (110) d Sydney Swans 14.9 (93)
Round 20, at the Gabba, August 17
Sydney Swans 14.6 (90) d Brisbane Lions 10.16 (76)
Round 21, at Stadium Australia, August 23
Collingwood 14.15 (99) d Sydney Swans 12.9 (81)
Round 22, at MCG, August 30
Sydney Swans 14.10 (94) d Melbourne 9.6 (60)
Qualifying final, Football Park, September 7
Sydney Swans 15.10 (100) d Port Adel. 13.10 (88)
Preliminary final, Stadium Australia, September 20
Brisbane Lions 14.16 (100) d Sydney Swans 8.8 (56)

games with the club from 1972-79) and traded with Collingwood to sign elusive half-forward Nick Davis, whose father Craig had played for Carlton, Collingwood, North Melbourne and the Swans. Davis also played a pivotal role in the Swans' climb to success and always will be remembered for his breathtaking final quarter in the 2005 SCG semi-final against Geelong.

The Swans also landed one of the bargains of the decade in nominating former Brisbane Lion defender Craig Bolton as the overall number three selection at the 2003 pre-season draft. Bolton quickly established himself as one of the most reliable players in the competition and not only played in the Swans' 2005 premiership side, but became a joint club captain. Four players made their VFL debuts in 2003, with mixed success. James Meiklejohn and Mark Powell had limited careers with the Swans, but Adam Schneider and Lewis Roberts-Thomson both played in the 2005 premiership side.

In what was to become a trademark under Roos' coaching, the Swans treated the pre-season competition (the Wizard Cup in 2003) more as preparation for the 2003 premiership season than a determination to land a trophy and the Swans went down to the Brisbane Lions by 32 points in the opening round at Stadium Australia. However, the Swans were well primed for their opening round match against Carlton there. The Swans opened their campaign in style, thrashing the Blues by 74 points, with Barry Hall kicking four goals and Adam Goodes racking up 28 possessions.

However, the Swans' early promise was cancelled by consecutive defeats by Fremantle, Adelaide and Hawthorn to leave them twelfth on the ladder. The Swans knew they had to turn their form around and did it in historic circumstances. In the first Anzac Day match played in Sydney, they defeated Melbourne by 24 points at the SCG. Daryn Cresswell was the Swans' best player with 26 possessions, with the consistent Jude Bolton picking up 24. The Swans debuted Schneider, who played with plenty of poise to kick three goals.

From there, the Swans went on a rollicking roll towards the top of the ladder. They defeated Collingwood, the Brisbane Lions and Geelong in consecutive matches to signal their finals ambitions and, after a loss to the Kangaroos, defeated Richmond, Essendon and the Western Bulldogs to sit fourth on the ladder at the completion of 12 rounds. The longer the season ran the more likely it seemed the Swans would make the finals, only for a report in round 16 to set the club back on its heels.

Although the Swans defeated Carlton by 31 points at Princes Park to climb into second position (behind Port Adelaide), Hall was reported for allegedly head-butting the Blues' Simon Beaumont. However, Hall was found not guilty and the Swans were able to concentrate on their run to the finals. They won just two of their next five games, but had to defeat Melbourne at the MCG to have any chance of finishing in the top four. It should have been a romp as the Demons had won just five games. However, they made the Swans fight all the way for a 34-point win after leading at half-time and trailing by just four points at the final change. Top side Port Adelaide did the Swans a favour in defeating Adelaide in their Showdown clash to push the Crows to sixth position and lift the Swans to fourth, behind Port, Collingwood and the Brisbane Lions.

This meant the Swans played Port Adelaide at Football Park in a qualifying final in the first week of the finals. The Swans were rank outsiders and classy forward Michael O'Loughlin had torn a hamstring in the final minutes against Melbourne and ruckman Jason Ball was missing because of a shoulder injury, with Jason Saddington and Ryan O'Keefe also absent because of injury. This meant the Swans were severely undermanned against a side notoriously difficult to topple on its home turf.

Roos did his homework well and instructed his team to restrict the Power's run. He noted that the Port midfield liked to run free through the middle and he told his players to lock down on their run. The Swans surprised the Power with their tackling and aggression to lead by eight points at the first break. Although Swan fans feared their side would run out of legs, the red and white produced a brilliant second quarter to race to a 40-point lead. Port was in shock and although they managed to reduce the margin to 24 points by the final break, the Swans only needed to hold firm over the final quarter. It was easier said than done as the Swans copped further injuries, to Tadhg Kennelly, Stephen Doyle and Brad Seymour, and were left with just 19 fit players.

The last quarter was a thriller, with the Swans holding firm against everything that the Power could throw at them. The ball seemed to be in the Swans' defensive zone for most of the quarter, but the visitors held firm to win by 12 points. It was one of the club's greatest wins since it shifted to Sydney in 1982 and midfielder Daryn Cresswell said after the game: "It was a victory for The Bloods today. We really dug deep, like the old South

Craig Bolton was an inspired pre-season draft selection.

Melbourne days." Cresswell was referring to the players' adoption of the club's old nickname of the Bloods to signify they would bleed for the cause. A legend was born.

The injury-hammered Swans needed the week's break before hosting the Brisbane Lions in a preliminary final under lights at Telstra Stadium. The Lions were the reigning premiers and vastly experienced finals campaigners, so the Swans knew their task would be tough. And that's the way it panned out, especially after the Lions kicked two goals from dubious free kicks very early in the match. Before 71,019 fans, the Swans trailed by 15 points at the main break, before rallying superbly to go into the final quarter trailing by just three points. However, injuries eventually took their toll and the Lions produced a six goals to one behind final quarter to win by 44

The Swans' Team of the Century

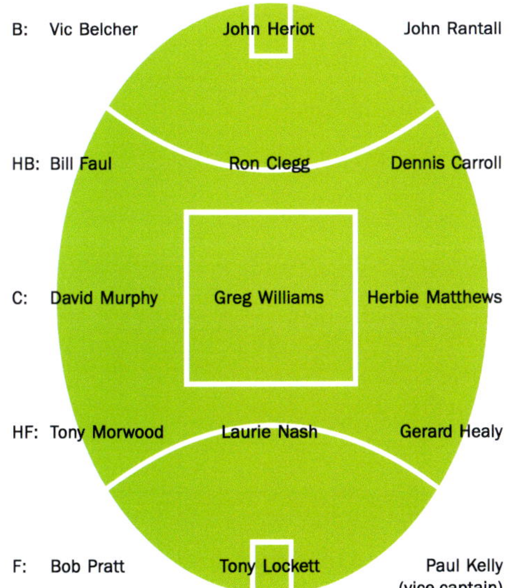

FOLL.: Barry Round, Peter Bedford, Bob Skilton (captain)
INTER: Billy Williams, Stevie Wright, Daryn Cresswell, Fred Goldsmith, Mark Bayes, Harry Clarke, Mark Tandy.
COACH: Jack Bisset

points before going on to defeat Collingwood by 50 points in the Grand Final.

It had been a magnificent season for the Swans, with one last highlight. The brilliant Goodes tied with Collingwood's Nathan Buckley and Adelaide's Mark Ricciuto to win a Brownlow Medal, each with 22 votes. Goodes said after his triumph that coach Roos deserved a lot of credit for turning the star's form around. Goodes, who took his mother Lisa May to the count, said: "He just told me to go out and play like I did at school." He also praised his mother in saying: "Being able to share this moment with her is sensational. She's been there in the other great moments in my life ... she's always been there for me, which is great." Goodes also was named in the All-Australian team, along with fellow Swan Paul Williams.

* * *

The Swans in 2003 named their Team of the Century at a glittering function in Sydney.

PLAYER	GAMES	GOALS
ABLETT, Luke	4	1
BALL, Jason	17	7
BARRY, Leo	24	0
BOLTON, Craig	24	0
BOLTON, Jude	24	13
CRESSWELL, Daryn	19	21
CROUCH, Jared	24	6
DAVIS, Nick	24	32
DOYLE, Stephen	4	2
FOSDIKE, Nic	24	9
GOODES, Adam	24	20
HALL, Barry	24	64
JAMES, Heath	2	0
KENNELLY, Tadhg	24	8
KIRK, Brett	24	9
MATHEWS, Ben	23	4
MAXFIELD, Stuart	22	10
McPHERSON, Daniel	3	1
MEIKLEJOHN, James	5	0
NICKS, Matthew	18	16
O'KEEFE, Ryan	16	17
O'LOUGHLIN, Michael	16	41
POWELL, Mark	5	0
ROBERTS-THOMSON, Lewis	16	5
SADDINGTON, Jason	14	0
SCHAUBLE, Andrew	23	1
SCHNEIDER, Adam	24	30
SEYMOUR, Brad	2	0
STEVENS, Scott	11	5
SUNDQVIST, Jarrad	8	1
WARFE, Rowan	13	0
WILLIAMS, Paul	23	20

POSITION: Third
COACH: Paul Roos
CAPTAIN: Stuart Maxfield
BEST AND FAIREST: Adam Goodes
LEADING GOALKICKER: Barry Hall (64)

Guests dined on Szechuan roasted marron tail, linguini, Angus beef tenderloin, lemon sorbet and dried fruits as they paid tribute to more than 70 nominees. Positions in the team were named from the backline, to rapturous applause.

2004

After such an exciting 2003 season, expectations for the Sydney Swans were high the following year. Paul Roos by now had established a reputation for himself as one of the best coaches in the AFL and his team was noted for its full-blooded commitment. They had won many admirers for their courageous qualifying final win against Port Adelaide in 2003 and, with Stuart Maxfield again captain, the Swans were among the premiership favourites for the new season as they had a developing list with plenty of class and depth.

The Swans, however, went into the 2004 season without midfielder Daryn Cresswell, who announced his retirement immediately after the preliminary final defeat by the Brisbane Lions. Cresswell had played 244 games for the Swans from 1992 after being recruited from North Hobart. Originally drafted by Geelong, he did not play a senior game for the Cats before returning to Tasmania and their loss was Sydney's gain as he was a wonderfully competitive footballer who did his best work at the bottom of packs. He won the club best and fairest in 1994 and was runner-up each season from 1997-99. All-Australian in 1997, he was named in the Swans' team of the Century. Reliable defender Daniel McPherson also retired after 111 games from 1994, while they traded Scott Stevens to Adelaide.

The Swans, at the national draft after the completion of the 2003 season, nominated Amon Buchanan at number 45 after he earlier had been delisted. Buchanan, who originally had been drafted in 2000 and had made his AFL debut in 2002, had been training with Carlton before the Swans gave him another chance. It proved a wise decision as Buchanan kicked the winning goal in the 2005 Grand Final against West Coast as an integral part of the midfield. With no trading for the first time since 1993, the Swans therefore went into the 2004 season with a settled squad. Just two players, local products Paul Bevan (Western Suburbs) and Jarrad McVeigh (Pennant Hills) made their debuts in 2004.

Again, the Swans treated the pre-season competition (Wizard Cup) largely as trials for younger players and went down to Carlton by a massive 102 points in a first-round clash at Telstra Stadium. The Swans used only a handful of senior players and newcomers and rookies included Daniel Hunt, Nick Potter, Aaron Rogers and Josh Willoughby. The Swans, however, felt they were well prepared for the opening of the premiership season, against the Brisbane Lions at the Gabba.

The Brisbane Lions might have been the reigning premiers, but the Swans wanted to make amends for the loss to the Lions in a preliminary final the previous season. The Swans took it up to the Lions from the first bounce and led by 17 points at half-time, only to go down by just two points. Paul Williams and Adam Goodes were brilliant for the Swans, while Nick Davis kicked four goals before being injured. It was an encouraging start to the season and, the following week, defeated Fremantle by 31 points at the SCG. Barry Hall kicked five goals and was awarded three Brownlow Medal votes for a best on ground effort.

With wins over Geelong (six points at the SCG) and the Kangaroos (51 points at the Manuka Oval, Canberra), the Swans were third on the ladder (behind St Kilda and Port Adelaide) at the completion of four rounds. Inexplicably, however, the Swans fell in a hole and went down to Essendon, Richmond and West Coast in consecutive matches to slide to seventh position and inside the top eight only on percentage from the ninth-placed Kangaroos. Although the Swans managed to hold off a fast-finishing Hawthorn to win by a point at the SCG in round nine, it was a lack-lustre effort against the bottom side.

The Swans might have been able to hold their place in the top eight in defeating Hawthorn and might have defeated the Western Bulldogs the following week, but faced a much greater challenge against the undefeated St Kilda at the SCG in round 11. The Saints had had their best start to a season but coach Grant Thomas gave his side a break during the week and, instead of training, the Saints went to see a movie. The Swans treated this as an insult and, fired up for a big challenge, defeated St Kilda by 36 points. The Swans' stars were defender Leo Barry and key forward Hall (five goals).

MATCH RESULTS

Round 1, at the Gabba, March 27
Brisb. Lions 11.14 (80) d Sydney Swans 11.12 (78)
Round 2, at SCG, April 4
Sydney Swans 15.12 (102) d Fremantle 10.11 (71)
Round 3, at SCG, April 10
Sydney Swans 10.13 (73) d Geelong 10.7 (67)
Round 4, at Manuka Oval, April 18
Sydney Swans 18.13 (121) d Kangaroos 10.10 (70)
Round 5, at Stadium Australia, April 24
Melbourne 17.9 (111) d Sydney Swans 15.9 (99)
Round 6, at MCG, May 1
Essendon 16.12 (108) d Sydney Swans 15.8 (98)
Round 7, at SCG, May 9
Richmond 10.7 (67) d Sydney Swans 8.6 (54)
Round 8, at Subiaco, May 15
West Coast 18.16 (124) d Sydney Swans 15.7 (97)
Round 9, at SCG, May 23
Sydney Swans 11.14 (80) d Hawthorn 12.7 (79)
Round 10, at SCG, May 29
Sydney Swans 12.21 (93) d Western Bull. 10.7 (67)
Round 11, at SCG, June 6
Sydney Swans 17.10 (112) d St Kilda 11.10 (76)
Round 12, at Football Park, June 13
Port Adelaide 20.12 (132) d Sydney Swans 8.12 (60)
Round 13, at Stadium Australia, June 26
Sydney Swans 13.7 (85) d Collingwood 11.13 (79)
Round 14, at Princes Park, July 3
Sydney Swans 15.5 (95) d Carlton 12.12 (84)
Round 15, at SCG, July 10
Sydney Swans 8.10 (58) d Adelaide 6.9 (45)
Round 16, at Kardinia Park, July 18
Geelong 11.11 (77) d Sydney Swans 9.8 (62)
Round 17, at Subiaco, July 24
Fremantle 18.10 (118) d Sydney Swans 14.7 (91)
Round 18, at SCG, July 31
Sydney Swans 12.11 (83) d Brisbane Lions 7.9 (51)
Round 19, at SCG, August 7
Kangaroos 17.16 (118) d Sydney Swans 18.4 (112)
Round 20, at Docklands, August 14
Sydney Swans 10.7 (67) d Melbourne 7.4 (46)
Round 21, at Stadium Australia, August 21
Sydney Swans 17.8 (110) d Essendon 12.18 (90)
Round 22, at MCG, August 28
Sydney Swans 16.12 (108) d Richmond 6.8 (44)
Elimination final, Stadium Australia, September 4
Sydney Swans 11.9 (75) d West Coast 4.10 (34)
Semi-final, MCG, September 10
St Kilda 16.11 (107) d Sydney Swans 8.8 (56)

From there the Swans always looked like making the finals, despite a terrible setback against the Kangaroos at the SCG in round 19. The Swans led by 40 points at the final break, but were shocked when they heard that highly popular head trainer Wally Jackson had collaped on the boundary fence and died of a heart attack. The deeply-concerned Swans stopped to a walk as the Kangaroos, in Glenn Archer's 250th game, stormed home. The Roos, thanks largely to a goal from a free kick after Jason Ball was deemed to have gone out of bounds deliberately, won by six points.

This heartbreaking defeat put the Swans in danger of missing the finals as, at the completion of round 19, they were eighth, ahead of ninth-placed Essendon and tenth-placed West Coast only on percentage.The Swans defeated Melbourne by 21 points at Telstra Dome the following week, but Essendon and West Coast also won to maintain the pressure. The Swans and Essendon clashed at Telstra Stadium in a mini-final in round 21, with the Swans putting the Bombers out of finals contention in winning by 20 points after trailing by 13 points at the first break. The Eagles defeated Fremantle but, with just one round to play, the Swans were sixth and a game and percentage ahead of ninth-placed Essendon.

Only a series of upset results could knock the Swans out of the finals, but they made sure of their place in thrashing Richmond by 64 points at the MCG. Essendon managed to climb into the final eight when the previously eighth-placed Fremantle went down to St Kilda and the Swans therefore were scheduled to play the seventh-placed West Coast in an elimination final at Telstra Stadium the following week.

The match started in torrential rain and, despite the Eagles leading by three points at the first change, the Swans produced brilliant wet weather football in the second quarter to score 5.3 to nil. However, lightning flashed around the ground and there were fears the game would have to be abandoned, Finally, however, the storm abated and the Swans slid to a 41-point win in atrocious conditions. The Swans went down by 51 points to early flag favourite St Kilda at the MCG in a semi-final the following Friday night to end their premiership dream for yet another season.

It had been a tough year for the Swans, apart from the sudden death of Jackson. Three players — Jason Saddington, Jarrad Sundqvist and the untried Nick Malceski — had knee reconstructions, while Davis (hip), Adam Schneider (hamstring), Andrew Schauble (hamstring), Lewis Roberts-Thomson (thumb and Achilles tendon) and Michael O'Loughlin (hamstring) missed large chunks of the season. Roberts-Thomson even was injured before a game, damaging an Achilles in the warm-up for the match against Carlton at Princes Park in round 14. As he had been named on the team sheet, he could not be replaced and the Swans therefore went into the match a man short. However, they won by 11 points in their last match at the ground the Blues had called home since 1897.

The big-hearted Brett Kirk was equal fourth (with the Bulldogs' Scott West) in the 2004 Brownlow Medal count with West Coast's Chris Judd the winner with 30 votes, well ahead of Adelaide's Mark Ricciuto (23) and Port Adelaide's Chad Cornes (22). However, Hall won the Swans' best and fairest and topped the club goalkicking with 74. Three Swans — Hall, Kirk and Barry — were named in the 2004 All-Australian side.

Ruckman Jason Ball, a former Eagle, leads West Coast's Chris Judd in the race for the ball.

PLAYER	GAMES	GOALS
ABLETT, Luke	21	2
BALL, Jason	23	3
BARRY, Leo	23	0
BEVAN, Paul	24	7
BOLTON, Craig	24	6
BOLTON, Jude	24	12
BUCHANAN, Amon	16	6
CROUCH, Jared	24	8
DAVIS, Nick	12	21
DOYLE, Stephen	19	5
FIXTER, Ben	3	1
FOSDIKE, Nic	13	3
GOODES, Adam	24	9
HALL, Barry	24	74
JAMES, Heath	11	1
KENNELLY, Tadhg	23	7
KIRK, Brett	24	10
MATHEWS, Ben	24	6
MAXFIELD, Stuart	24	8
McVEIGH, Jarrad	20	6
MEIKLEJOHN, James	1	0
NICKS, Matthew	17	14
O'KEEFE, Ryan	24	33
O'LOUGHLIN, Michael	18	38
POWELL, Mark	3	0
ROBERTS-THOMSON, Lewis	7	0
ROGERS, Aaron	2	0
SADDINGTON, Jason	10	7
SCHAUBLE, Andrew	10	1
SCHNEIDER, Adam	12	9
THEWLIS, Josh	2	0
WARFE, Rowan	1	0
WILLIAMS, Paul	21	9

POSITION: Fifth
COACH: Paul Roos
CAPTAIN: Stuart Maxfield
BEST AND FAIREST: Barry Hall
LEADING GOALKICKER: Barry Hall (74)

2005

The Sydney Swans started the 2005 season with high hopes after going down to St Kilda in a semi-final the previous season. The Swans started the season with Stuart Maxfield as captain and Paul Roos as coach, but Maxfield retired during the season and the captaincy then was shared by the player leadership group. The only player to retire at the end of the 2004 season was defender Rowan Warfe, although several players were delisted. The most significant newcomer was ruckman Darren Jolly, who joined the Swans from Melbourne in an enormously beneficial trade deal, handing the Demons number 15 draft choice at the 2004 national draft in return. The Swans, after having a 3-4 win-loss ratio after seven rounds eventually achieved their long-awaited premiership dream and here, round by round, is their progress to the club's greatest day in 72 years.

ROUND 1

Sunday, March 27

The Swans opened the season against Hawthorn, which had finished above only Richmond in 2004. The Swans therefore were raging favourites to defeat the Hawks in this Sunday afternoon clash in warm conditions at the SCG, and that's the way it turned out. The Swans, with Darren Jolly dominant in the ruck, defeated the Hawks by 63 points. Nick Davis kicked four goals and Paul Williams polled three Brownlow Medal votes. The Swans eased up over the final 10 minutes, happy to chip the ball around in cruising to victory. The big win put the Swans on top of the ladder with a percentage of 214.55.

Sydney Swans	4.1	9.4	12.8	18.10	(118)
Hawthorn	2.1	3.4	4.5	8.7	(55)

GOALS: N. Davis 4, Jolly 3, Hall 3, Doyle, Schneider, O'Keefe, C. Bolton, J. Bolton, Bevan, Williams, McVeigh.
BEST: Jolly, Williams, Mathews.
CROWD: 27,274, at SCG.

ROUND 2

Saturday, April 2

The Swans were brought back to earth in going down to the Kangaroos by 23 points at the Manuka Oval, Canberra. The Swans' kicking for goal, especially over the first half was atrocious and the Roos made the most of their opportunities. Former Swan Shannon Grant kicked three goals for the Roos, while the Swans had no multiple goalkickers. Luke Ablett was the Swans' best player and polled two Brownlow Medal votes. The defeat pushed the Swans down to fifth position, inside the top eight on percentage, with only Collingwood, Essendon and Hawthorn yet to win in 2005.

Kangaroos	2.5	4.8	7.9	12.10	(82)
Sydney Swans	2.5	4.11	7.14	7.17	(59)

GOALS: Buchanan, Jolly, Bevan, Hall, Crouch, N. Davis, Kirk.
BEST: Ablett, Buchanan, Hall.
CROWD: 13,481, at Manuka Oval, Canberra.

ROUND 3

Saturday, April 9

Although the Swans looked to be in a hopeless position against the Brisbane Lions at the Gabba, the red and white stormed home to win by six points. The winning goal was kicked by Barry Hall with a shot after the siren. The Lions had controlled most of the first three quarters but, after leading by 18 points at half-time and by 32 points at the final break, the Swans were irrepressible over the final 30 minutes and attacked in waves to score seven goals to one. The Swans' best was Jude Bolton

History awaits the Swans as they take the field for the 2005 Grand Final.

(two Brownlow Medal votes), while Hall kicked five goals. The win failed to improve the Swans' position on the ladder as they remained in fifth place, but now a game clear of the ninth-placed Western Bulldogs.

Sydney Swans	1.3	2.4	6.6	13.9	(87)
Brisbane Lions	1.5	4.10	10.14	11.15	(81)

GOALS: Hall 5, Goodes 2, O'Keefe, Ablett, Bevan, J. Bolton, Williams, Buchanan.
BEST: Hall, J.Bolton, Ablett.
CROWD: 33,960, at the Gabba.

ROUND 4

Sunday, April 17

It was back to the SCG for the Swans' round four clash, with modern nemesis club Adelaide. The Swans had defeated the Crows at the SCG in 2004, but always seemed to have trouble containing physically strong Adelaide sides. Although the Swans led by a goal at half-time, the Crows kicked eight final quarter goals to win by 41 points in Tyson Edwards' 200th AFL game. Ryan O'Keefe,

Swan forward Michael O'Loughlin at full stretch for a mark in the Grand Final.

Barry Hall, Michael O'Loughlin and Adam Goodes kicked two goals each for the Swans, with Luke Ablett named the club's best player. The defeat pushed the Swans down to eighth position, half a game clear of ninth-placed Carlton, which drew its round four game with Port Adelaide.

Adelaide	4.3	6.5	10.11	18.12	(120)
Sydney Swans	4.2	7.5	9.8	11.13	(79)

GOALS: O'Keefe 2, Hall 2, O'Loughlin 2, Goodes 2, Ablett, Mathews, Maxfield.
BEST: Ablett, J. Bolton, Kirk.
CROWD: 30,478, at AAMI Stadium.

ROUND 5

Saturday, April 23

In an SCG match paying tribute to Anzac heroes, Melbourne led from start to finish to defeat the Swans by 34 points. The Swans had trouble breaching the Demon defence and Melbourne's Brad Miller was able to shut the Swans' Barry Hall out of the game. Melbourne also controlled the midfield and the Swans' only multiple goalkickers were Hall and Ryan O'Keefe, who kicked two goals each. The media named Jude Bolton and Brett Kirk as the Swans' best players. For the first time in 2005, the Swans were out of the top eight, in tenth position, behind the eighth-placed Western Bulldogs on percentage.

Melbourne	4.5	6.6	10.10	14.10	(94)
Sydney Swans	2.3	3.10	6.12	7.18	(60)

GOALS: O'Keefe 2, Hall 2, Schneider, N. Davis, O'Loughlin.
BEST: J. Bolton, Kirk, Goodes.
CROWD: 29,099, at SCG.

ROUND 6

Saturday, April 30

No one would have guessed it at the time, but the Swans' round six match against West Coast at Subiaco was a prelude to the Grand Final. The Swans might have controlled play in the opening quarter, but kicked poorly for goal to lead by just four points at quarter-time. The Eagles took charge from there to defeat the Swans by 45 points. The Swans, with Barry Hall kicking three of their eight goals, slipped to twelfth position on the ladder. Just five days after this defeat, the Swans were rocked by Stuart Maxfield's resignation as captain for personal reasons. The Swans now were a game and percentage out of the top eight.

West Coast	1.2	7.5	12.10	15.14	(104)
Sydney Swans	1.6	4.6	6.9	8.11	(59)

GOALS: Hall 3, N. Davis 2, Crouch, Kirk, Goodes.
BEST: Kirk, Crouch, Barry
CROWD: 39,687, at Subiaco.

ROUND 7

Saturday, May 7

Just two days before the Swans played Essendon at Telstra Stadium, the club announced that Brett Kirk would lead the Swans against the Bombers. The Swans controlled most of the play over the first half, but Essendon's phenomenal accuracy in front of goal gave it an 11-point half-time lead. The Swans fell further behind to trail by 16 points at the final break, but then produced a stunning final quarter to win by six points. Kirk led the Swans superbly as acting captain, while Luke Ablett picked up two Brownlow Medal votes. Barry Hall kicked four goals for the Swans and Michael O'Loughlin three. The win lifted the Swans to tenth position.

Sydney Swans	3.5	7.8	9.11	13.16	(94)
Essendon	4.0	10.1	13.3	14.4	(88)

GOALS: Hall 4, O'Loughlin 3, O'Keefe 2, Buchanan, Moore, Goodes, Vogels.
BEST: Kirk, Goodes, Hall.
CROWD: 31,668, at Telstra Stadium.

ROUND 8

Sunday, May 15

In the week leading up to the Swans' round eight game against Port Adelaide at the SCG, the club announced that Brett Kirk, Leo Barry, Jude Bolton, Adam Goodes, Barry Hall and Ben Mathews would rotate the captaincy over the rest of the season. The Swans defeated the Power by 24 points in a dour, defensive game, with Michael O'Loughlin kicking three goals for the Swans. However, it was not enough to push the Swans into the top eight as they were still tenth, but behind eighth-placed Adelaide only on percentage.

Sydney Swans	2.4	3.8	6.12	9.15	(69)
Port Adelaide	1.2	2.6	4.8	6.9	(45)

GOALS: O'Loughlin 3, Hall 2, Goodes 2, Ablett, Vogels.
BEST: Barry, J. Bolton, Kennelly.
CROWD: 24,226, at SCG.

ROUND 9

Saturday, May 21

The Swans jumped back into the top eight (to sixth position) in defeating the Western Bulldogs by 13 points at the SCG in round nine. The Swans started slowly but controlled most of the play over the final three quarters. Michael O'Loughlin kicked five goals and first-year player Luke Vogels impressed with three goals. O'Loughlin's effort earned him three Brownlow Medal votes, while Jude Bolton polled two and Brett Kirk one. The AFL billed the round as Community Weekend and the most significant event was the last game at Princes Park, in which Melbourne defeated Carlton.

Sydney Swans	1.4	5.7	11.9	13.11	(89)
Western Bulldogs	4.3	5.7	7.12	10.16	(76)

GOALS: O'Loughlin 5, Vogels 3, Hall 2, O'Keefe, Crouch, Goodes.
BEST: O'Loughlin, Hall, Kirk.
CROWD: 22,358, at SCG.

ROUND 10

Saturday, May 28

The Swans' spluttering season suffered yet another setback in round 10 when the red and white went down to St Kilda by 43 points at Telstra Dome. The Swans were never a chance and only the good play of Adam Goodes and Barry Hall (three goals) made the margin respectable. The Swans had difficulty containing Saint full-forward Fraser Gehrig, who kicked seven goals., The defeat pushed the Swans down to ninth position, behind eighth-placed Fremantle on percentage.

St Kilda	4.1	5.5	9.8	15.11	(101)
Sydney Swans	1.0	3.1	6.6	8.10	(58)

GOALS: Hall 3, O'Loughlin 2, O'Keefe, Crouch, Nicks.
BEST: Hall, Goodes, Ablett.
CROWD: 37,014, at Telstra Dome.

ROUND 11

Saturday, June 4

Although round 11 opponent Carlton was on the bottom of the ladder with just two wins and a draw, the Swans found the Blues difficult opponents at Telstra Dome. The Blues several times looked capable of taking the match points before the Swans kicked six final quarter goals to win by 25 points. Barry Hall kicked five goals and Michael O'Loughlin four, while Jude Bolton polled three Brownlow Medal votes. The win lifted the Swans to sixth position and a game inside the top eight.

Sydney Swans	6.1	8.4	12.6	18.8	(116)
Carlton	2.1	5.3	11.7	14.7	(91)

GOALS: Hall 5, O'Loughlin 4, O'Keefe 2, Ablett 2, Buchanan, N. Davis, Goodes, Jolly, Malceski.
BEST: Hall, J. Bolton, Ablett.
CROWD: 30,973, at Telstra Dome.

ROUND 12

Sunday, June 12

The Swans were never in trouble in the round 12 match against Fremantle at the SCG and cruised home by 38 points. Barry Hall continued his good run with four goals, along with Michael O'Loughlin. The Swans collected all Brownlow Medal votes, Amon Buchanan three, Tadhg Kennelly two and Paul Williams one. The Swans again were rated a potential top four side as the win cemented their place in the top eight. They were sixth, but behind fourth-placed Adelaide only on percentage and a game and a half inside the top eight.

Sydney Swans	5.3	8.4	14.9	16.13	(109)
Fremantle	3.2	5.8	8.10	10.11	(71)

GOALS: Hall 4, O'Loughlin 4, McVeigh 2, N. Davis 2, Buchanan, Mathews, Saddington, Goodes.
BEST: Williams, Buchanan, Barry.
CROWD: 24,922, at SCG.

ROUND 13

Saturday, June 25

The Swans were fortunate in defeating Collingwood by a point in the round 13 game at Telstra Stadium as the Magpies stormed home after trailing by 17 points at the final break. It was the Swans' sixth win in seven games since Stuart Maxfield stepped down as captain and reconfirmed the club as a flag contender. The Swans now were fifth on the ladder and had the hard-working Brett Kirk to thank for their narrow escape against Collingwood as he was one of the best players on the ground. Barry Hall kicked three goals.

Sydney Swans	2.3	5.6	9.10	11.11	(77)
Collingwood	3.5	4.7	6.11	10.16	(76)

GOALS: Hall 3, O'Loughlin 2, Goodes 2, N. Davis 2, O'Keefe, Mathews.
BEST: Kirk, Williams, Barry.
CROWD: 44,387, at Telstra Stadium.

ROUND 14

Saturday, July 2

The round 14 game against Richmond looked as if it would be disastrous for the Swans as Barry Hall injured a groin and an ankle early in the match. He managed to return to the ground, but could not twist and did not score a goal. The Swans seemed shell-shocked seeing Hall in so much trouble and trailed by 33 points at the final break. The Swans produced some of their best form of the season over the final quarter, but failed by just one point. With Hall injured, the Swans shared their 12 goals between eight players, with Michael O'Loughlin and Nic Fosdike each kicking three.

Richmond	2.4	8.8	12.12	12.13	(85)
Sydney Swans	2.3	3.6	7.9	12.12	(84)

GOALS: O'Loughlin 3, Fosdike 3, Buchanan, McVeigh, Williams, Goodes, N. Davis, Crouch.
BEST: O'Keefe, Fosdike, Crouch.
CROWD: 34,572, at MCG.

ROUND 15

Saturday, July 9

The Swans rebounded from the narrow loss to Richmond in thrashing Geelong by 54 points at the SCG in round 15. Barry Hall proved his fitness to take his place in the line-up and kicked five goals. As the Cats were regarded as one of the flag favourites, the big win boosted the Swans' rating as a premiership danger. The win also pushed the Swans one rung higher on the ladder, to fifth. The Swans' stars against the Cats were Hall, Ryan O'Keefe and Adam Goodes. Although fifth, the Swans had cut the third-placed Cats' advantage to percentage only, with Melbourne fourth on the same number of match points.

Sydney Swans	1.1	10.3	13.6	16.9	(105)
Geelong	1.4	3.5	6.7	7.9	(51)

GOALS: Hall 5, O'Keefe 3, N. Davis 2, Kirk 2, Ablett, O'Loughlin, Crouch, Goodes.
BEST: Hall, O'Keefe, Goodes.
CROWD: 28,185, at SCG.

ROUND 16

Saturday, July 15

The Swans' round 16 match against Melbourne at Telstra Dome was one of their most important games of the season. They were fortunate the game was played at Telstra Dome as Demon fans did not appreciate travelling from their MCG home and there were more Swan than Demon fans at Docklands for the big clash. Although Melbourne pressed hard, the Swans were far too good over the second half and won by 26 points. Barry Hall kicked seven goals and Brett Kirk polled three Brownlow Medal votes. More importantly, the Swans jumped above Melbourne on the ladder to claim fourth position and poised for a genuine crack at the premiership.

Sydney Swans	6.2	8.5	14.5	16.8	(104)
Melbourne	4.3	6.7	8.11	11.12	(78)

GOALS: Hall 7, N. Davis 2, Goodes, O'Keefe, Buchanan, Mathews, O'Loughlin, Jolly, Kirk.
BEST: Hall, Goodes, Kirk.
CROWD: 28,749, at Telstra Dome.

ROUND 17

Sunday, July 24

After pushing Melbourne aside, the Swans faced an even greater challenge in the round 17 match against West Coast at the SCG. The Eagles were on top of the ladder with just one defeat and this game would tell whether the Swans could mount a serious challenge. The lead changed several times before the Swans edged clear over the final quarter to win by 21 points. Tadhg Kennelly polled three Brownlow Medal votes and, finally, the Swans were rated one of the Eagles' dangers for the flag. The Swans, in defeating the Eagles, climbed into third position and inside the top four by four match points.

Sydney Swans	3.2	5.7	9.9	13.10	(88)
West Coast	1.5	6.8	7.11	9.13	(67)

GOALS: O'Loughlin 3, Schneider 2, Jolly 2, Hall 2, J. Bolton, N. Davis, Buchanan, Ablett.
BEST: J. Bolton, Roberts-Thomson, Kennelly.
CROWD: 37,071, at SCG.

ROUND 18

Saturday, July 30

Just as the Swans were feeling good about their 2005 chances, they fell to their old nemesis Adelaide at AAMI Stadium in round 18. The match was a dour, defensive affair and the Swans found it difficult to breach the

Oh the joy of it all! The Swans have won the premiership and Tadhg Kennelly embraces Leo Barry, still holding the ball after THAT mark.

tight Crow defence. Adelaide led by 17 points at the final break, but a magnificent final quarter effort by Adam Goodes almost won the game for the Swans. The Crows won by seven points and the Swans slipped slightly to fourth position. With West Coast, Adelaide and the Swans in the top four, there were Victorian fears there again would be an "all interstate" Grand Final.

Adelaide	1.0	3.2	8.4	8.6	(54)
Sydney Swans	2.1	4.4	5.5	6.11	(47)

GOALS: O'Loughlin 2, Goodes, N. Davis, Mathews, Buchanan.
BEST: Goodes, Kirk, Roberts-Thomson.
CROWD: 45,629, at AAMI Stadium.

ROUND 19

Saturday, August 6

Although the Swans started slowly against a phenomenally accurate Essendon at Telstra Stadium in round 19, the red and white gradually got on top to win by 20 points. The Swans' heroes were Barry Hall (seven goals and three Brownlow Medal votes) and Ryan O'Keefe (three goals and two votes). Other good players included Adam Schneider and Luke Ablett. The Swans, in victory, retained fourth position, but ahead of the fifth-placed Kangaroos only on percentage. With just three rounds to play, the Swans were almost assured of a finals berth as they were two and a half games inside the top eight.

Sydney Swans	3.2	8.3	13.5	18.10	(118)
Essendon	5.0	10.1	13.6	15.8	(98)

GOALS: Hall 7, O'Keefe 3, Goodes 2, Fosdike, O'Loughlin, Vogels, Ball, Buchanan, Ablett.
BEST: Hall, O'Keefe, Schneider.
CROWD: 41,629, at Telstra Dome.

ROUND 20

Sunday, August 14

The Swans produced their best form of the season in thrashing the Brisbane Lions by 84 points at Telstra Stadium in round 20. The huge win ensured the fourth-placed Swans would play in the finals and, more importantly, it put them a game and a wide percentage margin ahead of the fifth-placed Kangaroos with just two rounds to play. Barry Hall kicked six goals for the Swans and Lewis Roberts-Thomson and Craig Bolton were superb in defence. The Swans now needed just one win over the final two rounds to grab a double chance in the finals.

Sydney Swans	6.1	11.5	14.6	19.10	(124)
Brisbane Lions	2.2	3.3	5.3	6.4	(40)

GOALS: Hall 6, O'Loughlin 4, O'Keefe 3, N. Davis, Kennelly, Mathews, Crouch, Buchanan, Jolly.
BEST: Hall. C. Bolton, Roberts-Thomson.
CROWD: 43,512, at Telstra Stadium.

ROUND 21

Sunday, August 21

With the Kangaroos snapping at the fourth-placed Swan heels in the penultimate round, the red and white produced the perfect result to end the challenge. They controlled the round 21 game at the SCG from the start to win by 37 points. The match was as good as over when the Swans led by 48 points at half-time. Nick Davis produced his best game of the season with five goals, while Tadhg Kennelly polled three more Brownlow Medal votes. The win assured the Swans of the double chance in the finals as they climbed to third position and two games clear of the fifth-placed Roos with just the final round to play.

Sydney Swans	7.2	12.3	14.8	15.11	(101)
Kangaroos	1.1	4.3	7.7	9.10	(64)

GOALS: N. Davis 5, Hall 3, O'Keefe 2, O'Loughlin 2, Goodes, Schneider, Fosdike.
BEST: Davis, Kennelly, Barry.
CROWD: 34,975, at SCG.

ROUND 22

Saturday, August 27

The Swans' final round game against Hawthorn at the MCG was little more than a romp. The Swans led by 49 points at half-time and cruised home to win by 54 points. Nick Davis continued his good form with four goals, while Barry Hall polled three Brownlow Medal votes even though he kicked just three goals. More importantly, there were no new injury problems. The Swans finished the premiership season in third position, behind Adelaide and West Coast, and were drawn to play the Eagles in a qualifying final at Subiaco. It looked a tough task on paper, but the Swans were heartened by Adelaide's eight-point defeat of West Coast there in the final round.

Sydney Swans	5.5	12.5	15.7	20.9	(129)
Hawthorn	1.2	4.4	6.9	11.9	(75)

GOALS: N. Davis 4, Hall 3, Goodes 2, O'Keefe 2, Schneider, Fosdike, Kirk, Buchanan, O'Loughlin, Vogels, Ball, Crouch, Ablett.
BEST: Hall, Kirk, O'Keefe.
CROWD: 31,891, at MCG.

QUALIFYING FINAL

Friday, September 2

There could be few more daunting tasks than crossing the nation to play West Coast at Subiaco against a backdrop of ferociously vocal local fans. Yet the Swans coped well against the Eagles in their qualifying final there and could have had the match wrapped up in leading by 14 points at the final break. However, the Eagles used their old ploy of moving Adam Hunter from defence to attack to get them back in the match. The Swans also were shattered by a vital free kick against defender Leo Barry which the AFL umpiring department later ruled was incorrect. To make matters worse, the Swans' Adam Goodes was running towards goal with his side trailing by less than a goal with only a minute or so to play when he was tackled from behind and, apparently, around the calves. No free kick was paid and the Eagles scrambled over the line by four points in a highly-controversial final. The Eagles therefore had a rest the following week while the Swans had to play Geelong in a Friday night semi-final at the SCG. The Swans' best against the Eagles were Brett Kirk, Nick Davis (three goals) and Tadhg Kennelly.

West Coast	4.1	5.4	5.7	10.9	(69)
Sydney Swans	3.1	5.2	8.3	10.5	(65)

GOALS: N. Davis 3, O'Loughlin 3, Hall 2, Schneider, O'Keefe.

BEST: Kirk, N. Davis, Kennelly.

CROWD: 43,3O2, at Subiaco.

SEMI-FINAL

Friday, September 9

The Swans looked flat in their semi-final against Geelong at the SCG and could manage just two goals to half-time. They trailed the Cats by 18 points and did not look like getting back into the match as the Geelong defence was water-tight. The Swans still trailed by 17 points at the final break and, early in the final quarter, the Cats extended their lead. The Swans' 2005 ambitions looked dead as the final siren loomed. However, Nick Davis bobbed up to kick three quick goals for the

Winners are grinners, and Paul Williams (left), Michael O'Loughlin (centre) and Ryan O'Keefe celebrate the Grand Final win.

Tadhg Kennelly's famous Irish jig after being presented with his premiership medallion.

Swans to leave them trailing by three points with just a minute or so to play. Davis then won the game for the Swans when he snapped accurately from just 15 metres after a clever ruck tap from Jason Ball. The Swans led by three points and the final siren blared just seconds after the restart of play. It was one of the most incredible wins in finals history. The Swans, in snatching an unlikely victory, had hit the front for the first time since the six-minute mark of the opening quarter. The Swans' best players, apart from the match-winning Davis, were Jared Crouch, Amon Buchanan and Jude Bolton. Apart from Davis, the Swans' only other multiple goalkicker was Michael O'Loughlin, with two.

Sydney Swans	2.2	2.6	3.12	7.14	(56)
Geelong	2.6	5.6	6.11	7.11	(53)

GOALS: N. Davis 4, O'Loughlin 2, O'Keefe.
BEST: N. Davis, Crouch, Buchanan.
CROWD: 39,079, at SCG.

PRELIMINARY FINAL

Friday, September 16

As St Kilda had defeated Adelaide by eight points in their AAMI Stadium semi-final to march straight into a preliminary final, the Swans and the Saints played off in the Friday night preliminary final, with West Coast scheduled to play Adelaide at Subiaco the following afternoon. The Saints were the overwhelming favourites as they had had a week's break after defeating the Crows, while the Swans looked sluggish in shrugging off the Cats in their semi-final. The Swans, however, took it right up to the Saints in the first quarter, with Barry Hall outstanding. The Swans led by 12 points at the first break, but there was consternation in the Swans' camp throughout much of the match as Hall had punched St Kilda defender Matt Maguire in the stomach.

St Kilda reacted to the Swans' great start by temporarily switching Fraser Gehrig from full-forward to mind Hall. The move had only limited success, but the Saints managed to reduce the Swans' lead to four points by the main break before taking control in the third quarter. It looked as if the Swans were tiring because of their heavy finals schedule and St Kilda fans were congratulating themselves when their side led by seven points at the final break. The Swans, however, had kicked a late goal in the third quarter to give them hope of overhauling St Kilda.

The final quarter saw the Swans overwhelm the Saints with seven goals to just four behinds. The Swans kept sweeping the ball forward and were rewarded with goals from Michael O'Loughlin and Adam Schneider to silence St Kilda fans. The Swans were irrepressible over the final quarter and won by 31 points to enter their first Grand Final since going down to North Melbourne in 1996. It also was the Swans' most realistic chance of winning a flag since its last, in 1933. The Eagles the next day struggled to shake off the Crows by 16 points and the Swans went into Grand Final slight betting favourites but the overwhelming sentimental favourite. Then, when Hall was cleared of a striking charge, the Swans looked good bets to win their first flag for 72 years.

The Swan rooms were strangely subdued after the match, with coach Paul Roos keeping his players behind closed doors. Outside, in the warm-up area, deliriously happy Swan fans tried to convince each other that the long drought was about to break. Former champion

Joy is written on every Swan face as the premiership cup is held high.

Here is it! The Swans had waited 72 years for this moment as coach Paul Roos holds up the 2005 premiership cup.

Swan winger David Murphy jumped onto a bench and started bellowing the club theme song and, after others joined in, there was a message from the players' room: keep a lid on it. Roos wanted his players to go into the Grand Final fully focused. The celebrations were put on hold.

Sydney Swans	5.1	6.3	8.6	15.6	(96)
St Kilda	3.1	5.5	9.7	9.11	(65)

GOALS: Hall 4, Schneider 3, O'Keefe 2, O'Loughlin 2, Williams 2, N. Davis, Buchanan.
BEST: O'Keefe, Hall, Crouch.
CROWD: 73,344, at MCG.

GRAND FINAL

Saturday, September 24

Grand Final week started brilliantly for the Swans through Barry Hall being cleared of a charge of striking St Kilda's Matt Maguire in the preliminary final. The Swans successfully argued that contact was made "in play" and Hall was free to play in the big match. Naturally, newspapers in both Sydney and Melbourne filled page after page with features, predictions and off-beat reports.

Former Collingwood star Mick McGuane, in his column "The Footy Professor" in *Inside Football* predicted: "The free-wheeling West Coast Eagles and the dour, accountable

Sydney Swans should turn on a classic contest. This year's Grand Final will have it all. Class, strength, courage, endurance and unpredictability are qualities both teams have in abundance." McGuane might have been accurate in his assessment that the game would be a classic, but he was wrong with his prediction of which team would win as he plumped for the Eagles. Of the 11 tipsters in *Inside Football,* only four tipped the Swans.

The big match opened at a frantic pace, with West Coast scoring the first goal through Mark Nicoski after just two minutes. The Swans did not score their first goal until ruckman Darren Jolly converted from a free kick six minutes into the match. It already was a tight, dour contest and the Eagles were dealt a savage blow when star midfielder Daniel Kerr was forced off the ground with a leg injury. The Swans' star was Lewis Roberts-Thomson, who kept ramming the ball forward from defence for the Swans to lead by two points at the first break.

The Swans scored the first goal of the second quarter through Michael O'Loughlin to lead by seven points and Swan fans hardly dared dream of victory, even though a Tadhg Kennelly goal stretched the lead. The Swans led by 20 points at half-time and, for about 10 minutes towards the end of the second quarter, looked capable of breaking the Eagles. However, the Eagles fought back in the third quarter and the Swans might have been fortunate to hold a two-point lead going into the final quarter as Eagle Adam Hunter missed an easy shot for goal 20 minutes into the third quarter.

After leading for most of the match, the Swans found themselves behind three minutes into the final quarter after Luke Ablett tried to pass the ball across goal to Leo Barry, only for Ben Cousins to intercept for an Eagle goal. Four minutes later, Hunter kicked another goal and the Swans, after looking comfortable at half-time, trailed by eight points and the premiership dream appeared to have turned to dust.

Although the Swans appeared to be wilting, Hall stepped up to kick a goal from outside the 50-metre arc to give his team hope. However, the Eagles still led by five points 16 minutes into the final quarter and the Swans desperately needed a lift. They got it from a set-play, with Jason Ball tapping the ball to Amon Buchanan who snapped a goal to put the Swans a point in front with about 12 minutes to play. No one knew it at the time, but it was the last goal of the match.

Both teams attacked frantically over the final minutes, with several acts of individual heroism. For example, Swan midfielder Brett Kirk dived headlong into a pack to knock the ball clear and Adam Goodes was knocked to the ground after taking a mark. The Eagles attacked relentlessly as the time-clock ticked past 30 minutes, with Swan fans wondering whether the siren would ever blare. With just 10 seconds left to play, the Eagles mounted one last challenge as Dean Cox pumped the ball forward.

A huge pack formed in the Eagle forward pocket about 25 metres from goal and, just when the Eagles' Mark Seaby appeared likely to take a big pack mark, there was a red and white blur across the front of the pack. It was Leo Barry, who flew to take a spectacular and courageous mark. It was THE mark, the mark that won a premiership. As he was going back for his kick, the siren blared. The Swans had won by four points for their first premiership since 1933.

The sound of the siren opened a floodgate of emotion. Long-time Swan fans broke down and wept openly, unashamedly. The MCG became a sea of red and white as scarves, beanies, caps and jackets were waved in jubilation. The win wiped out 72 years of pain and misery. It was time to celebrate. Appropriately, former club champion Paul Kelly presented the premiership cup to Roos and Hall.

Players, coaches, administrators, sponsors and supporters celebrated the victory at the Crown Palladium, while South Melbourne's Clarendon Street was awash with red and white and the raw emotion of a long-awaited premiership. The Melbourne *Sunday Herald Sun* the next day featured Hall and the premiership cup on its front page, with the headline AT LAST. The caption, in large type read: "Barry Hall holds up the Cup after yesterday's Grand Final win, a victory that ended the Swans' 72-year premiership drought."

The *Sunday Herald Sun's* lift-out sports section had THAT mark on the cover and the large-type caption read: "Leo Barry grabs the ball and the Swans grab the cup." Inside, Jon Ralph wrote under the headline GRAND PROMISE INSPIRES SWANS: "Sydney coach Paul Roos last night revealed the motivation for his players in yesterday's breakthrough win was his iron-clad guarantee they would win if they committed their bodies for the Grand Final against West Coast. Roos said he had never (previously) made such a promise to his players, but felt after the experiences that they had gained in the past two finals series, his team had been perfectly placed to win yesterday's Grand Final."

Newspapers ran features on Barry, who said he "could not believe" he took THAT mark, on Hall, on O'Loughlin — on just about every player. There was a poignant photograph of

Swan legend Bob Skilton embracing O'Loughlin and another of Nick Davis celebrating with an empty beer cardboard carton on his head.

The faithful, thousands and thousands of them, gathered at the Lindsay Hassett Oval (near the Lake Oval), the following morning and *The Age's* Greg Baum wrote under the headline THE MORNING AFTER — A SEA OF RED, AND EYES TO MATCH: "Drinking, blinking, stumbling, mumbling. Red and white T-shirts, red and white eyes. Red and white is the colour of dawn; this one was 72 years in breaking. The heroes of an epic Grand Final were greeted by a crowd estimated by police at 10,000, who gathered at the Lindsay Hassett Oval, home to South Melbourne District, who are also the Swans and also sing the Swans' song. Some old South Melbourne jumpers, some old South Melbourne folk, plenty of old South Melbourne sentiment. 'About bloody time,' read one giant banner."

However, the Swans are a team with two homes, two hearts. As the pre-match Grand Final banner suggested, one team, two towns. There was a parade through the streets of Sydney, with thousands lined up to greet their heroes. *INSIDE FOOTBALL'S* cover read BLOODS – GUTS & GLORY. Underneath, it read: SPIRIT OF SOUTH INSPIRES THE SWANS.

The images of the 2005 Grand Final will live forever in the hearts and minds of all Swan fans. There was THAT Barry mark, Hall's magnificent long goal in the final quarter, Kirk's heroism, Jude Bolton's helmet to protect a head injury, the blood-stained bandage around Jason Ball's head, Kennelly's Irish jig after being presented with his premiership medallion, and the tears — countless buckets of tears. All tears of joy. Images no Swan will forget, ever. It all was encapsulated in a Mark Knight cartoon published in the *Herald Sun.* It featured the Swan players surrounding former club great Laurie Nash, in his South Melbourne guernsey, drinking from the premiership cup. The caption poignantly had Nash saying: "Thirsty? It's been 72 years between drinks!"

Sydney Swans	3.0	6.3	6.5	8.10	(58)
West Coast	2.4	2.7	5.9	7.12	(54)

GOALS: Hall 2, Goodes, Schneider, Buchanan, Kennelly, O'Loughlin, Jolly.
BEST: Roberts-Thomson, Fosdike, Barry, Crouch, Kirk, J. Bolton.
CROWD: 91,828, at MCG.

THE 2005 PREMIERSHIP TEAM

B:	Craig Bolton	Leo Barry	Jared Crouch
HB:	Ben Mathews	Lewis Roberts-Thomson	Tadhg Kennelly
C:	Paul Williams	Adam Goodes	Sean Dempster
HF:	Ryan O'Keefe	Barry Hall (Capt.)	Jude Bolton
F:	Nick Davis	Michael O'Loughlin	Amon Buchanan

FOLL.: Darren Jolly, Luke Ablett, Brett Kirk
INTER.: Jason Ball, Paul Bevan, Nic Fosdike, Adam Schneider

PLAYER	GAMES	GOALS
ABLETT, Luke	25	9
BALL, Jason	21	2
Barry, Leo	26	0
BEVAN, Paul	15	3
BOLTON, Craig	26	1
BOLTON, Jude	24	3
BUCHANAN, Amon	26	14
CROUCH, Jared	26	8
DAVIS, Nick	23	38
DEMPSTER, Sean	22	0
DOYLE, Stephen	1	1
FOSDIKE, Nic	11	6
GOODES, Adam	26	23
HALL, Barry	26	80
JOLLY, Darren	24	10
KENNELLY, Tadhg	26	2
KIRK, Brett	26	6
MALCESKI, Nick	5	1
MATHEWS, Ben	25	6
MAXFIELD, Stuart	5	1
McVEIGH, Jarrad	13	4
MOORE, Jarred	5	1
NICKS, Matthew	9	1
O'KEEFE, Ryan	26	31
O'LOUGHLIN, Michael	23	52
ROBERTS-THOMSON, Lewis	25	0
SADDINGTON, Jason	7	1
SCHAUBLE, Andrew	4	0
SCHNEIDER, Adam	16	11
SPRIGGS, David	5	0
VOGELS, Luke	11	7
WILLIAMS, Paul	19	5

POSITION: Premier
COACH: Paul Roos
CAPTAIN: Stuart Maxfield
BEST AND FAIREST: Brett Kirk
LEADING GOALKICKER: Barry Hall (80)

2006

Most critics were convinced the Sydney Swans would have a premiership hangover in 2006. The club celebrated its first premiership in 72 years long and hard, but it was back to normal well before the first bounce of the new season. The Swans played an exhibition match against the Kangaroos in Los Angeles and then went down to the Roos by 31 points in an opening round pre-season NAB Cup match at the Manuka Oval, Canberra. The club, of course, again had Paul Roos as coach with Barry Hall, Brett Kirk and Leo Barry as co-captains.

The Swan list for 2006 was updated because of the retirement of several stars, including premiership ruckman Jason Ball, who had been enormously influential in the Grand Final win over West Coast. Stuart Maxfield had retired during the 2005 season, while Matthew Nicks also had retired, while Jason Saddington had been traded to Carlton. This meant there were numerous places up for grabs on the Swans list and, in an effort to to maintain their place at or near the top of the ladder, they traded with Essendon to sign the versatile Ted Richards and Geelong ruckman Paul Chambers.

Replacing Ball was a priority and, after Hawthorn rejected all bids to trade for Hawk ruckman Peter Everitt, the Swans were left with little experienced ruck cover for Darren Jolly. Also, as the reigning premiers and the trade for Richards, the Swans had only late draft selections and nominated Matthew

Swan forward Barry Hall is carried from the ground after his 200th AFL game.

MATCH RESULTS

Round 1, at Docklands, April 1
Essendon 17.6 (108) d Sydney Swans 12.9 (81)
Round 2, at SCG, April 9
Port Adel. 15.16 (106) d Sydney Swans 11.14 (80)
Round 3, at Docklands, April 15
Sydney Swans 12.9 (81) d Carlton 11.8 (74)
Round 4, at SCG, April 23
Melbourne 15.7 (97) d Sydney Swans 13.14 (92)
Round 5, at Stadium Australia, April 29
Sydney Swans 15.17 (107) d Geelong 13.7 (85)
Round 6, at the Gabba, May 7
Sydney Swans 15.12 (102) d Bris. Lions 10.10 (70)
Round 7, at Docklands, May 13
Sydney Swans 28.12 (180) d Richmond 9.8 (62)
Round 8, at SCG, May 20
Sydney Swans 17.14 (116) d Western Bull. 14.6 (90)
Round 9, at MCG, May 27
Sydney Swans 19.5 (119) d Hawthorn 7.12 (54)
Round 10, at Manuka, Oval, June 4
Sydney Swans 16.9 (105) d Kangaroos 14.14 (98)
Round 11, at SCG, June 10
St Kilda 7.10 (52) d Sydney Swans 7.8 (50)
Round 12, at Stadium Australia, June 24
Collingwood 14.11 (95) d Sydney Swans 11.16 (82)
Round 13, at SCG, July 1
Sydney Swans 12.19 (91) d Fremantle 9.4 (58)
Round 14, at SCG, July 9
Adelaide 15.11 (101) d Sydney Swans 8.14 (62)
Round 15, at Subiaco, July 15
West Coast 9.13 (67) d Sydney Swans 9.11 (65)
Round 16, at SCG, July 22
Sydney Swans 14.17 (101) d Richmond 7.11 (53)
Round 17, at Football Park, July 29
Sydney Swans 10.17 (77) d Port Adelaide 7.8 (50)
Round 18, at SCG, August 5
Sydney Swans 17.14 (116) d Essendon 11.7 (73)
Round 19, at SCG, August 12
Sydney Swans 14.11 (95) d Melbourne 10.3 (63)
Round 20, at Kardinia Park, August 19
Geelong 14.6 (90) d Sydney Swans 9.9 (63)
Round 21, at Stadium Australia, August 26
Sydney Swans 14.13 (97) d Brisbane Lions 6.4 (40)
Round 22, at SCG, September 3
Sydney Swans 21.10 (136) d Carlton 6.8 (44)
Qualifying final, at Subiaco, September 9
Sydney Swans 13.7 (85) d West Coast 12.12 (84)
Preliminary final, at Stadium Australia, September 22
Sydney Swans 19.13 (127) d Fremantle 14.8 (92)
Grand Final, at MCG, September 30
West Coast 12.13 (85) d Sydney Swans 12.12 (84)

It's a second Brownlow Medal triumph for Swan star Adam Goodes.

Laidlaw, Kristin Thornton and Ryan Brabazon. They also promoted Heath Grundy, Luke Vogels and Earl Shaw from the rookie list. Of this trio, only Vogels had played senior football, with 11 games as a temporary promotion from the rookie list in 2005.

Although the Swans were favourites to defeat Essendon at Telstra Dome in the opening round, the Bombers shocked the red and white with a nine-goal opening quarter burst. Matthew Lloyd kicked four of these goals and, from there, the Swans were always under pressure. Although they reduced the margin to 27 points by final siren, thanks to seven goals from Barry Hall, it was a disappointing start to the season.

The Swans played Port Adelaide at the SCG in round two, with the club scheduled to unfurl its 2005 premiership flag. Port coach Mark Williams promised his team would rain on the Sydney parade, and he was as good as his word. The Swans, after a moving unfurling ceremony, started slowly against the Power. They trailed by 38 points at half-time and eventually went down by 26 points. The reigning premiers had yet to open their account for 2006 and were above only Melbourne and Richmond on the ladder. Almost every critic wrote or said the Swans were "gone" and started writing epitaphs, only for the Swans to bounce back to defeat Carlton by seven points at Telstra Dome in round 3. It was hardly an inspirational win, but it at least put the Swans on the board.

Melbourne defeated the Swans by five points in their Anzac Day weekend clash at the SCG in round four and the football world wondered if the Sydney club could lift its game to even make the finals, let alone repeat its

AFL
CHARLES BROWNLOW TROPHY
ADAM GOODES

Dear Adam,
On behalf of the Australian Football League we congratulate you on your success in winning the Charles Brownlow Medal for the year 2006. We wish to express our admiration for the splendid sportsmanship and superb skill which you displayed throughout the season, qualities which gained for you the award for the fairest and best player in the Australian Football League. We convey to you every good wish and trust that you will long continue your active interest in our National Game.

Yours sincerely

Chairman AFL Commission Chief Executive Officer

SYDNEY SWANS

Adam Goodes' illuminated address as the 2006 Brownlow Medal winner.

PLAYER	GAMES	GOALS
ABLETT, Luke	24	8
BARRY, Leo	25	0
BEVAN, Paul	9	0
BOLTON, Craig	24	3
BOLTON, Jude	25	12
BUCHANAN, Amon	24	13
CHAMBERS Paul	12	0
CROUCH, Jared	12	3
DAVIS, Nick	17	23
DEMPSTER, Sean	18	5
DOYLE. Stephen	7	1
FOSDIKE, Nic	24	7
GOODES, Adam	25	25
GRUNDY, Heath	6	9
HALL, Barry	25	78
JOLLY, Darren	25	2
KENNELLY, Tadhg	22	1
KIRK, Brett	25	8
MALCESKI, Nick	17	9
MATHEWS, Ben	14	5
McVEIGH, Jarrad	25	21
MOORE, Jarred	2	0
O'KEEFE, Ryan	25	32
O'LOUGHLIN, Michael	25	47
PHILLIPS, Simon	4	1
RICHARDS, Ted	23	4
ROBERTS-THOMSON, Lewis	24	3
SCHMIDT, Tim	2	0
SCHNEIDER, Sdam	25	22
VOGELS, Luke	3	2
WILLIAMS, Paul	12	4

POSITION: Runner-up
COACH: Paul Roos
CAPTAIN: Barry Hall, Leo Barry, Brett Kirk
BEST AND FAIREST: Adam Goodes
LEADING GOALKICKER: Barry Hall (78)

2005 success. From there the Swans won their next six games, against Geelong, Brisbane, Richmond, the Western Bulldogs, Hawthorn and the Kangaroos to climb into fourth position. In round 11, Swan full-forward Barry Hall faced 2005 preliminary final rival, St Kilda's Matt Maguire, and was restricted to just five possessions as the Saints won by two points at the SCG.

The Swans spluttered over the next couple of rounds and, after they went down to Adelaide by 39 points at the SCG in round 14, veteran Paul Williams announced his retirement after 306 AFL games. Williams had been an important player for the Swans after crossing from Collingwood as he added speed and quality to the Swan midfield and was one of the best in the 2005 Grand Final. He had played 117 games with the Swans after crossing from Collingwood in 2001 and won the club best and fairest in 2001-02.

At the completion of 21 rounds, the Swans were fifth, but desperate to finish in the top four for a realistic chance of winning back-to-back flags. The last premiership match, against Carlton, was vital as the Blues were last on the ladder and, with a win and Fremantle or Melbourne losing, the Swans could jump to that vital fourth position. The Swans demolished the Blues by 91 points and Adelaide defeated Fremantle by 30 points at AAMI Stadium. The Swans were fourth and scheduled to play bitter rival West Coast in a qualifying final at Subiaco.

There was no love lost between the teams, especially as they had played another close match during the home and away season, the Eagles defeating the Swans by two points at Subiaco in round 15. This final again was a thriller, with the Swans squeezing past the Eagles by one point, thanks to a late, late goal from Michael O'Loughlin. To add insult to the Eagles' injury, O'Loughlin let a group of West Coast fans near the goals know what he had achieved, adding further spice to the eventual Swans-Eagles Grand Final.

The qualifying final win gave the Swans a week's break before playing Fremantle in a preliminary final at Telstra Stadium. The Swans might have been raging favourites, but the Dockers made them work hard for success. The Swans managed to kick away to lead by 17 points at the main break, but managed to increase this by just three points to the final change. Every time the Swans looked like breaking free, the Dockers would hit back, mainly through Matthew Pavlich. The Swans eventually won by 35 points, with Hall kicking six goals. Next day, West Coast defeated Adelaide by 10 points in the other preliminary final at AAMI Stadium. It again would be a Swans-Eagles Grand Final.

Over their previous 11 meetings, the Swans held a six-five advantage. Remarkably, the margins in their previous four encounters had been four points (Eagles), four (Swans), two (Eagles) and Swans (one). No one therefore would have predicted that this one also would go right down to the wire. The Swans started terribly to trail by 25 points at half-time. Although they fought back strongly and looked the likely winner early in the final quarter, the Eagles managed to hold on to win by a point. It had been the first time the Swans had made consecutive Grand Finals since they played four in a row from 1933-36, yet again could not land back-to-back flags.

Ted Richards was one of the Swans' best in the 2006 Grand Final.

The big consolation for the Swans was that Adam Goodes on the Monday night before the Grand Final won his second Brownlow Medal. He polled 26 votes to defeat the Western Bulldogs' Scott West by three votes, with the ineligible West Coast's Daniel Kerr polling 22 votes and teammate Chris Judd 21. Goodes did not poll a vote over the first five rounds, but was judged best on ground in four of the next five matches. He led by just one vote going into the final round, but most fans knew he already had the Brownlow in his keeping as he had played sensationally against Carlton with 26 possessions, nine marks and four goals. Goodes polled three votes and became the club's second multiple Brownlow winner, with Bob Skilton (three). Goodes also was named a 2006 All-Australian, along with teammates Craig Bolton and Ryan O'Keefe.

2007

Following the heart-breaking one-point loss to West Coast in the 2006 Grand Final, the Sydney Swans were tipped to slide the following season. Most media critics argued that the Swans had done well to make two consecutive Grand Finals but, overall, lacked the class of other teams. It was an inexplicable argument, especially as most of the critics would have been hailing the Swans as one of the great teams of the modern era if they had won back-to-back flags. As it was, the Swans had to prove themselves all over again, with basically the same list as it had in 2006.

The major loss was midfielder Paul Williams, who retired in 2006 following a collarbone injury. Otherwise, the Swans merely tinkered with their player list, cutting several inexperienced players. They also traded with Hawthorn to secure the services of veteran ruckman Peter Everitt. The man known as "Spida" had wanted to join the Swans before the start of the previous season, but the Hawks refused to even discuss the possibility of a trade. The Swans also drafted several youngsters, including Jesse White, but none of their 2006 national draft selections played a senior game in 2007.

Paul Roos was coach for his fifth consecutive full season, with Barry Hall, Leo Barry and Brett Kirk reappointed for a second full season as co-captains. As usual under Roos, the emphasis in the pre-season competition, the NAB Cup, was on the

Ruckman Peter "Spida" Everitt joined the Swans in 2007.

MATCH RESULTS

Round 1, at Stadium Australia, March 31
West Coast 11.8 (74) d Sydney Swans 10.13 (73)
Round 2, at MCG, April 7
Sydney Swans 13.10 (88) d Richmond 11.6 (72)
Round 3, at SCG, April 15
Sydney Swans 13.18 (96) d Brisbane Lions 10.9 (69)
Round 4, at Football Park, April 21
Adelaide 9.7 (61) d Sydney Swans 5.14 (44)
Round 5, at SCG, April 28
Sydney Swans 17.7 (109) d Melbourne 8.12 (60)
Round 6, at Docklands, May 5
Kangaroos 16.15 (111) d Sydney Swans 14.11 (95)
Round 7, at Docklands, May 12
St Kilda 15.7 (97) d Sydney Swans 11.5 (71)
Round 8, at SCG, May 20
Sydney Swans 17.16 (118) d Port Adelaide 13.9 (87)
Round 9, at Manuka Oval, May 27
Sydney Swans 15.10 (100) d Western Bull. 8.9 (57)
Round 10, at SCG, June 2
Essendon 11.8 (74) d Sydney Swans 11.7 (73)
Round 11, at MCG, June 9
Sydney Swans 11.9 (75) d Hawthorn 9.12 (66)
Round 12, at Stadium Australia, June 23
Collingwood 10.16 (76) d Sydney Swans 8.9 (57)
Round 13, at Kardinia Park, June 30
Geelong 13.9 (87) d Sydney Swans 10.9 (69)
Round 14, at SCG, July 8
Sydney Swans 11.23 (89) d Fremantle 9.7 (61)
Round 15, at SCG, July 15
Sydney Swans 25.12 (162) d Carlton 15.10 (100)
Round 16, at Subiaco, July 21
West Coast 16.16 (112) d Sydney Swans 15.10 (100)
Round 17, at SCG, July 28
Sydney Swans 21.12 (138) d Richmond 10.12 (72)
Round 18, Manuka Oval, August 5
Sydney Swans 17.10 (112) d Melbourne 9.10 (64)
Round 19, at Stadium Australia, August 11
Sydney Swans 12.10 (82) d St Kilda 9.11 (65)
Round 20, at the Gabba, August 18
Sydney Swans 8.15 (63) drew with Bris. Lions 9.9 (63)
Round 21, at MCG, August 25
Collingwood 15.11 (101) d Sydney Swans 11.10 (76)
Round 22, at SCG, September 2
Sydney Swans 22.9 (141) d Hawthorn 10.9 (69)
Elimination final, at MCG, September 8
Collingwood 18.17 (125) d Sydney Swans 13.9 (87)

Club legend Bob Skilton congratulates Brett Kirk after his 2007 best and fairest triumph.

development of younger players. It therefore was no surprise that the Western Bulldogs defeated the Swans by 27 points in an opening round match at Telstra Dome. Youngsters used in the match included Ryan Brabazon, Daniel Currie, Peter Faulks, Matthew Laidlaw, Sam Rowe, Earl Shaw and Jonathan Simpkin. Senior players rested included Hall, Barry, Jude Bolton. Jared Crouch, Darren Jolly and Michael O'Loughlin.

The AFL, after noting the ferocious rivalry between the Swans and the West Coast Eagles over the previous two seasons, scheduled a Grand Final "replay" at Telstra Stadium for the opening round. The match had extra "spice" as Eagle star Ben Cousins was in the United States as part of his drug rehabilitation. Also, former Carlton premiership player and coach Robert Walls suggested in his column in *The Age* that the Swans-Eagles clash was a case of "good versus evil". The Eagles had been painted with the one brush and were determined to prove their critics wrong, even though star ruckman Dean Cox was a late withdrawal from the side because of a thigh injury. It mattered little as the Eagles dominated early and led by 36 points at half-time.

Although the match attracted an attendance of 62,586, Swan fans made little noise until their team started overhauling the Eagle lead in the third quarter. The Swans trailed by 23 points at the final break and, despite a frantic late challenge, fell short by one point — the same margin as when the Eagles defeated the Swans in the previous year's Grand Final. The Swans' only multiple goakicker was Nick Davis, with two. It was yet another remarkable Swans-Eagles game and

Defender Lewis Roberts-Thomson played just two games in the 2007 season because of injury, and was badly missed.

PLAYER	GAMES	GOALS
ABLETT, Luke	20	8
BARLOW, Ed	4	1
BARRY, Leo	18	4
BEVAN, Paul	17	3
BOLTON, Craig	23	3
BOLTON, Jude	23	6
BRENNAN, Luke	5	0
BUCHANAN, Amon	16	6
CROUCH, Jared	8	3
DAVIS, Nick	18	33
DEMPSTER, Sean	14	3
EVERITT, Peter	23	15
FOSDIKE, Nic	23	6
GOODES, Adam	23	9
GRUNDY, Heath	8	1
HALL, Barry	20	44
JACK. Kieren	2	0
JOLLY, Darren	23	16
KENNELLY, Tadhg	13	1
KIRK, Brett	23	8
LAIDLAW, Matthew	1	0
MALCESKI, Nick	23	14
MATHEWS, Ben	23	8
McVEIGH, Jarrad	23	11
MOORE, Jarred	2	1
O'KEEFE, Ryan	23	23
O'LOUGHLIN, Michael	23	40
PHILLIPS, Simon	1	1
RICHARDS, Ted	23	2
ROBERTS-THOMSON, Lewis	2	0
SCHMIDT, Tim	14	11
SCHNEIDER, Adam	21	27
VOGELS, Luke	3	2

POSITION: Seventh
COACH: Paul Roos
CAPTAIN: Barry Hall, Leo Barry, Brett Kirk
BEST AND FAIREST: Brett Kirk
LEADING GOALKICKER: Barry Hall (44)

the media was quick to point out that the total winning margin over the clubs' previous six encounters had been just 13 points, with one-point results in the last three of these games.

Fortunately, the Swans were able to kick-start their season the following week against the undermanned Richmond. Yet the Swans found it tough going against the tenacious Tigers. The red and white led by just four points at the final change, but managed to kick away through goals from Jolly and Tadhg Kennelly to win by 16 points. It was hardly an inspiring result but, when the Swans defeated the

Michael O'Loughlin thanks fans after breaking John Rantall's club games record.

Brisbane Lions by 27 points at the SCG the following week, some critics were starting to eat their words.

Yet, despite their wealth of experience, the Swans found it difficult to string together more than two consecutive wins. Going into round 17, they looked as if they might miss the finals altogether and needed a strong finish to the season. They thrashed the Tigers by 66 points at the SCG, demolished Melbourne by 48 points in Canberra and then defeated St Kilda by 17 points at Telstra Stadium before a draw with the Brisbane Lions at the Gabba in round 20. The draw proved costly as it cost the Swans fifth position at the end of the season. Instead, the Swans finished seventh, half a game behind fifth-placed Hawthorn and sixth-placed Collingwood, but with a much better percentage than either the Hawks or the Magpies.

The Swans were desperately unlucky against the Lions as they led for most of the night and seemed certain winners until the dying moments. With just 25 seconds to play and the Swans leading by six points, star Lion forward Jonathan Brown took a contested mark 55 metres from goal. Not the most reliable shot for goal, Brown kicked accurately and the final siren blared just a second after the ball was returned to the centre of the ground. Despite the loss of two match points, the Swans virtually had a finals berth in the bag with two rounds to play. Although they went down to Collingwood by 25 points at the MCG in round 21, they were in seventh position and a game and a big percentage margin ahead of ninth-placed St Kilda. The Swans then thrashed Hawthorn by 72 points in the final round to at least march into the finals with optimism and confidence.

The problem was that they faced a cut-throat elimination final against Collingwood, their nemesis club over recent seasons. Although the Swans' Adam Goodes kicked the first goal of the match, Collingwood soon took control and led by 31 points at the first break. The Magpies' tackling and determination not to allow the Swans to break free took its toll, even though the Swans fought back to cut the margin to 10 points by half-time.

Despite the brilliance of Michael O'Loughlin (four goals) up forward and the all-round class of Goodes around the ground, Collingwood won by 38 points. The critics had predicted a Swans' slide and they were proven right, even if the red and white had made the finals for a fifth consecutive season, the club's best run since a run of five finals series from 1932-36.

Kirk won his second club best and fairest award, but Goodes was the Swans' leading vote-winner in the Brownlow Medal count, with 20. The medal was won by Geelong's Jimmy Bartel (29 votes), but Goodes was ineligible anyway as he had been found guilty of striking Melbourne's Simon Godfrey in the round five match at the SCG. Goodes managed to avoid suspension, but the guilty verdict made him ineligible for the Brownlow. He originally had been suspended one match, but won an appeal against the suspension and ended up with a reprimand.

One of the highlights of the season was star forward O'Loughlin setting a new club games record. He broke John Rantall's record of 260 games (from 1963-72 and 1976-79) in the round 14 match against Fremantle at the SCG. Although the Swans struggled at times, they finished strongly to defeat the Dockers by 28 points to help O'Loughlin celebrate a magnificent milestone. O'Loughlin, who had joined the Swans as a shy 17-year-old in 1995, became one of the club's most decorated players. He won the best and fairest in 1998, topped the goalkicking in 2000-01, was All-Australian in 1997 and 2000 and played in the 2005 Swans' premiership side.

2008

The disappointing loss to Collingwood in the 2007 elimination final had most critics suggesting the Swans were too old and too slow and that they needed to rebuild the side. The Swans reacted by trading two 2005 premiership players — Adam Schneider and Sean Dempster — to St Kilda. Ruckman Stephen Doyle, whose career had been hampered by one injury or another, retired and several players were delisted. The Swans picked up Northern Knights youngster Brett Meredith through the Schneider-Dempster deal and also drafted another Knights player, Patrick Veszpremi. Two players — Adelaide's Martin Mattner and Geelong's Henry Playfair — joined from rival clubs through trade deals and youngster Craig Bird was listed as a NSW/ACT scholarship player.

Bird, in fact, became the first NSW/ACT scholarship holder to graduate to senior action as he was selected for the opening round match against St Kilda at Telstra Dome. The Swans went into this match as underdogs, partly because it again had been knocked out of the pre-season competition, the NAB Cup, in the first round. The Swans, playing a young side, had been defeated by Hawthorn at Launceston's Aurora Stadium, but were extremely competitive in going down by two points.

The defeat was bad enough, but there was worse as Swan defender Nick Malceski damaged an anterior cruciate ligament and coach Paul Roos was hauled before the AFL to explain a comment he made to midfielder Jarrad McVeigh late in the game. Malceski had a knee reconstruction, but elected to have controversial and revolutionary surgery in which a synthetic tendon was attached to the knee. This allowed him to return to action much sooner than anyone would have expected, in round eight. The Roos controversy hogged headlines for days as his comment to McVeigh, of "don't kick a goal" in a tight finish, was interpreted in some quarters as proof that the Swans did not want to win. In reality, Roos was making a joke at McVeigh's expense as the midfielder over the previous season sometimes had been wayward with his kicking for goal. Roos eventually was cleared and the controversy waned.

Jarrad McVeigh had a superb 2008 season to win the best and fairest.

St Kilda jumped the Swans in the opening round to lead by 20 points at the first break. Although the Swans drew level by half-time, the game developed into an arm-wrestle, with both defences on top. St Kilda won by two points, but a miss by Jarred Moore in the final minutes could have given the Swans victory. The Swans had no multiple goalkickers, but midfielder Amon Buchanan picked up a

MATCH RESULTS

Round 1, at Docklands, March 22
St Kilda 6.15 (51) d Sydney Swans 6.13 (49)
Round 2, at SCG, March 30
Sydney Swans 22.14 (146) d Port Adel. 11.12 (78)
Round 3, at the Gabba, April 5
Sydney Swans 13.10 (88) d Bris. Lions 10.11 (71)
Round 4, at Stadium Australia, April 12
Sydney Swans 16.11 (107) d West Coast 5.15 (45)
Round 5, at Kardinia Park, April 19
Geelong 16.18 (114) d Sydney Swans 10.12 (72)
Round 6, at Docklands, April 27
Syd. Swans 8.16 (64) drew with North Melb. 9.10 (64)
Round 7, at SCG, May 4
Western Bull. 18.4 (112) d Sydney Swans 14.10 (94)
Round 8, at Stadium Australia, May 18
Sydney Swans 21.17 (143) d Essendon 7.10 (52)
Round 9, at Football Park, May 24
Sydney Swans 16.9 (105) d Port Adelaide 14.10 (94)
Round 10, at SCG, June 1
Sydney Swans 21.13 (139) d Richmond 8.9 (57)
Round 11, at Subiaco, June 7
Sydney Swans 12.11 (83) d West Coast 11.12 (78)
Round 12, at SCG, June 14
Sydney Swans 14.18 (102) d St Kilda 9.13 (67)
Round 13, at Manuka Oval, June 22
Sydney Swans 17.12 (114) d Melbourne 11.8 (74)
Round 14, at Stadium Australia, July 5
Collingwood 11.13 (79) d Sydney Swans 6.14 (50)
Round 15, at MCG, July 13
Hawthorn 15.16 (106) d Sydney Swans 10.15 (75)
Round 16, at Docklands, July 20
Sydney Swans 18.13 (121) d Carlton 18.11 (119)
Round 17, at SCG, July 26
Adelaide 11.11 (77) d Sydney Swans 6.17 (53)
Round 18, at Manuka Oval, August 3
Western Bull. 17.11 (113) d Sydney Swans 14.13 (97)
Round 19, at SCG, August 9
Sydney Swans 17.10 (112) d Fremantle 15.18 (108)
Round 20, at Stadium Australia, August 16
Geelong 20.13 (133) d Sydney Swans 14.10 (94)
Round 21, at Docklands, August 23
Collingwood 18.10 (118) d Sydney Swans 10.13 (73)
Round 22, at SCG, August 30
Sydney Swans 17.12 (114) d Bris. Lions 6.17 (53)
Elimination final, Stadium Australia, September 6
Sydney Swans 17.8 (110) d North Melb. 11.9 (75)
Semi-final, MCG, September 12
Western Bull. 16.10 (106) d Sydney Swans 9.15 (69)

Nick Malceski had radical knee surgery to bounce back in 2008.

Brownlow Medal vote, while Mattner made an impressive debut in the red and white.

The Swans, who found it difficult to breach the St Kilda defence in the opening round, the following week scored 22 goals in defeating Port Adelaide by 68 points at the SCG. Barry Hall kicked five goals and Michael O'Loughlin four to suggest the Swans would be in the mix at season's end after all. They followed up with a 17-point defeat of the Brisbane Lions at the Gabba in round three, but ran into a storm of controversy in the round four match against bitter rival West Coast at ANZ Stadium.

Although the Swans had opened brightly to suggest a big win for the home team, Hall threw a punch which sent a groggy Brent Staker to the ground. The incident took place behind play and the television cameras caught it for the world to see. It was as inexplicable as it was sudden. The Swan key forward later broke a bone in his wrist when he ran into an advertising hoarding, but it didn't matter as he was suspended for seven matches. The Swans defeated the Eagles by 62 points, but the result hardly made a ripple in the media as all attention was on Hall and his left-handed swing at Staker.

The Swans therefore had to contend without Hall over a large chunk of the season and there even were some doubts whether he would return to AFL action as there were suggestions he would turn to a boxing career. The Swans, without their most important forward, went down to Geelong by 42 points at Skilled Stadium the week after Hall was suspended and then played an exciting and controversial draw with North Melbourne at Telstra Dome in round six. The Swans looked as if they had won as a result of a late shot by Brett Kirk. Swan supporters behind the goal went up as one, only for the goal umpire to rule that the ball had been touched on the line.

Then, as if controversy was dogging the Swans, the Roos mid-week complained that the Swans had an extra man on the ground over the dying seconds. Jesse White, in his AFL debut, was the "extra" man, but he was well away from the action and his interchange mistake had no effect on the play or the result. Besides, the Roos said immediately after the match that they had no complaints. The result stood and the sharing of the match points probably hurt the Swans more than the Roos as they had had the last six scoring shots and were swamping their opponents at final siren.

The Swans had their chances in going down to the Western Bulldogs by 18 points at the SCG in round seven and then won their next six matches. There was life after Hall after all and the thrashing of Richmond by 82 points at the SCG was particularly impressive as the Swans kicked 13 goals to Richmond's one over the first half. The Swans, after these six consecutive wins, were fourth on the ladder and regarded as serious flag contenders. Hall had returned for the 35-point win over St Kilda in round 12, but ran into further trouble in the round 14 match against Collingwood at ANZ Stadium.

Hall took a swipe at Collingwood defender Shane Wakelin and although there was little or no contact, the AFL Tribunal suspended the Swan forward for another week. The Swans imposed a penalty of their own and suspended Hall indefinitely. Collingwood defeated the Swans by 29 points and Hall's club suspension lasted two games as he returned for the round 17 loss to Adelaide at the SCG. The Crows defeated the Swans by 24 points in the middle of a horror run for the red and white. The Swans won just two of their last six home and away games to finish sixth. However, the Swans at least had a home game in the first

PLAYER	GAMES	GOALS
ABLETT, Luke	22	3
BARLOW, Ed	7	6
BARRY, Leo	20	2
BEVAN, Paul	24	10
BIRD, Craig	21	8
BOLTON, Craig	24	2
BOLTON, Jude	24	11
BRABAZON, Ryan	1	0
BRENNAN, Luke	4	1
BUCHANAN, Amon	20	15
CROUCH, Jared	7	1
DAVIS, Nick	3	3
EVERITT, Peter	16	2
FOSDIKE, Nic	1	0
GOODES, Adam	21	29
GRUNDY, Heath	10	2
HALL, Barry	15	41
JACK, Kieren	23	11
JOLLY, Darren	24	15
KENNELLY, Tadhg	22	0
KIRK, Brett	24	9
MALCESKI, Nick	11	6
MATHEWS, Ben	2	1
MATTNER, Martin	24	4
McVEIGH, Jarrad	24	32
MOORE, Jarred	23	25
O'DWYER, Matt	2	1
O'KEEFE, Ryan	23	23
O'LOUGHLIN, Michael	16	36
PLAYFAIR, Henry	11	10
RICHARDS, Ted	24	4
ROBERTS-THOMSON, Lewis	24	4
SCHMIDT, Tim	1	1
SMITH, Nick	2	1
VESZPREMI, Patrick	6	9
WHITE, Jesse	2	0

POSITION: Fifth
COACH: Paul Roos
CAPTAIN: Leo Barry, Craig Bolton, Brett Kirk
BEST AND FAIREST: Jarrad McVeigh
LEADING GOALKICKER: Barry Hall (41)

week of the finals, against North Melbourne at ANZ Stadium.

There was considerable ill-feeling between the clubs following the Roos' claims that the Swans, playing an extra man late in their Telstra Dome match earlier in the season had robbed them of two match points. However, the public was less than impressed and just 19,127 fans rocked up for the night final. Although the Roos looked by far the better team early to lead by 14 points at the first break and then by 10 points at half-time, the Swans took control with an eight-goal third quarter. The red and white cruised home by 35 points, with Hall, Kieren Jack and Adam Goodes kicking three goals each.

As Hawthorn had defeated the Western Bulldogs by 51 points in another qualifying final, the Swans played the Bulldogs in a semi-final at the MCG. Although the Swans trailed by just four points at half-time, they could not control their quicker opponents over the second half and the Bulldogs won by 37 points to end the Swans' season. Hall kicked four goals and he and Kennelly were their side's best players.

Although Goodes was ineligible for the Brownlow because of suspension during the season, he polled 21 votes, with the Bulldogs' Adam Cooney taking football's most prestigious individual honour with 24 votes. Goodes had been suspended one match for "rough contact" in the round 13 match against Melbourne. The Swans, hampered for much of the season by the Hall suspensions, also had to play the final six premiership games and its two finals matches without star forward Michael O'Loughlin, who severely injured an ankle in the round 16 defeat of Carlton at Telstra Dome.

The Swans in 2008 gave six players — Bird, White, Veszpremi, Ryan Brabazon, Matt O'Dwyer and Nick Smith — their AFL debuts and, for a team considered too old and too slow, the Swans did well to inject youth and make the finals for a sixth consecutive season.

2009

The Swans had to tinker with their leadership group for 2009, with veteran defender Leo Barry relinquishing his co-captaincy role in what he announced would be his last season. The vacancy was filled by dual Brownlow Medal winner Adam Goodes, with Paul Roos again coach. Roos, to the end of the 2008 season, had coached the Swans in 156 games, a club record, and four more than Rodney Eade's 152 games from 1996-2002.

Underrated midfielder/defender Ben Mathews retired at the end of the 2008 season after 198 games in the red and white from 1997 after being recruited from Corowa-Rutherglen. Mathews, who played in the 2005 premiership side, filled a number of roles throughout his long and successful AFL career and was always one of the Swans' most committed players.

Veteran ruckman Peter Everitt, who had given the club two years' service after playing with St Kilda and Hawthorn, also retired, while enigmatic forward Nick Davis, who had been so important in the 2005 semi-final defeat of Geelong, was delisted. Collingwood's Rhyce Shaw was the only player from a rival club to join the Swans for 2009, but the club drafted promising youngsters Daniel Hannebery, Campbell Heath and Lewis Johnston, and promoted Matt O'Dwyer and Nick Smith from the rookie list. These youngsters, and others, will take the club forward as part of the club's proud 135-year history and heritage.

The future of the Sydney Swans is represented by players like Patrick Veszpremi.

Cheer, Cheer!

All Sydney Swan fans are familiar with the club theme song, played before all matches and, in victory, post-match. "Cheer, cheer the red and the white" was played over and over again at the MCG after the 2005 Grand Final win, and no one in red and white would have complained if it had been played until midnight, or even longer. It now is a vital part of the club's proud tradition, almost as significant as the red and white itself. Yet the song was introduced only in the early 1960s after long negotiations with the owners of the original theme — the University of Notre Dame in Indiana, USA. Until then the club's theme song was based on an old 1930s hit, "Spring time in the Rockies", by "the singing cowboy" Gene Autrey.

The South Melbourne Football Club early in 1961 decided it needed a more vibrant theme song and was inspired by the 1940 movie "Knute Rockne — All American", which told the story of the famous Notre Dame coach. The Notre Dame Victory March was played throughout the movie, which starred Pat O'Brien as the legendary Rockne and future US president Ronald Reagan as one of the Notre Dame footballers. The Swans sent a letter to Notre Dame on April 10, 1961, asking for permission to use the song, with change of words to suit the VFL club.

Notre Dame's Vice-President (Business Affairs), Father Jerome J. Wilson, wrote back on May 22, 1961: "After reading your letter I have written to the Melrose Music Corporation who have the licensing right for our song for some time into the distant future. We note that you have already put the music into use; therefore, we hesitate to decline the use of this song and we are asking the Melrose Music Corporation to grant the right to you to use the music." Father Wilson thanked the Swans for their "courtesy" of presenting Notre Dame with a South Melbourne membership ticket and indicated it would go on display at the university.

The Swans on May 31 were contacted by Australian music publisher Allan & Co to report that it held the Australian rights for the Notre Dame Victory March under licence from the Melrose Music Corporation. The company

University of Notre Dame
Notre Dame, Indiana

Vice-President - Business Affairs

Cable Address "Dulac"

May 22, 1961

Mr. Lynn Lawrence
Committee
South Melbourne Football Club
C/-312 Albert Road
South Melbourne
Victoria, Australia

Dear Mr. Lawrence:

Your letter of April 10, 1961, concerning the South Melbourne Football Club's use of our Notre Dame song reached my office while I was traveling through Europe. After reading your letter I have written to the Melrose Music Corporation who have the licensing right for our song for some time into the distant future. We note that you have already put the music into use; therefore, we hesitate to decline the use of this song and we are asking the Melrose Music Corporation to grant the right to you to use the music. However, it is within their rights to turn you down and if they choose to do so, we will be sorry but there is nothing we can do. They are the only ones who can furnish or tell you where to secure the sheet music for the song. I am sure they will be getting in touch with you shortly.

The University of Notre Dame's Father Jerome Wilson first wrote to the Swans on May 22, 1961.

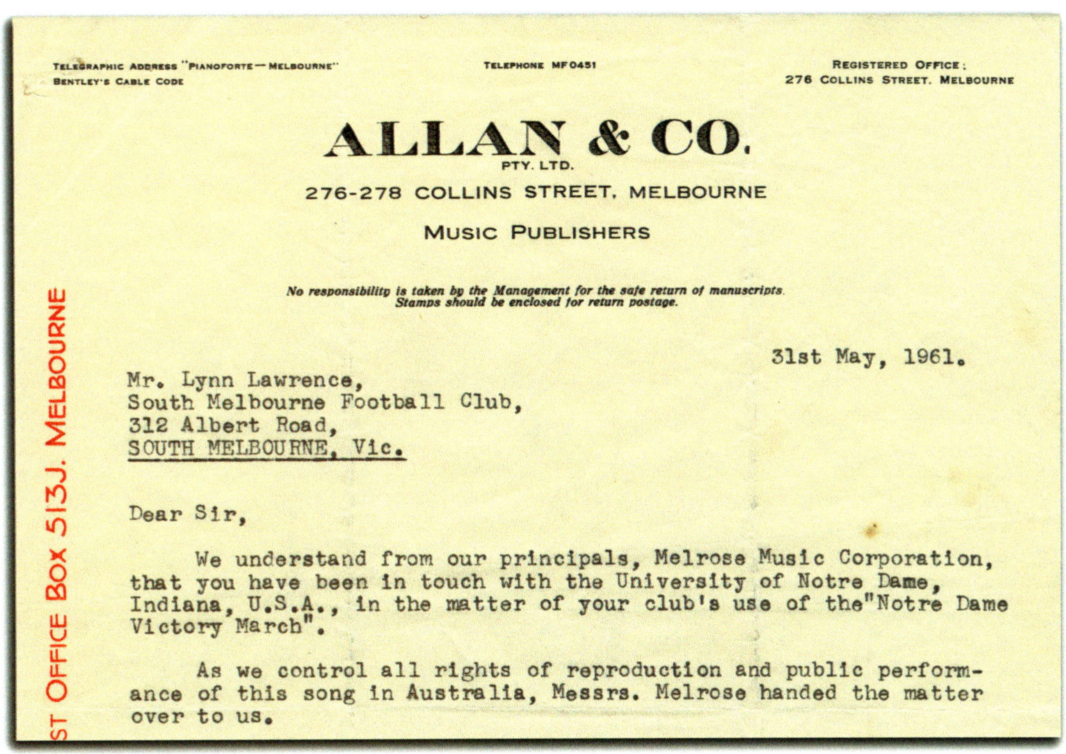
TELEGRAPHIC ADDRESS "PIANOFORTE—MELBOURNE"
BENTLEY'S CABLE CODE

TELEPHONE MF0451

REGISTERED OFFICE:
276 COLLINS STREET, MELBOURNE

ALLAN & CO.
PTY. LTD.
276-278 COLLINS STREET, MELBOURNE
MUSIC PUBLISHERS

No responsibility is taken by the Management for the safe return of manuscripts. Stamps should be enclosed for return postage.

31st May, 1961.

Mr. Lynn Lawrence,
South Melbourne Football Club,
312 Albert Road,
SOUTH MELBOURNE, Vic.

Dear Sir,

We understand from our principals, Melrose Music Corporation, that you have been in touch with the University of Notre Dame, Indiana, U.S.A., in the matter of your club's use of the"Notre Dame Victory March".

As we control all rights of reproduction and public performance of this song in Australia, Messrs. Melrose handed the matter over to us.

ST OFFICE BOX 513J. MELBOURNE

Music Publishers Allan & Co granted the Swans permission to use the theme song in this letter of May 31, 1961.

wrote to the Swans: "We have to say first of all that we do not, in principle, approve of any of our copyright songs being parodied or modified in any way and that, strictly speaking, by using this song in a parodied form without having obtained written permission from the copyright owners amounts to an infringement of copy."

There then was the all-important rider: "However, considering the circumstances, we do not want to create any difficulties and are prepared to authorise the use of the NOTRE DAME VICTORY MARCH by John F. Shea and the Rev. Michael Shea in conjunction with the words entitled "The Red and the White".

The Swans wrote a letter of thanks to Notre Dame and Father Wilson replied on August 8: "We appreciate your letter of thanks and we are happy that you will be able to use our NOTRE DAME VICTORY MARCH as you have adapted it. We want to assure you that we do not do this for any of the schools in America and therefore our granting of the permission is an act of friendship on our behalf." Father Wilson also indicated that the university would be "happy to hear from you to know how your football club is progressing".

So, let's hear the club song, based on the Notre Dame Victory March:

Cheer, cheer the red and the white,
Honour the name by day and by night.
Lift that noble banner high,
Shake down the thunder from the sky.
What though the odds be great or small
Swans will go in and win over all
While her loyal sons are marching
Onwards to victory.

* * *

The Shea brothers, Notre Dame graduates, wrote the theme song in 1908 and it first appeared under the Notre Dame copyright in 1928.

The original Notre Dame chorus goes:

Cheer, cheer for old Notre Dame,
Wake up the echoes cheering her name.
Send a volley cheer on high,
Shake down the thunder from the sky.
What though the odds be great or small
Old Notre Dame will win over all
While her loyal sons are marching
Onwards to victory.

AUTOGRAPHS

AUTOGRAPHS

Autographs

Autographs

Autographs

Autographs

Autographs